Dooley Noted

Books, plays, and screenplays by Ken Dooley

MBA: Management by Auerbach

The Murder Trial of John Gordon

The Auerbach Dynasty

Ups and Downs

Bellevue Avenue

Love Nests

Kistallnacht in Cranston

Ghosts Over Providence

My Brother's Keeper

Drums Along the Blackstone

From White to Black, with Bill Russell and Sam Jones

Dooley Noted

Tales of an Ordinary Man Fortunate Enough to Meet a Lot of Extraordinary People in His Life's Journey

KEN DOOLEY

With a Foreword by
Dr. Patrick T. Conley,
Historian Laureate of Rhode Island

Rhode Island Publications Society
East Providence
2021

ISBN: 978-0-917012-14-3

For information contact:
Rhode Island Publications Society
1445 Wampanoag Trail, Suite #201
East Providence, RI 02915
Tel: 401–272–1776

Printed in the United States of America by Lakeside Book Company

Contents

Foreword

At age ninety, Ken Dooley, noted Rhode Island Heritage Hall of Fame playwright, author, publisher, political consultant, and raconteur decided, with a nudge from his admirers, to compose a series of brief essays recounting his varied life experiences. His observations, based on first-hand involvement, bear the appropriate title *Dooley Noted.* His insightful recollections are notable indeed!

During his long and eventful career, Ken has encountered the famous and infamous, the literati, scholars, athletes, politicians, clergy, the military, and those who led an ordinary life, except for an extraordinary encounter with Mr. Dooley.

Long ago, in the late 1890s, a humorous writer and social critic named Finley Peter "Dunne created a wise and insightful Irish-American character whom he called "Mr. Dooley." In a series of brief, compact volumes, Dunne, through Mr. Dooley, commented on the morals and manners of America and the issues of the times. Social historians writing today about that era often spice their narrative with Mr. Dooley's pithy words of wisdom.

In the present volume, a real Irish-American character named Dooley offers the reader vignettes that illustrate the history and temper of our own times. These essays are more personal, local, and detailed than those of Finley Dunne, but just as revealing regarding human nature. One can easily and correctly assess Ken Dooley's book of escapades as very well done!

Patrick Conley
Historian Laureate
of Rhode Island

Preface

The definition of an autobiography is simple: it is a history of a person's life told by that person. I have always believed that autobiographies should be written by people who have made major contributions in medicine, history, music, politics, writing, theater, or industry. I certainly do not qualify in any of those areas. When I graduated from La Salle Academy in 1949, I was unofficially designated as the "most forgettable" member of the class. It is a label I carry to this day.

I read *The Autobiography of Benjamin Franklin* when I was in fourth grade at Eden Park Grammar School. I liked the size of the book, which fit neatly behind whatever book my class was reading at the time. We had graduated from "Dick threw the ball to Jane," but I was still bored with most of our reading. I was fascinated as Benjamin Franklin explained how he rose from a lower-middle-class youth into one of the most admired men in the world. Next, I read *The Autobiography of Mark Twain*. The book is a classic in scope, imagination, laughter, and tragedy. It reveals all the different roles Twain had in life—family man, author, son, brother, and friend.

Years later, I was spellbound with *The Diary of a Young Girl* by Anne Frank. She was a Jewish girl who, along with her family and a few friends, went into hiding during World War II. She describes her emotional roller coaster, her opinions on other people's behavior, and her loneliness. Her diary ends shortly after her fifteenth birthday when she dies in a German concentration camp. The reality is that Anne Frank has more to say in her 15 years of life than I do in my 90. So please do not consider this book an autobiography, which should be reserved for people who have something to say or made significant contributions.

The idea for a book started while I was having dinner with my good friends, Patrick and Gail Conley. Pat and I were engaging in our usual story game of "Can You Top This" when Gail suddenly said, "You should write a book about some of the fascinating people you have met."

"Great idea," Pat said. "And you should call it *Dooley Noted*."

Writing a story about other people does not fall into the category of an autobiography. Anyone who profits from the experiences of others writes biographies, not autobiographies. No one benefited more from the people I met more than I did in this book. I am merely an observer, reporting on some interesting people and events that shaped my life.

"A good teacher will teach you something that you will remember for a day, but a great teacher will teach you something you remember for the rest of your life." I do not know where that quote came from, but it makes me remember my fifth-grade teacher, Mrs. Phillips, who was the catalyst who inspired me to become a reporter, film and drama critic, editorial director for a major publisher, playwright, and screenwriter. (The Early Years)

I was never prouder of my sister Eileen than the day her photo appeared in *The Providence Journal* at the exclusive Bailey's Beach. (The Prettiest Girl on the Beach)

An act of kindness by the owner of a local shoe store allowed me to feel like one of the boys. (A Special Discount)

When I met John Dinneen in 1944, I was 13, and he was 12. A year difference in those days usually puts the older boy in the driver's seat. It did not work with John, who lived right next door to me. (The Wallet)

I was five years old when I saw Errol Flynn as Captain Blood and later as Major Geoffrey Vickers in *The Charge of the Light Brigade.* I remember crying hysterically after Flynn was killed in his role as General George Custer in the final scene of *They Died With Their Boots On.* (A Love Affair With Movies)

One of the disadvantages of having children is that they eventually get old enough to give you presents they made at school. My father had to deal with this when I made him a tie holder (Memories of My Father)

My first official job ended disastrously, but I learned something about business morals that stayed with me my whole life. (My First Job)

I came up with a creative plan for my confirmation name. Unfortunately, I got overruled. (Choosing a Confirmation Name)

Fr. John F. Sullivan was pastor of St. Matthew's Church in Cranston, Rhode Island. He was my great uncle, brother of my grandmother, Margaret Kenneally. We never liked each other. (A Priest in the Family)

The pastor at St. Paul's tried to deny a Mass of Christian Burial to a young man who committed suicide at the age of 15. (A Parish Revolt)

It was only a two-minute conversation between two 15-year-olds, but it may have been the last one that Frankie Hanson ever had with anyone (Still Missing)

I got dumped by my first girlfriend in fourth grade, the first but not the last time I was shown the door (Early and Late Dating)

I learned that not all adults in this world are good people—and that mothers are always there to protect us. (The Bad Seed)

I might be delivering books instead of writing them if not for the kindness of a friend at Providence College (A Guy Named Joe)

I lost two good friends in the Korean War, while the invading Chinese Army trapped a brother and close friend. (Korea)

I was in Manhattan for a meeting when somebody brought up an illegal escort service called Cachet. The lady in charge once worked for me. (The Mayflower Madam)

Every town needs a person like Margaret Coffee, who was always there for the sick and needy (She had a Love Affair with Humanity)

Gary Lutender was the closest version of a son that I ever had. (A Connecticut Knight of the Roundtable) Two young men by the names of Matthew and Clifford Satell are honorary grandchildren, and no grandfather could be prouder of them.

Regret the illnesses that created more pain than he ever let us know. Regret the fact that he was taken from us much too soon. But have no other regrets about the life of Paul Arthur Dooley. (My Brother Paul)

When the United States Air Force changed its contract with me, I thought I could resign. A major explained that I would not be going anywhere for the next four years. (Early Air Force)

The only romance in my mother's life was my father, Leo P. Dooley, who died at 51 when my mother was 47. (The Men in My Mother's Life) A mother's job is to provide the support, motivation, discipline, empathy, and love her children need. According to my mother, Marion Veronica Kenneally Dooley, she should not receive any special recognition for simply doing her job. (Mother's Day)

It was a night the six Dooley boys would never forget—August 15,

1971, the opening of Schaefer Stadium in Foxborough, Massachusetts, the new home of the New England Patriots. (Nightmare on Rt. 1)

Those old radio shows bring back so many memories of my family gathering around the radio to listen to Jack Benny, Bob Hope, or Bing Crosby. (Old Time Radio)

I used to play hockey and baseball with Brad Boss, President of Cross Pen & Pencil. (A Rhode Island Treasure)

Rhode Island has made its share of mistakes in electing or appointing people to high office. The best example of selecting the right person for the right job was naming Dr. Patrick T. Conley as the first-ever Historian Laureate in 2012. (Historian Laureate of Rhode Island)

It took me many years to appreciate my great fortune in joining the Dooley family on October 22, 1931. (Joining the Family)

Tim Cohane and Holy Cross basketball—the famous panty raid. (Like Father, Like Son)

My favorite news program of all time is *60 Minutes*, especially in its early years. (Meeting Morley Safer)

I grew up in three neighborhoods: 15 Hayward Street in the Auburn section of Cranston, 92 Massasoit Avenue in Edgewood, and Buttonwoods, a summer colony located on Narragansett Bay in Warwick. (The Neighborhoods)

Dr. Patrick T. Conley describes his wife Gail as his "navigator" in his book *A Historical Cruise Through the Ocean State*. I cannot entirely agree with his assessment. (Madame Advisory Council

It was just a breakfast club, meeting once a week, but it became so much more. (The Breakfast Club)

Every Tuesday night for about 15 years, the tennis group met at the Old Saybrook Racquet Club to play doubles. The group consisted of Bob Klimek, Carl Luntender, Bill Hostnik, and Earl Greenho. (The Tennis Group)

Shortly after joining a B-17 Bomber Squadron with the Eighth Air Force in England in 1944, Bernie Schwarz and three other Jewish pilots were invited to a meeting with an intelligence officer. (My Name is Bernie Schwarz)

I had no idea that Ambassador Middendorf lived in Little Compton, Rhode Island, until Pat Conley, President of the Rhode Island

Heritage Hall of Fame, suggested I nominate him for entry into the RIHHOF. (The Renaissance Man: J. William Middendorf)

Agnes Rooney spoiled mother-in-law jokes for me forever. She was one of the kindest, most thoughtful people I have ever known. (A Woman Named Agnes)

Dick Bruno and I attended the world premiere of "The Goodbye Girl" in Manhattan in 1977. (Neil Simon and Richard Dreyfuss)

I was honored when Susan Hostnik asked me to deliver the eulogy for her husband and my close friend and tennis partner, Bill Hostnik. (A Celebration of the Life of Dr. William J. Hostnik, "Dr. Bill."

Over the years, I have received many complimentary letters referring to books, plays, or articles that I have written. Only one is framed and sitting on my dresser. (The Greatest Sportscaster of All Time)

As Editorial Director for a division of Prentice-Hall. I had two rules: don't hire journalism majors and avoid job jumpers. (Breaking the Rules)

I used to walk around at cocktail parties with soda water and a twist of lemon, hoping it would give me cover and make me feel like one of the crowd. (The Wrong Drink)

I had long been an admirer of Andy Rooney for both his books and his role in "A Few Minutes with Andy Rooney" on *60 Minutes*. (Shootout in Philadelphia)

I knew quite a bit about the doctor who was going to operate on me for colon cancer before our first meeting. Dr. Victor Pricolo was described to me as one of the best surgeons in New England. What I did not know was that he had done some research on me as well. (Brotherly Love)

Richard Prentice Ettinger was the co-founder and chairman of Prentice-Hall when I joined the company as an editor in 1960. (Mr. Chairman)

In 1975, I was approached by a friend who had recently gone to work for Harcourt, Brace & Jovanovich in Manhattan. There was an opening for an editorial vice president, and he felt I had all the qualifications for the job. (Duluth, Minnesota).

William Vareika's Fine Arts gallery in Newport, Rhode Island, has grown into one of the largest and most respected galleries in the country. (Art Connoisseur, Philanthropist, and all-around Good Guy)

John Joseph appeared in about 70 of the documentary films I wrote and directed in the 1970s. He also played Fagin in Oliver and King Arthur in Camelot, two plays I produced with Dick Bruno at the Ivoryton Playhouse in Essex, Connecticut. (My Favorite Actor)

The movie *When Harry Met Sally* made a lasting impression on me. Harry (Billy Crystal) and Sally (Meg Ryan) meet when she gives him a ride to New York after they graduate from the University of Chicago. (Female Friends)

It began in 1972, shortly after Charles Toussaint sued Blue Cross of Michigan for wrongful discharge. It resulted in a personal experience for me. (Fire Me and I'll Sue)

When I went to work for Pieter Van Bennekom in Malvern, Pennsylvania, my first thought was that he could fire me in five languages and until he got to English, I wouldn't even know. (Meeting the Flying Dutchman)

I never met Frank Sinatra or Mia Farrow, so I was not surprised that I did not receive a wedding invitation when they married in 1966. (Honeymooning With Frank and Mia)

"Ken, we have a serious situation here. Invoices in the amount of over $400,000 have been paid to this company over the last few years. There is no telephone listing for that company. Get over to Groton and check it out." (Fraud and Theft)

In my early career as a freelance writer, I was paid by the word, an arrangement that motivated me to add as much extraneous language as possible. When I was writing for the detective story genre, victims never died quickly, even from a gunshot wound to the head. They lingered for four or five paragraphs as the word count mounted. (My Career as a Freelance Writer)

In 1998 I went to work as Senior Editor for Progressive Business Publications in Malvern, Pennsylvania. Ed Satell, the founder and CEO, called me into his office a few months later. He had an idea for a new publication that he thought I should write. It was to be a 24-page booklet filled with stories and quotes—nothing religious, political, or off-color. (Good Stuff)

My daughter Alicia chose a sleepover to celebrate her fifth birthday. So I spent the weekend with 10 of her classmates from the Old Lyme public school. (The Sleepover)

I was in the third grade at Eden Park Grammar School when the Hurricane of 1938 devastated Rhode Island on September 1, 1938. I was still in the United States Air Force, stationed at Kelly Field in San Antonio, Texas, when Hurricane Carol hit Rhode Island on August 31, 1954. (A Tale of Two Hurricanes)

In 1991, I moved to Bristol, Rhode Island, and through my friends, Herb Browne and Tom Breslin, I was introduced to Halsey Herreshoff, grandson of Nathanael Herreshoff, builder of six America Cup Defenders. (The America's Cup Hall of Fame.)

Owen was my first friend who owned a car. We met at La Salle Academy as sophomores and developed a friendship that lasted more than 50 years. He was from Fall River, Massachusetts, and drove to La Salle every day from the age of 16. (A Man Named Owen)

When I was living in Sarasota, Florida, we had a post office right on site. There were two handicap spots out front. One morning as I exited the post office, a black Cadillac drove up and parked horizontally, taking up both handicap spots. (Hyphenation)

When I reflect on my mother now, I don't know of any individual who believed in the American system more than she did. She sent six sons off to serve during wars (at least five of them in harm's way) because her country needed them. It was the right thing to do to protect our freedom and our American way of life. (Jury Duty)

In 1980, I became a member of the Board of Directors of the Ivoryton Playhouse, the second oldest summer stock theatre in the country. It was best known as the theater in which Katharine Hepburn made her stage debut. (My Brief Friendship with Katharine Hepburn)

After finishing my Air Force career in May of 1955, I returned to Rhode Island in a Ford convertible and a few thousand dollars in my pocket, resulting from weekly poker games with my service buddies. I planned to have a lovely summer before returning to Providence College in September. Unfortunately, my brother Bob had other ideas. (Lifeguarding)

There were four poodles in the litter, and three of them ignored us completely. The fourth, a little white ball of fire, would not leave us alone. When we left about 30 minutes later, Lilly, named because she resembled a lily pad, sat in the back seat in Sarah's arms. (The Song of Love)

"I really like my P-51. It's my idea of a fighter—it's lighter and plenty fast but tricky on landing," he wrote to Mary. However, he assured her that the combat assignments were not much to worry about. "It's nearly all ground support, which is interesting but not dangerous." It was the last letter Mary received from her husband, George Morgan (Love Story in the Middle of a War)

The theater was packed for opening night, and I felt we got off to a good start. I had a line in scene 3: "Mr. DePina, we have to go into the cellar and make the fireworks." As I moved stage right to the door, it wouldn't open. A beam had fallen, and the door was blocked. After trying to open it for several seconds, I turned to Mr. DePina and said: "Mr DePina, you have locked us out of the cellar again." (My Last Stage Appearance)

"Beginning on April 24, 1915, with the arrest of Armenian intellectuals and community leaders in Constantinople by Ottoman authorities, one and a half million Armenians were deported, massacred, or marched to their deaths in a campaign of extermination." (My Armenian Friends)

I had always been able to relate to kids much better than to their parents. Some of my most enjoyable moments occurred when I directed children in a musical or coached a girls' softball team. (Mentoring)

On May 24, 1984, a man walked up to his estranged wife in a divorce court, pulled a gun from his jacket, shot her six times, and muttered, "Now I can sleep at night." (Murder in the Courtroom)

Immediately after the Boston Celtics drafted the first African American player in 1950, a special meeting was called in Philadelphia. (NBA Owners and the "White Dollar" Quota System)

The first president I ever saw in person was Harry S Truman, who made a whistle-stop by train in Providence, Rhode Island, during his election campaign in 1948. I can still remember standing with my sister Peg as Truman waved to us—and about 5,000 other people—from the caboose. (Presidents and Elections)

During the past 64 years, I have cast votes for candidates rang members. Some of my selections turned out to be success stories, while others became disasters. In reflecting on my voting record, my wisest choice was John McCauley, who ran for President of the senior class at La Salle Academy in 1949. (A Man Called John McCauley)

Dick Bruno and I sold out every seat at the Ivoryton Playhouse and still lost thousands of dollars. (Oliver)

I knew a lot about George Plimpton before directing him in a film in 1990. He was famous for competing in professional sporting events and then recording the experience from the point of view of an amateur. (Journalist, writer, actor, and amateur sportsman)

I don't think Sammy Cahn and Julie Styne realized it when they wrote "Poor Little Rhode Island," but their song sums up a statewide inferiority complex that began during Revolutionary times and continues today. (Poor Little Rhode Island)

It was 1984, and I had rented a home on Martha's Vineyard for the summer. I rented a small rubber raft with a 1.5-hp outboard engine. It was ideal for boating in the outlet, but we ran into difficulty around when trying to use the boat to get to a nearby beach that was on the ocean. (Ocean Rescue)

My friends and I took great pride in our acceptance of African Americans in our culture, reacting in horror when the Ku Klux Klan stories made the headlines in *The Providence Journal*. The truth was that we had no African American friends growing up in Rhode Island. (Race Relations)

A college classmate approached me in 1958 about a job opening in a restaurant where he worked as a busboy. It was an upscale place called "Fore & Aft," located in Bristol, Rhode Island. My friend said the work was easy, and the money was good. (One-Night Stand)

I told my first little white lie when I was in third grade, and it started a habit that has stayed with me for more than 80 years. (Little White Lies)

I met Wes Forcier in 1945, shortly after my family moved to Edgewood. We remained best friends for more than 70 years. Wes was a voracious reader and listener, and there were few subjects in which he did not have in-depth knowledge. With the mind of an investigative reporter, it was said that Wes would learn everything about a new acquaintance, including birth weight, within five minutes of an introduction. Meanwhile, new acquaintances would be fortunate if they escaped with anything more than a name. (My Second Family)

In December of 1954, I took a part-time job with the local Sears & Roebuck in San Antonio. I might have flourished if I had been assigned to men's clothing or even the furniture department. But I was sent to the hardware department, even though I did not know the difference between a Phillips head and a standard screwdriver. (Creativity Beats Experience)

The philanthropic saga of the Hassenfeld family is inseparable from the story of their company, Hasbro Corporation. Begun in 1923 as a cotton waste material recycling operation in Central Falls, Rhode Island, it has grown into both a massive presence and a moral and ethical beacon in the global toy industry. (A Family of Philanthropists)

I never met Patrick B. McGinnis, the late President of the New Haven and Hartford Railroad, but I certainly knew his voice. When I got out of the Air Force in 1955, my uncle, Leo Kenneally, was the Director of Public Relations for the New Haven Railroad. He was credited with helping McGinnis gain control of the railroad in 1954, after a bitter proxy fight with former President Frederick C. Domain, Jr. (A Modern Railroad Robber Baron)

In the summer of 1996, I met with Hyman Golden, Arnold Greenberg, and Leonard Marsh, the founders of Snapple, to discuss a book. (The Snapple Boys).

I went to a local bar in Manhattan to watch the New England Patriots.

A loud conversation was going on, led by a character who could have played the role of Cliff Clavin on Cheers. Cliff was the resident barfly and know-it-all. John Ratzenberger, who played Cliff expertly, was only filling a role. The character I was listening to was for real, chastising his friends for not knowing the answers to his often-obscure questions on football, baseball, boxing, basketball, and hockey. Finally, he threw out a question that caught my attention. "Who was the first African American to play in the NBA?" he asked, after warning everyone to stay off their cell phones. No one came up with the answer, so he blurted out: "Chuck Cooper of the Boston Celtics."

I called out, "You're wrong." (The Bet)

I had never heard of Tom Sullivan, a blind entertainer who sang the National Anthem before Super Bowl X. Tom delivered our National

Anthem with more feeling and enthusiasm than I have heard before or since. Four years later, I met Tom Sullivan in person. (If You Could See What I Can Hear)

Although he never owned the property, people still refer to it as "Tommy Brent's Theatre-by-the-Sea." I think that title has a nice ring to it. (Tommy Brent: Theater-by-the-Sea)

I met Red Auerbach in September of 1981 when I directed him in a film entitled *Dedication and Desire, The Story of Red Auerbach.* When he finally got the team he needed, he did a lot of winning. Eleven NBA Championships in 13 years is a record that will never be broken. Red left a much more important legacy. In 1950, his first year as head coach of the Boston Celtics, he drafted Chuck Cooper, the first African American player to join the NBA. In 1998, I met another man who had a lot of the qualities of Red Auerbach. Ed Satell's game is publishing, not basketball. But his philosophy is similar to Red's. (Red Auerbach and Ed Satell)

In 1960, I was hired as an editor for Prentice-Hall, a publishing giant based in Englewood Cliffs, New Jersey. I met Seymour Katz, another editor, for the first time. I have no idea why a Jewish kid from New London and an Irishman from Rhode Island bonded quickly, but we immediately became good friends. (Meeting Sam Katz)

On the surface, it would appear that two prominent Rhode Island residents, Alan Hassenfeld of Bristol and David Maloof of Middletown, should be on opposite sides of the Israeli-Palestine debate. Hassenfeld, retired chairman of Hasbro, is Jewish, while David Maloof is a Christian Arab-American. Yet the two men have a great deal in common, especially in their efforts for a peaceful solution to a 57-year old conflict. (Two Rhode Islanders for Peace)

To be 90 years old in the United States is to have lived through more than one-third of its life. It has special significance for me since most of the nuns of my childhood predicted I would be executed by the age of 21. I am now a member of the fastest-growing age group in this country, 85 years or older. (What I Have Learned in My 90 Years)

The other stories range from people like Red Auerbach, voted by the press as the greatest NBA coach of all time, to Lee Iacocca, Chairman of Chrysler, to Fred Lewis, owner of the Parkway Tavern in Warwick, Rhode Island. I interviewed Earl Lloyd, the first African

American to play in the National Basketball Association, shortly before he died in 2016. Earl's stories about his amazing mother Daisy are fascinating. (Earl Lloyd) Bob Cousy explained his relationship with Chuck Cooper, the first African American drafted into the NBA in 1950.

After interviewing K. C. Jones, Sam Jones, and Bill Russell, we wrote "From White to Black," a screenplay based on the first African American basketball players. It was a journey that began with the Harlem Rens and the Harlem Globetrotters in the 1930s and culminated with African American players being acknowledged as the best.

I helped carry two little girls onto a Avianica Airline in Lajes, Azores in 1954. A few minutes later I stood and watched the plane burn after striking a mountain on takeoff. All 30 passengers and crew were killed. (The Wrong Turn)

When my friend Carl Lutender, owner of the Hideaway restaurant in Old Lyme, Connecticut, lost his entertainer for New Year's Eve, I pinch-hit. (My Role as a Stand-Up Comic)

In 2010, I wrote a play, *The Murder Trial of John Gordon*, based primarily on information I received from Dr. Patrick T. Conley and Dr. Scott Molloy, two of the greatest historians in the country. During the play, I met Newport State Representative Peter Martin, who introduced the bill that led Governor Lincoln Chafee to issue a pardon for a man who was executed in 1845. (John Gordon)

While researching a book about Bob Thorpe, a P-47 pilot, and brother of my close friend Gill Thorpe, I interviewed members of the 39th Fighter Squadron, which fought in New Guinea in WWII. Bob had been captured by the Japanese, tortured, used for target practice, and beheaded. For more than 60 years, our government listed Bob Thorpe as "missing in action" and sealed the records of the trial of the Japanese officers who had tortured and executed him. (Bob Thorpe)

I was also able to interview people like Lew Lockhart and Fred Tobi, who flew with Bob on that fateful mission. Lockhart and Tobi broke regulations and went in search of Thorpe with zero visibility at takeoff. Chuck Sullivan, another 39th Squadron member, told me an incredible story about being captured by headhunters after bailing out over the dense New Guinea jungle. (Faith, Determination, and a Bit of Irish Luck)

Jack Frost explained how former isolationist Charles Lindbergh taught 39th pilots to almost double the range of their P-47s. (See Lucky Lindy and the 39th). It was Jack Frost who stole the lumber intended for General Douglas MacArthur's headquarters in the Philippines to build a mess hall and recreation area for noncommissioned officers. (The Purloined Lumber)

I never met Captain John D. Steed, a member of the Australian Board of Inquiry investigating war crimes after the Japanese surrender, but I certainly appreciate his work. It was Steed who broke the cover-up of Japanese officers claiming that Bob Thorpe died of malaria. (The Cover-up).

Not all the characters I met or wrote about were admirable. Abe Saperstein kept African American players out of the National Basketball Association for years. Eddie Gottlieb, the owner of the Philadelphia Warriors, came up with the quota system that limited African American players to one or two for each team. Both men were inducted into the NBA Hall of Fame.

A con man sold my mother bogus subscriptions to her Catholic publications. She refused to give me his description because he was a family man, and she did not want to get him in trouble. A high school friend went to jail for receiving bribes while working for the City of Fall River. (Owen). A friend and co-worker embezzled $400,000 from my company through a series of forgeries. (Fraud & Theft) Another high school friend, Ray Lyons, became a ranking member of the Raymond Patriarca crime family (A Tale of Two Raymonds)

I was one of the few people who knew the real story about Bill Dillon, who served a year in prison for "insider trading." Bill was guilty, but a government cover-up prevented the whole story from being told. (Insider Trading)

My experiences with *60 Minutes* legend Morley Safer still fills me with guilt. Morley was one of the great ones, and I wish I had kept my mouth shut about his smoking. (Morley Safer) I would not change one thing about my confrontation with Frank Sinatra at the Griswold Inn in Essex, Connecticut. He was honeymooning with Mia Farrow and demanded that all diners leave the dining room for his wedding party. I left only after being ordered out by my friend, Bill Winterer, restaurant owner. Despite frequent calls and apologies from Bill, I stayed away for three years. So, I guess you can say I did it my way. (Frank & Mia)

Bill Russell was recently acknowledged as the greatest athlete in the history of Boston sports. Sam Jones has 10 NBA Championship rings, second only to Russell's 11. I was cut in the second practice of my high school team. I made it that far because the head coach was sick and missed the first practice. Yet the three of us combined to write the screenplay "From White to Black: the Painful journey of African American Players into the NBA." (Three Members of the National Basketball Hall of Fame and a 5′7″ who couldn't make his high school team)

I helped found the Girls' Softball League in Old Lyme, Connecticut, in 1980. The Old Lyme Youth Service Bureau was not overly receptive to the idea. The boys played Little League in a wonderful stadium complete with state-of-the art uniforms. We were given no uniforms and a field that lost second base when the tide came in. So, I wrote a musical, "Darn Yankees," and the whole town became involved in the production. Mothers danced and sang with their children to tunes such as "When You Know the Way to Swing" and "I've Grown Accustomed to their Braces." The musical was a huge hit, and the Girls' Softball League gained credibility. (Writing a Musical)

Some members of the Old Lyme Students Against Drunk Driving approached me about doing a movie in 1981. I was given a script that included crashing planes, helicopters, and a lot of very expensive special effects. I simplified the script, and we produced "I Can Walk, I Can Talk, I Can Drive, I Can Die," another scenario in the book. The film was shown in many schools throughout the country with very positive results.

In 1998, I took an editorial job with Progressive Business Publications in Malvern Pennsylvania. Actually, I got a whole family. (Meeting the Satells)

My daughter Alicia and my granddaughter Sarah are the reason why I still get up at 6:30 a.m. and write for seven or eight hours every day. They are my inspiration, and words cannot describe my love for them.

My brother Jack and cousins Tom and Ed Dooley were all members of a football team that joined the United States Marine Corps three days after December 7, 1941. (Swan Song)

It's surprising how many of my memories are built around things I barely noticed at the time. Some of them may make you laugh. Others may move you. Hopefully, they will keep you turning the pages on a very forgettable guy who met a lot of fascinating people on his journey and, in 2018, was fortuitously inducted into the Rhode Island Heritage Hall of Fame.

Acknowledgements

For Gail Conley, who came up with the idea for this book and Pat Conley, who gave me the title. For the two lights of my life, my daughter Alicia and my granddaughter, Sarah; Josh Peacock, Sarah's husband and Trace Kicklighter, Alicia's finance; my father, Leo P. Dooley, and my mother, Marion; my sisters, Eileen and Peg; my brothers, Jack, Bill, Bob, Larry and Paul; John and Linda Travers, Leo P. Kenneally, Ann Kenneally, Jane Kenneally, Margaret Kenneally, Bill and Joan Kenneally; my wonderful copy editor and friend, Margaret Stay, and her husband, Doug; my adopted grandsons, Matthew and Clifford Satell; my nieces, Kathy, Ann, Candy, Patti, Colleen and Marnie; my nephews, Scott, Jeff and Michael Dooley and Mike Ashley; Peter Martin; Regina and Bill Lennox, Pieter Van Bennekom, Curt Brown, Jen Erb, Michelle McGovern, Kerry Isberg; Wayne Muller, Dick Bruno, Red Auerbach and his daughters, Nancy and Randy; K. C. Jones, Sam Jones, Bill Russell, Bob Cousy; Bill Middendorf, Philip and Andrew Bilden, Tim Cohane, Rick Wolff, Wes and Loring Forcier, Herb and Chris Browne, Brad Boss, Gill Thorpe, Jack Swan, Jack Manning, Al Curtin, Howard, Ed, Bill and Ray McGinnis, John Dinneen, Ted Barrows; Arlene Violet, Pamela and Jeff Gill; Piyush and Vivek Patel; Scott Molloy, Russ DeSimone, Al Beauparlant; Susan Hostnik, Lois Lutender, Carol Klimek, Elaine McGirr; Dave and Barbara Preston; Avery Manco, Peter Martin, Vince Arnold, Mike Slein, Angela Vars, Vin and Peg Murray, Tony and Gloria Cercena, Francoise Pomfret, Lorraine McBride; Kevin O'Neil and all my friends whose stories are told on these pages.

What I have learned in my 90 years

To be 90 years old in the United States is to have lived through more than one-third of its life. It has special significance for me since most of the nuns of my childhood predicted I would be executed by the age of 21. I am now a member of the fastest-growing age group in this country, 85 years or older.

"There is no cure for birth and death, save to enjoy the interval," George Santayana said. "Age imprints more wrinkles in the mind than it does on the face," Montaigne wrote. My favorite age-related quote comes from Damon Runyon: "All of life is 6 to 5 against."

Like Frank Sinatra sings in his opening verse of "I Did It My Way," I've lived a life that's full. I consider the rest of the song arrogant and selfish. "Regrets I've had a few but then again too few to mention," Sinatra tells us in a later verse. Like Frank, I have had regrets, but I cannot dismiss them as easily as he does. I have had a failed marriage, the loss of a beloved daughter, the early death of my father, saying goodbye to four brothers and two sisters, the loss of most of my dearest friends, and the awful feelings associated with letting your friends and family down.

I walked away from the first girl I ever loved because of ambition and religion. I did the same thing about 30 years later, passing up a chance to grow old with a woman I truly loved. Not once did I get any consolation from the fact that I did it my way. On the contrary, it only exacerbates my guilt feelings.

When I was born on October 22, 1931, there were 48 states, the population in the United States was approximately 123,000,000, life expectancy for males was 63 years, and Mercurochrome was the miracle drug. Penicillin was about eight years away, and the Salk polio vaccine did not become available until 1955. I remember how infantile paralysis (polio) struck every summer of my youth. Between double features at the Park Theater, lights would come on as ushers walked up and down the aisle collecting money for "The March of Dimes," the nonprofit established to fight polio. The disease crippled more than it killed. Newsreels showed children in huge metal cylinders called iron lungs. No one knew how the virus passed from victim to victim. Water was considered a possible suspect, so beaches and pools were placed off-limits to many children. The Dooley family continued to summer at Buttonwoods because my father felt salt water would kill the virus. I do not remember one person in that beach community coming down with polio.

In the 1930s, measles killed or impaired thousands of children. Most of my family and friends contracted measles before reaching 15 years of age. About 400 to 500 deaths were reported each year nationally, and thousands more suffered from encephalitis, a swelling of the brain caused by the virus. I can still remember "quarantine" notices placed on the front doors of families suffering from measles. In 1963, an effective vaccine was developed for measles. In 2,000, the CDC declared measles as eliminated in the United States. But in 2019, almost 1,300 cases of measles were confirmed in 31 states. All of the cases came from people who did not receive the measles vaccine.

Whooping cough was another severe disease of my childhood. It would begin as a regular cold then develop into a severe and life-threatening illness, especially for babies. An effective vaccine is available to prevent the disease, but new cases are reported every year for the same reason—failure to vaccinate.

Now we have the same problem with COVID-19, the worst pandemic this country has ever faced. At least three effective vaccines have been developed to wipe it out. Yet, we fail to gain critical herd immunity because so many refuse to roll up their sleeves to get the vaccine. Some states now offer lotteries rewarding people for showing up to possibly save their own lives. I am appalled that health care professionals in Texas are suing their hospitals for requiring them to accept one of the vaccines before returning to work. I am pleased that all of the colleges in Rhode Island require vaccinations for students before allowing them to return to campus.

I'm sometimes bewildered when members of the present generation talk about the quieter, gentler times of the 1930s, often referring to us as the "Silent Generation." Indeed, we did not have TV, cell phones, Internet, ATMs, credit cards, HBO, or Netflix. But we grew up in the most significant recession this country has ever known. We came out of it because of a war that killed more than 73,000,000 people, including 6,000,000 Jewish men, women, and children. After WWII ended, we lived under the threat of a nuclear exchange with the Soviet Union. Then, in 1950, we became involved in a "police action" in Korea. More than 50,000 young Americans died before a cease-fire in 1953. Tell my friends, Ed McGinnis and Donald White, both killed in action in Korea, or Bobby Vickers, who returned with a 100% disability because of a Chinese shell, that this was a "Silent Generation."

I completely agree with Tom Brokaw, who came up with "The Greatest Generation" to refer to those born in the 1920s. Many of them fought in WWII or worked in industries that contributed to winning the war. My brothers Jack and Bill fought in Europe and the Pacific while my sisters Eileen and Peg traded in typewrites for welding torches and made pontoons used during invasions in Europe and the Pacific.

"The Lost Generation" was named by writer Gertrude Stein, and it refers to the post-World War I generation. "Lost" is supposed to refer to the disoriented, directionless spirit of many of the war's survivors in the early postwar period. It applies more to the generation of writers, artists, musicians, and intellectuals than the general public. Ernest Hemingway made it famous in his novel *The Sun Also Rises.*

Our "Silent Generation" was followed by the "Baby Boomers," the people born from 1945 to 1964. This generation witnessed the civil rights movement, women's empowerment, and the moon landing. I have no idea whether the other generations were named aptly—Generation X, Millennial, and Generation Z. I am impressed that Generation Z has never known a world without the Internet. They are expected to become the most educated generation in the world with the highest student debt. As a father and a grandfather, I am firmly behind the "Me Too" movement of this generation. For too many years, male predators demanded sexual favors in return for job security or advancement. I rejoice with every lost job or prison sentence.

I had friendships with African Americans such as Earl Lloyd, the first American to play in the National Basketball Association, and KC and Sam Jones and Bill Russell, three members of the National Basketball Hall of Fame. I remember the anguish of K. C. Jones when he told me about a cross being burned on his lawn, or Sam Jones describing how he was 21 before he ever sat in the same room with a white person. So I did not need the Black Lives Matter Movement to alert me to the terrible sufferings African Americans have received in this country. I also understand why taking down statues or renaming schools of known racists is a step in the right direction.

Tom Yawkey was the owner of the Boston Red Sox for many years. He was a philanthropist and helped establish the Jimmy Fund, an organization battling childhood cancer. Yawkey Way, a street named in his honor, was recently renamed because of Yawkey's racist past. The Red Sox were the last team to integrate, and Jackie Robinson was denied a contract after a workout. Yes, Yawkey did a lot of good things, but nothing could make up for his racism.

I cannot entirely agree with all of these renaming efforts. George Washington is a perfect example. There is no question that he was a slave owner. Does that mean we should take down the Washington Monument or change the name of our capital? Washington should be judged by the contributions he made during his lifetime, not only for his slaveholding. He was the only substantial slaveholder among the Founders to free his slaves voluntarily. We cannot allow our history to be destroyed by applying modern standards to people who lived hundreds of years ago.

Meanwhile, I still can get lost in a closet, misplace my car keys and forget where I park my car. All of these are considered early signs of dementia. But as my daughter Alicia points out, my terrible sense of direction and absent-mindedness has plagued me all of my life. Age has brought on physical ailments, but I seem to have mentally what I always had, which may not be much.

I get up at 6 a.m. and write for six or seven hours every day. Writer's block is conquered by the variety of the subjects I write about. Yes, I do end sentences with prepositions. When a proofreader reminded Winston Churchill that he was ending a sentence with a preposition, he replied: "This is one of those rules of English grammar up with which I will not put." If I run into a block while writing a business story, I switch to one of the screenplays I always have in the pipeline or a stage play or maybe a letter to the editor for a local paper.

I have written for newspapers, books, pulp magazines, stage, screen, and radio. My favorite story is always the one I am currently writing. My play, *The Murder Trial of John Gordon*, led to an official pardon for a man executed in 1845. I will never forget the compliments I received from Nancy Collins, Red Auerbach's daughter, or Celtic greats such as K. C. Jones, Tom Heinsohn, John Havlicek, and Bob Cousy when they attended my play, "The Auerbach Dynasty." I am now writing a television series, "White to Black," with Bill Russell and Sam Jones, telling the long and challenging journey of African American players in the early days of the National Basketball Association.

I was finally able to bring closure to my friend Gill Thorpe who spent more than 60 years trying to learn the truth about the death of his brother, Bob Thorpe, who was captured by the Japanese in 1944, tortured, and beheaded. The Thorpe family was lied to by both the Japanese and our own government about what happened to their brother and son. I was able to tell the story after getting 1,200 pages of court-martial records from 1948 in my book *Relentless Pursuit.* Researching this book led me to some incredible members of the 39th Fighter Squadron, Bob Thorpe's squadron based in New Guinea.

Probably my greatest challenge was writing a book with former Secretary of the Navy J. William Middendorf entitled: *The Great Nightfall: How We Win the New Cold War.* I learned about weapon systems, cyber warfare, artificial intelligence, and situations that may spark WWIII accidentally. It is a lot more enjoyable to write a television series with Arlene Violet, the former attorney general of Rhode Island, telling the story of Newport from 1905 to 1980.

William Faulkner once accused Ernest Hemingway of never using a word that might cause the reader to check with a dictionary to see if it was used properly. Hemingway replied that the simpler the words and the fewer, the better his readers understood them. I agree with Hemingway. I have always felt that the job of a writer is to tell entertaining stories. I do not feel I have the intelligence to educate anyone.

I share the last part of my life journey with my beloved daughter, Alicia, my granddaughter Sarah, and their spouses, Trace and Josh; with my brother Bob and nephews Scott Dooley, Jeff Dooley, Michael Dooley, Jeff Malone, Don Malone, Mike Ashley, and my nieces, Colleen Crawley, Marnie Dooley, Patti Concannon, Kathy Ashley, and Ann Brown, and my cousins, Bill and Joan Kenneally.

I have the pleasure of interacting with people like Margaret and Doug Force, my adopted grandsons, Matthew and Clifford, Ed Satell,

Pat and Gail Conley, Arlene Violet, Heather Bennett, Herb and Chris Browne, Scott Molloy, Russ DeSimone, Bill Middendorf, Dick Bruno, Peter Martin, Wayne Muller, Rick Wolff, Pieter and Christine Van Bennekom, Angela Vars, Peg Murray, Tony and Gloria Cercena, Lorraine McBride, Peg Murray, Ed Achorn, Al Beauparlant, Brad Boss, John Coffee, Bill and Anne Quirk, Brian McCallum, Jim and Mary Brown, Steve Meyer, Phil Ahr, Curt Brown, Tim Cohane and Bill Vareika. My cup runneth over!

Memories of friends like Wes and Loring Forcier, Bill Hostnik, Bob Klimek, Carl and Gary Lutender, Bill Crofton, Bob Plant, Jack Manning, Ray McGinnis, Jerry Roque, Al Curtin, Peter Sheridan, Peter Bowen, Paul Flaherty, Jerry Roque, Jack Swan, Bill Dowling, Gill Thorpe, Stu Hobron, Ruth Nagle, Arthur Halligan, John and David Dinneen, Ed McGinnis, Andy Fitzpatrick, John Demetri, Tom Comeaux, Susan Hostnik, Lois Lutender, Carol Klimek, Elaine McGirr, Biffer and Pat Kelley, Ralph and Helen McGonigle, and Lee Rixon will remain with me forever.

"Our worst fear isn't the end of life but the end of memories." That quote from Tom Rackman has special meaning for me. I have so many great memories of the people I have met these past 90 years. I share many of them with you in the following pages.

The Prettiest Girl on Bailey's Beach

My sister Eileen had the summer off when she was attending the Edgewood Secretarial School in 1939. I heard my mother tell my father that Eileen had taken a summer job as a parlor maid for Mrs. Rosalie Dolan at her Newport mansion, "Seaweed," just across from Bailey's Beach. "I don't think that's a good job for Eileen," my father said. He was right.

Eileen got off to a great start and became very friendly with Mrs. Dolan's daughter, Rose. One of the few fringe benefits of the job for the servants was the use of Bailey's Beach, a private area reserved for Newport Society. One afternoon when Eileen was swimming at the beach, a photographer for *The Providence Journal* approached and asked for permission to take her photo. Eileen was 18, dressed in a white bathing suit, and more than willing to pose for the picture.

That Sunday, the photo was published in the "Brown" section of *The Sunday Providence Journal.* The caption correctly identified her as Eileen Dooley from Cranston, not as a member of any Newport society family. The reaction of Newport society was instantaneous, predictable, and fierce. Why would the *Journal* publish a photograph of a maid instead of one of the young society debutantes swarming around Bailey's Beach? When questioned by the managing editor of *The Providence Journal,* the photographer explained that he was told to take a picture of the prettiest girl on the beach. And that's exactly what he did.

To her credit, Mrs. Dolan supported Eileen, saying that she had every right to swim at the beach. About two months into the job, Mrs. Dolan called Eileen in and told her how much she enjoyed having her in the household. "But you have to stop what you're doing," she warned. When Eileen refused, she was fired. My father was actually proud when she returned home and explained the reason for her termination. Eileen had been trying to unionize the servants, who, at that time, worked six-and-one half days a week for little money.

The most interesting part of the story was the friendship that developed between Eileen and Rose, Mrs. Dolan's daughter. They exchanged letters for more than 70 years, even though Rose had moved to Paris, France, after WWII. I can remember how delighted Eileen was when she received a letter from Rose.

About eight years after Eileen's death in 2003, I decided to write a Newport version of the very successful TV drama *Downton Abbey*. An article appeared in the *Newport Gazette* announcing the film and stating that casting would begin. I got a telephone call from a woman named Arnie Bern who explained that she was an actress interested in trying out for a role in the film. I was about to give her the name of our casting director when she said something that caught my attention. "I grew up on Bellevue Avenue and knew some of the children and grandchildren you may be writing about. She explained that she was the great-great-granddaughter of Mrs. Dolan, the same woman my sister had worked for briefly in 1938. "That's interesting," I said. "You want to be in my movie even though your great-great-grandmother fired my sister." The poor woman was speechless.

When I met Arnie Bern, I liked her very much. If we had made the movie, I am sure she would have had a part. She called me the next week and invited me to dinner at Bailey's Beach so I could meet her mother, Mrs. Dolan's granddaughter, Rosalie Brainard. It was the only time I was ever in the restaurant at Bailey's Beach, and we had a lovely dinner.

Rosalie was named after her great-grandmother and was close to her great Aunt Rose. She remembered Rose discussing Eileen and their long friendship. Rosalie's great-grandfather, Thomas Dolan built "Seaweed" the family's summer home in Newport for 102 years. Rosalie was also related to the Wetmores, who built and lived in "Chateau Sur Mer," now a museum run by the Preservation Society of Newport.

Rosalie told me that she was devoted to horseback riding, showing, and fox hunting. She seemed to enjoy hearing about my sister's relationship with her great-grandmother and great-aunt, Rose. She impressed me as a fiercely independent and adventuresome woman who lived life to its fullest. Less than a month after our dinner at Bailey's Beach, Rosalie died after sustaining injuries in a horseback riding accident n Bridgewater, Connecticut, on Sep. 11, 2014.

The Wallet

When I met John Dinneen in 1944, I was 13, and he was 12. A year difference in those days usually puts the older boy in the driver's seat. It did not work with John, who lived right next door to me. He had the most extraordinary persuasive powers I have ever encountered in another human being. If I suggested an activity, John would never come out with a flat refusal. But he would patiently describe the pros and cons of each possibility, and, almost always, we would follow his plan.

There was one activity that didn't appeal to either of us—scouting. Neither one of us cared for camping out or doing all those little things to earn merit badges. The fact that John's father, Ed Dinneen, was the head of the boy scouts in Edgewood complicated the situation. When parental pressure got too great, John and I joined the Boy Scouts.

We were only members for a few weeks when the telephone company transferred the scoutmaster of our troop. I don't remember much about him, other than his name, Mr. Lodge. We raised $16 for a going away gift, a wallet. As the oldest member of the troop, I was given the money and assigned to pick up the wallet from the Rhode Island Luggage Company.

A few days later, John came up with an impossible idea. Why don't we take the train to Boston and go to Fenway Park for a Red Sox game?

"And where are we going to get the money?" I asked.

"You know my birthday is next Tuesday," John said. "My grandmother always gives me $20 for my birthday. So we'll use the wallet money, then replace it after my birthday. The going-away party isn't until Saturday. So we'll have plenty of time to get the wallet."

I resisted for two days. But when John set a goal, he usually reached it. After telling our families that we were leaving early to play baseball and then take in a movie at the Palace Theater, we took the train for Boston. I had an uneasy feeling as I exchanged the wallet money for two round-trip tickets to Boston. My mood brightened as we sat in the bleachers at Fenway Park. There was no problem, according to John. He would be getting the $20 from his grandmother, and no one would ever know about our temporary embezzlement.

It was my second trip to Fenway Park. In 1939, I went to my first game with my brothers, Jack, Bill, and Bob. Ted Williams, Bobby Doerr, Johnny Pesky, and Dom DiMaggio were all playing. Except for Doerr, those Red Sox greats were all in the service in 1944, as were my brothers, Jack and Bill. The only other players I remember from that day were Joe Cronin, Jim Tabor, and Tex Hughson, the starting pitcher.

Neither the Red Sox nor the Yankees were particularly good that year, with the Yankees finishing third and the Red Sox fourth. The St. Louis Browns won the pennant and later beat the St. Louis Cardinals in the World Series. In 1953, the St. Louis Browns moved to Baltimore and became the Baltimore Orioles.

About halfway through the game, I began to get nervous again as four hot dogs and two drinks cut further into our vanishing bankroll. John sensed my mood and immediately went into the story about how his grandmother had never failed to give him a $20 bill on his birthday for as long as he could remember. And John had a long memory. Why would she fail him now? Feeling positive again, we celebrated with peanuts and ice cream.

We were a little late returning from the movie, but John had come up with a cover story that worked. A few days later, an incident occurred that gave me the same feeling a crooked bank clerk would experience at the arrival of a bank examiner. My mother told me that Mrs. so and so (I don't remember her name) had called and asked why I hadn't picked up the wallet. I made a quick trip to John's house and left with a great alibi. We worked together on a merit badge and planned to pick up the wallet on Wednesday, the day after John's birthday. The party wasn't until Saturday. The message was relayed, and all inquiries stopped. Why was I worried? John was in control.

Tuesday night, the telephone rang, and a trembling voice said, "She gave me a sweater." It was John. His grandmother had visited Ireland the previous month and returned with an Irish sweater. "That was it," I said. "We'd better confess and throw ourselves at the mercy of the court."

With thoughts of his father passing judgment, John came up with another plan. "This hand-made sweater is worth a lot more than $20," he said. "We'll go to the Outlet Company (a Providence Department store) return it and split the profits." The next day we went to the customer service department at the Outlet. A clerk looked at the sweater and said her store didn't carry that brand. "No department store in Rhode Island carries sweaters like that. So, you'll have to go to Ireland to exchange it," she added with a laugh.

"That's it," I said. "No more stories. The party is Saturday, and we've got nothing."

"Let's calm down," John said. "I was in Liggett's (a drug store chain) and saw wallets for 99 cents. I've got a nice box left over from Christmas. We'll put the wallet in it, and no one will know the difference."

John's confidence was so reassuring that I had a bounce in my step when we walked into Liggett's. It disappeared when I saw about ten plastic wallets on a card. The lights filtered right through the one we picked.

"It will look a lot different when we put it in the box," John said. He was so reassuring that we spent our last 50 cents on two coffee milkshakes.

We put the wallet in John's box and tied it with a bright red ribbon. "We don't want anyone else opening the box before Mr. Lodge," John explained.

We had a nice lunch, complete with a cake that Saturday. The hostess signaled me to give the wallet to the guest of honor. He smiled, opened the box, and took out the plastic wallet. As he was saying "nice wallet," the hostess summoned me to the kitchen. "That wallet didn't come from the Rhode Island Luggage Company," she said

I told her what I had done with the money but didn't mention John's role. It was then that I learned another of John's qualities—loyalty. I stood speechless as John took a position beside me. He took full responsibility for coming up with the plan for the Boston trip. Yet somehow he was able to shift the blame for the failure of his plan on his grandmother. If she had come through with her normal present, Mr. Lodge would have his wallet. As a final plea, John offered to give his new sweater to Mr. Lodge.

Phone calls were made, and our families came up with the funds to get the original wallet. A few days later, Mr. Dinneen sent for me to announce our punishment. John and I were both kicked out of the Boy Scouts. Since neither one of us ever completed the work for one merit badge, our exit rank was "Tenderfoot." Mr. Dinneen knew how crushed we would be at the verdict. He did his best, but our crime was too heinous to justify any other verdict. John and I stood solemnly as our judgment was pronounced. Then, when we were alone, the reality of the judgment set in. No more scout meetings. No more discussions about merit badges or excursions into the woods, which we both hated. "Crime can pay under the right circumstances," John said.

John never lost his persuasive qualities. We stayed in touch while I was serving in the U.S.A.F. and John was a student at Brown University. He later attended Georgetown Law School and graduated second in his class. I was a student at Providence College when John got married in 1959. I didn't know it then, but it was one of the last times I would ever see John. He was practicing law in Barnstable on Cape Cod, and I was living and working in Connecticut.

In 1963, the whole Dinneen family was invited to my wedding. I was hurt and shocked when none of them showed up. A few weeks later, I stopped in Edgewood to see my mother. She asked me if I was going to say hello to the Dinneens. "No," I replied. "They had all accepted wedding invitations and never showed up. I was finished with the whole family."

At this point, my mother began to cry. "John is dying of leukemia. He didn't want you to know before the wedding."

I was out the door and made record time getting to Barnstable. His wife, Ann, greeted me at the door. His brothers, David and Donald, were also there. I walked into the bedroom and saw John, a giant of a man at 6′3″ tall, lying in a hospital bed. He smiled and said something that I had to lean over to understand.

"Tell Ann the sweater story," he said. He smiled as I recounted that wonderful day at Fenway Park.

John died the next day at age 28.

I used to feel a sense of sadness when I thought of John Dinneen and how his potential was never realized because of cancer. Then I remember. Over the years, I have met many strong people. None was more persuasive than my childhood friend, whose memories will be with me forever.

My First Job

I had been self-employed as a newspaper delivery boy, a lawn cutter, and a snow-shoveler. Then, at age 13, I got my first job working for a big company as a clerk in the meat department at the local First National grocery store in Pawtuxet, RI.

There was no such thing as a minimum wage in those days, so I was hired at the princely sum of 40 cents per hour. I worked two hours after school Monday through Friday and all-day Saturday. The war was still on, and an essential part of my job was collecting the ration coupons that had to be given with each meat order (red stamps) or grocery order (blue stamps.) Every person had a ration book, even my four-year-old brother Paul.

A man by the name of Bob B. ran the meat department. He spoke in a controlled "yell" and wasn't the most pleasant man I had ever met. One of my first customers asked me the price of the shrimp. I glanced through the glass partition and told him 29 cents per pound. The "1" in front of the 29 was obscured so he got two pounds of shrimp for 58 cents instead of $2.58. After witnessing the transaction, Mr. B. banished me to the backroom to perform a function known as "boning." It involved scraping the last particles of meat off the bones and placing them in a bin holding cheap hamburger.

It got busy in the afternoon, so I was sent back on the firing line. One lady picked out an expansive cut of steak and asked me to grind it, explaining that her husband had difficulty chewing. The grinder was in the back room, so I went there with the steak. Mr. B. followed me and took the steak out of my hand just before I put it in the grinder.

"Listen carefully," he said as he put the steak on a scale. "Weigh the steak carefully, then replace it with an equal amount of this hamburger. Don't return the steak to the cooler until the customer has left the store."

The hamburger he referred to was about half the price of the steak. I did as he instructed and repeated that same process throughout the afternoon. It gave me an uneasy feeling, but Mr. B. was the boss, so I did it.

When I mentioned it to one of the older butchers, he smiled and told me it was time I understood the facts of life. Cheating the customers was not restricted to the meat department. The First National was within walking distance of the Rhode Island Yacht Club. Many boat owners would come to the store to stock up on groceries for the weekend. There would always be a few cans of expensive canned goods sitting on the counter. If the customer didn't notice, they would be charged for the order. If an objection was raised, the clerk would point to the items explaining they were assumed to be part of the order.

That night, my mother asked me how my day had gone. I told her the story about the bargain-priced shrimp. Then I explained the hamburger substitution and the "extra" cans at the checkout counter. My mother sat silently and then told me not to go to work that next Monday.

I wasn't there when the confrontation happened, but I certainly heard about it from my next-door neighbor, Cliff Reading, a clerk at the store. It was Cliff who got me the job in the first place. My mother showed up that Monday morning and left Mr. B. speechless. She told him he should be ashamed of himself for such behavior. She also said her son would not be returning to work again. I'm sure Mr. B. accepted that news with delight, as the other clerks had already warned him about my questions concerning the steak-hamburger switch.

I suspect that Mr. B. had some anxious moments, wondering if my mother would alert First National management about the practices of some of its managers. He had nothing to worry about. My mother's strong sense of right and wrong was only exceeded by her ability to forgive. I'm sure Mr. B. received many of her prayers. I will never know if her prayers worked for him, but they didn't help the First National chain, which went out of existence in 1978.

I do think my mother was responsible for the subsequent national trend of moving meat grinders from the backroom to the front counter where customers have a clear view.

A Love Affair With Movies

My father was a great believer in that old aphorism " An apple a day keeps the doctor away." There was always a bushel of apples on the porch outside our backdoor. After seeing my first movie, "Snow White," his theory was put to the test in 1937. The queen's poisoned apple made such an impression on me that I refused to eat an apple for the next year. But it did not keep me from developing a life-long love of movies.

I was five years old when I saw Errol Flynn as Captain Blood and later as Major Geoffrey Vickers in *The Charge of the Light Brigade.* I remember crying hysterically after Flynn was killed in his role as General George Custer in the final scene of *They Died With Their Boots On.*

In 1939 I saw *The Wizard of Oz* with my brothers Bob and Larry at the Albee Theater in Providence. Seventeen-year-old Judy Garland was on a national tour promoting the film, and she made a brief appearance before it was shown. I can still remember how thrilled we were when she waved to us. My brothers and I got the impression that every time we went to the movies from that time on, the star would make a personal appearance. In the thousands of films, I have seen since that time, I never again saw the star on the stage before the performance.

During the week, the price of admission to the Park Theater was 10 cents. On Sundays, it jumped to 17 cents. Two films were presented, an "A" which featured stars, and a second "B" film with casts of unknowns. In my early days as a critic, I remember liking some of the "B" films more than the "A" films.

The film that made the greatest impact on me was *Gone with the Wind,* in 1940. Many critics objected to the film, claiming it celebrated slavery and perpetuated many stereotypes attributed to African Americans. It had the opposite effect on me. I remember leaving the Park Theatre that day with strong feelings about the evils of slavery. I loved the character of Hattie McDaniel, who received an Oscar for best supporting actor. A Black field hand saved the life of Scarlet O'Hara when a white man attacked her.

One scene made an impression that stayed with me forever. It began with Scarlett and Rhett Butler at the bottom of the staircase, where he begins to kiss her, refusing to be told "no" by the struggling Scarlett. He finally carries her upstairs to the bedroom. But, of course, the scene ends at the bedroom door. The following scene the next day shows Scarlett smiling and content. Many critics objected to this scene, claiming it reinforced a false notion about forced sex, that women secretly enjoy it.

The National Legion of Decency, a United States Catholic organization, rated films according to their estimation of suitability for viewing, assigning their ratings with A (suitable for all audiences), B (adults only), or C (condemned for all audiences) Legion-organized boycotts made a C rating harmful to a film's distribution and profitability. Billy Wilder cut scenes from one of my favorite movies, *The Seven Year Itch*, to avoid the C rating. Elia Kazan cut four minutes from the classic *A Streetcar Named Desire* for the same reason.

Every year at St. Paul's School in Cranston, Rhode Island, students were required to recite an oath pledging their promise to follow the ranking designations of the Legion of Decency. A few years earlier, I had seen *Two-Faced Woman*, Greta Garbo's last film, which The Legion of Decency condemned as immoral and un-Christian. I disagreed with the League's designations and stood silent as my classmates recited the oath.

One young lady whose name I will omit because we later became friends noted my silence and turned me in to Sister Mary Edwards, who sent me to the principal, Mother Dunstan. It was not my first trip to see the principal.

"What did you do now," she demanded.

Instead of giving her a summary, I asked a question. "Which is worse, Mother? To recite an oath that you have no intention of following or to remain silent and keep your integrity?" She agreed with me and sent me back to the classroom without any extra work or detention.

Although I objected to censorship, I never used foul language in any of the screenplays, books, or plays I have written. I remember watching Red Skelton, the famous comedian, respond to a question about the use of foul language by today's comedians. "I can't understand why people pay good money to listen to language they can read on any public restroom wall," Skelton said.

Early and Late Dating

I decided not to write a "tell-all" book about my experiences with the ladies in my life. I am not being particularly noble—there is not that much to tell. Grouch Marx once said that he would never join any country club that would have him. I do not plan to reveal the identities of any ladies who were kind enough to go out with me. This list is not particularly long.

I learned relatively early that I would not be a big hit with the ladies. I was like the second male lead in a Hollywood film—everyone thought I was funny and filled with personality, but I never got the girl. I can still remember in fourth grade when Joan S. told me she liked another boy better. A girl turned me down for my junior prom at La Salle Academy because she "wouldn't be able to wear her heels." I'm 5′7″ and shrinking.

At the age of 16, I developed my first serious crush on a girl. I met her through her mother, a frequent customer of Henry's, a store I worked in during high school. The experience taught me something that I dealt with all of my life—mothers liked me more than their daughters.

I can still remember the first time Barbara P. came into the store with her mother. She was the most beautiful girl I had ever seen.

After much encouragement from her mother, I finally asked Barbara to the movies. No one prepared more for a first date than I did. My brother Jack agreed to loan me his car for the occasion. I washed and waxed it, and it was the first time the inside of that car was ever vacuumed.

I knew that Barbara's father was a stockbroker working in Providence. I read the latest issues of *The Wall Street Journal* and was ready to discuss the *Dow-Jones Index* with him or the latest mergers and acquisitions. Barbara and her mother greeted me at the door and took me into the living room where Mr. P. was sitting. He stood as we shook hands. He studied me carefully and then asked me to step into the kitchen for a minute. I was elated. Mr. P. was about to tell me how impressed he was and would encourage me to become a frequent visitor at his home. I marveled at how perceptive he was to come up with that favorable opinion so quickly.

"You did not finish dressing," he said to me as soon as we were out of earshot of his wife and daughter. I glanced down quickly and saw that my fly was wide open. My initial reaction was to hope that the kitchen floor would suddenly give way so I could escape through the cellar. After I zipped up, we returned to the living room, said our goodbyes, and left.

As soon as we got into the car, Barbara asked me about the discussion with her father. I said something about not staying out too late and was silent for the rest of the trip to the theater. We saw the movie *The Bachelor and the Bobby Soxer*, with Cary Grant and Shirley Temple. Barbara seemed to enjoy the movie while I sat uncomfortably, refusing to do anything that would require me to open the zipper on my pants. Every time I looked at Cary Grant, I saw the face of Mr. P.

The experience did not affect my friendship with Barbara's mother, but I never did ask for a second date. I used to see Mr. P. from time to time, and he was always friendly. In 1955, shortly after I completed a four-year hitch in the Air Force, I was waiting for a friend at a restaurant in Providence. Suddenly a man sitting at a table waved to me. It was Mr. P., sitting with his wife and another couple.

I was introduced and sat with them for a few minutes before my friend arrived. Mrs. P. brought me up to date with Barbara, who was now married with two children.

Suddenly Mr. P. began to laugh hysterically and asked if he could tell the story of our first meeting. We all had a good laugh, especially when Mr. P. explained that he could not allow his daughter to go out the door with a guy with an open fly.

About 30 years later, I saw Barbara at the funeral of a mutual friend. She smiled, and I could tell that our first date had become part of her family's history. "You hurt my feelings," she said to me. "You never asked for a second date," I explained that I was too embarrassed because of the circumstances.

I met a tennis friend in Sarasota, Florida, more than 50 years after that experience with Barbara. His first wife had died about two years earlier, and he always spoke highly of her. We were the only bachelors living in a compound filled with many widows. We had no trouble getting dates, but neither one of us was particularly interested in getting married again.

"You don't want to get married because you're afraid you will never find anyone like your first wife. I don't want to get married again because I'm afraid I might," I said to him one night.

I began dating a widow who was attractive, intelligent, and much fun. I also knew that she wanted to get married again, something that was not in my plans. For once, I decided to do the noble thing. We were having dinner that night, and I was determined to tell her that it was over. It was easier said than done. Just after we finished coffee, she looked at me and said, "Ken, I don't want to see you again."

I was shocked. "What do you mean?" I demanded. "I thought we always had such good times."

"Understand this," she said. "I have more fun with you than any man I have ever dated. We share a love of books and music and even seem to like the same people. It would be very easy for me to fall in love with you. I also know that you have no intentions of getting married again. I do."

I couldn't argue with that. We parted as friends, and she remarried a few years later. I do not know the groom, but he got a very nice lady. Meanwhile, I have not had a date in the last ten years.

THE MAYFLOWER MADAM

In 1970, I was the editorial director of a division of Prentice-Hall with offices in Waterford, Connecticut, and Manhattan. My assistant was Wayne Muller, a Wesleyan graduate, and an excellent writer and editor. An educational publisher, A.C. Croft, came on the market, and on my recommendation Prentice-Hall bought it.

Wayne Muller became the editorial director of Croft. I was impressed with most of the editors we acquired in the sale. One of the best was Amby Burfoot, a runner who won the Boston Marathon in 1968. Amby was an excellent editor, but he left us to become senior editor of *Running World Magazine*. One of the editors, a man named Don Barrows, let me know in the first five minutes of our introduction that his family was part of the Biddle clan that came over on the Mayflower in 1620. The family settled in Philadelphia, Pennsylvania, and became prominent in the business, political, and cultural affairs of the city.

I visited Croft on occasion, but Wayne Muller was fully capable of running the division independently. He called me one day and told me that Don Barrows had asked about the possibility of summer employment for his daughter, Sydney Biddle Barrows. Wayne emphasized the "Biddle" just as Don had in discussing his daughter. I called Personnel, and we hired her as a relief telephone operator.

About a week later, a young lady walked up and introduced herself as Sydney Biddle Barrows. Again, the emphasis was on "Biddle." She seemed to be a charming girl, but I would not classify her as a great beauty. I do not recall ever seeing her again that summer. I had my hands full running the other division. A few months later, Wayne told me that Don Barrows had resigned because he wanted to return to Manhattan. Neither one of us saw it as a significant loss. Don's Mayflower connection did not qualify him as a great editor.

I never thought of the Barrows family again until February of 1984. I was in Manhattan for a meeting when somebody brought up an illegal escort service called Cachet. Police had invaded the apartment of the prostitution ring's office and arrested a woman who identified herself as Sheila Devin. Later it was discovered that Sheila Devin was an alias for Sydney Biddle Barrows, our former telephone operator at Croft.

I called Wayne, and he was just as shocked as I was. It turns out that Sydney Biddle Barrows ran a highly successful prostitution ring. Cachet served a clientele of corporate executives and Arab sheiks. Services were $200–$400 per hour, with a deluxe overnight option including dinner, dancing, and a show for $2,000. Discipline was essential to Sydney, and she fined employees for gaining weight or being late for appointments. She also required her escorts to get regular medical checkups.

In July of 1985, Sydney Biddle Barrows, who had been given the name "Mayflower Madam" by the Manhattan media, pleaded guilty to promoting prostitution. "I was in the wrong kind of business, but I did it with integrity," she told the Court. She could have received a maximum of seven years in prison if convicted after a not-guilty plea. Instead, she received a $5,000 fine and no prison time.

Some of the Biddle family in Philadelphia tried to distance themselves, claiming she was not related to them. They were wrong. Sydney Barrows' grandfather, Donald Barrows, a Philadelphia real estate developer, married a Biddle, Sydney's grandmother. Her mother, Jeannette Ballantine, was descended from two Pilgrims on the Mayflower.

I told Wayne Muller that we had hired the wrong editor from the Barrows family. Sydney Biddle Barrows wrote several successful books, including *Mayflower Madam: The Secret Life of Sydney Biddle Barrows.* It tells the story of how she combined business and sex to create an escort service for the rich and powerful. She was able to adopt modern management techniques to the world's oldest profession. Wayne and I like to think she may have learned some of those business skills while working for us as a telephone operator.

CHOOSING A CONFIRMATION NAME

Choosing a confirmation name was a significant event in the Dooley family, probably because it was the first independent decision we were allowed to make. It took on special significance for us because our uncle, Fr. John F. Sullivan, was pastor of St. Matthew's in Cranston, R.I. All confirmation names had to be run by him for approval.

Confirmation was preceded by months of instruction from a group of nuns, Sisters of Mercy. My immediate instructor, Sister Mary Joseph, was a lovely nun who did not believe in physical punishment. She was sweet, and everyone loved her, which, of course, made her a perfect target for me.

One morning I asked, "Sister Mary Joseph, can God do anything?"

"Oh yes," Kenneth," she replied. "God can do anything."

"Can He make a rock so heavy He can't pick it up?"

She just stared at me, unable to come up with a suitable answer.

Another time I asked, "Can God make a square circle?" I got the same bewildered expression. Before our next session, I was called into the office of Mother Rose Marie, who was in charge of the convent. She was to the ruler what Billy-the-kid was to the six-gun. I stood before her anxiously, awaiting my punishment.

The ruler did into come into play. In a not very pleasant tone, she said, "If you have any questions, come to me. You're confusing Sister Mary Joseph."

Every week as Confirmation drew nearer, my mother would ask, "Kenny, have you chosen a name yet?' I would go into one of my long speeches about the significance of the decision and how I would have to live with it my entire life. Actually, I was stalling for time. I had already chosen a name, but I wanted to wait until the last possible day to reveal it. The less time my family had to consider it, the better.

The Friday before the ceremony, my mother took a firm stand. "You will be confirmed on Sunday. We need your name today."

"St. Ulrich," I replied.

I have never heard of a Saint Ulrich," she answered.

I had done my homework. "Saint Ulrich of Augsburg was the first saint canonized by a pope. Pope John XV elevated Ulrich to sainthood on July 4, 973. Until that time, all saints had been canonized by local authorities," I explained to my mother. "What better name for a young man from Cranston, Rhode Island," I pleaded.

My mother didn't answer. She had the same expression on her face when a family friend asked, "Which one of your six sons will become a priest?"

"If one of my sons becomes a priest, it will be his decision," she would answer firmly.

I went up to my room and was reading when my mother knocked, then entered. "I know what you're up to," she said. "You will not be taking that name for your confirmation," she added."

I was shattered, wondering how I was going to tell my friends. They had shared my secret for weeks. My middle name is Raymond. If I had been allowed to take Ulrich as my confirmation name, my initials would have been K.R.U.D., spelling Krud.

My confirmation name is Patrick.

MY BROTHER PAUL

August 31, 1989, Old Lyme, Connecticut

It is now over a year since I first promised my sister-in-law Marie a written version of Paul's eulogy. I knew it would not be an easy task since I had only rough notes to reference. So, I sat down shortly after the funeral on August 2, 1988, while the thoughts were still fresh in my mind. I sat, and I sat.

As one who has made a living for most of his adult life by putting words on paper, I am well aware of that malady called writer's block. But this was different from any form of the disease I have ever encountered. I went through all the techniques that I'd used successfully to overcome it—tape recorder, word processor, and finally, my old mechanical Royal. All the results were essentially the same—extremely poor.

Some of the thoughts came back to me, but they were disjointed, lacking any unifying theme. The harder I tried, the stronger the block became. Then finally, just before I was ready to confess my failure to Marie, the answer came to me. It was there all the time, so apparent that I'm embarrassed to reveal it.

When I walked out on the altar that day, I was not sure what I would say or whether I would have the strength to say it. As I passed by the casket, I said, "Paul, please help me." And he did. A strange calm came over me as I began to speak.

"If he helped me once, why not again?" I said to myself. So, I said a little prayer to Paul, and suddenly all of the thoughts came rushing back. I sat down with a tape recorder, and you are about to read a transcription of the results. There are some additions and deletions, but I think those who heard the original will agree that its integrity has not been lost.

Many kind words have been spoken to me about Paul's eulogy. They must be taken in perspective. My words only describe what Paul was. In no way were they responsible for making him what he was. I was nothing more than a projectionist in the theater booth, flashing images on the screen. I didn't create, write, or direct them. If it was a beautiful eulogy, it was because it was about a beautiful life. Only one person deserves credit for it. And we all know who that is.

Paul Arthur Dooley: A Life Worth Remembering

Regret the illnesses that created more pain than he ever let us know. Regret the fact that he was taken from us much too soon. But have no other regrets about the life of Paul Arthur Dooley.

I will not make more of our brother in death than he was in life. But those of you who did not call him brother, father, or husband may not be aware of the unique individual whose life we celebrate today.

How do we evaluate a person's life? Wouldn't it be nice if we could do it the same way we consider a business? We take a balance sheet, and through a series of debits and credits, we arrive at a bottom-line figure that tells us whether we have a good or a bad business.

Unfortunately, this wouldn't work too well for most of us. We have too many gray areas, items that could go on either side of the ledger. This was not true with Paul. The only debts in his life came under the heading of illnesses over which he had no control. The credits are too numerous to mention. Suffice it to say that his bottom line would have made IBM and General Motors combined look like the corner grocery store.

To begin with, Paul Dooley was the most courageous person I have ever known. I'm not referring to the military type of courage or that one reflex action that earns a person the title of hero. No, I'm talking about the most difficult form of courage, the grinding day-in, day-out type. You see, Paul had to be a hero every time he opened his eyes and learned that something else had been taken away.

Relentlessly, insidiously, the disease took away his ability to walk, sometimes to talk, sometimes to see—to perform the simplest function that we all take for granted. Ultimately, it won the physical battle. It took away his life. But it never won the more important battle. It was never able to change him from the loving, caring person that he always was. It was never able to undermine his faith.

Paul was not a famous doctor, scientist, or politician. And yet, in another sense, God gave him the greatest gift of all: a gift of faith that enabled him to accept pain and suffering that would have done justice to any martyr of the church. While most of us would have raised our fists against heaven or given way to bitterness, cynicism, or even despair, Paul never did.

I wish I had answers for you today that could help explain why this good and just man was chosen for so much pain and suffering. But I have questions, not answers. Paul seemed to ask so very little of life—to live simply with his beloved Marie and his five sons. He had no blinding ambition, nor was he taken up with the materialism that affects many of us today.

Was it asking too much that he be allowed to walk or to work? To roughhouse with his sons at the beach on a warm summer day or build a snowman with them on a cold winter afternoon? I do not think so, and I question now as I did then. But it does not matter whether I question, or you question. The critical point is that Paul never questioned. He was the greatest example I have ever seen of "Thy will be done."

Paul was also the most compassionate person I have ever known. One of the things that he resented most about his illness was the fact that it placed him in the spotlight too much. He was always happier on the sidelines, offering encouragement and help to others.

I remember one night in particular when I visited Paul in the hospital. I had driven in from New York and arrived quite late but was allowed to see him because he was so sick. As I walked into the room, I could not help but notice how sick he was. He looked so fragile, his face the color of the sheets that surrounded him in the bed.

He smiled when he saw me, as he always did, and then tried to say something. But I could not understand him until I moved closer and closer and, finally, with my ear pressed almost against his mouth, I understood his message. He thought I looked very tired, and he hoped that I was not working too hard. And he certainly didn't understand why I would drive all that way to see him.

You must never think of Paul with sorrow or pity. He was one of the happiest individuals I have ever known. When he was a little boy, he used to sit in another room reading or watching television. Suddenly he would break out in gales of laughter, and soon everyone within hearing would end up laughing too, without really knowing why. That humor never left him throughout his illness, which is why a visit to Paul was always an uplifting experience. Since he never felt sorry for himself, there was no way he would allow his family or friends to do so.

Shortly after he developed multiple sclerosis, I read an article claiming that acupuncture could help arrest the disease. I called Paul immediately, and we both went to Brookline, Massachusetts, the only area in New England where acupuncture was allowed at that time. When we returned to my mother's home after the initial treatment, we lost our balance as we struggled up the stairs, and I ended up on my back with Paul effectively pinning me to the steps. As we lay cheek-to-cheek and just as I was beginning to wonder what I was going to do, Paul suddenly whispered in my ear: "We have to stop meeting like this—the neighbors will talk."

After the treatments were concluded I turned to Paul and said, "I'm sorry."

"For what?" he asked.

"For holding out all those false hopes. The treatments did nothing," I said.

"Oh, don't say that. The treatments showed me that my family loved me, and that's the best treatment I could ever have," Paul said. He was right about his family loving him. My brothers Bob, Larry and Jack installed a swimming pool for Paul at our old home on Massasoit Avenue in Edgewood. We all got a big lift as we watched Paul splash about in the pool, free of his wheelchair.

Paul, like his brothers, was a great fan of the Boston Red Sox. When the Sox lost the playoff game to the Yankees in 1978, I made a special trip to RI to cheer him up. When I made a remark about his up-beat mood, he said, "I learned something yesterday—God is a Yankee fan."

Paul was shortchanged in many things in this life, but love wasn't one of them. In fact, he was the best-loved person I have ever known. And why not? What was there not to love? In his entire life, I never heard Paul make a mean, disparaging remark about anyone. He expected love, kindness, consideration, and empathy because that's all he ever gave—that's all he had to give. I used to marvel at how he was able to keep his disposition in the face of adversity that defies description. Now I have the answer.

I firmly believe that God, recognizing that Paul would be with us for such a short time, decided not to impose on him the foibles that torment the rest of us. So, Paul could go through his life without being afflicted with jealousy, rage, vengeance, pretension, meanness, or other negatives that preoccupy many of us.

From a quantitative point of view, Paul's life was short. He was the last to join the family and the first to leave. But he had more quality years than most of us could amass in two lifetimes.

Now I would like to say a few words to our nephews, the sons of Paul and Marie Dooley. I wish I had the eloquence to paint for you the verbal portrait your father deserves. But I know I don't have to do a great selling job where your dad is concerned. There are, however, a few misconceptions that I would like to straighten out. To begin with, your father was the best baseball player in the Dooley family, despite what your Uncle Bill tells you. He was so good that, at least on paper, he was the youngest employee at the Narragansett Electric Company. Your Uncle Bob had him listed as an employee so he could play on the company softball team. I think it was the only way Bob's team ever won a game.

So, Adam, your smooth swing and batting eye come directly from your father. I wish he could have demonstrated that swing to you himself. I know there are many things considered to be part of the normal father-son relationship that your father couldn't do with you.

He couldn't throw a baseball, a basketball, or a football or skate or swim with you. But I promise you that in a much more important way, you could not have had a better father. No one will ever have to explain to you the meaning of words such as loyalty, fidelity, kindness, courage, strength, support, sacrifice, charity, faith, and love—especially love. You have lived as an integral part of the most incredible love story I have ever seen.

I know the pain of his absence will be deep, but I promise you that the pleasure of his memories will be deeper. A wise person once said that memory is the first great gift of nature and the last to be taken away. It is memory that will keep your father alive for you forever. We have seen his hand on you and know that you will grow into fine young men.

What can we say about your mother and our sister, Marie? Without her constant support and strength, we would have had this ceremony many years ago. I remember an incident that occurred after one of Paul's lengthy hospital stays. I was there when a doctor told Marie that she could no longer care for Paul, that he had to be placed in a nursing home. She gave her answer, with those dark eyes flashing:

"Paul Dooley is a husband and a father. He will remain in his home while he is able to draw breath." And he did. Because of Marie, Paul was able to maintain his sense of dignity and self-worth.

Psychologists have a technique they use when interviewing candidates for a job or promotion. They ask candidates to come up with five words to describe themselves. I would like to pick out those five words for Paul.

In a world with too many cynics, he was TRUST.
In a world with too many doubters, he was FAITH.
In a world with too many haters, he was LOVE.
In a world without enough role models, he was INSPIRATION.
In a world in which it is in such short supply, he was GOODNESS.

Trust, faith, love, inspiration, and goodness. That is the legacy of Paul Dooley, and that's why I say that he died the wealthiest man that I have ever known. His estate is not measured in terms of dollars and property. It's not subject to inflation or mismanagement. But I submit to you that if J. Paul Getty or Henry Ford could exchange estates with Paul Dooley today, they would do so without hesitation.

So, what is the bottom line of Paul Dooley? He was one of the three finest human beings that I have ever known. The other two were his aunt, Ann Kenneally, of whom enough has never really been said, and his mother, Marion Veronica Kenneally Dooley, of whom enough can never be said. And I take great consolation in the knowledge that they are together today.

God bless you, Paul. I will always consider it to be one of the high points of my life that I am able to call you, brother.

There is an old Chinese proverb that tells us that when we enter this world, we are crying while those who are there to greet us are smiling. Conduct your life in such a way so that when you leave, you are smiling while those who are there to say goodbye are crying. I cannot think of a more fitting epitaph for Paul Dooley.

THE EARLY YEARS

There's an area of Cranston we used to call "Sweedsborough" because of the large Swedish population. It was also the home of my first school, Eden Park Elementary. It has been 75 years since I set foot in that school, but I can still remember every one of my teachers: Miss Vaughn, kindergarten; Miss Lodge, first grade; Miss Lynch, second grade; Mrs. Ball, third grade; Mrs. White, fourth grade; Mrs. Phillips fifth grade and Mrs. Pierce, sixth grade. Mrs. Pierce was also the principal.

I had two advantages when I arrived in kindergarten. I could read and touch type. My sister Eileen worked with me on the reading. At the time, she was a student at Edgewood Secretarial School. She had a Royal typewriter complete with an instruction manual. When she was at school, I would study the keyboard and was soon able to touch type. There was no homework in kindergarten, so no one knew about my typing skills.

I first met Mrs. Pierce when I was in kindergarten with Mrs. Vaughn. Every morning I would walk to the second floor and deliver the attendance book to Mrs. Pierce. Then, I would walk into the class and announce in a very loud voice, "Good morning Mrs. Pierce." Everyone would laugh, except my sister Peg, who was in sixth grade at the time.

My ability to read got me in trouble in those early grades. I would become bored as we plodded through the standard reading books. Their size did offer one advantage. My older siblings were reading interesting books, such as *A Tale of Two Cities*. The pocket-sized version slipped inconspicuously between the covers of the latest Jack and Jill book. While my classmates were reading about Jack throwing the ball to Jill, I learned about Madame Defarge and the French Revolution. I got discovered when I started to cry while reading Sydney Carton's final words, "It is a far, far better thing I do than I have ever done before," as he walks to his execution. I laid low for a while and then began to slip interesting books between the covers of whatever book the class was reading. I then learned how to multitask, keeping up with Jack and Jill while reading about Jim Hawkins and Treasure Island.

Sometimes I drive to the site of my first school, and the memories come flooding back. It has been many years since that old wooden structure was razed, but it is indelibly stamped on my memory. Names of old friends roll out—my first girlfriend—Joan S.—although she was not aware of it at the time. In fourth grade, she told me that she liked another boy better, but it sounded like I was at least in the running. That early experience prepared me for a lot of second place finishes with the ladies in my life.

My best friends were Tom Barry, Donald Thompson, Ray Murphy, Bill Considine, Bill O'Connor, John Clayton, Vincent Quinn, Dick Bell, Harry Grattage, Peter La Salle, Armand Tartarian, and Ellsworth Maine. Peter invited me to his home one day and showed me his chemistry laboratory where he made soap. I was surprised because everyone at the school felt that Peter was slow because of his reading problems. I am convinced now that Peter had dyslexia, an unknown condition at the time. Years later, I learned that Peter had earned a Ph.D. from the Massachusetts Institute of Technology.

I lost touch with Tom Barry and Donald Thompson, but the others have all died. Ellsworth Maine, one of my favorites, received his Ph.D. from the University of Rhode Island in Marine Biology. He died of leukemia at the age of 32. Armand Tartarian joined us in fourth grade. He had epilepsy, and I still remember how terrified we were when he had his first seizure in class. After that, we became good friends, and I used to hold his hands during a seizure. He told me that it helped him regain control. Armand also appreciated that I became his protector when a few bullies picked on him because of his illness. More than one of them went home with a black eye or a bloody nose after picking on Armand.

I still remember how sad we were when my family moved to another part of Cranston, and we attended different schools. Neither one of us knew that it would be the last time we would see each other. That summer, Armand went out in a canoe on Blackamore Pond, had a seizure, and drowned. It would never have happened if I had been around.

I felt that all my teachers were terrific, but I had a special feeling for Mrs. Phillips, my fifth-grade teacher. I wrote my first play that year, and Mrs. Phillips allowed me to put it on for the class. Of course, I was the director and usually got the leading role. She liked several of my plays so much that she had me put them on for the school.

In sixth grade, I wrote a song that was sung just before the "Star Spangled Banner." It was 1943, and we were deeply involved in WWII. I stole the music from George M. Cohan (another Rhode Island resident) and wrote the following lyrics to the tune of *Yankee Doodle Dandy*:

We're all in this fight for freedom
So come on Yankees and let's fight
Let's make our Uncle Sam a proud old Man
And keep our land free and bright.

There were four other stanzas, but I do not remember them. At that time, I learned an important definition: steal from one source and its plagiarism; steal from many sources, and it is research. Robert Benchley was my first writing hero. I used to go to the local library to read his stories in *The New Yorker*. Occasionally, one of his short films was shown at our local theater. One of them, "How to Figure Income Tax," appealed to me, and I adapted it for a play. It was so successful that we put it on for the whole school. I stole from Benchley again with his short movie entitled *An Evening Alone*. Robert Benchley died very suddenly at the age of 56. He wrote more than 600 essays, 45 short films, and many feature films. Yet, he is now best remembered for his grandson, Peter Benchley, author of *Jaws*.

One morning Mrs. Phillips said to me, "Kenneth, I don't know exactly how, but someday you will make your living by putting words on paper." Her words came back frequently to me over the past 75 years as I pounded on an old Royal typewriter before graduating to an Apple computer. Making a living through writing can be uneven and challenging. But I have never regretted my decision.

I don't think that teachers fully realize how much they impact the feelings and hopes of their students. Those ladies at Eden Park contributed more than they will ever know. I thought of Mrs. Phillips the night my play, "The Murder Trial of John Gordon," opened at the Park Theater in Cranston. She had been gone for many years, but I felt her presence that night and later when Rhode Island Governor

Lincoln Chafee signed a pardon for a man hanged in 1845, because of my play.

I started seventh grade at Valentine Almy, another excellent public school. We moved, and I switched to St. Paul's, a Catholic school also in Cranston. For years, I had heard stories about how Catholic schools were so much more advanced than public schools. After my first class, I relaxed and sat back for the next two years. We were covering arithmetic that I had learned in fifth grade at Eden Park.

I never really understood nuns. Fortunately, during my lengthy Catholic education career, I only had nuns in grades eight and nine and after-school instruction at St. Matthew's. I never considered them bad people—I did not think of them as people at all. Hiding in their black habits, emotionless and humorless, they usually swung into action only when transgressors—usually students like me—broke one of their rules. The nuns who taught me in junior high were the exact opposite of the Christian brothers I had in high school or the Dominican priests at Providence College.

I still remember how much the nuns loved to diagram sentences—subject, verb, and object—over and over. They did not like creative writing or thinking, areas in which I excelled. Instead of commenting on my stories, they took great delight in having me break the paragraphs apart to diagram the sentences. I don't think that Edgar Allen Poe's wonderful short stories would have survived their scrutiny. While my public-school friends were enjoying *Julius Caesar*, we were still diagramming sentences. Of course, I had read most of Shakespeare's plays while still in grammar school.

Things changed abruptly when I got to La Salle Academy. No sports or other activities for students from St. Paul's, we were informed the first day of school. We had to do much catching up in algebra and science. We may have excelled at diagraming sentences, but that skill was not of great interest to our English teachers at La Salle.

EARLY AIR FORCE

In April of 1951, I joined the USAF with my close friend Charlie Lafferty. We attended junior high and high school together. Charlie enrolled at the University of Rhode Island while I attended Providence College. We both passed the physical and mental requirements for acceptance into pilot training. After completing basic training at Sampson Air Force Base in New York, we would be going to Lackland AFB in San Antonio, TX, for pilot training. Then a funny thing happened on our way to getting our wings.

When we joined in 1951, the requirements for pilot training specified one year of college. Three weeks into basic training, the college requirement was increased to two years. We were both devastated. But I told Charlie not to worry, that we would be eligible for immediate discharge since the Air Force had broken its contract.

I spoke first to our drill Sergeant, a man by the name of Corporal Maples. He had been in the United States Army Air Force during WWII and had attained the rank of Master Sergeant—four times during his career. Unfortunately, a series of court-martials had taken away his stripes, usually the result of alcohol.

When I explained our contract situation, Maples listened quietly. Then he shook his head and asked, "Are you f***king nuts?" Ever the guardhouse lawyer, I explained to Mapes that he could not block my appeal to our commanding officer. That afternoon, I had a meeting with Captain Miller, our CO. I thought I made a good case about how the Air Force had broken its contract with us and why we should be allowed to resign and go back to college. His response was not as vulgar as the first one, but it was just as final. "No one resigns from the Air Force," he said. "Get back in that barracks and keep your mouth shut," he shouted.

We returned to the barracks and resumed basic training. Most of our fellow airmen were from Georgia, Florida, Alabama, and Tennessee. One of them asked me my age when I got my first gun. I explained that I had never owned or even fired a gun. The word went around the barracks quickly, and I became the butt of many jokes when we began receiving training on the carbine, the rifle of choice for the USAF. After a few weeks of training, we were required to shoot for record.

Again, the insults started. "Don't stand near Dooley, or you might get your ass shot off," was one of the more polite warnings. Two days later, the results were posted on the bulletin board. Only one person had shot expert, and it was Kenneth R. Dooley. Some of my roommates who had guns before they could walk were still trying to qualify when basic training ended. Never a gracious winner, I made life miserable for some of them.

At the end of basic training, Charlie was shipped to Biloxi, Mississippi, for electronics training. I was sent to Colorado State College of Education in Greeley, CO. My only dangerous assignment came when I dropped a typewriter on my foot while changing a ribbon. The top graduate in the class was awarded a stripe, so after three months in the Air Force I was a corporal. It took my brother Jack four years of brutal combat with the First Marine Division to attain that rank.

I volunteered for overseas duty and was sent to Camp Kilmer, New Jersey, for deployment. Instead of flying to my assignment, I was put on an old tub, the USS Darby, for transportation to Europe. On the first day on the ship, everyone was assigned to a work detail. I was on the "F" deck, the very bottom of the vessel. As a corporal, I was able to pick my bunk which was over Pvt. Bill Lake, who had been in the service for 18 years. Like my drill sergeant, he had lost his stripes during various court-martials, usually for drinking. I found out very quickly that his drinking days were not over. He showed me his duffle bag, which held bottles of rye and gin. I turned down his offer for an eye-opener and explained that I didn't drink. He was delighted because it meant he would not have to share any of his liquor on the long journey to Germany.

Shortly after we were squared away, a lieutenant walked into our compartment and asked if anyone knew how to run a film projector. Pvt. Lake raised his hand immediately, got the job, and was told to pick an assistant. The team would be showing six movies a day throughout the trip. When Lake selected me, I explained that I had never run a projector, but he told me not to worry. A short time later, we were in the ship's theater, getting ready for our first show. I stood in front of the projector, awaiting instruction. Then Lake told me he didn't know the first thing about running a projector. Meanwhile, troops were already in line for the first showing.

Merchant marines, not navy personnel, ran the ship. One of them came in to show us where the films were stored. Fortunately, he knew how to run the projector and gave me all the instructions I needed. Our first movie, *Here Comes the Groom*, starring Bing Crosby and Jane Wyman, was on the screen within minutes. By the time we reached Bremerhaven, Germany, 19 days later, I could play every role in the film.

Not only did Lake refuse to give me any help, but he was also disruptive. He would sit in the back of the theater sipping on one of his bottles. More than once, he made me run the film upside down for 5 or 6 minutes until the protests from the audience became too strong. Finally, one of my merchant marine friends told me that Lake was selling drinks in the back of the theater. I suddenly realized I had two stripes to his none, and the bar closed.

When he was sober, he related some exciting stories, primarily when he was stationed in the Philippines before WWII. He told me about a small town that had one Catholic Church and one whorehouse. The men used to form a line in front of the whorehouse that extended around the Catholic Church. The nuns used to have to break through the line to get to the school. Lake said if you got to the front of the line and didn't have an erection, you had to go all the way to the back of the line.

I never saw Pvt. Lake again after we docked in Bremerhaven. Months later, I developed a friendship with a sergeant who had access to all personnel records for all airmen stationed in Europe. For the first time, I learned that Pvt. Lake had been captured in the Philippines and took part in the infamous Bataan Death March. He had also received the Purple Heart and a Bronze Star for his actions again the Japanese shortly before the American forces surrendered. However, he never once mentioned his capture or incarceration at one of the worst Japanese prisoner-of-war camps.

A few days after landing in Bremerhaven, I was put on a train and sent to Sonhaoen, a small town on the Swiss border. We stayed in what was a former Hitler Youth Camp. Less than a week later, I was back on another train to Wiesbaden. It was a beautiful town, undamaged by WWII since it had no strategic industry. I was stationed at a camp referred to as Y-80, which housed the 2058th Air Weather Wing. I would have been happy to stay in Wiesbaden for my whole career. Unfortunately, the Air Force had different plans. I was sent to Rheine Maine, an airport in Frankfort, to travel to Wheelus Field in Tripoli, Libya.

A friend from basic training, Chester Baczyznski, stayed with me at a large hotel in downtown Frankfort. We were allowed to leave the hotel but had to check in every four hours for the flight schedule. Chester headed for the bars, but I was determined to see downtown Frankfort. I walked around barriers that warned in German and English to keep out. I later regretted it. Block after block was devastated. Outside of each building was a sign including names and photographs of people who had been killed in the bombing. War to me had always been John Wayne fighting in the Pacific and Errol Flynn taking care of the Nazis in Germany. Only the bad guys got killed. Looking at photos of deceased five and six-year-olds, I had to wonder what they did to qualify as the enemy. I walked for several miles, and the scene never changed. My face was wet, and I realized that I was crying. Then it began to rain, and I returned to the hotel

The food at the hotel was awful, so Chester and I decided to go into the city to a restaurant. An army sergeant who was returning to his home in Alabama joined us. We had a wonderful meal and then stayed to listen to the music. I had pointed out to my friends that the weather was awful, so no flights would be going out that night. When we returned to the hotel, we found out differently. All three of us missed flights, and we were told to report to Captain James Felton the following day. He opened the meeting by notifying us that we had betrayed our country and our service by our actions. If it were wartime, he would have had us shot. Then he and a sergeant walked us to a bombed-out section of the hotel, with bricks and beams nicely stashed at one end of the corridor. "When I return on Monday, I want to see that pile of bricks and beams on the other side." Then he and the sergeant left for the weekend.

The three of us got into fatigues and started moving the pile. After a 10-minute struggle, reality set in, and I told my two friends to stop what they were doing. "The weather is good, and chances are we will all be out of here today or tomorrow. So, let's put the debris back to where it was originally."

"What if there are no flights?" the soldier asked.

"Think about it. We're not the first guys to miss a flight. That pile has been moving back and forth, probably since the end of the war. They won't even remember what side it was on by Monday."

Chester thought it was a marvelous idea and, with a bit of urging, our soldier friend joined the conspiracy. We went into town but checked back every four hours for flights. No flights Saturday. No flights Sunday. As ordered, we reported to Captain Felton on Monday morning. He and the first sergeant walked with us to inspect our work. We were all a little nervous as Captain Felton went from one pile to the other, looking for any shortcomings in our work. Then he said in a gruff voice, "Back to the orderly room!"

At this point, I began to face the reality that Captain Felton had seen through our plan. If he was going to shoot us for the original transgression, what would he do now? As we stood at attention, the scowl on his face suddenly disappeared. "Boys, do you think I enjoy giving out assignments like that? I realize the physical work you had to put in to move all that rubble. But you had to be taught a lesson early in your military career. Rules must be followed, and violations have to be punished."

Actually, he did give me a strategy that I followed throughout my military career. You could get away with anything if you were creative and able to keep a straight face while doing it.

On Monday afternoon, I boarded a C-54 for a flight to Tripoli, Libya. I checked into a transit barracks that afternoon and was asked if I wanted to go to the beach in downtown Tripoli. I had spent much time on R.I. beaches and never had to worry about sunburns. Why would it be any different in Libya? It is. After three hours in that sun, I was driven to the hospital with bad burns and a fever.

The nurses were extremely kind to me, and I felt a lot better the next afternoon. Then a lieutenant walked into my room and began yelling. "You have committed a court-martial offense that will be dealt with," he shouted. "Your body belongs to the United States Air Force, and you had no right to abuse it."

One of the nurses disappeared and returned with an older-looking nurse. "Sonny, get the hell out of my hospital now,'" she screamed at my tormentor. "I am a lieutenant in the USAF, and you will not speak to me in that tone," he replied.

"I am a colonel in the USAF, and you will not disturb my patient." At this point, she nodded to two orderlies who escorted the still protesting lieutenant out of the hospital. Later I learned that her bite was more ferocious than her bark. The lieutenant was transferred to a remote base called Sidi Slimane.It seems in just a few days I had met the worst and best of what the USAF offered.

THE MEN IN MY MOTHER'S LIFE

My mother had six sons: Jack, Bill, Bob, me, Larry, and Paul. The list expanded to seven when her nephew John came to live with us after Jane, my mother's youngest sister, died and left two children. John was always more of a son than a nephew or cousin. Janie became her third daughter, joining Eileen and Peg.

The only romance in my mother's life was my father, Leo P. Dooley, who died at the age of 51 when my mother was 47. A number of men came to her door in widowhood. She had two bakers, two vegetable men, and a milkman. A great deal of time was spent scheduling so that the various vendors would not bump into each other. Each of the vendors believed he was the sole source of whatever products he was selling.

It wasn't possible to determine the products being sold by the title of the vendor. For instance, one of the bakers also sold furniture. My mother was pleased with a coffee table she purchased along with three loaves of bread and a couple of cakes. The vegetable man also sold over-the-counter medications. It was common to walk into my mother's kitchen and listen to a man describing the benefits of a home remedy over a head of lettuce or a basket of tomatoes. The other vegetable man also sold cleaning supplies. These were not simply door-to-door salespeople. They were true entrepreneurs, laying the groundwork for the conglomerates that sprang up in the 1960s.

I was always fascinated by the prices my mother paid, especially to the two vegetable men. If the purchase didn't include furniture or cleaning supplies, it was always $2. I raised this coincidence to my mother, but she dismissed my objection immediately. Whatever the product being sold, her vendors were the most honest and trustworthy. And they always gave her the lowest price possible, which was probably true.

Everyone loved my mother. And for a good reason. Marion Veronica Kenneally Dooley did more kind things on a slow Tuesday than many of us accomplish in a lifetime. She sent two sons off to the military in WWII, four sons in the Korean conflict, and one son during Viet Nam. In case you think my math is off, Bill, who served in the Army in WWII and was called back for the Korean War. He wasn't happy about it at the time but now likes to be identified with his hero, Ted Williams, the great Red Sox baseball player who also served in WWII and Korea.

Jack, a member of the First Marine Division, was wounded during the landing at Peleliu in the South Pacific. Bill fought in Italy and Germany during WWII. Bob was trapped when the Chinese came into the battle in Korea and had to be evacuated from North Korea. My mother didn't have to waste any of her prayers on me. I fought the Korean War in Europe and Africa with a typewriter. I never saw a shot fired in anger.

Saint Jude and the rosary were always big in my mother's life. She always felt that her sons came back successfully because of all her prayers and novenas. She did follow the old Irish rules about sons and daughters. Her sons were never allowed to cook a meal or make a bed. That burden fell on my sisters, Eileen, and Peg. The men cut the grass, shoveled the snow, and took care of any heavy work. I still feel my sisters, Eileen, and Peg, got the short end of that approach. I never made a bed until I joined the USAF in 1951 and still can't boil an egg.

It was particularly frustrating because my mother was a superb cook. She could turn the simplest ingredients into a five-star meal. I can remember sitting in some of the finest restaurants in Manhattan and thinking I would trade the entire menu for one plate of my mother's beef stew. If she had a shortcoming, it was in her belief that her sons could do no wrong. Believe me, we did. If one of us had committed an act of murder, she would help bury the body—as long as you promised to go to confession immediately. The only rule she ever enforced was mass attendance. She never really accepted the role of the evening mass. She believed that Mass should be celebrated in the day, lest prayers become lost in the darkness.

She never spent one day in college, but she had a sense of wisdom and fairness that can't be taught. I remember being sent to the store when I was about ten years old. Shortly after I returned, my mother came into my room, apologized, and said she had forgotten an item. I went back to the store and then returned to my room. A short time later, she came to me again. "Oh dear, I'm so sorry, but I need you to go to the store again."

I erupted. "How unfair, how unfeeling." I was the most mistreated boy in Cranston. She listened patiently until my rant ended. Her response has stayed with me for more than 70 years. "Kenny, you're a good boy, and I know you're going to do what your mother asks. So, if you're going to do something, don't take the good out of it."

I thought at times that my father really didn't appreciate my mother. That thinking changed shortly before his death in 1945. My house was always the gathering place for our friends, probably because of my mother. One Saturday the house was filled with family and friends when my father walked in. The only person missing was my mother, who had gone to a sick neighbor with some soup. My father scanned the crowd, then asked, "Where is everybody?"

We all loved her dearly and did a number of good things for our mother. I remember one trip I made to New York with my wife, mother-in-law, and my mother to attend a performance of *No, No, Nanette*. We stayed at the St. Regis and had dinner one night at Cote Basque, the French restaurant that Jackie Onassis used to call home. My mother was perplexed when she gazed at a menu with no prices. Many of the better restaurants only gave the gentleman a menu with prices. It was a challenge for my mother, who usually made her selections based on price and not the dinner being offered.

My mother died in 1981 at the age of 83. She had one prayer that she recited frequently. "Jesus, Mary and Joseph be with me today." Actually, I think that prayer was unnecessary. She was never far from those three in her entire life.

Mother's Day

Andy Rooney, the great writer, and host on *60 Minutes*, told me that too many medals were awarded to people who simply did what was required of them. Instead, medals should be awarded for actions that go beyond what is expected, according to Andy. He used his own Air Medal as an example. He was flying a mission on a B-17 in 1944 when the radio operator was seriously wounded in an attack by a German fighter plane. Andy stopped the bleeding, and the operator lived to fight another day. Andy accepted the Air Medal for his actions because he did not want to start a controversy. "I only did what any reasonable person who do under the circumstances. It should not have entitled me to a medal."

Andy's feelings about medals remind me of my mother's perspective on Mother's Day. She often referred to it as the holiday that "Hallmark, restaurants, and flower shops created." A mother's job is to provide the support, motivation, discipline, empathy, and love her children need. According to my mother, Marion Veronica Kenneally Dooley, she should not receive any special recognition for simply doing her job.

Her eight children felt differently. There were so many "beyonds" in my mother's life. I remember how she held my father in her arms as he collapsed after reading a telegram that my brother Jack was missing in action in WWII. When my father refused to allow my brother Bill to register for the draft when he turned 18, she quietly but firmly changed his mind. My father died in 1945, at the age of 51, while my mother was 47. They had a wonderful marriage, and I know she missed him terribly. But she never let her grief get in the way of mothering eight children, one only four years old. Money was tight, but not one of her children ever went to bed hungry or without the realization of her unconditional love.

When I was 13, my younger brother Larry was two inches taller. My mother convinced me there was a lot more to a person than his height. Fortunately, I accepted her argument because I topped out at 5′7″, the only male in the Dooley family not to reach 6′. The only time I ever heard my mother raise her voice to a guest at our home involved a man we called Bomby, the husband of my mother's cousin,

Mae O'Brien. He was a nice guy, and we all liked him. But he teased me about my height, pointing out that my younger brother Larry was already taller. He would end his remarks with a question: "Kenny, when are you going to grow?" I usually just smiled and said nothing. Poor Bomby could not believe it one Sunday when my mother charged in from the kitchen and told him that was the stupidest comment she had ever heard. "He doesn't have a switch to control his growth," she said. "I never want to hear a comment like that again." And she didn't.

I remember my first Mother's Day in 1935 when I was four years old. While we were shopping at the A&P that Saturday, I complained that I did not have a Mother's Day present for her. She told me to pick one out, and I selected a package of Hostess cupcakes. I wrapped them in a brown paper bag and wrote "Happy Mother's Day" on it. She responded with a hug and a kiss when I gave her the present the next day. I opened the package and ate both cupcakes, probably in front of my brothers.

My mother was always self-conscious about any attempts to make too much of her. She preferred to remain on the sidelines while the spotlight was turned on to her children and grandchildren. Unfortunately, the rest of the family did not share her disdain for Mother's Day. It was a special time to honor a person who gave so much to us.

I remember one Mother's Day when I took my wife, mother, and my mother-in-law, Agnes Rooney, to Manhattan for the weekend. We stayed at the St. Regis Hotel and went to Cote Basque, one of Jackie Kennedy's favorite restaurants, for dinner. My mother whispered an immediate problem to me—there were no prices listed on her menu, a custom observed by Manhattan's best restaurants. The prices were listed on my menu, the only male in the group. Price was always a serious consideration when my mother ordered dinner. This was one time when she was not able to use her system.

That evening we attended a performance of *No, No Nannette* on Broadway. It was pouring rain when we exited the theater, so I left Agnes, my mother, and my wife, Rosemary, in the lobby as I went in search of a cab. After a successful hunt that included a $50 bribe, I returned in a taxi. I screamed, "Agnes, Mom, Rosemary, without success. Suddenly, the crowd standing outside the theater took up the chant, and the ladies emerged.

On our return to Connecticut the next day, we stopped at the Red Coach Grill in Darien for lunch. This time, the prices were on all menus. When I suggested my mother order the roast beef, she said she would not let me pay $12.95 for lunch. That was about half of what her salad cost the previous evening.

Yes, my mother firmly believed that Mother's Day was a made-up holiday. But, regardless of how she felt about it, I know I find myself missing her most on that special day. I would like to bring her flowers and gifts and take her to an expensive restaurant where they don't print the prices on the menu. She would undoubtedly express her arguments about the "holiday," but she could never change my mind about that special day that comes the second Sunday in May. Requiesce in pace, Mom.

MEMORIES OF MY FATHER

Although monumental battles marked 1944 during World War II, some involving my two older brothers, my family still refers to it as the year of the tie rack and the lamp. I was 12 years old and enrolled in the local junior high school.

In those days, students were placed in divisions one, the highest, through six, the lowest, allegedly based on intelligence. The one subject in which there was no division was woodworking. If students had been separated in that class according to ability, I would have been placed in division seven. It took me three months to make a simple tie rack for my father, which I gave to him for Father's Day.

I heard him tell one of my uncles that he could shave with one end and barely get a tie around the other Meanwhile, Sal, one of the boys who was in division six in everything, made lamps, bookcases, and other furniture that could have sold in one of the local furniture stores.

The rule was that you could take home anything that you made as long as you paid for the wood and the hardware. Sal's furniture never left the school because he didn't have the money to pay for the materials. One of his creations, a lovely pump lamp, caught my eye and sparked what I thought was a win-win situation for both of us.

"That lamp isn't doing you any good sitting on the shelf," I said to Sal. "You need to pay $1 before you can take it home. So I'll give you two dollars, and you give me the lamp. Then you can pick out a gift for your mother."

Sal jumped at the idea. So the next day, I gave him $2 and took the lamp home. I walked into the kitchen and put it on the table. "Where did you get that beautiful lamp?" my mother asked.

"I made it," I said.

My mother couldn't believe how much progress I had made after the tie rack episode. She left the lamp on the table so she could surprise my father. I heard him ask about the lamp as soon as he came in the door. There was a long silence after she told him that I had made it. He came into my room and asked a direct question: "Where did you get that lamp?"

Lying to my mother was one thing. Lying to my father was another.

So I told him the truth. "Do you know where Sal lives?" he asked.

"Yes," I said reluctantly, realizing that the lamp was about to be returned to its rightful owner.

"Pick up the lamp and get in the car," he said.

On the way to Sal's house, I began plotting how I would get my money back from him. My father ended my planning with one sentence: "You're already in trouble for lying to your mother. If I hear of you trying to get any money back from that boy, you'll really be in trouble."

When Sal came to the door, I thrust the lamp into his arms. "Here's your lamp, and I want you to know you got me into a lot of trouble," I snarled. Poor Sal had a bewildered expression on his face as he stood in the doorway, the lamp in his hands. Dad and I drove in silence until we pulled into the driveway. "Don't you think that Sal would have liked to give that lamp to his mother?" my father asked.

Unfortunately, my father died very suddenly the following year when I was just 13. It occurred months after we had received a telegram that my brother Jack, a member of the First Marine Division, was missing during the invasion of Peleliu, a Japanese-occupied island in the South Pacific. Jack was later found wounded, but my father never recovered. I will always feel that he was a victim of WWII.

No one loved July Fourth more than my father. We would set rockets and all sorts of fireworks off at the beach at Buttonwoods as soon as it turned dark. He would allow us to ignite the wicks, but under his close supervision. On July Fourth, 1945, my sister Peg, my brother Bob and I went to Rhode Island Hospital to visit my father. Immediately after we left, the hospital called to inform us that my father had died. When we got to his room, his bed had been removed. I behaved badly, running up and down the hallways screaming for my father. It was a difficult way to learn that he was gone.

His death became even more frustrating when my friend, J. William Middendorf, former Secretary of the Navy, explained that the invasion of Peleliu was a mistake because the island had no strategic importance. Like Wake Island, it should have been bypassed.

For years, I hated the fact that my father died on one of his favorite holidays. I do not feel that way now. Now every time I hear a firecracker go off or watch a rocket dart into the sky, I think of my father. Over the years, my children and grandchildren have asked me what type of man my father was. I tell them the "lamp" story, and I don't have to say anything else to describe the character of Leo P. Dooley.

NIGHTMARE ON RT. 1

It was a night the six Dooley boys would never forget—Aug. 15, 1971, the opening of Schaefer Stadium in Foxborough, Massachusetts, the new home of the New England Patriots. The team was playing an exhibition game against the New York Giants. I called in a few favors and was able to get six tickets for one of the biggest games in Patriot history. We met at my mother's home in Rhode Island and left in plenty of time for the 8:30 p.m. kickoff. Except for the occasional bachelor party, wedding, wake, or funeral, it had been a few years since all six brothers were together in one vehicle. There was no shortage of conversation as we made our way to the new stadium. We did not know at the time that the night would become known as "The Nightmare on Route 1."

The new stadium had been built in less than a year for about $7 million. Compare that to the $325 million Gillette Stadium, which the Kraft family (owners of the Patriots) built to replace Schaefer Stadium twenty years ago. Most of the seats at Schaefer were bleacher-style, and it lacked basic comforts offered by other NFL stadiums. As humble as it was, most Patriot fans were delighted that the team finally had a home. Previously, it played its home games at Boston University, Fenway Park, Boston College, and, ultimately, Harvard. Billy Sullivan, the Patriots owner, wanted to build a new stadium in Boston, but the city rebuffed his proposals. His decision to move to Foxborough was seen as a last-ditch effort to keep professional football alive in New England.

We made good time on Rt. 95, then took Rt. 1 to the stadium and were stopped about 2½ miles from the stadium by a massive traffic jam that extended for miles. At first thought, it was a temporary parking problem that would clear in plenty of time to get us to our seats before kickoff. We listened to the pre-game radio broadcast and remained optimistic that we would be moving forward shortly. We had been sitting for almost an hour when my brothers Bob and Bill got out of the car to get some information. They returned soon, and the news was not good. Bob said the line hadn't moved for two hours and some vehicles had overheated, and some were out of gas. We listened to the kickoff on the radio and didn't move an inch during the whole first half. Billy Sullivan delivered an emotional speech at half time during which he broke down and cried.

As the third quarter began, it became apparent that we would not be getting into the game that night. We agreed that we should turn around and go home. Unfortunately, we were pinned in by several diehard fans who said they were not going anywhere. My brother Jack (6′2″, 225 pounds) got out of the car and conversed with a van driver parked directly behind us. I'm not sure what Jack said, but the van driver pulled back enough to allow me to get out and return to Rt. 95.

Surprisingly, not one of us was upset. It had been some time since we had been together in one place, and the conversation flowed with new stories and happy memories. I do not think we even listened to the rest of the game, which ended at 11:15 p.m., with the Patriots winning by a score of 20–14. Thousands of fans never made it into the stadium. Many who did were stuck in parking lots until 2:30 a.m., and some of did not get home until dawn.

Later we learned that traffic was only part of the nightmare of opening night. Plumbing issues caused scores of stadium toilets to not flush or to overflow. The problem was exacerbated by the fact that beer was selling for $1. The Foxborough Board of Health shut the stadium down until the plumbing was fixed. Columnist Ray Fitzgerald of the *Boston Globe* described the scene in sci-fi terms the following day: "Route One looked like the last road out of town, after the announcement that Godzilla had just swallowed City Hall and was looking for dessert."

This year marks the 50th anniversary of the "Nightmare on Rt. I," and it has been forgotten in time and the success of the Patriots, winners of six Super Bowls. I have attended several of those Super Bowls and countless other Patriot games. Yet my most memorable Patriots game is the one I never saw. That night, sitting with my five brothers will always be my favorite. If we had made it to the stadium and had seen the entire game, some of those stories so etched in my memory would never have been told. I can still remember the car rocking with laughter despite the overheated cars and frustrated fans. Paul, the youngest, was diagnosed with multiple sclerosis the following year. He never left a wheelchair until he died fifteen years later. Larry, Bill, and Jack are all gone. Only Bob and I remain from the original six.

There is one final story connected with that night. Bill Sullivan, owner of the Patriots, declined to say whether there would be any refunds for fans who could not get to the stadium. I sent him a short note, referring to his emotional speech at halftime:

"Dear Mr. Sullivan. While you were crying on the inside, I was crying on the outside."

I got a refund.

OLD TIME RADIO

I subscribe to Sirius radio to listen to classical music and old-time radio programs. Those old radio shows bring back so many memories of my family gathering around the radio to listen to Jack Benny, Bob Hope, or Bing Crosby. My father would listen to the newscaster Gabriel Heater every night, especially during the war years when he had two sons in the service. He would seem to relax after he heard Gabriel's opening words, "There's good news tonight." Of course, Gabriel would never say that if either of my brothers had fallen in harm's way. Children's shows on early radio included action heroes like Superman or The Green Hornet or western stories about Hopalong Cassidy, Gene Autry, or Roy Rogers. Many of my friends watched these programs faithfully. However, action heroes or cowboys did not appeal to me, especially after seeing a photo of Bud Collyer, who played Superman on the radio show. Superman is described as faster than a speeding bullet, more powerful than a locomotive, and able to leap tall buildings in a single bound. Collyer did not look capable of clearing a low hurdle, never mind a tall building.

I was five years old when I began listening to *Lights Out*, a half-hour radio show featuring horror programs. The show came on at midnight, and I was the only member of the Dooley family listening. Everyone else was sleeping, unaware that I had sneaked out of my bedroom and had my ear against the speaker of the only radio in the Dooley household. As a result, I learned early in my childhood that I could get by with just six hours of sleep. It was true at age five and remains so at age 90.

One of the first stories I heard on *Lights Out* was "Burial Service," about a paralyzed girl buried alive. It scared the hell out of me, but I was hooked. The friendly host, Raymond, introduced each program with a squeaking door in the background. He would warn listeners to turn off their radios if they felt their constitutions were too delicate to handle the frightening tale about to unfold.

Providence native H. P. Lovecraft wrote one of the stories, "The Dunwich Horror." He only lived for 46 years, but Lovecraft is now known as one of the great horror writers of all time. The more I learned about Lovecraft, the less I like him. He wrote a series of stories and poems belittling immigrants and describing African Americans as inferior people. Lovecraft wrote 100,000 letters in his lifetime. I doubt that any of them would have been addressed to me. Pen pals would never be a possibility for us.

Lux Radio Theatre began with a one-hour adaption of Broadway shows in 1934, but it soon switched to films. Cecil B. De Mille, the famous director, and producer, was the host when I began listening in 1936. The show featured many of the stars who had appeared in the original films. One of the first programs I remember was "The Legionnaire and the Lady," with Marlene Dietrich and Clark Gable. My early favorite was "The Thin Man," featuring Myrna Loy and William Powell. Fred Astaire, Jack Benny, George Allen, Shirley Temple, Spencer Tracy, Cary Grant, James Stuart, Ingrid Bergman, Henry Fonda, Judy Garland, and John Wayne were among the early stars on the program.

I did have a problem listening to the *Lux Radio Theatre*. It came on every Monday at 9 p.m., one hour past our bedtime. My two older brothers and two older sisters were allowed to stay up. Bob and Larry fell asleep as soon as their heads hit the pillow. So, I would slip out and go quietly to the bottom of the stairs and listen.

I heard Abbott and Costello's famous skit, "Who's on First," on the Kate Smith show in 1938. I thought it was a lot funnier on radio than it ever was on television. I began to listen to *I Love a Mystery* in 1939. It was about three friends who traveled the world in search of adventure. The central characters, Jack Packward, Doc Long, and Reggie York, met as mercenary soldiers fighting the Japanese in China. They opened a detective agency in San Francisco with a motto, 'No job too tough, no adventure too baffling." I traveled along with them on Mondays and Wednesdays at 8 p.m.

It was through this show that I learned the horror of suicide. Walter Paterson, who played Reggie, my favorite character, committed suicide in 1942. I was so afraid that another actor would take over the role. But the creator, Carlton Morse, felt as I did, so Reggie was written out of the series.

I began to listen to *Suspense* in 1940, a show that focused on thriller-type scripts usually featuring leading Hollywood actors of the era. One story, "Sorry, Wrong Number," was about a bedridden woman (Agnes Moorhead) who panics after overhearing a murder plot on a crossed telephone conversation but cannot persuade anyone to investigate. It was made into a film in 1948. I still recall the terror I felt as I listened to "The Hitch-Hiker," in which a motorist, Orson Welles, is stalked by a man who keeps appearing on the side of the road.

Alfred Hitchcock produced "The Lodger," for *Suspense*, a story based on the notorious "Jack the Ripper." Hitchcock never revealed if the "lodger" was really "Jack the Ripper." I was sure he was.

My all-time favorite show on *Suspense* was "Three Skelton Key," a story narrated by Vincent Price about a man trapped on an island as man-eating rats surrounded him. More than 70 years later, I can still feel the terror expressed by Price as the rats closed in on him.

One of the first war movies I ever heard on the *Lux Radio Theatre* was "Wake Island." It told the story of the Japanese invasion of the island shortly after Pearl Harbor and the heroic fight put on by American forces defending it. Against all odds, the defenders repelled the invaders for about two weeks. Instead of recapturing the island, the U.S. Navy established an effective blockade, and most of the Japanese on the island died of starvation. After the war ended, the United States Navy took control of the island and built an airfield to refuel military and commercial aircraft.

As a member of the U.S. Air Force, I was on a C-54 that landed on the island in 1954 for refueling while on a mission to Japan. I recalled the voices of Brian Dunlevy and Robert Preston, two stars of the movie and radio program, as I walked around the island, noting the rusting Japanese landing craft that had been destroyed 13 years earlier and abandoned Japanese pillboxes and fortifications. I read a translation of a diary kept by a Japanese officer describing the isolation and horrendous conditions as most of the men starved to death. However, he failed to mention the most memorable event during the Japanese occupation of the island.

On October 5, 1943, American naval aircraft from the aircraft carrier Lexington bombed Wake Island. Two days later, fearing an imminent invasion, Japanese Rear Admiral Shigematsu Sakaibara ordered the execution of the 98 captive American civilian workers who had been kept to perform forced labor. They were taken to the northern end of the island, blindfolded, and executed by machine gun fire. One of the prisoners (whose name has never been discovered) escaped, apparently returning to the site to carve the message "98 U.S. PW 5–10–43" on a large coral rock near where the victims had been hastily buried in a mass grave. The unknown American was recaptured, and Sakaibara personally beheaded him. I read the inscription on a rock at the site of the execution. Sakaibara was executed by hanging in Guam on June 18, 1947.

Sometimes, I watch a movie and get halfway through before I realize I have seen it before. The plot or the actors had made no impression on me. Yet I can recall almost every word of "The Doctor Prescribed Death," with Bela Lugoski, or "Donovan's Brain," starring Orson Welles, both on *Suspense* in the early 1940s.

Why have those early radio shows stayed with me for more than 80 years while contemporary movies, with all their special effects, disappear so quickly? I believe the word "imagination" is the answer. When I listened to, *I Love a Mystery*, *Lights Out,* or *Suspense*, I was forced to create the background circumstances with my imagination. No special effects could create the same horror I felt as I visualized the rats closing in on Vincent Price. I think it is a shame that today's children may never share in that creative adventure.

A Rhode Island Treasure

I was in Red Auerbach's office to sign a contract with Macmillan Publishing for a book we planned to write together entitled *Management by Auerbach*. Red reached for a gold Cross pen on his desk to sign the contract. I took out my Cross pen and told Red I used to play football, baseball, and hockey with Brad Boss, President of Cross Pen and Pencil.

"Why is the company named Cross and not Boss?" Red demanded. Questions like these made Red Auerbach the greatest coach in professional basketball history, a title given to him by the National Basketball Hall of Fame. A representative from Macmillan and a photographer waited impatiently as I gave Red the Boss family background. But I did not know where the Cross name came from. Red did not like incomplete answers, either on or off the basketball court. The next day while driving to Hellenic College where the Celtics practiced, Red said something that indicated he had investigated my insufficient history of the Boss family.

"You're right," he said. "The Boss family owns it now. But the company was started by a guy named Cross who sold it to the Boss family. I still think the company name should be Boss, not Cross. But they make a helluva pen," Red conceded.

That same due diligence attitude enabled Red to draft a college player in his junior year. "You can't draft him. He's not a senior," one of the NBA owners objected when Red announced his selection. "Look at the draft rules," the owner demanded. "No, you look at them," Red countered. Red was right. There was no provision preventing a team from drafting a player before his senior year. The owners closed that loophole before the next draft, but not before Red stole Larry Bird, one of the greatest players in NBA history and now a member of the NBA Hall of Fame. Larry was a junior at Indiana State University when Red selected him.

It was not the first time I had seen a gold Cross pen and pencil set on the desks of prominent people. Cross pen and pencil sets were in the Oval Office at the White House, in Buckingham Palace, and the offices and homes of national leaders throughout the world. I remember watching television as President Lyndon Johnson signed the Medicare bill into law with a Cross pen. One of the first things I noticed when I interviewed Lee Iacocca, Chairman of Chrysler, was the Cross pen and pencil set on his desk. Even singer Tom Sullivan, blind since birth, used a Cross pen when I directed him in a documentary film.

I lived most of my adult life outside Rhode Island in Connecticut, Manhattan, Philadelphia, Sarasota, and Savannah. Yet, I am always proud to say I am a Rhode Islander. We practiced freedom of religion, elected our political leaders, and were a democracy long before our New England neighbors. Yet we still suffer from an inferiority complex, probably because of our size and Massachusetts referring to us as "the sewer of New England." We were called "Rogue Island," welcoming outcast people like Roger Williams, Ann Hutchinson, and Samuel Gorton. But there was one claim that no other New England state could make. We were home to Cross Pen & Pencil, manufacturers of the finest writing instruments in the world.

I enjoyed showing the Cross ads in the Wall Street Journal to my friends. Some of them worked on Madison Avenue as advertising executives. They were surprised when I told them about my childhood friend, Brad Boss, now President of Cross. I particularly enjoyed pointing out that another friend, Tom Hazlehurst, was a partner in the Rhode Island advertising agency handling the Cross account. The ads were simple—just a picture of a Cross pen with a minimum of verbiage. I believe that was what made them so effective.

While we were only casual friends, the fact that I grew up in the same neighborhood as Brad Boss was a great conversation opener. I met Brad in 1944 when I was 13, and he was 11. We used to play football and hockey together in an area we called the "Meadows." Brad may have developed his lifelong love of hockey there. Ron Boss, Brad's brother and later President at Cross, was a few years younger, so we never knew each other. Brad and I did share close relationships with friends like Gill Thorpe, Herb Browne, Jack Swan, and Bill and Bob Considine. Jack Swan lived in Manhattan when I was there, and we frequently had dinner together. Jack sailed at the Edgewood Yacht Club with Brad, Gill, and Herb Browne.

George Plimpton made a comfortable living running around the world impersonating professional players in football, basketball, hockey, and automobile racing and writing about his experiences. I directed George in a documentary film and heard a lot of his experiences first-hand. Meanwhile, Russell Boss Jr., father of Brad and Ron, did not have to impersonate anyone. He was a world-class automobile racer, sailor, and President of Cross. He attended the 1929 Indianapolis 500 and stayed involved in racing as a competitor and later as a timer, scorer, and starter in the New England area.

After gaining control of the company in 1964, when his brother Ellery retired, Russell Boss moved it to Lincoln and expanded the workforce to 300. He developed a management philosophy that made Cross the Rhode Island employer where everyone wanted to work. Wages and benefits were among the highest in the state, and there were handsome year-end bonuses. Promoting from within and hiring employees' family members and friends became standard policy. This philosophy led to a battle with an investor who claimed the company was squandering money on high wages and employee bonuses instead of distributing it to shareholders. The problem was resolved when the company went public in 1971.

Russell met with his sons, Brad and Ron, and made an intriguing offer—"Do you want to sell the company and go sailing?" Next to making a quality writing instrument, sailing played an essential role with the Boss family. I wrote and directed a documentary film in 1992 based on the Herreshoffs, the great boat builders in Bristol, Rhode Island. Nathanael Herreshoff designed and built every defender of America's Cup from *Vigilant* in 1893 to *Resolute* in 1920. Halsey Herreshoff, Nathanael's grandson, told me at that time that Russell Boss had been one of the best sailors on Narragansett Bay. Russell raced in the Herreshoff S-Class; a relatively small 27-foot yacht still being raced in Narragansett Bay more than 100 years after it was first launched.

It was what Russell Boss did onshore that impressed 15-year-old Herb Browne. "He was such a great tactician," Herb said. "I went up to him one day when I was about 15 and asked, "Mr. Boss, could you explain that move you made today?" He said, "First of all, don't call me Mr. Boss. I'm "Pappy" to you and all the other young sailors at this club." He gave Herb a detailed explanation of his tactics.

"He was a great race-car driver, a wonderful sailor, and the president of one of Rhode Island's leading companies. But he always had time for all the young sailors. We would gather around Pappy and ask him questions after a race. One day I asked him why he had given way to another sailboat, even though he had the right-of-way. His answer stayed with me my entire sailing life. 'Sailing is a competitive sport,' he said. 'But there's nothing worse than a collision between sailboats. If you must choose between the right of way and avoiding a collision, take the safe route.' According to Herb, Pappy usually won, even when he gave up the right of way. "I always looked at him as a father figure. So did all my friends," Herb added.

Brad and Ron appreciated their father's offer, but they turned it down, fortunately for many Rhode Island families. After graduating from the University of Rhode Island and serving as a Naval officer, Brad joined the company and was immediately thrust into a customer-service role. "My father greeted me that first day with a box filled with customer complaints and inquiries. 'I want you to answer these,' he said. It was excellent training for Brad. "I had to go out to dealers to get the information I needed to respond to customers properly. It taught me a lot about the guts of the company and dealing with customers. It was a beautiful way to get involved," Brad said. He soon headed up marketing and sales and eventually became CEO of Cross.

After Ron Boss graduated from Dartmouth and finished his service as a U.S. Coast Guard officer, he joined the company in 1965 and soon oversaw production. At that time, Cross was thought of mainly as a producer of gift products for the Christmas season. The company was busy from October to December, with business falling off after the holiday season. But the 12-carat gold-filled pen with a matching pencil was starting to be thought of as a year-round gift product. In 1971, the company was flourishing with annual sales of $20.2 million and 700 employees. The company went public and was listed on the American Stock Exchange. By 1989, Cross had yearly sales of $250 million and 1,100 employees.

Brad and Ron believed in their father's philosophy that if employees are considered extended family, they will reciprocate with steadfast loyalty. They also inherited their father's love of sailing. Ron continued his father's legacy when he won the S-Class Championship

ship with *Argument* in 1967, the same S boat his father introduced in Narragansett Bay in 1942. The brothers also continued their father's tradition of giving back. Brad donated the Boss Hockey Arena at the University of Rhode Island in honor of his father's role in the growth of youth ice hockey. Ron presented the Alexis Allen Boss Tennis Center at Dartmouth College to honor his daughter. An outstanding tennis player and Ivy League Champion in both singles and doubles, Alexis died of a brain tumor in 1995 at the age of 24.

Their creativity, ingenuity, business acumen, and benevolence toward their employees earned W. Russell Boss Jr., Brad Boss, and Ron Boss a 1980 induction into the Rhode Island Heritage Hall of Fame, the highest civic honor that can be conferred upon a Rhode Islander.

Russell Boss also initiated the family's long affection for automobile racing, starting in 1929 when he attended the Indianapolis 500. Four years later, he started driving himself, primarily sports carts at the many road courses then dotting the East Coast. He competed at Sebring until 1959, and his fascination for racing was contagious. His son, Brad, raced MGs, and Alfa Romeos and attended many races in Indianapolis, the Thompson Speedway in Connecticut, and many others. Brad's three sons, Geoff, Andy, and Peter, all raced competitively. Geoff won Formula Fords championships on three occasions and drove 12 races in Indy cars.

I have had a personal relationship with a special Cross pen for more than 63 years. I write all my plays and screenplays using a computer program called Final Draft. But all my initial character descriptions are handwritten with a Cross pen given to me by the mother of my best friend, Wesley Forcier, when I graduated from Providence College.

Sometimes when the words do not come easily, I abandon the computer in favor of my Cross pen. I used it to write the play "The Murder Trial of John Gordon" in longhand. Later I watched Rhode Island Governor Lincoln Chafee sign a pardon with a Cross pen for John Gordon, a man executed in 1845. That same pen has played a significant role in all the books, plays, and screenplays I have written over the years. It remains the greatest weapon I have against writer's block.

Historian Laureate of Rhode Island

Rhode Island has made its share of mistakes in electing or appointing people to high office. The best example of selecting the right person for the right job was in naming Dr. Patrick T. Conley as the first-ever Historian Laureate in 2012. His appointment was renewed in February 2020. He is the author of thirty-two books, most of which focus directly on Rhode Island history and dozens of similarly themed scholarly articles. He has served as chairman of the Rhode Island Bicentennial Commission, chairman, founder of the Providence Heritage Commission, chairman of the Rhode Island Heritage Hall of Fame, founder of the Rhode Island Publications Society, and founder of the Rhode Island Heritage Commission, which has now merged with the Rhode Island Heritage Preservation Commission. He also served as chairman of the Rhode Island Bicentennial Foundation, chairman of the U.S. Constitution Council, and founding president of the Bristol Statehouse Foundation.

I graduated from Providence College in the same class as Dr. Patrick Conley in 1959. As a noted athlete, everyone knew who Pat Conley was. No one knew who Ken Dooley was aside from a few friends like Joe Paolino, Peter Bowen, Gerald Roque, and Paul Flaherty. It was not until I moved to Bristol in 1992 that I really became friendly with Pat and his wife, Gail. Whenever I mention that I graduated from college with Pat, he is quick to point out that I am eight years older, having served in the military during the Korean War.

I left Rhode Island shortly after graduation for jobs in Connecticut, Manhattan, Philadelphia, and Florida, returning to my home state in 2010. For many years, I had considered writing a play about John Gordon, an Irish immigrant hanged in 1845 for a crime he did not commit. I called Pat, and we met for lunch at the Fabre Line Club that included a delightful restaurant he and Gail had opened on Conley's Wharf. I gave Pat the first draft of the John Gordon play I had written. He made some corrections and added some wonderful insights. He also gave me an essay written by one of his students, Dr. Scott Molloy, a professor at the University of Rhode Island. Scott's essay gave me the final reason why John Gordon did not murder Amasa Sprague, a wealthy Cranston mill owner.

Conley's civic involvement, especially the Sesquicentennial of the State's famed Dorr Rebellion, led to awards and recognition from many groups, especially the military. The most unusual honor bestowed on Conley occurred in 1976 when Alabama governor George C. Wallace commissioned him an honorary Colonel in the Alabama State Militia.

Dr. Conley believes his title as Rhode Island History Laureate goes beyond delivering patriotic speeches at Fourth of July celebrations. His opinion pieces frequently appear in *The Providence Journal.* Here is one about a referendum to eliminate "Providence Plantations" from Rhode Island's official title.

> I am not a racist. I make this candid statement to avert such an unfounded charge against me in response to the position I will herein assert against changing the formal historical name of our State by deleting the words "Providence Plantations."
>
> Despite my well-documented lifetime of anti-racism and racial harmony, I oppose the deletion of "Providence Plantations" from the State's name because I also have spent a lifetime as a historian and, therefore, oppose the rewriting of history to cater to present trends or sensibilities, regardless of how tragic or unsettling they have been. Presentism is History's cardinal sin.
>
> In 17th century terminology, the English word "plantation" merely meant a settlement. Pioneers "planted" a town or colony. This act had nothing to do with slavery, despite the later use of the word to describe an agricultural enterprise that held its laborers and their families in bondage.
>
> The Providence Plantation was benevolent and interracial. Members of the Wampanoag Tribe gave refuge to its founder Roger Williams in the harsh winter of 1635–36 as he sought to settle beyond the bounds of the intolerant Plymouth and Massachusetts Bay colonies. In gratitude for this Native American hospitality, Williams later wrote:
>
> *I've known them to leave their horses and mato lodge a friend or stranger*

When Jews and Christians oft have sent
Christ Jesus to the Manger.

When Williams finally established his plantation in late spring 1636, he was welcomed by the leaders of the Narragansett tribe, Canonicus, and Mianinomi. The original deed to the Providence Plantation, signed by these Sachems on March 24, 1638, confirmed earlier verbal grants. "Not a penny was demanded by either," wrote Williams. "It was not price nor money that could have purchased Rhode Island. it was purchased by love."

Williams was so grateful to his Native American enablers that in 1643 he wrote and published A Key into the Language of America," the first English language dictionary and ethnography of Native American people. He believed that better communication would produce a bond of friendship between the natives and the English settlers. He also believed that the natives, and not the English king, held title to the land.

The Providence Plantation was not only a promising venture in interracial harmony. It also had an even greater significance. Williams admitted that with "a sense of God's merciful providence unto me in my distress, I called the place Providence." His Providence Plantation became the birthplace of religious liberty in America. Williams's plantation became a haven for persecuted religious dissenters and "a lively experiment" in church-state separation. According to its "Plantation Agreement" of 1640, the government of this settlement was allowed to rule "only in civil things." This agreement also reaffirmed "liberty of conscience" as the plantation's founding purpose. Two of its 39 signatories were women, indicating that such liberty extended to them.

Two great historical ironies weaken the case of the Providence Plantation deleters. First, there were no Blacks in 17th century Providence. Secondly, and more importantly, when the colony was temporarily split by William Coddington's vain attempt to make Newport and Portsmouth his proprietorship, the two mainland settlements—Providence Plantation and Samuel Gorton's town of Warwick—joined in 1652 to pass America's first anti-slavery ordinance. Unfortunately, after the reuniting of the colony, dominant Newport took a position that rendered this law obsolete.

The Providence Plantation, named for God's Divine Providence, had momentous beginnings: it was the birthplace of religious liberty and separation of church and state; it made an all-too-brief attempt at inter-racial harmony; it allowed women a voice in governmental and religious affairs; it helped to enact America's first anti-slave law; and it was founded and named for God's Providence by one of the greatest Americans, ever! The produce of William's plantation was not cotton or rice or the crops grown in the 18th century on our own South County slave farms, but rather religious liberty and interracial justice.

History is immutable. Historical writing should acknowledge that fact. Hysterical tinkering with our state's name ignores it.

We should vote to reject Referendum No. 1 and retain our State's historic and hallowed name as a reminder not of slavery but of freedom, or as Roger Williams called it, "soul liberty"

Conley's 31st book, *Historical Cruise Through the Ocean State,* includes thirty-three essays described by reviewer Dr. Scott Molloy, Professor Emeritus, University of Rhode Island, as a brilliant summary of the state's history. Here is Dr. Molloy's review:

In 2001, the State's foremost constitutional scholar, bookworm, real estate magnate, and orator—Dr. Patrick T. Conley—purchased a century-old building on Allens Avenue in Providence. The four-story structure, like most waterfront buildings from that era, served many purposes over the years. Constructed in 1899 by the Providence Gas Company, its adjacent state pier later morphed into Rhode Island's immigrant intake center from 1913 to 1934. Newcomers from Portugal and the Mediterranean region, especially Italy, graced our shores. This point became their disembarkation to the New World.

The Fabre Line gave Rhode Island its ethnic diversity. Conley's Club celebrated that diversity. By the time Conley bought this hidden jewel, it had featured more broken glass on the perimeter of the building than in its windows. Conley, with his wife Gail, proceeded to rehabilitate the old place from the broken shards into a diamond.

Within a few short years, the bottom floors housed a small colony of active artists with the Gail Cahalan Gallery, first-floor front, donated by the Conleys for them to exhibit their contents. The fourth floor went from a caterpillar to a butterfly. A steamboat theme on that top "deck" reflected the old maritime immigration route to Providence with a majestic view of the Bay as if you were on the boat itself.

Before Club events, I used to get there early, have a Margarita, and watch the stream of automobile traffic along I-95 on the west side/and the upper harbor of the Providence River on the east of the building. Exquisite craftsmanship turned the abused fourth story into a facsimile of a luxury liner—way beyond what our relatives experienced on their frill-less trans-Atlantic journey. Conley, known for his wiseacre humor, built a 30′6″ long conference table that trumped Donald Trump—then a mere television celebrity—and his famous 30′ piece of office furniture. The ever politically correct Conley used rehabilitated yellow pine salvaged from a demolished Bristol mill to construct the table and highlight the 8000 square feet of space on the fourth floor.

The greeting in the frontispiece to this mammoth book (over 500 pages) captures the magical kingdom that rose from the ruins on Allens Avenue. For seven years, it was a "cultural Camelot" using the metaphor of the great tables—one round (Arthur's), and one rectangular (Conley's). It would be easy to dub Conley as King Arthur or Lancelot, and Gail, the beautiful Guinevere. Like those knights who searched old England for the Holy Grail, Conley attempted to create an intellectual fortress to embrace knowledge and education in a world more akin to that recently broken glass than to the glories of an earlier age. How close he came with his wizardry, magic, sagacity, and sorcery.

If you listen carefully while reading the remaining paragraphs, you should be able to hear the notable steam blast whistles of those original ships that transported our forebears to these shores and appreciate Conley's attempt to transform the area from a perennial eyesore to a bustling perennial champion. His passion for that spot and the surrounding streets where he grew up in mid-century South Providence reminds me of the 1933 jazz hit, "I Cover the Waterfront," made famous by Billie Holiday.

By the time he completed the artistic table, conference center, and adjacent dock in 2006, Conley had scheduled a blistering lineup of academic and popular presentations, performances, amusements, and lectures which he conducted over the next seven years. Conley formed a club of over 400 dues-paying members (his Knights of the Rectangular Table) who not only imbibed the entertainment but partook of a smorgasbord of ethnic heritage buffets and dinners. The aptly named Fabre Line Club, from its inception in 2007 to the sorry murder of the organization in 2013, hosted dozens of amusements, spectacles, and cultural events.

A Praetorian guard of intellectual stars spoke above the wharf in the conference center, arguably featuring as many dignitaries and scholars as the venues along College Hill. Distinguished, award-winning constitutional scholars, justices, historians, and professors, kept the diverse audiences spellbound. More importantly, ordinary folks with a penchant for some of these academic sorties as well as a deep knowledge of sports, labor unions, politics, and ethnicity—also had a chance to present their own expertise. One might say that the sight of Rhode Islanders from all walks of life speaking and participating in such a venture was truly inspiring. Proletarians conversing with the literati: an unusual tandem in any quarter.

The Club hosted 60 book signings, another 60 lectures, sightseeing trips on nearby waters on the club's tour boat Providence Piers, a visit of the Liberty ship John W. Brown and the ill-fated Bounty, the Newport-Providence Ferry, a gymnastics show, and so many other wonderful things. The reappearance of a lost world devoid of any of yesterday's snootiness, those 41 ethnic heritage feasts, and buffets would require a professional waiter, hostess, and maître d' to prepared and explain the delicacies. The scope of these meals extended from our original citizens—Native-Americans—to the latest waves of immigrants—Hispanics and Southeast Asians. You would be hard-pressed to name a group that did not have its name on some feast.

Dr. Conley is a man of letters, someone for all seasons. He operates on a lot more floors than the four in his reconstructed building. He sought to celebrate diversity and history. Just as importantly, he sought to provide a living legacy of his beliefs in a bold attempt to reconstruct the Allens Avenue waterfront, north of Thurbers Avenue, into something special and financially viable. A mixed-use emporium of activities related to sea and land that would turn a wasteland into a garden. He set the stage for such a huge development with a building that made it onto the prestigious National Register of Historic Places, using the skill of general contractor Al Beauparlant.

The blending of financial revitalization and intellectual endeavor is never an easy union. Despite the shabby nature of the area before Conley's arrival, others had profited by polluting the space as bunkers for industrial waste and scrap metal. Just like the savvy Merlin fighting a recurrent enemy—Mordred—who protected the corrupt old ways, Dr. Conley battled the obstructive influence of corporate wealth and political bribery. Promet Shipyard, one of the villains, sold our State Pier No. 1 (Rhode Island's Ellis Island) to Sims Metal Recycling Company. Promet acquired the historic property during the Great Recession from the state for $1.38 million and miraculously resold State Pier No. 1 for $12.8 million a year later to Sims. Conley's dream of hotels, residential condominiums, medical centers to serve the nearby hospital complex, a marine terminal, and other tourist activities has been buried by tons of salt piles and towering scrap heaps.

A wayward and politically corrupt concept of revitalization triumphed. Conley sardonically called Allens Avenue "the Scrapplachian Trail," easily visible from Route I-95 in blatant violation of federal highway law. Sadly, the last event on December 17, 2013, celebrated the publication of the history of the Fabre Line by Conley and his student, Dr. William Jennings. The date was exactly the 100th anniversary of the first arrival of a ship from the Fabre fleet to Providence's newly built State Pier No. 1.

In the famous musical, the ending line echoed, "Don't let it be forgot, that once there was a spot, for one brief shining moment that was known as Camelot." Conley and his historical Knights have already rebuilt an inland version of the original concept, albeit without the marine framework or square footage. The output, especially its Rhode Island publications, continues unabated. Visions die hard. Our trans-Atlantic ancestors held on for dear life. We move forward.

When sufficiently provoked, Dr. Conley rises to the challenge. Here's a letter he wrote to Jorge Elorza, mayor of Providence:

March 29, 2021
Mayor Jorge Elorza
35 Deborah Street
Providence, RI 02909

Dear Mayor Elorza,

I have not seen the Providence racial injustice report that you commissioned (but would like a copy). However, I have seen the Journal's summary. The participants in the project did not include the state's historian laureate; the published historian of the City of Providence; the author of the only detailed study of South Providence's history; the founder of the now-defunct multi-ethnic and racial Providence Heritage Commission; the captain of one of the city's first integrated baseball teams; a long-time resident of the city and an 82-year resident of the state; its largest Providence landowner ever in terms of separate parcels owned; the creator of the Hispanic-American, Cape Verdean, Native American and Black Heritage subcommittees of the state bicentennial commission (ri76); the principal policy advisor to Providence's longest-serving mayor; the creator of the Rhode Island Heritage Commission (now merged with the Historical Preservation Commission); the general editor of the 15-pamphlet Rhode Island Ethnic Heritage Series; and the founding president of the Heritage Harbor Foundation, a non-profit that has given several substantial grants to Hispanic, Black, Native American, and Asian-American programs. These were not twelve people—but only one, namely me. Is such omission discriminatory?

Had I been a participant in this worthwhile project, I could have corrected at least one aspect of the report—the assertion that the construction of I-95 displaced Blacks in South Providence in the late 1950s and early 1960s. On the contrary, that highway took the line of least resistance from Point Street, where South Providence begins, to the Harbor Junction Railroad spur, where it ends.

After dislocating a few Irish, Italians, and Swedes near Coro and the adjacent Jewelry District, I-95 curved eastward around the hospital complex and then southward through a sloped, sparsely inhabited stretch between Eddy Street and Allens Avenue known as the Badlands because of its desolation. At what is now the Thurbers Avenue Curve, I-95 turned westerly, obliterating the city dump and adjacent Kay Street where my grandparents lived. Its westerly course parallels the Harbor Junction rail line necessitating the demolition of the houses on the south side of Byfield Street (including mine) and the south side of Detroit Avenue. This strip contained most of the homes in South Providence that were demolished by the construction of I-95. To my recollection, no Blacks lived on this strip. It was inhabited mainly by Irish and Jews.

Noted historian Christian McBurney describes another Conley book, *Democracy in Decline*, as "the finest Rhode Island history book ever written." In his book *Rambles through Rhode Island and Beyond*, Conley describes his relationship with the late Providence mayor Buddy Cianci. Conley served as Cianci's chief of staff when the mayor was reelected in 1978. His assessment of Buddy's character is based upon the interactions the two had from 1966 through early 1993, when their relationship was interrupted for a decade. Here is how Conley summarizes his relationship with Buddy Cianci.

I always said of Buddy that when he attended a wedding, he wanted to be the bride, when he attended a birthday party, he wanted to jump from the cake, and when he went to a wake, he wanted to be the corpse. On February 6th and 7th, 2016, he got his wish. He laid in state in Providence City Hall, with hundreds of truly sorrowful people paying their respects, as befitting the city's longest-serving mayor. On a cold and soggy Monday, February 8th, after a somber procession from City Hall to the Cathedral of SS Peter & Paul, where Bishop Thomas Tobin offered his funeral Mass, the energizer Buddy was finally put to rest.

On the basis of my contacts with Buddy, and my knowledge of Rhode Island history, I can state with assurance that Buddy

Cianci was the most charismatic Rhode Island political figure in its history. He had great talent and ability, which outweighed his several significant flaws. To liken him to other controversial American politicians, one might say he had the quick wit, sense of humor, and popular appeals of Louisiana Governor and Senator Huey P. Long; the boldness, persistence, and audacity of Boston Mayor James Michael Curley; and the flamboyance of New York Mayor Jimmy Walker. He will rank among the most dynamic, interesting, and controversial city mayors in all American history.

I can speak of his attributes because others, especially the local media, have incessantly focused on his flaws. Ironically, our last encounter occurred in November 2015 when I had the honor of serving as principal speaker at the Federal Hill resection that followed the unveiling of his portrait at City Hall. To paraphrase Marc Antony, I came to praise him, not to bury him.

Some people liked to hate buddy Cianci. I hated to like him. It is the mark of all great persons that they inspire both adulation and contempt. By that standard, Buddy was certainly great. He might be called the quintessential rogue of Rogue Island.

The role of Historian Laureate is an honorary title in most states, similar to what Gov. George Wallace did when he commissioned Dr. Conley an honorary Colonel in the Alabama State Militia in 1976. Dr. Conley defines that role differently, acting as the State's conscience on particularly challenging subjects.

Here's one of his recent essays concerning the efforts of Narragansett tribal leaders to remove the statue of the Rev. William Blackstone from tribal land.

A Monumental Mistake

Reverend William Blackstone was an Anglican clergyman who became Boston's first settler in 1625 on Beacon Hill. Then Puritans, led by John Winthrop, Sr. arrived in the so-called "Great Migration" of 1630. Because of territorial and theological disagreements with his new neighbors, who were determined to "purify" Anglicanism of its "Romish" residue, Blackstone moved west to the banks of a river (the Pawtucket) that now bears his name to live in relative peace and solitude. His new home near the present-day village of Lonsdale in Cumberland made him the first resident of what has become Rhode Island. He chose a site that he erroneously thought was outside the bounds of Plymouth Colony, whose "Pilgrim" settlers advocated complete separation from his Anglican Church. He called his new home Study Hall.

Blackstone's religious doctrines made him a self-imposed outcast from the anti-Anglicans who were settling in the surrounding colonies of Massachusetts Bay, Plymouth, Connecticut, and New Haven. He played no role in their land-grabbing wars against the area's Native American tribes. Blackstone died on May 25, 1675, nearly four weeks prior to the outbreak of King Philip's War on June 20. That conflict is the focus of the campaign against the erection of a Blackstone statue in Pawtucket. The most recent history of that war by Lisa Brooks won the 2019 Bancroft Prize in History. She makes no mention of William Blackstone in her 431-page study, titled *Our Beloved Kin*. This solitary, devout clergyman was certainly not a war provocateur yet, according to objectors, he shares the guilt for this bloody conflict.

The opposition of some Narragansett tribal leaders to a statue on Wampanoag land is misguided. This area was the historical domain of the Seaconke Tribe of the Wampanoag Nation. Several years ago, my wife Gail and I donated over 50 acres of land near Blackstone's home to that tribe which was then under the leadership of Chief Wilfred "Eagle Heart" Greene, my lifetime friend and the godfather of my son Thomas. Unfortunately, the town frustrated the tribe's efforts to remediate and utilize this property. In his bucolic surroundings, Blackstone read from his extensive library, conducted missionary work, and engaged in horticultural pursuits. He has been credited with developing the first American variety of apples and conducting the first Anglican religious services in Rhode Island by preaching to natives and others who listened voluntarily.

> In 1659, Blackstone married Boston widow Sarah Stevenson, who bore him one son. The eccentric cleric sometimes visited Providence for supplies, books, and other necessities, traveling to and from while perched on the back of his large white bull. The current vociferous opponents of the Blackstone monument know more about the potato chip that bears his name than they know about Reverend Blackstone himself. Their misguided crusade has chosen the wrong target. In doing so, they seriously undermine local Native American efforts to address continuing injustices such as Brown University's greedy grip on the Mount Hope lands in Bristol in defiance of Pokanoket claims to that tribal domain.
>
> The premise of the statue's detractors is that some whites abused Native Americans, therefore, all whites are guilty and evil— even an eccentric, bookish, and isolated minister such as Reverend William Blackstone. This is classic guilt by association—no matter how tenuous. It is an unhistorical bill of attainder, equivalent to the droppings of Blackstone's famous white bull.

Dr. Conley has an ability to write humorously about controversial issues that make others seethe with anger. While most of his humor is subtle and not always picked up immediately by his readers, it is always there. By combining humor and irony, he can defuse many of the issues dividing society today. A good example is his treatment of former Olympic runner Norman Taber in an article for *The Providence Journal.*

Your Turn

Patrick T. Conley

Guest columnist

> With the Tokyo Olympics now in the spotlight, it is fitting to fix the beam on an early and overlooked Rhode Island born Olympian who went the distance faster than anyone in his era of competition. That athlete, a Providence native, who starred first at

Providence's Hope High School and then at Brown University, was Norman Stephen Taber.

In 1968, when the newly created Rhode Island Heritage Hall of Fame held an induction of Rhode Island Olympic medalists, its then sports-minded directors ignored Taber. Not until 2004, when I scheduled a second Olympic induction to coincide with the Athens Games, did Taber get his due.

At the 1912 Stockholm Olympics, Taber won a gold medal in the 3,000-meter team relay and bronze in the 1,500-meter run. He is a leading candidate for the title of Rhode Island's greatest homegrown track star. In addition to his exploits at Brown and the Olympics, Taber is best remembered as the world record holder in the mile run. In 1915, paced by quarter-milers at Harvard Stadium, Taber broke the world mile record (established inl886) with a clocking of 4:12.6, a standard that stood until 1923, when the great Paavo Nurmi ("The Flying Finn") ran the distance in 4:10.4.

Since the days of Taber and Nurmi, the mile record time has been repeatedly lowered. Today it stands at 3:43.13, run by Hicham El Guerrouj of Morocco. Even the Rhode Island high school record leaves Taber in the dust. On June 13, 2009; Andrew Springer of Westerly High School posted a time of 4:02.7. Many developments explain that progression. Taber ran on a rough, unstable cinder track, whereas modern running surfaces are made of smooth synthetic rubber bound with latex or polyurethane installed to a depth of a half an inch on an asphalt or concrete base to ensure stability and more spring in the stride. Technology has resulted in well honed, carbon-plated spikes; the ringlet, a one-piece tight uniform that decreases wind resistance; and lighter, cushion-soled shoes.

Of even greater importance are the vast improvements in conditioning, nutrition, and training, and especially, dedication and focus. The casual approach to track and field, as beautifully depicted in the 1924 Olympics by the movie *Chariots of Fire*, is a thing of the past. Running has been transformed from an intermittent, pleasurable pastime to an all-consuming passion.

It is said (mainly by coaches) that sports competition teaches us life's lessons. Using that premise, let us compare those vast improvements in the mile run over the past century to the commendable improvements by Americans in their views and actions toward race and gender.

Some presentistic accounts of American History condemn Washington, Jefferson, and Madison for slaveholding, while ignoring the fact that in their time slavery was global and an accepted practice, whether in America, Africa, or Asia. These Founders were born and raised in the slave culture of Virginia.

Northerners such as John Adams, Ben Franklin and Alexander Hamilton are denounced for their belief that women should not be part of the political system. Adams, who deeply loved, admired, and took counsel from his amazing wife, Abigail, declared in a 1776 letter that women should be excluded 'because their delicacy renders them unfit for practice and experience in the great business of life, and the hardy enterprises of war, as well as the arduous cares of state."

If we choose to denounce these Founders for being people of their time, we, should also scold George Washington for not taking a plane from Mount Vernon to the original capital, New York City, to avoid being nearly two months late for his 1789 inauguration.

Such ridiculous criticism is no more absurd than the claims of those hysterical (not historical) ideological manipulators of our country's past who hold our Founders to the evolving standards of the present on such key issues as race and gender.

As my brief history of the mile run indicates, times change.

Dr. Conley does not always win, as evidenced by the removal of "Plantations" from Rhode Island's official title. The important point is his willingness to put his name and reputation on the line when it matters most. Historians warns us that unless we examine the mistakes of the past, we will repeat them in the future. Rhode Island is fortunate to have a Historian Laureate who can point out these errors while offering positive recommendations for the future.

Joining the Family

Do you ever have that feeling that something wonderful happened, but you were not perceptive enough to realize it at the time? It took me many years to appreciate my great fortune in joining the Dooley family on October 22, 1931. In those early years, I remember envying my friends who were part of small families or who had doctors, lawyers, or successful businessmen as fathers.

Dick Bell's father was a physician, and both of Tom Breslin's parents were medical doctors. Sherm Strickhauser's father ran a division of U.S. Rubber in Providence, and Wes Forcier's father headed Wilson Meats in New England. Bill Considine's father was the head of Narragansett Brewery, while Bill O'Connor's father ran the financial side of the same company. Ed Dinneen, the father of my close friend John Dinneen, ran his own building supply company. Jack Swan's father was sales manager for General Electric. Brad Boss's family-owned Cross Pen & Pencil and Gill Thorpe's father founded a successful pharmacy that later grew into a chain of five stores. Bob Arabian's father owned Imperial Jewelry, a significant costume jewelry manufacturer in Providence.

There was no question that the Dooleys were the lowest income family in the upscale neighborhood of Edgewood, Rhode Island, particularly after my father died in 1945. I have always felt that my father died as a result of my brother Jack's being reported missing in action during the invasion of an island called Peleliu in the South Pacific. My father had a stroke after the telegram arrived and died a few months later. Years later, I developed a close relationship with J. William Middendorf II, the former Secretary of the Navy. He told me that Peleliu should never have happened. The island had no strategic importance and should have been bypassed, he said. Yet, because of the vanity of a Marine Corps General, more Americans died or were wounded during that invasion than any other battle in American history.

Despite the financial handicaps, the Dooley house was the social hub of the neighborhood. I don't know exactly why, but it became the gathering place for all of our friends. Bob, Larry, and I each had our own circle of friends. Bill and Jack were older, and Paul was a baby. It wasn't unusual for 10 or 15 of us to be in the living room while planning the activities of the day. The gang knew there would never be any complaints from my mother, who always subscribed to the "room for one more" philosophy. There were very few meals that didn't include several of our friends.

I remember being at a cocktail party in Manhattan some years ago. The hostess, a very wealthy but snobbish lady, began to ask me questions about my background. She tuned me out after learning I was not Ivy League. (I did not tell her that I had been accepted at Brown University in 1949.) She came up with one final question. She asked me where I was born, and I replied, Providence, Rhode Island. "How dreadful," she said. "Why did you choose such a city?" "I wanted to be close to my mother," I answered.

It drew a laugh from the other guests, but there was a great deal more in that comment than they realized. I was so fortunate in having Marion Veronica Kenneally Dooley as my mother and Leo Patrick Dooley as my father. I only had him for 13 years, but I can still close my eyes and hear his voice or the touch of his hand on my shoulder.

When I arrived, five siblings were already in place—Eileen, Jack, Peg, Bill, and Bob. Later, I was joined by Larry and Paul, the baby in the family and everyone's favorite. I now look back and realize how truly fortunate I was to join that family. Only two of us are left now—Bill, 94, died on January 26, 2021. Bob is 92, and I'm 90. Eileen, Jack, Peg, Bill, Larry, and Paul are all gone, but their memories are so strong. A united group, we were all so different. I credit it to my mother, who always treated us as individuals.

Eileen was the oldest, the most difficult, and the most opinionated. She was a feminist long before Gloria Steinem. She got fired from her first job because she objected to the working conditions of the servants laboring for wealthy "cottage" owners in Newport, Rhode Island, and tried to form a union. In 1948, she was arrested for picketing a W.T. Grant store in Providence, Rhode Island, because the chain wouldn't serve Blacks in Mississippi. She conducted life-long campaigns for animal rights and started a successful national effort ending hunts where dogs destroyed foxes.

My brother Jack was my hero and remained so until his death at the age of 86. He was the strongest man I have ever known and yet the gentlest. He was by far the best athlete, an outstanding football player, and a boxer. He was the heavyweight champion of the First Division of the Marine Corps and hoped to start a career in boxing after the war ended. As much as he loved boxing, my mother hated it, so he postponed his professional debut for a few years. Even then, he fought under the name of Jack Ryan, so my mother wouldn't know. He was in his early 30s and not able to train professionally. He had some early wins and then retired after losing to a young and upcoming heavyweight. He was very proud to have sparred with Rocky Marciano, who trained and fought his early bouts in Providence.

By age 10, I was the runt of the litter. My brother Larry, almost three years younger, was about 2 inches taller. I was the shortest boy in the fourth grade and became the object of a bully by the name of Dick. (I will leave out his last name, as we later became good friends.) Dick sent me home one day with a bloody nose. Jack noticed and took me aside for boxing lessons. He taught me that punching began with the legs, not the arms, and showed me how to slip punches, jab, and load up for a heavy punch. About a week later, I challenged Dick to a fight. We met after school, and a lot of the other kids accompanied us to a small park. I slipped all of his punches and began to counter-punch, just as Jack had taught me. Dick had never seen a left jab or a right cross. I left him bleeding and crying and impressed a lot of people that day.

For the next couple of weeks, it was payback time as I got even with many of my former tormentors. Word got back to my brother Jack, and he was not happy. He explained that he had taught me how to box for defensive purposes. I hung up my gloves then, but those early boxing lessons saved me during a few confrontations in my service career. I remember the surprise on one 6-footer's face after he had pulled a book out of my hands and made a nasty remark. I hit him with a left jab and a right cross. He went down, shook his head, picked himself up and handed me my book, and muttered, "I'm sorry."

Some of my friends asked me why Jack had never married. There is a straightforward answer. After his discharge, he returned to a home with five brothers and two sisters. Eileen and Peg both worked, but

Jack bore the financial burden of the family. He worked in construction all of his life and was so proud that he was the oldest member of the Providence YMCA when he died in 2009.

One of my favorite Jack Dooley stories involved my first automobile purchase. I was 19 and had saved $450 to buy a used car in 1950. I went to a dealer by myself, fell in love with a blue 1942 Mercury with a rumble seat, signed the bill of sale, and began to drive the car home. I say "began" because the car overheated, and liquid poured out of the radiator a few miles after leaving the dealership. It was towed to a local garage, and I got an almost immediate diagnosis—the block was cracked.

A mechanic drove me back to the used car dealer, and I soon learned the meaning of the words "as is," which the dealer had written on the bill of sale. "The sale is final," he said to me. My brother Jack had a different idea when I told him what happened to the car and the dealer's reaction. The dealer, a hefty man, was sitting in his chair when we walked into his office. He began to say, "I told you already," but he was interrupted when Jack pulled him out of his chair, put him against the wall, and waved his fist under the man's chin. "Are you going to give the kid back his money?" Jack demanded. The poor man, unable to speak, nodded his head in agreement. After Jack put him down, the man took out his wallet and counted $450 into my hands. "He's got a towing bill," Jack snarled. Another twenty was added to my total, which resulted in a $10 profit since the garage only charged me $10.

In 2007, I was living in Sarasota, Florida. There was a major bookstore where I was a faithful customer. One day, I learned that Lou Gorman, former General Manager of the Boston Red Sox, was doing a book signing. We went to the same high school, La Salle Academy, but Lou was two years ahead of me, and I did not know him. I picked up four books and got in line.

"You don't know me, Lou," I said when I got to the front of the line. "But you were the quarterback when my brother played football for the Swan Club."

"What was your brother's name?" Lou asked.

"You knew him as Red Dooley," I said.

Lou stood up from the desk where he was sitting and bellowed.

"Red Dooley. He was the greatest football player Rhode Island ever produced. He saved my ass more than once." Lou wrote the following message in Jack's book: "To Red Dooley, the greatest football player in the history of Rhode Island." I think that Lou believed every word, but Jack did not when I gave him the book. "How about Pat Abbruzzi?" Jack asked, referring to an All-American professional football player and coach.

As much as I loved him, Jack could be trying at times. In 1961 I bought my first new car, a Ford Falcon. A few months later, Jack borrowed the car on a Saturday night. The car was in the driveway the next morning as my mother and I approached it on our way to Sunday Mass. We got within 15 feet of the car and were almost overcome by a burning odor. When I opened the door, the back seat was missing. When I confronted Jack, he had no idea about the missing back seat. My brother Bob quickly solved the puzzle.

"Did you pick up any hitchhikers on your way to Providence?" he asked Jack. Jack admitted that he had and acknowledged that the person was smoking when he got into the car. Bob concluded that ash from the cigarette had landed on the back seat and started the fire. He called the Providence Fire Department and asked if there was any report of a burning car the previous night. He got the location, and we were able to recover the seat that morning. It took a few months before the burning smell left the car and even longer for me to forgive Jack.

In 2009, I was living at my brother Bob's summer home in Narragansett. Jack spent much time with me as I was writing a play, *The Murder Trial of John Gordon*. Patience was not one of Jack's virtues. He would stand in the doorway, waiting for me to finish the next page of the play. I told him more than once that I needed a little time to think, but he never changed his routine. Because of him, the play was written in record time. Regretfully, he died the year before *John Gordon* opened at the Park Theatre in Cranston. I take comfort in the fact that he was the first to read the play, even before my excellent editor, Margaret Satell, or Pat Conley and Scott Molloy, historians who gave me so much background information on John Gordon.

Whenever I think of my sister Peg, I think of Ginger Rogers and dancing. Peg was the best dancer I have ever seen outside of the professionals. She loved life, people, and dancing. And how the boys loved her. Peg had this marvelous personality that attracted boys. We had a summer home in Buttonwoods, a small colony with a wonderful beach. Buttonwoods was divided into what we called the "rich side," wonderful homes right on the water, and the campgrounds, small homes without running water or indoor bathrooms. We thought the small home we had for about six years was wonderful. On the last day of school, we would leave for Buttonwoods and not return until after Labor Day.

Right across from our summer home was a small structure that Peg, and her friends turned into a dance hall. A nickelodeon was installed, and for 10 cents, we danced to the music of Glen Miller, Tommy Dorsey, and Harry James. The dance hall stayed open until 11 p.m., but Bob and I had to be home and in bed by 9 p.m. I can still remember falling asleep to Glen Miller's "Moonlight Serenade" or "A String of Pearls" ringing in my ears. No one danced more or better than my sister Peg.

Peg was always upbeat and happy. The glass was always full. Sometimes with Eileen, there wasn't even a glass. I never remember seeing my sister Eileen attend one dance. A story best illustrates the difference between my sisters. I was in high school, and my mother was so excited because Eileen had a date. It was with an assistant professor at Brown University. My mother and I were both impressed when he came to the door. They were going out for dinner and a movie. Less than an hour later, we heard a car door slam, and Eileen stormed into the house.

"What happened?" my mother asked.

"Stupid fool!" Eileen said. "Telling me that Marlowe wrote Shakespeare's plays." We never saw the professor again.

Eileen and Peg became involved in an episode right out of the famous play *Cyrano de Bergerac*. Cyrano, a dashing officer of the guard and romantic poet, fell in love with Roxane. He believed that Roxane would reject him because of his large nose. So, he resorted to writing letters to her on behalf of one of his cadets, Christian. Roxane fell in love with Christian because of Cyrano's letters.

In 1944, a family from Detroit named Link stayed with us while they visited their son stationed with the Navy at Quonset Point,

Rhode Island. Alvin Link met Peg shortly before he shipped out to the Pacific. He began a steady stream of letters to Peg, who wasn't particularly interested in starting a correspondence with him. She also didn't want to hurt him or his family. So, Eileen answered the letters in Peg's name. Like Roxane and Cyrano, Alvin fell in love with Peg through Eileen's letters. The matter resolved itself when Peg became engaged. Poor Alvin didn't even get a "Dear John" letter from the right girl. Unlike Roxane, who entered a convent after her lover Christian was killed in battle, Peg never thought about becoming a nun.

The boys loved Peg, but she was very selective. She worked at Standard Machinery in Cranston with an engineer by the name of Jack. (I'll leave out his last name). He repeatedly asked Peg out without success. One afternoon, he followed Peg into a dark room where she made copies of blueprints. He asked for a date, and when Peg turned him down again, he slapped her. Peg came home in tears and blurted out the story.

Jack sat at the table and said nothing. The following day, Jack confronted the other Jack, also a good-sized man. A fight ensued, and Jack made quick work of it, leaving Peg's tormentor in the parking lot with facial cuts and a back injury. Jack was arrested and charged with assault. The judge dismissed the case after learning all the circumstances. Jack still had to pay the medical bills, which amounted to several thousand dollars. Fortunately, Jack had not fought professionally at that time. If he had, he would have been charged with assault with deadly weapons, his fists.

Peg met a young man by the name of Donald Malone and married him in 1949. After graduating from Notre Dame, Don got his law degree and began practicing in Sacramento, California. Like her mother, Peg had eight children. Don died at the age of 46 in a courtroom during a trial. Peg was the same age as my mother when my father died, leaving eight children, Don, Pat, Kevin, Jeff, Brian, Candy, Kathy, and Ann.

Age was a big thing to Peg. Although she was about eight years older, she always introduced me as her older brother. The deception carried over, even in death. The date of birth on Peg's tombstone is listed as 1937, six years after I was born. Her wonderful daughters, Ann, Kathy, and Candy were responsible. They also buried their mother with her credit cards to Nordstrom, Bloomingdales, and Saks Fifth Avenue.

Peg moved back to Rhode Island after Don died and bought a house in Cranston, just a few miles from my home on Massasoit Avenue. Jack became close to Peg's youngest daughters, Ann, and Kathy. Later in life, the girls formed their own successful company in Sacramento, and they never forgot Uncle Jack. They even took him on a trip to Ireland, where he was able to visit the birthplace of our grandmother, Margaret Kenneally.

I've written some books, a few plays, and a lot of screenplays, so people logically assume that I hold the title for the best storyteller in the Dooley family. I don't. The best storyteller in the Dooley family was my brother Bill, the fourth member of the Dooley family, following Eileen, Jack, and Peg.

Because they were closer in age, Bill and Jack bonded while Bob, Larry, and I formed the second team. Paul arrived when I was 10. Because of WWII and Korea, he didn't spend too many of his formative years with his brothers. That may have contributed to the fact that he was the kindest and most loved of all the Dooley boys.

Bob, Larry, and I shared a bedroom with Bill. We would go to sleep listening to his wonderful stories about the Katzenjammer Kids, a comic strip we all loved. We also heard new stories about Terry and the Pirates and radio shows like *I Love A Mystery*.

Bill made the characters come alive for us, taking on new adventures and stories never imagined by the creators of those comic strips and radio shows. But, of course, his best stories were the ones he created himself. We would implore him to forget about the comic strips and take us on his creative journeys, frequently involving space travel and gold treasures. Buck Rogers may have influenced him, but his space adventures preceded Star Wars or any of the other storytellers. He had us on the moon long before the Apollo mission.

Along with storytelling, Bill had another great talent—sports trivia, especially baseball and boxing. His fascination with the Boston Red Sox led to confrontations with his younger brothers. Every night, Jim Britt, the Red Sox announcer, had a 15-minute radio show reporting the daily results in baseball. We were a one-radio home, and Jim's program came in the middle of adventure stories we listened to every night. My poor mother had to work out a system rotating the station between baseball and *I Love a Mystery*.

The stories stopped after Bill entered the United Army in 1944. There was a little drama related to Bill's being drafted in 1944. My father had decided that sending one son, Jack, off to war was enough, so he would not let Bill register for the draft. My mother intervened, pointing out that Bill could go to jail for failure to register for the draft. About two months after he registered, Bill was drafted.

After serving in WWII, Bill was recalled for the Korean conflict in 1950. He had just gotten a job with New England Telephone and was suddenly yanked away. Two years later, he returned from Germany to be discharged at Camp Kilmer, New Jersey. My brother Bob had returned from Korea and was at the same camp when they bumped into each other. A battle-hardened Master Sergeant almost wept when he saw the two brothers unite.

Years later, I worried that Bill's sports expertise would get me in serious trouble with my good friend, Red Auerbach, president of the Boston Celtics. I was writing a book with Red, and he invited Bill and me to join him for dinner and a game with the Celtics.

On our trip to Boston, Bill began describing what trades and cuts the team should make to continue its storied past. All I could think of was what would happen if he pushed too hard with Red. It brought back a memory of my first meeting with Red. It was in 1978 when Prentice-Hall commissioned me to write and direct a documentary film about Red. The opening scene was to take place in Red's office at Boston Garden. We were scheduled to begin shooting at 10 a.m., but Red didn't show up until noon. He offered no apologies as he strode into his office and began to light a cigar. I walked over, took the cigar out of his hand, and said, "Red, you're already two hours late. If you light that cigar, the smoke will go into the lights, and we won't be able to shoot today."

Red's face got ashen, but he didn't say anything. In the background, I could hear Red's Secretary, Mary Faherty, whispering under her breath, "Jesus, Mary and Joseph." I came to the office early the following day, and Mary delivered a message. "I thought he would throw you out of the window when you took that cigar out of his hand. When you left yesterday, he said to me, 'He's a tough little bastard, isn't he?'" Of course, I had never offered Red any advice about running a basketball team. Bill is 6′2″, and I'm 5′7″, so I knew who would go through the window first.

Red gave Bill a warm handshake when I introduced them. Bill mumbled something and then took a seat at the back of the office. It was like he was trying to blend into the woodwork. Red and I continued the interview for the book while Bill sat in absolute silence.

During one of the breaks, Red tried to engage Bill in a conversation.

"Are you a sports fan?

"Yes, sir."

"Have you been to many games at the Garden?"

"Yes, sir."

"Do you know who Lou Pieri is?"

"Yes sir. He owns the R.I. Reds and the auditorium in Providence."

"Did you ever go to any of the games in Providence?"

"Yes, sir."

After this series of short answers, Red was glad to get back to the book. We ended at about 5 p.m., then made plans to meet Red for dinner and the Celtics game that night.

As soon as we got out of earshot, I attacked Bill. "What the hell is wrong with you? Red has to think you're retarded."

'I couldn't help it," Bill said. "I was scared. That was Red Auerbach."

Fortunately, Bill loosened up when we met the Celtics owners at dinner, along with Larry Bird, who was rehabbing. It turned into a nice experience.

When my play *The Auerbach Dynasty* opened in Boston, John Havlicek, Tom Heinsohn, Jan Volk, former Celtics General Manager, and Bob Cousy came to opening night. Bill sat next to Bob Cousy, and they had a wonderful conversation going back to George Kaftan and Joe Mullaney and the Holy Cross team. Bob Cousy's daughter told Bill how much her father had enjoyed the conversation.

Bill made a good choice when he married Patricia Hackett in 1957. They had five children, Patti, Billy, Jim, Kathleen, and Bryan. Billy was killed in a tragic skateboarding accident at age 15. Bill's memorable laugh, which could captivate a whole room, disappeared after his son died and never returned completely. Pat died in December of 2020.

My mother had an expression she used when referring to her third-born son: "My poor Bob." He earned every word. Bob was always there for everyone., starting with his family and extending to his friends. I think he has the record for being "best man" at weddings with eight. Bob has more friends than anyone I have ever known. He also does more good things on a slow Tuesday than most of us accomplish in a lifetime. I could write a book about his kind acts, but one, in particular, demonstrates all you have to know about Bob Dooley.

It was a Saturday on a hot August day in 1956. I was sitting on the porch writing a report for a history class at Providence College. Jack was cutting the grass, and Bill was watching a Red Sox game. Suddenly a moving truck followed by a car pulled up across the street. A couple and five children climbed out and began moving furniture into a house directly across the street from the Dooleys. Suddenly Bob swung into action. "We have to help that family move in," he said. So, four of us crossed the street where Bob was already talking to Jack and Ann Donahue, our new neighbors.

Jack Donahue had already started to unload the truck when Bob stopped him. "It would be better if we did the bedroom sets first," he explained. "They will take the most effort, so we should do them when we have the most energy," he said. He was right. Carrying mattresses and heavy beds up three flights of stairs took much effort. We ran into a slight problem when we began to move the living room furniture into the house.

The Donahues had sketched out a plan showing where they wanted the couch and chairs placed. Bob disagreed, pointing out things like the afternoon sun and the best use of space. Bob was gracious enough to reach a compromise with the Donahues. Meanwhile, Jack. Bill and I stood impatiently, holding a heavy couch. The Donhues agreed to Bob's new placement plan for the kitchen, so we only had to make a few moves.

A few months after they moved in, Ann confided in me. "Jack and I were worried that Bob might not let us occupy the same bedroom," she said. "I asked Jack if our marriage certificate was in the truck."

While my mother liked the Donahues, she did not always agree with Ann's concepts of raising children. Ann was very bright, a graduate of Pembroke. She took a "hands-off" approach to child-rearing. Her five children climbed and hung over the edge of the third floor on more than one occasion. They rode their bikes into the street, often in front of cars. My mother's complaints to Ann fell on deaf ears. The children were lovable, especially one by the name of Paul. He was my mother's favorite, often stopping in for milk and cookies. Paul was also the most daring, climbing and hanging from all parts of the roof or darting into the street on his bicycle without looking for cars.

Three years later, Jack Donahue was transferred by his company, and the family moved to Connecticut, near a lake. A few months after they left, I found my mother crying in the kitchen. She had received a letter from Ann Donahue telling her that Paul had drowned in the lake.

Bob was in the United Army in Korea when the Chinese communists entered the war. He was trapped in the ensuing battle and had to be evacuated by the United States Navy from Pusan. I learned about the furious and dangerous fighting his unit went through from other sources because Bob never talked about the experiences that earned him a Bronze Star. "The real heroes are buried there," he said when I tried to question him.

Bob was 40 years old when he married Nancy Donahue, 13 years younger. They had a wonderful marriage with three great kids: Jeff, Colleen, and Scott. They had a solid relationship, yet they were two entirely different people. Nancy was slow and deliberate, while Bob was quick and decisive. I once said that it took Nancy 15 minutes to butter a piece of toast. By the time her toast was ready, Bob would have finished breakfast and did one of his many daily chores.

Because Nancy was so much younger, Bob always asked me to help her make decisions when he was gone. Sadly, and unexpectedly, Nancy died at the age of 63. Bob has always been a strong Catholic, and it is his faith that pulled him through the loss of his beloved Nancy. She did get to meet her first grandson, Joe, but not the three other grandsons who joined the family after she died. Bob's oldest, Jeff, is the voice of the Hartford Yard Goats, a minor league baseball team based in Hartford, Connecticut. He is also the voice of the University of Hartford basketball team. K.C. Jones, the Celtics great, served as Jeff's color commentator for years. Jeff introduced me to K.C., who contributed so much to a screenplay I wrote with Bill Russell and Sam Jones about African American players coming into the National Basketball Association.

Bob's other son, Scott, is an I.T. genius. He is always there to help me find new research material or set up fulfillment services for my books. His daughter Colleen is a special education teacher known for her compassion and patience.

Bob is argumentative and opinionated but never judgmental or mean-spirited. Unlike most of the Irish, it is impossible for him to carry a grudge. He thinks the best of everyone and firmly believes that the process of forgiving or being forgiven is the basic requirement for living a good life. It took me many years to realize it, but my brother Bob is the finest human being I have ever known. I can make this assessment objectively, recognizing that I lack most of the qualities that distinguish Bob.

About nine years after John Kennedy was assassinated, two of his closest friends, Dave Powell and Kenneth O'Donnell wrote *Johnny, We Hardly Knew Ye*, that title would be appropriate for my brother Larry. Of all my siblings, Larry was the most mysterious. It wasn't that he ever did anything so secretive. It was just that he was so independent and private, utterly different from his loud and opinionated siblings.

I think he was the brightest of all of us. He was undoubtedly the best read. To say that he marched to the beat of a different drummer is an understatement. He didn't care for rules and regulations, and he paid for it in numerous ways. Larry was a tall, good-looking man, and the ladies were attracted to him. He was the office manager for a major moving company for a number of years—until he stole the boss's girlfriend. He was out of the office the same day and out of the relationship a few months later. Larry did not believe in long-term commitments.

Through my brother Bill, Larry was hired by the phone company. He soon got a reputation for being one of the best troubleshooters at the company. When a complex problem erupted, Larry would come to the scene and resolve it almost immediately. He was respected by his co-workers, but Larry never developed many friendships. He preferred to keep to himself and read.

After my mother died in 1981, Larry became even more withdrawn. I was living in Connecticut at the time, but I talked to my brothers Jack, Bill and Bob frequently. Larry wouldn't answer phone calls or visits. He would remain behind a locked door, even when his car was in the driveway. Matters came to a head when Larry stopped going to work. Bill, who was well connected at the telephone company, did everything possible to save his job, but Larry simply decided he was done working.

I confronted Larry, and he agreed that he needed some help. I set up an appointment with a local psychiatrist and agreed to pick Larry up for the session. I was in the driveway of Larry's apartment on the day of the appointment. No Larry. I went to the local library, one of his favorite places, but was not able to find him. I drove back to Connecticut, deciding that I would wash my hands of this different and difficult brother. It's a decision that I will always regret. He needed help, and I should not have given up on him so soon.

Jack, Bill, and Bob repeatedly tried to see Larry. He would stay in his apartment behind closed doors and would not answer the telephone. My father always hated smoking, a feeling he conveyed to his children. It didn't work with Larry, who smoked at least two packages of Camels every day. I pleaded with him to switch to filtered cigarettes, but he never did. Fortunately, the last years of Larry's life were a lot happier. He moved in with Jack, and the two of them got along quite well.

He seemed more relaxed and comfortable with himself. Shortly after I accepted a job with a Philadelphia publisher in 1998, I got together with my brothers for a farewell dinner. It was like old times as we sat around an Irish pub in Providence and revisited great memories.

A few months later, Bob called to tell me that Larry had suffered a stroke. I never really got the chance to say goodbye, as he remained in a coma when I visited him the next day. He died about a week later.

Sometimes, when I think of Larry, I'm reminded of a story that involved my mother. It was a snowy day when I was 13, and I had just returned from a day of shoveling snow. I remember placing the money I had received on the fireplace mantle, as was the custom for all the Dooley boys—except Larry. He returned just as wet and exhausted as I was—without a dime. He had spent the day sledding or throwing snowballs with his friends David and Donald Dinneen.

"It's not fair," I complained to my mother. "I work all day to make money. Larry just plays, but you never say anything to him."

My mother would never make a negative about any of her children. She looked at me and said, "I guess I expect more of you, Kenny."

Maybe that was the problem with Larry. We had a different set of expectations. I was not an easy act for him to follow in school. Loud and frequently obnoxious, everyone knew exactly who Ken Dooley was. When I began writing plays in the fourth grade, I became quite popular with my classmates looking for roles.

There is another aspect of my relationship with Larry that I have come to appreciate. I was not the ideal older brother. I tormented Larry in so many ways. When I was 15, I was 5′7″. Larry was 6 feet tall and considerably stronger. Yet, he never tried to get even with me for any of my earlier transgressions. Larry was introverted, quiet, and private. He did not make a lot of friends and was quite content to stay in his room with his beloved books. Yes, the two of us could not be more different—but I miss Larry every day of my life.

There was no question as to Larry's favorite brother. Paul was at the top of the list for all of us. When Paul was stricken with multiple sclerosis, Larry and Jack put in a pool on Massasoit Avenue. Almost every day, Paul got to swim, one of the few enjoyments left to him after that awful disease put him in a wheelchair and eventually took his life.

Paul arrived in 1941, an event my mother always referred to as a "late blessing." It seems his mission in life was to spread good feelings and joy. He didn't receive any extraordinary intellectual or physical gifts, although he turned into one of the best baseball hitters in the family. It was his personality and love of people and life that set him apart. I never heard Paul make a disparaging remark about anyone. He saw only the good qualities in people and always looked past any faults.

He married his beloved Maria in 1965 and fathered five sons,

Steven, Michael, Peter, Patrick, and Adam. I remember Adam's birth in particular. Paul was already in a wheelchair with multiple sclerosis when Adam was born, two months prematurely. After I got the news, I drove to the hospital and went immediately to the pediatric intensive care unit. A nurse confronted me and said only parents were allowed to enter. I told her that I was Paul, the father of the newborn. Adam was barely the size of a coke bottle, weighing in at 2 pounds, three ounces. He grew to be six feet tall, five inches taller than me, and I was a full-term baby.

I guess my mother felt her family was complete when Paul was born. It didn't turn out that way. Her younger sister Jane married Clem Travers, a Navy veteran, in 1945. They had two children, Jane and John, in the next few years. Clem died of cancer in 1950, and Jane died about seven years later. Jane became my mother's third daughter and John, her seventh son. No one took my mother's death harder than John.

The only drawback to a large family is that it is so difficult to say goodbye. I have delivered eulogies for Paul, Larry, Peg, Eileen, and Jack. I am told that my living brother, Bob, gets very nervous when I return to Rhode Island.

It took me a long time to realize it, but the best things in life are the people you love, the places you've been, and the memories you made along the way. Of course, my most treasured heirlooms are the sweet memories of my family.

I frequently drive by 15 Haywood Street in Cranston, where I spent the first 12 years of my life. I close my eyes and watch as Larry, Bob, and I come down the stairs on Christmas morning. I have no idea how my parents did it, but none of my friends got more presents than we did.

Then I swing by 92 Massasoit in Edgewood, my home, for the next 20 years. In the summer, I drive to Buttonwoods, a place filled with so many great memories. The dancehall still stands, although it has not been used for that purpose for a number of years. When I close my eyes, I still hear the wonderful sounds of Frank Sinatra and Bing Crosby. I hear my sister Peg's wonderful laugh as she dances to the music of Glen Miller.

In 1941, a sign was erected in the hall listing all of the members of the armed forces from Buttonwoods during WWII. It is faded now, but I can still read the name, "John J. Dooley." I still marvel at our former house. It was about the size of a three-car garage. It had no indoor plumbing, and water had to be fetched from a nearby well.

Sometimes when I'm dining in one of those expensive French restaurants, it occurs to me that I would trade the whole menu for one plate of my mother's beef stew. She turned out all those wonderful meals on an old black cast iron stove with no temperature controls and a leaking oven.

Neither of my sisters inherited my mother's cooking skills. Peg explained that she would ask my mother to explain one of her recipes. "You put in a pinch of this and a dab of that," my mother would say. Take it out of the oven when it's finished."

A wise person once said, "Memory is the first great gift of nature and the last to be taken away." As long as I have memory, all of my wonderful family will be with me forever.

LIKE FATHER, LIKE SON

I enjoyed telling people that I was a Tennis Hall of Fame member when I lived in Newport, Rhode Island. Of course, anyone who watched me would soon realize a significant difference between being a member who can play on those extraordinary grass courts and being enshrined in the Hall of Fame building next door.

Every Saturday and Sunday, I played at a round-robin with other members. The teams rotated, so you were not stuck with the same player all morning. On one of my first days, I was paired with a very confident, positive lady who gave continuous and loud advice to me, even while the ball was in play. When we lost the point (frequently), she would give me an analysis of what I did wrong—being out of position, not covering her, volleying when I should have lobbed—the list was endless.

All of this would have been acceptable if her play had been at the same level as her instruction. She was terrible. Her serve was soft, and our opponents' sent screamers past me or drove the ball into corners where she would either swing and miss or send popups over the net, which my grinning opponent would put away with great glee.

More painful than the lost point was the analysis that followed. "You should have poached, you shouldn't have poached, you should have allowed the ball to go through to me, you served to our opponent's strength." The list was endless. She did make up for her poor play with her calls, which were among the worst I had ever seen. According to the rules of tennis, if you don't see the ball out, it is in. She reversed that rule, the only thing that kept us in the game.

What made matters worse was the grin of one of my opponents, especially after being chastised for another error that cost us the point. It was more of a smirk than a smile. He was a tall, gangly guy who had the movements of a good athlete, and he took great delight in blasting her serves past me. If I poached, he went down the line. If I stayed in position, he hit a deep return which my partner would miss entirely or put up a weak return that he would put away.

After the point was over, he would move quickly to the net as my partner explained what I had done to cost us the point. His smirk told me that he didn't miss a word. I decided I liked him only slightly better than my partner. Things came to a head when she called a ball that was clearly in, out. I overruled her. She said it was her call. I told her the only thing worse than her calls was her play. I said she was a disgrace to the game of tennis. Play stopped around us as she stalked off the court. Feeling a little sheepish, I tried to slink away as fast as I could.

My path was blocked by my tall opponent, whose sheepish grin had broken into a huge smile.

"What's your name," he asked, extending his hand.

"Ken Dooley," I said. "I'm glad I gave you such a good time," I added sarcastically. "And who are you?"

"Tim Cohane," he replied.

I stopped dead in my tracks.

Tim Cohane was one of my boyhood heroes. I knew at an early age that I wanted to be a writer, so I tried to read all of the great authors, from novelists like John Steinbeck and Thomas Wolfe to sportswriters like Tim Cohane, the sports editor for *Look Magazine*. To describe him as a sportswriter is like labeling Jack London a journalist. Tim Cohane was a journalist and a poet. He coined the phrase "The Seven Blocks of Granite" when describing Fordham University's great football line in the 1930s. It included the legendary football coach, Vince Lombardi. I remember reading his book, *Gridiron Grenadiers: The Story of West Point Football* while still in high school. Tim was an advisor to Red Blaik, a pallbearer for Grantland Rice, and a close friend of Vince Lombardi. There was no way this grinning guy could be related. The apple could not have fallen that far from the tree.

Yes, he was Tim Cohane Jr., named after my boyhood idol. We walked off the court together, and I told him about the great respect I had for his father. I did not say it, but I could not help but think that his father would have been a little kinder on the tennis court. Tim called me the following week, and we had lunch together. He was particularly interested in my friendship with Red Auerbach, mainly since he had attended Holy Cross on a basketball scholarship.

A light went off in my head as we talked—Tim Cohane and Holy Cross basketball—the famous panty raid. Tim played basketball as a freshman at Holy Cross in 1961. Following a game against St. John's in the NIT in New York City, Tim and two of his teammates took part in a panty raid at Manhattanville College, an exclusive school for young women. None of the ladies involved felt the least bit threatened by the intrusion and described the invaders as "gentlemen."

There was a lot of humor connected to the event, except for the Jesuits at Holy Cross and his parents in Scarsdale. Tim and his friends were suspended from school for a year. More than 30 years after the event, Holy Cross President, the Rev. Philip Boroughs, S.J., issued an official pardon to Tim Cohane.

After working as a truck driver for a year, the Naval Academy, one of 10 colleges that had recruited Tim out of high school, asked if he would be interested in the Navy. Tim entered Annapolis as a Plebe in 1963. He led the team in scoring his freshman year and later held All-American Dick Snyder in check as Navy upset Davidson, coached by Lefty Driesel and ranked second in the country. After a solid basketball career at Annapolis, he volunteered for Viet Nam.

Tim never talked much about his experiences in Nam. Like most guys who had stories to tell, he was quiet. As a former investigative reporter, I swung into action and got a copy of the citation that awarded him the Bronze Star Medal. It read in part:

> On 30 March 1969, Lt. Cohane was Patrol Officer of a mobile patrol force, consisting of a Monitor and an Armored Troop Carrier when the patrol suddenly came under heavy enemy rocket and automatic weapons fire from both riverbanks of the upper Van Co Tay River. The Monitor on which he was riding sustained four direct rocket hits, causing an intense fire aboard the craft and rendering all radios inoperative. Although Lt. Cohane received shrapnel wounds in his right arm, he disregarded his wounds, organized a fire-fighting party, and attempted to extinguish the flames. When the danger from exploding ammunition became too grave, Lt. Cohane assembled his men on the fantail for their own protection. When a River Patrol Boat came alongside to extract the crew, he was the last man to leave the burning craft, and then his only concern was accounting for all his men and ensuring the wounded received first aid.

Vice-Admiral E. R. Zumwalt, Commander of U.S. Naval Forces, signed the citation.

When Tim left the Navy, he took a job as basketball coach at Iona Prep, a team that had gone 1–17 the previous year. Three years later, the team went to the state quarterfinals. In 1974, he started a men's team at Manhattanville, the same college of the infamous panty raid that cost him a scholarship at Holy Cross. Tim built it into a solid Division III program that earned two NCAA berths.

In 1979, he took the head coach's job at Division I Dartmouth. The school was more interested in football than basketball, and Tim suffered his first failure as a coach. He left for Wall Street, hoping to work for Salomon Brothers, the Wall Street brokerage. At age 40, Tim was considered too old for Salomon's training program, so he became a trainee without a salary. He worked on the trading floor for two years before starting his own company—Cohane Rafferty Securities in 1985, a firm that acted as an agent in banking transactions.

Then the coaching bug struck again. He accepted a job as coach of the Merchant Marine Academy at King's Point, Long Island. The year before he took over, Kings Point had a record of 8–17. In his first season, they went 25–3 and reached the second round of the Division III tournament. He never got over his goal to coach a major college in a Division I school, which led him to leave Kings Point and accept assistant coaching roles with Army and Boston College.

In 1993, he became head coach at the University of Buffalo. He won three of his first four games as coach, including a stunning upset of Niagara. The team won 10 games the first year, double its total from the year before. In less than two full seasons under Cohane, the basketball team met all the University of Buffalo's goals.

A new athletic director, Robert Arkeilpane, and a disloyal assistant coach, Eric Eisenberg, turned things around abruptly in 1999 when Tim was accused of violating NCAA rules by watching uncommitted recruits play pick-up basketball in the University of Buffalo gym, a minor infraction even if true. One of the students who initially supported the school's position later recanted his testimony, saying that the school threatened to withhold his degree unless he supported the college's claims. Cohane was forced to resign, and the NCAA sanctioned him with a "show cause" label. It took two years for Cohane to convince the NCAA Appeal Board to reverse the finding, but his coaching career was over by that time.

In 2002, he sued the NCAA for a violation of due process. To prevail, Cohane would have to overcome the famous U.S. Supreme Court decision against legendary Coach Jerry Tarkanian when the Court determined the NCAA was not a State Actor and could not be held to the Constitution's due process standards. A victory by Cohane would rock college athletics for years to come.

Cohane graduated from Roger Williams Law School in 2005, specializing in Constitutional lawsuits. In 2010, the United States Supreme Court supported a Second Circuit decision and Cohane's theory that if the NCAA acted in concert with the State University of New York at Buffalo, it became a State Actor and subject to Constitutional due process. The case was remanded to the District Court in Buffalo. The NCAA argued that because Cohane had overturned the "show cause" section in the NCAA Administrative hearing, he was never legally punished. In 2015, the Second Circuit concurred with the NCAA argument. Even though Cohane had overturned the Tarkanian ruling, the NCAA wiggled out. Not to be dismayed, Cohane now represents Coaches Against the NCAA and has been Adjunct Professor at Roger Williams University Law School, specializing in Due Process.

The Cohane case reminds me of one of the protections that led the USA Gymnastics Board to make a secret payment to gold medalist McKayle Maroney to cover up the sexual abuse she suffered at the hands of Dr. Larry Nasser. He was sentenced to 175 years in prison after pleading guilty to sexual assault. How could members of the USA Gymnastics board cover up the sexual abuse of children? It's a question that organizations such as the NCAA or the USA Gymnastics Board will never have to answer, as long as they continue to be protected by our court system. Unfortunately, Tim Cohane never coached again after being forced out of the University of Buffalo, a sad ending to an otherwise illustrious coaching career.

When I asked Tim if he remembered our first meeting on the tennis court, he sent me the following email:

Yes—I remember it well. You were the first to tell her off. She later went to Del Ray Beach and has not been seen up here for ten years.

The Club is happy you both have left.

I'm sure Tim had his familiar smirk as he wrote that last sentence. Tim later founded the Newport Breakfast Club, which comprises many former jocks or successful businesspeople. I did not qualify in either category, but Tim waived the rules to get me in. He has since apologized to other club members for doing so. I have responded by initiating three petitions for his impeachment as president. The sole mission of this Club is to make sure every member has a few people to attend his final services.

Basketball player, coach, Navy hero, entrepreneur, lawyer, Tim Cohane has had a full and interesting life. When I compare his life to his father's, my boyhood hero, I have to agree—the apple doesn't fall far from the tree.

A Connecticut Knight of the Roundtable

When most young men are thinking about girls and games, Gary Lutender was confronting radiation and chemotherapy. The small lump in his neck turned out to be lymphoma, and only aggressive treatment could stop its deadly growth. While his friends worried about SAT scores, 16-year- old Gary worried about blood cell counts. He had to drop out of school because the treatments left him tired and weak. Family and friends were relieved when it appeared the disease had been arrested, and he returned to school. I still remember the phone call I received from Gary's mother Lois about six months later telling me that cancer had returned, and Gary was back in the hospital. More importantly, he had announced to the family that he did not want any further treatment.

Lois said I could cheer Gary up and asked if I would visit him. Gary and I had bonded a few years earlier when I gave him some instruction on hitting a baseball. We must have made an interesting contrast as we stood together in the batter's box. Gary was 6′1″ at the time while I checked in at 5′7″. The instruction worked, and Gary became one of the better hitters on his team.

I was in his hospital room that same day after Lois's call. His skin was the color of the sheets on the bed, but he struggled to tell me how great he was feeling. He did not want to have any more treatments. Instead of arguing, I told him the story of Sir Gary Lutender, an Irish knight who had fought against the English invaders of Ireland. He had been seriously wounded in battle and crawled into a cave to die. But he suddenly stood, and raising his sword and said, "I am Sir Gary Lutender, and I am hurt, but I am not slain. I'll lay me down to bleed a while, and then I'll rise to fight again."

I told Gary that Sir Gary healed and lived for another 50 years. When he asked me what became of him, I explained that Sir Gary drowned after falling into a vat of beer at a local brewery at the age of 98. I can still remember Gary's laugh when I told him that the knight got out of the vat at least three times to go to the bathroom. Gary agreed to another round of chemotherapy and radiation that finally eradicated the cancer.

I was the only non-family member at his graduation from the University of Rhode Island. He then started his own construction company and built a magnificent home for his parents on Mt. Archer in Lyme, Connecticut. When he was 29, Gary gave a luncheon for everyone who had helped him during his cancer treatments. Dr. Dick Benton, his oncologist, and all the nurses involved were invited. I was the only non-medical, non-family member invited to the celebration. One thing that was clear that day—I was not alone in my love for this young man. We rejoiced that afternoon, realizing that Gary was cancer-free and on his way to a successful and happy life. I never had a son, but Gary and a couple of other young men from Pennsylvania—Matthew and Clifford Satell—filled in admirably.

With a growing reputation as a builder of fine homes and a new girlfriend, Sondra, his future looked bright. Then suddenly, without warning, Gary suffered a heart attack. The doctors said the massive radiation Gary had received during his radiation treatments weakened the heart muscles. He spent a week in a coma at Yale-New Haven Hospital, awaiting a new heart. On the day that a suitable heart became available, Gary's vital organs began to shut down, removing him as a candidate for a heart transplant. He died on March 17, 1998, on St. Patrick's Day. I have never been able to celebrate that Irish holiday since Gary's death.

Gary gave us so many positives in life, and now there is one we can return to him. There was no suitable heart available when Gary was first stricken. I hope that every young person who reads these words lives to be 100. I also hope that they fill out an organ donor card in case God has a different timetable.

Gary endured more pain before his 17th birthday than most of us confront in a lifetime. Yet, he never talked about it because he did not want his family and friends to suffer with him. Perhaps a severe illness at such a young age helped him develop a sense of values that allowed him to distinguish between the important and the mundane. But no one should ever believe that cancer forged the character of Gary Lender. Instead, Gary's character enabled him to confront the disease in all of its ramifications without surrender or complaint. It cost him his health and, ultimately, his life. But it never won the more important battle. It was never able to alter his loving, caring nature or undermine his tremendous zest for life. It never caused him to develop a "why me?" attitude or cast himself as a victim.

Cynics who claim that the American family is in decline should have spent time in the coronary care unit of Yale-New Haven Hospital, where the Lutenders never left Gary's bedside. The love and devotion they showed sustained and comforted Gary during his final days. Those who feel that today's youth are callous and uncaring would change their thinking if they watched as Gary's friends rallied to show their love and support. They came not for a visit but to keep a bedside vigil for their dying friend. Shakespeare never wrote a more moving tribute than was delivered by one friend who whispered in Gary's ear that his beloved Bruins had defeated the hated Rangers.

Gary was only with us for 31 years, a relatively short time from a chronological perspective. But they were quality years because Gary lived every minute to its fullest. No knight could have exhibited more courage on a quest than Gary did during his battle with cancer. John Donne could have been writing about Gary more than 300 years ago when he wrote the wonderful poem, "Death Be Not Proud."

The same qualities that made it so difficult to say goodbye to Gary make him impossible to forget. I shall remember him as Sir Gary the Gentle, protector of goodness, trust, kindness, charity, and humor. In the center of his coat-of-arms is a large red heart representing both his tremendous capacity for love and his unlimited courage. Instead of weapons and symbols of war, his shield is covered with flowers and carpenter tools, for Sir Gary was a builder, not a breaker, a humanitarian, not a warrior.

As he takes his place at King Author's Roundtable, Sir Lancelot, Sir Galahad, and even Merlin had better beware, for Sir Gary is bringing the same magic to Camelot that he always brought to us.

A Guy Named Joe

In 1949, I bought a 1938 Dodge from a neighbor for $250. I overpaid. I could outrun the car from a standing start, and once the speedometer passed 50, the car would shudder and shake. The problem resolved itself when the speedometer broke and never worked again. I could tell exactly how fast I was going by the shaking and shimmering.

I was a freshman at Providence College that fall, and the car did get me there every day, overcoming some of the hills in the area. There were other challenges to be met during the cold months, jump-starting a dead battery, or getting my brothers up to give a hand-push to start the car.

I had to get a push from another vehicle more than once when my engine quit for no apparent reason. One morning the transmission went, and the cost for a replacement was $125, half of what I paid for the car. The car went into dry-dock, and I began to take two buses to get to school every day.

I remember one particular January day. It was slightly above zero, and all the buses were late. When I arrived in the cafeteria, ice cycles were hanging from my hair. I had struck up a casual friendship with another freshman, Joe Paolino. We didn't have any classes together—Joe was a business major, and I was majoring in English and history, but we began having coffee or lunch together in the cafeteria for some reason. Joe shook his head in disbelief as I sat shivering at the table, my frozen hands trying to grip a coffee cup.

"What happened?" Joe asked. "You look like you've been out in the cold all night."

When I explained about the late busses, Joe asked me about my car. I told him about the transmission problem that was going to keep it in permanent dry-dock.

"What will it cost to get it fixed?" Joe asked.

I told him about the $125 repair and thought that would end the conversation. It didn't. Joe came up with a plan. He would loan me the $125, and I could come up with any repayment plan that fit my budget. I turned him down kindly but flatly.

I had gone to La Salle Academy and spent three years with many of the freshmen at Providence College. Joe had gone to a private school, so I had only known him for a few months. I liked and respected him, but there was no way I could take a loan of that magnitude from a guy I hardly knew.

Joe seemed to accept my decision and didn't bring it up again—until one morning, I arrived at the cafeteria frozen and frostbitten. He was at another table as I struggled with books and frozen hands. I still remember the expression on his face as he walked up to the table. He handed me an envelope with $125 in it. "Get that car fixed," he said. His voice had that resolve that helped him become one of the most successful real estate developers in the history of Rhode Island.

I got the car fixed and repaid Joe on the installment plan. After the final payment, Joe and I had lunch at Oates Tavern. I joined the U.S.A.F. during the Korean conflict and didn't graduate from Providence College until ten years later. I lived in Connecticut and New York and never saw or spoke to Joe again.

I was not surprised by his tremendous success as a real estate developer. Joe had success written all over him as a college freshman. He was a natural leader who listened more than he talked, but when he said something, people listened. Joe ended up changing the face of downtown Providence forever.

I think we all have milestones that have a profound effect on our lives. Over the years, I've written a number of books, plays, and screenplays. I cannot help but think that if not for the kindness of a man I barely knew, I might be delivering books instead of writing them.

There was one final incident in my relationship with Joe Paolino. As a board member of the Rhode Island Heritage Hall of Fame, I was able to vote for Joe's induction in 2013. It was a belated thanks to a man who had been so kind to me. But gratitude had nothing to do with my vote. Joe's history of philanthropy and tremendous efforts in preserving historical Providence qualified him for induction. Later I voted for his son, Joseph R. Paolino Jr.'s induction in 2017. I joined the Paolinos when I was inducted in 2018.

So, two guys who used to drink coffee together more than 70 years ago at Providence College now hang together in the R.I.H.H.A. I could not be in better company.

Meeting Morley Safer

My favorite news program of all time is *60 Minutes*, especially in its early years. Every Sunday, I sat in front of the TV and listened to people like Mike Wallace, Dan Rather, Harry Reasoner, Ed Bradley, Andy Rooney, and Morley Safer as they exposed fraud and corruption, giving voice to whistleblowers.

I particularly enjoyed Morley Safer, a mainstay of the program for almost five decades, profiling politicians, opera stars, writers, homeless people, waterfront crime, Swiss bank accounts, and the Viet Nam war. He was one of the few reporters who went out with the troops during the Viet Nam War. One of his reports infuriated President Lyndon Johnson, who ordered Safer investigated as a possible Communist. He was cleared.

In 1983, Safer produced an investigative report in which he cited new evidence that helped free Lenell Geter, an African American engineer sentenced to life in prison in Texas for an armed robbery he did not commit. In contrast with the abrasive Mike Wallace, Morley Safer also produced exciting programs on the lighter side of life, including Tupperware parties, children's beauty pageants, and croquet games.

I lived in Connecticut when a friend told me that Morley Safer had moved to Chester, Connecticut, and joined the Old Saybrook Racquet Club, where I was also a member. Naturally, I was looking forward to meeting him on the tennis court. But, unfortunately, our first meeting occurred off the tennis court in a rather unpleasant encounter.

One of my favorite restaurants was *Restaurant du Village*, located in Chester, CT. It was owned by a husband-and-wife team, Michel and Cynthia Keller. Restaurants at the time had to offer both smoking and non-smoking sections. I had always hated smoking, so I was seated in the non-smoking area. As I studied the menu, my date nudged me under the table and motioned to the adjoining table. Morley Safer was being seated with his wife, Jane, and another couple.

Andy Rooney, another featured member of *60 Minutes*, always warned viewers to "let him eat his dinner if they saw him in a restaurant." I decided to offer Morley and his guests the same respect. I didn't even glance over at them—until all four members of the group lit cigarettes. I was almost blinded by the smoke that wafted into my eyes. Finally, I thought I would take the high road, and I turned to Morley and said very politely, "Mr. Safer, I'm sure you don't realize it, but you are sitting in the non-smoking section."

No response. My complaint was not even acknowledged. The conversation and smoking continued, and so did the smokescreen. Finally, I got up, sought out Chef Michel, and pointed out what was happening in the non-smoking section.

"Do you know who that is?" Chef Michel asked.

"I recognize Morley Safer," I answered. "But he has to respect the smoking rules like everyone else."

"I will be happy to move you," he said.

"He is the one who should be moved," I insisted as I returned to my table and watched as a busboy removed the dishes from my table. I demanded that he stop, and soon Chef Michel joined us. "You have to move or leave," Chef Michel warned. Meanwhile, my date pleaded with me to move to another table. It was a "first" date that turned out to be a "last" date. I majored in "first" dates for most of my life.

I chose to leave and told Chef Michel what he could do with the check for the dinners sitting at the table. The commotion had drawn the attention of most of the diners, except for Morley Safer's group. The conversation and smoking continued, and I wasn't even acknowledged.

Just before we left, I turned to Morley Safer and shouted, "Now I know how Jeffrey Wigand felt." It got Morley's attention, and for the first time, I was acknowledged, not with words but a withering glance. Wigand was the most famous whistleblower who appeared on *60 Minutes* and warned, "We're a nicotine delivery business." He was the former director of research for Brown & Williamson, the country's third-largest tobacco company. He was hired to develop a safer cigarette but was fired after clashing with his bosses. Wigand said his company was aware of the addictive product it was selling, despite its CEO's testimony before Congress to the contrary.

His interview with Mike Wallace was put on hold when the legal department ordered *60 Minutes* not to run the story. Wigand was thrown under the bus by *60 Minutes*. In 1999, *The Insider*, a movie starring Russell Crowe, chronicled both the infighting at CBS and the efforts by Brown & Williamson to silence its former employee. Wigand later said that he was disappointed that *60 Minutes* had wavered on getting his message out.

Morley Safer had nothing to do with his bosses' decisions that delayed the airing of the most important story ever reported by *60 Minutes*. It was an extremely sensitive subject for anyone connected to the program, as shown by Morley's reaction to my statement about Wigand.

Should I have said it? No, it was a cheap shot. My big mouth has cost me jobs, relationships, friendships, and more than a few fat lips. I like to think that I might not have said it if I had gotten the slightest bit of reaction from Morley. I never saw Morley Safer in person again, but I continued to enjoy him every Sunday.

I also never dined at *Restaurant du Village* again. But I did learn something that caused me to understand Chef Michel's decision that day better. Morley Safer had invested in the restaurant, so he was part-owner when I asked him to move.

Nothing that happened that night has made the slightest bit of difference in my feeling about Morley Safer, the journalist. Instead, it was his powerful close-ups of firefights and events that affected my thinking about the Viet Nam War. His helicopter was shot down on one occasion, but he was back in the air the next day.

He toured China in 1967, posing as a Canadian tourist because Western reporters were barred. He covered the war in the Middle East, the fighting in Northern Ireland, the Soviet invasion of Czechoslovakia, and Nigeria's civil war. He was a great interviewer, asking questions the man in the street might pose.

Morley Safer and I have one thing in common. It is not in writing, although we both supported ourselves by putting words on paper. My accomplishments pale in contrast to Morley's, who won many awards, including Emmys, Peabodys, and the George Polk Award for career achievement. But we were both born in 1931, in the middle of the Great Depression.

CBS ran an hour-long special, "Morley Safer: A Reporter's Life," when he retired on May 11, 2016. He died the following week. In it, Morley revealed that he had not liked being on television. "It makes me uneasy. It's not natural to be talking to a piece of machinery. But the money is good," he said.

You were the best, Morey Safer. I wish I had kept my big mouth shut that night at the restaurant.

The Neighborhoods

"Friends come into your life for a season, a reason, or a lifetime." I tried to track the author of that quote, but it is listed as "anonymous." It is appropriate in describing the friends I made along the way. I grew up in three neighborhoods: 15 Hayward Street in the Auburn section of Cranston, 92 Massasoit Avenue in Edgewood, and Buttonwoods, a summer colony located on Narragansett Bay in Warwick. I was always so fortunate to make a lot of good friends in all three neighborhoods. Some of them disappeared after grade school and high school. Others lasted until marriage or out-of-state moves. A few close ones disappeared after my divorce. Just as splitting couples divide the material assets, friends usually end up with either the bride or groom. I know I lost a few good friends in that process.

I still remember my earliest friends from Eden Park Grammar School: Tom Barry, Bill Considine, Bill O'Connor, Tom Kiernan, Dick Hoar, Dick Bell, Bob Ballinger, Herb Willis, Don Thompson, Harry Grattage, Vincent Quinn, Harold Hamlin, John Clayton, Armand Tartarian, Tom Barry, Peter La Salle, and Ray Murphy. Some lasted a season. Others, like Ray Murphy and Tom Barry, became lifetime friends. It was at 92 Massasoit Avenue in Edgewood where I developed most of my lifetime friendships. I met John Dinneen, my next-door neighbor in Edgewood in 1944. Only his early death from cancer separated us. He was a brilliant lawyer, recently married with a daughter, when he lost his battle with leukemia.

I feel so incredibly fortunate to have spent most of my formative years in Edgewood. Early friends were Peter Sheridan; Wes and Loring Forcier; Charlie Lafferty; Jack Casey; Bob Plant; Peter Bowen; Jack, Joe, Tom, and Lefty Manning; Al Curtin; Arthur Halligan; Jerry Roque; Howard, Bill, Ed, and Ray McGinnis; Paul and Joe Flaherty; Sherm Strickhauser; Jack Swan; Gill Thorpe; George Chouinard; Ken Sullivan; and Herb Browne. Brad Boss, who grew Cross Pen and Pencil into one of Rhode Island's largest employers, was a casual friend. Our friendship grew exponentially with the success of his company. I remember telling my friend, Red Auerbach, that we were best friends.

Five members of that neighborhood are now members of the

Rhode Island Heritage Hall of Fame. "Pappy" Boss, legendary race car driver and president of Cross Pen & Pencil, his two sons, Brad and Ron, Sherm Strickhauser, a great radio talk show host, and last and least, Ken Dooley.

I have spent a great deal of my life living outside of Rhode Island, in Connecticut, Manhattan, Philadelphia, Florida, and, more recently, Savannah, Georgia. Yet, I am and always will be a Rhode Islander. I frequently drive around the three neighborhoods of my youth, pausing before the homes of my friends. Almost all of them are gone now, but their memories will be with me forever. Wheeler Avenue in Cranston was the home of Wes and Loring Forcier, two of my dearest friends. Some of the memories are especially sad, such as when I drive by the McGinnis home and remember my friend Ed who was killed in Korea. Arthur Halligan was one of the nicest guys I grew up with, but he could not get his alcoholism under control and died before 40. George Horn committed suicide at age 15. David Dinneen died of cancer at age 28.

My neighborhood trips always end at 92 Massasoit Avenue, my home, for more than 20 years. I look across the street and remember Mrs. Lake, a great lady, and neighbor. The Hough family was next, and I remember Walter, a good friend of my brother Paul. Mrs. Carpenter lived right next door, a gracious and kind lady. Directly behind us lived the Reading family, with Clifford, George, Louise, and Mildred.

On the day that my brother Jack died, I parked in front of the house so long that the owner came out to greet me. He was very gracious after I identified myself as a Dooley and even invited me in to see the changes he had made. It was the wrong day for that, so I declined graciously. But I told him how pleased I was with the house's appearance. The swimming pool that my brothers Jack, Larry, and Bob installed after my brother Paul developed multiple sclerosis is in good shape. So are the rock gardens that Jack planted in 1945, soon after returning from WWII. I can still see Peg coming down the staircase when she married Don Malone in 1949. My father is watering the lawn, and my mother is in the kitchen preparing those great meals we all took for granted then.

Yes, tears have run down my face during some of those trips down memory lane. But then the smiles come as I recall some of those experiences and realize that I grew up in the most extraordinary family ever, surrounded by so many outstanding friends. My cup runneth over.

MADAME ADVISORY COUNCIL

Dr. Patrick T. Conley describes his wife Gail as his "navigator" in his book *A Historical Cruise Through the Ocean State.* I cannot entirely agree with his assessment. Navigators follow courses that have been plotted for them. A more accurate description of Gail is "tactician," a critical role during America Cup races. A tactician must plot the course of the ship, finding winds that elude other boats. Gail had to deal with two gigantic winds, Pat Conley and Ken Dooley. Trying to get a word in edgewise with those two would be a challenge for Cicero.

During their frequent dinners together, Conley and Dooley would trade stories about accomplishments, events, and people, always with a challenging "Can you top this?" approach. Gail would usually sit quietly as the two combatants jockeyed for position. Conley had many more accomplishments, but Dooley tried to offset them by namedropping people like Red Auerbach, Bill Russell, Lee Iacocca, or Andy Rooney. But like that New York stock exchange firm, when Gail talked, we listened. She gave us insights on recommending future board members of the Rhode Island Heritage Hall of Fame and counsel in so many areas. There is a very good reason why she serves as chairperson of the Rhode Island Heritage Hall of Fame Advisory Council.

Gail had a diverse and interesting business career, especially in real estate. At one time, she owned more individual parcels of real estate in Providence than any other woman in the city's history. She had all the credentials to challenge Dooley and her husband in the "Can you top this category." On her first visit to Poland in the 1980s, she met and was photographed with Lech Walesa, the Polish liberator. She was the guest of the Governor-General of the Province when she visited Quebec. Dr. Conley likes to point out that no dignitaries were on hand when she visited St. Petersburg, Russia, in 2015.

Gail and Patrick Conley have donated a total of several million dollars in monetary gifts, books, art, and real estate to an array of universities, colleges, and local schools, libraries, social service organizations, heritage foundations, churches, land, and environmental trusts. In addition, Gail has been especially active in supporting Native American tribes.

Here is a recent editorial she wrote for *The Providence Journal.*

In 2007 my husband and I bought the so-called King Philip House on Bristol's Mount Hope, the former summer home of Rudolph Haffenreffer, Jr. It sat on a two-acre parcel surrounded by about 450 acres of additional land the Haffenreffers gave to Brown University via several donations in the 1950s.

Our intent was to renovate the well-worn structure for the use of and eventual ownership by the Pokanoket Tribe of the Wampanoag Confederacy. We even named the road leading to the house "Pokanoket Place," but our road sign has since been removed.

Our house was less than 100 yards from the famous King Philip's Chair, a natural depression in a large quartz outcrop called by authoritative colonial historian Thomas Williams Bucknall "the most important Native American geologic site in New England."

We found the base of the chair, where Chief Sachem Metacom (aka King Philip) held tribal councils, littered with debris and a small, dilapidated shack. We asked Brown University's aid in joining us to clean up its site. The response was slow and reluctant.

When the Great Recession foiled our grandiose plans for house and site renovation, our mortgage on the property was foreclosed by Newport Bank in 2015. The purchaser at the mortgagee's sale was Brown University. Since that date, the house remains virtually unchanged.

In recent years, the reconstituted Pokanoket Tribe has made repeated efforts to regain at least a portion of its Mount Hope Land. The Heritage Harbor Foundation presided over by my husband Patrick has funded the publication of a booklet about the Pokanoket and their heritage to advance the tribe's goal of reacquiring the land of its ancestors. Brown University has curbed their claims and has delayed decisive action on a compromise agreement made with the Pokanoket in September 2017 regarding the use and disposition of the property.

Given my brief outline of this needlessly complex situation, I was annoyed to read the story in *The Providence Journal* of Thursday, February 4 titled "New study of slavery and taking of Native Land." It told of a $4.9-million grant to Brown and two other academic collaborators "to study historical injustices and the relationship between colonization of America by Europeans and racial slavery and European taking of Native American Lands in New England." This study should begin at Mount Hope, that huge parcel donated to Brown by the Haffenreffers and held tenaciously against the desires and demands of the Pokanoket.

Anthony Bogues, director of Brown's Center for Study of Slavery and Justice, the grant's major recipient, states that "our nation was founded on two major acts of deep historical injustice: racial slavery and Native America dispossession." Slavery was ended in 1865. Native American dispossession still exists in 2021 on the Mount Hope lands.

The purpose of the $4.9-million grant is to "study, teach and publish" in essence to generate words without deeds. Brown has made a habit of doing just that where Native Americans are involved. In 2015, using the historically fallacious ground that the religiously devout Columbus countenanced Native American slavery, Brown proudly renamed Columbus Day "Indigenous People's Day" while tenaciously maintaining its control over the lands at Mount Hope.

I suggest that Brown put its newly found grant money and some of its $4.7-billion endowment where its mouth is. Transfer the bulk of the Mount Hope acreage back to the Pokanoket, not in trust but free and clear, while returning and upgrading the existing Haffenreffer Native American Collection and Research Facility. For good measure, it should donate and renovate the King Philip House as a visitor's center for King Philip's Chair.

This gesture to the Pokanoket, a tragic victim of the ingratitude, greed, and land hunger of the sainted Pilgrims would dispel the hypocrisy from Brown's noble declarations and well-funded studies.

To date, Brown University has not responded to this opinion piece. But it has generated a positive response throughout the region. Gail's call to action was strongly endorsed by Hall of Fame and Heritage Harbor Foundation directors. It also prompted additional letters in the Bristol Phoenix. Most important, however, was the Pokanoket response. The tribe commissioned its attorney, Robert Watt, to meet with her and Dr. Conley. They suggested to Watt that the Pokanokets develop a plan for their use of the property and commit to restoring the King Philip House as a visitors' center for King Philip's Chair. Watt endorsed those suggestions and further stated that the Pokanokets would attempt to entreat other New England tribes such as the Narragansett, the Nipmuc, the Pequot, the Wampanoag, and even the Abenaski of Maine to unite in support of this reclamation effort. Time will tell.

Unlike her two loquacious friends, Madame Advisory Council Chairperson walks gently but carries a big stick.

THE BREAKFAST CLUB

When I moved back to Rhode Island in 2010, I decided to find a house in Newport. I was looking for a rental because I didn't know how long I would be staying. I planned to complete the book I was writing about Bob Thorpe and the 39th Fighter Squadron and finish the play about John Gordon. I had begun to write the Gordon play the year before when I was staying at my brother Bob's summer home in Narragansett, RI.

I found a house on Green Place, a quiet, dead-end street that was ideal for writing. I was in the house a few days when my doorbell rang, and I met my next-door neighbor, Vin Murray, for the first time. Vin turned out to be one of the most interesting people I have ever known. He served on three destroyers and one cruiser during WWII, taking part in many of the decisive sea battles in the Pacific. His ships received eight battle stars for heroic action against the enemy.

After his discharge in 1946, he went to work for General Electric in Lynn, Massachusetts, as a janitor. He worked days and attended night school at Suffolk University. However, his education was interrupted when the U.S. Navy recalled him during the Korean War. After his second Honorable Discharge, Vin returned to General Electric, where he was selected for the prestigious Management Training Program. After 21 years at GE, Vin was hired by Raytheon and made plant manager of the Portsmouth, RI facility. He became known as a "turnaround specialist" and was appointed as general manager of the Raytheon plant in Bristol, Tennessee, with more than 2,000 employees. He had been retired for about ten years when we met.

Vin spoke glowingly about his wife, Peg, and insisted that I meet her. Peg, who was more than 20 years younger than Vin, turned out to be everything that Vin had promised. She was energetic and highly motivated, and I once described her as making coffee nervous. (I stole that line from a movie.)

It was Peg who introduced me to Angela Vars, a lady I like to describe as Newport's answer to Mother Teresa. An excellent cook, Angela delivers healthy meals to many of her infirmed friends weekly. But, like the post office, no one can keep her from her appointed rounds. She is, beyond a doubt, one of the kindest people I have ever known.

Angela always sees the glass as full. Before her eyesight failed and she could still drive, she ran a personal "meals on wheels" for her friends. Angela made a wonderful beef stew which she delivered on a weekly basis. On one occasion, she forgot to put her car in "park," and it rolled into her friend's garage door while she was making a meal delivery. I did not care for his reaction, in which he demanded that the door be fixed. Angela, of course, had the door repaired immediately. She was back delivering meals to him right after she had the garage door repaired.

Tony Cercena is a male version of Angela. A career naval non-commissioned office, Tony spends every winter in the Philippines as a medical missionary. About this same time, I was introduced to Francoise and Bob Pomfret. Vin suggested that we form a breakfast club, so every Wednesday morning, Vin, Peg, Angela, Tony, and Francoise and Bob met for breakfast at Newport Creamery in Newport.

Francoise and Bob Pomfret were early members of the club. They had met in Paris in the 1950s and got married there. Next, we added Gloria, who married Tony in 2016. That marriage was a major concern for the breakfast club because Gloria was about 40 years younger than Tony. She was also a very beautiful young lady. While the rest of the breakfast club had concerns, Angela had none. Angela saw Gloria as an attractive young lady who would be just right for Tony. She was absolutely right. Gloria turned out to be a wonderful partner for Tony, helping him to get over the loss of his first wife, who had died of cancer a few years earlier. Angela reminded us that Peg was 20 years younger than Vin when they married.

I had an unusual experience with Tony concerning J. William Middendorf, the former Secretary of the Navy. Tony found out that I was assisting Bill Middendorf in a book he was writing about the threats facing the United States. He had a photo of himself standing with Secretary Middendorf at a naval event. He handed me the photo and requested that I have Secretary Middendorf sign it. I was prepared to identify Tony and explain the circumstances behind the photo when I met with Bill. I took the photo out of the envelope, but before I could say anything, Secretary Middendorf said, "Oh, Tony!"

It was just a breakfast club, meeting once a week, but it became so much more. I had some serious health issues, including colon cancer. I didn't have to go through it alone because of the breakfast club. When I could not eat because of the chemotherapy, Angela hand-fed me baked potatoes. Those and her beef stew kept me alive. Peg, Francoise, Tony, and Gloria kept in constant touch while I was recovering.

Yes, there were some sad times when Bob died, and Vin followed a few years later. But we always rallied, and pain soon turned to laughter. When I had a play open, the breakfast club was there. When I had a book signing, the breakfast group was there. When Gloria became a citizen, the group was there. When I was inducted into the Rhode Island Heritage Hall of Fame, the breakfast club was there.

Later the breakfast club expanded to plays and movies. There were some additions, including a lovely widow by the name of Lorraine McBride. Her husband had died the same week as Vin Murray, and Peg met her at a grief resolution meeting.

Things did not always go smoothly with the breakfast club. One night Francoise's cell phone went off in the middle of a play. It was a new phone, and she didn't know how to turn it off. I finally silenced it and warned Francoise that she would never go to a movie or play with me again. She responded by telling me that I was the meanest man on earth. The following week we sat together at a movie.

I left Newport in 2017 and now live in Savannah, Georgia. I returned to Rhode Island last year and met with the breakfast club. A scheduled meeting in 2020 had to be postponed because of the pandemic. While we haven't had any official meetings for over a year, we still stay in touch regularly. When we talk, it always seems like we're picking up from last week's meeting. Some friendships are just too precious to be affected by time or distance.

The Tennis Group

Every Tuesday night for about 15 years, the tennis group met at the Old Saybrook Racquet Club to play doubles. The group consisted of Bob Klimek, Carl Luntender, Bill Hostnik, and Earl Greenho. Bill Hostnik was the best of the group, and I was the worst. So, Bill was always stuck as my partner. Bill was quiet and deep, and I am noisy and shallow. He had this killer serve that was so difficult to return. If it came back at all, it would be a little duck over the net. I would usually put it away and then strutted about like John McEnroe. Bill would make ten great shots in a row. If he missed the eleventh, I would glare at him and say something like, "Are we giving this match away, Doctor?" And Bill would apologize to me. If I returned three shots in a row, it was unusual.

I don't know how good the tennis was, but the one-liners and the camaraderie were wonderful. One night I was serving at set point, and Carl called over to me: "Dooley, I could eat spaghetti off your head." I still don't know what that means. Carl did enjoy pointing out that I am vertically challenged. I double-faulted and lost the set. A short time later, Carl was serving at match point. I yelled, "Carl, do you know that a Lutender in London is a guy who cleans the bathrooms?" He aced me and won the match.

We were all competitive and did everything possible to win. Yet, when the match was over, we went out for pizza and beer, and the shots or contested calls were never brought up again. I think we all realized that we got a lot more out of those evenings than exercise and tennis. Those Tuesdays helped me through many trying times. In those years, I lost my film company, my wife, and my health.

I was the first to leave the tennis group when I moved in 1986. Yet, the memories of those four friends are still so strong more than 30 years later. Bob Klimek was one of the nicest, kindest men I have ever known. He was quiet and serious, and I don't think he ever really understood clowns like me. He had a wonderful laugh, and we did everything possible to encourage it. I told Bob that I once thought seriously about becoming a doctor.

"What made you change your mind?" he asked.

"I scored too high in my SATs," I answered. I can still remember his laugh.

No one was more competitive on the tennis court than Bob. And no one treated his patients and friends better than Dr. Bob. Wayne Muller, my friend of more than 50 years, told me a story about Bob seeing his wife on Sundays when she developed severe eye problems. I called Bob when my daughter Alicia developed hemorrhaging problems behind her eyes. Laser surgery was new at the time, and I was more than a little nervous when doctors recommended it. I called Bob, and he told me that laser surgery was the best option for Alicia. Her eyesight remains excellent 30 years after the surgery.

I still remember Bob and Bill Hostnik visiting my wife Rosemary after she had breast surgery in 1981. Dr. Lena, the surgeon, had just delivered some bad news. He told me that cancer had spread to 13 lymph nodes, not a good sign for long-term survival. Bob and Bill Hostnik were there for me when I needed them most.

Bob was the youngest of the tennis group but the first to die in 2013. I don't have the words to match the ones his children, Rob, Serena, and Alison wrote about their father for the funeral service:

> It was a perfect day for sailing. It was August. 5, 2013, and there was a consistent dry northwesterly wind blowing at a steady 12 to 15 knots. These were ideal conditions for *Reverie*, his beloved sloop of nearly 30 years. Bob felt most at ease while behind the helm and relished in the splendor and speed that his vessel provided.
>
> The winds held true, and his children's grateful smiles beamed about as they finished the day by sailing back to port. This was his spectacular day, a day capped by a view of the sunset sky over Hamburg Cove, sipping a Mount Gay rum and tonic all while listening to a little Oscar Petersen.
>
> Robert Klimek sailed into this world January 20, 1941, in Middletown and was raised in Meriden, Connecticut. His mother became head nurse at the New York Eye and Ear Infirmary and worked there for nearly 40 years. This was to be his catalyst for his chosen profession of ophthalmology. Bob graduated from La Salle Military Institute in 1958, Manhattan College in 1962,

and Southern University of New York Medical School in 1960. Following medical school, he interned at Greenwich Hospital. He returned to New York for his residency at the New York Eye and Ear Infirmary in 1967, when he was chief resident.

Carol Pearson, a Canadian "Doris Day," caught his eye during his last year of residency. In 1969, they were married along with her sister, Margo and her husband Don, in a double ceremony at St. Marks' Catholic Church in Prescott, Ontario. As winter rolled in, Carol hinted that the two of them should go to Europe for a ski vacation. Carol, having skied in Colorado, was the more avid and agile skier. In true Bob fashion, he perfected this new craft and was soon able to tackle the double-blacks of Telluride. Skiing became his sole winter pursuit, and Telluride would eventually become his second home.

After the birth of their son, Rob, in 1970, the two decided to leave the glass and metal skyline of Manhattan for New London, Connecticut, where Bob became a partner of Dr. John Gager. After Dr. Gager's death, Dr. Jack Reilly partnered with Bob, and the Shoreline Eye Group was formed. Bob was the chief of ophthalmology at Lawrence Memorial Hospital until the formation of the Constitution Eye Surgery Center East in 2001. He was one of the founding members and president.

Bob's passion for his patients and his staff was second to none. He strived for excellence and perfection, one of the many reasons he was respected by all. Bob was precisely balanced. When not attending to the needs of his endearing patients, he tended to his family and the community of Old Lyne, where they lived for 18 years. They eventually settled in Lyme overlooking Hamburg from its eastern prow. It was from this location that he would blast the sunset cannon, a tradition instilled from his memberships in the New York Yacht Club and the Cruising Club of America.

During the rearing of his three children, Rob of Colorado, Serena of New Canaan, and Alison of Boulder, Colorado, he took it upon himself to ensure that they had an upbringing that was sans peril. He invested in their minds, their pursuits, and their unlimited love of family and friends. That was what he bestowed upon his wife, children, four grandchildren, and patients. Bob lived every moment of his life with conviction and purpose. His legacy will continue even though his life was cut short. On August 18, 2013, he died at home surrounded by his family after a brief illness.

Sometimes I read a book or see a movie and reach for the phone to call Carl Lutender. Then reality sets in. The only time I ever got the last word in any conversation with Carl was when I delivered his eulogy. Carl and Lois Lutender were among the first families we met when we moved to Old Lyme. They had five children, Laurie, Keith, Gary, Lynn, and Gale. As my daughter Alicia says, it was always fun going to the Lutenders. They had the only pool in the neighborhood, and Carl and I would frequently go for a swim after Tuesday night tennis.

I was particularly fond of Gary, who died of a heart attack on March 17, 1998. Doctors said the massive radiation Gary received during his battle with Hodgkin's disease weakened his heart muscles. He spent a week in a coma at Yale-New Haven Hospital, awaiting a new heart that never arrived. A light went out when Carl and Lois lost Gary, and I never saw it again.

Gary died on St. Patrick's Day, which was also the birthday of his sister, Lynn. She vowed she would never celebrate her birthday again since it marked the day of Gary's death. I wrote her the following letter a few days after the funeral:

Dear Lynn:

When Abraham Lincoln was in the White House, he received a letter from a young "leap year" girl. She complained that she wanted to have a birthday every year, like her brothers and sisters. Instead of delivering a lecture on how she should accept her lot in life, Lincoln did the unexpected. He gave her his birthday in exchange for her leap-year date. He said it would allow her to celebrate every year, while his new birthday would keep him younger since it would only occur every four years. I want to do the same thing for you. Henceforth I will celebrate my birthday on March 17, while you will blow out the candles on October 22.

Love,
Ken Dooley

One thing that was never lacking between Carl and me was conversation, especially during tennis night. I think we enjoyed competing against each other on the tennis court. That changed when the Lutenders visited me when I was living in Sarasota and bought a house less than half a mile from mine. We played tennis four and five days a week, frequently as partners, and then enjoyed Lois's wonderful meals. Carl could have claimed me as a dependent during those years, considering the number of meals I had at his house. Those were among the best days of my life.

Earl Greenho is still with us, so I have to be careful of what I say. After delivering two eulogies and attending the funerals of three former members of the tennis group, I understand Earl goes into hiding when he hears that I am coming to Old Lyme. It was Earl who asked me to write and direct a film for Students Against Drunk Driving in Old Lyme. Both of his sons, Jim, and Brian, appeared in the film, and his home was the location of many of the key scenes.

Not a day passes without a fond memory of Bill, Carl, Bob, or Earl. Those evenings at the Old Saybrook Racquet Club were, and always will be, a source of humor and friendship for me. Some wise person once said you could judge a person by his friends. I have been incredibly lucky in my lifetime to be able to consider high-quality people like Bill, Carl, Bob, and Earl as my friends. I'm fortunate enough to believe that they saw some value in my friendship.

MY NAME IS BERNIE SCHWARZ

Shortly after joining a B-17 Bomber Squadron with the Eighth Air Force in England in 1944, Bernie Schwarz and three other Jewish pilots were invited to a meeting with an intelligence officer.

"I guess you know that Germans don't like Jews very much," the officer said. 'A number of our pilots are forced to bail out after their planes are hit by flack or attacked by German fighters. Some of them make it back with help from the underground, but many end up in German POW camps. So you'll be treated a lot better if we give you some new IDs with Christian names."

"My name is Bernie Schwarz," Bernie responded. "It always has been, and it always will be," Bernie told the officer. He flew with the same dog tags he had been issued when he first joined the Army Air Force and was assigned to a B-17 squadron with the 8th Air Force in England.

The 8th Air Force was the largest in personnel, aircraft, and equipment when Bernie was assigned to it in 1944. It had reached a total strength of more than 200,000 people, with forty heavy bomber groups, fifteen fighter groups, and four specialized support groups. It dispatched 2,000 four-engine bombers and 12,000 fighters on a single mission to multiple targets. These missions, however, carried a high price. The Eighth Air Force suffered more than 47,000 casualties with 26,000 deaths. Seventeen Medals of Honor went to Eighth Air Force personnel during the war.

The reason for the high casualty rate was apparent. While the Royal Air Force (RAF) conducted high-altitude, night bombing, 8th Air Force bombers struck during the day at altitudes between 6,000 and 8,000 feet. German anti-aircraft fire was considerably more accurate in the daylight—so were the American bombardiers who destroyed the German oil industry and helped the Allies gain control of the air war in Europe. The German Luftwaffe fielded two of the best fighters in WWII—the Messerschmitt B-109 and the Focke-Wuft 190. The two planes inflicted heavy damage on B-17s and B-24s, especially during 1944.

Bernie, like many WWII veterans who have the most to tell, seldom talked about his experiences during WWII. I met Bernie in the 1970s when we both lived in Old Lyme, Connecticut. Bernie's son Peter and my daughter Alicia attended grammar school together. I would see Bernie and his wife, Karen, at school events or social events. Bernie and his brother had just sold the EIS Automotive Group in Middletown, Connecticut when we first met. It was obvious that Bernie was going to have a comfortable retirement. He was a big-time boater and had a fantastic yacht, *Miss Karen*. We were always cordial when we met, but I cannot say we ever became close friends.

The first insight I had about the type of person he was came from my friend, Carl Lutender. Shortly after Carl's son Gary was diagnosed with cancer, Bernie went to Carl and offered to pay all medical bills. Carl graciously declined, but I will never forget that gesture. Other than that one incident, I knew very little about Bernie Schwartz in those early years. I learned about his role as a B-17 pilot from his close friends, Bob Klimik and Bob Miller. The next time I saw Bernie, I questioned him about his experiences with the 8th Air Force. He didn't open up immediately, but my training as an investigative reporter worked. He told me about some of his experiences, starting with that name-change story.

Bernie flew his B-17 during daylight at low altitudes when the flack was so heavy that crew members claimed they could get out and walk on it. He described watching some B-17s, filled with friends he had been with the previous night, exploding from enemy ground-fire or German fighter planes. On more than one mission, his aircraft returned from one of those daylight runs shredded by anti-aircraft fire or the guns of enemy planes. A photo shows Bernie and his crew standing in front of their B-17, which had just crash-landed. The wings and the fuselage were filled with holes from enemy ground fire.

Major General Jimmy Doolittle, well known for bombing Tokyo in 1942, was in charge of the 8th Air Force when Lt. Bernie Schwarz arrived. Although trained as a B-24 pilot, Bernie quickly switched over to B-17s. Bernie flew a number of bombing missions over Germany at a time when the Luftwaffe was strong and German anti-aircraft fire deadly.

He also took part in raids against refineries in Leuna, Germany, where most of the synthetic fuel for jet aircraft was refined.

I left Old Lyme in 1992 and didn't speak to Bernie again until six years later. I called him after I had received a contract to write a book about the 8th Air Force. He shared his air records and many photos of his plane and crew. He spoke proudly about his reunions with his original B-17 crew, who he kept in touch long after the war. Unfortunately, I developed prostate cancer and was out of action for the following year. I contacted Bernie when I recovered, but he was quite ill and died shortly after. Without Bernie, my motivation for writing the book disappeared.

Winston Churchill, British Prime Minister during WWII, once said about the Royal Air Force, "Never have so many owed so much to so few." That same honor applies to the pilots and crewmembers of the 8th Air Force who destroyed the German Luftwaffe and won the air war in Europe. It's understandable why newscaster Tom Brokaw called men like Bernie Schwarz part of "the greatest generation."

A Parish Revolt

The Horns were among the most devoted Catholic families in St. Paul's parish in Cranston, RI. When I worked at Henry's, a small convenience store directly across the street from St. Paul's, I frequently saw George Horn attend daily mass. He owned a fuel oil delivery service and was one of the most respected people in Cranston.

Mrs. Horn was a frequent customer at Henry's, and she was one of the kindest people I have ever known. When my father died suddenly in 1945, she gave me a big hug and said she was praying for my whole family. Her daughter Elaine, a year ahead of me in school, was among the prettiest and most popular girls in her class.

I got to know George Horn Jr., who worked with me at Henry's on weekends. George was 14 and extremely tall and thin. Height wasn't the only thing we didn't have in common. George was very quiet, and I was very noisy. So, I usually did the talking for both of us. As different as we were, we became good friends.

Sometimes when we were unpacking boxes or putting gallons of milk into the freezer, George would suddenly grow pale and have to sit for a couple of minutes. I would run to get him a cold drink and, after a few minutes, his color would return, and he was back to normal. He asked me to please not mention the problem to Henry, the store owner. George was especially concerned that his parents did not know about these episodes. I was never known as a quiet person, but I did not divulge a secret if a friend swore me to silence.

I never did find out the cause of George's problem. I did know that it was excruciating. His whole body would shake and go into convulsions. It wasn't epilepsy I knew because I had dealt with that a few years earlier with my friend Armand Tartarian. When Armand had a seizure, he would groan and have difficulty breathing. George never displayed those symptoms. And it didn't happen all the time. Sometimes George and I would work together several Saturdays in a row without incident.

One morning Elaine went into the basement to retrieve a pair of stockings she was drying near the furnace. It was 1946, and there were no home dryers at the time. She found George hanging in a half-cellar. He was so tall, he had to bend over to choke himself to death.

The tragedy spread quickly throughout the parish. The Horn family was liked and respected by all. I had a first-hand seat as to what transpired next. Henry's was right next door to the Knights of Columbus, where George Sr. was a prominent member. Other Knights came into the store and discussed, in hushed tones, that Msgr. Cannon, the conservative pastor of St. Paul's, had announced that George Jr. couldn't receive a Catholic mass or be buried in a Catholic cemetery because he had committed suicide.

Because of its Irish, Italian, and French residents, Rhode Island had the highest percentage of Catholics in the country. They were also the most conservative. When Pope John decreed that the mass should be celebrated in the country's language where it was being held, Catholics in Woonsocket continued to celebrate the mass in Latin. They only changed when threatened with excommunication. That's why what amounted to a parish revolution at St. Paul's was so extraordinary.

It started with a small delegation calling on Msgr. Cannon and asking him to reverse his ruling and allow George Jr. to receive a Catholic burial. They were turned down flatly. "The church's ruling on suicide had been in place for hundreds of years," Msgr. Cannon told them. "They were wrong for even calling it to his attention," he said.

Judging from the emotions of the conversations that I overheard for the next few days, I knew the controversy was far from over. The backlash crossed religious lines, with a number of my Protestant friends questioning Msgr. Cannon's decision.

A 3-man delegation from St. Paul's called on Bishop Keough the following day, and the result was a complete reversal of Msgr. Cannon's order. The bishop ruled that George would receive a Catholic mass and internment in a Catholic cemetery.

Over the years, I have attended many funeral masses and delivered many eulogies for family and friends. None was sadder than the one I attended for George Horn Jr. While the Horn family was devastated, I know they drew comfort from the fact that George received a Catholic burial.

I will always regret that I had not informed his parents about George's health problem. Questions remain as to whether they might have prevented the tragedy of a 14-year-old taking his own life. Why this young man received so much pain that he took his own life will always bewilder me. But I remember George with a great deal of affection.

A favorite Christmas movie of mine is *It's a Wonderful Life*, which is about a man who wants to commit suicide and is presented with many reasons not to do so. Over the years, I've read a lot about suicide. I don't think most people who consider suicide want to die. I think George wanted to eliminate the pain he was going through.

George only died once on that fateful day. But he left behind family and friends who will never forget that day and ask why?

WRITING A MUSICAL

The town of Old Lyme, Connecticut, went all out for its Little League. It included a state-of-the-art baseball field and uniforms that rivaled Yankee pinstripes. But unfortunately, the support did not extend to the girls' softball league, which I had helped form and served as a coach. No uniforms were provided, and we lost second base when the tide came in on the field we were given.

I went before the Parks and Recreation Committee and requested a new field and uniforms. We got nothing. When I suggested we be allowed to use the Little League field, I was dismissed with prejudice.

I knew we weren't going to get anywhere going through town channels. So, I took a different approach, writing a musical called *Darn Yankees*. I stole the storyline from *The Music Man* and the music from *My Fair Lady, Damn Yankees, Peter Pan, Bye-Bye Birdie, and The Sound of Music*. Instead of selling musical instruments, the main character in our musical sold uniforms. Like the original music man, he falls in love with the town librarian and mends his ways.

The musical opened in blacklight, with 30 girls wearing illuminated barrels and carrying illuminated bats, singing new lyrics to "Take Me Out to the Ballgame." As the lights come up, they make their way to the stage where a town meeting is taking place. Then they sing the last stanza:

"Take us out of these boards, please
Buy us some pants and some shirts,
It's no way to play the game,
When you slide, it really hurts."

The "music man" makes his first appearance singing about the danger of children hanging around bars in Southview, a local beach area filled with bars and nightclubs and totally out of step with the rest of the town. His goal, of course, is to get the town to buy softball uniforms, which he never plans to deliver.

After a lot of confusion and shouting, the town council agrees to schedule a game between the boys and girls. If the boys win, the status quo remains. If the girls win, they get a new field and uniforms.

The coach of the girls' team is frustrated as she tries to teach fielding and hitting skills. Finally, she breaks into song:

When you know the way to swing,
You can hit most anything.
Throw, the way to get an out,
Catch, the other side of throw.
Strike, a ball across the plate,
Ball, a pitch to high or low.
Slide, you have to miss the tag,
Force, you only tough the bag.
Home run, a might mighty blow,
That will bring us back to . . .

With apologies to Julie Andrews, that song was a showstopper. 'I've grown accustomed to their braces" was a close second.

Ella Grasso, the first female governor of Connecticut and the second in the nation, played a prominent role in the musical. In our version, a Woman's Liberal Group meets weekly and sings the following song in front of a huge photo of Ella Grasso.

We Love you Ella
You showed the way,
Because of Ella, we've got a say,
We're moving forward each day,
Oh Ella, you're okay.

The lyrics go on for another five stanzas, all to the music stolen from *Bye Bye Birdie.*

Ella came to the final performance, even though she was undergoing chemotherapy for cancer. An unbelievable set of circumstances came together that night. First, the last performance fell on Ella's birthday. In the final scene of the play, a whiffle ball comes over the fence, indicating that the girls have won the rights to new uniforms and a decent field. The ball actually ended in Ella's lap. To this day, some residents think that I was responsible for landing the ball in Ella's lap.

The musical was a great success, and we came up with the funds for new uniforms. One lady, Mrs. Martin, came to every performance, telling me that she liked it better than anything she had seen at the Goodspeed Opera House. "Why don't you take it to Broadway?" she asked. If I had, I would probably be sharing a cell with the late Bernie Madoff for copyright infringement. Some think Bernie and I would have made good cellmates.

I hesitate to name names, as I worry about leaving someone out. But I have to cite assistant director, Dick Bruno, John Joseph, Jerry Gordon, Missy Lynch, and Harry Cross, cast members; Susan Anderson, Susan Hostnik and Bill Hostnik, makeup; Liz Lynam and Sandy Tolderland, costumes; Vicki Dill, choral director; Pat Loiacono and Lynn Greenho, choreography; Nancy Manville, Barbara Romeo, and Sue Knirsch, associate producers; Ed Manville, set design; Marie Hall and Susan Hostnik, advertising, and Lois Lutender and Red Anderson for providing the music.

More important than uniforms or fields was the fact that the whole town got behind the musical. Mothers sang and danced their way across the stage with enthusiasm and skill. Others helped build sets, made costumes, sold tickets, or provided transportation for rehearsals.

I still have a note Ella Grasso sent me for "turning a bad day into a good one." Sadly, Ella died a few months later. However, I will always remember the smile on her face as the cast sang "We Love You Ella" and the audience serenaded her with "Happy Birthday."

The villain in the musical, Big Ed Hook, was played by Dave Miller, a fine actor who appeared in many of my documentaries. We were good friends but enjoyed cutting each other up a bit in conversations. Bill Hostnik, my plastic surgeon friend, had made "Big Ed" a special nose to illustrate his evilness.

On the night of the cast party, Dave made a reference to the fact that the musical was successful despite my weak writing. I turned to him and said that he should treat me with great respect since I had made him famous.

"What do you mean?" he asked.

"It's the first time in history that a plastic surgeon ever made an ugly nose for a Jew," I answered. Dave was speechless, the first time in our history.

I have had other plays professionally performed in Providence and Boston. *The Murder Trial of John Gordon* prompted the governor of Rhode Island to issue a pardon for a man who was executed in 1845. Jeff Gill, the actor who played the lead in my Boston play, *The Auerbach Dynasty*, received an award for the outstanding performance of the year.

But nothing I have done will ever give me that same feeling I had on the opening night of *Darn Yankees*.

THE RENAISSANCE MAN: J. WILLIAM MIDDENDORF II

I have had the privilege of meeting men such as Red Auerbach, Lee Iacocca, George Plimpton, Richard Ettinger, and William Yavonovich. As brilliant as they were, not one met the definition of a Renaissance Man, a person with many talents and areas of expertise. I did not meet a true renaissance man until I was introduced to J. William Middendorf II in 2015.

I remember reading about Ambassador Middendorf when he was Secretary of the Navy during the Ford administration. I also read his book, *A Glorious Disaster,* which described his experiences with Barry Goldwater during the 1964 presidential campaign. I had no idea that Ambassador Middendorf lived in Little Compton, Rhode Island, until Pat Conley, President of the Rhode Island Heritage Hall of Fame, suggested I nominate him for entry into the RIHHOF.

I met Bill's wife, Isabelle, before I met Bill. We stood in her kitchen, surrounded by religious posters and notices of Bible study groups. In the first few minutes of our conversation, Isabelle told me she conducted Bible study classes. She looked me full in the face and asked if I was saved. I hesitated because I was not sure of the answer myself. I blurted out something about never killing anyone or cheating people out of a lot of money. I did remember getting quite creative with some of my expense accounts when I was a division head for Prentice-Hall Publishing. Would such activities disqualify me from reaching the "saved" status that was so important to Isabelle? I was not sure. In the next few months, I was a frequent visitor at the Middendorf home.

Bill entered the room at that time, and we moved to his studio. After a few minutes of conversation, I realized I was dealing with a true renaissance man. As Secretary of the Navy and Ambassador to The Netherlands, Ambassador Middendorf served as an advisor to five presidents: Eisenhower, Nixon, Ford, Carter, and Reagan. He was 90 years old when we met and had a long career in business and public service. Middendorf received a letter from the New York Giants baseball team inviting him to spring training during his early career at Harvard. A week later, he enlisted in the U.S. Navy and joined the V-12 Officer's Training Program. Following his commission, he served in the Pacific on a landing support craft. After the war, he received a degree from Harvard, where he was active in the Hasty Pudding Club with George Plimpton and Jack Lemmon. Following his graduation from Harvard, he became a commercial banker on Wall Street. In 1961, he joined with Austen Colgate to form Middendorf Colgate and Company, a prominent Wall Street firm and a member of the N.Y. Stock Exchange.

In 1969, he left his investment firm and accepted the role of U.S. Ambassador to The Netherlands, and in 1974 became Secretary of the Navy. Recognizing the direct threat to our security in the Cold War with the Soviet Union, Secretary Middendorf immediately upon his appointment engaged in an all-out effort to procure the long-term lead time weapon systems needed to win the Cold War, the apogee of which he and Admiral Holloway the CNO, estimated would be reached a decade or so later. These systems, The Trident submarine program, which would carry 70% of America's nuclear warheads, the AEGIS missiles systems, and its fleet of Arleigh Burke cruisers, the F-18 fighter plane, and the CH53-E Marine Corps Heavy Lift helicopter, he sponsored through Congress in the four years of his tour. These weapons systems played a crucial role in the "Peace Through Strength" American victory in the first Cold War 15 years later.

Upon Ronald Reagan's election in 1980, Ambassador Middendorf was asked to chair the Finance Committee for the Inauguration. He also wrote the inauguration march, "Thumbs Up America," with Sammy Cahn writing the words at the president's request. Middendorf also became chairman of Reagan's C.I.A. Transition Committee, which reorganized the senior levels of the agency.

As Ambassador to the Organization of American States, he joined Constantine Mengis to present a Grenada Rescue Plan to the National Security Council. The Soviet Union, aided by Cuba, was building a 9000-foot-runway for their cargo planes in Granada. After several meetings of the National Security Council, a carrier with marines liberated the area and removed the Soviets and Cubans after brief combat. Following his four-year tour at the O.A.S., Ambassador Middendorf was confirmed as Ambassador to the European Economic Community (now called the European Union), where he was involved in wall-to-wall trade negotiations, most of them successfully won by his team.

In 1991, as communism was collapsing in the Soviet Union, President Yeltsin invited a team from the Heritage Foundation, including Secretary Middendorf, to write a constitution for the New Russia. Yeltsin realized that transferring state-owned facilities to private sector owners was the only way the new Russia could survive. Unfortunately, communist members of the Duma prevented many of the key recommendations from going into effect. A small group of oligarchs obtained control of a dozen major industries, and massive corruption, economic collapse, and inflation followed.

From his earliest days, Middendorf had intense interests in Visual Arts, literature, and music. He attended night school for five years at the Art Students League. He made several pilgrimages to Ripton, Vermont, to develop a friendship with Robert Frost, the great poet. The Ambassador has many fragmented and unpublished poems by Frost, who gave him a handwritten version of "Stopping By Woods on a Snowy Evening," one of his most famous poems. With C. Waller Barrett, who created The Clifton Waller Barrett Library of American Literature Library at the University of Virginia, he helped sponsor several visits by Frost to the Grolier Club in New York, where Frost recited his poems.

Ambassador Middendorf is a prolific artist and has made several thousand sketches of leaders and associates and 150 drawings of Art Historian friends, and over 1000 drawings of his children, grandchildren, and great-grandchildren. Recently, he and his daughter Franny, an incredible artist and art teacher, have exhibited their paintings in New York. Ambassador Middendorf also taught an art class for the prisoners at the Bristol County House of Correction in Massachusetts for five years. Sheriff Hodgson, head of the facility, said the program was significant in reducing recidivism at the facility.

At their home outside of Washington, D.C., he and his late wife Isabelle, a registered nurse, took into their home 28 foster babies. In meetings with Naval Admirals and Marine Generals, Secretary Middendorf felt he was not always as sharp as he should be, having been up at night burping babies and changing diapers. He volunteered to serve as chairman of the Harlem Facility of the Boys Club of New York for many years.

Ambassador Middendorf has always had an active interest in

sports. In the 1963 World Championships of Men's Field Hockey in Lyon, France, he played on the U.S. National Team. The Ambassador has been a lifelong rower. His father, his inspiration for rowing, was a legendary Harvard oarsman whose crew won the Grand Challenge Cup in 1914 at the Royal Henley Regatta. Fifty years later, his winning Harvard crew of 1914 reassembled and rowed The Henley Course again in 1964. The Ambassador has been active in many rowing contests, having won both a U.S. National Masters and a World Masters Rowing Championship. He stroked the victorious Thames Rowing Club Crew in the famous Vogalonga 20-mile regatta race around Venice in which 4,000 boats participated. In 2020, at the age of 96, the Ambassador competed in seven virtual Regattas (because of the pandemic), including one in Japan. These International Rowing Regattas, against worldwide competition, averaging 3000- 5000 meters each. In the over 85 categories, he placed 1st in the world in all but one, the famous Head Of The Charles Regatta, where he placed 2nd to a rowing colleague of the Rocky Mountain Rowing Club. Through April 2021, he has completed over a million meters on the Erg machine, and in January 2021 competition, he completed 154,000 meters.

Ambassador Middendorf is a member of The Council of American Ambassadors and an Honorary Member of The Society of Cincinnati. He has been elected to the Rhode Island Heritage Hall of Fame and selected to join the 50 Greatest Living Rhode Islanders. At this point in his life, he feels his most important mission is to warn America about the greatest threats to its survival. His book, *The Great Nightfall: How We Win the New Cold War,* explains what we must do to counter the threats from China, Russia, North Korea, Iran, and terrorist groups.

I helped the Ambassador research the book and was a frequent visitor in his home for next year. Isabelle and I always spent a few minutes together before and after my meetings with Bill. One morning, she turned to me and said, "Ken, you have been saved." Isabelle had a reputation for always speaking her mind and telling the absolute truth. A few months after giving me that good news, Isabelle died suddenly. I think of her with great fondness and will always cherish her final message to me.

A Woman Named Agnes

Agnes Rooney spoiled mother-in-law jokes for me forever. She was one of the kindest, most thoughtful people I have ever known. We became close while I was courting her daughter, Rosemary.

I only met Henry Rooney, a successful Boston attorney, once before he died at an early age. I decided he must have been a bright guy to have attracted a woman like Agnes. I should have been as lucky.

I was working in Connecticut at the time, but I journeyed to Winchester, Massachusetts, every weekend to see Rosemary. I would end up spending more time with Agnes than I did with Rosemary. While Agnes and I would watch one of the Boston teams on television, Rosemary would be shopping or having her hair "done."

Evenings would be spent with her friends, usually involving dinner and much drinking. I should have realized then that Rosemary and I had nothing in common. I don't think either of us was in "love" when we became engaged.

I was 31, and Rosemary was 25. Most of her friends were married or engaged, and I think we both worried too much about time slipping away.

So I gave her a diamond, bought through her jeweler, and we began to plan a honeymoon with the help of the Rooney family's travel agent.

There were some bumps in the road. I remember when Rosemary came to meet my family for the first time. Bill was married, but Jack, Bob, Larry, Paul, and my cousin John (my mother's seventh son) and her niece Janie were there for Sunday dinner.

Rosemary's only comment on the way back to Winchester was, "I'm marrying you, not your family." She made it clear that she was not too impressed with my family. It was a mutual feeling. The silence from my brothers delivered a message. I had to push my mother for an opinion, but she finally said, "I don't think she's the right girl for you."

About a month before the wedding, Rosemary and I went to Connecticut to look for a rental. Unfortunately, she did not like any of the places we were shown. On the way back to Winchester after a fruitless search, she said, "I'd call the wedding off, but I already bought the gown."

Why I did not cancel the wedding plans right then is beyond me. But when we got to Winchester, Rosemary either went to bed or got on the phone with her friends. Agnes and I talked about world events or sports, two subjects that Rosemary and I never discussed.

I shared an apartment with my friend Wayne Muller in New London. He came to Rosemary's home for a weekend and went out with one of her friends. Wayne was the strong silent type, so when he talked, I usually listened. However, on the way back to Connecticut, he advised me not to go through with the wedding. "You have nothing in common with her," he warned.

Years later, I delivered the same message to him when I felt he was marrying the wrong girl. He ignored my warning and lived to regret it. His marriage was only slightly better than mine, but it did not end in divorce. Wayne had a higher pain threshold than I did.

There was one major blowup about a month before the wedding. I had tickets for the Boston Pops on a Saturday night. When I arrived, Rosemary told me that we would be going to a birthday party at the Winchester Country Club instead of the Pops.

For once, I stood up. "I'm going to the Pops," I said. "If you do, the wedding is off," she screamed. I remember getting into my car and driving to the concert. When I left Boston, I was singing an aria from "The Barber of Seville." If you have ever heard my voice, you will understand why it was fortunate that I was alone.

Instead of driving to Connecticut, I spent the night at my mother's home in Cranston, Rhode Island. My mother was at her usual station at the stove when I got up the next morning. I gave her a hug, and she exclaimed, "You seem so happy today."

Then I got very serious and told her the wedding was off. Her answer has stayed with me for almost 60 years—"Thanks be to God."

My friend Sam Katz was delighted when I told him the news. Rosemary had not endeared herself to my group of Connecticut friends during a few brief meetings.

It was over. The only thing I had left was a string of payments for a diamond I really could not afford. Then the phone rang—it was

Rosemary. The conversation started all right, but she suddenly began to cry. I agreed to come to Winchester for a talk. It was a mistake because the marriage was back on. Rosemary has many good qualities and could have had a successful marriage with many men—just not with me.

The wedding was followed by a large reception at the Sheraton Hotel in Boston. We left for a honeymoon in San Juan and St. Thomas. The first week went well, but things took a wrong turn in St. Thomas. We were staying at a place called "Yacht Haven," bordering on the most beautiful port I had ever seen. All of the accommodations had been made through the Rooney's travel agent.

I rented a Jeep, and we drove to "Bluebeard's Castle," a spectacular hotel overlooking the entire bay. After lunch and cocktails, Rosemary turned to me and said, "I want to stay here."

I told her that it wasn't possible, that we had already prepaid everything at Yacht Haven. Her reaction was a preview of what was to come in the future. "My father would make the change for me," she cried. We sat in silence. Finally, I told her I was going back to Yacht Haven. "She climbed in beside me but not before saying, "What have we done. It's a mistake."

Things remain calm for the next several days until we returned to San Juan and boarded the plane for a flight to Boston. Unfortunately, the weather forced us to land in Manhattan instead of Boston, which meant an overnight stay.

I had about $100 left, and there were no credit cards in those days. The cab fare to Manhattan was about $25, so I had $75 left for a hotel room. There was a moderately priced hotel, The Grosvenor, where I frequently stayed in my single days in Manhattan. It certainly wasn't the Plaza, but it was clean and, more importantly, in my price range.

Rosemary complained from the minute we walked into the lobby. "My father would never allow me to stay in a flea-bag like this," she screamed. Instead of arguing, I began to plan. After listening to whines about the mattress, the bathroom, the room décor, and my snoring, an escape plan began to take shape.

Agnes picked us up the next day in Boston, and we were to stay overnight in Winchester before driving back to Connecticut on Monday morning. Rosemary seemed calmer in her home surroundings and was even civil to me over dinner. I swung into action with the first step of my emancipation plan. "Next week is going to be very busy for me," I explained. "I have meetings with authors, editors, and production people scheduled night and day. I think Rosemary should stay here, and I'll come and get her next weekend."

Even as I said it, visions of annulments and divorce were running through my mind. When I escaped Monday morning, nothing could drag me back to Massachusetts, not even Agnes or my beloved Red Sox.

Rosemary didn't object, so I thought I was home free. Agnes sat silently, and I assumed she had bought my plan. Rosemary went to bed (it was about 9 o'clock, an hour past her usual retirement).

After she left the room, Agnes turned to me. "When you leave here tomorrow morning, Rosemary will be sitting next to you," she said. "Now, let's see if the Red Sox are on." It was clear that Agnes had seen through my entire plan.

Agnes visited frequently, and no son-in-law was happier to greet his mother-in-law. Every once in a while, when Rosemary did something particularly annoying, Agnes would mumble to me, "Why don't you give her a slap-in-the-ass."

We lost Agnes to cancer in 1977. I will always regret that I ended our relationship with a lie. Agnes had just lost her left leg because of complications from heart disease. After the operation, it was discovered that she had terminal stomach cancer and had only a few weeks to live.

Her brother-in-law, Dr. Charles Rooney, saw no reason to tell her the diagnosis.

On the last night of her life, Agnes turned to me and asked, "Ken, do I have cancer?"

"No," I answered. So, I did what Charlie suggested. But I will always regret that my last message to this wonderful lady was a lie.

In 1984, Rosemary left Old Lyme for a summer on Martha's Vineyard. She never came back. I don't think there were any regrets on either side.

I was living in a six-bedroom, six-bathroom house at the time. I used to take a shower in a different bathroom each day for variety.

Although we didn't formally divorce until 2002, we both dated frequently. Even in our separation, there were some light moments. Rosemary was dating a man named Joe for a couple of years. My daughter Alicia told me he was a nice guy. I was living in Bristol, Rhode Island when I got a call from Joe explaining that he thought Rosemary was cheating on him.

"Do you see any humor in the situation?" I asked Joe. "You're telling me that my wife is cheating on you." We both laughed. By the way, Joe was right—enter Gordon.

It wasn't a happy marriage. But without it, I would not have my daughter Alicia or my granddaughter, Sarah. The joy they bring me overcomes the pain of a wrong choice made by both of us so many years ago.

Occasionally, I read about couples remaining as friends after a divorce. Rosemary and I were never friends during the marriage, so we can hardly be expected to develop any ties now. In a sense, there's nothing I wouldn't do for Rosemary and nothing she wouldn't do for me. We've been doing nothing for each other for the past 30 years.

My Roles as a Stand-Up Comic

I could tell my friend, Cark Lutender, was upset when he joined me for lunch at his recently opened restaurant, "The Hideaway" in Old Lyme, Connecticut. The restaurant got off to a good start when it opened in October 1990. Advertisements promised a prominent New York comedian as entertainment for New Year's Eve, and reservations poured in. Then, on Dec. 30, 1990, the comedian called and told Carl that he would not keep the date. No doubt he got a better-paying gig closer to home.

"What should I do?" Carl implored. "I called the booking agent who got me this guy, and he had no one else available. I'm afraid many people will be upset. Should I pay for a radio advertisement to let them know there will be no entertainment?"

"No, I said. "Don't do anything. I will go on."

"You! What do you know about being a comedian?"

Carl was one of my best friends and knew a lot about me—but not everything. I told him about my early days as a stand-up comedian in Texas when I was in the Air Force. I don't think the term stand-up comic existed in those days. It started when a few friends opened a bar in San Antonio, Texas. At first, I just introduced the musicians, but I always added a few comments about topical subjects of the day. I was talking nothing about nothing. It was a Jerry Seinfeld approach years before his famous TV show.

Jerry and I had another thing in common. Neither one of us used foul language, even though I was urged to do so. I always saw my mother sitting at one of the front tables, saying the rosary. So my act could have been performed for The Little Sisters of the Poor.

I told Carl that I got a lot of laughs, which was true. But I did not reveal the real reason. The audience laughed at my Rhode Island accent. It didn't matter what I said—"Good evening" and "welcome"—would bring the house down from my largely Texas audience. The more they laughed, the longer my routine.

Finally, I decided to do a set based on my experiences in Texas. It started out on my premise as to why the United States should secede from Texas. It was filled with some disparaging remarks about Texas women and cattle. There was an eerie silence as I got into the routine, and the audience realized I was disrespecting Texas. Halfway through the set, murmurs grew in intensity. A bartender escorted me off the stage before the bottles started flying. That night ended my stand-up career in Texas.

Of course, I did not share this experience with Carl. He already had enough to worry about. He distributed flyers announcing Ken Dooley would be the entertainer for the evening. We were both pleased when the announcement did not result in any cancellations.

I appeared in a tux and installed a sound system for the evening. I had much inside information, and the routine drew many laughs. For instance, there was always a contentious relationship between the towns of Lyme and Old Lyme over the need for a new high school. Lyme is one of the wealthiest towns in Connecticut, and residents send their children to private schools. The two towns shared the local public high school. So Lyme residents consistently voted against a new public high school that would raise their taxes, as their children attended private schools.

In my routine, I pointed out that Lyme residents came to Old Lyme for one of three reasons:

To go to the library.
To go to the Old Lyme Beach Club.
To vote against a proposal for a new high school.

Then I took on the Old Lyme Zoning Board, which was legendary for turning down requests for variances. "The last plan approved by the Old Lyme Zoning Board was for gallows to hang violators," I reported.

A few years earlier, I had written a musical, "Darn Yankees,' in which I stole music from the greatest shows of all time, including "The Music Man," "Damn Yankees," and "The Sound of Music," so plagiarism was a natural part of my act. "Steal from one source, and it's plagiarism; steal from many sources, and it's research."

The comment that caused problems for me at home involved the Old Lyme Beach Club. One of our friends had proposed the Dooley family for membership in the Old Lyme Beach Club. That didn't get in the way of my act. "The people in the Old Lyme Beach Club are so boring that one day the tide went out and refused to come back in," I said. That line got a lot of laughs, except from the President and the Treasurer of the Old Lyme Beach Club, who were in attendance. The chairperson of the Zoning Board was also there.

"I grew up with five brothers. I never got to sleep alone until I got married." That line didn't go over too well with Rosemary, my wife (and now former wife). "I understand we have a few deadbeats here tonight. Carl has placed a limit on their purchases. So if there's anyone at your table who isn't buying a lot of drinks, you'll understand why."

A few days after my performance, I received a telephone call from the lady who had nominated us for membership in the Old Lyme Beach Club. She had spoken to the president and warned me that there was no way the Dooleys would be admitted. I also got word that I should never apply for an exemption for anything to the Old Lyme Zoning Commission.

The important thing is that Carl was grateful for my act. He said not one person walked out on a check, which told me it was a subject of concern for him.

Not being admitted to the Old Lyme Beach Club was not seen as a tremendous setback. I always followed that Grouch Marx line. "I wouldn't join any country club that would have me."

I left Old Lyme shortly after that performance. No one has asked me to do another stand-up act since. It is probably just as well. Those acts cost me Texas, Connecticut, a few friends, and possibly a wife.

Carl ran the restaurant successfully for more than 20 years. He and his wife, Lois, visited me in Sarasota and bought a home almost next door to mine. Carl and I played tennis four and five days a week, and I enjoyed Lois's cooking.

One night when we were reminiscing, Carl told me something I never knew. The biggest day business-wise in the "Hideaway " history was Dec. 31, 1990, when I delivered my stand-up routine. Maybe I should come out of retirement.

The Bad Seed

The Wilsons were my favorite customers for my grass-cutting/snow-shoveling services. Although they lived in the middle of my route, they were always the first served, especially after winter snowstorms. Mr. Wilson was in a wheelchair, and Mrs. Wilson had some health issues. They were also my highest-paying customers, $5 for each visit, while the average for my other customers was $2.

I earned that extra $3. The Wilsons had a huge lawn on Narragansett Boulevard with a steep driveway leading to a 2-car garage. Although neither one was still licensed to drive, Mrs. Wilson said they wanted to keep the driveway cleared for their son, Fred, when he was on leave from the U.S. Army.

She was my kindest customer, bringing me lemonade on hot summer days and hot chocolate as I struggled with the ice and snow. Mr. Wilson enjoyed talking to me about the Boston Red Sox and whether they would ever win a World Series. Then, a few months after the war ended, Fred Jr. moved in. I wondered if I would keep the job since he was a large, husky man. But Mrs. Wilson assured me that my services would still be needed. Cutting grass or shoveling snow was not of interest to her son.

I cannot say that Fred Jr. was ever rude to me. When we were introduced, he nodded and said nothing. If Fred saw me, he walked by, usually on the way to the garage to get his father's car. He didn't seem to have any desire to return to work and spent his days moping about. He would stretch out in a backyard hammock, shooting me annoying glances when the sound of my lawnmower disturbed his sleep. Other times, he would stand impatiently as I shoveled out the driveway.

I speculated that he might have developed psychological problems from some wartime experiences. Later I learned he spent his entire military career at a supply depot and never left the United States. Then, after a few months, I heard raised voices as Mr. Wilson was growing tired of his son's behavior. Suddenly Fred Jr. and his father's car disappeared. Mr. Wilson died that year, and I did not see Fred Jr. at the funeral.

The following year Mrs. Wilson died, and Fred Jr. did show up at her funeral. The house was dark for a few months, then the lights went on, and Fred Jr. was back. We had a blizzard the next week, and I knocked on Fred's door to see if he wanted me to shovel him out. "Of course," he said, annoyed that I would even ask. The driveway was particularly brutal because freezing rain followed the snow. Fred Jr. didn't appear with any hot chocolate as I shoveled. I went to the door, but he came out for an inspection instead of simply paying me. Fred said nothing but appeared to be satisfied. He reached into his wallet and gave me $1. I explained that the job always paid $5. Instead of answering me, he raised the garage door, got in his car, and drove off.

I watched as his car disappeared onto Narragansett Boulevard, then went into action. First, I pinned his $1 bill to the driveway with a piece of ice. Then, I spent another hour repacking the driveway with ice and snow. There was about a six-foot wall in front of the garage door when I finished.

As I walked home, freezing rain fell. I took comfort in the fact that my blockade would be further enhanced by frozen snow and ice. When I got home, my face was flushed, and my feet were frozen from the cold. My mother made me sit as she poured a hot chocolate. As I began to thaw, I knew I had better tell my side of the story first. I was unsure when Fred Jr. was coming home, but I knew there would be problems when he did. It seemed I just finished the story when the doorbell rang. Fred Jr. stood in the doorway, too upset to speak. My mother stood patiently as he finally blurted out, "Do you know what your son did?"

"I certainly do," my mother said. "And I know what you did–paying him $1 for all that work. Your parents were lovely people. In your case, the acorn fell too far from the tree." Then she slammed the door in his face. That was not the end of the story.

The following week there was another snowstorm. I walked right by the Wilson home on my way to another customer. The door opened, and Fred Jr. caught up with me.

"Ken, I want you to shovel me out," he said. It was the first time he had ever called me by name. He also handed me a $5 bill in advance. Then he asked how my mother was. "You're lucky to have her," he said. After that, he became a customer again, although we had what I would call an uneasy truce. I would do the work, he would pay me, and that was it. No conversation.

The following year, a "For Sale" sign went up on the lawn, and the house sold quickly. Fred never said goodbye, and I had no idea of his new address. It did not matter because neither one of us would have exchanged Christmas cards. Finally, my friend Arthur Jalbert, who lived near the Wilsons, told me Fred had moved to Boston. I was surprised when I got a telephone call from the new owners. Fred had given them my name along with a strong recommendation for my work. A few months later, Arthur called me with some news. Fred Jr. had blown his brains out the previous day.

My mother was upset when I told her. And I had a few sleepless nights myself. Maybe I should have been aware that Fred Jr. had some psychological problems. I think I learned then, at age 15, not to be too harsh or jump to conclusions when it comes to dealing with human beings. I always loved that quote—"Before you judge a man, walk a mile in his shoes." I wish I had applied that rule to Fred.

Neil Simon and Richard Dreyfuss

Dick Bruno and I attended the world premiere of *The Goodbye Girl* in Manhattan in 1977. Neil Simon wrote the screenplay, and since Dick was on the original Board of Directors of the Eugene O'Neill Theater in Waterford, CT, we felt obligated to go.

The movie starred Marsha Mason, who later married Simon, and Richard Dreyfuss. It was a Wednesday evening, the night before Thanksgiving, when Dick parked his car in a Manhattan garage. Neither one of us noticed a sign warning that the garage closed promptly at 12 p.m.

George White, the founder of the Eugene O'Neill Theatre, greeted us as we walked into the theater a few minutes before the movie began. The story opens with former Broadway dancer Paula McFadden, (Marsha Mason) and her ten-year-old daughter Lucy (Quinn Cummings) living in a Manhattan apartment with her boyfriend, Tony DeForrest. Tony deserts her to go and act in a film in Italy. Before he leaves and unknown to Paula, Tony subleases the apartment to Elliot Garfield (Richard Dreyfuss), a neurotic and aspiring actor from Chicago. Elliot shows up in the middle of the night, expecting to move in. Paula is demanding and neurotic and clarifies from the start that she doesn't like Elliot, but he allows her and Lucy to stay.

Paula struggles to get back into shape to resume her career as a dancer. Meanwhile, Elliot has landed the title role in an off-off-Broadway production of Richard III. The director wants him to play the character as a gay person. Elliot agrees to play the role reluctantly, despite knowing it may mean the end of his career as an actor. Many theater critics from television stations and newspapers in New York City attend the opening night, and they all savage the production, especially Elliot's performance. The play quickly closes, much to his relief.

Elliott gets a job as a bouncer in a sleazy Manhattan nightclub. The 5′5″ Dreyfus is miscast in that role, even for a Neil Simon play. He gets beaten up on his first night on the job, and Paula nurses him back to health. Despite their frequent clashes, the two fall in love. However, although she loves Elliot, Paula sees the affair as a repeat of Tony's story. Elliot convinces Paula that he will never abandon her or Lucy.

Elliot gets an acting job at an improvisational theater where he is seen by a well-known film director. He is offered a role in a new film, the only catch being that the job is in Seattle and Elliot will be gone for four weeks. Paula is scared that Elliot is leaving her, never to return, like all the other men in her life.

Later, Elliot calls Paula from the phone booth across the street from the apartment, telling her that the flight was delayed. Elliot invites Paula to go with him while filming the picture and suggests Lucy stay with Paula's mother until they return. Paula declines but is happy because she knows that Elliot's invitation is evidence that he loves her and will return. Before hanging up, Elliot asks Paula to have his prized guitar restrung, which he had deliberately left at the apartment. She sees this as further proof that he will indeed return and that he does love her.

As the movie ended, I thought I should get a $245 refund on my $250 ticket. Immediately after the film was shown, we attended a dinner accompanied by George White, Neil Simon, Marsha Mason, Richard Dreyfuss, and supporters of the Eugene O'Neill Theatre in Waterford, CT.

After dinner, Dreyfuss walked to each table, asking for opinions on the film. We had to listen to comments like "Academy Award winner," "wonderful acting," and "amazing screenplay." Comparing this movie to films such as *The Odd Couple* or *Barefoot in the Park* is sacrilegious to Neil Simon lovers.

When Dreyfuss arrived at our table, he had a satisfied expression that quickly disappeared as he heard our answers. In response to his question, Dick said, "lousy." I told him I couldn't give a knowledgeable answer because I had fallen asleep at the film's beginning. He looked stricken for a moment and then began to laugh as he realized that we had set him up.

My reaction wasn't as contrived as he thought. I was shocked when the film was nominated for best picture, best screenplay, and best male actor. Dreyfuss deserved the Academy Award for best actor, the only award the film received. I agreed with a review in the *New Yorker* where critic Pauline Kael said, "It's not Neil Simon's one-liners that get you down in *The Goodbye Girl*. It's his two-liners."

The real drama for the evening occurred when we returned to the parking garage and learned it was closed. Unfortunately, it was also going to be shut for Thanksgiving Day, which meant we wouldn't get the car back until Friday.

We tracked down a nighttime employee, and Dick gave an academy award performance which, accompanied by a $100 bill, released his car.

The Goodbye Girl was shown recently on Turner Classic Movies. I fell asleep immediately after the scene with Dreyfuss playing Richard III. I guess I still have the same opinion of the film 42 years after that opening night.

A Celebration of the Life of Dr. William J. Hostnik, "Dr. Bill"

Delivered by his friend Ken Dooley at Christ the King Church Old Lyme, Connecticut, Friday, December 7, 2018

Lately, I have been thinking a great deal about my freshman year in college. It was shortly after the end of the civil war—at least it feels that way. It was 1949, and I was 18 years old and on the campus of Providence College. I wasn't particularly happy about being there. When I entered La Salle Academy in Providence a few years earlier, I had one goal in mind—Brown University. I knew that I wanted to be a writer, playwright, screenwriter, and Brown had a great group of professors in the English and History departments. I can still remember how happy I was that previous April when I received a letter of acceptance from Brown. But for reasons then, which are just as stupid as now, it was decided that Brown was not the right school for me.

Providence College was founded by the Dominican Order, disciples of St. Dominic. The first great theologian, St. Thomas Aquinas, was a member of that Order. He wrote the Summa Theological, which Catholic students were required to study for four years. I remember thinking at the time that I was grateful there were approximately 800 years between St. Thomas and myself because we had some serious disagreements. I remember St. Thomas's definition of love—I paraphrase now, but he said to love someone was to wish good things for them. Please remember that I was 18 at the time, and the hormones were running wild. Love to me was far more than wishing good things for another person.

Love was walks on the beach; love was holding hands; love was dropping your date off at 9:30 and calling her a half an hour later to make sure she had not met another boy; love was plotting and planning events, 99% of which never happened; love was a combination of delight and joy followed almost immediately by depression and loss, at least in my case. I still remember in 5th grade when Joan S. told me she liked another boy better. I carried my juvenile impression of love for longer than I should have, which may explain why I have lived alone for more than 30 years. It is only in this past 10-year period that I came to know the real meaning of love.

Love is when your husband of 62 years sits across from you and asks, "Do you know where my wife is?" Instead of shaking her first against heaven, Susan holds Bill's hands, smiles and replies kindly and lovingly, "Bill, I am Susan, I am your wife, and I am here."

Love is when the father of your children asks who the young people are in the dining room, and instead of crying in anguish, Susan says, "Bill, they are your children, Chuck, Heidi, Steven, John, and Susan." Love is when Susan opens the refrigerator door and finds things with no earthly reason for being there. She smiles and follows that old Abe Lincoln rule: "It hurts too much to laugh, but I'm much too old to cry."

Alzheimer's is a terrible disease, taking away its victim's past, present, and future. As insidious as it is, it can do nothing to destroy the memories that Susan has of her husband, the children have of their father, the grandchildren have of their grandfather, the patients have of Dr. Bill, and people like me have of my dear friend.

"A good physician treats the disease—a great physician treats the patient who has the disease. "Those words of Dr. William Ousler sum up the medical career of Bill Hostnik. He had a knack for making each patient feel that he or she was the most important person he would treat that day. The only people who loved Dr. Bill more than his patients were his family.

I remember an incident when Bill visited me in my office in Waterford when I still worked for Prentice-Hall. Suddenly a young woman, Linda, from Personnel came into the office and gave Bill a big hug. She explained to me how her three-year-old son had suffered a horrible burn on his face. When she met him in the Emergency Room, she was hysterical. He held her hands and said, "Give me six months, and you won't know that he had been burned." Of course, Bill kept his promise.

A lawyer I worked with by the name of Stan Maran came to me and asked a favor. He had a 14-year-old son who had some social problems at school. He had finally figured out that other kids didn't like him because of his protruding ears. When they went to see Bill, he refused to operate. "There's nothing wrong with your ears," he said to the young man. My friend asked me to go to Bill and ask him to reconsider.

Bill turned me down flatly, the first time he had ever done so. Then he explained why. "What if I operate on this young man, and in six months, he still has no friends? I would be taking away the only crutch he has." Instead of an operation, the young man saw a psychiatrist. Not only is he a doctor today, but he's also a psychiatrist.

One Saturday, Bill and I were playing a tennis match in North Haven. Bill was operating at the clinic at Yale-New Haven Hospital, and I was to pick him up at 4 p.m. When he got into the car, I could tell he was preoccupied. So, I went into my spiel about focus and how we had to beat those guys. He smiled and then said he was moved by something a nurse had said. He had operated on a four-year-old African American girl with a cleft palate. When he finished the operation, one of the nurses turned to him and said, "Dr. Hostnik, today you changed this child's life."

Bill was always ready to give to the community. When we started a girls' softball league, the town gave us nothing. We lost second base on the field they gave us when the tide came in. So, we wrote a musical and raised the money for uniforms and got a decent field. Bill made an excellent plastic nose for the villain in the play, Big Ed Hook. When I wrote and directed a film for Students Against Drank Driving, Bill donated his services again. Not even Alfred Hitchcock can say that he had a board-certified plastic surgeon as his make-up artist.

Bill loved to make people laugh. I remember he told me a story about a group of young physicians who were being counseled by an older doctor as they got ready to go into practice. One of the new doctors asked a pertinent question: "What do I do if a patient walks into my office, I give him a clean bill of health, and he falls dead on the sidewalk on his way out." "The first thing you do is run out and arrange the body, so it looks like he was walking in," the older doctor said.

Long before his illness, Bill had a terrible time with names. A mutual friend named Larry came to me once and complained that Bill always called him Dave. I went to Bill and told him about Larry's complaint. "I'll try to do better," Bill said. "But thanks for calling it to my attention, Stan," he said.

The Hostniks and Dooleys had ski houses in the same community in Vermont. Once, we were driving to visit his son Chuck, a junior at Dartmouth. I offered to drive, but Bill insisted. He drove down the 10 minutes to town, stopped, and said, "Now it's your turn." I drove the other 3½ hours and all the way back.

Bill fought so hard against this awful disease. He reminded me of that great poem by Dylan Thomas:

Do not go gentle into that good night,
Old age should burn and rave at close of day
Rage, rage against the dying of the light.

In the early days of the disease, Bill would apologize and tell me that he had a memory disorder. "I know I must repeat myself, and it has to be annoying." I would take him on drives, and we would visit familiar places—the Beach Club, Cricklewood, where our children learned to ride, and the Old Saybrook Racquet Club, where we spent so many wonderful evenings.

I would recite the familiar names—Bob Klimek, Carl Lutender, Earl Greenho, and Buzz Robertson—and sometimes there would be a glimmer of recognition, and he would be back with me. After a few minutes, the darkness would return. Sometimes, I would hear him counting as he sat next to me—one, two, three, four, trying to reconnect with that wonderful brain that enabled him to graduate number one in his class from Johns Hopkins and do the New York Times crossword puzzle every day at breakfast. Other times I would hear him recite the name of his children—Chuck, Heidi, Steven, John, and Susan.

Regret the pain and anguish that Susan and the children felt as they watch a man they loved so much drift into the darkness. Regret Bill's frustration as this brilliant man lost the ability to perform the simplest takes. But have no other regrets about the life of William John Hostnik. Every hat that he wore, he wore with great distinction: son, brother, husband, father, physician, and friend.

I have delivered eulogies for three brothers, two sisters, countless friends, and two members of the tennis group, Carl Lutender and now Bill. It's reached a point where people duck me, thinking I may be sizing them up for my next gig. I understand that the final member of the tennis group, Earl Greenho, goes into hiding when I come to Old Lyme.

I recognize that I have probably talked for too long. I can almost see Bob Klimek, Carl Lutender, and Bill Hostnik nodding in agreement and asking, "So what's new?"

The Greatest Sports Broadcaster of All Time

Over the years, I have received many complimentary letters referring to books, plays, or articles that I have written. Only one is framed and sitting on my dresser. The letter is not addressed to me. It was written by the late Bob Wolff, the longest-running broadcaster in television and radio history, to his son Rick, my friend of more than 40 years. The letter's subject was a play I had written about Red Auerbach, the legendary coach, general manager, and president of the Boston Celtics. In describing the play, Bob Wolff used language like "I really nailed it, or "I couldn't put it down."

Bob had insights about Red Auerbach that were particularly helpful. He and his wife Jane had been friendly with Red and his wife Dorothy during their early years in Washington, D.C.

Bob Wolff was 89 when I met with him, his wife Jane, and Rick at the Algonquin Hotel in 2009. Rick had been my editor at MacMillan when I wrote a book with Red Auerbach in 1991. So I was well aware of Bob Wolff's many accomplishments as a sports broadcaster. What I learned at our first meeting was his absolute humility about such an outstanding career. He used words like "luck" or "being in the right place" to describe his many successes. He reminded me of that old Lucille Ball quote: "The harder I work, the luckier I get."

Bob tried to help me bring the play to Broadway, but a problem developed when a play about Vince Lombardi and the Greenbay Packers opened the same season. Two sports plays on Broadway wouldn't be practical, we were told.

Bob's reaction to the play motivated me, and it later opened to critical acclaim in Rhode Island and Massachusetts. The experience also introduced me to one of the giants in the field of sports broadcasting. He and the late Curt Gowdy are the only two broadcasters to be honored by the Baseball and Basketball Halls of Fame.

Bob Wolff became the voice of the Washington Senators in 1947, and he moved with the team to Minnesota in 1961. He was selected as a World Series broadcaster in 1956 and called Don Larsen's perfect game that year. He also was on NBC Radio for the World Series in 1958 and 1961. In 1962, he joined NBC as the play-by-play man on the TV Baseball Game of the Week.

Among his classic broadcasts was the 1958 NFL Championship Game between the New York Giants and Baltimore Colts, frequently called "The Greatest Game Ever Played." In addition, he was television's play-by-play voice for eight teams in five different sports—the New York Knicks and Detroit Pistons of the NBA, the New York Rangers of the NHL, the Washington Senators/Minnesota Twins of MLB, the Baltimore Colts, Washington Redskins and Cleveland Browns of the NFL and soccer's Tampa Bay Rowdies of the North American Soccer League.

Bob Wolff called Jackie Robinson's last major league hit that won Game 6 of the 1956 World Series. He was also the New York Knicks' TV voice when the team won championships in 1970 and 1973. In addition, he was the play-by-play telecaster for all events originating from Madison Square Garden, including the Westminster Kennel Club Dog Show and the National Horse Show. On the collegiate scene, he broadcast the Rose Bowl, Sugar Bowl, Gator Bowl, and many others.

Bob Wolff had a reputation as being the most ethical broadcaster of all time. He would never go after a sportscasting job if a colleague was already holding it. He frequently sent out complimentary notes to sportscasters who had done an outstanding job.

When Bob Wolff died on July 15, 2017, Madison Square Garden and MSG Network released the following:

"Bob Wolff was not only one of the seminal figures in American sportscasting, but he was a part of the very fabric of Madison Square Garden, the New York Knicks, and the New York Rangers for more than six decades. In addition to leaving behind an unmatched body of work, his spirit carries on in the hundreds of broadcasters he mentored and the millions of fans he touched. His legacy will live forever."

I attended a celebration of Bob Wolff's life at Madison Square Garden a few months after his death. Speakers included Mike Breen, head announcer for the New York Knicks; Keith Olbermann of ESPN; Richard Sandomir, who covered TV radio sports for *The New York Times*; Maury Povich; and Kevin Maher, the sports anchor at News 12 Long Island, and several members of the Wolff family. Rick Wolff was master of ceremonies for his father's memorial, and his brother, Dr. Robert Wolff, was one of the speakers.

While each speaker covered a different aspect of Bob Wolff's life, they were united by a common theme: Bob Wolff was the kindest and most ethical person they had ever known. His son Bob described his early problems with kindergarten and how his father hid in the next room until he made the proper adjustment.

"My Mom and Dad always did the right thing," son Rick said. "My Mom was trained as a Navy nurse and even worked in the White House during WWII. But as my Dad's career took off, she became his business partner and accountant. She and my father commuted daily from their home in South Nyack, New York, to News 12, Woodbury, Long Island for more than 25 years. Mom did all of the driving while Dad prepared his newscast during the 90-minute drive."

Rick talked about his father's compassion after his promising major league baseball career was wiped out by a knee injury. His father encouraged Rick, at the age of 38, to return to the minor leagues as an active player for the South Bend White Sox (Midwest League). Over three games, he went 4–for–7 with three RBIs and a double. His .571 average was the highest among all players in the White Sox organization that year, and Rick was awarded a championship ring as South Bend won the league title that season.

In 2012, the Guinness World Records honored Bob Wolff for having the longest career of any sports broadcaster. He also deserves the highest honors for being an outstanding son, brother, husband, father, and friend.

BREAKING THE RULES

As Editorial Director for a division of Prentice-Hall., I had two rules: don't hire journalism majors and avoid job jumpers. Journalism graduates were good at observing the rules about who, why, where, when, and why. But most of them were too superficial about digging into complex issues that had to be addressed in business journalism.

One resume violated my job jumper rule. Harry Cross had a five-year history that included a string of jobs, not one lasting more than six months. I was puzzled why a Yale graduate had such a hard time finding the right career. Nevertheless, I liked him the first time he walked into my office for a job interview. He was tall and broad, resembling a tackle on an NFL team. I learned later that he had set a record at Yale for the shot-put that stood for years.

He was articulate and easy-going, and we had a great meeting. But, of course, I ignored asking about his frequent job changes, critical information I should have demanded. I had made up my mind to hire Harry, and I didn't want to uncover anything that would get in the way. For the first six months, Harry did well. He was intelligent and a natural writer. We were about to start a film program, and Harry would play an essential role in launching it.

One morning I walked into Harry's office and found it empty. I checked with Personnel and learned that Harry had not called in sick. When he was still missing at noon, I drove over to his house. I rang the doorbell but got no answer. Finally, I walked over to a window and saw Harry sprawled out on a couch. An almost empty bottle of liquor was sitting on a table next to him. After pounding on the window for a few minutes, Harry finally came to the door. I walked into his home, and Harry did not try to hide his displeasure. We sat staring at each other. After an uncomfortable silence, Harry finally asked, "I'm fired, right?"

"Wrong," I answered. "Today, I got the answer to something that has bothered me since our first meeting."

"What's that?" he asked.

"Your job record," I answered. "Three months here, four months there. You're bright and a good writer. But now I understand what's going on. You work for three or four months, disappear, and go home to live with Mommy and Daddy. Then, when your parents get sick of your lying around, you find another job and repeat the process. I'm not going to contribute to your well-organized scheme. So sleep it off today, and I'll see you tomorrow at 9 a.m. If you're not there, I'll be here! Understood?"

Harry didn't look happy. But he took my warning to heart. He was there for the next 16 years and became my right-hand man. There were occasional lapses, but his absenteeism was not any worse than any of my other editors—just for different reasons. Harry didn't know it at the time, but I had some interesting background information on him. My brother Bob's father-in-law, Joe Donahue, worked for Harry's father, the Rhode Island Tool Company president, for more than 25 years. Harry had worked there summers while in high school and college, and Joe liked him. However, he also acknowledged that Harry had been a disappointment to the family.

One night I got a call from the police chief in New London, Connecticut, a friend. Harry had been arrested that night for throwing a sailor through a plate glass window of the Crocker House, a local hotel. Fortunately, the sailor was only bruised and not cut in the incident. Harry had some problems, but violence was not one of them. "If Harry did it, there had to be a reason," I told the chief. I also pointed out that Harry had been drinking, but he was not drunk when arrested. Harry claimed that two sailors had attacked him outside the Crocker House. He was released in my custody, and I agreed to bring him to a court hearing that next day.

I did not come alone. Gus, the bartender from the Crocker House, accompanied me to the hearing. "Harry had been sitting in the bar quietly, watching television and quietly sipping a drink," Gus told the prosecutor. "Two sailors came into the bar and started harassing Harry, making unkind comments about his weight. Harry finally turned to me and said, 'I think I'll call it a night, Gus.' He walked out into the street, and the two sailors followed him. I called the police and then followed them. One of the sailors came at Harry and threw a punch. Harry blocked it, then picked him up and threw him through the window. The police arrived at that time, and Harry was arrested. They got the wrong guy."

Harold Dean, the New London prosecutor, agreed. After hearing

Gus's testimony, a representative of the Navy did not object when the case was dismissed. Harry and I never discussed the incident again.

Without Harry, we would never have produced more than 70 industrial films over the next 17 years. Harry contributed to the writing and was instrumental in overseeing all the technical aspects of filming. The only dispute we ever had involved my daughter Alicia, five years old, on the set for one of the films. It had been an awful morning, with actors blowing their lines and nearby trucks wrecking our sound recordings.

Finally, we had a long scene going smoothly when suddenly a sound of Niagara Falls interrupted the filming. I yelled "cut" and tried to find the source. There was my daughter Alicia sipping from the water bubbler that interrupted the filming. I was about to unload when Harry stepped in front of her. "She didn't do anything wrong," he said. His tone made me stop immediately. I was happy there were no windows on the set, or I might have gone through one of them.

I was delighted when I learned that Harry began dating another employee at Prentice-Hall, Liz Schaffer, a divorced mother of two. I always liked her, and she was good for Harry—no more midnight phone calls or sailors going through plate glass windows. Unfortunately, Harry's mother, Regina, was not delighted with the match. I know her objections kept the two from getting married. I have to put Regina's feelings into perspective. Her husband was the founder of one of the most successful companies in Rhode Island. He was the former President of the Agawam Hunt Country Club, one of the more prestigious establishments in Rhode Island. It was not easy for her to accept Liz, a divorcee, into the family.

The situation came to a head when Liz was placed in intensive care with a serious illness. Harry was stunned when he was not allowed in her room since he was not a family member. They were married a few weeks later, and it worked out well for both of them for the next 24 years. Harry called me after my first bout with prostate cancer. He said something I found particularly touching. "You and Liz were the two most important people in my life."

Even after I left Prentice-Hall to start my own film company, Harry and I remained close friends. Harry left Prentice-Hall in 1980, and he inherited a beautiful home on Cape Cod from his parents. In 1992,

Harry developed kidney disease, and I offered him one of my kidneys. He already had a match with Liz, and that operation bought him another ten years. Harry died in 2000 at the age of 63.

Dr. Seuss wrote, "Sometimes you don't know the value of a moment until it becomes a memory." I feel Dr. Seuss's comment is a perfect description of my first meeting with Harry Cross more than 50 years ago.

THE WRONG DRINK

I have always preferred ice cream drinks to any form of alcohol. Gin, vodka, whiskey, and all other hard liquors had no special appeal. The few times I tried wine, I ended up with headaches. I did enjoy a beer after tennis, but I soon learned that it detracted from my writing. If I had even one beer, no writing would be done that night.

I used to walk around at cocktail parties with soda water and a twist of lemon, hoping it would give me cover and make me feel like one of the crowd. A funny thing happened in 1978. I decided to end the charade and had my last drink of alcohol that year. Cold turkey. No AA meetings, counseling, or withdrawal symptoms. Before giving me too much credit, please understand that I was never more than a moderate drinker.

I did not make any public announcements about my decision, but it soon became general knowledge. There was one immediate response that took me off guard. The wife of a close friend asked me to talk to her husband. "Sure," I replied. "What do you want me to talk to him about?"

A little flustered, she told me that Phil was drinking too much. It was evident that she thought I was in a program that her husband should join. No one loves to give speeches more than I do. I could see myself standing in front of all those people, announcing that my name was Ken Dooley, and I am an alcoholic. The only problem was that it would be a big lie. It would be like having me lecture someone about smoking. I used cigarettes for defensive purposes and never inhaled one in my life.

Several other ladies approached me with the same request before word got out that I was a fraud. I stopped drinking because of choice, not because of a job or life-threatening reasons. I never had one withdrawal system or felt any regrets about my decision. It would have been much harder for me to give up Ben and Jerry's ice cream.

About 20 years later, I had a funny incident involving non-alcoholic beer. I used to enjoy an O'Doul's, a non-alcoholic beer made by Budweiser. I was shooting a game of pool with my good friend Ted Barrows in his home in Bristol, Rhode Island. Ted was drinking Rolling Rock, a beer that came in a green bottle similar to O'Doul's. After several games, Ted went into the kitchen to retrieve a couple of beers. He returned with a stricken expression. "Ken, I screwed up," he said. "You just drank Rolling Rock instead of an O'Doul's."

"Don't worry about it," I replied. A few minutes later as I was lining up a shot, I turned to Ted and in a trembling voice asked for a shot of Scotch. "If you don't have Scotch, anything else will do—but I've got to get a hit,"

"What have I done," Ted said in anguish. He was so upset that I could not carry out the hoax as I began to laugh. That afternoon was one of the few times I ever defeated Ted on the pool table. So technically, I have to admit that in the past 43 years, I have had one beer.

Shootout in Philadelphia

I had long been an admirer of Andy Rooney for both his books and his role in "A Few Minutes with Andy Rooney" on *60 Minutes*. Ed Satell, President of Progressive Business Publications, invited other staff members and me to a meeting of the World Affairs Council at the Union League in Philadelphia on Oct. 20, 2000, at which Andy Rooney was the guest speaker. I was delighted with the prospect of meeting one of my heroes.

Since Ed was sponsoring the event, Andy sat at the head table two seats from me. Sitting next to Andy was Michelle McGovern, an excellent writer and friend. Twenty years later, she still remembers what she describes as the "shootout between Rooney and Dooley."

Before the meeting, I wondered if all the stories I had heard about Andy being a curmudgeon were true. Ten minutes after he sat down, I realized that reputation had was understated. He sat without really acknowledging anyone, including Ed Satell, who had paid thousands of dollars for his appearance.

Every person at the event had received an autographed copy of *My War,* Andy's book about his experiences as a reporter during WWII. Some people came to our table and asked Andy to personalize copies of the book for a friend or relative who had served in WWII. He brushed them all aside with a warning that "he had been signing books for two hours before the event and no one was going to get anything extra."

Our table sat silently as Andy chased the last victim away. We all breathed a sigh of relief when the waiter began taking orders for lunch. Andy looked at the three luncheon meals being offered, scowled, and shouted, "These are not luncheon meals. Lunch should be a sandwich and a glass of milk."

Ed told Andy to order anything he wished, but our guest of honor would have none of it. He accepted only a glass of water and sat glumly as the rest of us began to order in an uneasy silence.

Finally, I asked Andy what he thought of authors who published a book, added a foreword written by a famous person, then came out with a "new" edition. I'm still intimidated by the memory of those bushy eyebrows and deeply circled eyes as Andy, face flushed, stared at me. Ed Satell asked me to explain. I picked up my copy of the book and said that I had read the first edition almost five years earlier. Tom Brokaw added a new introduction, describing what he called "the greatest generation."

Andy asked who I was. I told him that we had one thing in common. He was a staff sergeant who wrote for "Stars and Stripes" in WWII. I was a staff sergeant who wrote for the United States Air Force publications during the Korean War.

The comparison stopped there, I told Andy, "You flew on bombing missions, covered the invasion of France in 1944, and won a Bronze Star for reporting under fire the battle of Saint-Lo in Normandy. You were among the first Americans to enter the concentration camp at Buchenwald, Germany."

I told Andy that I fought the Korean War in Europe and Africa with a typewriter and never saw a shot fired in anger. I did receive the Berlin Occupation Medal in 1953, although I was never in Berlin. I was also hospitalized with sunburn after spending too much time on a beach in Tripoli, Libya, in 1952. No Purple Heart.

After explaining that the second edition wasn't his idea, Andy seemed to soften. I asked him to tell us the origin of one of his most famous *60 Minutes* episodes. He had taken a can of mixed nuts and compared the contents to the pictures shown on the label. The peanuts far outnumbered the cashews and other desirable nuts illustrated on the outside of the can.

The story behind the episode was even more impressive. The *60 Minutes* brass decided at the last minute that Andy's projected episode for that week didn't live up to his standards. They sent a camera crew to his home in Rowayton, CT, to film a new segment.

Andy sat in his office without a single idea for the replacement show. Then, just before the crew arrived, Andy's eyes fell on a can of mixed nuts on his desk. Everyone loved the new episode except the owners of Planters Peanuts.

Once Andy warmed up, the stories poured out: "What about wash and wear shirts that you can wash but not wear? Why do they make two-prong plugs in a three-prong society? Why are cereal boxes so big but contain very little cereal?"

Andy also explained that he didn't like any music he couldn't hum.

His other dislikes included New Year's Eve, waiting in line for any reason, and the bursars at whatever colleges his children attended.

By the time Ed introduced Andy, the atmosphere was considerably warmer. His descriptions of the landing at Normandy and the subsequent battles were spellbinding. It also allowed him to express some of his other feelings. "We give too many medals for ordinary acts. Medals should be for heroic acts. I was given the Distinguished Service Cross for bandaging a wounded gunner during a bombing mission. I didn't deserve a medal for doing what was expected of me." Andy received a standing ovation when he concluded his remarks.

He returned to the table and actually had coffee. Then he asked if I had any relatives in WWII. I explained that I was one of six boys. Two of them served in WWII, four in the Korean War and one in the Viet Nam War. My brother Jack, a Marine, was wounded during the invasion of Peleliu. My brother Bill fought with the Army in Europe in WII and was later recalled for the Korean War. My brother Bob was evacuated from Pusan after the Chinese entered the Korean War.

I had two books on the table for my brothers. Andy reached for them, took out his pen, and personalized each book. I think I was the only one to receive that treatment.

I never saw or spoke to Andy Rooney again after that meeting, but I never missed an episode of *60 Minutes*. Occasionally Andy crossed the line and was even suspended by CBS a few times. The dramatic drop in TV ratings kept those suspensions short.

Andy Rooney lived life on his own terms. During his final appearance on Oct. 2, 2011, he made a plea to viewers. "If you see me in a restaurant, just let me eat my dinner." He also said he had lived life luckier than most. "I wish I could do this forever."

So do we.

Brotherly Love

With Dr. Victor Pricolo

I knew quite a bit about the doctor who was going to operate on me for colon cancer before our first meeting. Dr. Victor Pricolo was described to me as one of the best surgeons in New England. He had an air of confidence about him as he told me he could promise a cure. What I did not know was that he had done some research on me as well.

"I understand you have written a number of books," he said after we finished discussing the operation. He asked me how much I knew about Italy's role in WWII. I was only 10 when the Japanese bombed Pearl Harbor, and we went to war with Japan, Germany, and Italy. I remembered being nervous when I learned that Japanese Americans were being placed in detention camps. Half of the population of Rhode Island, including some of my best friends, would have been behind barbed wire if that same ill logic had been applied to Italians.

As a history buff, I knew quite a bit about Italy's role in WWII. But Dr. Pricolo told me stories about his father and uncle that changed my perception of how Germany treated Italian soldiers who refused to fight for Hitler. His father, Dr. Vittorio Pricolo, was born on January 18, 1910, one of 10 children, in a small town of 2,000 people in Frosolone, Molise, a mountainous region of central-southern Italy. The town was known for its main trade of artisans making knives and scissors. Felix and Mike Mirando, Vittorio's first cousins, emigrated to Rhode Island and founded Imperial Knife in Providence. Very successful, they provided bayonets for the U.S. Army in WWII.

After completing a classical high school education, Vittorio went to Medical School in Parma, graduating in 1936. He became a specialist in oncology and started his surgical career at the National Cancer Institute in Milan in 1939. He went on to become a Professor of Surgical Pathology and Clinical Surgery at the University of Milan.

His brother, Major Alphonse Pricolo, was fighting in Yugoslavia in 1943 when the disastrous 20-year fascist experiment imposed on Italy by Benito Mussolini was approaching its inevitable end. The Allies had invaded and were routing combined German and Italian armies across Italy. The Italian government arrested Mussolini, described by King Vincent Emmanuel III as the most hated man in Europe.

In September 1944, an armistice was reached with the Allies. But for thousands of members of what had been the Italian army, the suffering had only begun. The soldiers, including Major Alphonse Pricolo, were placed in German concentration camps, and their only ticket to freedom was to agree to fight for Germany. Fewer than 10% decided to do so. More than 90 percent of them remained in concentration camps for the duration of the war.

Italian prisoners were not afforded protection specified by the Geneva Convention because they were labeled as traitors, not prisoners of war. They received ow rations, no medical treatment, and little heat. An estimated 50,000 died from forced labor, disease, malnutrition, and executions inside the camps.

The Waffen SS, under the command of the notorious Colonel Walter Rauff, established Gestapo headquarters in Milan in 1944. Rauff had been in charge of a group of mobile gas vans that executed thousands of Jews in the early days of the war. He was sent to Milan to hunt down Jews and partisans. Only about 8,000 Italian Jews out of an estimated 50,000 had been turned over to the Nazis. More German soldiers were stationed in Milan than in any part of Italy in 1944. The city had industrial plants producing tanks, vehicles, and ammunition for the Germans. It became a primary target for Allied bombers. More than once, stray bombs struck the hospital where Dr. Pricolo performed critical operations under very trying conditions.

One of Dr. Pricolo's best friends in Milan was a Jewish dentist named Ben Steiner, who had changed his name to Giorgio Spinelli in the early days of the war. He was a favorite of many German high-ranking officers and was able to get information about Alphonse Pricolo as he moved from concentration camps from Yugoslavia to Germany.

Dr. Victor Pricolo got me a translation of a diary kept by Col. Francesco Grasso, who described his good friend Alphonse Pricolo and the inhumane treatment they received from Col. Heinz Muller, Commandant at Tschenstochau Concentration Camp. One of the entries describes Muller executing an Italian soldier who refused to sign an oath to Hitler. Other entries detail prisoners dying of starvation and mistreatment and being denied access to the Red Cross parcels sent to the camp. In addition, the prisoners covered up the deaths of friends to continue to collect their rations.

Dr. Pricolo learned of his brother's internment at Tschenstochau through his Jewish dentist friend with an Italian name. By bribing German guards, he was able to send his brother food and medicine. The German guards removed cash as a special bonus for their participation. The diary mentions how Dr. Pricolo's medical supplies helped set up a clinic at the camp.

All contact between the two brothers was lost when Alphonse was moved to Dachau, the first Nazi concentration camp located in southern Germany. Thousands of Italian prisoners were sent there after refusing to fight for Hitler. Dachau was initially a camp for political prisoners; however, it eventually evolved into a death camp where countless thousands of Jews died from malnutrition, disease, overwork, or execution. In addition to Jews, the camp's prisoners included members of other groups Hitler considered unfit for the new Germany, including artists, intellectuals, the physically and mentally disabled, and homosexuals.

The Nazis also used Dachau prisoners as subjects for brutal medical experiments. Italian prisoners were used as guinea pigs in a series of tests to determine the feasibility of reviving individuals immersed in freezing water. For hours at a time, prisoners were forcibly submerged in tanks filled with ice water. Some prisoners died during the process. Alphonse Pricolo got in much trouble with Col. Muller when he refused to participate in the experiments with German doctors.

A German patient of Giovanni Spinnelli reported that Alphonse was a prisoner at Dachau. Before Dr. Pricolo could even send any packages, word comes that Alphonse had been transferred to a concentration camp at Nuremberg, about two hours from Dachau. Alphonse had been pleasantly surprised when he learned that Col. Muller has been transferred to the eastern front because of his inability to convince Italian prisoners to fight for Hitler. He was replaced by the more humane Major Hilmar Weiss, a medical doctor. Red Cross packages were distributed to the prisoners that same day.

The brothers were not able to establish any connections when Alphonse got to Nuremberg. Through his relationship with the "Italian" dentist, Vittorio did learn that Alphonse survived a major bombing attack on the Nuremberg camp. Vittorio had his hands full with nightly bombing attacks on Milan and shortages of medical suppliers. During one of the bombing attacks, Vittorio refused to leave the operating room where he was operating on a 15-year-old boy, Orazio Pizzigoni, shot by a fleeing German soldier. He completed the operation and saved the boy's life.

On Oct. 28, 1945, Benito Mussolini and his mistress, Claretta Petacci were executed by the Partisans. Their bodies were beaten and hung from a metal girder above a service station on the square. An American team recovered the bodies and brought them to the Milan Cancer Hospital, where Vittorio Pricolo performed an autopsy on both bodies. He was told that the Americans had a theory that Mussolini suffered brain damage from syphilis. There was no indication of brain disease, according to the report. "Mussolini had signs of multiple gunshot wounds to his chest, abdomen, neck, and thighs. One bullet struck him in the right forearm, indicating he was not blindfolded before his execution," the report read. A photo was found in the pocket watch hidden in the brassiere of Claretta Petacci. The photo was of Mussolini, and he signed it, "I am you, and you are me. Ben." Those words are right out of *For Whom the Bell Tolls*, written in 1940 by Ernest Hemingway. The photo was returned to the Mussolini family after the war ended.

On May 25, 1945. The people of Milan flooded the streets to welcome the arrival of Allied troops marking the end of the German occupation. Shops and workplaces closed as the civilians went wild, greeting American soldiers with flowers, wine, and embraces. Dr. Pricolo's joy was clouded by the fact that he had not heard from Alphonse for over a year. He was told that his brother had survived a major bombing raid on the camp. But there had been other raids, and his Jewish dentist had left the area, so Dr. Pricolo was left in the dark. On June 15, 1945, Dr. Pricolo was interrupted on his rounds by a visitor—his brother. Alphonse was extremely thin, and it took many months for him to recover from the harsh treatment he had received in the German concentration camps. After he recovered, he became a successful owner of pharmacies.

Colonel Walter Rauff, the man responsible for the deaths of more than 100,000 people in WWII, was arrested in 1945. However, he escaped and was never tried for his war crimes. He died in Chile in 1987, and former Nazis attended his funeral. Shortly after the war ended, Dr. Vittorio Pricolo was married to Bruna Marudi in a ceremony conducted by Cardinal Schuster. They had two sons, Cosimo, an attorney in Piacenza, Italy, and Victor, Chief of Surgery in Southern Massachusetts and Professor at Brown Medical School in Providence, RI.

Fifty years after they had first met, Orazio Pizzigoni, the 15-year-old Dr. Pricolo had operated on during a bombing raid in Milan in 1944, visited the now-retired Vittorio Pricolo. The doctor had not been able to stand up unassisted, having survived stomach cancer and a stroke. At the sight of Orazio, he stood and touched Orazio on the cheek. "Professor I'm here because of you. You saved my life," Orazio said. "I relived that day when I was shot. I'm so glad I had a chance to thank you for saving my life. I have always wanted to do that. But I also wanted to thank that German soldier for sparing my life. He shot me because I had a gun pointed at him. He fired before I could. He was defending himself. He could have finished me off, but he didn't. Before he leaned over me, I had only seen a uniform an enemy uniform. Maybe he had only seen a gun pointed at him. But when he leaned over me, I saw a defeated mature man, and maybe he saw a naïve young man. At that point, he had to survive, and I had to survive. I wish I could find out what happened to him, talk to him, thank him too."

After surviving the gunshot would, Orazio graduated from high school in 1949 and studied Political Science in Pavia, Italy. He started his career as a journalist in 1950 and is the author of 10 books, including one that recounts his encounter with the German soldier and his operation.

MR. CHAIRMAN

Richard Prentice Ettinger was the co-founder and chairman of Prentice-Hall when I joined the company as an editor in 1960. Publishers of books and business and professional information services, he and Charles Gerstenberg formed Prentice-Hall in 1913, taking the company's name from the family names of their mothers.

Ettinger liked to tell the story about how an early disaster for the young publishing company turned into an economic boom. He and Gerstenberg wrote a book on Federal taxes that became obsolete overnight when Congress voted for new regulations. That inspired the partners to bind future manuals on taxes in loose-leaf, so they could be updated when necessary. The company had annual sales of more than $120 million with 3,400 employees in 1960.

I met Ettinger briefly when he came to Waterford, CT, to dedicate a new building housing a division of P-H, the Bureau of Business Practice, in April of 1960. However, we did not meet again until two years later, when I was editorial director of the division. Ettinger had a policy of meeting with division presidents and editors-in-chief of each division annually to review results, discuss strategies and go over budgets for the upcoming year.

Dave Silberstein, my division president, and I met with Mr. Ettinger in Englewood Cliffs, New Jersey, company headquarters. I went to the meeting confidently since we had the highest growth rate of any division in P-H. About 45 minutes later, I staggered out, feeling that I had just gone through a sparring session with Muhammad Ali. Ettinger didn't like my plans for new publications. He particularly objected to my budget request, telling me I had not done my homework correctly. He also said I was not taking advantage of the opportunities, just waiting for an intelligent and ambitious editorial director to pluck them. Unfortunately, he did not name any of those "opportunities" that I was overlooking. Before I could even mount a defense, Ettinger suddenly stood, indicating our meeting was over.

Dave Silberstein and I sat in silence for the first part of our trip back to Connecticut. Suddenly Dave turned to me and said, "RP (the nickname given to him by company executives) really liked you." I didn't answer immediately. Finally, I said, "How would he have treated me if he didn't like me?" Dave did not have an immediate answer, but he told me that what I had gone through was typical for one of Ettinger's review sessions. Maybe Ettinger liked me, but I knew one thing for sure—I did not like him. I also decided that day that Prentice-Hall was not a fit for my long-term goals. I was getting married that next year and wanted to be settled in a new job before tying the knot.

I decided to be selective and turned down several job offers for the next ten months. Then I was contacted by a recruiter for a job as publications director for Aetna Insurance in Hartford. I liked the vice president I would be reporting to and the whole team at Aetna. The job included a $10,000 raise from my current salary with P-H. So, I accepted the position and only had one more assignment for my old job. Dave and I were scheduled for our performance review session with RP. I had decided to hold up on giving my notice to Dave until after the meeting.

The meeting began in the same negative fashion as the first one. Ettinger had circled every overhead figure that reflected an increase in the previous budget.

"How do you explain these outlandish numbers?" he demanded.

"Mr. Ettinger, if you want me to decrease those particular numbers, you will have to get the United States Congress involved. Those numbers you have signaled out represent the recent increases in social security taxes. Perhaps I could refer you to the P-H tax service."

Ettinger said nothing, but his body language indicated that he would love to reach out and strangle this brash, sarcastic editor. Dave Silberstein sat in stunned silence.

Ettinger decided to take a different approach. "Your division had a good year. How do you explain it?"

"The reason for the success of our division is that the people who read our publications do not pay for them, and the people who pay for our publications do not read them," I said.

Ettinger stared at me and said nothing. Finally, he stood, ending the meeting. No congratulations, no good-byes. As we left Ettinger's office, Dave Silberstein spoke in a shaky voice. "I don't know if I can save your job," he confided.

It was then that I told him about my new job and gave him 30 days' notice. We were walking towards the car during the conversation. "Is that decision final?" Silberstein asked. When I confirmed it, Dave said he had to return to the office and make a phone call. So, I waited in another office until he returned. "RP wants to see us," he said.

When we entered his office, RP said nothing. We sat silently, then suddenly he broke into uncontrolled laughter. "Paid for by people who don't read them. Read by people who don't pay for them." That's the funniest—and most accurate assessment I ever heard. " Even Dave Silberstein risked a smile.

After the laughter ended, the conversation got serious.

"What's this company offering you?" Ettinger said.

"A vice-presidency and a $10,000 raise," I responded, realizing that the penny-pinching Ettinger would never match it.

"Okay, you get the title and a $15,000 raise to stay, Ettinger said. "But I need a decision before you leave this office."

I elected to stay with P-H. The fact is I liked my present job. We were doing a lot of new things, including setting up a film division. I always wanted to write screenplays and direct. I did both for the next 14 years. Dave Silberstein was quiet during our trip to Connecticut. Later I found out why. He had been with Prentice-Hall for almost 25 years. I had three years of seniority when Ettinger offered me that deal. Yet Dave and I were making the same salary after that historic day.

Ettinger died in 1971, but we had seven successful meetings while he was still chairman. They always ended with compliments and congratulations as our division continued to exceed expectations. I can honestly say that I grew to like RP.

THE CON MAN

The Dooleys were never a wealthy family, particularly after my father died in 1945. I don't know how she did it, but my mother saw that we never went to bed hungry. She ran a tight ship, and every dime was accounted for, except in one area—Catholic magazines and newspapers. So, our mailbox was filled with the *Providence Visitor, Catholic Digest, The Voice of St. Jude, The Angelus*, Maryknoll, *St. Anthony Messenger*, and *U.S. Catholic*. George, the mailman, a staunch Baptist, told me he thought all the Catholic propaganda he was delivering was an attempt by my mother to convert him.

My mother was excited one afternoon when I returned from school at Providence College. "Wait until I show you all of the money I saved," she said. She read me a list of all of her subscriptions, noting savings of between 40% and 50%.

It was all the result of a lovely Catholic man who had knocked on her door that morning. He was such a wonderful man, caring for his sick wife and a Downs Syndrome child. Then, I suddenly remembered a warning I had read in *The Providence Visitor*, a weekly Catholic newspaper. A man was going door-to-door in the diocese, passing himself off as a sales representative for Catholic publications. He had no credentials and gave a receipt available from any stationery store.

When I asked my mother for a receipt, my suspicions were confirmed. A boiler-plate receipt acknowledged the payment of $65 for a long list of Catholic publications. When I told my mother that she had been cheated, she refused to believe it. "He was such a nice man, caring for his sick family."

I got out the article, and it even listed a phone number to call if approached by this culprit. After my mother read the article, reality set in.

I called the number listed, and the person answering asked for a description. I turned to my mother and asked for a few facts. Silence. Was he short, tall, fat, thin? Silence. I asked again, and she shook her head. I told the person at the *Visitor* I would call back.

"Mom, you're trying to cover for a con man. He is cheating people who can't afford it. You can help put a stop to it. Now tell me what he looked like."

"I'm sorry that he is forced to live like this," she said. "But I'm not going to get him into more trouble than he already has." A representative from the *Visitor* called back later that day. Unfortunately, I had no additional information to give him.

I don't know if he was ever apprehended. We never talked about the incident again. One thing I know—he got a lot more than $65 from my mother. I'm sure he was the recipient of a few rosaries and a lot of other prayers from my forgiving mother.

One of my mother's favorite parables was the one about the lost sheep. "Which of you, if you had 100 sheep, and lost one of them, wouldn't leave the 99 in the wilderness and go after the one that was lost. When he found it, he called together his family and friends, saying to them, 'Rejoice with me, for I have found my sheep which was lost.' I tell you that even so there will be more joy in heaven over one sinner who repents than over 99 righteous people who need no repentance.' "

Since I am a sinner in need of repentance, I appreciate that my mother was so fond of this parable.

Duluth, Minnesota

In 1975, I was approached by a friend who had recently gone to work for Harcourt, Brace & Jovanovich in Manhattan. There was an opening for an editorial vice president, and he felt I had all the qualifications for the job.

The group publisher interviewed me and explained the job in detail. All of the company's publications were printed in Duluth, MN. If I got the job, I would be expected to travel to Duluth every few months to ensure a smooth operation. I told him that would not be a problem. The initial interview seemed to go well, and he set me up to meet with other key executives. After about two weeks, I was offered the job, providing I cleared one last hurdle. Chairman William Jovanovich himself made the final decision on all executive positions.

When I was ushered into his office, I wasn't sure if I was expected to genuflect. I had dealt with other CEOs, but none was treated with the deference shown by this man's executive staff. They referred to him as "the Chairman" in reverent tones. The Chairman had my resume spread out on his desk, together with what I assumed to be comments about me from other executives.

I waited for him to question me about books and publications I had developed in my 20-year career in publishing. Instead, he commented on my printing experience.

When I got out of the Air Force in 1955, I took a part-time job with the Providence Lithography Company as a "gofer," a person who loaded paper onto the presses or who cleaned them after a color change. When my boss found out I could type, he decided to teach me how to run a Linotype machine. It was a metal system that cast blocks of metal type for posters, magazines, and newspapers from the 19th century to the 1960s. The system was replaced by photo and computer typesetting in the 1970s. I explained to the Chairman that I had no experience with either of those new systems.

The day after my interview with the Chairman, I was told it was successful, and the job was mine. I made several trips to Manhattan, met with my new secretary, and even picked out the rug color for my office. In a final touch, I put family photos on my new desk.

My wife and I began looking at houses in the Westport area of

Connecticut. Fortunately, we had not located the right house in our price range. I say fortunately because of an abrupt change in the plan. The week before my start date, I made a trip to Manhattan. I was greeted in my office by my new boss, who told me there had been a slight change in my assignment. Because of my background in printing, the Chairman reversed the original plan. Instead of being headquartered in New York and traveling to Duluth several times a year, I would be stationed in Duluth with occasional trips to Manhattan.

"Is this decision final?" I asked. "Absolutely," he said. "It came directly from the Chairman."

I began taking the pictures off the desk and sliding them into my briefcase.

"What are you doing? he asked.

"Packing up. I'm not taking the job."

"You can't do that," he said

"Watch me," I replied.

"What am I to tell the Chairman?"

"Tell the Chairman I'd rather deal with him than tell my wife she will be living in Duluth, Minnesota."

He called me several times over the next few days and asked me if I had changed my mind.

"Has the Chairman decided to go back to the original plan?" I asked.

"No. Once he makes a decision, he never changes it."

"Neither does my wife," I replied.

We never spoke again.

Not long after that, the Chairman made another decision that had more impact than the loss of an editor. He decided to invest 40 percent of the pension fund to build a new headquarters in Orlando, FL. In 1983, the U.S. Department of Labor ruled against the use of these funds for that purpose. The Chairman left his post in 1990, and the publishing company is now simply Harcourt-Brace, the original name of its co-founders.

The First African American to Play in the NBA

Chuck Cooper was the first African American player to be drafted into the NBA when Red Auerbach chose him in the second round in 1950. Because of the schedule, Earl Lloyd, drafted by the Washington Caps in the 9th round, was the first African American to play. I used to needle Red a little bit about that draft. While Cooper was a good NBA player, Lloyd was an all-star and became the third African American head coach in NBA history.

My friend, Sam Jones, set up a telephone interview with Earl Lloyd just months before his death in 2015. This is Earl's story, in his own words.

Every Halloween night, I get lots of calls from friends, former players and simply fans reminding me about another Halloween night, October 31, 1950. I took the floor for the Washington Caps that night, playing against the Rochester Royals in Rochester, New York, the first African American to play in NBA history.

I still get many questions concerning the drama of the game. Was there tension in the arena as I took the floor? Were the fans hostile, or did I get any resentment from my teammates or opponent? Did the event make the national news, together with a lot of pictures and comments about me?

Some people—especially reporters—are disappointed when I answer "no" to all of the above. I didn't hear any racist remarks from either the fans or opposing players. My teammates accepted me completely, as did my coach, Bones McKinney. Newspapers, both before and after the game, made little mention of me.

One of them mentioned that I scored six points and grabbed ten rebounds in a losing effort to Rochester. An article before the game described me as a Negro guard from West Virginia State. Not one story mentioned my first game as a historic event.

There probably would have been more drama if I had made my debut in St. Louis or Ft. Wayne, both racist cities. I was lucky to begin in a completely integrated city like Rochester.

Maybe the rest of the world didn't notice, but I'll never forget hearing my name called in the starting lineup that night. Coming from a segregated background, going to a small Black school, and being the second African American drafted into the pros was overwhelming.

The following night, Chuck Cooper took the floor for the Boston Celtics, and "Sweetwater Clifton started for the New York Knickerbockers four days later. Each of us recorded a first: I was the first to play; Chuck Cooper was the first drafted, and "Sweetwater" Clifton signed the first contract with an NBA team. Within one week, the three of us had ended the four-year reign of the original WNBA—the White National Basketball Association.

My next game, the Caps' opener against the Indianapolis Olympians on Nov.1, was a lot more memorable. I scored eight points, and the Washington Post credited me and a teammate, Bill Sharman, with turning a close game into a win.

My parents attended the second game, and there was an incident I'll never forget. There was only one Black player in the whole building. When they announced the starting lineups, a white man sitting in front of my mother asked his friend, "Do you think this nigger can play any basketball?" Before the other man could answer, my mother, steps in and says, "Trust me, the nigger can play basketball."

I ran into my first problem with segregation during my first game in Fort Wayne, Indiana. I was allowed to stay in the hotel, but the restaurant was off-limits. As I sat in my hotel room waiting for room service, I had a guest. Bone McKinney, my coach, walked in and told me he wanted to enjoy room service with me. I'll never forget Bones for doing that, a very classy act from a very classy person. Bones McKinney grew up and played all of his game in segregated schools. Yet, the man didn't have a prejudiced bone in his body.

When the Washington Caps folded, Bones caught on with the Boston Celtics. He volunteered to room with Chuck Cooper, and Red Auerbach approved his request. So Bones McKinney coached the first Black to play and roomed with the first Black drafted.

My biggest obstacle in becoming a professional Black player didn't have anything to do with racism, on or off the court. It came from within, a nagging sense of inferiority resulting from growing up as a Black kid in a segregated system.

I was raised in Alexandria, Virginia, about eight miles from Washington D.C., but about a thousand miles away in terms of segregation.

There were no Black cops, no Black mailmen, no Black anything. It was an era when you were told you were inferior so much that you began to believe it: Back of the bus, upstairs at the theater, no service at the restaurants. I never sat next to a white person until I was twenty-two years old.

My mother, Daisy, and my father, Theodore, tried to give the right values to my two brothers and me. My father worked in a coal yard, a good job for a Black male. He could never attend any of my high school games because he always worried about being fired. My mother was the most significant influence in my life. If she had gone to college, she probably would have become the first female president, Black or white. She instilled the importance of attire, hygiene, and punctuality in me and my two brothers, qualities that stayed with us always.

I started playing neighborhood basketball, sharing one ball, and playing on dirt courts. By the time I got to high school (Parker-Gray) I was a pretty good basketball and baseball player. I was extremely lucky to have Lewis Johnson as my high school coach. He never raised his voice, never cursed, but he was the man. If you didn't do what he said, you could hang up your uniform and go home. Coach Johnson game me the values that helped me throughout my NBA career.

I also became a pretty good pitcher on the baseball team. While I could throw the ball through a wall, I didn't always know where it was going. In 1950, I got an offer to play for a Pittsburgh Pirates minor-league team. Coach Johnson convinced me that basketball was my sport, and he helped get me a scholarship to his college, West Virginia State. I was the tallest kid on campus at six-foot-six, so I got the nickname "Moon Fixer," which has stayed with me all my life. The idea was that if the moon went off-kilter, I was tall enough to straighten it out.

The basketball coach, Mark Caldwell, had the same coaching philosophy as Coach Johnson, so I had the advantage of spending eight years in the same system. During my college career, the team went 80–14, and the 1947–48 team went unbeaten throughout the CIAA regular season and postseason tournament and became the Black intercollegiate champion.

The following year, we won thirty-two regular-season games and repeated as Black intercollegiate champs. I made the CIAA all-conference and all-tournament teams in 1948, 1949, and 1950.

I get many questions about when Black players first started talking about playing professional basketball. I can tell you it wasn't during my college career. You don't talk about something that's not available to you. Our only opportunity to play pro basketball was with the Harlem Globetrotters.

Bob Wilson, a college teammate, spent a little time traveling with the Globetrotters after graduation. Fortunately, we heeded a warning from Coach Caldwell and didn't commit to the Globetrotters. It wasn't hard for me to turn down. I liked the players but not the grind. I also noticed the owner, Abe Saperstein, stayed at the best white hotels where Blacks weren't allowed. He wasn't exactly free with the money, either. The salary I was offered was less than I could make as a schoolteacher.

Then fate stepped in the form of a tryout offer with the Washington Caps. Harold Hunter, a point guard for North Carolina College, was also invited. Coach John McLendon of North Carolina State drove us to Uline Arena for the tryout. Twenty-four white players, already practicing, froze as Hunter and I walked onto the court. It was the first time that Black players were ever in an NBA training camp. We didn't run into any problems from the players and received a fair tryout. John Norlander, a guard with the Caps, played with Hunter and me against three other players. We more than held our own.

Bones McKinney told me later he was impressed with my ball-handling skills, unusual for a guy my size. He also liked Hunter's speed which allowed him to run by players for lay-ups. After the workout, the two of us went upstairs with Bob Foster, the general manager, to sign contracts. Foster said that since Hunter was about seven inches shorter than me, he should sign the first contract. So Hunter beat me out of signing an NBA contract by about 10 seconds. I didn't realize at that time that I would be registering a more historic first in just a few months.

Events were taking place in Washington that gave me the idea that the Caps might be integrating. It was more a result of economics than any moral sense on Mike Uline, owner of the Caps. During the 1940s, Uline chose to ban Black people from all events other than boxing matches held at his arena. In 1948, Uline agreed to allow Blacks to attend any events held in the area, but his basketball team remained Lilly-White.

In 1950, the team suffered from low attendance levels, so Uline decided to add some Black players to attract fans from the growing Black population. I was picked in the ninth round of the 1950 draft while Hunter was taken in the eleventh round. The Caps made Dick Schnittker from Ohio State their first-round choice and took Bill Sharman of Southern California in the second round. I didn't know about it at the time, but Bones McKinney, the coach, and Bob Foster, the general manager, warned all white players that Blacks would be joining the team. They offered releases to any white players who objected.

I'm proud to say that not one white player left the team. I still had a significant problem to overcome before I reported to training camp. It was another hangover from my segregation days. Was I good enough to play with Dick Schnittker, a college player of the year, or Bill Sharman, another all-American?

I was still living at home and didn't have a car, so Bill Sharman would pick me and drive me to practice. Bill told me at the time that he didn't realize that the NBA had no Black players since he had played with and against Black players in high school and college. There was no NBA team on the west coast at the time, so he assumed that Blacks were playing in the league.

I was awestruck when I started scrimmaging with all of those great players. After a few days, I had a defining moment. I was just as good as these guys. I had no problem keeping up with Sharman, Schnittker, and all of those great athletes. Some of the veterans had trouble keeping up with Hunter, who ran like the wind.

Hunter had a good camp, but he was a victim of size. He was only about five-foot-nine, and the Caps cut him, not because of a lack of ability but more for lack of size. I made the team and never had a problem with teammates or opponents the first year.

I played in only seven games that first year because I was subjected to another draft—into the U.S. Army during the Korean War. The Washington Caps folded while I was away for two years, and the Syracuse Nationals selected me in a dispersal draft. It was a good situation for me when I joined the team in 1952. The team was filled with good people with a great owner, Danny Biasone, and a good coach, Al Cervi. I spent six years with Syracuse as a mobile power forward.

My specialty was defense, which meant I always got saddled guarding guys like George Mikan and Bill Russell. Playing against Mikan was like trying to guard a truck. He was 6′10″, about 245 pounds, with sharp elbows and exceptional strength. I don't think George ever got the credit he deserved. He could shoot with either hand and had tremendous moves for a big man. No one could guard Bill Russell.

Bill and I used to laugh in those early days because we always ended up guarding each other. The other few Blacks in the league usually ended up guarding other Blacks. The owners felt the fans would accept Blacks as long as they didn't get tough with the white players.

The game was slower in those days because there was no 24-second clock with people tripping and elbowing. No fines for fighting meant there were all kinds of tripping and gauging which sometimes resulted in bench-clearing brawls. The league was more compact, extending no further west than Minneapolis or south than St. Louis.

When we played exhibition games in some Southern cities, I couldn't stay with the team. So I'd check into a Black hotel or stay with a Black family. It wasn't always easy to find restaurants that would serve me. So sometimes, I'd walk into a restaurant with my teammates and be turned away. Any time that happened, my teammates walked out with me—every time.

In 1954, Jim Tucker joined the team, so I was no longer the only Black player on the Syracuse Nationals. Jim came from a small, segregated town, Paris, Kentucky, so I tried to help him adjust to the NBA. I reminded him that he had to be especially careful, both on and off the court.

I guess my advice paid off because we became the first Black players on a Championship team when we beat Fort Wayne 92–91 in the seventh game of the 1955 NBA Finals. Jim and I enjoyed that victory because we had to listen to much name-calling from those Fort Wayne fans, such as "pork chop," "Satchel Paige," and a lot of other derogatory names.

That was also the first year of the 24-second clock, a move that probably saved the NBA. Not many fans were interested in paying to see games where the ball was frozen for much of the game, resulting in scores like 25–23.

I frequently get asked who should get the credit for opening the NBA to Black players. Certainly, Bones McKinney and Bob Foster deserve much credit. But my two heroes are Walter Brown, owner of the Boston Celtics, and Red Auerbach, his coach. If they hadn't had the courage to draft Chuck Cooper, I don't think the Caps would have had the guts to be the first team in the league to draft a Black player. I always told Chuck that although I was the first to play, he was the first drafted and opened the door for all of us.

Art Connoisseur, Philanthropist, and All-around Good Guy

William Vareika's Fine Arts gallery in Newport, RI, has grown into one of the largest and most respected galleries in the country, specializing in important 18th, 19th, and early 20th century works of art. What makes the story more remarkable is that Bill Vareika intended to become a lawyer, not a gallery owner. Raised in Brockton, MA, Bill majored in political science at Boston College. In the Fall of 1971, he took a class in 19th-century art mainly to fulfill a school requirement. One day, he slipped into Boston's Trinity Church to research a topic for his art class. Vareika saw the elaborate murals around the sanctuary, works by Nineteenth-Century American artist John La Farge. His class project turned into a lifelong endeavor.

As part of an independent study on La Farge, Bill visited Newport, Rhode Island, during his senior year. La Farge lived from 1835 until 1910—much of the time in Newport—and is America's most famous stained-glass maker. As a result of his visit, Bill was drawn into a struggle to save Newport's Congregational Church, with its La Farge stained-glass windows, from being bulldozed. Bill decided to devote his summer before law school to a "Save-the-Church Campaign," which turned into six years of unpaid community organizing and negotiating among church members and developers. Meanwhile, Bill worked as a part-time janitor at a local art museum and as an art "picker," trolling yard sales and thrift shops for items and reselling them to galleries. The church battle was eventually won, but Bill never entered law school. Instead, he became an art dealer, and in 1987, Bill and his wife, Alison, established William Vareika Fine Arts Ltd. on historic Bellevue Avenue, next to the landmark Casino building and the Tennis Hall of Fame.

From the beginning, the Vareikas defined the mission of their business as twofold: it would serve to provide a public viewing space for influential historic American art, and it would be the vehicle through which they could support charitable causes. For almost 30 years, the Vareikas used their gallery to raise awareness about a variety of causes. They have also donated over one million dollars, as well as numerous artworks, to various institutions, such as the Newport

Art Museum, Newport Hospital, Hasbro Children's Hospital, Martin Luther King Community Center, and the Newport Historical Society. Bill also established the William Vareika Award for Arts and Public Policy conferred annually on a Salve Regina University graduate with a demonstrated appreciation for art, as well as social conscience.

Bill has served on numerous boards and has received many awards for his efforts. Four years ago, he was honored by the Rhode Island Council on the Humanities with the "Honorary Chairs Award for Lifetime Achievement in the Humanities," a tribute to his dedication to the preservation and appreciation of historic art and architecture in Rhode Island. The Vareikas also led an effort to raise funds to acquire, restore, and install thirteen La Farge stained-glass windows in the Our Lady of Mercy Chapel on the Salve Regina University campus. He received an honorary Doctorate of Humane Letters from Salve Regina University for his contributions as a preservationist and philanthropist.

In 2017, I had the pleasure of nominating Bill for membership in the Rhode Island Heritage Hall of Fame. His photo and biographic information now hang next to his mentor, John LaFarge, also a member of the Rhode Island Heritage Hall of Fame.

Bill Vareika exemplifies the art of giving. Some individuals stand out because of their unique talents and abilities. In this respect, one thinks of athletes or entertainers. It is rarer when a person stands above the crowd because of such qualities as integrity, earnestness, demeanor, and charity. Bill Vareika is such a man.

Faith, Determination, and a Bit of Irish Luck

"You can't write a book about the 39th Fighter Squadron during WWII without interviewing Chuck Sullivan," Lew Lockhart advised me after I reached out to him in 2012. Lew, John Dunbar, and Fred Tobi were the first three pilots from the 39th I interviewed for my book, *Relentless Pursuit: The Untold Story of the 39th Fighter Squadron.* Lt. Charles P. Sullivan was one of the early aces of the 39th, and I looked forward to interviewing him.

The interview began with the standard information. In February 1941, after graduating from Northwestern University with a degree in business administration, Chuck Sullivan enlisted in the Army Air Corps Flying Cadet program. He learned to fly at the Spartan School in Tulsa, Oklahoma, Randolph Field in San Antonio, Texas, and Brooks Field in Brooks, Texas. Upon receiving his commission and pinning on his silver wings at Brooks Field on September 21, 1941, 2d Lieutenant Sullivan was transferred to Mitchell Field, New York. In January 1942, he was shipped to Australia and assigned to fly P-39s in combat with the 35th Fighter Group's 39th Fighter Squadron.

While flying a P-40 fighter (a P-39 export variant) near Port Moresby on June 17, 1942, Sullivan scored his first aerial victory, a Japanese bomber. But it wasn't until after the 39th Fighter Squadron transitioned to P-38s that Sullivan began his steady climb to ace status: He downed a Ki-43 near Gasmata, New Britain, on January 6, 1943; a Zero over Lae on March 3, 1943; a Zero probable over Huron Gulf on March 4, 1943; a Betty near Port Moresby on April 12; and, finally, a Ki-43 near Lae on July 26, 1943.

On September 20, 1943, he was flying one of sixteen 39th Fighter Squadron P-38s, escorting V Bomber Command B-24s on a raid against the Japanese base at Wewak. He led a four-plane flight when his plane developed engine trouble, and he tried to return to Port Moresby. Here is his dramatic story, told in his own words.

After I left the formation, I had not gone far before the engine began running fine, so I turned back to rejoin my squadron. Then I looked into my rearview mirror and saw an unmistakable image: a Japanese fighter in firing position. He was so close I didn't bother to look over my shoulder, and I didn't have time to be afraid!

Instinctively, I shoved the P-38 into a violent dive, dropping my auxiliary line tanks as I went. It was then that I felt the shudder of bullets striking my plane. He had hit my left engine, which began spraying oil that started a smoky fire. I raced for the clouds below at speeds of nearly 500 miles per hour. The plane shuddered and shook from the strain. I looked back. I was pulling away from the Japanese fighter, but he was still stalking me. Oil began to spray on my windshield, obscuring my vision. I thought about parachuting right then, but instead, I cut off the flaming engine and feathered the propeller, which stopped the fan and turned the blades so they would cut through the air with minimum drag. The fire in the left engine went out, and my windshield cleared—but the stalker was still with me.

At about 3,000 feet, I entered fleecy clouds, but they had gaps between them. I sailed through the first cloud, emerging into the clear, and saw that the stalker was still there. I went into a second cloud, then out into the clear air again. The stalker was still trailing me. To make matters worse, I was beginning to lose my precious dive speed now that I was on one engine. The third cloud loomed up. I needed to vary the program, or eventually, he would nail me. So, while in the third cloud, I put my plane in a spiral and came out underneath the cloud, then flew beneath it for some time.

While I was in the third cloud, I thought about how clever it would be of me if I could circle behind the stalker and shoot him down. But wisdom said, 'What if you miscalculate and come out right in front of him?' Wisdom won! I quickly dismissed that idea. When I came into the clear again, my pursuer was nowhere in sight. I had eluded him! Or perhaps he was low on gas and had turned for home.

I had radioed my squadron that I was hit and on fire, but the fire was now out, and I was on a course for Port Moresby at 3,000 feet. But there were complications. With my left engine cut off, I had lost my plane's only generator, causing my batteries to give out. As a result, I lost radio contact with Port Moresby. I berated Lockheed and the Army Air Force for not spending a little more money to put a generator on the right engine, too.

As soon as I was sure I had lost the stalker, I began to think about the long flight home—at least two more hours in the air—and the necessity of climbing to at least 7,000 feet to get through a pass in the mountains. But this was not to be. The right engine began heating up, and white smoke was soon trailing from it- most likely because of a Prestone leak in the coolant radiator. I decided to try the left engine again. Somehow I got it cranked up and running, so I feathered the right engine and shut it down. I flew for about five minutes before the left engine began to smoke again. So, with black smoke streaming from the left engine and white smoke streaming from the right, I decided to either make a forced landing or bailout.

I had been flying over tall trees for some time and did not wish to parachute, as I had friends who had parachuted and landed in tall trees, with the result that they sustained everything from broken legs to broken backs. I elected to set the plane down. I was at the end of the road! Both engines were dead, the props were feathered, and I was sinking rapidly. As l lined up on an open area, I jettisoned the canopy, pulled down my goggles, and rode it in at about 130 miles per hour. The P-38 acted like a giant lawnmower, cutting off small trees, kunai grass, and brush.

I came to a screeching, sizzling halt. The engines sounded as if they would explode. I had hit my head on something in the cockpit; it split my cloth flying helmet and gave me a deep head wound. With blood pouring from my head, I thought I was mortally wounded, but the shock spared me some severe pain. It was only a scalp wound, which I quickly bound up. My right elbow was also hurt, but not seriously. I grabbed my parachute, survival pack, and the one-man raft in the seat. I was still wearing my Mae West inflatable life vest. I took off with hardly a backward glance, for I feared the Japanese might have seen me come down and because the engines were so hot they might explode or start a fire.

I went down at high noon about 5 degrees, 30 minutes south of the Equator. The air was stifling and the silence oppressive in the kunai grass, which stood ten to twelve feet tall. A few moments earlier, I had been sailing along at about 180 to 200 miles per hour. Now I was on the ground, feeling lonely and sensing that I had been thrust back five hundred years in time. Home was nearly four hundred miles away. To the west were mountains, which I hoped to cross to an outpost airstrip named Bena Bena.

It took me three or four hours to slice my way through the tall, swaying grass to the shelter of some trees, a distance of probably no more than seven hundred yards. I tried cutting the kunai with my machete, but it was futile, so I high-stepped and fell forward time and time again. I finally reached the trees and shade, but I was exhausted. I found a bit of a clearing, where I cut up my parachute to make a tent and hammock of silk. Such luxury!

The first night in the jungle was terrifying because of the strange noises and shrieks of birds and small animals. It later rained almost every night starting about 1600 hours, but I was spared that first night, the only night of my travels that it did not rain. I stayed the second day among the trees, peering out frequently toward my plane, which I could not see.

At the time, the Fifth Air Force's air-sea rescue efforts were meager, to say the least, especially in the interior of New Guinea. Rescue efforts on my behalf probably consisted in their entirety of instructions to all pilots: "Look for Sully somewhere down in the jungle." Indeed, they did look for me the next day—from about 25,000 feet, then went home and reported, "No sign of Sully." The following day the instructions were, "Don't forget about Sully; he's out there someplace." Flying once again at 25,000 feet, they did not see me. On the third day, the talk went to, "Too bad about ole Sully." And that's the way it happened!

I watched for rescue planes all day from below my canopy of trees. Then I ventured out to see what was around me. Water, which I had needed the previous afternoon badly, was hardly seventy-five yards from where I slept. It was so welcome! I filled my faithful little emergency drinking can (about one-pilot capacity) and ate some of my chocolate bar. I was still a bit jumpy and watched closely for Japanese troops or natives.

I wasn't really frightened, but the jungle was new to me, so I felt I could not take chances. I was very lonely but full of hope, and I wanted to get somewhere before my head injury gave me trouble. I put sulfa powder on the wound, which I bandaged with my field dressing.

I slept relatively well the second night, but I frequently awoke to check noises. The moon was on the wane but still quite large. On the third day, I decided I was gaining nothing staying where I was. I thought of my trip ahead and optimistically concluded I could be home in four or five days. Little did I comprehend the power of the jungle and the difficulties that lay ahead.

I hid the remnants of my parachute at the edge of the kunai grass and covered or otherwise obliterated most of my camp markings. Wisely or unwisely, I did not spread my chute above the top of the kunai—I reasoned that the Japanese had as much chance of seeing it as my friends did. I felt that I was indeed on my own because I didn't think the friendlies could pluck me out of the woods.

I gathered my possessions—the tent, the hammock, the one-man raft—took a heading of 135 degrees for Port Moresby, and bravely set off. When I crossed my drinking stream, I took off all my clothes and shoes to wade across the twelve-foot wide, four-foot-deep run. On the other side, I dressed back up in my long-sleeved khaki shirt, long khaki trousers, woolen socks, ankle-top GI shoes, and cloth flying helmet. Then I took up my course of 135 degrees again. The going was much easier here than in the thick kunai grass; it was all trees, thickets, and grass.

At about 0900 hours, I heard a radial-engine plane. I thought it was a Japanese fighter, which was mostly radial-engine aircraft, but it turned out to be an American single-engine A-24 dive bomber, with a crew of a pilot and observer or gunner. I tried in vain to start a fire in the damp underbrush. I searched for my matches in my waterproof container and came up with a good, old farmer-type match. But the kunai grass was too wet. Frantically, I searched for tracer ammunition for my trusty Colt .45-caliber automatic pistol. The A-24 was then only a quarter of a mile from me, flying at about 100 feet. It was so close I could see the pilot and the observer, who had his canopy rolled forward to see better. Moments later, the A-24 was gone, out of sight. It was disappointing, but not overwhelmingly so. After all, this was only my third day down. So I struggled on.

The path was hard, but I found some trees that had been chopped down sometime before. This greatly encouraged me. The path led to an abandoned grass hut- an exciting discovery! My thoughts raced from one idea to another. Was this just a way station for a native hunting party? When had people last been here? I found some discarded fish bones, but it did not appear that anyone had been in the hut for some time. I continued, crossed another small stream, and then came to another shelter on the bank of another stream. I crossed this stream and continued along the path, which was marked by crocodile footprints.

Losing the trail where wild pigs had rooted up the path, I returned to the last stream, set up my hammock, cleared an area, and retired for the night. I always retired at sundown because the dangers of wandering about in the dark jungle were apparent to me. It began to rain about midnight, and the downpour continued all night. I was drenched and frequently rose to exercise by simulating skipping rope and shadowboxing until I was warm, then I went back to sleep. What an uncomfortable night it was.

I suspected a river nearby, so I elected to leave my hammock, Mae West, one-man raft, and a box of .45-caliber ammunition at my camp while I searched for the river. I found the river, but when I tried to retrace my steps to my camp, I became lost, confused, and bewildered. I intended to come back and retrieve the heavy stuff. I blazed a trail as I went along, breaking off small branches and cutting into the bark of trees to leave marks. I could not recognize my trail-blazing effort.

The jungle closed in on me oppressively. I panicked. I wanted to run blindly away, anywhere—just run and run. It was a terrible feeling that I had never experienced before or since. Somehow, faith and reason prevailed. I knelt and prayed earnestly: "Mary, conceived without sin, pray for us who have recourse to thee. Never was it known that anyone who sought your help or intercession was left unaided."

Mary was listening and interceded with God. I stood up, now calm and confident. I resolved to take a compass course, which I believed would take me back to the river. I did not deviate from the course. In about twenty minutes, I was back at the riverbank, but it was not the same spot where I had first come upon the river. The jungle had won. I was not about to try to find my heavy equipment

Now my problem was getting across the river without my Mae West life vest or the raft. Undaunted, I looked for trees with which to build a raft. I began to flail at small trees with my twelve-inch machete, but the trees were tough, and the job was arduous. I gave up that idea and began collecting limbs and logs from along the river bank. I tied seven or eight logs together with a parachute cord and confidently set sail. It was not to be.

The logs were soaked through, and the raft would not fully support me, so I just lay on it, half in and half out of the water. I drifted with the current, kicking my feet for a little extra stability. All seemed to be going well; at least I was still afloat. Then I came to a bend in the river where the current quickened, and I was swept against a muddy bank about four feet above the water level. The swift current swung my raft around, and it hit me in the back. I lost the raft, and, like the proverbial drowning man, I frantically grasped for anything around. I kept my pistol in my right hand and above the water all the time I was flailing. Then, Providence came to my aid! I saw a vine hanging down from the side of the bank, grabbed it, and steadied myself. The makeshift raft floated merrily on, disappearing downriver.

I surveyed my precarious position. In the current, I was in deep water, but the swift part of the current was narrow. I realized that I would cross the swift current and soon be in shallow water if I shoved off from the bank. After reaching the shallow, pebbly shore, I decided to wash my clothes. I had had enough for one day, so I prepared for the night. Beneath a huge tree only a few feet from the river, I fashioned a little shelter, using sticks to support huge banana leaves that served as my roof. Then I booby-trapped my little area, using a parachute cord as a cordon, hoping that any intruder would trip over my alarm system and awaken me.

Branching into my river was a beautiful mountain stream, which I planned to explore the next day. Bridging the juncture of the river and the stream was a fallen tree, which I believed was used by the natives to cross the river. It rained most of the night, but my tree and banana leaf roof shelter served me quite well. I was tired and slept soundly!

I awoke, ate the last square of my chocolate bar, looked to the east, and got ready to start up the mountain stream. A sandbank on the left of the stream extended for a short distance and appeared to lend itself to easy walking. As I approached the sandbank, I was startled to see a solitary human footprint in the sand–just one footprint. I looked on either side of the print for another footprint. There was none. It was baffling. I thought of when Robinson Crusoe discovered his man Friday's footprint in the sand.

The footprint was pointing up the mountain stream. In the distance, I detected a clearing on the side of the mountain. We had been told that the natives girdled a tree near the base, so the tree would eventually die and fall over. It was in such clearings that the natives planted their gardens. The mountain stream seemed to lead in the direction of the clearing—hopefully a garden tended by friendly natives.

We had had good luck with the coastal natives in the Port Moresby area. Indeed, natives had helped several of my comrades in the 39th Fighter Squadron back to our camp after being shot down. So up the middle of the sparkling stream, I proceeded. The stream varied from knee—to waist-deep. The bottom was rocky and uneven, but I never fell.

After proceeding up the stream for about an hour, I began to shout periodically in the hope of attracting the attention of the "friendlies." About 0900, a movement on the right bank caught my attention. I stopped dead in my tracks. Gradually, the figure of a man appeared from behind the tree cover. He had a weapon, a spear or bow and arrow, which he lowered. I felt he had drawn a bead on me from behind his cover.

I raised my hand and waved, smiled, and tried to appear very friendly. Under such circumstances, I could be very friendly, but at the same time, my right hand moved ever so close to my trusty .45, which was holstered on my right hip. I advanced very cautiously, gun hand at the ready, smiling, and constantly trying to appear relaxed and friendly. I reached the bank, which was about three or four feet above the water. The native extended his hand and helped me up the bank. We went back into the trees a few feet, where on the ground lay a freshly killed wild pig. Nearby was a young native woman. My host indicated that l should sit down, which I did, and he proceeded to dress his pig.

He laid the pig on its back and chopped it open through the chest cavity with a stone ax. I noticed the woman had a bunch of ripe bananas in a fiber bag. I indicated by munching actions that I was hungry, and I pointed to her bananas. My host told her to give me some bananas, and she gave me two or three, which were delicious. She was timid and giggled a little, but my host was stern and businesslike as he continued with his task. I was fascinated when he sopped up blood from the pig's chest cavity with spongy leaves and then squeezed the blood into a three or four-inch diameter bamboo tube. I was to see more of the bamboo tube later.

Soon the dressing of the pig was complete, and it was obvious we were ready to depart the area. I then saw New Guinea chivalry at its best. My host (I was to learn later that his name was Tootaroo) loaded the pig on the shoulders of his mate, gathered his spear, bow and arrows, and headed for the stream. Very shortly, we were at the bank of the stream. Tootaroo took the pig from the woman's back, and she got down into the water. Then Tootaroo loaded the pig on her back again. Next, he got down into the water, and I followed. We walked downstream for about fifteen minutes before coming to a path on the left side, where the bank was almost level with the water. Tootaroo and his mate started up the path, and I began to follow at a tactful and respectful distance.

Suddenly, Tootaroo turned to me and pointed emphatically back down the stream, whence I came. I protested and indicated by my motions that I wished to continue with them. He shook his head angrily and again pointed downstream. By sign language, it came out: "Go back downstream." I said, "No, I go with you ' " and he replied, "No, you don't." To which I responded, "Yes, I do!" After a couple of these exchanges, he simply turned away and started up the path. I hesitated, then followed. I expected him to turn on me again, but he did not, though it was apparent he did not want me to come along.

Quietly, we plodded on for perhaps thirty minutes before Tootaroo stopped and began to shout as if to warn someone that he was bringing a stranger home for dinner. My heart sank. What should I do? I considered my options: either leave them and go back to the known loneliness of the jungle or continue with them to an unknown but at least human company. I reasoned that if I left them, they would still know I was out there, someplace. The thought of more food and what I hoped were friendly natives won the debate. Apprehensively, I followed.

Shortly, we arrived at a small, level clearing. There were old campfire remains and a strange-looking stick placed in the fork of a short vertical stick that had stuck upright into the ground. Tootaroo started a fire and cooked some pig meat in a cylindrical earthen vessel. He later placed some whole bananas in the ashes and baked them. In about a half-hour, my feast was ready. Bananas have never tasted so good. Meantime, I was aware that little dark faces were beginning to appear from behind the bushes and foliage. Soon the faces materialized into bodies of men, women, and children. They approached me cautiously.

Still, on my best behavior, I smiled and did nothing to excite them. They were curious about all my possessions and poked at my pockets. One youth was inquisitive and wanted to see everything in my pockets, which were loaded with compasses, parachute cord, ammunition, and a small can. The can was similar to a sardine can and had contained my field bandage. The bandage was now wrapped about my head and tied under my chin. I had my cloth flying helmet, split in the crash-landing, perched on my head with my flying goggles still attached.

I sensed that the curious boy was a little retarded, but he looked happy, and his companions appeared most tolerant of him. I must have been a bedraggled-looking curiosity. More and more natives began to appear and disappear, seeming to bring back a whole new audience each time. Twice men who were chiefs arrived to look me over from a comfortable distance.

The chiefs wore beaded bands around their foreheads, and all the men appeared to have little sticks in their noses and ears. The men's hair was different from the bushy hair style of the Port Moresby-area natives; it was twisted into many small, tight braids. Each time a chief or newcomer arrived or left, I was frightened. For all I knew, they would bring Japanese soldiers.

The afternoon passed this way. I was the new sideshow in town. During the early part of the afternoon, I tried to determine the meaning of the strange sticks, the older fire, and a small shelter that was open on all sides. It was obvious someone had camped here before. I pointed to the shelter, fire, and sticks and, by sign language, questioned the natives.

One man held up three fingers and pointed to me as if to say that three men like me had been there. I made signs: did they go that way (toward suspected Japanese-held areas), or did they go that way (toward Australian- or American-held territory)? The native pointed down at the ground! Now there was a discomfiting thought: the three like me had not left the area; they had died or had been killed!

As twilight approached, the audience had dwindled to five or six people, never more than ten at a time. By implicit invitation, I accompanied Tootaroo, his mate, and several others into a nearby area containing two thatch-covered huts. I concluded that they did not consider me a threat, so they took me in for the night. It was an exciting family affair. I believe these were two families of three men in all, including one chief, Tootaroo, and a new acquaintance named Sego, plus two women—Tootaroo's mate, Sego's mate, and three or four children. The other natives I had seen during the day.

The women prepared dinner: more pig, yams baked in the ashes, and lima-type beans cooked in blood. They also got out the bamboo tube that contained the blood from the dead pig's chest cavity. After putting some herbs or leaves in, they held the tube over the open fire. Presently, when the mixture was bubbling nicely, they proceeded to take the contents into their hands and ate it with great gusto. As we sat around the campfire circle, I was served food on a giant banana leaf. Occasionally, a dog tried to run through the circle to get a morsel of food.

Eventually, we arrived at names for the major players. I explained I was Charlie, which they thought was pretty funny. Tootaroo was the native I had found with the pig, Sego was another young man with a mate and a boy of five or six, and the chief was either Lulawai or "Headman."

It was a pleasant, light-hearted, jovial evening. After dinner, we were joined by other natives from the area. I tried to explain my presence among them. I simulated a plane (a "balus" in their language) flying high in the sky with engine sputtering, then crashing to the ground. I made signs to show me crashing forward in the cockpit and injuring my head. Strangely enough, my story got through, except to my dismay, they all laughed when I pointed to my head. Then one native took over and retold my story in his native tongue, accompanied by appropriate gestures. Again, they all laughed at the crash landing and my injured head. Perhaps they laughed in relief that the mighty flying "balus" was indeed vulnerable.

They had a pet, which was cute but a pest. It circled the group around the fire, came up behind me, and began pecking my back. I tolerantly pushed it away a couple of times, but it was persistent. So I backhanded it with my right band, knocking it back a bit. My hosts loved that; they laughed merrily. Everything seemed so congenial and friendly.

When it became dark, the women and children went inside a rectangular thatched hut while the men remained near the fire with me. At length, they gave me a small hollow log to sleep in or on. It was about four feet long and wide enough for even a very heavy-set person. I lay near the fire in my log, with my right hand placed comfortingly near my holstered .45. I was alert for any strange behavior or action, but it became apparent to me that I had nothing to fear. Occasionally during the night, one or another of the men stirred and replenished the fire. It was evident that they had to keep the fire burning. I suspect they started fires by friction or sparks from stones. I awoke each time the fire preserver got up to tend the fire.

The night passed without incident. At dawn, the small village began to stir. It appeared that Sego's mate, their son, and Headman were planning to travel. Perhaps I wanted to go with them? I made signs about departing, hoping to convey that I wished for a plan or route to go home. They seemed to get the idea and mentioned several places or names of people. I copied these on the back of my map. There were such names as Masaro, Lowy Kowy, and Bena Bena.

I tried to write the words phonetically, then repeated them back to Sego. I had heard of Bena Bena, which I knew was somewhere across the mountain range from my suspected location. It occurred to me that a relay system to get me home could be arranged. The names I had been given were locations or contacts along the way. This sounded encouraging, for earlier that morning, I had had a sinking feeling that I would not be able to escape the area and perhaps have to spend my life in the jungle wilds. That was a sobering thought, but the more we exchanged signs, the more hopeful I became.

Not wishing to waste time, I signed, "We go." Strangely enough, they were ready also, so we turned to leave the village. I suspected then that Sego, his family, and Headman were returning to their village, located some distance away. Before we left, I gave Tootaroo the small field-dressing can as a farewell gift. He received it stoically. Not too impressed, I thought. Shortly after we left Tootaroo's home, we began a rather arduous climb. I thought I was in fair shape but began to tire. At one point, about an hour after starting, Headman approached me and signed that he wanted my big machete knife. I thought he was leaving us for good and desired a souvenir, so I shook my head, "No!" He disappeared into the trees, but he returned in about twenty minutes with freshly cut stalks of sugar cane, which we sucked on for a time. It was delicious and refreshing. I felt a bit of remorse at not giving him the knife to cut the cane for all of us.

We started on again, and in about another hour, we all stopped when Sego pointed out a small pitfall in the path that had been covered with light branches and leaves. It appeared to be a security measure for a nearby village. Thoughtfully, they detoured me around it, and shortly we stopped again as they shouted a warning to unseen natives that they were bringing in a stranger. In a few minutes, we arrived at the top of a lightly forested ridge. It was about noon and a most pleasant day, sunny and nice. A few locals came out to look me over, and the overall atmosphere was relaxed. When we arrived in the village, Sego cooked some food, which was unremarkable compared to the feast I had the night before.

It seemed to be a lazy day. I decided to rest, perhaps share another meal with them, and depart early in the morning for that faraway place called Port Moresby. The villagers left me alone, except for Sego's little son, an alert and happy child. I tried to amuse him as best I could as I took off my shirt to better enjoy the pleasant sunshine. I also cleaned my .45. At Tootaroo's village, I had made signs for something with which to wipe my gun, and my idea got through. I had been rewarded with fibers impregnated with lard or some other grease, which I now used. I was constantly amazed and pleased at how effective sign language could be when you worked at it.

I was enjoying myself, but my idyllic afternoon came to an abrupt end. Sego came and led me to meet two new natives, and it was as if a calm wind and dark clouds permeated the scene. Suddenly, I had a sense of impending danger. However, I tried to seem confident and cheerful as my sign language indicated how I hoped to be relayed over the hills to friendly territory. The apparent leader of these two visitors was named Aidee, but Aidee's partner did not give his name, so I named him "Grinning One" or "Grinny." Facetiously, I thought he had cut cards early in the afternoon for my knife and won. I did not like his attitude and distrusted both of them.

Standing toe to toe in the clearing, Sego and Aidee had a violent argument. Finally, Aidee grabbed two spears and thrust them violently into the ground as he appeared to read Sego the riot act. And Sego acquiesced to whatever Aidee wanted of him. I was standing nearby throughout the argument, and I felt compelled to say something to ease the tension. In what I hoped was a light-hearted manner, I said, "What is the matter, Sego? Did you take his spears?" Of course, I knew that the natives did not understand my words or care about my opinion. I was later to conclude that my ultimate fate was the subject of the argument, that Sego had tried to defend me and lost. Sego appeared crestfallen as we all turned away from the scene of the fight.

As twilight approached, the waning moon came out, and the villagers began to prepare dinner. Gone was the hospitality and friendliness of the previous village. I wandered about, but no one asked me to eat with them, not even Sego. I walked up to one family campfire and made signs of eating. I was no longer hungry, but I wanted to see whether they would give me food. They handed me something but did not ask me to sit down on the ground with them. I wandered away, not knowing what to do.

Aidee and Grinny suddenly appeared beside me and started a small fire. Nearby was a thatched-roof hut with a tiny doorway. As I sat down near the fire, facing the rising moon, Aidee and Grinny took up positions on the other side of the fire and stared at me without showing any emotion. I felt I was being stalked! To show my nonchalance, I sang every popular and college song I could think of. I was determined not to show fear or undue concern. Earlier in the day, Aidee had conveyed the idea that he had been to the coast, and he did seem to be a more worldly person than the others. As we sat around this fire, he pointed to the moon and indicated that I perhaps had arrived at the wrong time of the month and that maybe he regretted it had worked out this way. These were only impressions, but the feeling that there was an impending threat was there.

After I had exhausted my song repertoire, I suppose Aidee thought it was time to move on with his plan. He and Grinny rose and slowly approached me. They sat down on either side of me, so close that they brushed my sides. This was too close and threatening for me, so I immediately stood up. I believe they were about to attempt to overcome me. As I cast about for an idea to ease the tension or provide them with reason to leave, I again noted the nearby hut and crawled through the doorway, taking with me a little grass mat the natives had given me. I crouched just inside the entrance, hoping they would go away, but this was not to be.

Aidee and Grinny approached the doorway, and Aidee reached inside to tug at my shoulder, a clear suggestion that I come out. Thinking that perhaps Aidee was simply envious of my attentions to Sego and his little boy, I stepped outside. Immediately, several natives, including Aidee and Grinny closed in around me. They were carrying spears, bows, and arrows. Without anyone jabbing me with a spear, I was prodded, not too subtly, along a path that led up a slight incline. Soon we reached a circular hut—the execution chamber? Above the doorway, I could make out in the dim light a stick device that reminded me of the stick symbol I had seen the day before, at the edge of Tootaroo's village. This symbol was a forked stick embedded in the ground with another stick placed across the fork. Whatever it was, I took it as a disturbing sign.

My escorts gestured that I go into the hut. I didn't see any alternative, so I bent down and entered. Four natives followed me in. One carried a firebrand and an empty but ominous-looking bamboo blood tube. My heart sank a little lower, and all signs were most foreboding. I felt maneuvered, but no course of action came to mind. Hoping against hope that things would get better, I continued to play their game. The native with the firebrand started a small fire in the middle of the hut, and another native handed me the grass mat again, suggesting by signs that I lie down and sleep, to which I replied aloud, "I always sleep sitting up." Simply responding audibly made me more confident, although I knew they understood little beyond what I could convey using my limited sign language.

I was about six feet from the door, wary, and sitting on my mat with my back against the wall. I realized I was in a very vulnerable position. If a melee ensued, they might block the door to prevent my escape, even if I shot some of them. When I pressed my hands against the bamboo wall at my back, I realized I could not easily break through it. The room began to fill with smoke, as there was no ceiling opening. Seizing on this situation, I began to cough and wave my arms to indicate the smoke was too much for me. A native stood up and began tearing a hole in the roof to let out excess smoke. Now or never, I thought, as this had created the diversion I needed.

From a crouching position, I bolted for the opening and came out of the hut just in front of the doorway. As I came out, I pulled my .45 automatic from its holster and chambered a round. The hammer was back, and the .45 was ready to fire. Then I slipped the safety switch on and dropped the .45 back in its holster. As I stood and waited for their next move, more natives appeared, so I elected not to make a run for it. Those in the hut followed me out, bringing the bamboo tube and the firebrand with them. Once again, by common consent, we moved down the path away from my "execution chamber" to a rectangular hut with a porch extension open on three sides. There we stopped. I was escorted inside and again given my grass mat along with a firm indication to lie down. I took the mat and sat down, facing the interior of the enclosure with my back vulnerable to the outside darkness.

The men stacked their bows, arrows, and spears against a post and started up the fire. Once again, we eyed each other as we all sat on the ground. Some of the men decided to smoke or chew betel nut. They made some square motions with their arms as if to say, "See, I have nothing to harm you with." They wanted me to see that they weren't making any overt moves. I let them smoke and chew. Most of the men who chewed took betel nut with some lime from a small gourd. They put a little lime on some betel leaves, chewed up a bit of betel nut, and then spit it out in one hand. After looking at the mess, they would put the betel nut combination back in their mouths. The Headman had a little fiber bag that contained a broken mirror. I suppose that made him the kingpin. He chewed with great dignity. After chewing for a while, he would reach into his bag and pull out the mirror. Then he would stick the mess out on his tongue and look at it to see if it was the right consistency or color. Because he had a mirror, he did not have to spit the betel mess into his hand.

Sego and his little boy were inside, too. The boy's job was to keep the fire going. It might have been sort of an initiation ritual for him. The boy was only about six years old and was there against his wishes. He kept crying. Suddenly, Aidee took a brand from the fire and stuck it right on the child's face. The little boy stopped crying and kept up the fire real well after that. That didn't make me like Aidee any better.

The contingent inside the hut included Sego, his son, Grinny, Aidee, the Headman, and a lookout who sat in the back of the hut. I could hear other natives rustling around outside the hut. I was afraid that someone on the outside might strike me with a spear if we sat there long enough. If I could manage to move to the doorway of the hut, they would all be in front of me. I got up slowly, walked toward the entrance, and sort of stooped over sideways by the doorway. I then took a firebrand and sort of flashed it in the back to make sure that there was no one in the back of the hut. My move placed all of them in front of me, so I was at least temporarily in command. Just to be sure, I took out my .45 and put it across my right thigh.

We sat there from about 2000 hours to about 2200. I threatened them with the strength of the Fifth Air Force: "The balus will come and boom-boom the hell out of your villages." But that didn't seem to bother them, though they did shrink down and repeat, "boom-boom!" a few times. They didn't like the idea, but I guess they didn't think the Air Force would get there.

Next, I thought I'd try a little religion on them, thinking that the missionaries might have contacted them. Since I was convinced, they would kill me, I didn't see any reason not to be frank about it. So I said, "God wouldn't want you to kill me." I think I spoke pretty convincingly. Aidee, who had been out to the coast, muttered a word that sounded something like "Lord." But after I had gotten all through, Aidee said, "No savvy talk." I answered, "You savvy this gun, don't you?" and shook the .45 right in his face. I sat there for over an hour with my gun trained on Aidee. The whole time, I snapped the safety on and off- click, click, click- to be sure he got the message. But this guy remained cool as a cucumber.

After a while, the home team began to get a little anxious. The Headman got up and sort of stretched as if to show that he was tired. Then he walked toward me, indicating that he wanted to go behind me into the hut. It was pretty obvious that if he went back there, I would have two fronts to cover. He got real close to me and motioned again that he wanted to go inside. I swung the .45 around on him and shouted, "Sit down!" Well, he withered right down beside me, clearly frightened.

This standoff had been going on for hours. I was in command—temporarily. If I can just get them in close, in sort of a semi circle, they won't shoot through their own people. I didn't know how I was going to get out of the hut, but I didn't want them to shoot me before I did. The Headman played right into my hands. He crouched right down beside me, which made Grinny unhappy. I thought that Grinny was showing some fear, so I reached out with my left hand and motioned for him to come in a little closer to protect me on the right. But before he did, he looked at Aidee, who was sitting right in the middle, sort of head on to me. Aidee blinked his eyes. I think that meant, 'Yeah, go ahead and humor him.'

Grinny moved a little closer but kept looking over his shoulder. He was sort of a sassy little guy, and I didn't like the way he grinned. So, with the gun in my right hand, I grabbed him by a shoulder with my left hand and sort of yanked him. The poor guy probably thought I was going to shoot him in the back because he was really scared.

At this point, I established a priority list of how I was going to take care of them. They all understood "Number One." I said, "Aidee, I get you number one. Grinny, I get you number two. Headman, I get you number three." I didn't go to number four because I didn't think it would last that long. Then I waved the .45 and described what it would do to them. Aidee sort of believed it. It all sounded rather grim, but I had to keep talking to try to make the point. Aidee was the only one who had not shown a bit of fear, but his team had not shown many initiatives.

Next, I motioned for Aidee to move to a position right in front of me. He was close enough that I could touch him with my left hand. I signaled, "Come in a little closer." He rose slightly and sat without moving forward. "No! Closer!" I said. I then reached out a little farther and motioned him in closer. I guess he thought I was off-balance, for he came right out of his crouching position and lunged at me like a tiger. He threw me against the wall, but I came to my feet naturally.

I had the gun in my right hand, but he grabbed both my wrists and pinned me back briefly. Somehow, I forced the gun down and shot him from a distance of about six inches—right through the chest. The shot sent him clear across the room.

A split second later, the Headman came at me from the left side. If he and Aidee had timed it a little better, they might have had me. The Headman came in from my left and went for both my wrists. He got my left wrist and grappled for my right. I pulled my gun back and shot him in the chest from my left side, WHAM! WHAM! Two shots, one to Aidee and one to the Headman, in the space of two seconds. It was practically all over. My grim prediction was almost accurate. I got number one, Aidee, skipped number two, Grinny, and got number three, the headman. I still remember it like it was yesterday. I can picture the dull glow from the fire, my smoking .45, and me standing there in a crouched position like it was Custer's Last Stand.

I thought they would come after me in waves, but they didn't. Instead, they ran off like a bunch of scalded dogs and left me alone. The Headman staggered outside and died. I then realized that no one was left in the hut but me. I ran out to the left as fast as I could, in the same direction as the staggering Headman, and cut back and made an end-run like football. I ran full tilt to the left, then back to the center, and then I tripped in the tall grass. This probably saved my life because if I had not fallen, I would have been still running. I slithered down into a bit of a depression.

Back at the village, the natives had lighted torches and were screaming and shouting. I could hear them answering from all the neighboring villages. I seemed to be surrounded by their war whoops. When the torches were lit, they started to come up the hill. After they found the two men I had shot, they had a mourning ceremony. They beat on the ground and wailed, sobbed, and shouted for about an hour. It was terrible to just lay there on the ground and listen. The mourning ceremony went on and on. I could see their shadows. Although I am usually optimistic, I couldn't see how I would possibly get out of there alive. As I lay there motionless with the .45 in my right hand and a fresh clip with six bullets in my left hand, I pondered the chances of my leaving alive. I knew the natives would not be kind to me after killing two prominent members of their tribe.

I prayed some more: "Dear Virgin Mary never was it known that anyone who sought thy help or intercession was left unaided. Inspired with that hope and confidence, I ask your intercession with God the Father, God the Son, and God the Holy Spirit." I prayed the Hail Mary, which ends with "Holy Mary, Mother of God, pray for us sinners now and at the hour of our death." The chilling thought hit me: "Now and at the hour of our death" had become the same for me!

What could I do? Should I save the last bullet for myself—a permanent solution to a temporary problem? I agonized over this decision. My faith and upbringing had taught me that suicide was wrong and the cowardly way out. But I dreaded torture. Then I remembered somewhere in Scripture it was said that God would not permit a person to be tempted beyond his will or capability to resist and that even Christ was tempted. So I decided not to save the last bullet for myself but to continue to fight to the end or escape alive. It was comforting when I realized I had weathered that trial of temptation.

After about an hour, the mourning ceremony stopped, and the natives went down into the lower end of the camp. Everything got real quiet. No fires, no voices, nothing. It was as still as death. A little hope trickled through my veins, but at about 0200, the natives came alive again. Up the hill, they strode, with torches held high. This time, the light seemed to penetrate my little hideout, and I thought surely they would see me. But they didn't. They went through the mourning ceremony again, beating sticks on the ground and all of that.

From the shadows, I spotted the figure of a woman coming toward me. It seemed as if she had guessed where I was. She walked straight toward me, closer and closer. I couldn't bring myself to shoot her, so I thought I would shoot at the ground, get up, and run. She got closer, now about two or three feet from me. I could have reached out, stretched a little, and touched her toes. She stood right over me, sobbing and wailing her heart out. After what seemed an eternity, she turned and walked back to the camp.

By 0400, everything became very quiet again. It was dark, no fires, no moon. Dawn was coming, and I knew I had to get out before first light. With a great deal of fear and trepidation, I stood up, fully expecting to become a human pincushion. But nothing happened, so I took a couple of steps while thinking perhaps they wanted a moving target. Still, nothing happened. Then I began to feel that I might get out of there after all. I tip-toed across an open area and climbed over a couple of little stone walls. I made up my mind to head for Port Moresby.

I had two compasses. One was a luminous compass that I could read at night. Having two compasses was a great consolation because you get to where you don't trust one compass. I ran the gauntlet past two open huts, but nothing happened. After I got by those, I went down a path. It was beginning to get tight. As I looked down the valley, I could see that a couple of natives were hunting. I immediately withdrew off the path, but as I did, I stepped on a twig. It snapped, and the sound reverberated like a shot across the valley.

The two hunters just froze in their tracks, like a couple of hunting dogs on point. They just stared at the spot at which they had heard the noise. They couldn't see me, but they had me pinpointed. Then one of them dropped out of sight. I knew I had to get out of there quickly because they would either circle around to investigate or go back to the village to get help. I pulled off the path and took off my shoes because I felt they had betrayed me by the noise of stepping on the twigs. I hung them around my neck and started crawling.

I crawled all morning. I was in such a desperate frame of mind that I hid my shoes under some bushes because they were making a clumping sound. I put them in there neatly like I was putting them in a closet or under a bed as if I might come back for them later. I was determined to make it difficult for the natives to follow me. I would crawl for three minutes and listen for two minutes, then crawl again. I did this for about two hours. I figured that if they were getting close, I would hear them during my rest interval.

I got to a tiny mountain brook clogged with bushes and fallen trees and had several waterfalls. Remembering Boy Scout training and lore, I walked in the water to hide my tracks. About mid-morning, I reached a rushing mountain stream. It took me about a half-hour to decide where to cross not to leave footprints on the banks. After I crossed the stream, I took off, almost running to get away from the area. My feet felt like they were cut to ribbons. I put my sulfanilamide powder from my jungle kit on them to keep them from getting infected.

When it seemed confident that I had gotten safely away, I stopped to build a shelter. I rested there for a couple of days, then moved on, built another shelter, and relaxed again. I went on this way for about three weeks, and by then, I was getting pretty weary. One time I built a big fire, hoping that someone from my squadron was still looking for me. I gathered a huge pile of logs and started a fire that burned all night, like a prairie fire. It must have burned off about half of New Guinea. In fact, I had to get down in a ditch to get away from the fire. The next day I had to walk through miles of burned stubble.

One day, I saw a shadow on the path and then noticed a figure coming toward me. It was a native woman. As soon as she spotted me, she started running away like a deer. I took off after her, but she left me in the dust. I spent a very uncomfortable night in an abandoned hut. I'm sure the natives were also uncomfortable that night, knowing I was out there.

My toothbrush, one of my few possessions, was a great consolation. I brushed my teeth but didn't have much to eat. I had a pamphlet that told about native foods, but it had gotten wet, and the ink ran all over it so that I couldn't read it. However, I did eat some papayas and small bananas. By then, I had been barefoot for about three weeks. But I put on my socks every night because the insects drove me wild. Without my cloth helmet, mosquito head net, flying gloves, and socks, I would have been in terrible shape.

One of my favorite respites each day was to climb a hill and try to figure out where I was. I wanted to get up into the mountains, but every time I got to the top of one mountain, there was another mountain, another valley, and another mountain ahead. Finally, I left the mountains and went back down into the plains. On my way down, while contemplating the panorama and the beauties of New Guinea, I saw a glimmer of light a few miles away. It turned out to be a reflection of a small, conical hill. I walked toward it, and late in the afternoon, I was able to see some human figures up there. I didn't think they were natives, but I couldn't tell if they were Japanese, Americans, or Aussies.

I was so desperate by this time that I thought, even if they were Japanese, I might sneak into their camp at night and steal food. The next day I honed in on the camp. I saw someone wearing an Aussie hat, but even that didn't convince me. Maybe one of those tricky Japanese was wearing an Aussie hat. I sneaked up closer and closer until I was about thirty feet from them. It was like playing hide and seek, where you come out from hiding and jump up to scare the seeker. I was so close to them that it was almost embarrassing to jump out and say, "Here I am!"

Finally, I came out from behind a tree and saw that they were indeed Aussies who had come down from their fortification for lunch. I just stood there and tried to think of something clever to say, but the only thing I could think of was, "Well, here's another one of those bloody Yanks." The Aussies didn't say anything; they just looked at me in disbelief. It was kind of awkward. Later, I learned that two weeks earlier, in a skirmish with the Japanese, they had lost a second lieutenant who was about my size and had the same color hair. That was why they were so surprised to see me. I was all bandaged up and looked so much like their lieutenant that they thought I was him, come back from the dead.

The Aussie soldiers gave me some food but warned me not to eat too much, or I'd get sick. Well, I did eat too much, and I did get real sick. However, after three weeks of not eating, you can't really eat too much. The Aussies had a radio and asked if I wanted to send a message. Of course, I wanted to let my squadron and the Fifth Air Force know that I was safe. I composed a concise message: "Captain Sullivan, 39th Fighter Squadron, arrived at this point. Injury slight. Please advise."

The next morning, there came a reply: "Captain Sullivan will proceed on when able." Some callous, headquarters type must have composed that thoughtless message because no one in the 39th Fighter Squadron would have been so inconsiderate. I thought, 'To hell with them. I'll stay here for the rest of the war; I'll never go back!.' Then I decided that I had better return.

The Aussies offered to send a native back with me across the mountains. I thought it over and quickly decided against the plan. They also suggested I might go with one of their patrols, which was planning to cross the river, although there was some danger of running into the Japanese. I decided that I had had enough of the natives and that I would go with the Aussies. I was with the Aussie patrol, in their camp, for two days. I felt guilty about eating their food because everything they had come in on their backs. They had no airdrops whatever but had lugged all of their food and supplies over the mountains. The first night out, we saw a big fire. The Aussies thought it might be the Japanese, who would sometimes advance behind the cover of a big fire. As the fire came toward us, I was afraid I had gone from the frying pan into the fire, but it was much better to be with twenty other guys than to be out there by myself. The threat did not materialize. I don't know who started the fire.

The Aussies were nice to me. They even carried my .45, which had become too heavy for me. They realized I was fragile. A couple of big Aussies on either side of me helped me along. Although they had said we wouldn't go too far, we walked about fifteen or twenty miles a day. Eventually, we got across the big river and soon arrived at a camp where there was a small observation plane. We had been walking for two days.

The pilot, Lieutenant Frederick, who wore glider wings, said to me, "Captain, I will save you a long walk if you get into my little airplane. We'll fly to another airstrip." I agreed and got in. It was a tandem arrangement, so I sat in the front, and Lieutenant Frederick sat behind me.

We didn't have any parachutes, and the plane didn't run very well. "It always runs better in the air," Frederick said. Famous last words, I thought. Somehow, we took off and flew for a bit. When we got up to about 1,500 feet, he asked if I wanted to fly. I said I would like to try. But when 1took control, it felt like I was holding it up in the air with my bare hands, so I gave it back to him. Soon after that, I saw that while the throttle was advancing and advancing, the engine wasn't reacting. Then Frederick announced, "I think we have to turn back." But as he turned it back in a big loop, the plane began to lose power. We had been flying over some real tall trees for a long time, and I knew first-hand what tall trees could do if you had to crash-land. Fortunately, the trees thinned out, and the pilot made a pretty good crash-landing in an open area. But the plane had fixed gear, so it flipped over on its back when it bit the grass.

I was hanging upside down by my seat belt. So I just pulled the buckle and fell about four feet to the ground. Frederick was very solicitous: "Are you all right? Thank God! I'm glad it wasn't the general." It turned out he had been flying an Aussie general around. I fired off three shots—the international emergency signal—waited, fired another three shots, and waited again.

Nothing happened, so we walked back to camp. The next day a C-47 transport plane picked me up at Dumpu airstrip. I spent a night in Nadzab, and the next day, October 20, I was flown home to Fourteen-Mile Drome, near Port Moresby, where my squadron put on a glorious welcome. I was back from a thirty-day mission!

During the welcome, one dear friend said, "I knew you would make it. Oh yeah, I'll bring back your razor in the morning." I was on cloud nine. I sent a cablegram to my beloved wife, Mareelee, advising her to pay back the insurance money. Ironically, as I learned later, one insurance agent had indeed tried to begin payoff procedures, but Mareelee politely threw him out! I sent a wire to my dear friend, Captain Tommy Lynch, who was on leave in the States: "Bring back my boots, you vulture." Tom had taken my favorite flying boots home with him. Tom was killed later, so I never got my boots.

Malaria struck me, which deprived me of following up on a suggestion made by one of the Fifth Air Force generals that I lead a revenge mission against the natives. My plan was simply to drop supplies to my Aussie commando friends and cause the natives no further harm. I was to direct the mission from a B-25 covered by four P-40 fighters.

Before I left Brisbane, Australia, for the States, I was advised that General Douglas MacArthur wished to see me and possibly decorate me. My weakened condition and the questionable condition of my uniforms motivated me to decline.

After arriving home, I spent Thanksgiving with Mareelee and our families. Following welcome rest and recuperation, I was assigned to a replacement-training unit in Santa Maria, California, to teach combat skills in my favorite airplane, the P-38. I was even able to give Mareelee a piggyback ride in a P-38. She literally rode on my shoulders.

Charlie Sullivan remained in the service and retired with the rank of colonel in 1968, after nearly thirty years of active duty. He and his wife, Mareelee had five sons. In September 1993, he learned that a pair of Australian aviation enthusiasts had located the remains of the P-38 he crash-landed in the middle of nowhere a half-century earlier. Col. Sullivan died on September 20, 2013, about a year after our interview.

My Favorite Actor

John Joseph appeared in about 70 of the documentary films I wrote and directed in the 1970s. He also played Fagin in *Oliver* and King Arthur in *Camelot,* two plays I produced with Dick Bruno at the Ivoryton Playhouse in Essex, Connecticut. John also played critical roles in a musical I wrote, *Darn Yankees*, and a film, *I Can Walk, I Can Talk, I Can Drive, I Can Die*. John was too busy supporting seven children to take that long and arduous route that might have resulted in a stage or screen career. His day job was steady and relatively lucrative, working as a biologist at Charles Pfizer in Groton, Connecticut.

John told me a story about his role on a research team trying to develop a new blood pressure drug. It had an unexpected side effect that led Pfizer to develop a lucrative new drug that had nothing to do with blood pressure.

Based on John's research, I wrote the following play that opened in Plymouth, Massachusetts, and Narragansett, Rhode Island, in 2016.

SIDE EFFECTS

INT. OFFICE – MORNING

CHARACTERS

CHESTER BACZYNSKI, AGE 55

DR. JEAN EDDINGTON, AGE 40S, extremely attractive doctor

SCENE: Hospital office. Jean sits at a desk, reading from a file. Chester shuffles in, shoulders bent, and stands silently in front of Jean. He doesn't see the glass as half empty or half full. To Chester, there is no glass. The years have not been kind to him, and he looks considerably older than 55. He stands patiently while Jean finishes reading from his medical records.

JEAN

Mr. Baczynski?

He nods.

She motions him to the chair.

JEAN

Please sit.
He sits awkwardly and stares at Jean. There's an uncomfortable silence.

JEAN
How are you today?

CHESTER
I thought you'd tell me.
She smiles.

JEAN
You're in general good health, except for high blood pressure. Which, of course, is why you're here.

CHESTER
Am I going to get a new prescription? That old one didn't seem to help. And I didn't like the side effects.

JEAN
If you're accepted for the clinical trial, you'll be receiving a new drug that may help regulate your blood pressure. Hopefully, without any disturbing side effects (she looks at record_ such as belching and ... whatever

CHESTER
It's the whatever that drove Carol from my bed. Carol is my wife. Do I have to pass a test to get accepted? I've never been very good at taking tests.

JEAN
It's not a pass or fail test, Mr. Baczynski. I'm just going to ask you a few questions to see if you're a good fit for our trial.

CHESTER
Questions. If I don't give you the right answers, I fail. Isn't that a test?

JEAN
Let's not call them questions. I just have to get some information. Please be comfortable and answer as honestly as you can.

CHESTER
It works both ways, you know. Maybe I'll decide your trial isn't a good fit for me.

JEAN
Touché.

CHESTER

I don't speak any foreign languages. I'm 100 percent American, so everything has to be in English. Maybe with a little Polish thrown in.

JEAN

All English then. I don't speak any Polish.

CHESTER

I think you should know this is a first for me.

JEAN

You mean you've never been to a woman doctor?

CHESTER

You got it.

JEAN

The fact that I'm a woman doesn't have anything to do with your acceptance into our pilot program.

Let's move on. I have to get some additional medical information. Have you ever had any chest pains or heart problems?

CHESTER

No.

JEAN

Have you ever taken any nitrate drugs for chest pain?

CHESTER

I just told you I've never had any chest pains. You're not doing too good on this test, Doc.

JEAN

(ignores him) Sildenafil—the drug you'll be taking in the trial—can cause a severe drop in blood pressure if taken with nitrate drugs. So I have to get some answers. Do you use any recreational drugs, such as poppers?

CHESTER

Smoked a little grass about 30 years ago. Nothing since. Tell me about this silda (he struggles with the pronunciation). Is it safe?

JEAN

Sildenafil. It has been safely tested in laboratory trials.

CHESTER

So if it didn't kill a rat, it's okay for me. I guess Carol would see the connection.

JEAN

How long have you been married?

CHESTER
About ten years.
JEAN
You married later in life.
CHESTER
No, I was 25. Carol was 23.
JEAN
I don't understand. You said you were married ten years and
Interrupts.
CHESTER
You know that application you asked me to fill out isn't very accurate. You told me to be honest. We were married for the first ten years. The last 25 we've been roommates—housemates is more accurate.
JEAN
In what way?
CHESTER
You've got those four categories: Single, Married, Divorced, Separated. I'm married and separated.
JEAN
The test is whether you're living under the same roof.
CHESTER
There you go with that test again. Look, you can live under the same roof with someone and still be separated. Hang around my house some night, and you'll see what I mean.
JEAN
You and Carol no longer sleep together?
CHESTER
You know, Doc, I was concerned about flunking this test. I'm getting worried about you. No, Carol and I no longer sleep together.
She studies his record.
JEAN
Some of those medications you took for your high blood pressure may have affected your libido.
CHESTER
I thought we were going to speak English.
JEAN
Libido refers to your sexual desire or ability to have sex.

CHESTER
The medications had nothing to do with my ability to get it up. Carol got rid of that long before I had any blood pressure problems.
JEAN
Were there any prostate problems involved? Those can seriously
He interrupts.
CHESTER
You're not listening again. Let me put it this way. You're an actor, and you got all your lines down, but you never get a role for opening night—do you think you might get tired of dress rehearsals?
JEAN
When did Carol lose her interest in sex?
CHESTER
I don't know that Lady Macbeth ever had any interest in sex. At least with me. Look, why does my sex life have anything to do with my getting into this program?
JEAN
I must develop a profile on everyone who is considered for the trial. Sex may play an important role in our evaluation. Have you ever been told you shouldn't have sexual intercourse for health reasons?
CHESTER
Only by Carol. She said she'll kill me if I ever come near her again. What do all these questions have to do with my high blood pressure? I thought I was here to get that down and not worry about getting anything else up.
JEAN
It's important that we be able to determine the possible effect of this drug on the sex lives of our participants.
CHESTER (angry, frustrated)
So I flunk. I'm not getting any now, and I won't be getting any after the study. So why are you wasting my time?
He starts to get up.
JEAN
There is no pass or fail here. Please let's continue. Can you tell me when you stopped. . . ?
CHESTER
(he sits) I can't give you an exact time. I can say it was at night because

Carol never allowed sex in the day. She blamed my snoring and asked me to move out of the bedroom. But we hadn't had sex for four or five years before she kicked me out. Snoring. That's a laugh.

JEAN

Snoring can be extremely annoying to a bed partner.

CHESTER

You don't have to sell me. No one snores louder than Carol. Even the kids complained about it.

She looks at the record.

JEAN

You didn't list any children.

CHESTER

I thought they only counted if they lived at home. They're both long gone. Pete moved out after college, and Lucy got married two years ago.

JEAN

Do you think you were a good father?

CHESTER

What does it matter? Fathers get honored once a year. Pickles get a whole week.

JEAN

Were you close to the children?

CHESTER

Not as close as Carol. Come to think of it, our sex life began to end after they were born.

JEAN

In what way?

CHESTER

Carol always worried that the kids would hear us.

JEAN

As you've said, the children have been gone for a long time.

CHESTER

But their memory lingers.

JEAN

You seem to blame Carol for the end of your sex life. Did you ever do anything to prolong the romance? Flowers or little gifts.

CHESTER

When Carol smells flowers, she looks around for a coffin. The only endearing words she likes to hear are "Let's eat out."

JEAN

It doesn't sound like you and Carol have much in common.

CHESTER

Nothing in common. We don't even hate the same people.

JEAN

Did she stop you from doing things that made you happy?

CHESTER

Carol never stopped me from doing anything—she just made sure I didn't enjoy it.

JEAN

Tell me a little bit about your childhood. Did you have siblings?

CHESTER

Five brothers and two sisters. You know I never got to sleep alone until I got married.

JEAN

You seem to have a negative outlook on life. Were you always like this?

CHESTER

You know that Chinese saying about a journey of a thousand miles starts with a single step. Mine started with a broken fan belt and a flat tire.

JEAN

You don't think life is very fair, do you?

CHESTER

If life was fair, Elvis would be alive, and all his impersonators would be dead. That's not original—I got it from Johnny Carson.

JEAN

The fact that you no longer have a sex life. Any other contributing factors?

He falls silent, and a serous expression comes over his face.

CHESTER

Donna Berkowitz.

JEAN

Who is?

CHESTER

My boss's wife at my former job.

JEAN

You had an affair with her?

CHESTER

A one-night stand's more accurate. Carol and the kids were visiting her sister in Chicago. Donna and I worked late one night and ended up on the office floor. A photographer walked in and caught us in the act.

JEAN

Photographer?

CHESTER

Morrie—Donna's husband who owned the company—was suspicious and hired a photographer to catch her in the act. It turns out that she had been entertaining the whole office. I was just unlucky enough to get on candid camera when my turn came up.

JEAN

Carol found out?

CHESTER

The whole city found out. Berkowitz vs. Berkowitz was right up there with Kramer vs. Kramer.

JEAN

I take it you lost your job?

CHESTER

Morrie offered to keep me on. Said he could never have gotten rid of Donna without me. Told me he'd call me if he had another unhappy marriage. But Carol said she wouldn't take me back unless I quit.

JEAN

So you separated after

(Interrupts)

CHESTER

If finding my clothes spread over the front lawn qualifies for a separation, yeah, we separated.

JEAN

How did your children react?

CHESTER

Lucy didn't speak to me for months, even after I moved back in. Pete was more understanding. We got a lot closer after the story hit the papers. Pete claims my bad reputation helped him get into his college fraternity.

JEAN

How long was the separation?

CHESTER

About a month after the trial, Carol called. We had lunch, and she invited me to move back in.

JEAN

But not into the bedroom.

CHESTER

Lucy was still living at home. So yes, I moved back into the bedroom.

JEAN

But no sex.

CHESTER

Just once. The night I moved back in, we had sex. After we finished, Carol looked at me and said, "Donna gave up all that luxury for this?" I had trouble getting it up after that.

JEAN

Any more affairs?

CHESTER

No. I was in a new job with much pressure. Then the high blood pressure started and ...

JEAN

No more office floors.

CHESTER

No more anything.

JEAN

You don't seem too upset about how things have turned out in your life.

CHESTER

I learned to accept that some days you're the pigeon, and some days you're the statue.

Jean picks up his record again.

JEAN

I think you should understand how the research study will proceed. You'll receive the first dose of Sildenafil today and for the next 30 days. If you have any side effects such as vision changes, ringing in

your ears, hearing loss, or irregular heartbeat, stop taking it immediately and call me at this number, night or day.
She hands him a card.
CHESTER
Do you mean I passed?
JEAN
You have been accepted into the research pilot.
She writes a prescription and hands it to him.
JEAN
Stop at Pharmacy and pick up the prescription.

SCENE 2: OFFICE—MORNING

Jean is sitting at her desk as JAMES TUTTLE, 40, tall and thin, enters with his wife, ELMIRA, 38. She is short and heavy, and her expression reveals her dissatisfaction with many people, especially James.
Jean stands and motions them to sit.
JEAN
Good morning. You must be Mr. and Mrs. Tuttle. I'm Dr. Jean. I believe you know why you're here.
ELMIRA
Some sort of new program We haven't made any commitments yet.
JEAN
Of course. (She picks up his medical records.) I'm sure you're aware that Mr. Tuttle's blood pressure is dangerously high. The drugs he's been taking have either been ineffective or have resulted in severe side effects. We are in the process of testing a new medication, and we think Mr. Tuttle would be a good candidate.'
ELMIRA
How much money is involved?
JEAN
If Mr. Tuttle is accepted, there will be no charge for the drugs.
ELMIRA
That's not what I meant. Will he be paid for taking part in the program?
JEAN
I will be able to offer him enough to cover his transportation expenses.

ELMIRA
'That's a laugh. You test these drugs on people like my husband, then make millions when you sell them to the general public.
JAMES
Elmira, I don't think
ELMIRA
That's the smartest thing you've ever said. You don't think!
JEAN
This discussion is premature. We don't even know if Mr. Tuttle will be accepted into the program.
ELMIRA
What does he have to do? He's got high blood pressure. The other drugs aren't working or make him impossible to be around.

SCENE 2: OFFICE—MORNING ONE MONTH LATER

Jean is sitting in her office when the phone rings.
JEAN
Dr. Eddington. (pause) Good morning Mrs. Baczynski. All right, Carol. (pause). Chester will be a little late? No problem. (pause) It doesn't really matter whose fault it is. (pause) No, Chester won't be dropped from the pilot program because of a little lateness. I'm sure that he would appreciate your willingness to accept blame, but it's not necessary. So please relax. Have you noticed any changes in Chester since he started taking the experimental drug? (pause) You're both a lot happier. Good. High blood pressure can cause mood swings and erratic behavior. Has Chester shared his pressure readings with you? (pause). I understand. I'll be able to get the information I need from his log. Thank you for calling. (pause. I assume he'll be home after our meeting. Thanks. Goodbye. (She hangs up with a puzzled expression.)
Chester strides into the office, animated with a big smile. He is dressed in a Ralph Lauren blue blazer with gray pants. His change from the round-shouldered, unsmiling man from a month ago is dramatic.
CHESTER
Good morning Doctor. So good to see you again.
She looks at him in disbelief, wondering who this confident stranger

is, replacing the pessimistic, down-in-the-mouth man she had interviewed a month ago.

JEAN

Good morning, Mr. Baczynski. I must say you seem like a totally different person.

CHESTER

I am different. Thanks to you. Sorry, I'm a little late.

JEAN

Carol called and already apologized. Said it was her fault.

CHESTER

She's right about that. Wouldn't let me out of bed . . . until . . . you know.

JEAN

(ignores) Did you bring your blood pressure chart? I'm anxious to find out if you're avoiding those dramatic ups and downs.

CHESTER

I've had more ups and downs than ever. It doesn't have anything to do with my blood pressure, though. (laughs)

JEAN

Please explain.

CHESTER

It started right after I took that first pill in the Pharmacy. Wow. It was like I was 16 again. I had to buy a newspaper and put it in my lap as a cover in the subway. If I hadn't found a seat, I probably would have been arrested.

JEAN

Are you telling me that the pill caused you to have an erection?

CHESTER

Not just one of those run-of-the-mill erections that appear quickly and then disappear. No, this one was good for 21 blocks. It was still there when I got home. Carol couldn't believe it when I walked into the apartment.

JEAN

She agreed to have sex?

CHESTER

Probably out of curiosity that first time. We spent most of the afternoon in bed. It was my first doubleheader since the Dodgers left

Brooklyn. I left to get the car serviced. When I got back, she had moved all my things back into the bedroom.

JEAN

What happened after you took the second pill that night?

CHESTER

Carol was supposed to go shopping with our daughter. She called our daughter and said she had a headache. She didn't act like she had any pain.

JEAN

And the next morning?

CHESTER

Carol got up early to get the water for my pill. Then she made me bacon and eggs. Said I couldn't keep this up without a good breakfast.

JEAN

It sounds like you and Carol are on a second honeymoon.

CHESTER

First. You have to understand, Doc. Carol's 53 years old. She can't go on like this. I can't give her all my business.

JEAN

Which means.

CHESTER

After I take the morning pill, I wear baggy pants to smuggle it out.

JEAN

You've found some willing partners?

CHESTER

Mrs. Murphy, the widow on the first floor, has been helping me out. I ran into her in the elevator one morning. She was impressed when I pushed the floor button without using any fingers. And Donna's back in the picture. I bumped into her at Dunkin' Donuts right after the morning pill.

JEAN

What happened?

CHESTER

We can't go to that Dunkin' donuts any more.

JEAN

I'm surprised that you would have anything to do with Donna after all the trouble she caused.

CHESTER

You have to forgive, Doc. When Donna told Morrie about my prescription, he borrowed one of my pills. He's offered me a full partnership if I can get him the pills on a regular basis. We could be on easy street if you —

JEAN

Don't even go there. You were part of a pilot study that may be able to resolve a serious health problem. You make me sound like some kind of pimp.

CHESTER

Relax, Doc. No one thinks of you that way. Carol, Donna, Mrs. Murphy, even Morrie. They all love you. And they're counting on you. I bought along a pair of baggy pants I can use after you give me my next set of pills. Carol even canceled her bridge club for today.

JEAN

You won't be getting any pills today. I have to compile the results of Pilot one before we can move on to Pilots two and three.

CHESTER

Maybe a little break is in order. I'm getting a little tired. But this guy is relentless. Right after I take the pill, he's agitating. "Come on, big boy let's go. We've got a lot of work to do." It's like he's a separate person. Sometimes, I feel like that guy who used to change personalities after

JEAN

Dr. Jeckyl and Mr. Hyde.

CHESTER

You got it Doc. But calling this guy Hide doesn't exactly fit. He's got no shame. He just sits there pretending to be in charge. I've even told him off a few things.

JEAN

What happens?

CHESTER

Carol gets angry. It was the same way when I tried to discipline the kids. She doesn't like me to speak mean to him. So maybe he should take a little breather. The rest of the guys in the pilot must have had the same results. How many are involved?

JEAN

There are 30 participants in the program. You were the first one accepted and the first one debriefed. I have meetings scheduled the rest of the week. Why didn't you call me when you started having these results?

CHESTER

You told me to call if I had any problems with vision, heartbeat, shortness of breath, or dizziness. I didn't feel any of those. The only side effect I've felt has been appreciated by everyone involved.

Jean glances at her deskbook, picks up the phone, and dials a number.

JEAN

to phone) Good morning. May I please speak to Harry Crosby. (pause) I see. Is Mrs. Crosby there. (pause) I understand. Would you please ask Mr. Crosby to call Dr. Jean Eddington when he returns? (to Chester)

He and his wife are on a second honeymoon.

CHESTER

You see what a wonderful thing you're doing Doc. If you can bring so much happiness to 30 men, what can you do for humanity?

JEAN

Let's not get ahead of ourselves. Two men don't make a study. (she looks at her directory and dials another number.)

JEAN

Mr. Mazza. Dr. Eddington from the research center. We're not scheduled to meet until tomorrow, but I'm wondering if you have time to answer a few questions on the phone. You're still in bed. I'm so sorry to wake you—I didn't wake you, I interrupted you. I see. You've answered my major question. I'll see you tomorrow. No, the pills are not available over-the-counter.

She glances at the record.

JEAN

James Mazza is 78 years old. He and his wife haven't had sex for 12 years. They've been in bed for two days, and she's up frying him eggs as we speak.

She looks in her directory again, then dials a number.

JEAN

Good morning Mr. Von Statts. This is Dr. Eddington from the clinic. I'm calling about (pause as she listens). Five hours. Mr. Von Statts, any erection lasting more than four hours is dangerous. A prolonged erection can result in priapism, a condition that may damage your penis. You have to get to (pause as she listens) Mrs. Von Staats, I appreciate the fact that you want to help. But Mr. Von Statts should be seen in the emergency room immediately. I'll call and tell them he's coming. No, I can't give him any more pills until we have a debriefing session. (pause) I can't give you any more pills at this time. Please leave for the emergency room immediately. (She hangs up and turns to Chester, not trying to hide her frustration.

CHESTER

We're on to something here Doc. It's bigger than both of us. You're going down in history Doc—right up there with Jonas Salk, Louie Pasteur, and Dr. Curie.

JEAN

It was an accidental discovery, something we never planned.

CHESTER

Penicillin was discovered by accident. I don't think any people it cured objected. The people in this study aren't going to trade this boner—I mean bonus—for normal blood pressure. Who cares if it's an accident?

Chester's cell phone rings, and he answers it.

CHESTER

Good morning Morrie. I'm with Dr. Eddington now. No, there might be a problem. It doesn't sound like I'm going to get any more pills today.

(he puts his hand on the receiver.

He wants to talk to you.

He hands Jean the phone.

JEAN

This is Dr. Eddington. (pause) No, you cannot be accepted into this pilot program. Naming opportunities? That's quite generous Mr. Berkowitz, but I have nothing to do with fundraising at the hospital. You'll have to contact the hospital building committee. No, I have no idea when or if the drug will receive FDA approval. Now I must go.

She hands the phone back to Chester.

JEAN

You had no right to share this drug would anyone outside of the program. You may have seriously compromised the entire study.

CHESTER
By making people happy. Carol's got a smile on her face, and Morrie and Donna are talking about getting back together. Mrs. Murphy's dating the doorman. You held a mirror up for all of us, Doc.
JEAN
I can't give you any more pills until we compile the results of Pilot 1 and move into Pilot 2.
CHESTER
Pilot one. Pilot 2. What the hell do I care. The best way to make your dreams come true is to wake up. Those pills are my personal alarm clock. Don't take them away.
JEAN
I change your life by turning you into the stud of the city.
CHESTER
Okay, I see what you're driving at. I'll give my business to Carol 100%.
JEAN
And Morrie?
CHESTER
I'm too old to be anyone's partner. So he's shut off too. One thing Doc. Is your company publicly traded? Because there's one other thing that's going to be elevated—your stock.
JEAN
Be careful. You could be found guilty of insider trading.
She reaches into her drawer, pulls out an envelope, and hands it to Chester.
JEAN
Thirty more days. Remember, Dr. Frankenstein regretted reviving the monster. Don't give me any second thoughts.
CHESTER
The wolf man's not a bad guy. You hurt his feelings when you call him a monster.

SCENE THREE

Jean's office, one month later.
Jean sits at her desk as the phone rings.

JEAN
Good morning, Mr. Bacynski. You sound bright and chipper. Yes . . . I guess it's good to start the day with a bang. You'll be happy to know that Pilot Three has been completed. No, there will be no Pilot 4. (pause) Don't be upset. The good news is that the drug has received FDA approval, so I'll be sending you a prescription today. No, Morrie will have to get a prescription from his own doctor. One more thing—don't ask for Sildenafil. The marketing department has come up with a new name—Viagra. Yes, it does have a nice ring to it. It was a pleasure working with you, Mr. Baczynski. Give my best to Carol, Mrs. Murphy, Donna and, of course, Morrie.

CURTAIN

FEMALE FRIENDS

The movie *When Harry Met Sally* made a lasting impression on me. Harry (Billy Crystal) and Sally (Meg Ryan) meet when she gives him a ride to New York after they graduate from the University of Chicago. The film jumps through their lives as they both search for love. Harry's marriage ends in divorce, while Sally goes through the breakup of a long-term relationship. Nevertheless, they keep bumping into each other and develop a close friendship. But they are confronted with a problem. Can a man and a woman be friends without sex getting in the way? According to Harry, it's not possible.

I can answer that question with an empathic yes! I first became comfortable with the mothers of my girlfriends, certainly more than with the girlfriends themselves. I got second or third dates because of the pressure exerted by mothers on their daughters. The mothers liked me more than the daughters, and I enjoyed the mothers more than my girlfriends. Sometimes I would be in the kitchen talking to "mother" while my girlfriend waited impatiently in the living room.

When I became Editorial Director of a division of P-H, I inherited a proofreader named Eleanor Lewis. It didn't take me long to realize how bright she was. Eleanor was much more than a proofreader. Yes, she caught the grammatical errors, but she also did much rewriting, improving the articles dramatically. There was a vast difference in salary between a proofreader and an editor. I got some resistance when I tried to promote Eleanor to the editorial staff, with a significant salary increase. But I stuck to my guns, and Eleanor became the first female editor in our division. Eleanor raised four daughters practically by herself. We remained friends until she died in 2007. I reminded her friends and family of her strong character and quick wit when I delivered her eulogy.

I also worked with a woman by the name of Ruth Nagle at Prentice-Hall. Long after I left P-H and moved from Connecticut, Ruth and I remained friends. She traveled from Connecticut to Rhode Island to see two of my plays, and we remained friends until she died in 2013. So I was very honored when her family asked me to deliver Ruth's eulogy.

Three of my favorite female friends were married to members

of my tennis group. Bob Klimek, Bill Hostnik and Carl Lutender. All three are gone now, but I remain close to Susan Hostnik, Carol Klimek, and Lois Lutender. Elaine McGirr, widow of my friend John McGirr, will always be a good friend, as will Carol German.

Peg Murray, Angela Vars, Francoise Pomfret, Lorraine McBride and Gloria Cercena are key members of the Newport Breakfast Club. We still meet whenever I am in Rhode Island. Regina Black Lennox has always been there for me during our 23- year friendship.

So I can happily tell Harry that yes, men can have female friends with no strings attached. Believing otherwise would have deprived me of some of the most incredible friendships of my life.

Fire Me, and I'll Sue

It began in 1972, shortly after Charles Toussaint sued Blue Cross of Michigan for wrongful discharge. In a performance appraisal before his termination, Toussaint was rated average and even received a raise. In explaining the reason for the termination, his boss told Toussaint he was an "okay" employee but felt he could do better.

When Toussaint was hired in 1967, he was given a "Supervisory Manual," which explained Blue Cross' personnel policies and procedures, including certain grounds and procedures for terminating employees. "You will be terminated only for just cause after the disciplinary procedure has been followed. " This policy spelled out a three-step procedure that included (1) oral warning, (2) written warning, (3) final warning. Toussaint was terminated without warning and was given no indication that his job was in jeopardy. A jury upheld his claim that the "Supervisory Manual" represented an implied contract. Toussaint was awarded $73,000.

Most states follow the employment-at-will concept that states that an employee can resign for any reason or no reason and that employers could fire them for any reason or no reason. Companies began to lose wrongful termination cases because of language in their policy manuals or employee handbooks. After reviewing the Toussaint case, I came up with an idea for two books: *How to Write a Company Policy Manual* and *How to Write An Employee Handbook*. We sold more than $5,000,000 of those books in the first year.

All of our books were on an approval basis. If the customer returned it during the trial period, no questions were asked. Very few customers took advantage of our return policy. One morning, our shipping supervisor came into my office with *How to Write A Company Policy Manual*. In returning the book, the personnel manager included a short note she had written to her secretary. "Can you believe this?" the shipping manager said.

The secretary was told to make a copy of the book and then return it in the note. She left the message in the returned book. The executive who issued the copying order was a member of the marketing department at Hilton Head. My family and I had stayed there several years and loved it. Her telephone number was listed on the note, so I called her directly.

"I want to say that my family and I have stayed at Hilton Head for the past three summers. We love it and recommend it as a wonderful vacation designation to our friends."

I could feel the question in her voice as she thanked me. "How did this nut get my telephone number?"

"Tell me, if I stay next summer and leave with the bedding and silverware, what would you think?" I asked.

"That would be stealing," she said.

"I'm glad to hear your feeling about stealing. You just stole something from me." I explained the note in her handwriting with the name of her secretary. She denied everything and was about to hang up until I delivered another message. "As soon as you hang up, I will be calling the president of Hilton Head—right after I fax him your note."

She did the only thing that would have stopped me from completing that call. It is a reaction that began in fourth grade when Nancy M. ate the cupcake out of my lunch. With chocolate crumbs still sticking to her lips, she began to cry when I threatened to tell our teacher. Young girls, middle age girls, and even old girls have used this defense successfully for a variety of reasons. When my Hilton Head bandit began to cry, I relented. A few days later, I received a check for the book.

MEETING THE FLYING DUTCHMAN

When I went to work for Pieter Weiger Van Bennekom in Malvern, PA, my first thought was that he could fire me in five languages and until he got to English, I wouldn't even know. Pieter was the editorial director for Progressive Business Publications (PBP) when I was hired as an editor in 1998. Born in the Netherlands in June of 1945, Pieter is fluent in Dutch, German, French, Spanish, and English.

In a writing career that began in the 1940s and continues today, I have met a lot of interesting people like Red Auerbach, Lee Iacocca, Bob Cousy, Tom Heinsohn, Bill Russell, John Havlicek, K. C. Jones, and Sam Jones. Pieter doesn't take a backseat to any of them. Even his name is historical—Pieter and Wieger were two uncles of Pieter who were killed on the last day of WWII in northern Holland during shelling by Canadian troops. Pieter's father had been in the resistance during the war, and most people knew him by his wartime alias, Jan van Beuzekom.

Pieter had held a string of top management jobs, including the presidency of United Press International, before joining PBP. We bonded immediately, and I had no worries about being fired in any language. Moreover, the job allowed me to work for one of the most unforgettable characters I have ever met. We developed a life-long friendship that continues today.

Like Pieter, I had held a succession of jobs, including editorial director for a division of Prentice-Hall, the presidency of Madison Productions, a film company, and a lot of freelance gigs in between. Pieter and I both love tennis, and he visited me frequently to go to the induction ceremonies of tennis greats into the Tennis Hall of Fame in Newport, RI.

When we got together, the stories would pour out as if we were playing a game of "can you top this?" For example, I told Pieter about the reaction of the other team owners in 1950 when Red Auerbach drafted Chuck Cooper, the first Black drafted into the National Basketball Association. Pieter countered with a story about a courageous decision by an editor that gave UPI the distinction of being the first news outlet to announce the death of Stalin in March 1953.

As president and CEO of UPI, Pieter interviewed more than 60 heads of state, including eight United States presidents. Yet one of my favorite Pieter stories had nothing to do with presidents or heads of state. It involved a young Chilean named Patricio Candia, who had just been hired as a news reporter for a UPI office in Columbia where Pieter was bureau chief. A day before his starting date, he went to the office to get checked out on the teletype transmitter he would be using to send stories to UPI headquarters in New York.

At this point, Patricio asked if he could practice on the teletype machine. After the power to the transmission channel was turned off, ensuring that nothing would be sent to the New York office, Patricio was encouraged to practice as much as he wanted. He spent the entire morning on the machine and then went to lunch. Meanwhile, an office boy saw that the machine was in an off: position and turned it on, unbeknownst to Patricio.

When Patricio got back on the machine, he decided to get a little creative, and he started typing, "Columbian President Alfonso Lopez Michelsen was assassinated today by Communist guerillas who fired at him from point-blank range with Russian-made AK-47 automatic rifles. Four bullets penetrated his skull." An editor in New York ran through the office screaming, "The President of Colombia has been assassinated."

Before the bulletin was corrected and "killed" about 10 minutes later, it had already caused quite a stir. Pieter tried to call President Michelsen to explain what happened and apologize, but a private secretary told him that the president did not wish to see him. That night Columbian radio and T.V. stations announced that the international news agency (UPI) had been banned from operating in Columbia. Cooler heads prevailed, and it was decided that UPI could resume operations in Columbia—on one condition: Pieter Van Bennekom had to be expelled from Columbia. He was transferred to Buenos Aires as chief correspondent for Argentina.

When I mentioned my meeting with Lee Iacocca, Pieter related stories about his experience with some of the conspiracy theories concerning the assassination of John Kennedy. Few events make such an impression that people remember exactly what they were doing and where they were at the time. For those old enough to remember, the assassination of President John F. Kennedy on Friday, Nov. 22,

1963, in Dallas, TX, was definitely such an event. Here, in his own words, Pieter tells the strange story of how the Kennedy assassination impacted his life.

I was still in the Dutch provincial capital of Middelburg, in my last year of secondary school. The shooting happened in the afternoon in Dallas, but because of the time difference, it was Friday evening there, the time our local chess club met at a hotel. The manager had strict instructions to maintain quiet—no T.V. or radio—since chess players needed to concentrate. So we all reacted angrily at first when the T.V. suddenly started blaring. But we all shut up when he heard what the announcer was saying. John F. Kennedy, wildly popular in Western Europe, had just been shot and killed in Dallas.

At the time, I didn't think the Kennedy assassination would affect me personally, but I was very wrong. About every ten years or so, new developments around the Kennedy assassination would come back to haunt me. It started only a few months later. Early in 1964, I had applied for a Fulbright exchange student scholarship to study in America for a year, and I was summoned to the United States Consulate in Amsterdam for a final interview with a young American. He asked me who I thought had killed Kennedy. I thought it was an extraordinary question. Hadn't all the newspapers said Lee Harvey Oswald had been the lone assassin who was subsequently killed himself?

In Holland, we didn't know any better. The American didn't let it go, asking if I thought that the antipathy shown towards Kennedy in the Deep South over his support for racial integration might have had something to do with his assassination. "I do know Dallas is in the South, but the newspapers said that the guy who killed him was a Communist who had lived in Russia. So it seems like it had more to do with the Cold War than with internal strife in the United States.

I had the distinct impression that he had serious doubts about the official version of the Kennedy assassination and was disappointed that I had swallowed the official version, but he didn't hold it against me, and I got the scholarship. It was strange that my first real exposure to America, in that American Consulate interview in Amsterdam, was all about the Kennedy assassination, the event that has intruded into my life with some regularity. I am not a crazy conspiracy theorist. I do not know who really killed Kennedy and why and I don't believe I, or anyone else, will ever find out. However, I do not agree with the conclusion of the Warren Commission that Lee Harvey Oswald was the lone assassin. I believe he was a pathetic little man set up as a patsy to take the blame. And before he could talk, he was himself killed inside a police station by a man with a shady past who happened to be dying of cancer who said he did it to spare Mrs. Kennedy the ordeal of a public trial. So that official version is just not believable.

Enough things happened to me over the years to convince me that the Warren Commission jumped to a convenient conclusion to tie things off with a neat ribbon, but that the absolute truth was much murkier. I did learn certain things over the years that throw serious doubt on the lone gunman theory, but I cannot connect the dots. And frankly, I do not want to pursue these leads anymore. The whole thing started giving me severe creeps over the years. Every time I got involved repeatedly, someone seemed to die, and I didn't want the next victim to be me. Sure, I hope the truth will come out someday, but I don't want to be involved anymore.

In early 1967, I was working in Winnipeg, Canada, as a reporter for the city's main newspaper, the Winnipeg Free Press. I was on the evening shift, the only reporter in the newsroom, available if any big local story broke. I wasn't too busy when the phone rang, and a caller identified himself as Richard Giesbrecht, as if I should know who he was. He told me to go to the newspaper's morgue (library of past issues) and look at a certain issue from about a year ago, and he'd call me back in 30 minutes. I found what he was talking about right away, a front-page story that quoted an anonymous person (who I suspected was Giesbrecht) as the source for a pretty fantastic tale. The source had described in great detail how he had been sitting in a quiet corner of the cafeteria at the Winnipeg Airport, waiting to pick up an acquaintance arriving on a delayed flight, when he overheard a conversation at a nearby table between people unaware of his presence. There was no mistaking what they were talking about, which was their escape from Dallas after the Kennedy assassination. Apparently, this group of people met regularly in different places outside the United States to discuss their ongoing efforts at avoiding detection in the investigation of the assassination.

At some point, Giesbrecht felt he had to get away from there, but as he tried to leave by a rear door, he heard footsteps. Giesbrecht was now running for his life and eventually managed to lose himself in a crowd at the airport, making it home safely. He told his story to Sergeant Pollock of the Royal Canadian Mounted Police (RCMP). They searched the airport but found no trace of the men Giesbrecht had described, filed a report to RCMP headquarters in Ottawa, which was forwarded to the FBI in Washington, where it died.

So why was Giesbrecht calling me a year later? He explained when he called back as promised 30 minutes later. The main story in that afternoon's newspaper had been a wire story from New Orleans, where District Attorney Jim Garrison had announced he had uncovered a plot to assassinate Kennedy, giving the names of some of the plotters and releasing their pictures. The plotters included a pilot, David Ferrie, who had rather distinctive features with fake eyebrows. Ferrie had been found dead in his apartment in New Orleans, an apparent suicide, just before Garrison's deputies were about to arrest him, and his photo was splashed all over the front page of our newspaper that day.

"That's one of the men I saw at the airport that day," Giesbrecht told me. "I am absolutely sure of it." Giesbrecht was a solid citizen not given to flights of fancy, middle-aged, and on the heavy-set side, of Mennonite stock, a devoted family man, an insurance salesman who didn't drink or smoke. He was not given to making up stories.

I wrote the follow-up story for the Free Press, revealing the local angle to the alleged Kennedy assassination plot uncovered in New Orleans. Garrison's investigation was later discredited, but at the time, he was the darling of the press, and everybody wanted to believe him. So I called the New Orleans DA office. I never got to speak to Jim Garrison himself, but I did talk to several attorneys in the following days. We would help them with any information from Canada, we said, and we hoped that in return, they could fill us in about how this Canadian angle fit in with the story. In retrospect, they did not hold up their side of the bargain. I provided a great deal of information to them, but they never gave me anything in return. I ran across a slew of loose details, but much it would have been highly libelous, and I had no idea how it all fit into a big picture.

Garrison's crew wasn't all that interested in the airport meeting witnessed by Giesbrecht. They said a small group of plotters would meet from time to time outside the United States, and Winnipeg, located just north of the North Dakota-Minnesota state line, was an ideal place. But they wanted something else from me. Their investigation focused on Clay Shaw, director of the New Orleans International Trade Mart, the only man ever to be charged with conspiracy to kill John F. Kennedy. At trial in 1969, Garrison's case had crumbled, and it took a jury less than an hour to acquit Shaw, but we didn't know any of that yet in the early days. The DA's people had laid hands on Clay Shaw's little black book of contacts with a significant number of names and addresses of people around the world. (Shaw was gay and most, if not all, names in the book were part of a worldwide gay network.) To check out Shaw's Canadian contacts, formally the New Orleans DA's office would have to forward a request to the FBI, which would forward it to the RCMP in Ottawa, which would then farm it out to local police forces, and any reports would be sent back through the same chain. It would take forever, but the main problem was that the FBI in Washington was not cooperating with Garrison because they held fast to the Warren Commission's conclusion that there was no plot. So the New Orleans Assistant DA asked me to check out some of Shaw's Canadian contacts.

My first assignment for Garrison was to check out a man in Vancouver. I had a friend who was a reporter for a Vancouver newspaper. I gave him the name and address from Shaw's little black book. My friend got back to me within hours, enabling me to give New Orleans a full report. My friend said he had felt rather uncomfortable disturbing the guy at home, asking if he had any idea why his name would appear in a notebook of a suspect in the Kennedy assassination. "Is this guy gay?" my friend asked me. He had been somewhat evasive, saying he might have known Clay in New Orleans, but declined to give any specifics. So if there was a story there, we couldn't figure out what it was.

There was, however, a surprising angle to the Clay Shaw contact in Toronto. This guy was a high school guidance counselor, but he lived with another Canadian named Robin Drury, who was somewhat famous—or infamous. In 1963 when he lived in London, England, Drury had been "business manager" for Christine Keeler, the British call girl who was the central figure in the Profumo spy scandal. Drury had peddled the lurid details of Keeler's affairs with both Britain's Conservative defense minister and the local KGB agent named Ivanov to the Fleet Street tabloids for money. The matter had just about brought down the British government.

The connection, however tenuous, between the Profumo scandal and the Kennedy assassination, two of the biggest stories of the decade, was pretty sensational stuff, but it didn't seem to fit the narrative being developed by Garrison. However, the New Orleans DA office put me in touch with a British lawyer, Michael Eddowes, who had also been offering his assistance from afar and who believed that the Kennedy assassination was part of a worldwide Russian plot to undermine and cripple Western democratic leaders, either by compromising them (Profumo) or assassinating them (JFK). Eddowes had credibility in the Unied Kingdom as the author of a book turned into a movie, The Killings at Rillington Place, about a miscarriage of British justice, the execution of an innocent man for a series of killings later proved to have been committed by someone else. It was the main factor that led Britain to abolish capital punishment. Eddowes figured in Kennedy assassination affairs for many years and even got an order to exhume Oswald's body from a Dallas cemetery to test his theory that a Soviet agent had been buried in his place. By then Eddowes had been discredited, like Garrison, and I was no longer in contact with him.)

At the time, I didn't know any of this yet, and Eddowes and I agreed to meet in Toronto to jointly further investigate possible connections between the Kennedy and Profumo affairs. Eddowes had no trouble setting up a meeting with Drury in the cafeteria of the Royal York Hotel, but he would not let me attend, saying that it would be too difficult to explain my presence and that he might get more out of Drury if he went alone. So I was only allowed to observe the meeting from a cafeteria counter stool. Eddowes later told me Drury had provided some more context for what had happened in the Profumo affair but claimed to know nothing about Clay Shaw or any connection to the Kennedy assassination through the guy he was living with. The whole Robin Drury connection turned out to be nothing more than an intriguing coincidence, and there was nothing more we could do on that front.

There were a couple of more names and addresses in Clay Shaw's notebook in Montreal, which I had not yet checked out, so Eddowes and I took a train to Montreal, where the plot thickened. One of the addresses was an apartment where the person we were looking for had moved out and left no forwarding address. But in yet another intriguing coincidence, the apartment was one floor below the flat of Gerda Munsinger, an East German Communist spy who had an affair with then Conservative Canadian Prime Minister John Diefenbaker in the early '60s.

Eddowes was fascinated by the coincidence, convinced that the Munsinger scandal was further evidence of the worldwide Communist plot to infiltrate and embarrass Western governments. Moreover, he believed the apartment immediately below Munsinger's had been occupied by an intelligence agent to gather compromising evidence of her activities with paramours. But since we had no way of knowing where this person had gone, or even if he had rented the apartment in his real name, we hit another dead end.

The second name in Montreal turned out to be interesting in a different way. We were invited in by an elderly couple, but the man we asked for was not there anymore. He had rented a room there for about a month, answering a newspaper ad and paying in cash in advance, but left without a trace and no contact information. The owners of the house remembered him well. He was apparently not one of Clay Shaw's gay network. He always had lots of cash on him, drove a big car with U.S. license plates, and had one of the first mobile telephones—they'd never seen anything like it—on which he held the strangest conversations. From what he told his hosts and from what they overheard on the phone, he was on a special mission to meet a Czech airliner en route from Prague to Havana, making an unscheduled stop in Montreal to let one passenger off the plane. The lodger would debrief him and route him to his eventual Western Hemisphere destination. Eddowes immediately concluded the lodger had been a CIA agent, and when we relayed our information to the New

Orleans DA's office, they agreed: "That man must have been CIA." But why was his name in Clay Shaw's address book? Did Shaw work for the CIA, too? Many questions—few answers.

I came across more explosive information in Montreal about JFK's infidelities with Judith Exner, who has also been the mistress of a mob boss. The liaison was revealed years later among many other affairs he had, but I knew about it way back in 1967. Apparently, the mysterious CIA man staying in that rooming house in Montreal had been sent at one point to escort her someplace. I tried to sell the story to the *National Enquirer*, but this was too lurid even for them, so that story went nowhere, either.

I was becoming increasingly frustrated with the Kennedy assassination business. Philip Shenon, a former *New York Times* reporter, wrote a 2013 book, *A Cruel and Shocking Act—The Secret History of the Kennedy Assassination*, in which he said, "I became a victim of the dual curse faced by anyone who tries to get close to the truth about the assassination—of too little information and too much."

Truer words were never spoken. I had run across much extraneous detail—way too much. I had no way of fitting it together into a cohesive pattern or even knowing which details were essential to the big picture or which were red herrings. Besides, the people I was associated with—no one can do this stuff alone—turned out to be big disappointments. Eddowes was looking for Communists under every bed, and Jim Garrison's office had used me as a leg man to get information on Clay Shaw's contacts but never got back to me with any helpful information on how it all fits together into a context that would give me a story, and his whole investigation was losing credibility. So I dropped the story and didn't think about it for years. But somehow, it didn't drop me, and it kept coming around to me every 10 years or so.

I left Winnipeg in the fall of 1968 and found a job in Mexico City, first on a couple of English-language local newspapers and later with the wire service, United Press International (UPI). I didn't realize at the time how central Mexico City was to Lee Harvey Oswald's movements in the weeks immediately before the Kennedy assassination, but during my years in Mexico City, I never ran into any of the figures whose names would later emerge in the investigations.

In 1972 I was transferred to UPI World Headquarters in New York as Latin American Editor, and three years later, I was transferred back to Latin America as bureau chief in Bogota, Colombia. After I was expelled over a 1976 incident that gave UPI's credibility a severe black eye, UPI wanted to make it up to the Colombians and scoured the payroll for the best candidate to succeed me. Ralph (Rafael) Bermudez, the bureau chief in Baton Rouge, LA, but a Colombian by birth, turned out to be the man. UPI announced with pride that it had found the ideal man with deep roots in the country and an impeccable journalistic resume. Unfortunately, it would be a few weeks before Bermudez and his family would arrive in Bogota while he wound up his affairs in Louisiana, and my boss, Vice President for News H.L. "Steve" Stevenson told me to monitor local reaction to the announcement.

The reaction wasn't as positive as Stevenson had hoped. A friend in the Colombian media put it this way: "We can't believe UPI can't find anyone better than the son of the prince of the homosexual community." Apparently, Rafael's father, Mario Bermudez, had come out of the closet as gay after fathering Rafael and his siblings, and had become a lord protector of the gay community in the country. Unfortunately, that had not endeared him to the local press lords with whom his son would have to deal as UPI bureau chief.

Stevenson asked me if I believed the rumors. I said I had no way of knowing. "Well, find out then," Steve said. "Get yourself invited to this guy's house. Check out who he is and if it even matters if his son becomes our bureau chief. You know, the sins of the fathers shall not be visited upon the children."

I had a friendly conversation with Ralph Bermudez's mother, Mario's wife. We laughed a little. She said she was sorry about my misfortune of being expelled from the country, but they were glad because the whole incident allowed them to be reunited with their son. We hit it off, and she invited me to their house the following Sunday for a midday meal. The house was an incredible mansion that would be worth millions in any American city. Old man Mario Bermudez was there, as was his wife, and I believe two younger women were Ralph's sisters. The father had worked in New Orleans for a number of years, where his three children grew up, and then retired back to Bogota, taking his wife and two daughters with him, but leaving Rafael (my designated successor) there. Mario looked like a family man, surrounded by his wife and some of his children, not at all like the "prince of the homosexuals." He appeared to be quite old and seemed to walk with some difficulty.

After a great meal, the women and the men separated. Mario Bermudez invited me into his library for an after-dinner drink. He felt very comfortable with me and seemed impressed that I had learned to speak Spanish like a native. My eye happened to fall on the spine of the book, American Grotesque, the account of the Clay Shaw-Jim Garrison affair by James Kirkwood, Jr., a book extremely sympathetic to Shaw that ridiculed Garrison for having brought the case against him. I picked it up and saw a dedication on the title page:

"To my best friend in the world"—signed Clay Shaw.

"So you knew Clay Shaw?" I asked.

"I worked for him for many years," Mario replied. "He was my friend and my boss. After that, I was the security chief for the International Trade Mart in New Orleans."

I didn't say anything about my dealings with Jim Garrison's staff. If he was Clay Shaw's best friend, Garrison was not likely to be a popular name in the Bermudez household. I simply said something to the effect that it must have been challenging to go through the trial. Then he said something that chilled me to the bone.

"Yes, it was," he said. "Jim Garrison tried hard to prove the connection between Clay Shaw and Lee Harvey Oswald, but he never could. That was because Clay never dealt with Oswald directly. He had me do that—I ran Oswald for him." He had slipped into English then, perhaps remembering dealings in New Orleans that took place in English, and he definitely used the word "run" in the sense that spymasters use for "running" their agents.

The implications of what he had said were staggering. It meant the American intelligence services (the CIA or the FBI—it wasn't till later that the FBI's counter-intelligence service became the only intelligence agency that could conduct operations on U.S. soil) had much closer ties to Oswald, and probably to Clay Shaw, than they had ever revealed, either to the Warren Commission or to the New Orleans DA office. In his quasi-documentary, JFK, film director Oliver Stone contends that the assassination resulted from a vast conspiracy of shadowy elements of U.S. intelligence and military services. The Vietnam War colored Stone's views, and he believes Kennedy was about to pull the plug on the war, while the U.S. military wanted to continue it.

The movie did have some fascinating snippets, such as the fact that Oswald had operated as a provocateur out of two sides of the same building on a street corner in the French Quarter of New Orleans. One day he distributed pro-Cuba leaflets telling the U.S. to keep its hands off Castro's Communist Cuba. The next day he would distribute different leaflets purportedly from a far-right organization urging the overthrow of the Communist government in Cuba. The leaflets had different addresses, but they were on two sides of the same building. Those kinds of operations were typical in intelligence. They would see who would show any interest in either cause and decide where they would lead with surveillance. Mario Bermudez said he had contact with Oswald as he was handing out leaflets on a sidewalk in New Orleans around the International Trade Mart building.

Mario was never interviewed by either the Warren Commission or Jim Garrison's staff. What he told me represented a whole new revelation, but what was I going to do with it? Almost ten years earlier, I had resolved not to get involved in Kennedy assassination matters anymore. Too many people on the fringes of it had died—I did not want to be next, and in a country like Colombia, people disappeared all the time without a trace. All official branches of the U.S. government still clung to the conclusion of the Warren Commission about one lone nut with no known ties to foreign or domestic organizations. I knew no one in a position of authority would be willing to listen to any more conspiracy theories. Eventually I decided to ignore it and get on with my life. New circumstances, however, never quite allowed me to do that.

In 1983 I made a series of trips to Havana to meet with President Fidel Castro. The previous year my employer, UPI, had changed ownership. The Scripps family trust sold it to two young entrepreneurs, Doug Ruhe and Bill Geissler, who had served a year in federal prison for refusing to be drafted to go to what he considered the illegal and immoral war in Vietnam. I knew one place where that would be regarded as a badge of honor. I had the idea that maybe it was time to see if we could break through the sugar cane curtain that separated the U.S. and Cuba. Castro had kicked all American news media out of Cuba in 1969, but it would be a real feather in our cap if UPI would be the first American news outlet to be let back into Cuba. Geissler enthusiastically embraced my idea.

I was based back in Mexico City as UPI Vice President for Mexico, Central America, and the Caribbean. I told the press department of the Ministry of Foreign Affairs in Havana that the new co-owner of UPI, who had done a year in prison for refusing to be drafted for Vietnam, would like to make a visit to Cuba, perhaps meeting with President Castro, and talking about reopening relations. Geissler and I were invited to Havana to attend the New Year's celebrations commemorating the anniversary of the Jan. 1, 1959, date when Castro had taken power in Cuba after dictator Fulgencio Batista had fled.

On the last day of our visit to Havana, Fidel came to see us in the seaside bungalow outside Havana, where they had put us up. Fidel arrived late, around 10 p.m., and stayed late, till about 4 a.m. We solved all the world's problems, touching upon most current world situations, and somehow the Kennedy assassination came up. We did bring up the fact that among the various conspiracy theories being advanced was one that he, Castro himself, had ordered the assassination in retaliation for the 1962 attempted overthrow of the Castro regime in the failed Bay of Pigs invasion. Castro reacted indignantly, saying that of all the things he had been blamed for, that was the worst. He did note that it had been revealed that the American CIA had tried to assassinate him several times, in bizarre plots involving an exploding cigar or a drug to make his beard fall out. He vowed that he had never retaliated. He said he liked Kennedy, and he thought the Bay of Pigs incident had been a case of far-right elements in the American government freelancing by themselves. He praised Kennedy for withdrawing support once he found out about it. He didn't seem bitter, either, about Kennedy having forced the Russians to withdraw their nuclear missiles from his island—he was much more critical of the Russians than of the Americans over the Cuban missile crisis. In general, he said he always had like Democratic presidents of the U.S. much more than the Republicans.

I eventually became President & CEO of UPI in 1990 after a whirlwind series of ownership changes. Finally, I had enough trouble keeping the company afloat against external and internal foes, so the last thing in the world I was thinking about was the Kennedy assassination. But one afternoon after I had returned from an appointment, my Vice President for Communications, Milt Capps, followed me into my office and closed the door behind him.

"Pieter, you'd better tell me what you have to do with the Kennedy assassination," he said. "You're now the face of UPI, and if your name is going to be all over the press in new revelations about the Kennedy assassination, I'd better know about it."

"Oh, no, not again," I said as I sank into my chair. "I'm trying to forget about that whole thing." Milt had intercepted a call from a man in Vancouver, Canada, who wanted to ask me about the Kennedy assassination. Capps urged me to call the guy back (I don't remember his name) and help him, but I was reluctant. I just didn't want to get dragged into the whole thing again. Besides, Kennedy assassination conspiracy theorists included so many kooks—and I wanted nothing more to do with them. Capps and I finally settled on a compromise. In 1984 a private institute had been founded in Washington, D.C., funded by public donations, the Assassination Archives & Research Center (AARC), to act as a repository for all legitimate information on the assassinations of John F. Kennedy as well as his brother, Bobby. The AARC was serious about separating the wheat from the chaff, the crazy, far-out conspiracy theorists. The archives started with new information unearthed by the House Select Committee on Assassinations that had re-investigated the Kennedy assassination.

Capps and I decided to ask the AARC Director, a well-known Washington lawyer named Bernard "Bud" Fensterwald, whether he had ever heard of this guy in Vancouver and whether he thought I should talk to him. If he recommended I speak to him, I would return his call. Fensterwald was a heavy hitter, having represented some notorious figures in significant political cases, like James Earl Ray, the guy hired to kill Martin Luther King Jr., as well as chief Watergate burglar James McCord. Fensterwald and I had a nice conversation, and he listened with great interest as I described my earlier peripheral involvements with the case, and he immediately recognized the name of the guy in Vancouver and strongly urged me to talk to him.

So I did return the call from Vancouver. The man had come across my name in newspaper clippings of Giesbrecht overhearing Kennedy conspiracy talk at the Winnipeg airport. Giesbrecht had died in the meantime, and the Vancouver sleuth wanted to see if I remembered any additional details. He tried some names on me of other figures in the supposed plot with descriptions of what they looked like to see if Giesbrecht had mentioned them in his airport meeting. Nothing, however, clicked.

A couple of days later, Milt Capps was waiting for me again when I arrived at the UPI office one April morning in 1991. He followed me into my office and closed the door behind him, carrying that morning's Washington Post, open to the obituary page. There was the story. Bernard "Bud" Fensterwald had died of a sudden heart attack at his home in Alexandria, VA, at 69. We were both shocked. I had just talked to the man a couple of days earlier. There was nothing wrong with him at the time.

"Now, do you see why I didn't want to get involved with the case all over again?" I finally asked Milt. "This is the kind of thing that seems to happen inevitably. People suddenly turn up dead. I don't want to be next on the list. I don't want anything more to do with it."

But it would not leave me alone. Early in 1992, I found myself in London, England, several times, trying to straighten out the many problems UPI had in Europe, Middle East, and Africa division. UPI was operating at the time under bankruptcy protection in a Chapter 11 reorganization, awaiting a cash infusion from a new owner. To relieve financial pressures in Europe, I decided to try something similar in the U.K., although bankruptcy laws were different. There was no Chapter 11 reorganization under British law, but I could try to negotiate a voluntary agreement with principal creditors to suspend payments on old debts until the sale of the company and pay only current charges going forward. Our main creditor was the British telecommunications authority, and at a meeting with some of their senior people, they were amenable to temporarily suspend payment on old debts to give us breathing room. It almost sounded like they were proud to do their bit to preserve freedom of the press, and the meeting appeared to be over.

"So who killed Kennedy then?" the lead British telecom official suddenly blurted out. I sat there dumbfounded, not knowing what to say. Why would that man out of the blue ask me that? Could he possibly know something about my (very reluctant) involvement? It turned out he didn't. It was just a subject that had intrigued him over time, and he wanted to take advantage of being with a prominent American journalist to get my view on the matter.

I begged off, saying that I had done some inconclusive investigations, which would take too long to explain. I promised that at any future meeting, we might be able to talk about more, but that in any event, I had no definitive answers about who killed Kennedy. He let it go at that. It was just another weird coincidence how the Kennedy assassination kept raising its head. It was uncanny how it would not leave me alone.

I sold UPI off to the brother-in-law of the then King of Saudi Arabia in a bankruptcy court auction later in 1992, and two years later started working for Progressive Business Publications in the suburbs of Philadelphia, where I soon became Editorial Director in charge of some 40 business newsletters. I thought I was out of the news game once and for all, and I thought I'd been able to leave the Kennedy assassination stuff behind me for good. But it was not to be.

Sometime in 2010, I got a call out of the blue from Donald H. Carpenter from Tennessee, a retired law enforcement official who had become an author and published a couple of books. Carpenter's latest book project was a biography of the late Clay Shaw, the only man ever to be formally accused of a plot to assassinate John F. Kennedy. Carpenter had been given access to old paper files of the New Orleans District Attorney's office on the Garrison investigation, and in those files, my name figured as a friendly foreign journalist pretty good at chasing down loose ends on Shaw's international connections. Carpenter wanted to see if I could tell him anymore. My memory was somewhat refreshed when he read me details of my efforts from the files. Carpenter did not appear to have a particular ax to grind. He simply felt that biographers or historians had not sufficiently explored the mysterious figure of Clay Shaw.

I decided Carpenter's book project was worthwhile, but the only thing I could add was my meeting with Mario Bermudez, in Bogota, Colombia, in 1976, seven years after Shaw's trial and acquittal. I had not reported that meeting to anyone, and in view of the ignominious demise of the Garrison investigation, no one else had appeared to be interested. Mario Bermudez had not been on Carpenter's radar screen in his research, even though I told him Bermudez might have been more important than he had realized. I told him Bermudez had encountered Lee Harvey Oswald handing out pro- and anti-Cuba leaflets on the sidewalk outside the International Trade Mart building. I related Bermudez's admission to me that he, and not Shaw, had run Oswald as an agent. Carpenter sounded incredulous. It did not fit with whatever else he had found out about Clay Shaw, and I had the distinct impression he did not believe me. I don't care. I know what I heard. Mario Bermudez was long dead by then, but I did point Carpenter to Ralph Bermudez, his son then running a P.R. firm in Baton Rouge, LA. I also knew Ralph would say he knew nothing about his father's work in New Orleans.

Carpenter's book was finally published in 2014, *Man of a Million Fragments: The True Story of Clay Shaw*. It wasn't a great seller and never had a second printing. I didn't buy it because I didn't think I'd learn anything new, and I didn't want to get involved all over again. Once again, I was hoping I would be able to put the JFK stuff behind me, but not quite.

In the spring of 2013, I got a call out of the blue at my office in the Philadelphia suburbs asking me about the Kennedy assassination, this time from a guy named Jason in Boise, Idaho. He was also writing a book about a possible JFK plot, and he had run across my name in old archives, and he wanted to talk to me. I was mildly curious—what's one more?—and I told him he was in luck. It just so happened that my better half Christine and I were planning a trip to Boise for a Davis Cup tennis match between the U.S. and Serbia. I had to be in Las Vegas for a business conference in the days immediately preceding the Davis Cup, and as long as we were out West, it seemed like a shame not to take in the tennis in Boise. Who would ever think that Boise could figure in an ongoing saga about the Kennedy assassination?

So as unlikely as that scenario appeared to be, there we were in Boise, Idaho, on Sunday after the Davis Cup matches were over, meeting Jason at a local coffee shop. I wouldn't say we hit it off. He said he was a "Christian" author, whatever that meant. He had an idea for a book in which the central figure, a reporter, would be investigating some loose ends in the Kennedy assassination, and some strange things kept happening to this guy. The central figure in the book, which would be fiction, could be someone like me. He wanted to get a good look at me to have a model for the central character. I wasn't sure that I wanted to collaborate with such a project, so I didn't tell him too much. Finally, he begged off, and I never heard from him again. Of all the things that happened to me over the years with Kennedy assassination events, the side trip to Boise was one of the weirdest.

In mid-May 2013, I had to go to Dallas, Texas, for a business conference. Christine had never been to the Dallas-Fort Worth area, so at the end of the conference, she flew out to Dallas for the weekend. I took her to Dealey Plaza, the site where JFK was shot. I had been there several times, but it is always a chilling experience. We stood at the spot where the motorcade had made the turn to head for the railroad underpass where he was shot. We stood on the grassy knoll, and of course, we gawked up at the 6th floor of the Texas School Book Depository building, from where Oswald had fired his rifle. We struck up a conversation with a guy from Montana who looked at the spot in the road where Kennedy was shot, then up at the 6th floor of the building and to the grassy knoll just in front of where JFK's limo had been when the fatal shots were fired.

"There's no way. I'm a good shot myself, but there's no way I could hit a moving target from way up there with such accuracy to hit him right in the head. If you wanted to make sure you got him, this is the place to fire from, right in front of him as the motorcade is coming toward you, just a short distance away," he said, pointing to the infamous grassy knoll, from where many eyewitnesses said they saw and heard shots being fired. The Warren Commission dismissed that testimony as coming from confused people. The sharpshooter from Montana sort of summed it all up for us—there's no way Oswald could have been the lone assassin.

Even though I had stopped actively investigating the Kennedy assassination, I could never entirely forget about it. I kept hoping the truth would eventually come out. I had pinned my hopes on Donald

Trump. I despised the man for his misogyny and xenophobia, but there was one campaign promise I actually liked. If he became President, Trump had promised he'd order some Kennedy assassination documents unsealed to let people know what the government had been keeping a secret for so long. After its latest investigations ended in 1992, Congress had ordered some documents sealed for 25 years, but that 25-year period was up in early in 2017, right after Trump's inauguration. I always assumed the documents dealt with Kennedy's extramarital affairs. It made sense that the Warren Commission would want to spare the Kennedy family that embarrassment. By 2017, only his daughter Caroline was still alive, and what were we still trying to protect? The stuff about Kennedy's women had already come out.

To my chagrin, Trump reversed himself. After hearing objections from the CIA and the FBI, he somewhat reluctantly agreed with them that there were still overriding national security considerations to keep the files sealed. Trump's reversal—and the reasons he gave—spoke volumes. The CIA and the FBI still don't want the truth out. The agencies had never fully revealed the ties they had to Lee Harvey Oswald and likely other figures around the assassination drama. They knew a lot more than they let on; they have kept their secrets all these years, and they intend to keep them even longer.

Will we ever find out the truth? I doubt it. If there was a plot, most people involved in it are surely dead by now, but I'm convinced there still are documents somewhere that could shed light on the affair. In any event, I'm out of it. Sure, I'm curious, and I would still like to know the truth. But I value my peace too much to get involved all over again. So let someone else do it.

I do, sort of, have a theory, but I can't prove anything. Two important facts are that both the FBI and the CIA knew a lot more about Lee Harvey Oswald than what they provided to the Warren Commission. Weeks before the assassination, Oswald made a bus trip from Dallas to Mexico City, where he visited both the Cuban and the Soviet embassies. Apparently, Oswald still was—or pretended to be, at someone's behest—a devoted Marxist, even though he had found life in the Soviet Union too stifling. At that time, he supposedly thought that Fidel Castro's new brand of revolution in Cuba might be something for him. So he applied for a visa to Cuba, and when they didn't immediately accept him, he also went to the Soviet embassy in Mexico City to have them vouch that he was a true Marxist and had loyally served the Soviet workers' cause during his years in Minsk, where he had married his wife, Marina. It seems that he was finally told "no" by the Cubans because Kennedy's support for the anti-Castro Cuban exile movement made it impossible to admit Americans to Cuba. Enraged by the refusal, Oswald supposedly left the Cuban embassy yelling, "I'm going to kill that guy Kennedy!"

The CIA knew this but never told anyone, least of all the U.S. Secret Service before Kennedy's visit to Dallas or the Warren Commission after the assassination. The CIA had a reason for withholding this information because they had both the Cuban and Soviet embassies in Mexico City under surveillance. They were afraid that by revealing the information about Oswald, they would admit they had the embassies bugged, something they did not want their Cold War enemies to know. Actually, neither the Russians nor the Cubans wanted Kennedy assassinated, least of all by an unreliable agent like Oswald, but they didn't tip off the Americans to watch him because they knew the CIA had wiretapped their embassies. So they thought there was no need to tell the Americans because they already knew. They didn't want the Americans to know that they knew they'd been bugged—such is the world of spydom.

Both the FBI and the CIA knew that as a Dallas resident, Oswald was a clear and present danger to Kennedy during his visit there, but neither organization told the Secret Service. Was this merely a question of misguided zeal to protect their own secrets (the sources of their information), or was it a case of failure to connect the dots? Or was there something more nefarious going on? Did the CIA and the FBI know that an attempt was probably going to be made on the life of John F. Kennedy, and did they let it happen, knowing that they'd be in the clear because a convenient scapegoat named Lee Harvey Oswald would be caught and would be blamed as the lone deranged killer—and that he would probably be killed himself before saying anything except that he was "just a patsy" in this drama?

Neither the CIA nor the FBI lacked a motive. J. Edgar Hoover, at the head of the FBI, despised Bobby Kennedy, who was nominally his boss, and Hoover didn't have much use for Jack, either. And the CIA was ramping up its involvement in Southeast Asia and wanted to have its little Vietnam War, a nice proxy war with the world's two Communist superpowers, the USSR and Communist China. Oliver Stone may turn out to be partly right that Kennedy was killed because he was about to pull the plug on America's involvement in Vietnam. If the FBI and the CIA decided to let Oswald go ahead, be the primary shooter and let himself get caught, perhaps they decided that they couldn't put all their eggs into that one rather unreliable basket. Just to make sure, they put a sharpshooter on the grassy knoll to finish off the job or help out in case Oswald missed.

Some of the details I ran across over the years do fit with that picture, although I can't prove any of it. David Ferrie, who moved in Cuban exile circles in New Orleans, was a getaway pilot for someone out of Dallas, perhaps for the backup shooter from the grassy knoll, and was overheard talking about it at the Winnipeg airport by Richard Giesbrecht.

And how does Clay Shaw fit into this? He had many international connections both as Director of the International Trade Mart in New Orleans and as the kingpin in a worldwide homosexual ring. The CIA wasn't above using someone with such contacts to keep tabs on lots of stuff. The CIA over the years used lots of anti-Castro Cubans for dirty jobs in the U.S. and elsewhere. Oswald dabbled in Cuban affairs in New Orleans, either trying to pretend to be a pro-Cuban agent and infiltrating anti-Castro groups or vice versa. In this shadowy world, sometimes you don't know who's who. It all sort of fits together, but let someone else find the truth. I'm out of it—and don't want to get back in.

After more than 50 years in the information business, Pieter retired to Vero Beach, Florida, in 2013. However, he keeps his name in the writing business with a weekly syndicated bridge column. In one of his better moves, he is now living with his former bridge partner, Christine Matus, who has managed to ground the flying Dutchman with a combination of kindness, charity understanding, and the knowledge that she has more Masterpoints in the American Contract Bridge League.

Honeymooning with Frank and Mia

I never met Frank Sinatra or Mia Farrow, so I was not surprised that I did not receive a wedding invitation when they married in 1966. Mia was 21 and Frank 50, already divorced from his first wife, Nancy, and second wife, Ava Gardner. However, I did have an experience with the newlyweds as they celebrated their honeymoon with a yachting trip throughout New England.

It was a July afternoon, and I had just ordered lunch with my friend Wayne Muller at one of my favorite restaurants, the Griswold Inn in Essex, Connecticut. Bill Winterer, the owner, was a good friend. Unfortunately, the service was a lot slower than usual, and just as I was about to complain, the waiter approached. He had a big smile on his face as he explained that Frank Sinatra and his wedding party would be coming into the room shortly.

"Fine, but what does that have to do with our lunch?" I asked.

"You have to move to the main dining room," the waiter said. "Mr. Sinatra wants this whole room."

"How many are in the wedding party?" I asked.

"I understand about 20."

"This room seats at least 100. We will move to the last table in the back. If Sinatra doesn't bother us, we won't bother him." The waiter left, and the next voice we heard was from the innkeeper, Bill Winterer. "Ken, please. move into the other dining room, and lunch is on me."

"I buy my own lunch, Bill. You know I always sit in this room. I'm not moving for some crooner. Besides, he divorced a woman I have loved for many years—Ava Gardner."

Bill begged me to move for the next few minutes. When I persisted, he finally had my table carried out by two large waiters. It was made clear that I would be moved, one way or another.

"Okay," I finally said to Bill. "But this is the last time I will ever come to this joint."

As we were leaving, Sinatra and his group came through the door. I'm sure he had been told about the reluctant guest. We glared at each other as I walked past his table.

Bill Winterer called me the next week and offered to buy me dinner.

I hung up on him. About two years later, after many phone calls and letters, I finally went back to the Griswold Inn. Bill was a good guy, and we later served together on the Board of the Ivoryton Playhouse. We never mentioned Sinatra again.

I caught Sinatra's appearance in Atlantic City in the 1980s. He had just gone through an incident where a Los Vegas bouncer punched him in the mouth, requiring surgery. Whether it was due to a missing tooth or a sore jaw, his performance was awful. Fortunately, I also attended "The Main Event" in Manhattan, and Frank was terrific.

When I lived in Manhattan in the 1960s, I met Mario Puzo through a writing group. He was working for the post office at the time, supporting his large family as he tried to develop a writing career. Like me, he wrote for a bunch of magazines with titles like "True Action," "Male," and "Swank." I can still remember when Mario told us that he had been asked to expand the Mafia story he had introduced in *The Fortunate Pilgrim*. It became *The Godfather*.

It had been ru mored that Sinatra had connections to organized crime, which allowed him to break a contract through the threat of violence. Nevertheless, Sinatra won an Oscar for his performance in *From Here to Eternity*. In Puzo's book, singer Johnny Fontane's career is helped by his connection to Vito Corelone, the Godfather.

Frank Sinatra hated *The Godfather* and publicly voiced his opinion. One night, Sinatra and Puzo were dining at the same restaurant in Beverly Hills. A mutual friend escorted Puzo to Sinatra's table for an introduction. Sinatra refused to look up from his plate and, instead, shouted a string of obscenities at the retreating Puzo.

Later, Puzo wrote about the meeting. "What hurt was that here he was, a northern Italian, threatening me, a southern Italian, with physical violence. This was roughly equivalent to Einstein pulling a knife on Al Capone. It just wasn't done. Northern Italians never mess with Southern Italians except to put them in jail or get them deported to some desert island."

The story reinforced my earlier feelings about Sinatra. He was a great singer who misbehaved in public, especially in restaurants.

Fraud and Theft

An ad from Foxwoods Casino, the resort and gambling center in Mashantucket, CT, promises, "We know you will find a lucky machine or discover one of your own in our 3500 machines. Have a seat and find out why slot play is better at Foxwoods."

This invitation may have enticed Yvonne Bell, a tax collector for nearby Ledyard, to leave town hall on a Friday in 1997 with a deposit and go directly to Foxwoods without stopping at the bank. She lost all of her own money and then used the bank deposit still in her purse. The more Bell played the slots over the next year, the more she tapped into taxpayer funds. By the time she was caught, Bell had embezzled $302,587 from Ledyard taxpayers.

The incident reminded me of a personal experience I had while working as the Editorial Director for a division of Prentice-Hall in Waterford, CT. I'm changing the names of the people involved because some of them are still living, and I don't want to embarrass anyone. The story began when an employee from the accounting department came to me with a question. She had received a call from Prentice Hall headquarters in New Jersey concerning a mistake on an invoice. Any invoice over $15,000 was paid from headquarters. There was no telephone listing for the company located in Groton, CT.

I told her to check with Fred H., the assistant treasurer who handled all invoices. She explained that Fred was on vacation, and the treasurer was out sick. Now I didn't want to do anything that would upset Fred. We had a bit of a sensitive issue concerning my expense accounts. Let me begin by saying I never misappropriated a dime from any of my expense accounts. But I had to get a little creative to make sure I did not have to dip into my pocket.

The co-founder of Prentice-Hall, Richard Ettinger, was rumored to have the first dime that he ever made. Ettinger had personally written the guidelines for expense accounts that put a ceiling on the "entertainment" for each guest. It probably worked out for the timeframe he wrote it in (shortly after the Civil War), but it fell far short of today's restaurant prices. Fred and I had some serious battles when I turned in an expense account after entertaining a couple of professors (and sometimes their wives) in a Manhattan restaurant. Then I discovered an attractive solution. Fred did not care about the check's total amount as long as it met the individual limit. So if I entertained two people, I would add two more to reach the per-person goal. I would take a couple of names off the roster of the people attending the conference I was covering. But it was essential that I maintain a good relationship with Fred so my plan could not be detected. Fred was impressed that I could get a table for ten at a busy New York restaurant. There were four of us that night.

Fred was also a decent guy, active in his church, and a great father to his teenage son. He didn't drink or smoke and was also the local scoutmaster. So we didn't have much in common. Shortly after I said that we would have to await Fred's return, my phone rang. It was from George Costello, Executive Vice President of Prentice-Hall. "Ken, we have a serious situation here. Invoices in the amount of over $400,000 have been paid to this company over the last few years. There is no telephone listing for that company. Get over to Groton and check it out."

I left with my assistant, Wayne Muller, and we drove directly to the Groton address. It was an empty storefront that looked unoccupied for a long time. I called George back, and he had more news for me. A New London law firm lawyer had called to set up a meeting in Waterford for the next day. George told me to sit in on the meeting with Dave Silberstein, our company president. He also said that the "old man" Richard Prentice Ettinger, co-founder of P-H, wanted Fred put in jail. I reminded George that we had just published a book, *How to Prevent Fraud and Theft in Industry*. "What would it do to our image if this story came out that we had been ripped off by one of our employees?" There was a long pause, then George agreed. "We won't prosecute if all of the money is returned. But it will be up to the bonding company to make a final decision."

Fred came in the following day with his lawyer, and he sat starring at the floor throughout the meeting. Fred would return the money immediately if we agreed not to prosecute, his attorney said. Dave Silberstein explained that the final decision about prosecuting would come from the bonding company. After the meeting, Dave told me to negotiate with the bonding company.

My initial conversation with a representative of the bonding company was not fruitful. He said his company intended to make an example of Fred. I asked to speak to his boss, who took a different position when I explained that all of the money would be returned immediately if no prosecution would occur. He agreed.

A few months after Fred was fired, I got word that he suffered a heart attack. He was only 42, and I was convinced that stress had caused the illness. I tried to see him, but his wife said he was not ready to see any of his former associates. She also thanked me for a letter I had sent to Fred right after he left. In that letter, I confessed my expense account scheme. I guess I was trying to convince him that we all have a little larceny in our hearts. I asked her to have Fred call me when he felt up to it.

A few weeks later, I called Fred, and we had lunch. I asked what he planned to do. "I would like to stay in this area," he said. "But I don't know if I can find a job." That same night I played doubles at a tennis facility located in Waterford. After the game, I asked one of the players, the president of a local company, if he had any openings in his accounting department. It turns out that his treasurer, who had been with the company for more than 40 years, had announced his retirement that week. I explained Fred's qualifications, a C.P.A. with more than 15 years of experience. "Send him in to see me," my friend said. "There is one other little piece of information you should have," I said. Then I explained the circumstances of Fred's dismissal.

My friend stared at me in disbelief. "We're a small company," he said. "An embezzlement like that would put us out of business."

"I'm going to make you a promise," I said. "Fred will never steal another dime."

"Did he tell you that?" he asked. "And why did he steal the money in the first place?

"I have no idea why he stole the money because I never asked him. And no, he didn't make any promises about future honesty. I'm convinced that he will never repeat that mistake."

"Send him in to see me," my friend said. "But I'm not making any promises."

A few days later, Fred called and told me he got the job. We continued to have lunch occasionally, and I was delighted by Fred's progress on the job. Within a few years, he was named treasurer. My tennis friend also thanked me over the years, saying that Fred had become a key employee.

I left P-H for Manhattan that next year and never saw Fred again. My friend, Wayne Muller, who had succeeded me at P-H, called to tell me that Fred had died of a heart attack. I went to the wake, and one of the first people who greeted me was Fred's boss, my former tennis friend. I will never forget what he said that night.

"I still don't know how you knew it," he said. "But you were right about Fred. I would have trusted that guy with my life."

My Career as a Freelance Writer

In my early career as a freelance writer, I was paid by the word, an arrangement that motivated me to add as much extraneous language as possible. When I was writing for the detective story genre, victims never died quickly, even from a gunshot wound to the head. They lingered for four or five paragraphs as the word count mounted. Later I switched to knives, poisons, axes, and hatchets as my weapon of choice. They all lent themselves to long, involved exits. No characters were described without long introductions describing their physical characteristics and their feelings on subjects ranging from politics to love to murder. Chain saws were not available at that time, so I missed out on a slow and very profitable murder weapon. Some of my words fell victim to the editor's red pencil, but enough of them survived to make my writing efforts profitable.

My career in freelance writing began in San Antonio, TX, in 1955, my last year in the Air Force. I answered an ad from a greeting card company from Dallas looking for birthday card verse. I sent in three suggestions and received a check for $75 a week later. It began a very profitable relationship for me, and I was soon making more money from birthday verse than my military pay. A few months into the arrangement, the company owner, Selly Belosky, wrote and asked me to write some verse for sympathy cards. I was about to tell him that normal death was outside my area of expertise until he told me I could earn double—$50—for each accepted verse. Messages like "He is only away" made me enough money to buy a one-year-old Ford convertible which I drove to Rhode Island in 1955 after the year of my discharge from the Air Force.

After graduating from Providence College in 1959, I took a writing job with Federal Products in Providence, RI, the manufacturers of precision writing instruments. After a few weeks, I knew that writing technical ads about dial indicators was not a career I cared to pursue. I decided to return to the newspaper business as a reporter The Hartford Courant in Groton, CT. My penchant for overwriting did not get me off to a good start with Joe DiBona, the bureau chief. Joe had spent his entire life in the newspaper business and felt that a reporter's job was to tell the story in the fewest words possible. We repeatedly clashed in those early days, gently at first but more forcefully later. One day, it came to a head as Joe was editing one of my longer pieces with an introduction right out of *Gone With the Wind*.

"Dooley," he shouted across the newsroom. "The Greatest Story ever told: 'And Jesus wept.' Three words." Joe was a good guy and a great editor. His message finally got through to me, but we had another problem. He firmly believed that writers should get paid for their work. At the time, I was doing a lot of pro-bono work for nonprofits such as "Mothers Against Drunk Driving" and hospital fundraisers.

"Dooley," he said to me one day, "writing is like prostitution. First, you do it for fun, then you do it for friends, and finally, you do it for money. Money is the important thing."

I got a taste of my own medicine while working in the Old Saybrook bureau of *The Hartford Courant*. The paper had a number of "stringers" who covered many of the towns in the immediate area. The stories included "Grange" news, school lunch menus, and minutes of various organizations. My job was to edit the articles with the various stringers, who would place them for pick-up on the railroad station in Clinton, Connecticut.

"Ruth" was the stringer for Clinton, and she represented a daily challenge. I understood her motivation because she was paid by the length of her stories. She could turn the birth of a cow or a special night at the local VFW into a three-part story if given a chance.

After one particularly aggressive effort in which I cut Ruth's story by about 80 percent, she called me back with a problem. "I won't be able to put my story on the train today. Sorry."

I did not feel that circulation would drop the next day because of the absence of the Clinton column. Almost as an afterthought, I asked, "Why?"

"There was a major train wreck in Clinton a few minutes ago. An Amtrak train derailed, and I understand a couple of people were killed," Ruth said. "But the station is blocked off, and I won't be able to get my story on the train."

I called Hartford immediately, and reporters and photographers were sent to the scene. It was the front-page story in the newspaper the next day.

The state editor sent Ruth flowers and a note of thanks for reporting the train wreck immediately. I have a strong hunch that if I had not asked Ruth for an explanation, she never would have told me about the train wreck.

An event in 1985 brought back memories of one of my rejected freelance stories 30 years earlier. In what has been described as the most fantastic April Fool's Day joke ever, George: Plimpton wrote a story about a Met's prospect, Sidd Finch, who could throw a baseball 168 mph. The article was published in *Sports Illustrated* on April 1, 1985. It brought to mind a story I had written 30 years earlier about a baseball pitcher who threw a fastball at 105 mph. In rejecting the story, an editor had written in red ink, "Not physically possible to throw a fastball in that range." Apparently, the editors at *Sports Illustrated* were a little more liberal because no one questioned Finch's 168-mph fastball.

Good Stuff

In 1998 I went to work as Senior Editor for Progressive Business Publications in Malvern, PA. Ed Satell, the founder and CEO, called me into his office a few months later. He had an idea for a new publication that he thought I should write. It was to be a 24-page booklet filled with stories and quotes—nothing religious, political, or off-color. Most of my stories had always violated one or two of these rules and, in some cases, all three.

I asked Ed what he planned to call it. He said *Good Stuff*, a title I thought was worse than the idea. There was already a similar publication called *Bits & Pieces* that had been around for years. I wasn't thrilled with the idea and didn't expect it to have a long life. I had learned in publishing that it is not the person with the bad idea who gets blamed for the failure. It is usually the editor who tries to execute it.

Twenty-two years later, I'm still putting *Good Stuff* together. I don't say "write," because the material all comes from other sources. The quotes and stories come from Churchill, Lincoln, Kennedy, Reagan, friends, books, former girlfriends, and a few favorite bartenders. The fact that we still have subscribers looking forward to each issue is sometimes bewildering to me. I have written books, plays, and screenplays that never attracted the fan mail I have enjoyed from *Good Stuff*.

A few years ago, I was on a flight returning from a conference in California. It was one of those three-seat arrangements, and I sat next to a couple. The woman suddenly took a copy of *Good Stuff* out of her purse and began to read it to her husband. She read it loud enough for some of the other passengers to hear. There were chuckles and smiles throughout our part of the plane.

Some of the other passengers asked her for information on how they could subscribe. She explained that she showed a copy to her mother who liked it so much she ordered a subscription for herself. After things quieted down, I said in a low voice, "I put *Good Stuff* together each month." She turned to her husband and told him what I had said. He looked at me and said, "Oh sure," not in a positive tone. I think it embarrassed his wife, so the conversation ended there. As we were getting ready to land, I took out another copy of *Good Stuff* and asked the lady her first name. I signed "To Mary, best wishes." She handed it to her husband, who saw that my signature matched the one on the inside cover of the book. "I want to talk to you," he said as I grabbed my bag from the overhead compartment. "You already have," I answered and made a quick exit.

There were other stories involving *Good Stuff*. I used to get fan mail from people telling me how the publication helped them through an illness or even a death in the family. One of my favorites involved a woman whose husband was dying of cancer. She used to visit him in the intensive care unit and read him *Good Stuff* during his final days. She had just finished reading him one of the stories when he died with a smile on his face.

I received a letter from a minister who counseled death-row inmates in San Quentin in California. The one subscription he had didn't last long as it was passed from convict to convict. He wanted to know if I could offer him a discount for multiple copies. So I began to send him five complimentary copies each month. Unfortunately, he shared the story with other death-row ministers. Soon I was sending out free copies to prisons in Florida, Texas and a number of other states that still had the death penalty.

Finally, the Editorial Director, Pieter Van Bennekom, called me in and asked about all those free copies. When I told him the story, Pieter shook his head and laughed. "I can see some poor soul walking to his execution carrying a copy of *Good Stuff* instead of the Bible," Pieter said.

I received a letter from Bill Keane, creator of the comic strip "The Family Circus," one of my favorites. He said he frequently got ideas for his comic strip from *Good Stuff*. His letter included a drawing of one of his characters, which I still cherish. His son, Jeff, continues to write "The Family Circus" following Bill's death in 2011.

The following message is in each issue of *Good Stuff*.

Dear Reader:

Warning! This little magazine is addictive. It will make you laugh. It will make you think. Sometimes it will move you. But it will always inspire you.

Every four weeks, Good Stuff delivers quotes and anecdotes you can use immediately. I'm confident you'll find something in every issue that will help you communicate better, enjoy life more, and achieve greater success.

I guess our message resonates with our subscribers because we have a high renewal rate and are still sending out issues after 22 years.

The Sleepover

My daughter Alicia chose a sleepover to celebrate her fifth birthday. So I spent the weekend with 10 of her classmates from the Old Lyme public school. Each year, I would write a birthday story that involved everyone at the celebration. It was usually the high point of a weekend spent reading stories, playing games, or otherwise relating to five-year-olds. The children always loved it when they heard their names mentioned in the story.

Dealing with five-year-olds for two days did take its toll, especially on the Monday morning after the event. It took on added significance when it fell on one of the Mondays that I have to communicate to our Manhattan editorial office, a journey I had to make twice a month.

I took the Amtrak train from New Haven at 6:56 a.m., the day after the party. Although I recognized many of the faces as I took my seat, a strict code of silence was part of the ritual. These veteran commuters buried themselves in their newspapers or briefcases, never acknowledging their seating companions. I struggled into a seat, still groggy after about six hours of sleep over the weekend. My traveling companion was already into her *Wall Street Journal*, and no acknowledgments were exchanged. It was not the first time we had sat next to each other, but we observed the same rule—sit in silence throughout the trip.

I watched as the woman in front of me, not a member of our inner circle, tried to start up a conversation with one of our veteran commuters. His withering gaze shut her down completely. A silence descended on the whole coach as the transgressor sat uncomfortably. Then, suddenly, a train passed on the other track startling us all back to reality. I turned to my seat companion and asked, "Did that Choo-Choo startle you?"

More than 40 years later, I can still recall the shock on her face. I saw her look about the coach for another seat, but not one was available. She put her face into the *Wall Street Journal* and never said another word until we pulled into Grand Central Station. I thought of explaining about two days with five-year-olds but decided against it. I had violated the rules, and there was no going back. I did sit in silence on my return trip that night on the Choo-Choo.

A Tale of Two Hurricanes

I was in the third grade at Eden Park Grammar School when the Hurricane of 1938 devastated Rhode Island on Sep. 1, 1938. It had rained hard on the previous four days, but it was bright and sunny that morning when I left for school. Ships along its path signaled the presence of a hurricane, but weather forecasters thought it had turned out to sea. No satellites were peering down on us from orbit to give warning of severe storms. The hurricane struck without warning late that afternoon while I was in school. I'm sure Mrs. Pierce, the principal, felt like she was making the right decision when she sent us home in the middle of the storm. It would have been more prudent if she had gathered us in the basement of the school.

I walked with my friends Ray Murphy, Tom Barry, and Dick Bell, and my brothers, Bob and Larry, as we watched trees uprooted by the strong winds and electric cables sparkle as the poles supporting them toppled to the ground. Bob, who was in sixth grade and the oldest of the group, warned us to stay away from the wires, some of which blocked our path. He always made wise decisions, even at the age of 10, a talent he exhibited throughout his life. Ironically, Bob later worked for Narragansett Electric for more than 35 years.

The wind was so strong that we had trouble moving as a driving rain splattered on us. Suddenly my father's car appeared, and he crammed all the children into the car. There must have been 10 or 12 of us by then, packed liked sardines. He was able to drop my friends off before we returned home.

I remember my mother was upset because she couldn't get my grandmother or Uncle Leo on the phone. Vivid memories of trees toppling and the sound of debris hitting the house in 120 mph winds remain with me to this day. Not one student from Eden Park was killed or seriously injured that day. But scores of people in Watch Hill, Charlestown Beach, Green Hill, and Matunuck were swept to their deaths during the first 20 minutes of the hurricane.

Seven schoolchildren in Jamestown perished in a great wave as the bus driver struggled to get them to higher ground. Misquamicut Beach suffered 41 deaths, and another 18 died in Narragansett. Damage in Jerusalem, Galilee, and Bonnet Shores was extensive in the beach areas, with many homes washed into the sea.

Newport's Ocean Drive was destroyed, and the storm enveloped Sakonnet Point cottages, and 18 people died at Highland Park. None of the huge "cottages," built by affluent summer vacationers such as the Vanderbilts and Astors, suffered significant damage. Hundreds of workers were marooned in downtown Providence office buildings, where people threw ropes from second-story windows to stranded pedestrians. Bronze markers on buildings note the water level reached 14 feet above normal at the height of the storm.

The Great Hurricane of 1938 has gone down in history as one of the most destructive storms to hit New England, with Rhode Island suffering the most. It took days to reach the final death count of 262 lives lost, as 2000 houses were swept from their foundations and 899 boats were destroyed. In Watch Hill, Misquamicut, Quonochontaug, Charlestown Beach, Green Hill, and Matunuck, whole families were swept to their deaths, all within a span of 20 minutes. Ten women attending a church social in Misquamicut perished when waves engulfed their cottage.

My friend Bill Considine's mother, Lillian, was stranded for two days in downtown Providence without being able to get in touch with her family. I don't recall how long we were without power, but I can still remember my mother boiling water on the stove for days.

I didn't understand the full force of the storm until my father drove us to Nausocket Beach, where we had a summer home. It had been lifted from its foundation and turned upside down. The following summer, we had a beach house at Buttonwoods, a scene of many of my fondest childhood memories. So, overall, the Dooley family suffered few losses in the 1938 storm. I was still in the United States Air Force, stationed at Kelly Field in San Antonio, TX, when Hurricane Carol hit Rhode Island on Aug. 31, 1954. In one hour, Carol destroyed thousands of homes, sank or damaged 2,000 boats and yachts, and leveled power and telephone lines throughout the state. It also cost the life of a good friend. One of my best friends growing up was Harry Grattage. Through Harry, I met Danny O'Brien, who was 15 at the time. Danny was one of those people everyone liked. A real good guy in every respect. We lost track of each other when we both went into the service during the Korean War. Later, Harry told me that Danny had become a Rhode Island State Trooper.

I had trouble getting through to my mother immediately after the storm. Telephone service was out for about a week. But my Uncle Leo sent me a telegram telling me that everyone in the family survived the storm. It was not until a week later that my mother told me that Hurricane Carol had taken a good friend.

Trooper O'Brien drowned in East Matunuck while warning residents to evacuate the area due to hazardous weather conditions from Hurricane Carol. He pushed a stalled car with two young boys across Potter Pond Bridge with his cruiser just before the bridge was blown away. When his cruiser stalled in the rising water, he radioed his barracks that he was abandoning his car and warning residents by foot. He went door-to-door, helping people in the increasingly urgent need to evacuate the area. A witness said he saw a giant wave crash over Danny and carry him out to sea, where he drowned. His body was found lying face down in debris near Post Road in the marsh in East Matunuck. The abandoned patrol car was found with just the siren sticking out of the water.

The morning of his death, Trooper O'Brien was sworn in for his second three-year enlistment in the Rhode Island State Police. He was 25 when he died. Colonel John Sheehan presented the State Police Service ribbon posthumously to him for "heroism displayed at the cost of his life while in the performance of his duty and engaged in the rescue of persons."

On May 24, 2012, 58 years after Hurricane Carol, the beach pavilion at East Matunuck State Beach was dedicated to the memory of Trooper O'Brien. I was living in Newport at the time, so I attended the event. One of the speakers was O'Brien's sister, Lois Cheney, and she told a "rest-of-the-story" tale. The parents of the two young boys reached out to inform her they had two grandsons, both named Daniel, in honor of her brother. Trooper Daniel O'Brien would have been proud.

America's Cup Hall of Fame

I grew up within walking distance of the Edgewood and Rhode Island Yacht Clubs in Edgewood, RI. Several of my friends, including Herb Browne, Gill Thorpe, Brad Boss, and Jack Swan, were avid sailors, but the Dooley family was more concerned about making mortgage payments than buying boats or yacht club memberships. Consequently, I never became a great sailor.

In 1991, I moved to Bristol, RI, and through my friends, Herb Browne and Tom Breslin, I was introduced to Halsey Herreshoff, grandson of Nathanael Herreshoff, builder of six America Cup Defenders. Halsey sailed on four America Cup Defenders as bowman, tactician, and navigator. He was also the founder of the Herreshoff Marine Museum in Bristol.

Halsey hired me to write and direct a documentary film based on the Herreshoff legacy. Later he offered me a job as a member of a capital campaign to enlarge the existing museum. I worked with a young man named Dave Guertin, who, almost 30 years later, is CEO of a successful fund-raising company.

Dave and I began to develop a list of prominent individuals, like Ted Turner, who had won the America's Cup in 1977 on Courageous, Ted Hood, who also won with Courageous in 1974, and Bill Koch, who won the Cup in 1992 on America.

We sent out many letters and brochures and made countless telephone calls, but the results were unimpressive. One morning Dave and I began to brainstorm some possible ideas to draw national attention to the museum. I said to Dave, "Why don't we establish the America's Cup Hall of Fame right here in Bristol." Dave thought it was a great idea, but initially, Halsey was less than enthusiastic. "The New York Yacht Club would never let us do it," Halsey said.

"The New York Yacht Club has a branch in Newport. It would certainly add to their prestige to have the America's Cup Hall of Fame within a few miles of their club," I said. "Your grandfather built the first great America's Cup Defenders right here in Bristol. It makes sense to establish the America's Cup Hall of Fame as part of his legacy," I argued. Halsey finally agreed to at least present the idea to members of the New York Yacht Club. We visited the New York Yacht Club in Manhattan, the first and last time I was ever there.

It was on that visit that I discovered the magic of the Herreshoff name. Members greeted Halsey like he was royalty, waiting in line to engage him in conversation. So I was not surprised when the New York Yacht Club gave its blessing to Halsey to establish the American's Cup Hall of Fame in Bristol.

We used the recently completed movie to announce our plans at Marble House in Newport in 1992, with more than 500 guests in attendance. Speakers included Gov. Bruce Sundlin and former America's Cup skippers Ted Hood, Bill Koch, and Rod Stevens, one of America's best-known sailors. Koch had just won the America's Cup with America a few months earlier.

Dave and I began to put together a list of potential large donors. Ted Turner was a prime candidate because of his wealth and the fact that he had won the America's Cup in 1977. Halsey was able to set up an interview with Turner, and we flew to his headquarters in Atlanta. I had some strange interviews in my life, but this has to go to the top of the list. When we finally were ushered into his office, Turner greeted us with a short but cryptic message. "I'm an environmentalist, and I don't ask you to contribute to my causes, so why should I contribute to yours? Besides, I hate what they're doing with the America's Cup these days. Spending millions of dollars for a boat race."

At this point, Turner put on an Indian headdress, picked up a hatchet, and began circling the desk while making threatening Indian war whoops. Turner was the owner of the Atlanta Braves, the reason he had the Indian headdress and hatchet in his office. I was now more concerned about escaping with my rapidly thinning hair than any possible donation. However, on the way out the door, Turner did agree to a $10,000 donation to cover our expenses.

A few months later, Turner showed up at the Herreshoff Marine Museum with his then-wife, Jane Fonda. Halsey and Ted got into deep conversations about some of the historic boats while Jane and I trailed them. I had heard all the talk about "Hanoi" Jane, but she was one of the most delightful people I have ever met. I told her about a speedboat at the museum that was a dead ringer for the one used in *On Golden Pond*, the movie she made with her father, Henry Fonda and Katharine Hepburn. I took her to the boat and her eyes filled with tears as she told me the story behind the film. She was estranged from her father when she saw the original play, *On Golden Pond*. She took an option on the play and brought it to her father and asked him to make the movie with her. He told her he would do it if she could get Katharine Hepburn to play his wife. The film resulted in three Academy awards for best male performance, Henry Fonda, best female performance, Katharine Hepburn, and best-adapted screenplay, Ernest Thompson.

Ted Turner was already a legend in my family long before he was inducted into the America's Cup Hall of Fame. He defeated the Australian challenger in a four-race sweep in September 1977. My nephew, Jeff Malone, a student at Northeastern, took a job as a bartender at the Black Pearl restaurant in Newport, about 100 feet from where the defender, *Courageous* and *Australia*, the challenger, were docked. Turner went to Jeff and two other bartenders who had been hired that day. He handed them an envelope with $5,000, told them to split it and make sure they took good care of his crew. The three bartenders never got to meet Ted's crew, because they quit the Black Pearl that same night.

After dealing with Turner, it was a pleasure to meet with a high-class individual like Charles Adams IV, son of Charles Adams III, who had defeated Sir Thomas Lipton's *Shamrock* while sailing *Resolute* in the 1920 America's Cup contest. Mr. Adams, chairman of Raytheon at the time of our meeting, spoke with such great respect about his father, a former Secretary of the Navy.

Moving from Charles Adams to Dennis Connor was a culture shock. Dennis Connor was the only person to have won the America's Cup four times as skipper, the first to lose the Cup, and the first to win it back. Conner's record as one of the greatest sailors in history speaks for itself. His off-the-water activities leave a lot to be desired, at least in my only experience with him.

I met him at a dinner hosted by the Herreshoff Marine Museum. When he rose to speak, it was apparent that he had already been over-served during cocktail hour. He began a long and rambling talk that seemed like it would never end. Paul Darling, best known as the America's Cup photographer, stepped forward to snap a few photos.

Connor screamed at Paul. "Get that fxxxing camera out of my face." Paul was humiliated and quickly left the tent.

At the time, I was seated at a table that included Louise Dainty Ball, about 22, beautiful, and Dennis Connor's finance. The morning after the dinner, I was standing with Halsey Herreshoff when Dennis Connor approached. When he got within ten feet, I said in a loud voice, "I really enjoyed meeting your daughter last night, Dennis." His face got a little red as he replied, "My fiancé, not my daughter."

Later, Halsey smiled and said, "You knew who she was, didn't you?

"Did you see what he did to Paul last night?" I replied.

Meanwhile, we moved on to target number 2—Bill Koch, who had spent more than $64 million dollars winning the 1992 America's Cup. Koch had told Dave Guertin how much he admired Larry Bird, one of the greatest basketball players of all time, and the legendary Red Auerbach, ranked as the best coach in the history of the National Basketball Association. Koch said he would love to bring his son to a Celtics game to meet them. Fortunately, I was in a position to make it happen. I called Red Auerbach and made the arrangements. Bill Koch was delighted as he snapped photos of his son standing with Larry Bird and Red Auerbach.

A few months later, I walked with Bill Koch to the tent where the first class of the America's Cup Hall of Fame was inducted. Bill told me that he planned to give one of the four boats he had built to defend the Cup to the new Hall of Fame. Before we got to the table, Halsey approached and welcomed Bill. At this point, Bill told Halsey about his planned donation of the boat. "We have too many boats right now," Halsey said. "We need money, not more boats."

Koch didn't reply, but his body language reflected his mood. When we were seated at the table, he turned to me and said, "So he doesn't want my boat. f--- him!" I explained that Halsey was nervous, there had been many logistic problems surrounding the first installation, and, of course, we would be delighted to have the boat.

When Bill made his acceptance speech, he mentioned Halsey's comment about the boat. However, he did give a $50,000 matching grant, about $450,000 less than what Dave and I expected. Halsey and I had an unpleasant exchange the next day, particularly after I quoted Bill Koch. I left the campaign that same day and moved from Bristol to Philadelphia a few months later.

Years later, I learned that the Board of Directors removed Halsey from his post as CEO of the Museum and Hall of Fame. I have no idea what prompted that decision. But I do know that Halsey was the heart and soul of the Museum and Hall of Fame. Without his presence, there is an emptiness that no outsider will ever fill.

After years of silence, Halsey and I reconnected through our mutual friends, Gail and Pat Conley. And yes, one of Bill Koch's boats is now prominently displayed at the museum.

A Man Named Owen

Owen was my first friend who owned a car. We met at La Salle Academy as sophomores and developed a friendship that lasted more than 50 years. He was from Fall River, MA, and drove to La Salle every day from the age of 16. His father was a physician and a prominent political figure in Fall River. The only time I ever saw Owen quiet and respectful was when I was a dinner guest at his home. Otherwise, Owen and I combined to keep our classmates in a constant state of laughter.

We stayed in touch those early years after graduating in 1949. Owen attended the University of Rhode Island, while I went to Providence College. I was in the United States Air Force in Germany when Owen got married. I visited him in Fall River after I returned to civilian life in 1955. Owen was teaching and coaching at De La Salle Academy in Newport at the time. We got together a few times, and Owen was then Chairman of the History Department at Tiverton High School. Later he told me that he had left teaching and was working for the City of Fall River.

We completely lost track of each other for the next 20 years. Then, I bumped into an old high school classmate in Providence in the 1990s, and he told me that Owen was in a federal prison in Danbury, CT, for allegedly taking a bribe. I was living in Old Lyme, CT, at the time, about 45 minutes from Danbury Prison. The following week I drove to Danbury Prison, went to the Visitor Center, and asked to see Owen. A guard noted that I was not on Owen's visiting list. I assured him that we were old friends, and Owen would be delighted to see me. He took my information and left for the prison. A few minutes later, he returned with the message that Owen didn't want to see me.

I guess I was a little hurt and stunned. Then reality set in—Owen didn't want to see me because he was embarrassed. So I wrote him a letter explaining that if the situation were reversed, I would see him. I also told him that only fortunate circumstances kept me from occupying a cell near him in Danbury. A letter arrived a few days later, and I was at Danbury that afternoon. Any worries I had about awkward moments disappeared in the first few minutes of our meeting. We discussed old times at La Salle and what some of our old friends were doing. The time passed quickly, and I left that meeting feeling that my old friend would handle the situation. After that, I saw him a couple of times a month until he finished his sentence.

Sadly, we lost contact again. A book I wrote about Red Auerbach, coach and president of the Boston Celtics, was published in 1991, and Owen called me about it. In 1999, I contacted him about our 50th reunion from La Salle Academy. I was living and working in Philadelphia, PA, at the time. He promised to get back to me, but that was our last conversation. He died in 2008, but I didn't learn about his death until a few years later.

After my first visit with Owen at Danbury Prison, my former wife asked, "Was he guilty?"

"I have no idea," I replied.

"You didn't ask him," she demanded.

"No. It would have been rude. Besides, we had more important issues to discuss."

So I have no idea about Owen's guilt or innocence. But there are many positives to remember about him. He was the founder of the New England Addiction Association of Fall River and later served as president of Steppingstone, an addict treatment center in Fall River. Those organizations helped thousands of addicted people return to useful lives. As an educator, he touched the lives of thousands of young people in Massachusetts and Rhode Island. As a friend, his memories will be with me forever.

HYPHENATION

The Americans With Disabilities Act (ADA) was passed in 1990, three years after the death of my brother Paul. He had been in a wheelchair for more than 20 years suffering from multiple sclerosis. There were certain aspects of the law that could have benefited Paul and me, especially handicapped parking.

I remember how difficult it was for me to find convenient parking when I drove Paul to acupuncture treatments in Brookline, MA. I would drop him in front of the clinic, then struggle to find a parking spot within 30 minutes of the treatment center. As a result, I have always had a soft spot for handicapped parking and have little patience for violators.

When I was living in Sarasota, FL, we had a post office right on site. There were two handicap spots out front. One morning as I exited the post office, a black Cadillac drove up and parked horizontally, taking up both handicap spots. A man of about 35 got out of the car and rushed to the door as I was exiting. I blocked his entrance as I starred at his vehicle.

"You can't park like that," I said.

"I'm only going to be a minute," he said.

"I don't care if you're going to be a second. Move the car," I ordered.

"Get out of my way," he responded. He was about five inches taller, 30 pounds heavier, and at least 30 years younger. But I wasn't going anywhere.

At this point, a small crowd gathered to watch the confrontation.

He moved quickly and went around me to enter the post office. He was out just as quickly when the postal worker refused to wait on him. Meanwhile, I had moved to the back of his car and wrote down his license tag as he stormed out.

"Do you want my name, too?" he asked.

"Not necessary I replied. "But tell me—do you hyphenate ass-hole?"

The crowd laughed hysterically.

He ran up to me like he was going to get physical. Some of the people in the crowd reacted. I didn't. I saw something in his eyes that told me he was all bark and no bite. Maybe he saw something in mine that prompted him to back away and get in his car, a good decision on his part. I was feeling something about my brother Paul at that moment. I also remembered when I put a 6′ drunk on the ground after he took a swing at me. If he tried to get physical, he might have been able to qualify for a handicap spot in the future.

I Can Walk, I Can Talk, I Can Drive, I Can Die

I have moved many times in the past 40 years, from Connecticut to Rhode Island, to New York, to Pennsylvania, to Florida, and now Georgia. Many items have been lost along the way. One treasured trophy still sits on a table in my office. It is an old, ripped sneaker that has been preserved and placed on a wooden platform. An inscription reads, "To Ken Dooley for writing and directing, *I Can Walk, I Can Talk, I Can Drive, I Can Die*, from the Students Against Drunk Driving, April 26, 1981.

The backstory began a few months earlier when my friend, Earl Greenho, asked me for a favor. His sons, Jim and Brian, were part of a group of Old Lyme students who wanted to do a film for Students Against Drunk Driving (SADD).

He gave me a script that included crashing helicopters, speeding car crashes, and an assortment of very expensive stunts usually associated with big-budget Hollywood films. At the time, I was president of Madison Productions, a company specializing in documentaries.

I agreed to write and direct a film without the expensive scenes included in the first screenplay. I think some of the students were disappointed at first, but they quickly adjusted, and the experience was rewarding for all of us. The students even got permission from The Police to use "Every Breath You Take" as the theme song for the movie.

The students played most of the roles along with the actors I used in my documentaries. I reached out to Ed Dimeglio, a filmmaker from Johnston, RI, my collaborator on more than 50 documentary films, and he agreed to provide the camera and editing work at cost.

The main character is Jim, a good student, and athlete who hopes to follow in the footsteps of the Celtics great, Larry Bird. One night at a party where alcohol is served, Jim becomes drunk and a little belligerent when a friend tells him he shouldn't be driving. We shot the film at the home of Earl and Lynn Greenho. He leaves the party with his girlfriend, loses control of his car, and strikes a tree. Jim is killed instantly, and his girlfriend is seriously hurt and ends up in intensive care.

The entire town of Old Lyme participated in the film. The fire department and the rescue squad all played key roles. Dr. Bill Hostnik, my good friend and a great plastic surgeon, served as make-up man. Not even Alfred Hitchcock can boast of having a board-certified plastic surgeon in that role. We shot the final scene on Town Woods Road, a dead-end street surrounded by giant maple trees. We picked a suitable tree for the crash scene, and everything went well as we finished shooting at about 11 p.m.

The following day, I thanked Doug Maynard, the owner of a car repair and body shop in Old Lyme, who had donated the car used in the crash scene.

Before I could say anything, Doug asked me if I had heard anything about the other accident. He took me into the shop and showed me an MG with the engine pushed back into the passenger compartment. When I said it looked like people had been killed, Doug nodded and replied, "The driver was killed, and his girlfriend is in intensive care."

Then Doug hit me with the real bombshell. The car had struck a tree less than 20 yards from our simulated crash on the same street. The story made the front page of *The New York Times*.

The film was distributed to schools across the country with many positive reviews. It's hard for me to realize that these students are now in their fifties as I turn 90. I only hope they feel the same sense of accomplishment that I do, 40 years after the release date.

THE MAN WHO SAVED CHRYSLER AND THE STATUE OF LIBERTY

I had just completed writing *MBA:Management by Auerbach* in 1991, a book in which Red Auerbach adapted his basketball coaching skills to the business world. The final question from the publisher was whether we should have a prominent sports figure or a business leader write the Foreword. When I brought up the name of Lee Iacocca, Red practically jumped out of his chair. In 1979 Chrysler was on the verge of bankruptcy until Iacocca secured $1.5 billion in federal loan guarantees and turned the company around. He paid off the loan seven years early, resulting in a profit of $350 million for the federal government. In 1980, President Ronald Reagan asked Iacocca to undertake a fundraising effort to restore the Statue of Liberty and Ellis Island. There was no question that Iacocca was a great choice to write the Foreword.

"How do you know him?" Red asked.

"I don't," I answered.

"Then why would he write the Foreword?" Red snapped.

"If you let me write a letter on Celtics stationery with your signature, I think he will do it."

Red agreed, and the letter went out that same day.

We heard nothing for a couple of weeks. Then Red got a letter back from Iacocca agreeing to write the Foreword. When we didn't hear anything for several weeks, I called the public relations director, whose name was listed on the letterhead. He made it clear that he had no intention of writing the Foreword. We should do it and then send it to him for approval.

I wanted to have a different style for the Foreword, so I reached out to my friend, Tom Condon, a terrific writer and former editorial pages director for the *Hartford Courant*. Tom did a great job, and we sent the Foreword off for Iacocca's approval a few days later. No response. Meanwhile, Rick Wolff, a close friend and senior editor at MacMillan, publisher of the book, kept pushing me for a completed manuscript. I called daily and heard nothing. The final deadline was approaching, and Rick told me to think of other possibilities to write the Foreword.

Finally, I got a call from the Chrysler PR Department. I would have to come to Chrysler headquarters and meet directly with Iacocca. I was on the next plane. The same PR director met me in the lobby. He pointed to his watch and said, "You've got five minutes."

I walked into Iacocca's office, and his expression told me that he had no idea why I was wasting his time. "Before I discuss the reason for my visit, I would like to thank you for helping to save the eyesight of my daughter, Alicia," I said.

"What do you mean?" he asked.

"My daughter is a Type One diabetic," I explained. "The bleeding behind her eyes was just corrected by laser surgery at Massachusetts Eye and Ear Hospital. The surgeon told me that research from the Iacocca Foundation helped develop the technique that probably saved my daughter's eyesight."

Iacocca's wife Mary had died of complications from Type 1 diabetes at the age of 57. He established the Foundation in her honor. He motioned me to a seat and began asking me questions about my daughter. When did her diabetes develop, how did she handle it, what kind of a student was she? He seemed pleased when I told him that Alicia was an honor student and competed successfully all around New England in horse shows. She never let diabetes define her as a person. He wanted me to tell her story to his daughter Kathryn, who ran the Foundation, but she was unavailable by telephone.

Every five minutes, the PR person walked into the office and pointed to his watch. Iacocca finally told him not to bother us again. A few hours later, I was on my way back to the airport in a limousine with Iacocca's written approval for the Foreword.

I was not surprised to read that Iacocca had two short-lived marriages after the death of Mary. His love for his first wife was so evident during our meeting. He donated 7 million dollars to the Iacocca Foundation from the royalties he received from his book, *Iacocca: An Autobiography*. The Foundation has funded more than $45 million in research to bring new hope to everyone living with Type 1 diabetes.

Here is the Foreword credited for the first time to Tom Condon, the actual writer.

FOREWORD

I used to hate Red Auerbach. Detroit got an NBA basketball team back in 1957. The Pistons moved here from Fort Wayne, Indiana. We expected great things. We knew damn well we were making the best cars in the world then. We wanted the best of everything.

Well, we had some great basketball players—like Dave Bing and Bob Lanier. But it took us over thirty years to win the NBA championship. That guy with the cigar from Boston kept showing up and beating our brains out.

A lot of people seem to think sports is somehow not connected to the rest of the world. Somebody once referred to sports as the country's toy store. Well, it isn't.

Professional sports is a business, just like manufacturing cars is a business. That means you've got to compete on a business level with other guys who are trying to bury you. You've got to be smarter and more imaginative. You've got to think of things before they do. Most importantly, if you're running the company, you've got to be the leader–the boss.

A lot of new management theories have been passed around in the last couple of decades. Some are okay, and some are crap. Red Auerbach understands what a manager is supposed to do. He's supposed to mold his people into a team and win with them.

Red's toughness and will to win were imbued within the men and teams he coached. He never asked his players to give more than they could—yet he demanded every bit of what they had, and he got it.

Red's greatest talent was knowing how to motivate men in a game situation. He would curse, cuddle, enrage, or do anything he thought would make his team perform better. The results were also unbelievable. Red would do anything within the rules to win. And if that wasn't enough, he was perfectly willing to bend those rules to give himself that little competitive edge that spells the difference between winning and losing.

Red, like me, is a son of immigrants and one who didn't stay in the family business. It took him seven years to win a title. That isn't the amazing thing, at least to me. The amazing thing was that he could keep doing it fifteen more times.

The way he did it is one of the key lessons of his life. He worked people hard and then convinced them they were good. They began to believe it. Then other people started to believe it. They call it "Celtics Pride." I call it great motivation.

Back at Ford and again at Chrysler, I've tried to hire the best, provide the best, and get us all working together. That's what Red did. He is the master. He also has a realistic sense of what loyalty is all about. Many managers demand blind loyalty, then go out and sell somebody down the river. Loyalty is a two-way street. Both people reach a hand toward the other. That's the only way there's any mutual respect. Red is able to be a boss without being a tyrant. That's the key. He'd listen to his people and test what they said against what he knew. Then—and this is so very important—he'd make a decision.

Every human being makes mistakes, and Red made a few doozies. I couldn't believe he drafted a guy in the first round one year who didn't fly. It reminded me of the "Edsel." But most of the time, he was right. The record bears that out.

Red was the most successful basketball coach of all time. No one else ever came close to his record, and the betting here is that nobody ever will. Like football's Vince Lombardi and baseball's Joe McCarthy, Red has become a legend.

As I went through this book, I kept finding myself saying, "Right." There's a part about dealing with the press where Red reminds managers that reporters don't know a business as well as the person who runs it. "If they did, they'd have the job. But they don't. You do." Exactly.

So, I used to hate this man, but now I like him. As you read this book, you won't find any highfalutin language or academic terminology. That's not Red. He's straight from the shoulder, no-nonsense, no bull. He makes it interesting, and he makes it fun.

Tom Condon
West Hartford, Connecticut

A Story of Two Raymonds

Anyone growing up in Rhode Island in the 1940s and 1950s did not have to wait to read Mario Puzzo's *The Godfather* in 1972 or see Martin Scorsese's film *Goodfellas* in 1990 to realize the existence of an organization called the Mafia. Throughout the 1940s, 50s, 60s, and 70s, Raymond Patriarca controlled New England organized crime from his office, the Coin-a-matic shop on Atwells Avenue in the Federal Hill section of Providence, RI. Patriarca came to power with the passage of the Volstead Act in 1919 and controlled liquor, gambling, and "white slavery," as prostitution was called then, for more than 50 years.

In 1930, Patriarca was behind an Easter Sunday break for two criminal cohorts serving sentences at Rhode Island state prison. In a shoot-out, two guards died. Patriarca was designated as a "public enemy," but he was never charged with the crime. One of Patricia's first moves after WWII was to take over the lucrative race wire business from Carleton O'Brien, an Irish gangster, who was shot to death in the driveway of his home. The "race wire" reported horse racing results from around the country, essential information for gambling interests. Although he was never indicted for the murder, there was little doubt that Patriarca ordered the hit.

At the height of his power, it was reported that Patriarca got a piece of the action on any illegal activity in New England. He resolved an Irish-Italian war in Massachusetts and arbitrated disputes among the Five Families in New York. He numbered Jimmy Hoffa and Meyer Lansky among his friends and was reportedly a silent partner in a Massachusetts horse track with Frank Sinatra and Dean Martin. He also understood that he needed more than muscle and violence to run a successful business. So he bribed politicians, judges, and cops to protect his illegal operations. Under his control, Providence lived up to its colonial reputation as "Rogue's Isle," a city of gamblers and hustlers.

Patriarca built a reputation as the Robin Hood of Federal Hill, financing scholarships so poor Italian youths could attend college. The Federal Hill section of Providence had the lowest crime rate in the city, mainly due to Patriarca's presence. When two druggies mistakenly broke into the home of Joseph Patriarca, Raymond's brother, they were brutally murdered. Patriarca had a reputation as a generous boss to those loyal to him or a vengeful sadist to anyone who dared to cross him.

One of his earliest "hits" was on a man by the name of George "Tiger" Balleto, a former enforcer and collector for Patriarca. It was reported that Balleto developed sticky fingers and made negative comments about Raymond and his brother, Joseph. On August 10, 1955, Balletto was murdered at a bar called the Bella Napoli Café. His assassin was a man by the name of John "Jackie" Nazarian. Two bartenders and about 60 customers crowded into the single bathroom at the time of the murder and saw nothing. However, one witness, Eddie Hannan, an ex-boxer, told friends that he had seen Nazarian execute Balleto. He was found a few days later strangled to death with baling wire.

In 1962, while Patriarca was ill, Nazarian made comments about taking over the Rhode Island Mafia. On January 17, 1962, he was shot to death by another enforcer, Louis J. Taglianetti. On February 7, 1970, Taglianetti, who was finally indicted for Nazarian's murder, was shot to death with his girlfriend at a Warwick apartment house. There is little doubt that Patriarca was behind all three murders.

After the Balleto murder, I was told a story that I relate for the first time more than 60 years later. It requires a little background information. When I attended La Salle Academy, I met another student by the name of Ray Lyons. Although we were only casual friends, Ray was very close to two of my best friends, Loring Forcier and Bill Crofton. Loring and Bill were two of the most honest, reliable friends I ever had. The same cannot be said of Ray Lyons, who joined the Patriarca crime family right out of high school and, if not for his Irish heritage, might have become a top figure in the Mafia.

Ray Lyons never carried a gun or took on any of the brutal aspects as a member of a crime family. He was extremely bright, had a photographic memory, and mentally recorded the bets he picked up on his "route" as a bookie that included stops in bars throughout Rhode Island and Southern Massachusetts. Bill Crofton owned the Standard Dental Laboratory in Providence, the largest and most profitable in Rhode Island.

Ray Lyons had been identified as a Patricia associate in The Providence Journal and had even served a prison sentence. There is no doubt that Ray had gained the trust and confidence of Raymond and Joseph Patriarca. He started as a bookie but quickly moved up, finally running the "race wire," which was critical for New England gambling. Unfortunately, not all of his childhood friends cared to continue the friendship. Bill Crofton was the exception. He was never judgmental, and they remained close friends right up to the time of Ray's death in 2007. Bill used to ride with him every Friday night as Ray made stops at bars in Providence and nearby Massachusetts, picking up bets or paying off winners. They usually started the evening at Bella Napoli Café in Providence. On the night of August 10, 1955, Ray drove right by the Bella Napoli. "Did you forget our first stop?" Bill asked. "This isn't a good night to visit that bar," Ray replied. Hours later, Balleto was shot to death while sitting at the bar at the Bella Napoli.

Bill told me that story after I promised never to repeat it. Bill and Ray are both dead, so I feel free to relate that story now. Over the years, I pumped Bill for other stories about Ray's involvement with the Mafia but got nothing. He said when Ray had serious business to conduct, he would ask Bill to wait in the car.

While I never met him personally, my brothers Bill and Jack had a confrontation with Tiger Belleto in 1948. Jack had started his career as a heavyweight boxer in Providence that year. He had been heavyweight champion of the 1st Marine Division in 1943. While Bill and Jack were sitting at the bar of a nightclub, the Ambassador, Tiger Bellato, without warning, punched Jack in the face knocking him off the stool. He jumped on top of Jack and began punching him. Bill broke it up by hitting Tiger with what was described as a "terrific right hand." Police entered the scene before the fight was resumed. It ended with Jack threatening to get Tiger in the future.

A few days later, Jack caught up to Tiger in Providence and challenged him to a fight. Balleto refused, saying that the two of them should become friends. Not too many kind words were said about Tiger at the time of his death. Later that week, I asked Jack where he was going as he was leaving the house dressed in a suit. "Tiger's wake," he replied. I told him to be sure to smile, as he would probably be photographed by the FBI at the funeral home. Jack also attended Tiger's funeral.

I never had any direct contact with Raymond Patriarca, but I did have an indirect one with his brother Joseph. My aunt had died several years earlier, and her daughter, Jane, and son, John, were being raised by my mother. When I returned from Providence College that day, a black Cadillac was parked in front of my home in Edgewood. When I got inside, my mother introduced me to Mrs. Joseph Patriarca, whose daughter was attending St. Pius School with Jane. The two had become good friends, and Mrs. Patriarca had driven Jane home after a social event at the school.

Of course, I didn't say anything while Mrs. Patriarca was there. But after she drove away, I gave my mother and cousin a brief history of Joseph and his brother, Raymond. Jane refused to believe it, claiming that Mr. Patriarca was a kind and generous man. My mother never really believed anything bad about anyone, so she probably just remembered this mob boss in her prayers.

In March 1970, Raymond Patriarca was convicted of the murders of Rudolf Marfeo and Anthony Meli. He was sentenced to 10 years in prison, but he continued to run his "family" while imprisoned. He died of a heart attack at the age of 76.

In 1971, the FBI released a list of names with links to the old Patriarca family. They included Raymond Patriarca Jr., Frank Marrapese, Robert De Luca, and Raymond Lyons, three Italians and one Irishman. So rest in peace, Bill and Ray. You were the odd couple long before Neil Simon wrote his famous play.

My Brush With Insider Trading

The Silo Inn was my favorite restaurant in Old Lyme, CT, where I lived for more than 25 years. The food was good, and I was friendly with the owners, Libby and Bob Dillon. Although I did not drink, I enjoyed eating at the bar to watch sporting events and converse with the friendly bartender, Bill Dillon, son of the owners.

Bill's wife, Diana, boarded a horse at the same barn where my daughters kept their ponies. She had hoped to train him as a jumper, but he developed a severe hoof disease and had to be retired. One night Bill asked me if I knew anything about a Rhode Island horse farm that took in sick or old horses. I told Bill I had never heard of it. The following week he said the woman who ran the farm had come to Connecticut, and Diana was impressed with her love and commitment to horses. She left with Diana's horse and extended an invitation for them to visit at any time.

About a month later, Diana and Bill drove to Rhode Island to see how her horse was getting along. They were surprised when the address took them into a residential neighborhood. They rang the bell repeatedly, but no one came to the door. Finally, a neighbor walked over and asked them if they were checking on a horse. After Bill told his story, the neighbor said there was no horse farm. The neighbor, who had moved abruptly, collected horses all over New England and sold them to slaughterhouses the same day. I did report the incident to my friend in the Rhode Island State Police, but the woman was never found. I don't know exactly why, but Bill confided in me that Diana blamed him for the murder of her horse.

I was surprised when Bill told me he was leaving the bar for a more challenging position—a stockbroker for a prominent investment firm. I have decided not to mention names, as I don't want to get involved with lawsuits more than 30 years after the event. While I liked Bill personally, I was surprised that he had even qualified for such a job. He had no business experience and even lacked a college degree. Of course, I wished him well in his new venture.

A few months later, a friend, a prominent New London architect, who will only be identified by his first name, Frank, approached me about joining an investment team that had been recently formed. I lost interest when he told me Bill Dillon handled the investments. For me, there was a world of difference between Bill Dillon, the bartender, and Bill Dillon, the investment broker. So I took a pass.

One night I got a call from Bill, who asked to see me right away. We met in a local coffee shop, and he told me a story that had not yet hit the papers. He had just been charged with insider trading and fired from his job. He admitted his guilt immediately. While tending bar at the Silo, Bill became friendly with two employees from the R.R. Donnelly printing plant in Old Saybrook, Connecticut, which printed Business Week. He paid them $10 to $30 each for advance copies of the magazine, which carried a column entitled "Inside Wall Street." He bought securities in about 129 companies mentioned favorably in the column, then sold them after the prices rose. He said a private investment firm he handled made about $94,000 through his insider trading. Members of his investment club included his mother, Libby, his wife Diana, and my friend, Frank.

There was only one part of the story that Bill disputed. Of course, the management of the investment firm said all the right things about being shocked and appalled by the actions of a rogue employee. Bill told me his manager knew all about his plan to get advance copies of Business Week. He even complimented Bill on his resourcefulness. Bill had memos that would prove his allegation. He pleaded with me to write an expose about the whole story. I told Bill I could not do anything without some documentation. He left the meeting with the promise to return with the evidence I needed. Later, I called my friend Frank, who confirmed that he had been charged with insider training. He had to retain a lawyer who eventually cost him more than $50,000. Libby and Diana had also been charged.

Bill called me the next day and said we had to meet immediately. I noticed a change in his demeanor as soon as he arrived. "You have to forget everything I told you yesterday," he said. "If that story goes public, my wife, my mother, and our friend Frank could end up in jail."

"What happened between yesterday and today that changed your mind?" I asked. "A member of the Securities Exchange Commission met with me this morning. Here's the deal. If I plead guilty, accept a deal for one year in prison, and keep my mouth shut, no one else will be prosecuted." I didn't try to argue with Bill. If my mother's freedom were on the line, I would have made the same decision.

Here is how Larry Rosenthal reported the story in the *Washington Post*:

"A former broker charged in the insider trading scandal involving leaked copies of *Business Week* magazine pleaded guilty today to one count of wire fraud. Bill Dillon, who entered his guilty plea under a bargain struck with federal prosecutors, did not make a statement during his brief appearance before U.S. District Judge Ellen B. Burns. The government contends that Dillon made about $94,000 through his insider trading. Neither Dillon's mother, Elizabeth, nor his wife, Diana, was charged due to the plea bargain."

While Bill was serving his prison sentence, his wife divorced him. R.R. Donnelly fired five employees from its Old Saybrook plant. I'm happy to say that Bill remarried, lived a good life, and retired in Florida. I spoke to him a few years ago, and he now refers to the affair as a learning experience. My only regret is that we missed out on a possible *60 Minutes* segment. I can just hear Mike Wallace cross-examining that local manager about his involvement in the scheme—especially if he had the documentation that Bill said he could furnish.

JOHN GORDON

I never met John Gordon. According to Rhode Island court records, John Gordon was a convicted murderer, executed in 1845 for the brutal murder of Amasa Sprague, a wealthy industrialist. But I certainly heard a lot about John, starting in my grandmother's lap in the 1930s. Granny Dooley used to lull me to sleep singing "The Old Spinning Wheel," "Danny Boy," and "Mother McCrea." Occasionally she would mix in some folk songs, including one about "Poor Johnny Gordon." I remember asking my mother about Johnny Gordon, and she said he was an Irishman who had been mistreated in Rhode Island.

I was about 10 when my sister Eileen told me the real story. John Gordon had been framed and executed for a murder he did not commit. Eileen never let me forget the Gordon story. She called me immediately after I had written a successful book with Red Auerbach, famed coach and president of the Boston Celtics. "Why are you writing books about sports when John Gordon lies in an unmarked grave as a convicted murderer for a crime he didn't commit!" she demanded. This was the same sister fired for organizing servants into a union while working for a Newport society woman at 19. Unfortunately, Eileen died in 2002, eight years before I wrote the play *The Murder Trial of John Gordon.*

My Uncle Leo Kenneally gave me some good advice when I was about nine years old. "Ken, try to surround yourself with people who are more intelligent than you are." It's a rule I had no trouble following all my life. So when I decided to write a play about John Gordon, I sought out an old classmate from Providence College, Dr. Patrick T. Conley. The author of 39 books, Pat Conley has forgotten more about Rhode Island history than most of us will ever know. Like Mark Twain, Dr. Conley always combines sage advice with a touch of humor. Pat and I had lunch at the Fabre Line Club in Providence during the summer of 2009. In about two hours, I had most of the information I needed to write the play.

A few days after the meeting, Pat sent me an article written by one of his former students at Providence College, Dr. Scott Molloy. I had not met Scott at that point, but he is now a close friend. Scott's article made a point that convinced me of John Gordon's innocence. John Gordon was an alcoholic, subject to blackouts. He probably never would have been charged if he had been able to account for his whereabouts at the time of the murder. John was also a Catholic who never missed Sunday mass, regardless of how much he drank the previous evening.

Fr. John Brady heard John's last confession just minutes before they walked to the scaffold together. In his final message, Fr. Brady said, "Have courage, John. You are going to join the noble band of martyrs of your countrymen who have suffered before at the shrine of bigotry and prejudice." Scott Molloy asked two questions in his article: "Would Fr. Brady have made such a statement if John Gordon had just confessed to murdering Amasa Sprague? Would John Gordon have gone to his death without confessing the mortal sin of murder? With his last words, John Gordon forgave everyone involved in his conviction and execution." His last words paraphrased those of Jesus on the cross: "I forgive them for they know not what they do."

I began to write the play in the summer of 2008 while staying at my brother Bob's summer home in Narragansett, RI. My brother Jack stayed was with me as I wrote the play. I can still see him standing in the doorway, waiting for the next page to be written. Sadly, Jack died a year before the play opened. However, with the input from my two historians, I put together the story that became the basis for my play.

On December 31, 1843, Amasa Sprague was shot and brutally bludgeoned to death. The gory incident touched off the Gordon murder trial, an event which became the Rhode Island version of the Sacco-Vanzetti case—but here, the defendants were Irish Catholic immigrants rather than Italians. Amasa Sprague was a powerful, wealthy, and influential man. He was administrator of the A & W Sprague industrial empire, a portion based in Cranston, Rhode Island. He personally supervised the Cranston complex at Sprague's Village (near the present Cranston Print Works) in the manner of a feudal baron, with several hundred Irish men, women, and children in his employ.

Amasa had a strong and forceful personality. Sprague's Village was his. He owned the plant, the company houses, the company store, and the farm which supplied that store. He even owned the church where the Protestant workers worshipped. William Sprague, Amasa's brother, was the United States Senator from Rhode Island and former governor. He and his brother had a disdain for the recent immigrants called the "low Irish." However, the brothers did not let their prejudice stand in the way of hiring Irish immigrants who toiled for meager wages in their textile mills.

On that fateful Sunday afternoon, December 31, 1843, 46-year-old Amasa left his mansion adjacent to his factory and began to walk northwest toward a large farm he owned in the neighboring town of Johnson, a mile-and-a-half distance, using a shortcut. Later that same day, Michael Costello, a handyman in the Sprague household, took the same route and came upon Sprague's bloodied body. Sprague had been shot in the right forearm and then brutally beaten to death. The sixty dollars found in the victim's pocket eliminated robbery as a motive, making the murder appear to be one of hatred or revenge.

Suspicion immediately centered on the Gordon family, a clan of Irish immigrants who were particularly hostile towards the strong-willed Yankee industrialist. The family's earliest arrival, Nicholas Gordon, had emigrated from Ireland sometime in the mid-1830s, settled in Cranston, and opened a small store near Sprague's Village, where he sold groceries, notions, and miscellaneous items. He then expanded his business by obtaining a license to sell liquor.

Liquor sales proved so popular in the dreary mill village that in 1843 Nicholas was able to finance the immigration of his family -mother, sister; three brothers (John, William, and Robert) and a niece—from Ireland to America. But Gordon's liquor sales also produced a confrontation with Amasa Sprague, who felt the intoxicating brew was adversely affecting the productivity of his factory hands. Thus Sprague used his political weight in June 1843 to block a renewal of Nicholas Gordon's liquor license.

Tempers flared and harsh words were exchanged between Nicholas Gordon and Amasa Sprague. "I'll get you for this," Gordon screamed at Sprague immediately after the verdict was announced. Because of this incident, Nicholas, William, and John Gordon were arrested the day after the murder. John and William were indicted for murder, and Nicholas was charged with being an accessory before the fact. Nicholas had been in Providence on the day of the murder, first at mass and later at a Christening at the time of the murder. The implication was that Nicholas planned the murder and imported his brothers from Ireland to carry it out.

The trial of John and William was conducted in the spring of 1844 before a 12-man jury, none of them Irish Catholic. At the outset, William Gordon definitely established that he was elsewhere when the crime was committed. Attorney General Joseph M. Blake and Prosecutor William H. Potter zeroed in on the hapless 29-year-old John Gordon, who could neither remember nor prove his whereabouts. The evidence was entirely circumstantial, starting with the fact that John's shoe size matched the prints in the snow found at the murder scene. Witnesses identified a broken gun found at the location as the one Nicholas kept in his store.

A Providence prostitute swore she had seen John Gordon wearing the bloodstained coat found at the murder scene earlier on the day of the murder. The "blood" was later proven to be the madder dye used in coloring textiles. Nicholas admitted that he kept a gun in the store but claimed it disappeared shortly after the murder. He denied that the gun found at the scene was his. The missing weapon was the state's most damaging evidence.

The Irish communities in Providence and Cranston rallied to the support of the Gordons and raised money for their defense. John P. Knowles, a Protestant attorney, agreed to defend the Gordons, a courageous decision that cost him his health and, later, his career. The Gordons proclaimed their innocence, and Knowles defended them brilliantly. He was also able to establish that the real murderer was Big Peter, a huge Irishman who had been fired by Amasa Sprague three days before the murder. He disappeared on the day of the murder and was never found.

One of the state's key witnesses, a known prostitute, Sally Field, claimed to be a close friend of William and John. She was the only person to connect John to the coat found at the murder scene. Knowles had Gordon try on the coat at trial, and it wrapped around him about three times, proving it belonged to a person much larger than the defendant. When Knowles asked Field to identify the two defendants, she became confused and pointed out John as William and William as John. *The Providence Journal* didn't point out this mistake and failed to report any damaging testimony against prosecution witnesses throughout the trial. The day after the murder, a headline appeared in the *Journal*: "The Guilty persons, the Gordons, have been arrested for the murder of Amasa Sprague."

This was not the first time that the Journal had taken a stand against Irish Catholics. When Irish Catholics campaigned to remove a restriction that required land ownership to become a qualified voter, the *Journal*'s publisher, Henry Anthony, declared his unyielding opposition to such a change, even for naturalized Irish-Catholic soldiers who had fought in the Civil War to preserve the Union. The bigoted Anthony warned in *The Providence Journal* that if the restriction is removed, "Rhode Island will no longer be Rhode Island when this is done. It will become a province of Ireland. St. Patrick will take the place of Roger Williams, and the shamrock will supersede the Anchor and Hope."

Anthony's close friend, Chief Justice Job Durfee, who presided at the trial, gave a charge to the jury in which he called the killing the "most atrocious" crime that had ever come to his attention." Durfee also distinguished the testimony of native-born witnesses and Gordon's "countrymen," implying that the latter Irish were less credible. The jury took Durfee's advice, leaving the box at 6:30 p.m. on April 17 and returning one hour and fifteen minutes later with a verdict of guilty for John and freedom for William. When John was sentenced to death, he turned to his brother and said, "William, it was you who have hanged me."

Two weeks before the execution, William Gordon went to John Knowles and admitted he had gone to the store after hearing about the murder and hidden Nicholas' gun. Armed with the actual weapon, Knowles appealed to the Rhode Island Supreme Court, but the Justices rejected it. Then Knowles petitioned the General Assembly for a reprieve and a commutation of sentence. The petition was rejected, but the narrowness of the margin indicated growing doubts concerning the fairness of the trial. Time was running out for John Gordon, and Governor James Fencer was not sympathetic to a stay of execution. When no reprieve was granted, John Gordon was hanged on February 14, 1845, in the state prison yard.

The funeral of John Gordon was attended by Irish from miles around, some journeying from New Hampshire, Massachusetts, and

Connecticut. According to observers, it took all day for the long procession to pass the home where John's body had been taken. Nicholas Gordon was later freed after two juries deadlocked on the question of his guilt, but he never recovered from the personal calamity of his younger brother's death or his confinement in the damp prison. Broken in health, he took to excessive drink and suffered premature death.

The execution of John Gordon had a permanent impact on Rhode Island law and politics, and it stands today as one of the darker episodes in its history. Seldom before or since has the cause of justice or the spirit of religious toleration implanted here by Roger Williams received such a severe jolt as it did on the day John Gorton was hanged. Numerous mass meetings were held in Providence to protest the continuance of capital punishment.

In 1852, just seven years after Gordon's hanging, and in large part because of it, Rhode Island became the second state in the nation to abolish capital punishment. The General Assembly would later reinstate mandatory death penalty for persons who commit murder while incarcerated. No one was put to death under those policies, though, and in 1979 capital punishment was declared unconstitutional by the Rhode Island Supreme Court. John Gordon remains the last person executed by the State of Rhode Island.

I finished the play in 2010 and reached out to the drama department at Salve Regina University, owners of a wonderful historic theatre that would have been ideal for the play. I met with a young lady, the head of the drama department, who talked more about her degree in theater than she did about the play. I listened to her impressive background (all theory and little practical experience) and asked her a couple of questions about the play. When she couldn't answer them, it was obvious that she hadn't even read it. I picked up the manuscript and left.

My following approach was to the Trinity Playhouse in Providence. I received some favorable comments but no interest in producing the play. At the time, I read a story about Piyush (Pi) Patel, owner of the Park Theatre in Cranston. It was an old movie house that Pi invested millions in to produce a first-class theater. The technology, seating, dressing rooms, and acoustics were on a level with any Broadway theater. I had a personal history with the Park Theatre, growing up about a block away on Hayward Street. Every Saturday and Sunday, I would go with my brothers to movies at the Park. Admission was 10 cents on Saturdays and 17 cents on Sundays.

I called Pi and received a call from Vivek Mistry, his assistant. Vivek read the play, had a positive impression, and set up a meeting with Pi. I do not think Pi ever read the play. But he liked the story and put his theatre and a considerable investment behind the play. I think Pi was also impressed that the Park Theatre was less than a mile from the spot where Amasa Sprague was murdered. It was an expensive play to produce, with 23 actors and expensive scenery and costumes. Pi never complained, even though he lost a considerable amount of money on the production.

One of the earliest supporters of the play was Vince Arnold, founder of The Museum of Newport Irish History. He made the arrangements for a whole busload of museum members to attend the play on opening night.

Someone once said that playwrights should never attempt to direct their own work. I began writing plays in the fourth grade at Eden Park Grammar School. Of course, I always directed and had the leading role. It's a little different at the professional level. I started out as the director but quickly relinquished the role to Pamela Lambert, an African American actress and director. Her husband, Jeff Gill, played defense attorney John Knowles and was magnificent. Jeff played the role of Red Auerbach in a later play I wrote and received the Massachusetts 2013 Best Actor Award.

We were fortunate enough to cast many good actors from Rhode Island and Massachusetts. Margaret Salvatore, a renowned costume designer, played a key role in the production. We even had a romance develop during the 23 performances. I attended the marriage of Chris Conte (William Sprague) and Tray Gearing (Sally Field) the following year. I treasure a comment Chris wrote on a Gordon poster I have framed in my office: "Thanks for changing my life."

During one of the early performances, a man walked up to me and said, "You really think that John Gordon was innocent, don't you?" It was State Representative Peter Martin. When I answered "yes," he asked me what I planned to do about it.

"He was executed in 1845," I replied. "It's a little late for a reprieve."

"It's never too late for a pardon," Martin said. Representative

Martin suggested that he introduce a formal resolution in the Rhode Island House of Representatives that would request that Governor Chafee grant a pardon for John Gordon. A petition to support that request was signed by over 4,000 people who attended the play.

A House Resolution was submitted and referred to the House Judiciary Committee. The facts of the case were reviewed in a hearing on May 4, 2011. Testimony regarding the trial was provided by Rhode Island historians Patrick Conley, Scott Molloy, and Don Deignan; legal experts John Hardiman and Michael DiLauro from the RI Public Defenders office; Director Pamela Lambert; and Playwright Ken Dooley. Many of the 23 actors who had appeared in the play attended the hearing.

The resolution to request the pardon was supported by the Committee on a 13 to 0 vote. On May 11, 2011, it was passed unanimously 70 to 0 by the full body of the House of Representatives and was transferred to the Rhode Island Senate for affirmation. On Wednesday, June 29, 2011, a ceremony was held at the Old State House in Providence, in the same room where John Gordon was tried and found guilty in 1844.

Governor Chafee signed a gubernatorial proclamation granting Gordon a complete pardon. "John Gordon was put to death after a highly questionable judicial process and based on no concrete evidence," the governor said. "There is no question he was not given a fair trial. Today we are trying to right that injustice. John Gordon's wrongful execution was a major factor in Rhode Island's abolition of and longstanding opposition to the death penalty," Governor Chafee added.

"I sponsored this bill because I came to understand that an innocent man was forced to suffer the terror, despair, and humiliation of a public execution and that society and government will remain complicit if the record of the judgment of that travesty of Rhode Island history is not corrected," Representative Martin said. "Today, we have righted a wrong, and we have done the just thing."

The pardon of John Gordon attracted worldwide attention. The story appeared immediately in over 500 news sources, including publications in Ireland, England, Russia, and Turkey. In addition, there was a celebration at the St. Mary's Cemetery in Pawtucket on Saturday, October 8, 2011. It was sponsored by the Friendly Sons of St. Patrick, and Fr. Bernie O'Reilly, who played the part of the priest in the stage play, gave the homily.

The following day there was a dedication of a granite flagstone in memory of John Gordon at a ceremony at the Rhode Island Irish Famine Memorial. The inscription reads:

John Gordon. Born in Ireland. Died 2/14/1845
in Providence, RI. This stone placed in his honor
by his fellow Irishmen and those who cared
to right a wrong done unto him.
Forgiveness is the ultimate revenge.
October 8, 2011.

The last line is taken directly from my play. A song, "The Ballad of John Gordon," was written and recorded by the Tom Lanigan Band. It was performed at the St. Mary's Cemetery celebration. A medallion was designed and manufactured by Ed Johnson of Universal Plating, Inc., River Street, Providence.

The day after the pardon was issued, I went to my sister's Eileen's grave, dug a little hole, and planted the medallion. "You did it, kid," I said. "Because of you, John Gordon is no longer considered a convicted murderer."

Jury Duty

Like most Irish Americans from Rhode Island, the Dooleys were solid Democrats. I can still remember sitting in my father's lap as Franklin Delano Roosevelt delivered one of his famous fireside chats. I was in Tripoli, Libya, when Eisenhower was elected in 1952. When he ran for reelection in 1956, I was back in college, living with my family in Cranston, RI. I can still remember my shock when my mother sported an "I like Ike" button shortly before the election. "Ike brought my boys back safely," she explained. Once her mind was made up, Marion Veronica Kenneally Dooley seldom changed it, despite severe challenges from my sister Eileen and my Uncle Leo. Both of them were big supporters of the Democratic challenger, Adlai Stevenson. So my mother rejoiced when Ike was reelected.

When I reflect on my mother now, I don't know of any individual who believed in the American system more than she did. She sent six sons off to serve during wars (at least five of them in harm's way) because her country needed them. It was the right thing to do to protect our freedom and our American way of life. She voted in her first election in 1920, right after the 19th Amendment passed, giving women the right to vote. She voted in every election up to the time of her death in 1981.

My mother's parents, Bill and Margaret Kenneally left Ireland in the 1880s and landed in Newport, Rhode Island. They were accompanied by my grandmother's sisters, Ann and Johanna Sullivan, and her brother, John J. Sullivan. John entered the seminary in Maryland shortly after the family arrived in Newport. My grandfather William worked as a stonemason on some of the "cottages" being built by members of high society on Bellevue Avenue. His name is listed on a roster of workers who help construct Marble House, the estate of William and Alva Vanderbilt.

The Sullivans were once wealthy landowners in Kinsella, and there is even a Sullivan Castle still standing in ruins in County Cork. We were able to locate it when my family and I visited Ireland right after 9/11. I think many of the stories my mother heard about the Irish Republican Army (IRA) and English retribution influenced her special feelings about American freedom.

In 1957, my mother was called for jury duty. No one ever answered that call with more enthusiasm and dedication than she did. My mother only drove a car once in her life. My father was attempting to give her driving lessons, but he frightened her so badly that she refused to get behind the wheel again. So while jury duty didn't inconvenience my other at all, it was a bit of a challenge for her sons who drove her.

My brothers and I took comfort in the fact that she might not even be selected. I listened as some of the candidates gave lengthy excuses why they could not possibly take time out of their busy lives to serve on juries. MV (Marion Veronica), as my friends liked to call her, would have none of it. She answered all questions and explained that she had absolutely no objection to serving on a jury. It did come as a surprise when she was selected.

I remembered reading a story about a young man killed after climbing over a fence guarding a railroad crossing and was struck and killed by a train. The family sued the New Haven Railroad for wrongful death, and my mother was selected for the jury that heard the case. At the time, my Uncle Leo Kenneally was the Director of Public Relations for the railroad. Immediately after the accident, my uncle had taken a strong position that the railroad was not at fault. "He ignored all of the posted warning signs, so he was responsible for his death," Leo said. Of course, he did not know then that his sister would be part of the jury that determined guilt or innocence.

I still remember my mother's reaction when he learned about her role on the jury. He started to explain his earlier opinion, but my mother cut him off immediately. "I'm not supposed to discuss this case with anyone," she snapped. Not many people were able to shut Uncle Leo up with a simple sentence. His sister did. Her silence extended to other family members. Every night we would ask her what happened during the trial that day. She would answer by asking if anyone else wanted another pork chop or more vegetables.

If my mother were typical of the other jury members, I would have bet against the railroad winning the case. My mother had a special love for children and a great deal of sympathy for the mother who had lost her son. After a very short deliberation, the jury ruled in favor of the railroad. My mother didn't talk about the case immediately after the verdict. But one night at dinner, she told us why the jury had voted unanimously to rule against the family. She got very emotional, and her eyes filled with tears as she explained. "The young man had climbed over the fence, ignoring all of the warning signs," she said. "There was no way that we could find the railroad guilty under those circumstances."

It was not an easy decision for her. But if she was to uphold the American judicial system, which she believed in so fervently, she had no other choice.

My (Brief) Friendship with Katharine Hepburn

In 1980, I became a member of the Board of Directors of the Ivoryton Playhouse, the second oldest summer stock theatre in the country. It was best known as the theater in which Katharine Hepburn made her stage debut.

Katharine Hepburn had grown up in Hartford, CT, and summered in an exclusive area in Old Saybrook, called Fenwick. She had retired to the Hepburn mansion in the late 1970s.

The theater had fallen on hard times and had even been closed for a few years. So what better way to promote the theater than to have Katharine Hepburn, a four-time Oscar winner, involved. Of course, everyone thought it would be a marvelous idea, except for Katharine Hepburn. She never responded to letters or phone calls offering tickets to the productions.

In 1982, I had a summer house in Martha's Vineyard, MA. One day I saw a sign in a local church announcing a play, "To Heaven in a Swing," written and performed by Katharine Houghton. She had two claims to fame. First, she was named after her aunt, Katharine Hepburn. Second, she gave a tremendous performance in the 1967 film *Guess Who's Coming to Dinner?*

To Heaven in a Swing is a one-person play based on the life of Louisa May Alcott, author of Little Women. It tells the story of the last days of Louisa May Alcott as she is dying in a private nursing home in Roxbury, MA. She reminisces about her life with her father, Bronson Alcott, a member of an Abolitionist circle in New England that included Ralph Waldo Emerson and Henry David Thoreau. She also describes her experience as a nurse during the Civil War.

Years later, I learned the difficulty of creating the illusion of dialogue with unseen characters while holding a stage alone. I wrote *The Auerbach Dynasty*, a one-person play based on the life of Arnold "Red" Auerbach, coach, general manager, and president of the Boston Celtics. All I had to do is write the play. Katharine Houghton was both playwright and actor, and she did an admirable job in both roles.

I contacted the Board of Directors, and we agreed to ask Katharine to bring the play to the Ivoryton Playhouse. I scheduled a lunch with

Katharine, and I had no idea if she would be receptive, considering the reluctance of her aunt, even to acknowledge our invitations.

She could not have been more charming or receptive and agreed to do to the play. The play was well-received, and we sold out for two weeks. It did not hurt that her father, Ellsworth Grant, was the former Mayor of Hartford. In addition, Houghton was Katharine Grant's maternal grandmother's maiden name.

Marion Grant, Katharine Hepburn's sister, and Katharine Houghton's mother were delightful and the most normal member of the Hepburn family. Her brother Dick Hepburn showed up for the performance in tennis attire, accompanied by his wife, his former wife, and his girlfriend.

The day before opening night, I still did not know if my plan to bring Katharine Hepburn to the playhouse would finally work. I had set aside two front-row center seats, but we had not heard from her. Then, the Saturday afternoon of the opening, there was much commotion, and a lady from the box office came looking for me. Katharine Hepburn had arrived.

I introduced myself, and she said, "Yes, Mr. Doo-lee, I have heard all about you." She sounded like the character she played in "The Good Earth," and I was one of her Chinese friends. She had broken her ankle in a fall a few months earlier and was using a cane.

I brought her to the front row center, where I had reserved her seats. "These are lovely," she said, "but they won't do." She hobbled to a side section and pointed to two seats right under the "Exit" sign. "You will be here, Mr. Doo-lee, at 1 minute before curtain to escort me to my seat. At the end of the play, you will take me to the dressing room to see my niece."

I didn't salute, but I followed her orders. Katharine gave a lovely performance, and everyone got quite emotional in the dressing room. Katharine Houghton kissed me. Mrs. Grant kissed me. Katharine Hepburn kissed me. We never did get Katharine Hepburn to the theater again. But the two-week run of the play was extremely successful. It also gave me the opportunity to solve a mystery.

I was always puzzled by Katharine Houghton's film career. She gave an academy-award performance in "Guess Who's Coming to Dinner," then disappeared. I asked her about it one night, and she told me a story with one requirement. I could never repeat it while Aunt Kate was still living. Katharine Hepburn died in 2003 in Old Saybrook.

The story: Katharine Houghton had just graduated from Sarah Lawrence, and she was visiting her aunt who was living with Spencer Tracy. A few days later, Spencer Tracy told Katharine Houghton that he wanted her to read for a part in a movie he and Katharine Hepburn were about to make.

Katharine Hepburn interrupted immediately and told Tracy that the role had already been cast. Tracy called the studio and asked that Katharine Houghton be allowed to read for the role. He was told it was too late, that the role had already been assigned. At that point, Tracy warned that if she weren't given an opportunity to read for the part, he and Katharine Hepburn would withdraw. Of course, Katharine Houghton got the role.

Spencer Tracy died suddenly of a heart attack right after *Guess Who's Coming for Dinner* was released. "Every door in Hollywood closed to me," Katharine Houghton told me.

"Your aunt received four academy awards and was nominated for another eight. Couldn't she have helped?" I asked.

"My aunt didn't think I paid my dues enough before I got that role," Katharine Houghton said.

Her story explained some of the tension I detected between Katharine and her sister, Mrs. Grant. The day before Katharine Hepburn finally showed up at the theater, I asked Mrs. Grant if her sister was coming. "She'd better be coming," Mrs. Grant said.

Mrs. Grant gave a lovely cast party, but her sister did not attend. The following week I saw Katharine Hepburn in a garden shop in Essex, CT.

"Good morning, Miss Hepburn," I said. She walked right by me.

Remembering Korea

Korea will not be forgotten by my Edgewood friends who served in the war or me. Frankly, I do not count because I fought the war in Europe and Africa with a typewriter and never saw a shot fired in anger. But two of my friends made the ultimate sacrifice. Don White was killed in the early fighting, and Ed McGinnis, a close friend and member of the First Marine Division, was killed by an incoming shell the day after he arrived in Korea. His brother Bill was with him that day and became a lifelong marine.

Friends like Bob Plant, Peter Bowen, Herb Browne, Charlie Lafferty, Bill Crofton, and John McGirr fought in Korea. My brother Bob had to be evacuated from North Korea when the Chinese came into the war. Other friends who served during the war included Ray McGinnis, Paul and Joe Flaherty, Wes and Loring Forcier, Bill Considine, Jerry Roque, Tom Breslin, Bill O'Connor, Al Curtin, and Brad and Ron Boss. Bob Vickers, one of the best athletes in Cranston, was permanently disabled after being struck by North Korean gunfire.

My brother Bill was recalled for the Korean War, although he had already served in WWII. Of all my friends, Bob Plant was the only one to conduct two tours in Korea. In November 1950, during the coldest winter North Korea had experienced in 100 years, Bob's army unit was surprised by 120,000 Chinese troops at the Chosin Reservoir. Bob was one of the few Army survivors who joined the 1st Marine Division in a desperate 78-mile journey to freedom.

Cut off from support, the Marines and army veterans were able to fight their way through 10 Chinese infantry divisions. The attitude of those who served at the "Frozen Chosin," as it was later called, set an example that is still remembered by Marines and soldiers who fought against what seemed like impossible odds.

For more than 40 years, Bob attended reunions of the "Chosin Few" held annually around the country. At one of the gatherings, a Marine first sergeant described Bob Plant as "Audie Murphy," the most decorated soldier in WWII, as Bob operated a machine gun and threw grenades to keep the attacking Chinese from overwhelming key positions. During that battle, Bob suffered frostbite in both feet, problems that plagued him all his life. He refused to accept the idea that he was a war hero, claiming that the real heroes were the men who died in Korea. Bob is gone now, as are all of my Korean my friends, with the exception of Herb Browne.

The ruling dynasty in North Korea was begun in 1948 by Kim Il-sung, passed on to his son, Kim Jong-il in 1994 and to his grandson, Kim Jong-un, in 2011. The fundamental idea is that North Korea can only survive by remaining separate and distinct from the world. The country's strength depends entirely on its godlike leaders, the Kim family. The vast majority of the population lives in terrified and impoverished misery.

In 2017, North Korea successfully tested an intercontinental ballistic missile capable of flying between 6,213 and 6,835 miles. At that range, Los Angeles, Denver, Chicago, and possibly New York, Boston, and Washington, D.C., are within range. Despite two U.S.-North Korean summit meetings, there has been no decrease in North Korea's weapons of mass destruction. On June 13, 2020, Kim Yo Jong, sister of Kim Jong-un, warned that the North-South liaison office in North Korea would be destroyed in retaliation for South Korea activists who are launching propaganda leaflets across the border. Two days later, the building was destroyed in a move that raises tensions on the Korean Peninsula.

Inter-Korean relations have worsened since the breakdown of the second summit between President Trump and Kim Jong-un. The negotiations fell apart when North Korea demanded the lifting of all sanctions before dismantling its nuclear weapons.

We will never forget the Korean War or the frustration of what it really accomplished, which remains questionable 67 years after the last shot was fired. Did people like Ed McGinnis, Donald White, and thousands of other young Americans die in vain for a war that accomplished nothing?

She Had a Love Affair with Humanity

We used to marvel at her normal workday. No matter what time we drove to Laysville Center, a convenience store in Old Lyme, CT, it always seemed that Margaret Coffee was behind the counter. We did not know that her workday did not end when she finally put the key in the door at night.

Margaret put her training as a nurse to good use, calling on the sick in the community, many of them old and alone. She did so quietly, efficiently, and lovingly, three words that best describe the character of Margaret Coffee. Her type of charity was not the subject of newspaper articles or charity balls. It was the Mother Teresa variety, except instead of laboring in the streets of Calcutta, she journeyed to the homes of sick friends in Lyme and Old Lyme, dispensing her unique blend of nursing and human relations skills. No one who called Margaret friend ever had to face a serious illness alone.

She had a deep faith in God yet was never judgmental about the beliefs and conduct of others. Long before George Bush talked about his "points of light" or Bill Clinton's volunteerism, Margaret Coffee was laboring in the trenches. In the more than 30 years that I knew her, I never heard Margaret Coffee make an unkind comment about anyone. She expected to be treated with kindness and respect because that was all she ever gave. A random act of kindness is an event today, usually worthy of media attention. Margaret Coffee's life was a series of "random acts of kindness." She performed more charitable works on a slow Tuesday night than most of us achieve in a lifetime.

She had personal tragedies, losing her husband Ken at an early age, leaving her to raise a large family on her own. She also suffered the ultimate tragedy for any parent, losing a daughter, a nun, to cancer. While both losses hurt her deeply, nothing could undermine her faith. Her children and grandchildren reflect the legacy of love, character, and responsibility that she instilled in them. She and Ken Coffee would be so pleased to see what her children and grandchildren have done to Laysville Center. It features the finest hardware store in the area and a first-class restaurant.

Margaret combined the tenacity of her Midwestern roots with the work ethic of a native New Englander that would make any Yankee proud. She had a wonderful sense of humor that can best be illustrated by an incident that occurred while her daughter was in the convent. No one believed in that old adage, "We are what we eat," more than Margaret. She used to read food labels the same way some of us study the sports or financial pages. Her warnings about food ingredients would have done justice to any FDA nutritionist.

As a great benefactor to the convent in Madison, Margaret would load her car with frozen dinners and pizzas for the nuns. It did concern her that the nuns were eating more frozen dinners than they should. One morning, I was in the store when a local fisherman delivered two gallons of Niantic Bay scallops that Margaret had ordered. "At last, the nuns are going to have some nice fresh seafood," Margaret said to me as she loaded the car for her trip to the convent.

"How did the nuns enjoy the scallops?" I asked Margaret the following week. Margaret shook her head as she told me. "They froze them so they can eat them this winter." Customers had to be puzzled when they came into the store and saw two middle-aged people laughing hysterically.

When my dear friends, Carl and Lois Lutender, lost their son Gary at age 31, Margaret went to their home and sat with them. "I don't remember what was said," Lois told me years later. "But her being there took away some of the pain."

Margaret died on April 29, 1997, 24 years ago. While it saddens me that I will never hear that laughter again, I feel blessed that I could share in it in the first place. Some wise person once said, "Memory is the first great gift of nature and the last to be taken away." As long as we have memory, Margaret Coffee will always be with us.

In the final hours of his life, Robert Frost was asked which poem he wanted most to be remembered by. "None of them," Frost answered. "Let this be my epitaph: 'He had a love affair with humanity.' "

This is a fitting epitaph for Margaret Coffee. Another would be, "She would rather light a candle than curse the darkness." Margaret would reject them both as being too flowery for her simple tastes. Since she would never accept recognition for her good works in life, we should not impose them on her in death.

Her son John said it best: "She was such a role model for us to grow up with, and we miss her love and presence."

Margaret Coffee always believed in actions more than words. The best way we can remember her is to offer each other the same kindness, consideration, and charity that she always gave to us. There are angels among us who impersonate people as they spread love, kindness, charity, and faith. Margaret Coffee was one of them.

LIFEGUARDING

After finishing my Air Force career in May of 1955, I returned to Rhode Island in a Ford convertible and a few thousand dollars in my pocket, resulting from weekly polka games with my service buddies. I planned to have a lovely summer before returning to Providence College in September. Unfortunately, my brother Bob had other ideas.

He had a friend, Jim, a high school teacher, who had a summer job teaching swimming and diving at the Agawam Hunt Country Club, one of Rhode Island's most prestigious clubs. Jim had a problem that year. The pool was going to open two weeks before his school closed for summer vacation. If he did not find someone to cover for him, the club planned to find a replacement.

I resisted. I had been swimming since the age of five, but I would never classify my form as classic. My diving skills were limited to a cannonball, jackknife, and Swan dive. There was no way I could pass myself off as a swimming instructor. But the real reason I turned down the job was my underlying dislike for the country club set. So I told Bob I was not interested.

Jim came to my house and explained that I would only be responsible for lifeguarding duties. There would be no swimming or diving instruction. He emphasized how important this job was to him financially. I reluctantly agreed to take the job. I went to the club the following day, and Jim showed me how to test the water and add the proper balance of chemicals. I also met the Club President, who seemed like a nice guy.

My first week on the job went quite well, and I enjoyed supervising young children. I was more of a babysitter than a lifeguard. Their mothers would drop them off and then leave to play golf. I started playing games with the kids, tossing a ball into the air as they dove into the pool. I supervised races and diving competitions and invented a lot of crazy games the children seemed to enjoy. More than one mother told me that "Jack" or "Jane" could not wait to get to the pool in the morning to play games with Ken.

There were basic rules I had to enforce., such as no running or horseplay in the pool. When I blew the whistle, the children stopped whatever they were doing. If they did not, the mothers backed me 100 percent.

The success of the first week gave me a sense of confidence. However, the second week got off to a rocky start. "Jack" was 15 and already six feet tall and about 150 pounds. I was seven inches shorter and 10 pounds heavier. A few days earlier, I talked to him about his rough treatment of some of the younger children. He just nodded, but I could tell he was not impressed.

I watched as he pushed some of the younger kids into the pool. After I fished the kids out, I told him he was out of the pool for the day. He looked down at me and announced he was not going anywhere. When I took his arm to lead him out of the poor area, he pushed me. I threw him over the pool fence, and when he landed, his courage seemed to evaporate. He began to cry and ran towards the golf course. One of the mothers sitting by the pool told me I had done the right thing. She also warned me that I would be hearing from Jack's mother.

A few minutes later, a golf cart drove up with Jack and his mother. "My son tells me that you hit him," she demanded. Before I could reply, the other mothers came to my rescue and explained what had happened and why Jack had been banned from the pool.

She turned to Jack and told him to return to the pool and behave himself. I stood in front of the two of them and said that Jack was not allowed in the pool for the rest of the day. The two of them left, but I had a strong feeling the incident was not over.

Just before the day ended, a tall, distinguished gentleman walked up and introduced himself as Jack's father. "You did the right thing in throwing my son out of the pool. If you ban him for the rest of the week, I will understand."

I let Jack in the pool the next day, and a strange thing happened. We became friends. By Wednesday, I felt comfortable that I would be able to finish the week. However, an event that day changed everything. It was late afternoon, and there were only a few people left in the pool. A group of caddies walked by the pool, and one of them asked if they could go in for a swim.

"Sure," I replied. About 10 of them left and returned in their bathing suits. They were having a great time in the pool when a woman drove up in her golf cart. "Do you see that young man," she said, pointing out one of the caddies. "He carried my clubs this morning."

"Well, isn't it nice that he is now able to cool off, and I'm sure he'll be able to carry your clubs tomorrow." It was not the answer she wanted. As I was closing the pool, the company president walked up to me. I understood his position that they could not open the pool to the public. That did not stop me from handing him the keys and quitting. At that point, I was not concerned about protecting Jim and his job. My brother told me later that Jim found a replacement and was able to keep the job.

I did learn one thing about the country club set. Yes, some snobs dislike people or activities they regard as lower-class. But there are many more nice people with respectful children.

THE SONG OF LOVE

I moved to Melbourne, FL, in 2003, about 45 minutes from my daughter, Alicia, and my granddaughter Sarah. I had a lovely house directly across from one of the most gorgeous beaches I had ever seen. It was a "55 and over community," and I quickly realized the significance of that term. My next-door neighbor introduced himself and invited me to join his group for dinner. I agreed, and he told me he would pick me up at 3 p.m.

"Isn't that a little early for dinner?" I asked.

"We always get the "early-early-bird-special," he said. "We save a lot of money."

"I'm sorry. I can't eat dinner that early," I replied. My reputation as a snob quickly spread throughout the community. It got worse when I attempted to join the tennis group. There was one court and many players waiting in line. Let me make one point perfectly clear—I was not a great tennis player. But for this group, I was a combination of Andrew Agassi and Roger Federer. My first serve blew right past my opponent. He looked at me and called, "I can't return that serve." My partner called over to me, "You had been served again, but not so hard."

Instead of answering him, I sent a second serve with the same result. Then a third and a fourth. We won the game 40-love, but my partner walked off the court, indicating he did not want to play with me again. Neither did anyone else. That was the last time I played tennis with that group. "A tennis bully" was added to my snob reputation.

When Alicia and Sarah visited me that first weekend, we went for a ride. I didn't want them to be aware of the hostility of my neighbors in the community. Sarah, who was ten at the time, spotted a sign offering Poodles for sale. We had lost three previous poodles, Gidget, Tiffany, and Chi-Chi. Each loss hit me hard, and I did not want to deal with it again. At first, I said "no," but I finally consented to go in for a look. I told them both I was firm in my resolve not to have another dog.

There were four poodles in the litter, and three of them ignored us completely. The fourth, a little white ball of fire, would not leave us alone. Alicia and Sarah fell in love quickly, but I stuck to my resolve—for about 10 minutes. When we left about 30 minutes later, Lilly, named because she resembled a lily pad, sat in the back seat in Sarah's arms.

We did not get off to a great start. The first night, Lilly chewed through the sheets in my rented condo. The next day, I took her to the beach, which meant crossing Rt. 1A, a jam-packed highway. It was February, and dogs were allowed on the beach. Lilly was about seven pounds, so I had no trouble keeping her under control. She lulled me into a false sense of security. Suddenly she bolted, pulling the leash out of my hands and heading for the staircase that would bring her onto a bustling highway.

I had just turned 70 and took off in pursuit. Just before Lilly reached the first step, I dove and got one of her rear legs. Out of breath and gasping for air, I was not very happy with Lilly. She sat on my chest and then did something that set the tone for our 16-year relationship. She looked me in the eyes and then licked my hand. "It's over," her eyes told me. "Let's move on."

I was happy to leave Melbourne and settle into an apartment at the *Renaissance,* a lovely condominium complex in Sarasota, FL. Lilly and I were on the 13th floor and had a gorgeous view of the Gulf. It was a dog-friendly community, and we quickly made many friends during our morning and afternoon walks. A few weeks into the lease, I received a letter from the building committee informing me that only condominium owners could have pets, not renters. I would have to give up Lilly if I were to stay. The owner had assured me that Lilly would not be a problem. I called him and read him the letter. He said he would do whatever he could, but I did not get his attention until I told him that Lilly and I would be leaving his condominium if the eviction stood. Fortunately, some of the friends I had made appealed to the building committee on my behalf. Lilly and I were "grandfathered" in, the first renters allowed to have a dog.

Lilly was about five years old before I realized she was the first female I had ever lived with successfully. She was a constant in the next eleven years as I moved to Orlando, Sarasota, Winter Garden, and Newport, RI. We became like an old married couple, adjusting to each other's idiosyncrasies. And we both had plenty. My former wife complained that I frequently went into spells when I seemed to enter a world of my own. I spent a good part of everyday writing, some for my job, which allowed me to avoid "early-bird specials" and to keep Lilly in the expensive treats she liked. Lilly was always a high-maintenance female—inexpensive dog treats didn't appeal to her. I also wrote plays and screenplays, most of which didn't go anywhere.

Lilly would fall asleep with her head on my shoe as I was at the computer. Sometimes we would both forget her presence and react with surprise when I got up abruptly. Lilly would give me one of her famous "how could you" looks, but she always forgave me. We developed a nighttime ritual before bedtime. Of course, Lilly always slept with me. I would hold her in my arms, look into her eyes and sing:

The song of love is a sad song,
Hi Lilly, Hi Lilly, Hi lo.
A song of love is a song of woe
Don't ask me how I know.
A song of love is a sad song
For I have loved and it's so
I sit at the window watch the rain
Hi Lilly, Hi Lilly, Hi-lo.
Tomorrow I'll probably love again
Hi Lilly, Hi-Lilly, Hi-lo.
A song of love is a sad song
Hi-Lilly, Hi-Lilly, Hi-lo.
A song of love is a song of woe.

The best example of my singing skills is illustrated by my membership in the Boys' Choir of St. Paul's Church in Cranston, RI, in 1946. The choir director was a nun by the name of Sister Muriel. She told me when I first tried out for the choir that I had a very unusual voice, and she would save me for special roles. She would point to me when she wanted me to sing, and otherwise, I was to remain silent, she warned. Sister Muriel never pointed at me in the two years that I was a member of the choir. I guess Lilly never came into contact with Sister Muriel, because she looked at me as if I were Luciano Pavarotti during our bedtime song.

I rented a house on Green Street in Newport, RI, in 2010. It was there that I wrote *Bellevue Avenue*, a Newport version of *Downton Abbey*. Lilly developed an annoying habit of barking at the postmaster whenever he walked on the old wooden porch. My daughter Alicia used a water squirt gun to keep her two cats under control. So I went out and bought a water gun, which I kept on my desk. I will never forget her expression the first time I shot her with the water gun. She gave me a "how could you look" then hid in the guest room. She wouldn't even go for a walk until I apologized. That one shot did not do the trick. So during the next week, she got hit three or four times a day.

One morning during a horrible barking episode, I reached for the water gun, and it wasn't there. I searched the entire house but couldn't find it. Then a strange thing happened—Lilly stopped barking despite the absence of the water gun. A few months later, I dropped a sock on the bedroom floor. When I reached down to pick it up, I saw something glittering under the bed. It was the missing water gun. Lilly had taken it off my desk, carried it up the stairs, and hid it under my bed. I threw the water gun in the basket, realizing that I had violated Lilly's rule of conduct. If I wanted her to change something, I should ask and not resort to punishment.

When Lilly was about 12, she began developing throat problems. I took her to a veterinarian on Park Avenue in Cranston, RI. The waiting room was crowded with dogs and cats when Lilly and I arrived. She sat quietly on the floor as we waited our turn. A very large lady with the biggest German Shepherd I had ever seen walked into the waiting room. The dog strained at the leash, barring his teeth as he tried to get to Lilly. I leaned over and picked her up.

"Don't worry," his owner called out to me. "My dog has been fixed."

"I'm not worried about your dog sexually assaulting me," I called back. "It's the teeth." The whole room rocked with laughter, except for the German Shepherd's owner.

Three years later, a different veterinarian gave me a somber diagnosis about Lilly's neck. She would require expensive surgery that may only buy her a short time. Considering her age, did I want to make such an investment?

Lilly was operated on the next week and made a rapid recovery. We were back to our evening rituals, and she was better than she had been for a long time. On July 17, 2018, I was awakened by Lilly's heavy breathing. I clicked on the light and then picked her up. She looked at me with those endearing eyes, licked my hand, and died. Later I realized that she had awakened me to say goodbye.

I moped around for the next few months. That line in the song—"Tomorrow I'll probably love again"—does not apply to me. Alicia and Sarah wanted to get me another dog. But I'm old enough to know that there are some people and pets who cannot be replaced. Lilly will be my last dog. I take consolation in the realization that Lilly was a lady, and ladies always know when it's time to go.

My Last Stage Performance

I remember reading about the conversion of an old knitting needle building into a theater in Chester, CT in 1982. I had no idea that I would be involved in the theater's first production. It began when an old friend, Susan Anderson, asked me to recommend a play for the opening production. She told me the roles would be performed by Chester residents, so I tried to select a play that was so inherently funny it could withstand amateur acting. So I recommended *You Can't Take It With You*, a play that opened on Broadway and was later made into a successful movie.

Written by Moss Hart and George Kaufman, it tells the story of a successful banker who has just returned from Washington, D.C., where he was effectively granted a government-sanctioned munitions monopoly, which will make him very rich. He intends to buy up a 12-block radius around a competitor's factory to put him out of business, but there is one house that is a holdout to selling. Kirby instructs his real estate broker to offer a huge sum for the house, and if that is not accepted, to cause trouble for the family. Meanwhile, Grandpa Vanderhorn, convinces a banker named Poppins to pursue his dream of making animated toys.

Kirby's son_Tony, a vice president in the family company, has fallen in love with a company stenographer, Alice Sycamore. When Tony proposes marriage, Alice is worried that her family would be looked upon poorly by Tony's rich and famous family. In fact, Alice is the only relatively normal member of the eccentric Sycamore family, led by Vanderhof. Unbeknownst to the players, Alice's family lives in the house that will not sell out.

Kirby and his wife strongly disapprove of Tony's choice for marriage. Before she accepts, Alice forces Tony to bring his family to become better acquainted with their future in-laws. But when Tony purposely brings his family on the wrong day, the Sycamore family is caught off-guard, and the house is in disarray. As the Kirbys are preparing to leave after a rather disastrous meeting, the police arrive in response to what they perceive as printed threats on flyers by Grandpa's son in law. When the fireworks in the basement go off, they arrest everyone in the house.

Held up in the drunk tank preparing to see the night court judge, Mrs. Kirby repeatedly insults Alice and makes her feel unworthy of her son, while Grandpa explains to Kirby the importance of having friends and that despite all the wealth and success in business, "you can't take it with you". At the court hearing, the judge_allows for Grandpa and his family to settle the charges for disturbing the peace and making illegal fireworks by assessing a fine, which Grandpa's neighborhood friends pitch in to pay for it. The judge repeatedly asks why the Kirbys were at the Vanderhof house. When Grandpa, attempting to help Kirby, says it was to talk over selling the house, Alice has an outburst and says it was because she was engaged to Tony but is spurning him because of how poorly she has been treated by his family. This causes a sensation in the papers, and Alice flees the city.

With Alice gone, Grandpa decides to sell the house, thus meaning the whole section of the town must vacate in preparation for building a new factory. Now, the Kirby companies merge, creating a huge fluctuation in the stock market. When Kirby's competitor dies after confronting him for being ruthless and a failure of a man, Kirby has a realization he is heading for the same fate, and decides to leave the meeting where the signing of the contracts is to take place.

As the Vanderhofs are moving out of the house, Tony tries to track down Alice. Kirby arrives and talks privately with Grandpa, sharing his realization. Grandpa responds by inviting him to play *Polly Wolly Doodle* on the harmonica that he gave him. The two let loose with the rest of the family joining in the merriment, and with Alice taking Tony back. Later, at the dinner table, Grandpa says grace for the Sycamore family and the Kirbys, revealing that Kirby has sold back the houses on the block.

Susan asked me to attend a casting call, and she was crushed when only two people showed up. One of them hoped to be a stagehand. The other was more suitable as an usher and not an actor. No one had been kinder to my family when my wife was recuperating from breast cancer. So I came up with a plan. At the time, I was making a lot of documentary films with some very capable actors. I called them together and suggested they volunteer for the stage production.

I put together a very capable team, including John Joseph, Harry Cross, Liz Cross, and some other good talent. Susan was supposed to direct, but at the first rehearsal, it was decided that I should take over. I felt we were in good shape for opening night, three days away. A dilemma developed when Dave Miller, who was cast to play Paul Sycamore, got hurt in an automobile accident and had to withdraw. I called the cast together and asked for suggestions for a replacement. "You know every line in the play," John Joseph said. "So you're playing the role."

The theater was packed for opening night, and I felt we got off to a good start. I had a line in scene 3: "Mr. DePina, we have to go into the cellar and make the fireworks." As I moved stage right to the door, it wouldn't open. A beam had fallen, and the door was blocked. After trying to open it for several seconds, I turned to Mr. DePina and said: "Mr DePina you have locked us out of the cellar again." We exited stage left and no one picked up on the problem. I can still hear my twelve-year-old daughter, Alicia, giggling when I appeared in Act Two in patched long johns. We got good reviews and the theater was sold out for the remaining performances.

The theater has been renamed the Terris Theatre and it now serves as the second stage for Goodspeed Musicals. The first two-time Tony Award winning theater in the nation, Goodspeed Musicals is renowned as the home of the American Musical. At the Terris Theatre, Goodspeed develops new musicals and nurtures emerging artists.

As humble as it was in contrast to what is happening in the theater now, I take great pride in my last performance as an actor and director.

I just hope they fixed that damn door!

LUCKY LINDY AND THE 39TH

Charles Lindbergh completed his solo transatlantic flight in 1927, four years before I was born. Unfortunately, his son was kidnapped in 1931, when I was a baby. The Lindberghs paid the $50,000 ransom, but, sadly, their son's body was found in the woods several days later. The ransom money was traced to a carpenter by the name of Bruno Hauptman. I can remember my father and Mr. Reynolds, who delivered eggs and chickens to the Dooley family weekly, arguing about Hauptman's guilt or innocence, a German immigrant like Mr. Reynolds. We were good customers with seven children, but Mr. Reynolds did not follow the old rule about the customer always being right.

I can still remember the tension between my father and Mr. Reynolds, our egg man when Hauptman was executed in 1936. Although the relationship was strained, Mr. Reynolds kept the Dooleys as customers until Adolf Hitler began to persecute the Jews and made preparations to start WWII. After that, the tension between my father and Mr. Reynolds became unbearable, and my mother started to buy eggs from the A&P.

Jack Benny, my father's favorite comedian, was Jewish. I can still remember sitting in his lap listening to Jack, Mary Livingstone, Rochester, Phil Harris, Dennis Day, and Don Wilson every Sunday night. Jack Benny had special significance for me also because the most money I ever earned at that time came through a 1945 contest on his show. In the contest, you were to complete this sentence in 25 words or less. "I can't stand Jack Benny because . . ." I completed the sentence with "because my Uncle Leo likes him and I don't like my Uncle Leo." Actually, Leo Kenneally was my favorite uncle. I can still remember the excitement when I got the letter with a check. Although no age restrictions were stipulated in the contest, my mother feared that they would take the check back if they found out I was only 14 years old. Jack Benny never asked me to return the money.

I never heard much about Charles Lindbergh during WWII. His name came up when I began to interview former 39th Fight Squadron pilots for the book I was writing about them. Lt. Fred Tobi never forgot his first combat mission. He and Lt. Bob Thorpe were given an orientation flight conducted by Lt. Lew Lockhart and then sent out the next day on an escort mission to protect U.S. ships from Japanese air attacks. The mission was under the command of Major Billy Anderson, who had "Nasty" for a nickname. His name had nothing to do with his disposition or combat experiences. He earned the "Nasty" title over a strategy he used in a game of Hearts.

The mission flew over the Owen Stanley Mountains with Tobi in "wing" position, the usual spot for new pilots. Tobi used his 200-gallon belly tank before switching to his main fuel supply. He called Anderson and reported his gas situation was getting low. Anderson merely told him, "You're all right." When Tobi landed, he was totally out of gas and had to climb out of his plane and run off the runway to avoid being hit by landing planes.

"When Bob Thorpe, Jack Frost, and I joined the 39th, veteran pilots like Lew Lockhart were still complaining about losing their beloved P-38s," Tobi said. "Bob, Jack, and I had been thoroughly trained in the P47s, so we were comfortable with the aircraft. But there was one argument we couldn't win. They were gas guzzlers which kept us from taking part in a lot of critical missions—until Charles Lindbergh got involved."

I asked Tobi to explain what he meant about Lindbergh's involvement. "We heard that Lindbergh had been at Guadalcanal working with the P-38 and Marine F4U squadrons there, teaching them how to reduce gas consumption and increase their flight range," Tobi said. "He first briefed a large meeting in Nadzab, and then came back for individual briefings with the 39th. He did not fly any missions with us because General Kenney issued orders that he was not to take part in combat," Tobi explained.

The Lindbergh method was to open the throttle wide and then reduce RPMs by increasing the propeller's pitch, which would leave the engine laboring heavily. Then the pilot would lean the fuel mixture, starving the engine for fuel and significantly reducing its power output. Leaning the mixture too much would produce vibration, which was corrected by making the mixture a little richer. At the correct setting, this would result in a 180-mph cruise speed at a very low altitude.

Lindbergh combined his teaching with combat flying, mostly unknown to the Fifth Air Force brass. On May 21, 1944, he flew a strafing mission at Rabual and, a few days later, a bomber escort mission from the Marine air base at Bougainville. In his six months in the Pacific, Lindbergh flew 50 combat missions, including one on July 28, 1944, when he shot down a Japanese observation plane.

There was a good reason why his role was not publicized during the war. When he proposed that a neutrality pact be negotiated with Germany during testimony before the U.S. House Committee on Foreign Affairs on January 23, 1941, he had gone too far for the Roosevelt Administration. The President described him as a "defeatist and an appeaser" at a White House press conference on April 25, 1941.

"When I read Lindbergh's speech, I felt that it could not have been better put than if it had been written by Joseph Goebbels himself," Secretary of War Henry Stimson said. "What a pity that this youngster has completely abandoned his belief in our form of government and has accepted Nazi methods because apparently, they are more efficient." Treasury Secretary Henry Morgenthau added, "If I should die tomorrow, I want you to know this. I am absolutely convinced that Lindbergh is a Nazi."

On April 28, 1941, Lindbergh resigned his commission as an Air Corps colonel, claiming he had no honorable alternative. The Japanese attack on Pearl Harbor shocked Lindbergh, although he had previously predicted that America's "wavering policy in the Philippines" would invite war there. In one speech, he warned, "We should either fortify these islands adequately or get out of them entirely." He had consistently advocated alertness and military strength while maintaining that defending the country from attack was the U.S. military's sole purpose. Now, the country had been attacked, and its best-known aviator wanted to rally to its defense, but would the defense establishment welcome his help?

When Stimson declined his request for a commission in what was then the United States Army Air Corps, he approached several aviation companies to offer his services as a consultant. First, Lindbergh was accepted at Ford Motor Company, where Henry Ford shared many of his views and contributed to troubleshooting early problems on the B-24 production line. Then he joined United Aircraft in 1943, first as an engineering consultant and later as a technical representative in the Pacific Theatre to study aircraft performances under combat conditions.

So much had changed in the 16 years since Charles Lindbergh took off from Roosevelt Field Long Island at 7:52 am on Friday, May 20, 1927, burdened with a record load of gasoline and hampered by a muddy, rain-soaked runway. He was not the best-known aviator attempting a non-stop trans-Atlantic flight. Five others had tried and failed before him. But 33 ½ hours later, when he landed at Le Bourget Airport, seven miles northeast of Paris, he became a worldwide hero who had transformed aviation.

He arrived back in the United States aboard the United States Navy cruiser Memphis. On June 11, 1924, a fleet of warships and multiple military aircraft flights, including pursuit planes, bombers, and a rigid airship, escorted him up the Potomac River to the Washington Navy Yard, where President Calvin Coolidge awarded him the Distinguished Flying Cross.

Two days later, a ticker-tape parade was held for him before enthralled crowds down New York's Fifth Avenue, and the next night he was honored with a grand banquet at the Hotel Commodore attended by some 3,700 people. On December 14, the Medal of Honor, usually only awarded for heroism in combat, was awarded to him by a special act of Congress. He was selected as the first Time magazine "Man of the Year," appearing on its cover on January 2, 1928. At age 25, Lindbergh remains the youngest individual to receive the designation. The massive publicity transformed the public's skepticism about air travel. By 1928, applications for pilots' licenses had tripled and the number of licensed aircraft quadrupled. Between 1926 and 1929, the number of U.S. airline passengers grew from 5,782 to 173,405.

Lindbergh's connections with the Army Air Corps began in 1924 with a year of military flight training with the U.S. Army Air Service. On March 5, 1925, he experienced his most serious flying accident. Just eight days before graduation, he was involved in a mid-air collision while practicing aerial combat maneuvers and had to bail out. But he graduated first in his class of 104 cadets and earned his pilot's wings and a commission as a 2nd Lieutenant in the Air Service Reserve Corps.

Years later, he attributed that year of training to his development as a focused, goal-oriented, skillful and resourceful aviator. At the time, the Army did not need any more active-duty pilots, so he returned to civilian aviation as a barnstormer and flight instructor. As a reserve officer, he continued to do some part-time military flying by joining Missouri National Guard's observation squadron, where he was promoted to 1st Lieutenant. Fame has its price, and in his case, it was the kidnapping and murder of his baby son. The circus atmosphere surrounding the trial of the century when the kidnapper was sentenced to execution disgusted Lindbergh, and he moved to Europe in 1930.

In December 1937, after years of living abroad, the Lindbergh family returned to the U.S. at the personal request of General "Hap" Arnold, Chief of the United States Army Air Corps, in which Lindbergh had risen to the rank of Colonel in the reserves. He accepted a temporary call-up to active duty to help estimate that service's readiness for a potential war. It included evaluating new aircraft types being developed, recruitment procedures, and finding a site for a new Air Force Research Institute and other potential air bases.

Assigned a Curtiss P-36 fighter, he toured various facilities in the U.S. and made several trips to Germany to report on the German Air Force, the Luftwaffe. Touring German aviation facilities, sometimes in the company of Luftwaffe chief Hermann Goring, Lindbergh became convinced that the Luftwaffe was the most advanced air force in the world. He was the first American to examine the Luftwaffe's newest bomber, the Junkers 88, and the frontline fighter, the Messerschmitt 109. Of the 109, he said that he knew "of no other pursuit plane which combines simplicity of construction with such excellent performance characteristics."

In Berlin, Lindbergh was lionized much as he had been in Washington nine years before. At a dinner held in his honor, Goring presented him with the Commander Cross of the Order of the German Eagle. The medal became controversial a few weeks later with the anti-Jewish rioting and violence of Kristallnacht, but Lindbergh declined to return it. "If I were to return the German medal, it seems that it would be an unnecessary insult. Even if war develops between us, I can see no gain in indulging in a spitting contest before that war begins."

Lindbergh warned in a secret memo that it would be "suicide" for Britain and France to oppose Hitler's violation of the 1938 Munich treaty. He contended that the French Army was incapable of stopping Hitler and that Britain's military, overly reliant on naval power, was outdated. Lindbergh apologists have argued that he was not so much pro-German as anti-Soviet. In an issue of the Reader's Digest in 1939, Lindbergh wrote, "Our civilization depends on peace among Western nations and, therefore, on united strength." Deploring the rivalry between Germany and Britain, he favored conflict between Germany and Russia.

By late 1940, he served as a spokesman for the antiwar American First Committee, addressing large crowds at Madison Square Garden and Soldiers' Field in Chicago. Rather than opposing Germany, he insisted, America's focus should be on upholding the Monroe Doctrine, preserving the Western Hemisphere from European conflicts.

Lindbergh's growing rift with Washington may have had as much to do with his stubbornness in his convictions and his inexperience in political maneuvering as with convictions themselves. A. Scott Berg, his Pulitzer Prize-winning biographer, points out that the American embassy had approved Lindbergh's acceptance of the German Eagle medal and that his non-intervention message and participation in the America First Committee had broad-based popular support.

What probably hurt him most in the public eye, according to Berg, was his willingness to make excuses for Hitler. In his diary on April 2, 1939, "I believe she [Germany] has pursued the only consistent policy in Europe in recent years. I cannot support her broken promises, but she has only moved a little faster than other nations in breaking promises. The question of right and wrong is one thing by law and another thing by history."

Lindbergh's contributions to pilots in the Pacific were not overlooked. "What he did for us was a lot more important than any role he could have supplied in combat," Tobi said. "Charles Lindbergh was the unsung hero of the war in the Pacific," General Mac Arthur added.

My Armenian Friends

"Beginning on April 24, 1915, with the arrest of Armenian intellectuals and community leaders in Constantinople by Ottoman authorities, one and a half million Armenians were deported, massacred, or marched to their deaths in a campaign of extermination."

Those words were part of a statement issued by President Joseph Biden on Armenian Remembrance Day, April 24, 2021. The president may have been alerting much of the nation to the atrocities suffered by the Armenians, but I already knew the story, told first-hand by one of the survivors, Henry Derderian. Henry was the owner of a small convenience store, similar to our modern 7-Eleven. My brother Bob went to work for Henry in 1945, and I joined him a year later when I was 15 and worked there through my senior year in high school.

Bob warned me that Henry never talked about his experiences in Turkish Armenia during the massacre, a word that was not used in history books when describing the events that took place in 1915. Turkey was a member of NATO, and no one wanted to offend a strategic ally. Until President Biden's statement, no American president had ever used the word "genocide" when referring to Turkish treatment of Armenians.

Always curious, I began to question Henry about his childhood in Armenia. He initially brushed off my questions, but, with the mind of an investigative reporter, I persisted. I hit a nerve when I told him that Turkish authorities insisted the so-called "genocide" never took place. He told me stories that gave me the same reaction when I read about the Nazi treatment of Jews in WWII.

His story began in Turkish Armenia when he was five years old. He watched as men, women, and children packed their worldly possessions onto mules and wagons and left their villages under the supervision of the Turkish police. Henry recalled seeing massacred Armenians along the roadways as he walked with his mother and a long line of displaced villagers. "The smell of death was everywhere," he said. Suddenly, the caravan was halted, and the Turkish police took all of the young men and marched them out of sight. Henry remembered hearing gunfire, and he never saw any of the young men again.

Henry and his mother were taken from the group and sent to

the home of a wealthy Turkish farmer. Henry's mother cooked and cleaned while he tended sheep and maintained the barn. His Turkish master beat him with a whip when he found Henry asleep in the pasture one day. Sadly, his mother, a Christian, died and was buried without a church service. A group of Armenians kidnapped Henry from his Turkish master and sent him to an orphanage. His older brother Arshag found him and told him the Turks had murdered their two sisters.

Shortly after Henry was transferred to an orphanage in Greece, he was contacted by his father, who had been living in America since 1900. His father wanted to return to Turkish Armenia and bring his family back to America, but WWI interrupted his plan. In 1927, at age 17, Henry finally came to America with his brother Arshag. In 1933, he married Bargeshd Stambolian in Providence, the daughter of a prominent doctor in Istanbul, Turkey, whom the Turks had killed in 1915.

Henry and his wife had two children, Kelum and Aroxie. I began calling his son Kelly, a name that has stuck with him for more than 70 years. He graduated from Brown University and now practices law in Boston.

The Derderians were only part of my Armenian family. When we moved to Edgewood, I became friendly with Bob Arabian while Albert Arabian became my brother Bob's best friend. Their father owned Imperial Jewelry, and the Arabians were extremely kind to us. They had a large summer home at Johnston Pond, and we were frequent guests. Fred Berdrosian operated Edgewood Pharmacy, right on the corner of my street. He became a family friend together with his daughters, Helen, a pharmacist, and Mary, a family court judge.

Ara Gelenian wrote an interesting booklet, "The Armenians in Rhode Island" for The Rhode Island Heritage Commission. The book includes a photo of the grand opening of Henry's Spa on March 6, 1947. The photo shows Henry and Bargeshd Derderian, Albert Arabian, and my brother Bob behind the counter.

My last interaction with the Armenian community occurred in 2013, shortly after I co-wrote a screenplay with Arlene Violet, former Attorney General of Rhode Island, *Bellevue Avenue*, an American version of *Downton Abbey*. Giovanni Feroce, CEO of Alex & Ani, reached out to us and expressed interest in financing the movie. We had several meetings with him and Carolyn Rafaelian, founder and chairman of one of the fastest-growing jewelry companies in the world. Giovanni told us that Alex & Ani would finance the film, and Carolyn's last statement to me was "Make a masterpiece." Giovanni was fired shortly after that, and the financing for the film disappeared.

It was embarrassing for Arlene, me, and Peter Martin, our site director, who had made arrangements for us to use some Bellevue Avenue mansions and a historic courtroom in Newport.

In the last few years, Carolyn Rafaelian has lost the company and about $900 million in her net value. I take no comfort in her demise. Alex & Ani was a significant employer in a state that can use all of the financial help it can get. Meanwhile, eight years later, Bellevue Avenue is drawing interest as a TV series.

MENTORING

In 1998, I was hired by Progressive Business Publications (PBP) as senior editor in Malvern, PA. Founded by CEO Ed Satell, it was one of the fastest-growing companies in the business information industry. Shortly after joining the company, Pieter Van Bennekom, Editorial Director, told me about a partnership the company had established with Cook-Wissahickson, a K-8 school located in Philadelphia. The company sponsored before-and-after-care classes and a mentoring program in which PBP employees worked with students who needed extra help. Once a week, mentors met with students at the school on a special one-on-one basis. In addition, each month, a bus transported students to PBP, where they would hang out with their mentors, be given special gifts and lunch.

I was unsure how to respond when Pieter asked me if I would like to join the mentoring program. At age 67, I didn't know if I had the patience to fulfill that role. I had always been able to relate to kids much better than to their parents. Some of my most enjoyable moments occurred when I directed children in a musical or coached a girls' softball team. Pieter referred me to Regina Black-Lennox, a vice-president of the company in charge of the mentoring program. She had tremendous organizational skills. WWII would have been over at least a year earlier if Regina had run the 1944 invasion of France. After a short conversation, I left her office with my first assignment—a student named Richard.

I met with Richard at the school about a week later. He was a very likable boy, and we bonded almost immediately. Everything seemed so normal that I didn't understand why Richard was even part of the mentoring program. Then we had our first reading session, and I realized where Richard needed help. He was in grade seven but was reading at a fourth-grade level. When I was editorial director for a division of Prentice-Hall, I had edited a course by Evelyn Wood, a recognized expert on speed-reading. I can't say I agreed with some of her techniques, remembering what Woody Allen once said on the subject of speed-reading. "I read War and Peace in 15 minutes. It was about Russia." But as I watched and listened to Richard read, I remembered what Evelyn Wood said about subvocalization, a process in which readers mouth the words as they read. Richard was not even aware of what he was doing until we began to fix it. Within a few months, Richard was reading at grade level. I remember how proud I was when he was selected as student of the month in grade eight, his last year at Cook-Wissahickon. After Richard graduated, I was anxious to take on a new assignment.

Because of my success with Richard, Regina told me I would be taking on a more challenging assignment. Charles's problems were more social and mental than educational. He suffered from Attention-Deficit Disorder (ADD). The school nurse frequently interrupted our sessions as she gave him Ritalin, a stimulant drug used to treat ADD. I never saw any positive results after Charles was given the drug. If anything, he became more restless and undisciplined.

We had our problems, especially when Charles didn't feel like reading or working on educational programs on the computer. But I never had any question about his brightness. He would make observations that would sometimes startle me. Occasionally, he would share some insights about his mother or one of her boyfriends. There were many, and Charles was not fond of most of them.

He also had problems with his classmates. Charles wore the same clothes almost every day, and his physical hygiene left much to be desired. He was the butt of many jokes from his classmates, but his retaliation was quick and decisive. One morning, I met the bus transporting students to PBP for lunch and activities. As Charles got off, he suddenly kicked the boy in front of him, who screamed and fell to the ground. I led Charles away for a time-out as the other boy received treatment for his leg. "Why did you kick that boy, Charles?" I demanded. "He told me I smelled," Charles answered.

There was another side of Charles that was utterly endearing. PBP had box seats for the Philadelphia Phillies baseball games, and Charles and I attended whenever we were invited. He was always enthusiastic and well-behaved on those occasions. It was on one of those trips when I got to meet his mother. She was a single parent, listed as "mentally challenged," which translated into a low IQ. She didn't even acknowledge me when Charles introduced us. No hellos or goodbyes as Charles got into my car. After that first meeting, Charles said something that gave me an early warning that something was wrong in his home situation.

Charles had told me about a radio he had in his room that suddenly disappeared. He blamed it on one of his mother's boyfriends. I can still remember the delight on his face when I gave him a new radio. However, a few weeks later, he confided that this radio had also disappeared.

"My mother's a good person," he said. "I don't care what anyone else says," he continued. He brought his mother up again the following week. We were having a reading session when he looked up and asked, "Did anyone from the school talk to you about my mother?" I shook my head no. "If they do, tell them that my mother didn't steal my prescriptions," Charles said. When I asked for more details, he shook his head, indicating we were through with that topic. I had no idea that this would be the last conversation I would ever have with Charles.

After returning him to his classroom, I asked to see the principal. I told her what Charles had said and asked for an explanation. She shook her head and replied that an investigation was incomplete and she couldn't share any information with me at this point. About a week later, I went to the school for an afternoon session with Charles. His classroom teacher referred me to the principal.

"Charles is no longer at this school," she said. "He is now in the custody of Pennsylvania and has been placed in foster care. She turned me down flatly when I asked for contact information. "You did a good job with Charles," she said. "Take comfort in that, but your role in his life is over." Later, I learned through the grapevine that Charles's mother had falsified his Ritalin prescription to attain additional pills, which she sold.

It seems hard to believe, but Charles is now 30 years old. I pray that he ended up in a good foster family and overcame a difficult beginning. Yes, we had our problems, but the good times far outweighed the bad. I think of him fondly and will always regret that I did not play a more prominent role in his life. My relationship with Charles reminds me of a line from a John Greenleaf Whittier poem:

Of all sad words of tongue or pen
The saddest are these: "It might have been."

MURDER IN THE COURTROOM

On May 24, 1984, a man walked up to his estranged wife in a divorce court, pulled a gun from his jacket, shot her six times point blank, and muttered, "Now I can sleep at night."

Kenneth Spargo a 53-year-old shipyard worker, was arrested and charged with killing his wife Priscilla, 44, who died on a hospital operating table shortly after the shooting. She had been sitting on a bench inside Norwich Superior Court awaiting a hearing in the couple's divorce proceedings. Although the courthouse had a metal detector at the front, Spargo had entered with a handgun through another door.

Spargo and his wife were waiting for court to start when the shooting occurred. The couple had been separated about six months, and Spargo believed his wife was having an affair with a fellow parishioner at their church, his attorney said.

"She was sitting in the gallery, and all the lawyers were ready, and he just walked around directly in front of her, didn't say anything, and just pumped her with the bullets," said attorney Griswold Morgan of New London, who was representing Spargo. The attorney characterized his client as a religious man who was a Lakes Pond Baptist Church member. He said Spargo was convinced his wife had left their upper-middle-class neighborhood to run away with another man. "We alleged that his wife disappeared or left the household about six months ago and went with another parishioner of the church to Oklahoma," Morgan said.

Spargo worked as a specialist in the steel trades administration department of Electric Boat Shipyard in Groton, which builds nuclear submarines for the Navy. I never met him, but the murder had an impact on my life. Our company treasurer was a woman named Carol who had two daughters and a husband, Danny. They were members of the Lakes Pond Baptist Church, where Ken and Priscilla Spargo worshipped. Danny and Ken Spargo went on proselytizing missions together, walking neighborhoods and distributing literature. I had a confrontation with Danny when he entered company premises to distribute religious materials. Carol was embarrassed when the incident almost turned physical. But Danny did not come on our property again.

Carol knew Priscilla and was very disturbed by the event. She also complained that Danny was ignoring his family and devoting all his time to the church. A few months later, she told me that Danny had moved out at her insistence, and she was filing for divorce. She was particularly upset one morning after a telephone conversation with Danny. She told me that Danny had finished the conversation by commenting that Ken Spargo had the right idea. An hour later, we were in the office of the chief-of-police in Old Saybrook, Connecticut, and a restraining order was taken out against Danny. To my knowledge, no other threats were issued, and the divorce was granted without further incident.

I did have one final experience with the Lakes Pond Baptist Church. I was invited to the ceremony when Carol's daughter graduated from Lake Pond High School. A guest minister from Arkansas delivered the commencement address. In the middle of his remarks, he asked everyone who had been saved to raise their hands. I didn't move. Then he asked for anyone who wanted to be saved to raise their hands. His process of elimination worked. He spotted me as the only unsaved person in the audience. During his remarks, he described visiting a parishioner in a hospital who was hooked up to a cancer machine.

As I left the ceremony, the minister was standing in the doorway accepting congratulations for his fire and brimstone address. Our eyes locked as I stood in front of him. I know that he was expecting a request for a private ceremony in which I could be saved. "Tell me?" I asked. "What is a cancer machine?"

I moved on before he could answer. By the way, Ken Spargo was sentenced to life in prison. And I still do not know the definition of a cancer machine—or if I have been saved.

NBA Owners and the "White Dollar" Quota System

I referred to Red Auerbach as the "Branch Rickey of basketball" in a script I wrote for a motivational film entitled *Dedication and Desire—the Red Auerbach Story*. He made me take it out. Red never wanted to be credited for opening professional basketball to African American athletes. He selected Chuck Cooper, the first African American athlete to be drafted into the NBA, because he was the best player available. He started five black players because they represented the best team he could put on the floor. He appointed Bill Russell as the first black coach because he was the best man for the job.

Regardless of Red's feelings, it is impossible to tell the story of African Americans coming into the NBA without referring to Red Auerbach and the Boston Celtics. It started with the 1950 draft when Walter Brown, President of the Celtics, stood and announced that the team was drafting Chuck Cooper. "Do you realize that Cooper is Negro?" one of the owners asked. "I don't care about the color of a ballplayer's skin," Brown said. "He can be black, yellow, or green, as long as he can put the ball in the basket."

Although it had been seven years since Chuck Cooper, Earl Lloyd, and "Sweetwater" Clifton joined the NBA, there was still an unofficial quota system in play. Right after the league was integrated in 1950, Eddie Gottlieb, owner of the Philadelphia NBA team, warned that players would be 75% black in five years. "You're going to do a disservice to the game," he warned.

Gottlieb argued that since most ticket-buyers were white, they would not pay good money to watch black players. Too many blacks would be bad for business and would hurt the league's image. He was not alone in his thinking, with one owner arguing that blacks would also be hard to coach.

Gottlieb's position may have been influenced by his close relationship with Abe Saperstein, owner of the Harlem Globetrotters. Like the other owners, Gottlieb relied on doubleheaders with the Globetrotters to boost the low attendance for league games. Saperstein ensured his pick of the best black players available by threatening to keep his Globetrotters out of any NBA arenas featuring black players. After learning about Clifton, Auerbach drafted Cooper and signed

Sweetwater Clifton to the Celtics. Commissioner Maurice Podoloff vetoed the Clifton contract with the Celtics but allowed Ned Irish, the New York Knicks owner, to sign Clifton. Although he made some verbal threats, Saperstein never attempted to punish the Celtics or Knicks for signing black players.

When a quota system was first suggested after the 1950 draft, Walter Brown and Red Auerbach spoke against it. Brown announced at an owners' meeting that he would sell the Boston Celtics if a quota system were established. Ned Irish threatened to pull his team out of the league if it was not opened to black players. While there might not have been a written agreement, there was an understanding between the all-white owners that prevented a team from having too many blacks on its roster. The number of black starters was also controlled.

Looking at the rosters from 1950 to 1965 certainly supports a quota being in place, whether it was official or not. The highest number of blacks on a team was four, and some teams had one or two during that period. In 1950, Chuck Cooper of the Celtics, Sweetwater Clifton of the New York Knicks, Hank DeZonie of Tri-Cities, and Earl Lloyd of the Washington Caps were the only Blacks in the league, and they represented less than 3% of the 135 NBA players.

Bob Wilson joined Milwaukee in 1951, but the percentage stayed the same because of the departure of Hank DeZonie. The percentage jumped to five in 1952 when Don Barksdale and Dave Minor joined the league. Ray Felix joined Baltimore in 1953, Ken McBride was drafted by Milwaukee in 1954, Jackie Moore became a member of Philadelphia, and Jim Tucker joined Syracuse. At this point, nine of 105 players were Black, representing a jump to nine percent.

Ed Fleming, Dick Rickets, Maurice Stokes, and Robert Williams joined the league in 1956, raising the average to 13% Black (13 of 99). In 1957, Bill Russell, Willie Naulls, Sihugo Green, Hal Lear, raising the average to 15% (15 of 99). In 1958, K.C. Jones, Bennie Swain, Wayne Embry, Shellie McMillon, Elgin Baylor, Boo Ellis, Andy Johnson, Guy Rodgers and Willie Sauldsberry joined the league, representing a jump to 25% (19 of 92).

In 1959, Maurice King, Tim Hawkins, Johnny Green, Cal Ramsey, Wilt Chamberlain, and Dick Barnett came into the league, bringing the percentage to 24% (24 of 99). In 1960, Tom (Satch) Sanders, Bob

Boozer, Oscar Robertson, Willie Jones, Fred LaCour, Lenny Wilkins, Al Attles, and Joe Roberts joined the NBA, bringing the percentage to 29% (27 of 93). In 1961, Walt Bellamy, Horace Walker, Joe Buckhalter, Ray Scott, Cleveland Buckner, Ed Burton, Al Butler, Sam Stith, Stacey Arceneaux, Cleo Hill, and Bob Sims came into the NBA, bringing the percentage of Black players to 32% (36 of 113).

In 1962, Charlie Hardnett, Bill McGill, Leroy Ellis, Gene Wiley, Paul Hague, Tom Stitch, Wayne Hightower, Howie Montgomery, Hubie White, John Barnhill, Zelmo Beatty, Bill Bridges, Chico Vaughn, Porter Meriwether, Chet Walker, and Bob Warley brought the percentage of blacks to 38% (45 of 117). In 1963, Gus Johnson, Tom Thacker, Reggie Harding, Eddie Miles, Jerry Harkness, Tom Hoover, and Nate Thurmond brought the percentage of Blacks in the league kept the percentage of blacks in the league at 38% (42 of 111). In 1964, Les Hunter, Walt Jones, John Thompson, Happy Hairston, George Wilson, Joe Caldwell, Walt Hazard, Jim Barnes, Emmette Bryant, Willis Reed, Lucius Jackson, Larry Jones, Paul Silas, and John Tresvant brought the percentage of Blacks in the league to 49% (56 of 115).

While Eddie Gottlieb's 1950 prediction that Blacks would occupy 75% of NBA rosters in five years never materialized, his warning that white fans would not buy tickets to watch largely Black teams was also inaccurate. NBA attendance has grown every year, and the caliber of the team and not its racial balance has always been the determining factor in fan support.

Bobby Douglas's statement to Red Auerbach on draft night of 1950 has proven to be much more accurate. "This is our game. We're taller, faster, better rebounders, and we dribble and shoot better than you guys. Our problem isn't playing the game. It's getting to play the game. You just opened the door," Douglas said to Auerbach. Douglas's prediction is substantiated by the African American Rookies of the Year starting in 1954 with Ray Felix and continuing with Maurice Stokes, 1956; Willie Sauldsberry in 1958; Elgin Baylor, 1959; Wilt Chamberlain, 1960; Oscar Robertson, 1961; Walt Bellamy, 1962. Tommy Heinsohn was the only white to break the list by earning the award in 1957.

While Blacks had come of age in professional basketball in those early years, some owners continued to worry about the effect they would have on the gate. There was an unwritten agreement that each team would have no more than two blacks, then three, then four, then five. They had to be starters, not benchwarmers, to make the roster. It wasn't anything that anyone talked about. It just happened.

The experience of Al Attles when he joined the Philadelphia Warriors in 1960 is a good example of the quota system in action. Philadelphia already had four Blacks on the roster when Attles was drafted: Chamberlain, Johnson, Rodgers, and Sauldsberry. Instead of making Attles the fifth Black on the team, Philadelphia traded Sauldsberry, who had been Rookie of the Year two years earlier.

The early players had to deal with prejudice, both on and off the court. They frequently could not stay with the team at hotels or eat with them in restaurants. They would also be assigned to guard each other, frequently leaving the game to be played with four white players on each team. Some white players refused to pass them the ball, as they did to Cleo Hill when he played for the St. Louis Hawks.

The St. Louis Hawks defeated the Boston Celtics in the NBA Finals in 1958, becoming the last team in NBA history to win a championship without a Black player on the roster. The series went six games but was actually decided in game three when Bill Russell severely injured his left ankle and was out for the rest of the series. A team picture features only eleven players because the twelfth member of the team, Worthy Patterson, a Black guard from the University of Connecticut, played only four games in the regular season for St. Louis and did not appear in the playoffs. He was deliberately left out of the team picture.

Red Auerbach, who opened the league to African-Americans in 1950, helped shatter the quota system in 1963 by starting five black players: Willie Naulls, Tom Sanders, K.C. Jones, Sam Jones, and Bill Russell. When Auerbach retired in 1967, he appointed Bill Russell as his successor, the first African-American coach in any U.S. Professional sport.

The American Basketball Association (ABA) came into existence in 1967, creating leverage for African-American players and real competition for the established NBA. It featured electrifying players like Julius Erving, Connie Hawkins, Ernie DiGregorio, Marvin Barnes, and Artis Gilmore. The ABA also offered a flashier style of play than the NBA, a 30-second shot clock (as opposed to the NBA's 24-second clock), and the use of a three-point field goal. The freewheeling style of the ABA caught on with the fans, but the lack of a national television contract spelled its doom as an independent league. The ABA pioneered the popular slam dunk contest at its all-star game in Denver in 1976, the last year of its existence as it merged with the NBA.

By this time, NBA teams were featuring all-African-American starting lineups. By 1972, the Western Conference All-Star squad had only two white players on the team, Gail Goodrich and Jerry West. Of 250 active players in 1972, only seventy-seven were white, and most were fringe players.

Bobby Douglas, often called the "father of black professional basketball," died in 1979, the year after Larry Bird joined the Boston Celtics. It's doubtful they ever met, but the two share a common belief about basketball being a Black man's game. Bird went even further with remarks concerning playing against other white players when he was president of basketball operations with the Indiana Pacers in 2004.

"I really got irritated when they put a white guy on me during my playing career with the Celtics," Bird said. "A white guy would come out, and I would always ask him if he had a problem with his coach. If he said no, I would tell him he had no chance of guarding me. It is a Black man's game, and it will be forever. The greatest athletes in the world are African-American," Bird asserted.

Presidents & Elections

The first president I ever saw in person was Harry S Truman, who made a whistle-stop by train in Providence, Rhode Island, during his election campaign in 1948. I can still remember standing with my sister Peg as Truman waved to us—and about 5,000 other people—from the caboose. All the pollsters in the country had Thomas Dewey winning in a landslide. The Chicago Tribune even printed an edition confirming that Dewey was the next president.

My favorite political story of all time was the result of Dewey's defeat. The day before the election, the confident Dewey asked his wife, Frances, how she would feel election night sleeping with the president of the United States. After learning of Truman's victory, Dewey sat alone in his study, seeking solitude after his stunning loss. Suddenly Frances burst into the room with a question. "Now dear, am I going to Washington, or is Harry coming here?

I only met one person who ran for president, Barry Goldwater, who faced off against Lyndon Johnson in 1964. Our meeting took place four years earlier, right after John Kennedy was elected president in 1960. I had just started working for Prentice Hall and was sent to cover a meeting of the American Management Association, which featured Barry Goldwater as principal speaker.

I was sitting in the pressroom with two other young reporters when Barry Goldwater walked into the room an hour early. If he had arrived on time, veterans from The New York Times, The Wall Street Journal, and weeklies such as Time and Newsweek would have pushed us to the back of the room. Goldwater, a Republican, was a U.S. Senator from Arizona.

I was immediately impressed by his friendliness. He pulled up a chair, poured himself a cup of coffee, and asked where everyone was. He smiled when we told him he was an hour early for the press conference.

I asked a somewhat naive question. "Senator, do you think the Catholic vote elected Kennedy?"

"Of course it did," Goldwater answered. I don't place any blame there. The country has never had a Catholic president until Jack."

One of my colleagues asked him how he liked living in Arizona.

"I like it," he replied. "But I just got a letter from the local golf club informing me that I'm not eligible to join since I'm Jewish. I wrote back and asked if I could play nine holes since I'm only half Jewish."

In the hour I spent with him, I got the impression that Barry Goldwater was an intelligent, sincere man. He was labeled "Mr. Conservative" and described as a trigger-happy militarist when he ran unsuccessfully for president in 1964. His honesty contributed to his defeat. He talked about the long-term burden of Social Security in Florida and attached farm subsidies in Minnesota, Nebraska, and Iowa.

The meanness and inaccuracy of political advertising were evident during this election. Advertising agencies began selling presidential candidates as if they were cars or soap. One ad showed a 3-year-old girl in a dress counting as she plucked daisy petals in a sun-dappled field. Her words were supplanted by a mission-control countdown followed by a massive nuclear blast in a classic mushroom shape. The message was clear—Presidential candidate Barry Goldwater was a genocidal maniac threatening the end of the world. Another ad showed Goldwater yelling at a distraught woman huddled with several children. The caption reads, "Go and inherit a string of department stores," an apparent reference to Goldwater's family business.

Another ad mocked Goldwater's statement about privatizing Social Security by showing a pair of hands ripping up a Social Security card.

"The whole campaign was run on fear of me," Goldwater said after the election. 'In fact, if I hadn't known Goldwater, I'd have voted against the s.o.b. myself."

More than fifty years after that election, I became friendly with J. William Middendorf II, a key member of the "Draft Goldwater" movement in 1962. He was Goldwater's campaign treasurer and, afterward, a significant force within the Republican Party

The former Secretary of the Navy and Ambassador to the Netherlands, Middendorf wrote *Glorious Disaster: Barry Goldwater's Campaign and the Origins of the Conservative Movement*. Middendorf points out that even though he lost to Lyndon B. Johnson by a landslide, Barry Goldwater's failed presidential run was a major turning point of the twentieth century. Without Goldwater's philosophy to pave the way—and, just as importantly, without the strategic and political infrastructure created by the "Draft Goldwater" movement that preceded it—there likely would have been no Reagan or Bush administrations, and possibly no Nixon administration either. The policy positions and electoral strategies of the Goldwater campaign became standard tenets of Republican politics.

A MAN CALLED JOHN MCCAULEY

During the past 64 years, I have cast votes for candidates rang members. Some of my selections turned out to be success stories, while others became disasters. In reflecting on my voting record, my wisest choice was John McCauley, who ran for president of the senior class at La Salle Academy in 1949.

I like to think that I had a lot to do with John's successful campaign. I was a member of a small group of eggheads, and I convinced members of the class to cast their votes for John. That's why it was particularly perplexing when in 2010, a neighbor, Peg Murray, told me about meeting John in the waiting room of a doctor's office. When Peg learned that John had graduated from La Salle in 1949, she brought up my name, and he said he never heard of me. I got John's phone number and called him.

"Is this the same John McCauley who was the president of La Salle Academy senior class in 1949?" I asked.

"Yes, it is," he replied.

"Then I want my vote back," I demanded.

I then went on to explain the valuable contribution I had made to his campaign. Matt Zito, his campaign manager, knew about the number of "egghead" votes that helped get him elected. Poor John was embarrassed and assured me that he remembered me. I let him off the hook by reminding him that I was chosen as the "Most Forgettable" in the class in 1949.

My friend, Tim Cohane, had recently established a breakfast club made up of successful athletes who had retired to Newport. I don't know exactly why or how, but Tim got the bylaws changed to include me. Tim was a great basketball player at the U.S. Naval Academy and later became a successful Division I basketball coach. He is best known for his participation in a panty raid at Manhattanville College in New York that got him kicked out of Holy Cross College. His father, Tim Cohane Sr., the great sportswriter, covered Army football at West Point when John served as an assistant coach. One of the other assistants was Bill Parcells, who later became one of the greatest football coaches in the National Football League. Parcells is godfather to one of John and Gerry's children.

John became an active member of the breakfast club, and we enjoyed many breakfast club meetings together. I also became friendly with his wife, Gerry, who is a great croquet player. John was an outstanding athlete in football and basketball at La Salle and went on to stardom at Boston College. He devoted his life to football, coaching at the high school level and later at West Point. After graduation, we went in different directions, and I did not see John again until that reunion in Newport. When we reconnected, our friendship blossomed. It allowed me to know John in a way that we never achieved at La Salle.

The last years had to be difficult for John because his aching knees restricted his movements. It must have been painful for one of the great running backs in Rhode Island history to use a walker. He never complained and kept his wonderful sense of humor. When John and I were attending a function together, I commented, "Thank God for Lou Cimini," a football coach at La Salle. John asked me why I said that since I never made the football team.

"Lou cut me that first day and my knees are great," I said to John. I can still remember his laugh. I always enjoyed telling John that we set records together at La Salle. John not only made every team he tried out for but was the star. Meanwhile, I was cut from every team, usually during the first or second day of practice. There just wasn't that much call for a 5′7″, 125-pound running back. I believe it was during that time that I decided to pursue a career in writing.

John McCauley used to ask me many questions about Red Auerbach's style of coaching. Red taught that there was nothing wrong with being a sore loser, that only losers accepted losing. John placed a lot more emphasis on building character than on teaching X and Os. No, John didn't follow the teachings of legendary coaches like Red and Vince Lombardi. He placed more importance on building the character of his players instead of increasing their speed or strength.

No one took more pride in his family than John. He was so fortunate to have Gerry as his life partner. What a team they made. Six beautiful children and many grandchildren. John cherished them all. When John died in 2017, his family asked me to deliver his eulogy. It was an honor I will never forget.

'OLIVER' WILL HAVE A LOCAL LOOK AT IVORYTON

By Tim Murphy
Day Staff Writer

IVORYTON—Actors straining to remember lines, stagehands scurrying over props, a harried director blocking a scene for the dozenth time—all the frenzy of a musical speeding toward opening night is being replayed once again at the Ivoryton Playhouse, where such scenes have been common for 50 years.

But you thought the Ivoryton was closed, right? Wrong. The playhouse's summer producer was forced to cancel his summer season after only three shows, but a new group with a crowd of impressive local talent has moved in and his busy preparing a production of "Oliver," scheduled for 11 performances beginning Sept. 11.

The producers, Richard J. Bruno of Waterford and Kenneth R. Dooley of Old Lyme, are hoping "Oliver" will be only the first in a series of theater events at the Ivoryton, which eventually could include a wide range of locally produced fare as well as touring professional productions.

The pair, who have been active in local theater for years, say traditional summer theater like that featured at the Ivoryton for a half-century is a thing of the past, the victim of high costs and low audience support. But they say the success of the Goodspeed Opera House, the Long Wharf Theater in New Haven, and other theaters has convinced them there still is a market for good theater, one which they hope to tap.

"There's an audience out there waiting for us," said Dooley, copartner with Bruno in the newly formed New England Productions. "If we can give them the quality they're looking for, there's no question that they'll support us."

In addition to "Oliver," the pair plans to present an old-fashioned melodrama in October, complete with a sinister villain and a pure-hearted hero. And they are hoping to convince the Ivoryton Playhouse Foundation, the local group which owns the theater, to install a heating system, making possible a steady series of productions through the fall and winter.

But now, the pair are concentrating on "Oliver," which they chose, says Dooley, "because Essex (where Ivoryton is located) just seemed like a community for "Oliver," with its rich English tradition."

The production will feature a sort of gathering of the clan of local talent, nearly all of whom have won local theater awards.

The cast of 42 includes John Joseph as Fagin, Linda Denne as Nancy, David Miller as Bill Sikes, Liz Shafer as Mrs. Sowerberry, and Mary Ann Liniak-Bodwell as the Widow Corney. Jerry Gordon is the director. Most of the cast have had professional experience and are familiar to those who frequent community productions.

Many of the children's roles in the show, including the main roles, will be played by members of "Great Jubilation," a professional show choir which has performed throughout the state and in the Catskills.

"People are going to go away from this show on a high," said Bruno. "They'll be seeing the best people in the area."

Bruno and Dooley, who are providing all the financial backing of the show, admit they are taking something of a risk, but they are confident that the audiences who see "Oliver" will want more and they hope to be able to provide it.

"It's a labor of love, anyway, working with people you really like being around," said Bruno during an interview at the theater.

Both Bruno and Dooley admit the publicity which surrounded the cancellation of the Ivoryton's season last month is an obstacle they will have to overcome. They say lack of advertising contributed to the season's demise and they plan to advertise heavily to spread the message that the theater is still alive.

They are planning a special performance Sept. 17 for anyone who held a ticket to one of the canceled Ivoryton shows, whether or not the person received a refund on the ticket. Other performances will be at 8 p.m. Sept. 11, 12, 13, 18, 19, 20, 25, 26, and 27, with a matinee Sept. 28 and a senior citizen's night Sept. 10.

And there is no question, they say, but that the show will go on.

"We can't promise much about the future, but we absolutely guarantee that 'Oliver' will go on as promised, even if I have to play Oliver and Dick (Bruno) has to play Nancy," Dooley said.

Two Rhode Islanders for Peace

On the surface, it would appear that two prominent Rhode Island residents, Alan Hassenfeld of Bristol and David Maloof of Middletown, should be on opposite sides of the Israeli-Palestine debate. Hassenfeld, retired chairman of Hasbro, is Jewish, while David Maloof is a Christian Arab-American. Yet the two men have a great deal in common, especially in their efforts for a peaceful solution to a 57-year old conflict.

As United States Chairman of the Jerusalem Foundation, Hassenfeld is committed to creating a pluralistic Jerusalem, one where "East and West, old and new, everything would come together, and people would live in harmony." He became acting chairman of the Foundation in 2001, believing "very idealistically" to be part of the peace process. That, he admits, was naïve. But there have been successes. The Foundation has built community centers, homes for seniors, and parks and sponsored many cultural events. His favorite Foundation project is the Hand-in-Hand School, where all classes are half Jewish and half Arab. Each class has a Jewish and an Arab teacher, and each day they teach half in Hebrew and half in Arabic. There are two principals, one Jewish and one Arab, and the parent-teacher council is half and half.

"I have great hope," he says. "If you can bring people together, they can learn together, work together and create together. It is a model for peace. But if you can't get people to sit at the table because they are always fighting, taking land, or firing missiles, it won't work. You don't make change happen by knocking down walls. Change must come from within, and you can't force it on people. We are desperate to keep the young people in Jerusalem, not just the religious but the very bright young people who might be going to great universities."

David Maloof, a Lebanese-American, has devoted years to attaining peace for the over five million Palestinians and the over 9.1 million Israelis. Maloof grew up on Long Island, where he attended Chaminade High School, followed by Columbia University. He modeled his negotiating style on his father's law partner, James B. Donovan, the subject of the Steven Spielberg film, "Bridge of Spies." Donovan arranged the trade of a Soviet spy for the U-2 pilot Francis Gary Powers and also negotiated the ransom of prisoners taken by Cuba in the Bay of Pigs invasion.

Maloof, a lawyer and former television investigative reporter, went to Lebanon for the first time in the early 2000s to donate sports equipment and coach basketball in a Christian refugee camp. He has a history of working with peaceful Palestinian leaders. He and his group, Churches for Middle East Peace, developed a plan to allow the President of the Palestinian Authority, Mahmoud Abbas, to address the student body at The Cooper Union, a prestigious university in New York City. Abbas was in Manhattan to address the opening session at the United Nations in November of 2014. When word of the proposed Cooper Union speech went public, there was outrage in some quarters, including death threats. Some student supporters of Israel developed an online plan to sabotage the entire event by purchasing tickets in a block, showing up early, and walking out when President Abbas was introduced.

Maloof reached out to some of the Jewish groups who, like him, were fighting for peace. An official of a Pro-Israel, Pro-Peace lobbying group promised to have replacement students ready to walk in if the other students walked out. Students from "Seeds of Peace," an organization dedicated to bringing Israeli and Palestinian students together, also promised to attend to hear President Abbas.

There were three separate levels of security on September 22, 2014, the day of the speech. The NYPD has undercover officers in street clothes mingled in the audience, there was Palestinian Security, and The Cooper Union hired a private security firm. The auditorium did not have an empty seat when President Abbas rose to speak. The mood was tense, as no Palestinian leader had ever addressed the U.S. public before in English.

Abbas defused the crowd with his opening lines: "Just as it took courage for Abraham Lincoln to stand at this very podium to argue for the end of slavery, I am honored today to stand in front of you at this very podium where eight men who were or became American Presidents have stood and announced their programs and platforms." No one walked out as Abbas pledged non-violence, freedom of religion, equality for women, and full recognition of Israel and a Palestinian state.

While no peace deal was reached, the words of the speech still resonate with idealistic people, including Maloof, who hope to be there when a fair and just peace between Israel and Palestine becomes reality.

The Parkway Tavern

Fred Lewis was the proprietor of the Parkway Tavern located in the village of Pawtuxet, Rhode Island. The tavern was a converted house and had no historical or architectural value. Yet, it filled a vital role for many of the young men in the area.

I never worked at the tavern officially, but Fred hired me to run the horse pool every Saturday afternoon. He liked the idea that I didn't drink and would probably run an honest pool, particularly given his other choices. He paid me the princely sum of $25 to officially conduct the horse pool. He got his investment back many times over because the horse pool attracted many customers that would drink before and after the race. Every Saturday, the main event of a featured race would be shown on national television.

There was nothing scientific about playing the horse pool at the Parkway Tavern. Participants did not have to consult The Morning Telegraph, the bible of horse racing, or any other daily scratch sheets predicting the winners for each race. The number of horses in each event ranged from eight to 15. I would place each horse's name in a hat and, after paying $5, the participant would draw a name. Some would immediately reveal the name of the horse selected. Others would keep it a mystery until the race was over.

One standard event that began before the race and then continued to closing time was Fred Lewis's crying about never having any luck. It was true. In the two years that I had been running the event, Fred never won once. "God damn it, Dooley," he would snarl before pulling a name from the hat. "Aren't you ever going to give me a winner?"

On this particular Saturday, the feature race included Kelso, one of the greatest racehorses of all time. Kelso usually won by 9 or 10 lengths. After he drew, I asked Fred the name of his horse.

"None of your God-damn business," he snarled with a slight smirk.

Kelso went off to an early lead and then won the race by ten lengths. Fred immediately put his ticket with the name Kelso written on it on the bar. "Pay up, Dooley. I finally won it." Then each of the other participants put their slips on the bar. They all had Kelso written on their slips. I had written that name 13 times—which, of course, meant no official winner.

Fred came around the bar, and I ran, peeling rubber as I left the parking lot, vowing never to return. Fred was about 6′5″ and had two moods—bad and ugly. When I didn't show up for the next horse pool, Fred called and asked me to come back. After he promised that he wouldn't kill me, I returned.

Years later, when I was working in Manhattan, I got a call from one of Fred's close friends. The two-pack-a-day cigarette habit Fred enjoyed for many years had finally caught up to him. His sister was married to a doctor at New York Hospital, where Fred was being treated for lung cancer.

I went to see him the next day. It was clear that he did not have much time left. He recognized me immediately and broke into a smile. I had to take a step back because I had never seen Fred smile. He tried to say something to me, but his voice was too weak, and I could not understand. A nurse bent over him, then looked up and said, "He wants you to tell me the Kelso story." As I told the story, the smile on Fred's face broadened. He died a few days later. Whenever I think of Fred, I begin with a frustrated man looking at 13 strips with Kelso written on each. Then I remember that last smile and things are right again.

Journalist, Writer, Actor, and Amateur Sportsman

I knew a lot about George Plimpton before meeting him for the first time in 1990. He was famous for competing in professional sporting events and then recording the experience from the point of view of an amateur. In 1963, I read his book, *Paper Lion,* which described his role as a backup quarterback during preseason training with the Detroit Lions of the National Football League. However, only the coach knew that Plimpton was a writer gathering material for a book and not a professional athlete trying to make the team.

In 1958, Plimpton pitched against the National League in an exhibition game. His experience was captured in the book *Out of My League*. Another sports book, *Open Net,* described his role as an ice hockey goalie with the Boston Bruins. His book, *The Bogey Man*, chronicles his attempt to play professional golf during the Nicklaus and Palmer ere of the 1960s.

Plimpton also tried his hand at auto racing, played basketball with the Boston Celtics, soccer with the Tampa Bay Rowdies, tennis with Poncho Gonzales, trapeze acrobatics with the Flying Apollo's, the Clyde Beatty-Cold Brothers Circus, stand-up comedy in Las Vegas, and as a percussionist on tour in Canada with the New York Philharmonic Orchestra under Leonard Bernstein.

I do not know how other coaches or owners regarded George Plimpton, but I can tell you that Red Auerbach, general manager of the Boston Celtics, was not a fan. It was not that Red disliked Plimpton personally. He enjoyed their conversations and told me that Plimpton was a good athlete but not a professional. Red took basketball seriously and objected to anything or anyone that would detract from his game.

In 1990, Prentice-Hall hired me to write a script based on Plimpton and direct him in a documentary film. He was the most fantastic storyteller I have ever met and kept me entertained every night at dinner. He told me about his comedy routine in Las Vegas with a script written by Woody Allen. He related a disastrous experience with the Cleveland Orchestra when he was brought in as a "guest" conductor. Even though Leonard Bernstein had trained him, he immediately lost control of the orchestra during the first rehearsal. Fritz

Chrysler, the resident conductor, told the orchestra to ignore Plimpton and play the music. George said it was his greatest failure.

He also gave me the background of one of his greatest pranks, an April Fools' story. On April 1, 1985, he published a story in *Sports Illustrated* about a pitcher named Sid Finch who threw a baseball over 160 mph. The prank was so successful that many readers believed the story, which resulted in Plimpton writing an entire book on Finch.

We were shooting the film at the Coast Guard Academy in New London, Connecticut. I was with George when the commanding officer of the Coast Guard Academy asked him to deliver a speech to the freshman class. George agreed, explaining that he had given commencement addresses at West Point, Annapolis, and the United States Air Force Academy. "This would complete the cycle," George said.

He asked the Captain to allow him to deliver an amnesty to the freshman class, forgiving them of any penalties incurred for minor violations. The Captain turned him down immediately. "Discipline is a serious matter," the pretentious Captain said, implying that the other academies were lax in wiping the slate clean because of a guest speaker.

Even after George explained that it was a tradition for visiting speakers to deliver amnesty at the other academies, the Captain would not relent. I saw an expression on George's face that told me that trouble lay ahead.

The next day, George and I sat at the head table as members of the freshman class marched in and sat at attention. George opened his remarks by relating the Captain's refusal to allow him to wipe the disciplinary slate clean. "It is a tradition at all of the other academies," George explained. "I think I was turned down for one of two reasons. You people are particularly evil, or I am not an important enough speaker."

There was no response from the officers at the head table or members of the class who were still sitting at attention. The room was silent until George finally said, "I cannot speak under these conditions." The Captain issued an "at ease" order, and George finished his presentation. It was funny, clever, and delightful. I led the applause, which was polite but not deafening.

A young cadet approached George with a small box in his hand. "I was hoping for a ceremonial sword," George said as he began to open the box. "This is probably one of those silly little paperweights." He opened the box to reveal a paperweight of *The Eagle*, Coast Guard Academy's training ship. Fortunately, we had concluded our filming at Coast Guard the previous day. I doubt that we would have been allowed on the campus again.

George and I had our final dinner that night, ready to finish shooting at another location the following day. If I had been able to keep my big mouth shut, I'm sure that George and I would have parted as friends. Unfortunately, after a lifetime of saying the wrong things, I could not change now. I loved George's stories, but there was one area that I found tiresome—the Kennedy family. George's voice always took on an almost religious quality when he talked about the Kennedys, especially Robert (Bobby) Kennedy. George was a classmate at Harvard and a close friend. He was walking directly behind Kennedy in the Ambassador Hotel in Los Angeles when Sirhan Sirhan fired the fatal bullet. In what he described to me as "behaving badly," George had the assassin in a headlock that probably would have been fatal if Rosey Greer, the ex-football player, had not been there to break the hold.

George was still emotional when he described the incident. I should have moved on. But, as one who majored in indiscretion for most of his life, I had to speak up. "It's too bad Bobby developed such an obsession for toppling the regime of Fidel Castro when he was Attorney General of the United States." When George asked me what I meant, I described the embarrassing failure of the Bay of Pigs invasion and how it became a personal matter between Bobby Kennedy and Fidel Castro. "Bobby Kennedy oversaw the covert Operation Mongoose, which was created to harass, overthrow or possibly kill the Cuban dictator," I said. I offered to loan George a book written by a former CIA officer explaining in detail Bobby's plans to remove Castro from office.

George stood and said good night. Except for some direction during the final day of the production, those were the last words I ever heard from George Plimpton. He left without saying goodbye the next afternoon. A few months later, I called George when I was in

New York and left him a message. Unfortunately, he never returned my call. Do I regret my criticism of Bobby Kennedy? Absolutely. I was in Manhattan in 2003 when George's sudden death led the news that day. It brought back a lot of pleasant memories.

The two greatest speakers I have ever heard are George Plimpton and Patrick T. Conley, Historian Laureate of Rhode Island. Giving either of these men a teleprompter would be like giving Hall of Fame baseball player Ted Williams four strikes.

POOR LITTLE RHODE ISLAND

I remember seeing the movie *Carolina Blues* at the Park Theatre in Cranston, RI, in 1944. It was a typical "Class B" movie starring Victor Moore and bandleader Kay Keyser. Victor Moore was the best-looking person in the movie, so that should tell you something about the cast. The movie is only remembered because it introduced the song "Poor Little Rhode Island." It was the first time I heard it, but certainly not the last. A number of Air Force people serenaded me with that song as soon as they found out I was from the Ocean State. The first stanza of the song is:

Poor Little Rhode Island
The smallest of the forty-eight
She's got no prairie moon
For which the coyotes croon.

I don't think Sammy Cahn and Julie Styne realized it when they wrote "Poor Little Rhode Island," but their song sums up a statewide inferiority complex that began during Revolutionary times and continues today. Some historians blame it on Rhode Island's reluctance to ratify the Constitution. Certainly, we are the runt of the litter, being the smallest of the fifty states. But size cannot be the determining factor, otherwise Napoleon, at barely five foot six inches, would never have become a world leader. So what is it that leads some to think that we Rhode Islanders suffer from an inferiority complex?

From its earliest days as a colony, Rhode Island was derided by its neighbors, especially Massachusetts. We were often referred to as the "sewer of New England," because we welcomed into our colony outcast people like Roger Williams, Ann Hutchinson, and Mary Dyer. They were expelled from Massachusetts for their religious beliefs. In Rhode Island, we practiced religious freedom and offered sanctuary for Baptists, Quakers, Jews and others. North America's oldest synagogue, Touro, was dedicated in Newport, Rhode Island, on Dec. 2, 1763.

The Bay Colony's Puritan (Congregationalist) tenants did not allow for free thinkers, so they cast them out to Rhode Island and called us a sewer. But it was the Congregationalists who burned women at the stake in Salem, Massachusetts, for being witches and hanged Mary Dyer upon her return to Boston for her religious beliefs. Today there is a bronze statue of Mary Dyer on the grounds of the state house on Beacon Hill as a testimonial to their religious intolerance. In Rhode Island religious freedom was a right but in Massachusetts the state taxed all its citizens in support of its state religion until 1833—57 years after the Declaration of Independence.

"It is well-known that Rhode Island did not attend the Philadelphia Convention to participate in the drafting of the Constitution," Dr. Patrick T. Conley, Historian Laureate of Rhode Island and former Chairman of the United States Constitution Council, wrote to celebrate RI Constitution Day on Sep. 17, 2020. "But some of our practices, especially religious liberty, federalism and democratic governance, influenced the Framers."

Dr. Conley, Dr. Scott Molloy, retired history professor from the University of Rhode Island, and Russell DeSimone, an expert on Rhode Island history, explained to me that Rhode Island brought much more to the colonies than religious freedom. Discussing Rhode Island history with those three is like taking baseball-hitting classes from Babe Ruth, Ted Williams and Willie Mays.

Here are the most important contributions Rhode Island made during the Revolutionary War.

1. The Burning of the *Gaspee*

The burning of His Majesty's schooner *Gaspee* and the wounding of her captain was really the first 'shot heard round the world,' since it occurred on the night of June 9, 1772, nearly three years before Lexington and Concord. It is considered to be the first major act of defiance leading up to the Revolutionary War.

Every year the burning of the Gaspee is celebrated with a parade in Pawtuxet Village, Rhode Island. A wonderful website tells the complete story.

2. The Siege and Battle of Rhode Island

The siege of Newport and the Battle of Rhode Island are significant for several reasons. The siege represents the first time the American Army planned a joint operation with the French. It was also the largest land operation in New England during the entire Revolutionary War. Another important fact is that the First Rhode Island regiment, a key force in the battle, marked the first time in U.S. military history that a black regiment fought for the new country.

3. Barton's Raid and the Capture of General Prescott.
Major General Charles Lee, second-in-command to General Washington, was captured by the British in December 1776. In response, a secret mission to kidnap British General Richard Prescott was planned, with the Americans hoping to exchange him for General Lee. A Rhode Island hat-maker turned patriot named Col. William Baton and a band of raiders kidnapped General Prescott on the night of July 10, 1777. Gen. George Washington called it one of the "finest partisan exploits of the war on either side." In his book *Kidnapping the Enemy*, Christian M. McBurney gives an excellent account of the planning behind the mission.

Rhode Island has to take the blame for not telling its history in a positive way to the rest of the nation. It is only one of three states that does not have a State Historic Museum to tell its rich history. In Hartford, CT, thousands of children in grades K–12 visit the Connecticut Museum of History each year to see exhibits and learn about the State's role in the development of the nation from the colonial era to the present. In Boston, the Massachusetts Historical Society's Education Department offers primary-source based workshops for K–12 students on a variety of topics. Participants become historians as they investigate a particular historical topic using a broad range of materials from the Society's collection.

In Rhode Island, where could educators take their students to learn about Rhode Island history? Right now, nowhere. In 2017, Dr. Patrick T. Conley, Historian Laureate of Rhode Island, tried to come up with a solution. He proposed an interactive learning center to be built in a new Heritage Hall of Fame Center in Bristol, Rhode Island. The center would have featured an interactive design that would engage students in a continuous dialogue to generate enthusiasm and pride in Rhode Island. Unfortunately, the plan did not draw interest or money from private donations or the General Assembly.

Meanwhile, Rhode Island lost more than $100,000,000 in a video game company proposed by a former baseball player. Maybe we should write a new stanza for "Poor Little Rhode Island."

OCEAN RESCUES

A sailor was heading from Alaska to Vancouver when his 30-foot sailboat lost its rudder and rigging in heavy seas and 50 mph winds. A video shot by the U.S. Coast Guard shows him tucking his cat into his clothing before jumping to the rescue ship. Another video shows a Coast Guard helicopter rescuing the captain of a yacht after he fell overboard during a race about 10 miles from the Bahamas. Four teenagers and four adults were in grave danger when their boat sank 12 miles off of Hawaii. One of them captured the rescue on his camera as a helicopter came into view, and we heard words like "We're getting rescued!" and "We're going to live!"

As I watched the program entitled "7 Amazing Rescues at Sea," I was reminded of a less dramatic yet life-saving rescue involving me and my daughter Alicia. It was 1984, and I had rented a home on Martha's Vineyard for the summer. The house was situated on a small inlet that led directly to the ocean. I rented a small rubber raft with a 1.5-hp outboard engine. It was ideal for boating in the outlet, but we ran into difficulty around when trying to use the boat to get to a nearby beach that was on the ocean. The small outboard did not have the power to buck the tides if conditions were not ideal. So our beach excursions took careful planning around the tides.

One morning, we had just made it to the beach when a young man came up to us screaming. He pointed to his friend, who was clutching to a capsized sailfish. "He's just learning how to use it," the young man said. "He fell a number of times, and he's too tired to get up. He's drifting out to sea."

"What's his name?" I asked as I jumped into the boat and headed for the sailfish.

"Dave," the other man said. I had no trouble reaching him because the tide was going out. Dave was totally exhausted and wasn't even able to speak when I reached him. My heart sank a little when I realized that Dave was a huge man. "Hang on," I said as I grabbed the mast of the sailfish and headed into shore. The little engine gave me everything that it could—but we were losing ground as the tide began to sweep us out to sea. I realized there was no way I could get to shore with Dave and the sailfish.

"We have to abandon the sailfish," I said to Dave. I grabbed his arms, got him partially into the boat, and headed for shore. For the first few moments, we held our own against the tide. Then slowly, we inched forward and finally got close enough to the beach for several people to drag us the rest of the way.

Dave was too exhausted to even talk. We sat around him as he slowly recovered. After about 20 minutes, he finally stood (he was 6′3″ tall) and clutched my hand. "I would never have made it without you," he said. "I couldn't have held on to the mast for another minute."

Then a funny thing happened. Not one boat was in sight when I went to get Dave. Suddenly many large boats with big outboard motors appeared. One towed Dave's sailboard to shore. Dave and his friend left the beach a few minutes later. Alicia and I were both reading when a woman walked up to us. She identified herself as a reporter for a weekly newspaper and wanted to get some facts about a rescue. I explained that it happened before we got there, and we knew nothing. She had a quizzical look on her face as she talked to some of the other people on the beach and looked back at me. By this time, Alicia and I were in the boat headed for home.

That night, Alicia said something to me that I still remember after 37 years. "Dad, what happened to us today reminds me of that story you used to read to me at bedtime. Except I would call it 'The Little Boat that Could.'"

A Priest in the Family

Father John F. Sullivan was pastor of St. Matthew's in Cranston, Rhode Island. He was also my great uncle, brother of my grandmother, Margaret Kenneally, who had little in common with her brother. She was one of the sweetest, nicest people I have ever known. No one ever accused Fr. John of being either nice or sweet.

We developed a dislike for each other that began when I was about six. Fr. John used to come to our home on Hayward Street for the Armistice Day ceremony that took place at a small park on the corner of Park Avenue and Rolfe Street. He would give the invocation at the beginning of the parade. Unfortunately, I never remembered him being there for the finish.

Our troubles began as I watched Fr. John playing solitaire on our dining room table. I studied carefully and then reported to my mother that Fr. John cheated. He moved cards around when they were not going his way.

My mother told me to be quiet and not tell my brothers or anyone else about what I had observed. It turns out that all the adults in the family knew about his cheating ways. He was always so happy when he "got it," they were delighted to look the other way. He had two moods—bad and worse. Anything to lighten his mood was acceptable to all the family members—except me.

He had a dominating personality, and not too many people challenged him, and never family members. I had nightmares about Fr. John standing at the Gates of Heaven pointing a downward finger at me as he explained, "Of course you're going to hell. Look at the things you said about me."

A priest in an Irish family draws the same respect as the Pope. The only time I ever saw him challenged was over an incident involving my brother Jack, a terrific football player. I was home when one of Jack's friends from the team came to the house looking for him. Fr. John was visiting, and my mother was hanging a wash on the clothesline in the backyard. When Fr. John answered the door, he told the young man to go away, that he shouldn't be there in the first place. Dick was a good friend of Jack's, and I saw the hurt on his face when the door was closed in his face. Dick was also Black.

Being the resident fink, I could hardly wait to tell my mother what had happened when she came back into the house. Her face got very red, and then she marched into the dining room and interrupted his game of solitaire.

"Dick is a very nice young man, and you had no right to turn him away. Now I'll thank you to get out of my house," she said. Revolutionary! No one ever talked to Fr. John that way. His face got very Red, and he stormed out of the house, slamming the door. He drove to my grandmother's house to report my mother's disrespect, and after hearing the story, she threw him out, too.

Prayers and the intercession of other family members got things back on track a few months later. Fr. John forgave everyone, including his favorite niece, my mother, or, as he always called her, Marion Veronica. He never did forgive me as he felt I was the source of much negativism about him. He was right. I was always on the lookout for any of his transgressions.

I was the smallest of all my brothers, extremely light on my feet with extraordinary vision and hearing. Somehow, I would blend into the woodwork and listen to conversations that we never met for my ears.

I learned that Fr. John didn't particularly like Italians, an extreme handicap because his parish was divided equally between Irish and Italian parishioners. His unwritten rule was that only the Irish could become Knights of Columbus. Italians had to join St. Rocco's Society.

Things came to a head when members of St. Rocco's donated a statue of their patron saint to St. Matthew's. From overheard conversations, I knew that Fr. John was not particularly happy about placing the statue in St. Matthew's. But he had little choice, and the statue ended up in a not particularly strategic place in the church.

A few weeks after St. Rocco made his debut, Fr. John made an announcement from the pulpit. He had received a letter from the company responsible for making the statue complaining that an invoice had not been paid.

About two weeks later, Fr. John said he had received a second letter and advised those responsible to pay the invoice immediately.

The following month, his face got very red as he issued a threat. "You all know I'm a baseball fan and, in baseball, you get three strikes.

I have issued two warnings about payment for this statue. Now we're at strike three." He turned to the statue and said, "Rocco-me-bucco, you will be paid for this week, or it's out you go."

Years later, my brother Bill met some priests when he was stationed in Europe during the Korean War. One of them asked about his parish in Rhode Island. When he identified it as St. Matthew's, the priest asked if the story about St. Rocco was true.

It was. I was there.

Fr. John did not have a happy ending. He developed what we called "hardening of the arteries," now labeled Alzheimer's. He spent the last ten years of his life cared for by my grandmother, my great aunt, Annie, and my Aunt Ann.

He never got over his love of cards, and my grandmother would urge me to play a few games with him when I visited. Fortunately, he had no idea who I was, which was probably good for both of us.

Shortly before he died in 1951, I took part in the dedication of St. Matthew's School with my mother, grandmother, and other family members. While the church remains open, the school closed about ten years ago after the nuns disappeared.

I can never understand how a man of God could be so prejudiced. Yet over the years, I have met parishioners who told me stories about how kind Fr. John was to their families, especially during the depression years. It makes me think that I may be too hard on him. My mother and his sisters and nieces loved him. I guess that should make up for a bit of card cheating.

RACE RELATIONS

My friends and I took great pride in our acceptance of African Americans in our culture, reacting in horror when stories of the Ku Klux Klan made the headlines in *The Providence Journal*. The truth was that we had no African American friends growing up in Rhode Island. I never attended a grammar school or junior high that had one Black student. At La Salle Academy, we had one Black student, Bernie Pina, who happened to be the best football player in Rhode Island.

I never related to any African Americans until I entered the United States Air Force in 1951. My first Black acquaintance turned into a lifelong friend until he died a few years ago. I met George Robinson when stationed with him in Wiesbaden, Germany, in 1951. His wife, Ethel, was a great cook, and I had many meals with them. I was transferred to Africa about six months later, but George and I kept tabs on each other for the next couple of years. Ethel was quite jealous when I got my orders to report to Kelly Air Force Base in San Antonio, Texas, in 1953. Ethel was from San Antonio and was hoping that she and George would wind up at Kelly.

Soon after I reported to Kelly Air Force Base, I got a letter from George with the good news—they were coming to San Kelly. George gave me his mother-in-law's address and said they would be staying with her until they got quarters on the base. I checked in regularly and learned the exact date when they would be arriving. I called George the day they came and announced I was taking them out for dinner—no argument.

"Where will we be going? George asked.

"Ethel is from San Antonio. She must know the best restaurants," I argued.

"We can't go to any of those restaurants," George said. Yes, George and Ethel were Black. I had seen the signs with separate restrooms and water fountains for Blacks. But the whole reality of segregation did not hit me until that day when I learned I could not go out to dinner with two of my favorite people. We could only eat together on the base. The same was true for movies. The theaters in San Antonio got the first run movies long before the base did. I remember telling George that I would sit upstairs with them to see a new film in a timely fashion. "Do you want to get us killed?" he said.

I became friendly with Texans like Tom Comeaux and Bill Donahue. They were both kind, educated people. I went with Bill Donahue to the University of Texas campus in Austin. It was a lovely city, and we spent three days there. Except for cafeteria workers and the janitorial staff, I did not see one Black in Austin. I am always amused now when I see Southern football teams with rosters featuring many African American players.

While I had minimum contact with African Americans during my early years, I certainly made up for it later. It began when I did a film with Red Auerbach, the great coach and president of the Boston Celtics. Red had opened the NBA for Black players when he drafted Chuck Cooper in 1950. Six years later, he made a trade that netted him Bill Russell, considered by many as the greatest player in NBA history. K. C. Jones, the great Celtics guard, and coach became a good friend. He introduced me to Sam Jones and Bill Russell, and we are now working on a TV series called "From White to Black: The story of the early African Americans Coming into the NBA." Two Hall of Fame basketball players and a 5′7″ guy who could not make his high school basketball team.

No one could be more dismissive of something he disagreed with than Red Auerbach. Nothing earned his withering, dismissive glance quicker than a comparison of his role in opening professional basketball to African American players to what Branch Rickey and Jackie Robinson did for professional baseball. Red's relentless focus was assembling the array of interlinking player talents that would create teams capable of winning an astonishing 11 NBA championships over 13 years. Along the way, this "Celtic Magic" would defeat teams with superior individual talents. Red knew there would be no way of achieving that magic while shunning the skills of African American players.

While he rejected any credit for selecting Chuck Cooper, the first African American drafted into the NBA by the Boston Celtics, Red played a key role in emancipating African Americans from the relentless segregation preventing them from playing professional basketball. Much is written about Red's selection of Cooper in the 1950

NBA draft, his first as Celtics coach. The real story behind the draft has never been explored. It began when a 16-year-old Red Auerbach went to Harlem to learn about playing and coaching basketball from Bobby Douglas, owner/coach of the Harlem Rens. The brash young man established a relationship with Douglas, whose team regularly beat the Harlem Globetrotters and any white teams that dared to play them. Douglas helped Red recover from two white man's diseases—he was short and slow—and helped him get a basketball scholarship to George Washington University.

It was Douglas who encouraged Red to seek his first professional coaching job with the Washington Capitals. When Caps owner Mike Uline refused to meet his salary demands, Red left the Caps to join the St. Louis franchise but ran into immediate problems with its owner, Ben Kerner, and resigned. Red was ready to resume his career as a high school coach in Washington, D.C., but Douglas convinced him to stay in professional basketball. Douglas set up a meeting for Red with Lou Pieri, the owner of the Providence Steamrollers, the worst team in professional basketball. Red advised Pieri to fold the team, a recommendation that impressed Pieri and led directly to Red's becoming the Boston Celtics coach.

While Auerbach opened professional basketball to African-American players, it was up to the players to deal with the prejudice they faced daily. The pace of integration was agonizingly slow, filled with stories such as Chuck Cooper not being allowed to play in a Southern arena and later being called a "Nigger" during an NBA game. While Bill Russell was cheered at Boston Garden, neighbors broke into his home and defecated in his beds while spraying hate messages on the walls. Russell drove a school bus filled with African American children during a bussing crisis in the 1960s. He held a clinic in Mississippi one week after Medgar Evers' assassination. Martin Luther King asked Russell to sit with him on the stage when he delivered his famous "I Have a Dream" speech.

The journey of African American players started in 1923 with the Harlem Rens, the greatest team in basketball at the time. The Rens played their home games in the Rensselaer Ballroom in Harlem. Entertainers like Duke Ellington, Louis Armstrong, Ella Fitzgerald, and Lena Horne sang or played before and after basketball games. In 1926, the Harlem Globetrotters performed and, like the Rens, played road games in segregated areas throughout the country. They couldn't stay in local hotels or eat in restaurants. Meanwhile, both teams defeated the best of the white teams.

I met Red Auerbach, legendary coach and president of the Boston Celtics, in 1978 when I directed him in a documentary film. Thirteen years later, we wrote a book together, *M.B.A. Management by Auerbach*. We remained close friends for the next 28 years, right up to Red's death in 2006. During one of the interviews, I asked Red a question about the 1950 draft, the one in which he selected the first African American drafted, Chuck Cooper, in the second round. There was no national television coverage of the NBA draft in those days. Owners and coaches met in a hotel suite where they were usually outnumbered by service personnel. Red had just joined the Celtics before the draft, and sportswriters and fans were angry that he was passing over Bob Cousy, the All-American basketball player from Holy Cross, a local college, in the first round.

"I know that most of the owners were upset when you chose an African American player," I said. "But Cooper was under contract to the Harlem Globetrotters when you drafted him. Then you signed another African American player, Sweetwater Clifton, who was the star player for the Trotters. Weren't you afraid of offending Abe Saperstein?"

Saperstein, the owner of the Harlem Globetrotters, had done more to keep Blacks out of the NBA than any Southern racist. The NBA depended on the tremendous gate appeal of the Harlem Globetrotters to keep their league afloat. When the Trotters appeared in their arenas, they played the featured game while the NBA game followed. Saperstein made it clear that the Trotters would boycott any owners who drafted Black players.

Red put down his cigar and gave me that famous Auerbach stare, one he reserved for officials or during negotiations with players. "Nobody ever asked me that question before," he said. "Let's just say I had inside information." Then he told me a story about Bobby Douglas, owner of the Harlem Rens, the most outstanding basketball team in the world in the nineteen twenties and thirties. I tried to tell the story in the book, but Red made me take it out. He just explained he was tired of this "black and white thing."

In 2005, I had lunch with Red at the China Doll restaurant in Washington, D.C. I brought up the Bobby Douglas story and said it was a shame that it would die with the two of us. "You can write about it when I'm gone," Red said. He died the following year, and five years later, I wrote and directed *The Auerbach Dynasty*, a play that opened in Cranston, RI, and later in Watertown, MA.

"From White to Black" is much more than a story about African Americans joining, then dominating the National Basketball Association. During this period, segregation in public schools ended, voting rights were enforced, and major Civil Rights legislation was passed. It was also the time when Emmett Till, a 13-year-old African American, was murdered, Medgar Evers was assassinated, Rosa Parks was arrested for refusing to give up her seat on a public bus, and Dr. Martin Luther King conducted his march on Washington, D.C.

Regardless of Red's feelings, it is impossible to tell the story of African Americans coming into the NBA without referring to Red Auerbach and the Boston Celtics. It started with the 1950 draft when Walter Brown, President of the Celtics, stood and announced that the team was drafting Chuck Cooper. "Do you realize that Cooper is Negro?" one of the owners asked. "I don't care about the color of a ballplayer's skin," Brown said. "He can be black, yellow, or green, as long as he can put the ball in the basket."

Although it had been seven years since Chuck Cooper, Earl Lloyd, and "Sweetwater" Clifton joined the NBA, there was still an unofficial quota system in play. Right after the league was integrated in 1950, Eddie Gottlieb, owner of the Philadelphia NBA team, warned that players would be 75% black in five years. "You're going to do a disservice to the game," he warned.

Gottlieb argued that since most ticket-buyers were white, they would not pay good money to watch black players. Too many blacks would be bad for business and would hurt the league's image. He was not alone in his thinking, with one owner arguing that blacks would also be hard to coach.

Gottlieb's position may have been influenced by his close relationship with Abe Saperstein, owner of the Harlem Globetrotters. Like the other owners, Gottlieb relied on doubleheaders with the Globetrotters to boost the low attendance for league games. Saperstein ensured his pick of the best black players available by threatening to keep his Globetrotters out of any NBA arenas featuring black players. After learning about Clifton, Auerbach drafted Cooper and signed Sweetwater Clifton to the Celtics. Commissioner Maurice Podoloff vetoed the Clifton contract with the Celtics but allowed Ned Irish, the New York Knicks owner, to sign Clifton. Although he made some verbal threats, Saperstein never attempted to punish the Celtics or Knicks for signing black players.

When a quota system was first suggested after the 1950 draft, Walter Brown and Red Auerbach spoke against it. Brown announced at an owners' meeting that he would sell the Boston Celtics if a quota system were established. Ned Irish threatened to pull his team out of the league if it was not opened to black players. While there might not have been a written agreement, there was an understanding between the all-white owners that prevented a team from having too many blacks on its roster. The number of black starters was also controlled.

Looking at the rosters from 1950 to 1965 certainly supports a quota being in place, whether it was official or not. The highest number of blacks on a team was four, and some teams had one or two during that period. In 1950, Chuck Cooper of the Celtics, Sweetwater Clifton of the New York Knicks, Hank DeZonie of Tri-Cities, and Earl Lloyd of the Washington Caps were the only Blacks in the league, and they represented less than 3% of the 135 NBA players.

Bob Wilson joined Milwaukee in 1951, but the percentage stayed the same because of the departure of Hank DeZonie. The percentage jumped to five in 1952 when Don Barksdale and Dave Minor joined the league. Ray Felix joined Baltimore in 1953, Ken McBride was drafted by Milwaukee in 1954, Jackie Moore became a member of Philadelphia, and Jim Tucker joined Syracuse. At this point, nine of 105 players were Black, representing a jump to nine percent.

Ed Fleming, Dick Rickets, Maurice Stokes, and Robert Williams joined the league in 1956, raising the average to 13% Black (13 of 99). In 1957, Bill Russell, Willie Naulls, Sihugo Green, Hal Lear, raising the average to 15% (15 of 99). In 1958, K.C. Jones, Bennie Swain, Wayne

Embry, Shellie McMillon, Elgin Baylor, Boo Ellis, Andy Johnson, Guy Rodgers, and Willie Sauldsberry joined the league, representing a jump to 25% (19 of 92).

In 1959, Maurice King, Tim Hawkins, Johnny Green, Cal Ramsey, Wilt Chamberlain, and Dick Barnett came into the league, bringing the percentage to 24% (24 of 99). In 1960, Tom (Satch) Sanders, Bob Boozer, Oscar Robertson, Willie Jones, Fred LaCour, Lenny Wilkins, Al Attles, and Joe Roberts joined the NBA, bringing the percentage to 29% (27 of 93). In 1961, Walt Bellamy, Horace Walker, Joe Buckhalter, Ray Scott, Cleveland Buckner, Ed Burton, Al Butler, Sam Stith, Stacey Arceneaux, Cleo Hill, and Bob Sims came into the NBA, bringing the percentage of Black players to 32% (36 of 113).

In 1962, Charlie Hardnett, Bill McGill, Leroy Ellis, Gene Wiley, Paul Hague, Tom Stitch, Wayne Hightower, Howie Montgomery, Hubie White, John Barnhill, Zelmo Beatty, Bill Bridges, Chico Vaughn, Porter Meriwether, Chet Walker, and Bob Warley brought the percentage of blacks to 38% (45 of 117). In 1963, Gus Johnson, Tom Thacker, Reggie Harding, Eddie Miles, Jerry Harkness, Tom Hoover, and Nate Thurmond brought the percentage of Blacks in the league kept the percentage of blacks in the league at 38% (42 of 111). In 1964, Les Hunter, Walt Jones, John Thompson, Happy Hairston, George Wilson, Joe Caldwell, Walt Hazard, Jim Barnes, Emmette Bryant, Willis Reed, Lucius Jackson, Larry Jones, Paul Silas, and John Tresvant brought the percentage of Blacks in the league to 49% (56 of 115).

Eddie Gottlieb's 1950 warning that white fans would not buy tickets to watch largely Black teams was totally wrong. NBA attendance has grown every year, and the caliber of the team and not its racial balance has always been the determining factor in fan support. Bobby Douglas's statement to Red Auerbach on draft night of 1950 has proven to be much more accurate. "This is our game. We're taller, faster, better rebounders, and we dribble and shoot better than you guys. Our problem isn't playing the game. It's getting to play the game. You just opened the door," Douglas said to Auerbach.

Douglas's prediction is substantiated by the African-American Rookies of the Year starting in 1954 with Ray Felix and continuing with Maurice Stokes, 1956; Woody Sauldsberry in 1958; Elgin Baylor, 1959; Wilt Chamberlain, 1960; Oscar Robertson, 1961; Walt Bellamy,

1962. Tommy Heinsohn was the only white to break the list by earning the award in 1957.

While Blacks had come of age in professional basketball in those early years, some owners continued to worry about the effect they would have on the gate. There was an unwritten agreement that each team would have no more than two blacks, then three, then four, then five. They had to be starters, not benchwarmers, to make the roster. It wasn't anything that anyone talked about. It just happened.

The experience of Al Attles when he joined the Philadelphia Warriors in 1960 is a good example of the quota system in action. Philadelphia already had four Blacks on the roster when Attles was drafted: Chamberlain, Johnson, Rodgers, and Sauldsberry. Instead of making Attles the fifth Black on the team, Philadelphia traded Sauldsberry, who had been Rookie of the Year two years earlier.

The early players had to deal with prejudice, both on and off the court. "It was an era when you were told you were inferior so much that you began to believe it," Earl Lloyd, the first African American to play in the NBA, said. "Back of the bus, upstairs at the theater, no service at the restaurants. I never sat next to a white person until I was twenty-two years old," Lloyd added. "Bill Russell and I used to laugh in those early days because we always ended up guarding each other." Blacks could not stay with the team at hotels or eat with them in restaurants. They would also be assigned to guard each other, frequently leaving the game to be played with four white players on each team. Some white players refused to pass them the ball, as they did to Cleo Hill when he played for the St. Louis Hawks.

The St. Louis Hawks defeated the Boston Celtics in the NBA Finals in 1958, becoming the last team in NBA history to win a championship without a Black player on the roster. The series went six games but was decided in game three when Bill Russell severely injured his left ankle and was out for the rest of the series. A team picture features only eleven players because the twelfth member of the team, Worthy Patterson, a Black guard from the University of Connecticut, played only four games in the regular season for St. Louis and did not appear in the playoffs. He was deliberately left out of the team picture.

Red Auerbach helped shatter the quota system in 1963 by starting five black players: Willie Naulls, Tom Sanders, K.C. Jones, Sam Jones, and Bill Russell. When Auerbach retired in 1967, he appointed Bill Russell as his successor, the first African-American coach in any U.S. Professional sport.

The American Basketball Association (ABA) came into existence in 1967, creating leverage for African-American players and real competition for the established NBA. It featured electrifying players like Julius Erving, Connie Hawkins, Ernie DiGregorio, Marvin Barnes, and Artis Gilmore. The ABA also offered a flashier style of play than the NBA, a 30-second shot clock (as opposed to the NBA's 24-second clock), and the use of a three-point field goal. The freewheeling style of the ABA caught on with the fans, but the lack of a national television contract spelled its doom as an independent league. The ABA pioneered the popular slam-dunk contest at its all-star game in Denver in 1976, the last year of its existence as it merged with the NBA.

By this time, NBA teams were featuring all-African-American starting lineups. By 1972, the Western Conference All-Star squad had only two white players on the team, Gail Goodrich and Jerry West. Of 250 active players in 1972, only seventy-seven were white, and most were fringe players.

Bobby Douglas, often called the "father of black professional basketball," died in 1979, the year after Larry Bird joined the Boston Celtics. It's doubtful they ever met, but the two share a common belief about basketball being a Black man's game. Bird went even further with remarks concerning playing against other white players when he was president of basketball operations with the Indiana Pacers in 2004.

"I really got irritated when they put a white guy on me during my playing career with the Celtics," Bird said. "A white guy would come out, and I would always ask him if he had a problem with his coach. If he said no, I would tell him he had no chance of guarding me. It is a Black man's game, and it will be forever. The greatest athletes in the world are African-American," Bird asserted.

ONE-NIGHT STAND

A college classmate approached me in 1958 about a job opening in a restaurant where he worked as a busboy. It was an upscale place called "Fore & Aft," located in Bristol, RI. My friend said the work was easy, and the money was good. Busboys got a share of the waitresses' tips. I told him I didn't know the first thing about being a busboy, but he said that wouldn't matter. The owner of the restaurant, Jeb Hanley had a unique system for training busboys, my friend said. I should have taken that as a warning.

Jeb Hanley was not at the restaurant when I arrived for an interview. Mrs. Hanley was very nice and told me to come in that evening at 6 p.m. Jeb Hanley was waiting for me when I arrived at about 6:10. "Punctuality is essential for all restaurant employees," he said as he looked at his watch. I almost told him I wasn't yet an employee but decided against it. My first impression of him was that he was a crank. I was wrong. He was a miserable crank.

He spent a few minutes showing me when and how to clear the table properly. "Nothing is done until the last guest finishes eating," he warned. "If they linger over coffee, you can begin clearing, especially during busy nights. It's a good way to let guests know that others are waiting to be seated," Hanley said.

He also emphasized that I was a "trial" employee, and my performance that night would determine my future at the Fore & Aft. I felt like an understudy for a Broadway show who had just been told he or she was "going on" that night. The only difference was that I didn't have a script to follow. So he had me follow another busboy for the first hour, then it got very busy, and I was forced to make my debut.

I did get a little flustered early on, but things went okay until I spilled a glass of wine on a furious lady. She calmed down when the waitress told her that the restaurant would pay to have the garment cleaned. When I returned to the kitchen, Hanley was waiting for me. "That cleaning bill will be deducted from your salary," he said.

Guests next to a table I was clearing were having a spirited discussion about J. Howard McGrath, RI Governor from 1940 to 1945. He had left Rhode Island for Washington, D.C., after President Harry Truman appointed him Solicitor General in 1945. One of the guests insisted that Truman fired him for corruption. Another argued that his firing had nothing to do with crime, that he wanted to return to Rhode Island so he could run for the U.S. Senate.

I paused in the middle of my clearing to resolve the issue. "President Truman asked for McGrath's resignation in 1949 because he refused to co-operate in a corruption investigation initiated by his department," I said. "He was never charged with corruption himself."

"How do you know so much about McGrath?" the guest, who had accused him of corruption, demanded in an unpleasant tone.

"My Uncle Leo Kenneally was McGrath's campaign manager during his first run for governor. He also graduated from La Salle with McGrath in 1922. They were lifelong friends."

Now while all this was going on, I was getting frustrating looks from other busboys and waitresses. While I was educating the paying customers, dishes and dirty tables remained uncleared. When I finally finished the table, Jeb Hanley waited for me as I went through the kitchen door. "What were you discussing with our guests?" he demanded.

"They were a little confused about one of our former governors. I was able to straighten them out."

His serious expression grew darker. "We do not educate our guests in this restaurant. We are here to give them a great dining experience. Therefore, their conversations are private and confidential. The job description of a busboy says nothing about monitoring conversations and offering advice. The only words you should have with guests is to answer questions about the location of our restrooms. Is that clear?"

I kept my mouth shut for the next half hour, but I still managed to get in trouble. It involved a $5 tip left on one of my tables. I gave it to Mary, a pretty waitress who had gone out of her way to be nice to me. Hilda, who could have been a nose tackle for the New England Patriots, stormed into the kitchen and demanded to know why I had given her tip to Mary.

After sorting it out, Hanley turned to me and said, "Another reason why you should not allow yourself to be distracted. You must be able to connect the tips to the correct waitresses you're bussing, or problems like this are bound to happen."

I left the kitchen with a new resolution. Tonight would end my career as a busboy. I did not like the work, and I had already developed an intense dislike for the restaurant owner. I knew I was not on his Christmas card list either.

Guests next to another table I was clearing were having a heated discussion about the Academy Awards, a subject dear to my heart. One of them said the best picture award for 1951 went to *Sunset Boulevard*. A second maintained that it was *Born Yesterday*. I put down my tray and told them they were both wrong. The best picture award went to *All About Eve*. The lady who backed *Sunset Boulevard* said that she knew that Gloria Swanson got the best actress award. I corrected her again by explaining that the best actress award that year went to Judy Holiday for *Born Yesterday*.

Of course, all of my instruction interfered with my busing. When I finally cleared the table and walked into the kitchen, Jeb Hanley was waiting for me. We were like two gunslingers getting ready to draw. He said, "You're," as I said, "I." I like to think of it as a tie. Regardless of whether "quit" came before "fired," the outcome was the same. I would do no more busing for Jeb Hanley—or anyone else!

Mrs. Hanley, whom I liked almost as much as I disliked her husband, called me a few days later and asked where she should send my check for four hours of bussing. I told her to give it to Mary. Then she lowered her voice and said something interesting. "Several of the guests who were here the night you worked asked about you. One of them said you were the brightest busboy she had ever been around." It was a nice compliment but did nothing to change my decision to never work in a restaurant again—except as a stand-up comic.

The Truth About Lies

I told my first little white lie when I was in third grade. One of my classmates, Gloria, had lost her eye in a household accident. Mrs. Ball, my third-grade teacher, told us we should be especially nice to Gloria when she returned to school. I was in a vulnerable position because Gloria sat right in front of me.

I noticed almost immediately that her new eye was slightly off-kilter. For whatever reason, it did not line up correctly with her other eye. I was not the only one who noticed. Gloria's cockeye was the main subject at recess.

Gloria was a quiet girl who usually kept to herself. Suddenly she turned around and asked me, "Can you tell the difference between my real eye and the artificial one?"

I looked her full in the face and lied. "They both look the same to me," I said. Now, about 80 years later, I do not regret that decision. But I have to admit it set me on a lifelong habit of telling little white lies. Most of them are harmless, and all of them are intended as acts of kindness for a person who is going through a difficult time.

"Have you noticed how much weight I've gained?"

"No. I would never have guessed."

"Does this new wig look natural?"

"I never would have known it was a wig if you hadn't told me."

"Do you think plastic surgery would remove the wrinkles?"

"What wrinkles? It would be a waste of money."

Whenever a situation arises where I can ease someone's pain by a little stretch of the truth, I'm ready with an assortment of white lies. Yet, I have to admit that it was a white lie that led to the ending of my marriage.

It's usually challenging to identify the exact timeframe when a marriage begins to unravel. But, because of a white lie, I am able to identify the time and place. It was in the fall of 1980. In those three months, my daughter Alicia was diagnosed with Type I Diabetes, my mother died, and my wife, Rosemary, was operated on for breast cancer.

Dr. Hugh Lena, the surgeon who operated on Rosemary, felt cancer had been detected early, and he did not expect any complications. I was sitting in the recovery room as Dr. Lena, accompanied by my good friends, Dr. Bill Hostnik and Dr. Bob Klimek, walked down the hall. I could tell by their expressions that all was not well.

Dr. Lena explained that the tumor was larger than expected. Thirteen lymph nodes were involved, and chemotherapy would have to begin immediately. I met with Dr. Richard Benton, oncologist, the following week. He explained an aggressive treatment plan that involved 18 months of chemotherapy. I explained to Dr. Benton that Rosemary was timid and would have difficulty dealing with such news. Could we soften the blow somehow?

Instead of telling her the truth, I offered a series of lies. "The operation was a success. Dr. Lena just wants you to have a little follow-up treatment to make sure the tumor doesn't return." We met with Dr. Benton on Christmas Eve Day of 1980. The meeting went smoothly until Dr. Benton mentioned that Tomaxafin would be among the drugs she would be receiving.

"Tomaxafin. That drug would make my hair fall out. So I won't take it," she said.

"Rosemary, I think you should understand one thing," Dr. Benton said. "We are in a life-threatening situation."

Instead of replying to him, Rosemary turned to me. "You lied to me," she said. For the next 18 months, I drove Rosemary to every weekly appointment. She lost her hair, her appetite, and sometimes her ability to even walk. But those treatments saved her life, and she is still around at the age of 83. Unfortunately, while she survived, the marriage did not. After her recovery, she left Old Lyme in 1984 and never returned. We were separated for 18 years before finally divorcing in 2002.

After having a couple of bouts with cancer myself, I realize how important it is to know the truth. I was wrong to lie to Rosemary and will always regret doing so. I also underestimated her inner strength. After we separated, she became a very successful advertising executive on Cape Cod, MA.

Did this experience cure me of my tendency to tell little white lies? Not really. First of all, I don't classify my lie to Rosemary as little. It was major and involved someone's life. But if a situation arises where my little white lie might help someone and bring no harm to anyone else, I'll probably tell it.

A Modern Railroad Robber Baron

I never met Patrick B. McGinnis, the late President of the New Haven and Hartford Railroad, but I certainly knew his voice. When I got out of the Air Force in 1955, my uncle, Leo Kennealy, was the Director of Public Relations for the New Haven Railroad. He was credited with helping McGinnis gain control of the railroad in 1954, after a bitter proxy fight with former President Frederic C. Dumaine, Jr.

McGinnis was unquestionably the most outspoken and controversial railroad executive of his time. He believed the ailing railroad industry's greatest handicap was its lack of modern thinking. He felt that if his ideas were accepted, he would revitalize the railroad industry in the whole country. He traveled throughout New England, delivering speeches warning that the industry's most significant handicap was its lack of modern thinking. He was a visionary, promising that his ideas, including the addition of high-speed trains, would lead the railroad into a bright future.

Uncle Leo was part of a team that went to Spain and bought a Talgo, a revolutionary train that traveled at high speeds with minimum track noise. The first Talgo train for the New Haven Railroad was delivered in 1954. It was named the "John Quincy Adams," and it traveled from New York City to Boston in record time.

McGinnis was a spellbinding speaker, and Uncle Leo decided his speeches should be recorded and used for press releases for newspapers, radio, and TV. Someone had to transcribe the tapes, and I ended up with the job. Leo gave me two big boxes filled with about 50 tapes to be recorded. I was to receive $55 for each recording.

I had difficulty with the first tape because McGinnis was a fast talker. Starting and stopping by hand led to a lot of missed words. Bill Kenneally, my cousin, who became a brilliant physicist, came up with a solution. He installed a foot pedal that allowed me to transcribe the speeches a few sentences at a time. It took about an hour for each speech that translated to $55 each, a considerable sum for a college student. I remember counting up the tapes and figuring that my immediate financial goals were set. Meanwhile, McGinnis was delivering two or three speeches every week, so the future looked bright, too.

From my early radio days, I made quick judgments about the characters on the programs being broadcast. I never liked Superman or any of the cowboy voices, but I loved people like Orson Welles and Vincent Price. After I finished the first tape, I knew I was not too fond of Patrick McGinnis. His words seem to tumble out without a lot of thought or meaning. He also had a derisive tone when describing his many detractors. I did not share these feelings with my Uncle Leo. Those tapes represented a considerable windfall for me.

While McGinnis was planning for the future, he let some things slide in the present. The union complained bitterly about a $12 million slash in maintenance funds that delayed or postponed indefinitely routine preventive maintenance. However, it did allow for a better P&L for stockholders, with an alleged $9,275,000 profit in 1955. Former President Dumaine claimed that McGinnis used cash reserves and income from subsidiaries to pad railroad earnings. Meanwhile, passengers complained about late trains, poor air conditioning in the summer, and not enough heat in the winter. Diesel engines stalled because diminished crews failed to drain condensation coils.

McGinnis was able to keep things under control until hurricanes Connie and Diane arrived in 1955. Connie hit on August 3, 1955, with bands of heavy rain and wind causing damage to thousands of miles of track. Days later, Diane made landfall, causing significant flooding throughout southern New England. Railroad tracks were washed away, and a reduced maintenance crew struggled for weeks to restore service.

Under intense pressure from the Board of Directors, Patrick McGinnis resigned as President on January 18, 1956. However, he was not out of work for long. Just days later, Patrick McGinnis was hired as President of the Boston & Main Railroad. He did not take his former associates at the New Haven Railroad with him. Those who remained were quickly fired when a new president arrived. My Uncle Leo was one of the first causalities. He never once criticized his former boss, but I know he had been hurt by McGinnis's indifference to all of his former associates.

About nine years later, Patrick McGinnis was in the news again. This time the heat wasn't coming from irate passengers, the union, or unhappy stockholders. In 1965, as President of the Boston & Maine, he and three other executives were accused by the Government of selling 10 of the B & M's passenger cars to the International Railway Corporation for $250,000 with the cars to be sold the next day to the Wabash Railroad for $425,000. McGinnis was to receive $35,000 in the deal.

I went immediately to Uncle Leo, trying to get a little inside information that I could use to sell an article about McGinnis. I did not doubt that Leo either knew or could find a little more background on the story.

Leo looked at me and shook his head. "Ken remember one thing—you can't kiss and tell." I know Leo was sad when McGinnis was sentenced to 18 months in prison for his part in the scheme. McGinnis was the topic of gossip throughout his career. One associate who never participated in criticizing him was Leo P. Kenneally. He believed, above all else, that you owed your boss loyalty. It seems to be a disappearing belief, but I like it—and I loved my Uncle Leo.

After my mother died in 1981 and the family home was sold, my brother Jack found a couple of boxes in the attic filled with the McGinnis tapes.

"Do you want these?" he asked.

"No thanks," I said. "You can take them to the dump."

My typed versions of the speeches probably suffered the same fate—only a lot earlier.

Patrick B. McGinnis certainly had a more impressive resume than Leo. He founded his own Wall Street investment firm and later served as President of the New Haven and the Boston and Maine Railroads. But he lacked two qualities that Leo had in abundance—integrity, and loyalty!

My Second Family

I met Wes Forcier in 1945, shortly after my family moved to Edgewood. I was playing hockey in Roger Williams Park when I noticed a figure skater making wonderful turns and jumps. He was the best skater on the ice. I asked some of the other players why Wes didn't play hockey with us. With his speed and skating ability, he would have been a natural. Wes didn't like team sports, I was told. He didn't play football, basketball, or baseball for the same reason. My friends said that Wes was a loner. He was also one of the best pool players in Cranston.

In one of the best decisions in my life, I introduced myself to Wes. For more than 70 years, we were best friends. A voracious reader and listener, there were few subjects in which he did not have in-depth knowledge. With the mind of an investigative reporter, it was said that Wes would learn everything about a new acquaintance, including birth weight, within five minutes of an introduction. Meanwhile, new acquaintances would be fortunate if they escaped with anything more than a name.

We were both teenagers when Wes said he was an atheist. I thought he just shared his feelings with me. But he suddenly stopped going to Sunday mass, which caused an uproar with his family, strong Catholics. I suggested that he leave on Sunday morning to let his family think he was going to mass. He would have none of it. "It would not be honest," he said.

When you befriended Wes, you got a lot more than one person. The Forciers became my second family in Edgewood. I didn't know Mr. Forcier that well. He was a vice president for Wilson Meats and ran the company for all of New England. He also died shortly after I met Wes. Hollis, the oldest, had married right after WWII, and we only had a casual relationship. But I bonded with Mrs. Forcier, Wes, Bruce, Beverly, and Loring.

The Forcier home was always particularly wonderful at Christmas. One glass of Bruce's eggnog was terrific. Two or more met you were staying the night, if not the week. Mrs. Forcier was a delight. She was always upbeat and so gentle. She really didn't understand her youngest son, Wesley, but no mother was more supportive.

Ginger, a cocker spaniel, was the family dog. One Christmas, Bruce gave his other a parakeet. I noticed that Ginger would follow the bird as it flew about the house, poised to attack. "Does Ginger bother the bird?" I asked Mrs. Forcier.

"No, Ken she replied. "Only when he flies low."

Wes and I spent one year together as freshmen at Providence College. He never did get his degree, but it did not stop him from achieving a successful business career. As a management consultant, he provided expertise in the beverage and jewelry industries for more than 60 years. He also served as Deputy Liquor Commissioner for the State of Rhode Island. His reputation for providing valuable advice for the business community was exceeded only by the support and help he gave to his many friends. If you could name Wes Forcier as a friend, you did not need much else in this life.

As Rudyard Kipling said in his poem "If," Wes walked with kings but never lost his common touch. His friends ranged from company presidents to blue-collar workers to the destitute. No one ever approached him without leaving with some good advice and, in many cases, some financial support. He also served as an unofficial employment agency, connecting out-of-work friends with business opportunities.

That Frank Sinatra song, "My Way," could have been written for Wes. He did not take the traditional paths that most of us follow. He lived with his partner, Patricia Plourde, for more than 65 years, without the benefit of marriage. When I asked Wes early in their relationship why they didn't get married, he said it was unnecessary. I know of no other couple more devoted to each other than Wes and Pat.

Wes was "best friend" to a number of friends, including Herb Browne, my friend of more than 70 years. Herb and I are the only survivors of the original Edgewood group. We speak frequently, and our conversation usually includes one or more Wes Forcier stories.

One of my favorites occurred when Wes and I were going to a dance in Boston. When I picked him up, he was dressed in a sweater and slacks. I told him a jacket and tie were required for admission. He said he understood and told me to drive. When we got to North Attleboro, he directed me to a men's clothing store. It was about to close when we walked in. Wes quickly picked out a shirt, jacket, and slacks. He asked the salesman to show him some ties.

"We don't carry ties," the man said. Wes starred at him. "You've got a choice," he said. "Sell me your tie or keep the jacket, slacks, and shirt." Twenty minutes later, we left the store with the jacket, shirt, slacks, and the salesman's tie.

Not all of our adventures had happy endings. In 1953, I was home on leave from the Air Force. Wes had made arrangements to meet a mutual friend, Bill, at the Celebrity Club in Providence. I had met Bill years earlier when we were both in grammar school. He was a nice guy, except when he was drinking. When we arrived, Bill was involved in an argument with the club manager. It was obvious that he had already had too much to drink, and the manager was asking him to leave. Bill refused. Wes tried to intercede, but Bill would have none of it.

About five minutes later, Bill was thrown into the back of a police wagon. Wes walked up to a police sergeant and asked where Bill was being taken. "Do you want to go with him?" the policeman demanded. I grabbed Wes on the arm and practically dragged him to my car. I also reluctantly agreed to follow the police wagon. Wes walked up to the same police sergeant who shouted, "You again. I told you to fxxx off. Now you can join him." As Wes was being led away, he shouted to me, "Call Bill's father."

The only problem was that Bill's father had an unlisted number. Someone did reach him because Bill's father was in court the next morning. Bill and Wes were fined for disorderly conduct. It was what happened after that remains in my memory. Bill's father told Wes he was a bad influence and to stay away from his son. Bridges were mended, and both Bill and Bill's father played essential roles in Wes's life.

Loring and I were always friends, but we drew close after I accepted a job with Prentice-Hall working in New London, Connecticut. Loring was the general manager with Wilson Meats, based in the same city, so we began to spend a lot of time together. When Loring introduced me to his fiancé, Joanne Dalton, I knew he had a winner. Nothing changed my mind over the years, as Loring settled in as a husband and father. While he was a late entry in both roles, no man ever approached them with more love, dedication, and joy. JoAnne deserves a great deal of credit for helping him make this transition effortlessly.

I can still remember his excitement when his son Hank was born. Then along came Heather, Gerard, Michael, James, and Thomas. While I'm not sure of the order of their births, no child was ever born into a more welcoming family. The joy in his voice as he announced each addition would stay with me forever. As the family grew, our conversations became shorter and fewer since Loring always seemed to be driving the children to some practice or activity. No parents ever showed more love and support than Loring and Joanne. It comes as no surprise that their six children turned into wonderful adults, blessing them with 18 grandchildren. God bless you, Joanne. Thank you for making my dear friend a loving husband and father.

Wes had already dealt with the loss of his mother, father, and two brothers, Hollis and Bruce. Loring's death was a lot harder for him to handle.

I was always pleased that Loring and JoAnne raised their family at the Forcier home on Wheeler Avenue in Edgewood. It was the favorite place of my youth where I spent so many beautiful hours talking to Loring's mother as I waited for my friend Wesley.

Wes battled throat cancer and heart problems later in life. I drove his sister Beverly to visit him at Hull, MA, where Wes and Pat had built a lovely home overlooking the beach. Wes had just returned from the hospital, but he still had severe health problems. Beverly said she would speak to her nephew Robert Forcier, a Catholic priest, about bringing Wes back to the church. I advised her it was not a good idea, but Beverly brought it up shortly after arriving.

"No," Wes said politely but firmly.

Wes always thought that he would die before his beloved Pat, but God had other plans. Pat had been born in Maine, and her background was French Canadian. She never did get rid of her strong accent, and it took me a long time to understand her. But you did not have to hear her words to appreciate her devotion to Wes. She was with him every step of the way as his health declined. I was honored when Wes asked me to deliver Pat's eulogy.

Things got very difficult for Wes after Pat died. Herb Browne and

Bill Considine, friends of Wes for more than 70 years, and I went to visit him shortly after Pat died. We were surprised when Wes seemed to accept our idea of moving into an assisted living facility. I had some experience with assisted living facilities after working in the publications department of Brookdale Senior living for three years. So Bill, Herb, and Wes agreed that I should take the lead in finding the best fit for Wes.

I set up an appointment at an assisted living facility based in Narragansett, Rhode Island. It was a good choice because it was close to Bill, Herb, and myself. We arrived for our appointment early, so Wes could get his own impression without listening to a sales representative. There were probably 100 residents sitting in the main building when an employee came through the hallway screaming, "Bingo time. Everyone in the library." Wes did not move. He looked at me, got up, and walked to the car. Our idea of Wes moving into assisted living died that same day.

Wes did not die a happy death. He was found in the driveway of his home one morning after collapsing in the driveway, probably trying to get to his car. He may have been there all night.

While Wes never had any children, he was particularly proud of his nieces and nephews, including Henry (Hank) Forcier, Heather Guttari, Gerard Forcier, Michael Forcier, James Forcier, Thomas Forcier, Mary Greene, Richard Forcier, Judith Sullivan, and Rev. Robert Forcier. I was honored when the children asked me to deliver Wes's eulogy.

We worried too much about what Wes did not believe in and did not appreciate the things he did believe in. He loved family and friends and had the strongest sense of ethics of any businessman I have ever known. The rest of us need rules, regulations, and commandments. Wes lived a good and honorable life based on his integrity.

Thank you, Wes, for being my best friend for more than 70 years. I am a better man because of you and the wonderful Forcier family. So as long as I have memory, all of the Forciers will be with me.

CREATIVITY BEATS EXPERIENCE

In December of 1954, I took a part-time job with the local Sears & Roebuck in San Antonio. I had two weeks of leave, so I decided to use them to pick up a little extra cash. If I had been assigned to men's clothing or even the furniture department, I might have flourished. But I was sent to the hardware department, even though I did not know the difference between a Phillips head and a standard screwdriver.

I was a disaster from the first day. My fellow workers helped me as much as they could, but things got hectic when the Christmas rush began. Every day I expected to get fired. The week before Christmas, the store manager came to the department and asked to see me at the end of my shift. I knew what he had in mind, so I shook hands with all my fellow workers and thanked them for their help. When I got to the manager's office, I was introduced to the vice president in charge of the entire Southeast area. I was impressed that a top executive was called in to fire me.

"We've been reviewing your sales records, and frankly, we're puzzled," the vice president said. "Most of your numbers are below average right across the board—except in one area," he said. "You led the country in sales of plungers, and we'd like to know how you did it." Delighted that I might be able to collect a few more paychecks, I explained my technique.

"When customers ask for a plunger, I show him or her the inventory, explaining the advantages of each style. After he makes a selection, I take two plungers in hand and head for the register. Almost all of the customers object at this point, saying that they only want one plunger. I try to have enough distance between us so that I have to raise my voice. Then I ask loudly, 'You mean you're going to use the same plunger in your kitchen sink that you use to unclog your toilet?" Usually, they buy the two plungers," I explained as the vice president and manager dissolved in laughter

I kept the job throughout the Christmas season.

The Snapple Boys

I met Donald Von Staats in 1981 when I leased a Mercedes Benz from his company, Essex Leasing. Thus began a friendship that ended with his death in 2018. Don was a fascinating man and a great storyteller. I enjoyed hearing him talk about his clients, including Ralph Lauren and three men he referred to as "the Snapple boys."

When a book I wrote with Red Auerbach was published in 1991, I gave a copy to Don with this message: "For Don Von Staats—without your help and guidance, this book could have been published four years earlier." I stole that idea from Mark Twain.

About five years later, Don called me with an idea for another book. He had sent his copy of the book to Hyman Golden, who, together with Arnold Greenberg and Leonard Marsh, founded Snapple in 1972. Golden had called Don and told him that his partners were interested in writing a book about their company. He invited Don and me to meet with them at his home in East Hampton, Long Island. After passing security, I looked up at a large, beautiful home right on the beach. I thought it was Golden's, but I was wrong. It was Steven Spielberg's. Golden's was next door, and it was twice as big as Spielberg's.

Don and I were seated at a table overlooking Long Island Sound as we waited for the partners to arrive. I still remember that strange feeling I had as I looked out at the water. A week before, July 17, 1996, TWA Flight 800 had taken off from JFK Airport headed for Paris. Twelve minutes later, it exploded over Long Island Sound, killing all 230 people on board. The suspicion of terrorism led to one of the most extensive investigations in aviation history. Twenty-five years later, questions remain about the crash, even though the NTSB concluded that a spark in the center fuel tank caused the accident.

Don had described the three owners of Snapple as interesting, good guys. He did not exaggerate. I liked Hyman Golden, Arnold Greenberg, and Leonard Marsh. We did not get off to a great start, however, when I asked permission to use a tape recorder as they told me the story of Snapple. I felt the tension, so I put the recorder away and agreed to take notes.

The company was founded as a part-time venture to supply fruit juices to health food stores. Unsure if the business would succeed, Greenberg continued to run his health food store in Manhattan's East Village, while Leonard Marsh and his brother-in-law, Hyman Golden, operated a window-washing business. Marsh told me he knew "as much about juice as he did about making an atom bomb."

They stumbled into the business by accident. A customer owed Marsh and Golden $25,000. He told them he was going to retire to Florida and gave them formulas for fruit juices. "You'll make a fortune," he predicted. The company owned no manufacturing facilities but instead made agreements with 30 bottlers across the country. In this way, Greenberg told me that Snapple was able to keep overhead low and payroll short.

They got their name "Snapple" from their first product, apple juice. An immediate problem developed when the first batches fermented in the bottle, causing the bottle caps to fly off. They resolved the issue quickly and were delighted when sales began to climb for a product "Made From the Best Stuff on Earth." They introduced their products in Manhattan by cutting a deal with hot dog vendors. They offered free products for the first week. Howard Stern and Rush Limbaugh helped promote the new company on their radio shows. Wendy Kaufman became known as the "Snapple Lady," chatting on-air with Oprah Winfrey and David Letterman.

Just before a national advertising campaign began, the company was sued by a Texas man who had registered the name "Snapple" several years earlier. Golden said the partners had nightmares about demands in the six figures. The man told the partners he would not negotiate—he would give them one price, take it or leave it. The owner's price was $5,000, and it was wired to him the same day.

The company enjoyed modest success with its natural sodas in the early 1980s, but after it introduced its iced tea in 1987, sales skyrocketed. Snapple was the only ready-to-drink iced tea promoted as having natural ingredients and being made from a real brewed tea. A national boom in health consciousness helped Snapple become a national brand.

The company experienced glitches in the early 1990s. The original graphic on the Iced Tea flavor, a depiction of the United States historical event, the Boston Team Party, was replaced due to protest groups claiming the ships on the packaging were slave-trading vessels. Through a media campaign with the NAACP, Snapple successfully fought back those rumors.

In 1984, sales were $4 million. By 1994, Snapple was available across the country, and sales ballooned to $674 million. Greenberg said the company had grown beyond their limited expertise and looked for a new owner to take it to the next level. In 1994, Quaker paid $1.7 billion for the Snapple brand, outbidding Coca-Cola and several other major beverage owners.

Snapple started as an almost amateurish company with poorly designed labels and mostly word-of-mouth advertising. It had little supermarket coverage, so it cultivated small distributors serving thousands of lunch counters and delis. Immediately after acquiring Snapple, Quaker Oats tried to take over 300 distributor accounts with supermarkets by offering them the right to distribute Gatorade. The distributors refused to give up the accounts they had worked so hard to secure. Most distributors held contracts in perpetuity, so no deal was ever reached.

Quaker also introduced Snapple in larger 32-and 64-ounce bottles. Consumers didn't buy them. They were looking for 16-ounce bottles they could finish with one sitting. Quaker also started running ads with slick production values, not in keeping with Snapple's initial image. It also fired Wendy, The Snapple Lady, and dumped Limbaugh and Stern, who took his revenge by urging listeners to stay away from "Crapple." In 1997, Quaker sold Snapple to Triarc Beverages for $300 million, a $1.4 billion loss that cost the chairman and president of Quaker their jobs.

How did Quaker Oats go so wrong? Business analysts have studied all the factors that led to one of the most significant failures in business history. Even the ones I can understand do not pinpoint the primary cause of the failure. It comes down to a single reason for me. A company can acquire formulas, trademarks, and proprietary information, as Quaker Oats did. It failed to capture the "soul" of Snapple, represented by Golden, Greenberg, and Marsh.

One of the most striking things about my conversation with Greenberg, Marsh, and Golden was their absolute delight in talking about their success and failures. They did not try to hide their mistakes in turning a small company into a national brand. Instead of carefully analyzing their advertising campaigns and market research, they talked of parties and parades, good times and bad. Some brands are born to have fun, and Snapple is one of them. While operating out of the back of Arnie's parents' pickle store in Queens, Greenberg, Marsh and Golden took on giants in the beverage industry and won.

I left the meeting that day with a notebook filled with stories about the successes and created a beverage giant. I listened as Golden told me about the three partners seated around a table with chemists doing taste tests for new products. Marsh told me about offering flexible work schedules to allow employees to care for children and elderly relatives. Snapple was considered a pioneer in introducing employee-friendly policies to corporate America. Greenberg said the three partners never got over their gratitude for accomplishing the American dream. They would kick off board meetings by singing "God bless America."

Some wise person once said, "Choose a job you love to, and you will never work a day in your life." I cannot think of a more fitting epitaph for three men who started a great company and had fun doing it. I left the meeting feeling we could write a great book about how they took on companies like Coca Cola and Pepsi and won.

However, I never spoke to the three founders of Snapple again after that 1996 meeting. I did receive a friendly letter from Arnie Greenberg, thanking me for my time but telling me that their wives were worried that a book might publicize their wealth and increase the chances of their children or grandchildren being kidnapped. I did not argue with the decision. But I would have enjoyed telling their story, notably after Quaker Oats acquired the company and made some significant mistakes.

Don Von Staats, Hyman Golden, Arnold Greenberg, and Leonard Marsh are all gone now. As far as I know, no relatives of the Snapple founders have ever been kidnapped. Snapple lives on under the ownership of Cadbury Schweppes, which paid $1.45 billion for Snapple in 2000. There is an important message for executives who are considering an acquisition: Go beyond economic analysis before making a decision. Give some thought to its soul as well, which in the case of Snapple was represented by three guys named Golden, Greenberg, and Marsh.

A Special Discount

Mr. Wolfe ran the Park Shoe Store, located on Park Avenue, Cranston, a short distance from my home. With six boys in the Dooley family, he saw us frequently. What we lacked in quality, we made up for in quantity. He was a kind, patient man and always took his time measuring our feet to get it right.

The country was still recovering from the Great Depression, so we didn't have discretionary funds for specialty items. That changed when I spotted a pair of boots in Mr. Wolfe's window. Many of my friends in the sixth grade at Eden Park Elementary School were already wearing them. The boots featured a pocket, holding a small knife not intended for any lethal purpose. It was just another selling point for an item I craved.

The price of the boots was $3.50, a large amount of money for what was considered a non-essential purchase in the Dooley family. I began to work on my mother, and finally, she handed me the princely sum of $3.50 to buy the boots. Before entering the store, I took a final look at the boots in the window. The price was now $4.50. Mr. Wolfe must have seen the disappointment in my face, and he opened the door and invited me in.

I explained that I had $3.50 to buy the boots and did not know about the price increase. He did not answer me immediately but had me sit as he measured my feet. Then, he left for the storeroom and returned with a pair of boots. It was a perfect fit, and I strode about the store, still wondering when I was going to get the other dollar.

"I saw you admiring those boots when the price was $3.50," Mr. Wolfe said. "I consider that a pre-existing order, so you are entitled to buy them at the former price," he said. I didn't understand his reasoning, but I left wearing those prized boots.

The following year, I was in the seventh grade at Valentine Almy Junior High School. One of my classmates was Sheldon Wolfe, Mr. Wolfe's son. Every morning we started the day by singing the Star-Spangled Banner and reciting The Lord's Prayer. Sheldon had a booming voice and really got into our national anthem. His silence during The Lord's Prayer came to the attention of our homeroom teacher, Miss Hazard. She told him that he should recite The Lord's Prayer.

Sheldon said he was Jewish, and his parents had instructed him not to join in as his classmates recited the prayer. Miss Hazard and Sheldon stared at each other until I broke the silence.

"If Sheldon's parents don't want him to recite the prayer, he shouldn't do it," I said. I think Miss Hazard was happy that I diverted the conversation to me. "Go to Mr. White's office now," she ordered.

Mr. White was the principal of Valentine Almy. Although early in the school year, we had already met several times, not always under the most pleasant circumstances. His secretary, Ida, greeted me as I walked into his office.

"What did you do now?" she asked. Before I could answer, Mr. White summoned me into his office. I explained the reason for my visit, and he listened quietly and didn't bring up the subject of detention, which usually followed one of my transgressions. I avoided trouble at home by telling my mother the school day had been extended by another hour. "Go back to your classroom now," he said. "Tell Miss Hazard I will speak to her later."

I don't know what message was delivered to Miss Hazard, but she never confronted Sheldon again as he remained silent during the prayer. I want to add that Miss Hazard was a wonderful teacher, and that episode with Sheldon was out of character for her.

Later that same year (1944), Mr. White's son was listed as missing in action. He was never found, and the designation was changed to killed in action. On D-Day, June 6, 1944, Mr. White announced the invasion on the school intercom. I moved that year and never saw Sheldon Wolfe again.

About ten years ago, I was in a branch of a New England hardware chain. There was a huge banner with the words, "If you're dissatisfied for any reason, call Sheldon Wolfe," and it listed a phone number. Yes, it was the same Sheldon Wolfe who was now the president of the chain.

I called my former classmate and told him the story about his father and my boots. He remembered my coming to his defense over the prayer issue. We also discussed our mutual friend, Ellsworth Maine, who died of leukemia at the age of 31. He had read a story in the Providence Journal about my plan to write a book about 2nd Lt. Robert E. Thorpe, the brother of his friend Gill. Bob Thorpe, a P-47 pilot, had been captured by the Japanese, tortured, and beheaded during WWII. Sheldon and Gill graduated together from Cranston High School in 1949.

Sheldon's assessment of his father was right on the money. "He was a real gentleman," Sheldon said. I proudly wore a pair of much-loved boots for three years because of his kindness.

THE BET

It was 2016, the year of Deflategate for the New England Patriots. Tom Brady, the great Patriot quarterback, was suspended for the first four games of 2016 for allegedly taking the air out of footballs (Deflategate) during the Patriots' victory over the Indianapolis Colts in the 2014 American Football Championship Game. The backup quarterback, Jimmy Garoppolo, was set to start his first NFL game against the Phoenix Cardinals on opening day, and I didn't want to miss it.

I was in Manhattan that Sunday getting ready for a conference that started early Monday morning. The game was not being shown on national television, so I made a few phone calls to find a local bar that carried it. I found one right around the corner from the hotel where I was staying. I took a seat at the bar directly in front of a TV that had a Patriots-Phoenix sign. I ordered a shot of Johnny Walker Black Label Scotch, and the bartender put it in front of me along with a beer chaser.

A loud conversation was going on, led by a character who could have played the role of Cliff Clavin on Cheers. Cliff was the resident barfly and know-it-all. John Ratzenberger, who played Cliff expertly, was only filling a role. The character I was listening to was for real, chastising his friends for not knowing the answers to his often-obscure questions on football, baseball, boxing, basketball, and hockey. I followed those sports all of my life, but I couldn't answer some of his questions.

Finally, he threw out a question that caught my attention. "Who was the first African American to play in the NBA?" he asked, after warning everyone to stay off their cell phones. No one came up with the answer, so he blurted out: "Chuck Cooper of the Boston Celtics."

No one challenged his answer. I called out, "You're wrong." The crowd was silent as attention turned to the stranger who had just challenged their recognized leader.

"Chuck Cooper was the first African American to be drafted into the NBA by Red Auerbach in 1950," I said. "But Earl Lloyd was the first African American to play in the NBA.

I did not tell him that Red Auerbach was a personal friend, that I had directed him in a play and a movie, and also wrote a book with him. I also did not mention that I had interviewed Earl Lloyd for a movie I was writing with Bill Russell and Sam Jones about African Americans coming into the NBA.

Mike (he had given me his first name) was not about to surrender, especially in front of all of his friends. "I'll take Cooper, and you can have Lloyd for a round of drinks for the house," he challenged.

I was not too fond of Mike at this point. He represented every loud, obnoxious punk I had met over the years. So I took the bet, and one of his friends read the answer from Google: "On Oct. 31, 1950, 21-year-old Earl Lloyd became the first African American to play in an NBA game when he took the court in the season opener for the Washington Capitals." The roar of approval that followed the announcement told me that Mike didn't have as many friends as he thought. Judging from the size of the crowd, I would say that Mike lost at least $150 on the bet.

The football game started, and I did not notice that Mike had left the bar shortly before his team, the New York Giants, took the field. I was very impressed with Jimmy Garoppolo that day as he led the Patriots to a victory. As the game ended, I had eight shots of Scotch with beer chasers strung out in front of me. When I asked for my check, the bartender shook his head in disbelief. "You haven't touched one of them," he said.

"I know," I said. "Would you distribute them to my friends along the bar. You see, I don't drink. I didn't want to come in here, take up a seat at the bar, and drink cokes all afternoon."

"But why in the name of God would you order Johnny Walker Black Label—it's the most expensive scotch we carry!"

"Because when I don't drink, I don't drink only the best," I answered as I walked out of the bar to a round of applause from the recipients of my Johnny Walker Back Label scotch.

I still think of Earl Lloyd with great fondness. I never met him personally, but I had several hour-long interviews with him. He was a real gentleman and had no bitterness about some difficult experiences when he could not stay with the team or eat with them. Instead, he focused on his white teammates, who always walked out with him when he was refused service in a restaurant.

Although Earl was chosen seven rounds after Chuck Cooper, he was by far the better ballplayer. Cooper lasted only a few years in Boston, and his career was over in five years. Earl Lloyd had a 10-year career, played on championship teams, and became the third African American head coach in history. He is also a member of the National Basketball Hall of Fame. I enjoyed pointing this fact out to Red Auerbach, who usually responded by blowing cigar smoke in my face.

Red showed me a letter that he had received from Earl Lloyd shortly after the 1950 draft. "If you had not taken Chuck Cooper earlier, the Washington Caps never would have taken me in any round. So I want to thank you and Mr. Brown (Celtics owner) for allowing me to play professional basketball." Earl Lloyd died in February of 2015, only a few weeks after our last interview.

I never went to that Manhattan bar again. But I'm confident the story about Mike losing that bet to a stranger who did not drink but ordered only the best Scotch is retold frequently.

"If You Could See What I Can Hear"

I attended Superbowl X played between the Dallas Cowboys and the Pittsburgh Steelers at the Orange Bowl in Miami on Jan. 18, 1976. It was a great game, with the Steelers getting the victory by a score of 21–17. Lynn Swann, Pittsburgh's great wide receiver, caught four passes for a Super Bowl record of 161 yards and won the MVP award. The two head coaches, Tom Landry of Dallas and Chuck Knoll of Pittsburgh, and the two quarterbacks, Roger Staubach of Dallas and Terry Bradshaw of Pittsburgh, are now members of the National Football League's Hall of Fame. In addition, the game featured players like future Hall of Famers Mel Renfro, Cliff Harris, Joe Greene, Jack Ham, Jack Lambert, and Mel Blount. And yet, my most memorable moment from that game had nothing to do with football.

The game was one of the first major national events of the United States Bicentennial celebration. Both the pre-game and halftime show celebrated the Bicentennial, and players on both teams wore special patches on their jerseys with the Bicentennial logo. I had never heard of Tom Sullivan, a blind entertainer who sang the National Anthem before the game. Tom delivered our National Anthem with more feeling and enthusiasm than I have heard before or since.

Four years later, I met Tom Sullivan in person. My film company, Madison Productions, had a contract to produce a safety film for Prentice-Hall. The movie's theme was eye safety, and it was intended to show the difference between someone who suffered blindness as an infant and one injured in an industrial accident.

When we were introduced, Tom Sullivan, calm and confident, looked directly into my eyes as he spoke. He could not possibly be blind, I thought. He held his hand out and said, "You must be Ken—I'm Tom Sullivan." We bonded immediately, especially after he learned I was a friend of Red Auerbach, the legendary coach, and president of the Boston Celtics. Tom was born in Boston in 1947, the son of a saloon owner. His premature birth caused him to need oxygen treatment while in an incubator. Unfortunately, he was given too much oxygen, which left him permanently blind. Tom grew up listening to Johnny Most, broadcaster of Celtic games, and could recite all the great memories associated with Bill Russell, Bob Cousy, Tom Heinsohn John Havlicek, Sam Jones, and K. C. Jones.

On the first day on the set, Tom knew everybody's name and could identify them by their footsteps. Lighting people, sound technicians, actors, key grips, and the director and cinematographer were all addressed correctly by their first names. Tom brought a calmness to the whole production. He kept us all entertained with his songs and humor in between scenes or at breaks or lunch.

When we had dialogue changes, we read them to Tom once. Not only did he have his lines, but he knew everybody else's. On more than one occasion, he told the screenwriter (Ken Dooley) that some dialogue contradicted something that had been said earlier. He also reminded the director (Ken Dooley) about a required scene change.

Tom never let his handicap stand in the way of a normal life. He continues to work as an author, composer, and singer, as well as an actor. Tom married Patricia Steffen in 1969 and fathered two children, Blythe and Thomas. He told me an incredible story about Blythe when she was three years old.

Tom was sitting in the swimming pool area outside of his home in Los Angeles. His wife had gone shopping, and a babysitter was watching the children. Tom heard the gate to the pool open, followed by a splash. He knew that Blythe had fallen into the deep end of the pool. Tom panicked, jumping into the pool and swimming back and forth in a frantic effort to find her. Suddenly he stopped thrashing about and put his head underwater and listened. His extraordinary hearing brought him right to his daughter. Tom later wrote "If You Could See What I Hear" to commemorate the event. In addition, his life story was made into a film with that same title.

We stayed in contact for a few years. Then we both got busy, and I haven't heard from Tom for more than 20 years. I have had a lot of "unforgettable" people come into my life. Tom Sullivan is right up there with the best of them.

Tommy Brent: Theater-By-the-Sea

After reopening the Ivoryton Playhouse by producing *Oliver* and *Camelot*, Dick Bruno and I faced a significant problem. Both busy with full-time jobs, we did not have the time or the money to produce three or four shows each summer. While those shows resulted in excellent reviews and sold-out audiences, we lost money on each of them. But, on the other hand, we did not want to see the playhouse go dark again.

When we discussed the problem, Dick came up with what I thought was a brilliant idea. His friend, Tommy Brent, ran the Theatre-by-the Sea in Matunuck, RI. Every summer, Tommy produced four excellent productions before sold-out audiences. Each show played for three weeks, and then the costumes and sets went into storage. "Why not bring those productions to the Ivoryton Playhouse after they finish their run at Theatre-by-the Sea?" Dick suggested.

While I didn't know Tommy personally, I attended many of his productions, starting in the 1960s. I remember seeing *Barefoot in the Park*, *LUV*, and *The Odd Couple*, three shows I had seen on Broadway. The sets and the costumes were not as elaborate as the Broadway productions, but they still represented great summer theatre.

Tommy had an extensive theater background, acting, directing, and performing PR work throughout the straw-hat circuit. Theatre-by-the-Sea had been dark for several years before Tommy showed up in 1967. Almost immediately, he developed a sense of what audiences wanted to see in summer theatre. Season ticket sales soared, and sold-out performances became the rule. Tommy could be the lightning rod the Ivoryton Playhouse needed.

Dick set up a meeting with Tommy at Matunuck. Tommy wasn't particularly enthusiastic when we presented him with the plan. His first question was who he would be dealing with at the Ivroryton Playhouse. Tommy had a completely free hand at Theatre-by-the Sea and controlled everything from play selection, costumes, casting, and directing. However, I sparked his interest when I pointed out the economics of the situation. Bringing in pre-packaged shows would allow us to pay a premium for each production.

We would need the approval of the Ivoryton Board of Directors, of which I was a member. Dick and I assured him we already had board members excited about the possibility of bringing his shows to Ivoryton. We were telling the truth, with one exception. There was a board member, Mrs. D, who took a negative approach to everything. She knew nothing about theater, and the only reason she was on the board was because of her wealthy husband. The large donations we all expected from him never materialized. Meanwhile, we were stuck with a stubborn and ignorant board member who didn't even attend performances at the Ivoryton Playhouse.

I was hoping she would not show up for the meeting we scheduled for Tommy to meet board members at the playhouse. Unfortunately, she was present when Dick and I opened the meeting. I thought we made a good presentation, outlining all of the benefits of the plan. Then we introduced Tommy, who gave a brief history of his theater background and shared his vision of what summer theater was all about.

The first question for Tommy came from our negative board member, Mrs. D. "Mr. Brent, you have failed to inform us where you received your degree in thear-ta," she asked.

Tommy paused for a moment, then lit into her. "My degree in thear-ta began when I ushered at the New Amsterdam Theatre in New York City. Later I did PR work throughout the straw-hat circuit. Finally, I graduated to acting and directing. I do not have the Ivy-league theatre degree that you obviously require. So I respectfully withdraw my unqualified name as a candidate to bring shows to your theatre." With that, he stalked out of the theatre.

The following week, Mrs. D resigned. I like to think it was because of what I said to her after Tommy left. Dick and I made one last attempt with Tommy, but he dismissed us. The following year, Tommy signed a lease with the Garde Theatre in New London, Connecticut, for a fall-winter season. *The Pirates of Penzance* closed after one night in the almost empty 1,500-seat theatre. Yes, Dick and I attended and welcomed our old friend to Connecticut.

Sadly, Tommy left Theatre-by-the-Sea in 1988, after a 21-year run. In 2003, the theatre went dark and remained closed for the next four years. In 2007, plans were made to demolish the theatre and build single-family homes in the nearly six acres the theatre occupied.

Tommy Brent helped broker a deal that led to Bill Haney purchasing the property and reopening the theatre. "Without my dear friend Tommy Brent, I would not have had the opportunity to purchase such a magical place. I will continue his legacy," Hanney said at the time of the purchase.

His first full season in 2008 included *Ain't Misbehaving*, *George M.*, *Evita*, and *The Producers*. *George M* will always have special significance for me, because I attended it with my brother Jack, who died the following year.

Tommy and Bill Haney remained good friends. Tommy was supposed to attend opening night on June 3, 2011, but he was taken ill. He died at home the following day at the age of 88.

Under Haney's direction, the theatre has enjoyed a string of successes. He air-conditioned the theatre without ruining the barn's rustic charm. The gardens have also been restored to their former pristine condition. The theatre closed in the summer of 2020 because of coronavirus but will reopen, offering *Mamma Mia!*, *Funny Girl*, *Footloose the Musical*, and *Kinky Boots*.

Although he never owned the property, people still refer to it as "Tommy Brent's Theatre-by-the-Sea." I think that title has a nice ring to it.

RED AUERBACH, ED SATELL, AND JAMES LEACH

Three of the most impressive men in my life are Red Auerbach, Edward Satell, and James Leach. I met Red Auerbach in September of 1981 when I directed him in a film entitled *Dedication and Desire, The Story of Red Auerbach*. I was warned that he was difficult to deal with, tough, and it was either his way or the highway. When it came to basketball, he lived up to his reputation.

Red taught his players that being a sore loser wasn't such a bad thing. Only losers accepted losing. During his first years as coach of the Boston Celtics, Red did a lot of losing. When he finally got the team he needed, he did a lot of winning. Eleven NBA Championships in a 13-year period is a record that will never be broken. Red left a much more important legacy. In 1950, his first year as head coach of the Boston Celtics, he drafted Chuck Cooper. When his selection was announced, an owner turned to him and snarled, "Don't you know that Mr. Cooper is a Negro?"

'I don't care if he's polka dot," Red replied. "He can play basketball." So Red Auerbach opened the NBA to African American players, much like Branch Rickey did for Jackie Robinson. Red never wanted any credit for what he did. In fact, he made me take it out of a book I wrote about him in 1992: *MBA: Management by Auerbach*.

Red never looked for stars, the guys who led the NBA in scoring. Despite all of their championships, no Celtic has ever led the league in scoring. He preached teamwork, and the result is that he has the highest winning percentage of any NBA coach in history.

There is another aspect of Red that few people know. He ran a basketball camp every year on Cape Cod. The manager at the camp complained that it was always in the red because of all the scholarships that were given out. Red never refused an inner-city kid who wanted to come to his camp. He also set up the Auerbach Foundation, which sets up basketball courts in the most challenging areas of Boston.

In 1998, I met another man who had a lot of the qualities of Red Auerbach, Ed Satell. His game is publishing, not basketball. But his philosophy is similar to Red's. Business is a team game, Ed always preaches. Give customers a quality product, and they will keep coming back. Ed started with a pots and pans business. He got into publishing almost by accident when he backed a publication called *The Selling Advantage*. The publication lost money steadily until a new editor took it over—Ed Satell. It became the flagship publication for Progressive Business Publications. After all these years, Ed still reads every word that goes into The Selling Advantage," one of the most successful publications of all time.

Like Red, Ed is decisive but not dogmatic. Red always listened to his players in the huddle, looking for some piece of information that might give him a competitive advantage. But when the game was on the line in those final seconds, everyone listened as Red dictated the final play.

Ed is a good listener, and he is always ready to accept recommendations to improve the quality and scope of our publications. He can also be decisive, and the company's success is a good reflection of his decision-making capabilities.

It is never a good idea to approach Ed with a plan that hasn't been thoroughly investigated and researched. He's a quick thinker and doesn't suffer fools graciously. I know from personal experience. On the other hand, no one shares success or compliments more than Ed.

Like Red, Ed is a philanthropist. We all know how much Ed contributes to worthy causes every year. In my first year at PBP, I because a mentor for a young man who had a reading handicap. He racked up two outstanding student awards and graduate reading at grade level. I've had a few accomplishments in my lifetime, but none was sweeter than my success with this young man.

Ed is also the founder of The Satell Institute, a nonprofit that creates long-term commitments between businesses and nonprofits. I have had the opportunity of interviewing CEOs of major corporations and the heads of nonprofits being supported. All agreed that the Satell Institute brings a new dimension to creating a better understanding of corporate gift giving.

So thanks for making me part of the team, Ed. Before you get too pensive about turning 85, remember that I am 90. I have no plans to retire. As George Burns said, "I can't go anywhere—I'm booked." Neither can you.

Peter Martin, site director for our proposed movie, *Bellevue Avenue*, introduced me to James Leach in 2013. James owned a Newport estate that would have made a great location for our movie, "Bellevue Avenue." After about a 10-minute conversation, James gave us blanket permission to use his estate in any way we wished. He even waived a fee. Unfortunately, the movie never moved to production status, but I will never forget James' kindness. I later found out that this was standard procedure for a very philanthropic man. He is a former Board Member and Chairman of the Providence City Planning Commission, serving for over 20 years. He is a trustee of the Providence Public Library and the Providence Children's Museum and Chairman of the Rhode Island PBS Foundation.

James Leach is Chairman of National trust, managing the interests of the Leach family, one of Rhode Island's oldest industrial families with investments in industrials, real estate, private equity, and technology. He pioneered the efforts of major retailers in the Northeast, including Wal-Mart, Stop & Shop, Loew's Home Improvement, and the Home Depot. The United States Environmental Protection Agency recognized him for the first-in-the-nation conversion of a superfund site into a major retail shopping center in Stratford. Connecticut.

As I reflect on the lives of Ed Satell, Red Auerbach, and James Leach, I am left with a question. How come three of the most impressive men in this Irishman's life are Jewish?

Still Missing

It was a two-minute conversation between two 15-year-olds. It became memorable only because it may have been the last conversation Frank Hanson ever had with anyone.

About 7 p.m. on Saturday, July 12, 1947, Frank Hanson walked into Henry's, a Cranston version of a 7-Eleven long before that chain was founded. I worked there five nights a week and on one of the weekend days.

I asked Frank how he had done earlier that day in a sailboat race at the Edgewood Yacht Club. Frank crewed for Herb Browne, one of the best sailors at the club. I was not surprised when Frank told me they had won again, because the Browne-Hanson team had the best record on Narragansett Bay.

Frank asked me if I was going to play baseball the next day. I told him I might have to work. He smiled and said, "Maybe I'll see you tomorrow."

Those words and that smile have stayed with me for the past 72 years, because I never heard his voice or saw Frank Hanson again. A little after 9 that night, Frank's father, Frank Hanson Sr., came to the store.

"Did you see Frank today?" he asked. I related my conversation.

He became agitated when I said I had no idea where Frank went after he left the store. "His mother is very upset, Kenny. Tell me where he is."

At this point, Henry Derderian, the store owner, asked what was going on. Mr. Hanson told him that Frank was missing, and I wouldn't say where he was. Henry asked me the same question, and I gave the same answer. Henry turned to Mr. Hanson.

"You know Kenny's a good boy," Henry said, "and if he knew, he would tell you."

Mr. Hanson left the store, still upset.

At about that same time, two Cranston police officers were at the Edgewood Yacht Club questioning Herb Browne. Herb told them Frank had left the club about 5 p.m. Herb had expected Frank to return that night for the awards ceremony and dance.

When I went to work the next day, the same officers were waiting for me. I got the impression they thought Frank's disappearance was temporary, that he was upset about something that happened at home and simply ran away for the night. They asked me about Frank's home life, did he have problems with his parents, and had he ever mentioned the possibility of running away. I said that Frank had always talked about his parents with love and respect. It was a brief conversation, and I don't think the officers felt I added anything of value.

Some of my friends came in Sunday afternoon and told me about searches being conducted by the Cranston police, Rhode Island state troopers, firemen from Warwick and Cranston, and Boy Scouts in the vicinity of Darby's Cove in the Pawtuxet River. Bloodhounds had led police to the abandoned trestle of the Buttonwoods Line, a railroad track that had once run from Providence through Cranston to Warwick. It was thought that Frank may have fallen off the structure, hit his head and drowned in the Pawtuxet River.

I was not surprised that Frank's scent was on the old trestle. He used it frequently as a shortcut to the new home his parents were building. The scent of a lot of Edgewood boys—including mine –was on that trestle.

Firemen dragged the river while police and Boy Scouts searched the shoreline. I asked Henry if I could leave work early, not wanting to miss all the excitement. I got to the site just before darkness set in and the search was ended for the night. It resumed on Monday with no results.

A report surfaced that a woman had seen Frank hitchhiking Saturday night. Mrs. Hanson dismissed it, saying that Frank would never get in a car with a stranger. My mother would have given the same response. The truth was that, too old to ride bicycles and not old enough to drive cars, we made hitchhiking our major means of transportation. Frank, like all of us, used his "thumb" frequently.

The Hansons came to the store and spoke with Henry during the early days of Frank's disappearance. Mrs. Hanson cleared up one puzzle that the press never ended up correcting. The *Providence Journal* and the *Cranston Herald* reported that Frank was missing from 9 a.m. on Saturday, July 12. Mrs. Hanson knew that Frank was racing with Herb Browne that day, and his parents did not become concerned until about 7 p.m. She also answered a question for Herb Browne. He had expected Frank to return for the awards ceremony and dance. Mrs. Hanson had told Frank to come home after the race, something Frank failed to convey to Herb.

On Thursday, July 17, the FBI became involved and the search for Frank went nationwide, with his picture posted throughout the country. I remember how disappointed Herb and I were that the FBI did not consider us important enough to interview. On July 26, 1947, three women reported seeing a body in the Pawtuxet River. Cranston police, divers and firemen resumed their search with powerful searchlights, but no body was found.

That same week, Mrs. Hanson came to the store and asked if I had ever heard Frank talking about stowing away on a tanker that had left Providence the day he disappeared. She asked several of his other friends the same question. We didn't want to dash her hopes, but there was no way the Frank Hanson we knew would have become a stowaway. The Hansons sent a radiogram to the ship, and a search turned up nothing.

Frank's neighbors started a fund offering a reward for any information about his disappearance. We set up a contribution jar at Henry's and had to empty it several times a day. I worked at Henry's for another two years and saw the Hansons and their daughter, Helen, frequently. It was during that time that I learned there are some not very nice people in this world. The Hansons began to receive letters from around the country. Some were supportive, but many were like the one they received from someone in Kansas City: "I think I saw your son last week. Send me $50 and I'll go back to search."

I never saw the Hansons again after I left Rhode Island in 1949.

Herb Browne, Gill Thorpe, Jack Swan and I talked about Frank's disappearance frequently over the next 50 years. Gill and Jack sailed in that same race on the day that Frank went missing. They were Frank's closest friends and used almost the same words in describing him: "Good student, very organized, always did his homework, friendly and dependable."

We asked the same questions over and over.

— Where did Frank go after he left Henry's about 7:15 that night?

- Why would he walk to the trestle shortly before nightfall?
- Could he have been hitchhiking to the Edgewood Yacht Club for the dance and awards ceremony and gotten in the wrong car?

We never came up with any answers, but we all agreed that Frank did not voluntarily disappear into the night. The Frank Hanson we knew would never have done that to his family.

There were other tragedies involving young men from Edgewood.

Bob Thorpe, Gill's brother, was reported missing in action in June 1944. When the war-crime trials started at Yokohama in 1948, we learned what had really happened. His P-47 fighter had been hit by ground fire during a mission against a Japanese naval base in New Guinea. He was captured by the Japanese, tortured, and beheaded.

Eddie Ballard died in a YMCA pool at age 16, and George Horn sparked a parish revolt when he committed suicide at 15. Monsignor Cannon, pastor of St. Paul's, had ruled that George could not receive a Christian burial because he took his own life. The bishop listened, and George received a Catholic burial from St. Paul's. Ed McGinnis and Don White were both killed in the early days of Korea. My close friend and neighbor, John Dinneen, graduated number two from Georgetown Law School and died of leukemia a few years later. His brother David died of cancer the following year.

As sad as all of these losses were, there was closure to each of them. There will never be closure to the disappearance of Frank Hanson. Files of the Cranston Police Department, Rhode Island State Police and FBI have been closed for years. There is no DNA, no "interested person" to interview. The name "Frank Hanson" is not even listed in a database of missing persons.

The questions that were asked in 1947 remain unanswered today.

Sadly, his parents died without learning the fate of their son and brother. Most of Frank's close friends, including Jack Swan and Gill Thorpe, are also gone, though his older sister, Helen, still lives in Warwick at age 93.

It is ironic that the two people who may have had final conversations with Frank are still here: Herb Browne and me. Both 90, we still talk about Frank and his mysterious disappearance. Herb is still racing on Narragansett Bay, but he traded his 12-foot Beetle for a 35-foot Hinckley.

People have suggested from time to time that Frank just ran away from home, like many troubled teenagers do, joining a legion of runaway boys roaming America's cities, not wanting to be found. So what—another runaway kid! We knew Frank well enough to know he would never do that. Whatever happened to him that night, Herb and I are convinced that it wasn't due to anything he did deliberately. He was not unhappy at home. He loved his parents and his sister, and he knew they loved him. He was comfortable with his school and his many friends.

Some 72 years after his disappearance, we must face the fact that we will never really know what happened to him. It's possible that he came to harm while hitchhiking that night—predators have been known to roam the roads looking for young boys.

Thoughts about what may have happened to him have haunted Herb and me since the night he disappeared. And we were only his friends. We did not give birth to him, raise him and watch him grow up to become a fine young man, the pride of his family. We cannot imagine what his parents and his sister went through all those years.

I reflect on a conversation I had with Herb, Jack, and Gill about 30 years ago. They all had sailed with Frank that day in what turned out to be his last race. "Frank spent the day with his best friend, Herb Browne, doing what he loved best—sailing," Jack said. "How many of us will ever be able to make that same claim in our final hours?"

THE SILENT GENERATION

I'm sometimes bewildered when members of the present generation talk about the quieter, gentler times of the 1930s, often referring to us as the "Silent Generation." Indeed, we did not have TV, cell phones, Internet, ATMs, credit cards, HBO, or Netflix. But we grew up in the most significant recession this country has ever known. We came out of it because of a war that killed more than 73,000,000 people, including 6,000,000 Jewish men, women, and children. After WWII ended, we lived under the threat of a nuclear exchange with the Soviet Union. Then, in 1950, we became involved in a "police action" in Korea. More than 50,000 young Americans died before a cease-fire in 1953. Tell my friends, Ed McGinnis and Donald White, both killed in action in Korea, or Bobby Vickers, who returned with a 100% disability because of a Chinese shell, that this was a "Silent Generation."

I agree with Tom Brokaw, who came up with "The Greatest Generation" to refer to those born in the 1920s. Many of them fought in WWII or worked in industries that contributed to winning the war. "The Lost Generation" was named by writer Gertrude Stein, and it refers to the post-World War I generation. "Lost" is supposed to refer to the disoriented, directionless spirit of many of the war's survivors in the early postwar period. It applies more to the generation of writers, artists, musicians, and intellectuals than the general public. Ernest Hemingway made it famous in his novel *The Sun Also Rises.*

Our "Silent Generation" was followed by the "Baby Boomers," the people born from 1945 to 1964. This generation witnessed the civil rights movement, women's empowerment, and the moon landing. I have no idea whether the other generations were named aptly—Generation X, Millennial, and Generation Z. I am impressed that Generation Z has never known a world without the Internet. They are expected to become the most educated generation in the world with the highest student debt.

As a father and a grandfather, I am firmly behind this generation's "Me Too" movement. For too many years, male predators demanded sexual favors in return for job security or advancement. I rejoice with every lost job or prison sentence. I had friendships with African Americans such as Earl Lloyd, the first African American to play in the National Basketball Association, KC and Sam Jones, and Bill Russell, three members of the National Basketball Hall of Fame. I did not need the Black Lives Matter Movement to alert me to the terrible sufferings African Americans have received in this country. I also understand why taking down statues or renaming schools of known racists is a step in the right direction.

Tom Yawkey was the owner of the Boston Red Sox for many years. He was a philanthropist and helped establish the Jimmy Fund, an organization battling childhood cancer. "Yawkey Way," a street named in his honor, was recently renamed because of Yawkey's racist past. The Red Sox were the last team to integrate, and Jackie Robinson was denied a contract after a workout. Yes, Yawkey did a lot of good things, but nothing could make up for his racism.

I cannot entirely agree with all of these renaming efforts. George Washington is a perfect example. There is no question that he was a slave owner. Does that mean we should take down the Washington Monument or change the name of our capital? Washington should be judged by the contributions he made during his lifetime, not only for his slaveholding. He was the only substantial slaveholder among the Founders to free his slaves voluntarily. We cannot allow our history to be destroyed by applying modern standards to people who lived hundreds of years ago.

PRIVACY RIGHTS

When I was born on October 22, 1931, there were 48 states, the population in the United States was approximately123 000,000, life expectancy for males was 63 years, Mercurochrome was the miracle drug, and Penicillin was about eight years away. In the 1930s, measles killed or impaired thousands of children. Most of my family and friends contracted measles before reaching 15 years of age. About 400 to 500 deaths were reported each year nationally, and thousands more suffered from encephalitis, a swelling of the brain caused by the virus. I can still remember "quarantine" notices placed on the front doors of families suffering from measles.

In 1963, an effective vaccine was developed for measles. In 2,000, the CDC declared measles as eliminated in the United States. But in 2019, almost 1,300 cases of measles were confirmed in 31 states. All of the cases came from people who did not receive the measles vaccine.

Whooping cough was another severe disease of my childhood. It would begin as a regular cold then develop into a severe and life-threatening illness, especially for babies. An effective vaccine is available to prevent the disease, but new cases are reported every year for the same reason—failure to vaccinate.

I remember how infantile paralysis (polio) struck every summer of my youth. The disease crippled more than it killed. Newsreels showed children in huge metal cylinders called iron lungs. No one knew how the virus passed from victim to victim. When Franklin Roosevelt started a foundation to fight polio, Comedian Eddie Cantor came up with the "March of Dimes," asking people to mail a dime to the White House. Between double features at the Park Theater in Cranston, lights would come on as ushers walked up and down the aisle collecting money for "The March of Dimes," the nonprofit established to fight polio.

The Salk vaccine did not become available until 1955. Dr. Jonas Salk decided not to patent his vaccine so it would be affordable for millions of people. That decision cost him an estimated 7 billion dollars. I still remember going to a fire station in Warwick with my five brothers to receive the vaccine. The mood of the crowd was jovial, and no protestors carried "privacy" signs.

Now we have COVID-19, the worst pandemic this country has ever faced. At least three effective vaccines have been developed to wipe it out. Yet, we fail to gain critical herd immunity because many refuse to roll up their sleeves to get the vaccine. Some states now offer lotteries rewarding people for showing up to possibly save their own lives. Governors in Florida and Texas threaten schools boards that mandate masks for students. Parents are attacking teachers for enforcing masking rules. Flight attendants are being abused for the same reason. I am appalled that some Rhode Island healthcare professionals protest the governor's mandate requiring them to be vaccinated before returning to work.

"Freedom of speech does not give one the right to stand in a crowded theater and scream 'Fire,'" U.S. Supreme Court Justice Wendell Holmes ruled. Privacy issues do not give anyone the right to spread a plague that can be resolved with simple vaccinations. For those who object to the vaccine on religious grounds, I am reminded of a verse from a WWII song: "Praise the Lord and pass the ammunition." Objectors who use the "My body, my choice" defense ignore a simple truth: Their right to privacy ends where their neighbors' right-to-life begins.

RICK PITINO AND THE BOSTON CELTICS

I had lunch with Red Auerbach at the China Doll restaurant shortly after Rick Pitino took over the Boston Celtics in 1997. I never met Pitino, but I was close to many people who worked with him briefly. I say briefly because Pitino fired most of the key people on the Celtics, including Jan Volk, General Manager.

Volk was the General Manager when the Celtics made probably the greatest trade in NBA history—Bob McAdoo for Kevin McHale and Robert Parish. He was there for the championship teams with Larry Bird, McHale, Parish, and Bill Walton. He also helped the Celtics recover when Len Bias was lost to a drug overdose in 1986, and Reggie Lewis died of a heart attack in 1993.

Celtics fans know the value that Larry Bird brought to the team. Few of them know that Volk uncovered a loophole that allowed the team to draft Bird while he was still a junior at Indiana State. Bird had already announced that he was going to play his senior year before entering the draft.

"We can't do that," Auerbach said when Volk told him about the possibility of drafting Bird early. Red finally agreed to reach out to David Stern, who was the league's general counsel at the time, for a ruling. Stern said that Volk's interpretation of the rule was correct, and the Celtics drafted Bird on June 9, 1978. The other owners grumbled and passed a rule prohibiting early drafting—but not before the Celtics had one of the greatest players of all time.

I was upset when Red confirmed that Pitino had taken his title as President of the Celtics. When I voiced my displeasure, Red would have none of it. Always the loyalist, he said that Pitino should be given a chance to turn the Celtics around. "If he needs the title of president, he should take it," Red said. End of conversation.

Red and Volk were not the only casualties of the Pitino regime. He took complete control of every facet of the team, even to the extent of reportedly ordering the toilet paper. I know for a fact that Red reached out to him early and offered help. He was ignored.

Red recommended two Celtics players to build the team around, David Wesley and Rick Fox. Pitino cut them both. Wesley signed with the Carolina Hornets and had an excellent career. Rick Fox joined the Los Angeles Lakers and played on championship teams. When he was finally removed, Pitino admitted that he had made a mistake with those two players. He whined that he didn't have anyone on the "inside" who could give him any advice, not mentioning that he had ignored Auerbach, considered by many as the greatest evaluator of talent in NBA history.

Although he was not officially named as General Manager until 1997, Pitino was in charge of the 1996 NBA Draft. He selected Chauncey Billups with the third pick. Midway through the season, Pitino grew frustrated with the rookie's development and traded him to Detroit. Billups eventually made five all-star-teams, won the 2004 NBA Finals MVP, and developed a reputation as one of the NBA's most challenging leaders.

Pitino tried to bring the same style of basketball to the NBA that made him so successful in college basketball—full-court presses and mass substitutions. "I saw Pitino adhere stubbornly to his system, shuffling guys like chess pieces, micromanaging every second of every game, sticking with presses the team couldn't possibly sustain over a full season—in short, slowly sucking the life from his players." Bill Simmons wrote these words in *ESPN The Magazine* in 2003.

Pitino went just 102–146 in three-and-one-half seasons as the Celtics Head coach, General Manager, and President. He made a statement to Boston fans to explain the failure of the team: "Larry Bird isn't coming through that door. Kevin McHale isn't coming through that door. Robert Parish isn't coming through that door." He should have added Red Auerbach and Jan Volk to the list. In 2001, he left the Celtics and returned to college basketball as coach of the University of Louisville.

One of my fondest sports memories occurred when Jan Volk, John Havlicek, Tommy Heinsohn, Bob Cousy, and Jeff Twiss, director of Public Relations for the Celtics, attended my play, *The Auerbach Dynasty,* at the Mosesian Theater in Watertown, MA. Red had been dead for four years, so I no longer had to worry about betraying any of his confidences. Johnny Most, the legendary Celtics broadcaster, was there in spirit as we ran his voice and dramatic incidents such as "Heinsohn stole the ball." I did nail Pitino in the play, describing his action in destroying a storied franchise.

I was pleased with the reaction of Havlicek, Heinsohn, Cousy, Twiss, and Volk, who told me that I had captured the story and personality of Red Auerbach. The common denominator in this group was the word character, best illustrated by Bob Cousy when I invited him to the play. "My wife, Missy, has Alzheimer's, Ken," he said to me. "I don't go anywhere without her." She came, along with their daughter, and sat quietly throughout the performance, still a beautiful woman dealing with that awful disease. She could not have had a better support system than her husband and daughter.

I was particularly pleased with the reaction of Jan Volk, who gave me a big hug after the play. Although he didn't mention it specially, I think he appreciated my treatment of Rick Pitino.

After leaving the Celtics, Pitino took over as head coach at the University of Louisville. In the 2005 season, Pitino led Louisville to its first Final Four in 19 years and became the first men's coach in NCAA history to lead three different schools to the Final Four—Providence, Kentucky, and Louisville. He guided Louisville to appearances in the Final Four in 2005 and 2012, and the school won a record 35 games in 2012–2013. There is no question that Pitino is a college coaching genius. His off-the-court antics included:

- The first and only vacated men's basketball national championship when Louisville was stripped of the title in 2017. An assistant coach, Andre McGee, was found to have paid escorts and strippers to entertain Louisville players and recruits in the basketball dorm on the campus.
- A five-game personal suspension from Atlantic Coach Conferences games in the 2017 season. Pitino never served the suspension because Louisville fired him before the season started.
- An FBI probe implicated Louisville in an Adidas scheme that would pay $100,000 to the family of recruit Brian Bowen for him to attend Louisville. Pitino was not personally tied to the strippers or the pay-for-play schemes.
- Pitino brings to mind a conversation I had with Red Auerbach when we were writing *Management by Auerbach*. We were discussing trades and free-agent signings. Red always believed that the best trades were the ones he never made. Sometimes

> he would reach out to players other teams had cut—Willie Naulls, Don Nelson, and Dennis Johnson—even as he passed over available superstars. Nelson became a great sixth-man for the Celtics, and Naulls and Johnson made significant contributions to championship teams., Red believed a player's character was more important than his skill set.

Red also objected to college coaches breaking their contracts to leave for better positions and not receiving any discipline from the NCAA. "If a player accepts a scholarship and then transfers to another school, he loses some of his eligibility. Coaches should be treated the same way when they break contracts," Red said.

Hindsight is always 20/20. Rick Pitino made the following statement recently about his time with the Celtics. "If I could have just stuck to coaching and not paid attention to anything else, it would have worked out." Red Auerbach, Jan Volk, and thousands of Celtics fans would agree.

WITH FRIENDS LIKE THESE

"One does not make friends. One recognizes them." Those words by Garth Henicek described my more than 80-year friendship with Bob Venditto. I don't think either one of us could come up with a date or even an anecdote on how we met. It seems like Bob was always part of the Dooley family. We all danced at his wedding when he married Sheila Lynch, the love of his life, and they were blessed with five children. They are still together after more than 60 years.

Bob is a tremendous artist, the former president of the Providence Art Club. He is also a terrific illustrator who did a lot of work for me when I was managing editor for a division of Prentice-Hall Publishing in Waterford, CT. I don't see him as much as I used to, but it always seems like I was with him yesterday when we do meet. We were always there for each other when Bob lost his two brothers and six members of the Dooley family passed away.

In between, there were many joyous celebrations when the Vendittos and the Dooleys meshed. One of my Bob's famous stories involved the tennis great, Andre Agassi. Bob's daughter Stephanie was an actress and a good one. She had several recurring roles in TV series and appeared in films made in Manhattan and Los Angeles. She was a close friend of Brooke Shields and a member of the wedding party when the actress married Andre Agassi, the great tennis player, in 1997. About a year later, Agassi's plane made a stop at the Warwick Airport in Rhode Island, only minutes away from the Venditto house. Brooke persuaded Andre to make a quick trip to visit the parents of her close friend, Stephanie. They asked a postman for the final directions, and he led them directly to the Venditto house. Bob said his mail delivery approved considerably, because the postman was a tennis player.

One of my fondest memories was a celebration of their 60th wedding anniversary at the Providence Art Club. The room was crowded with family and friends when Bob got up to speak. I was sitting at a table with my brother Bob and some of Sheila's relatives I met for the first time.

Bob was quite emotional when he got up to speak. He described Sheila as the love of his life, and then went on to his wonderful family.

His voice suddenly broke and tears streamed down his face as he fought to regain control. More than one lady in the audience had tears in her eyes as Bob recounted stories about Sheila, the love of his life, his friends and family. It was a wonderful, moving tribute to a great family. The sweetness of it made me uneasy, a problem I faced all of my life.

After the applause died down, I turned to one of the lady's and asked, "Did Bob's remarks sound genuine to you?" She was offended, as were several others at the tale. "Of course, they did," she answered. "Why wouldn't they?"

"I am relieved to hear you say that," I responded. "I was a little nervous because of something that happened earlier in the day. I had gone to the men's room and heard someone sobbing behind one of the doors. I knocked and Bob opened the door. "What's wrong Bob?" I asked.

"Oh nothing Ken," he said. "I'm just rehearsing"

What I thought was a funny story didn't impress my table group. Only my brother Bob, well aware of some of my antics, remained quiet. His facial expression told me he was not happy with my remark. Sheila's relatives sat in silence, first disbelief, then anger on their faces. Finally one of the ladies got up and made a beeline to Sheila. I couldn't hear what was said, but Sheila had a serious expression on her face when she turned to Bob. and whispered in his ear. Bob turned to me and suddenly burst into laughter. It had no impact on my table where members sat quietly wondering why this insensitive person was even invited to the celebration.

The reason for their happy marriage was obvious. Sheila thought that Bob was America's greatest artist while Bob thought that Sheila was the country's greatest woman.

I have been blessed with the many friends I have made over the years. Most of them are gone now, but their memories remain. I tell their stories in other sections of this book. Herb Browne, my friend of almost 80 years is alive and well. One of my favorite stories about friendship took place on the day that Herb got married. Chris Gorsinski, the bride, was beautiful and intelligent and Herb could not have made a better choice. She was also a Polish Catholic, while Herb was a strong Protestant, particularly proud of his Scottish heritage.

They had a whirlwind courtship, engaged only months after meeting at the University of Rhode Island. Tall, good looking and extremely personable, Herb had many ladies in his life before meeting Chris. His closest friends, Wes Forcier, Tom Breslin, Bill Considine, and I all worried about the short duration of the courtship before Herb proposed. We were not the only people concerned. I met Chris's parents, Stephanie and John Gorsinski, shortly before the wedding. John went out of his way to talk to Wes, Tom and myself at the bachelor party. We all remarked on his friendliness and the interest he seemed to be taking in the lives of Herb's friends. I didn't really understand his intent until the day of the wedding.

After a lovely reception, a small group returned to the Gorsinski home with the bride and groom. I was talking with Wes Forcier and Tom Breslin when John Gorsinski joined us. "We were worried when my daughter told us that she was going to marry Herb after such a short courtship. The day after the bachelor party, I told Stephanie not to worry. If Herb could attract friends like these, he is right for our daughter." It is one of the nicest compliments I have ever received.

A few years ago, I attended their 60th wedding anniversary. I shared a story with their children and grandchildren that day. Just before they left for the Honeymoon, Herb took me aside at the Gorkinski home and asked a question. "Tomorrow is Sunday, he said. "Do you think Chris will get out of bed to go to Mass?" I didn't have an answer then, and I don't have one now. What I do know is the Browne-Gorskiski marriage is one of the happiest unions ever.

I was six years older than most of my classmates when I returned to Providence College after serving in the military during Korea. So I did not establish many close friendships by the time I graduated in 1959. The once exception was Paul Dunphy. He and his wife Marilyn have been friends for more than 60 years.

I met Stu Hobron in 1959 when I went to work for Federal Products in Providence, RI. Stu was my boss and a great guy, but I knew that writing about precision measuring instruments was not going to work for me. About a year later, I went to work for Prentice-Hall Publishing in New London, CT. Stu went to work for me, and we remained close friends until he died in 1978. I had a similar experience with Bill Dowling. A Ph.D. from Harvard, Bill was my first boss at

Prentice-Hall. Three years later, I was appointed Editorial Director, with Bill reporting to me. We remained close friends until he died prematurely at age 55.

I hired Wayne Muller in 1963, and he replaced me as Editorial Director when I left the company in 1977. We have been close friends for more than 60 years. The best advice I ever received from anyone came from Wayne. He told me I was making a mistake when I became engaged to Rosemary. I ignored him. Five years later, I gave him the same warning, which he disregarded. The fact that he is still married is more of a testament to his ability to absorb punishment than his choice as a marriage partner.

Bill Quirk was a vice president with the American Management Association when we met in 1975. He and his wife, Anne, became good friends. I met Rick Wolff in 1984 when he was the editorial director for Alexander Hamilton Institute in Manhattan. I had been hired by the president, Jim Jenks. Rick was a Harvard graduate and a terrific athlete. If not for a serious knee injury, he had a great chance of playing major league baseball. We have been good friends for almost 40 years. After Rick left, I worked for Brian Zevnik and Schuler Jenks, Jim's son. Brian and Schuler did their best, but Alexander Hamilton went the way of many small publishers when it eventually folded.

When my wife was operated on for breast cancer in 1981. Dave Preston came to the hospital and sat with me. Dave and Barbara remain my good friends after more than fifty years. I was on his Board of Directors when Dave took over a struggling box manufacturer, Scott & Daniels, and turned it into a major company. I was delighted, but not surprised, when they showed up for my induction into the Rhode Island Heritage Hall of Fame.

When I moved to Pennsylvania in 1998, I rented an apartment from a young man by the name of Avery Manco. I was adopted by his whole family, which included Dr. Michael Manco, his wife Stephanie, sister Melanie, and her husband, Joe. About 10 years later, I served as Avery's best man when he got married.

Some of the nicest people I ever met are working at Progressive Business Publications. Jen Erb, the Art Director has been a great friend for 23 years. I still work with Colin Drummond, Michelle McGovern, Rich Henson, Scott Ball, Jenny Weiss, Fred Hosier, Jennifer Azara, Renee Cocchi, Emma Chou, Tom D'Agostino, Sharon McHugh, Lori Kappel, and the editorial director, Curt Brown. Curt's father, Jim Brown, a senior vice president at Progressive and his wife, Mary, remain close friends. Regina Black Lennox, Ed Satell's right hand, and her husband, Bill, are two of the nicest people I have ever met. They threw a surprise 80th birthday party for me that I will never forget.

I am the only editor who writes directly for Ed Satell, the founder of Progressive Business Publications. Lori Kappel, Ed's secretary, makes it all work. I met friends like Kerry Isberg, Phil Ahr, Tom Schubert, Steve Meyer, Brian McCallum, John Hiatt, Ron McCrea, Patti and Amy Jacoby, Ed and Nicole Riegel, and Dave Dombrosk at Progressive. Pieter Van Bennekom, Editorial Director when I joined the company, remains one of my closest friends.

I love the idea that people might judge me by my friends—they always made me look better than I am.

Abe Saperstein and the NBA Basketball Hall of Fame

In April 2018, John Henry, owner of the Boston Red Sox, filed a petition with Boston's Public Improvement Commission requesting that "Yawkey Way" be renamed its original "Jersey Street." Henry told the Commission he was haunted by the team's racist past when Tom Yawkey was the Red Sox owner. The Red Sox were the last team to hire an African American player and even refused to sign Jackie Robinson after a tryout. The Commission voted unanimously in favor of the name change. While Yawkey did many good things for the City of Boston, there is no question he was a racist.

Meanwhile, a member of the National Basketball Hall of Fame personally kept African Americans out of professional basketball for years. There is strong evidence that Abe Saperstein mistreated, lied to, and cheated African American players when he was the owner of the Harlem Globetrotters.

In 1948, the Globetrotters defeated the Minneapolis Lakers, known as the best basketball team in the world at that time. Many of the white teams refused even to schedule the Globetrotters. At this point, Saperstein came up with a plan that led to the Globetrotters becoming the most entertaining basketball team ever and helped the all-white National Basketball League survive.

Saperstein noticed how the crowd laughed when Marques Haynes went into his dribbling routine, or Goose Tatum went into his antics under the basket. The crowd laughed and forgot that the Globetrotters were embarrassing their home team.

The new team was wildly successful, and fans lined up at the arenas of the new National Basketball Association (NBA) teams. The Globetrotters always played the second game, and the crowd usually didn't filter in until the first game was almost over. No one was more appreciative of the Globetrotters than Maurice Podoloff, NBA Commissioner. He was more than receptive to Saperstein's demand that no NBA team draft an African American player. Saperstein made it clear that the Globetrotters would boycott any team that broke his "no-draft" rule.

His rule was tested by Red Auerbach, Celtics coach, and Walter Brown, Celtics owner, in 1950, when the team drafted Chuck Cooper, an African American, in the second round. Before Saperstein could ban the Celtics, Walter Brown announced that the Globetrotters were no longer welcome in Boston. Saperstein went directly to Podoloff when Auerbach signed Sweetwater Clifton to a contract. Podoloff voided the contract, allowing Saperstein to sell Clifton's contract to the New York Knicks for $25,000. Saperstein, who had agreed to split the contract sale with Clifton, said the deal was for $5,000, cheating the player out of $7,500. It was not the first time that Saperstein lied to his players or paid them meager salaries while he reaped millions. Ironically, when Clifton retired years later, Red Auerbach and Walter Brown bought him a taxi, which he drove around Chicago until he died in 1990. Clifton had never played one day for the Celtics.

The mission of the Basketball Hall of Fame is to honor players who have shown exceptional skill at basketball as well as great coaches, owners, referees, and other significant contributors. While writing a screenplay with Sam Jones and Bill Russell about African American players coming into the NBA, I learned why Bill Russell refused entry into the NBA Hall of Fame for years. He did not want to be in the same organization as racist owners and people like Abe Saperstein, who mistreated African American players.

Eddie Gottlieb, owner of the Philadelphia Warriors, who came up with a quota system for African American players in 1950, is also a member of the Hall of Fame. So is Maurice Podoloff, NBA Commissioner from 1949–1967, who supported Saperstein's efforts to keep African Americans out of the NBA.

The question remains: Is Abe Saperstein, a person who made a travesty out of James Naismith's original game of basketball, mistreated and lied to Globetrotter players, and kept African American players out of the NBA for years worthy of induction into the NBA Basketball Hall of Fame?

THREE MEMBERS OF THE NATIONAL BASKETBALL HALL OF FAME AND A 5′7″ WHO COULDN'T MAKE HIS HIGH SCHOOL TEAM

Bill Russell was recently acknowledged as the greatest athlete in the history of Boston sports. Sam Jones has 10 NBA Championship rings, second only to Russell's 11. I was cut in the second practice of my high school team. I made it that far because the head coach was sick and missed the first practice. Yet the three of us combined to write the screenplay "From White to Black: the Painful journey of African American Players into the NBA."

It was a journey that began a few years earlier when I met K.C. Jones through my nephew, Jeff Dooley, who was the voice of the University of Hartford Basketball team while K.C. was his color analyst. KC came to my play, "The Auerbach Dynasty," and we began to talk about collaborating on a book. Later that year, I met with K.C. and Sam Jones in St. Augustine, FL, to discuss a book and possible screenplay. Unfortunately, K.C. became ill with Alzheimer's and had to withdraw from the project.

I had never had much luck connecting with Bill Russell. I was given his personal number when I co-wrote a book with Red Auerbach, but no calls were returned. Sam Jones, probably Bill's best friend, unlocked the door. I was soon talking with Bill and his wife Jeannine, a former professional golfer, and the screenplay became a reality.

I was fortunate enough to be around during those years when the Boston Celtics dominated the NBA. I even attended Celtics games at the Rhode Island Auditorium, a building owned by Lou Pieri who was instrumental in bringing Red Auerbach to Boston as coach. Walter Brown, Celtics' owner, needed $50,000 to keep the team going. Pieri agreed to provide the money if Brown hired Auerbach as coach.

Bill Russell arrived in the NBA as an All-American, key to the University of San Francisco winning 55 straight games and the NCAA college championship two years in a row. Red Auerbach had to make a series of trades to draft Russell with the second pick in the draft. Russell became an immediate starter for the Boston Celtics.

Sam Jones played at North Carolina College in Durham in the segregated South, and no one knew who he was when the Celtics drafted him in 1958. Red Auerbach learned about Sam from one of his former players, Bones McKinney, who described Sam as the best basketball player in the State of North Carolina. Sam sat on the bench for much of his first two years, behind people like Bob Cousy and Bill Sharman.

Cousy, Hall of Fame guard for the Celtics, called the drafting of Jones one of the best moves that Red Auerbach ever made. "He was a steal, better than anyone could have dreamed he could be. He was six feet four, big for a guard in those days, and lanky and athletic, too. He was a great shooter, often using the backboard in ways no one had ever done before,"

Russell came into the NBA with a reputation for being outspoken, complicated, opinionated, and profound. He embraced his African roots and challenged the nonviolent tenets of the civil rights movement. Sam Jones grew up in Laurenberg, NC, a city that reflected the South at that time, with segregated schools and facilities. He was quiet and respectful, especially during his early years with the Boston Celtics.

When Bill Russell joined the Celtics in Dec. of 1956, there were only 15 blacks in the league. It had been six years since Red Auerbach, coach of the Boston Celtics, drafted Chuck Cooper, a black player from Duquesne. The NBA remained lily-white, probably the result of a warning from Eddie Gottlieb, owner of the Philadelphia Warriors of the NBA.

Immediately after Cooper and Earl Lloyd, another black player, joined the league in 1950, NBA owners held an emergency meeting in which Gottlieb said the teams should set up a quota system or the league would be 75% black in five years.

"The majority of our fans are white. How long do you think they'll pay good money to watch colored players take over our game?" Gottlieb asked. When Gottlieb stressed that each team be limited to two black players, Auerbach and Walter Brown, walked out.

"What we're talking about goes beyond the number of coloreds on the roster," Gottlieb said. "We have to be careful how we use them. We don't want a colored player guarding one of our white stars. Try to have coloreds guard each other. It will keep our white fans from getting upset." Gottlieb added.

Before joining the Boston Celtics, Russell led the University of San

Francisco on a 55-game winning streak and two NCCA championships. When Russell played his first game for the Boston Celtics on December 22, 1956, radio announcer Johnny Most said, "I think we just witnessed the birth of a star and the start of a bright new era in Celtics basketball."

Most had a reputation for being a "homer." The Celtics never committed a foul while opposing players manhandled them. But his comments about Russell were right on the money. Though not the first Black player, Bill Russell was the first Black superstar. He became to basketball what Jackie Robinson was to baseball. When Russell joined the Celtics, Boston was a two-sport city—baseball in the summer, hockey in the winter. The Boston Patriots (later the New England Patriots) were not founded until 1959.

The Celtics, like the rest of the league, struggled financially, playing to half-empty arenas. Sell-outs occurred only when the Harlem Globetrotters came to town and played an exhibition after an NBA game. Abe Saperstein, president of the Globetrotters, warned NBA owners he would boycott their arenas if they drafted a black player. He kept Blacks out of the NBA for years until Red Auerbach and Walter Brown stood up to him. Russell initially refused entry into the NBA Hall of Fame because it had inducted people like Saperstein.

Not everyone shared Red Auerbach's opinion of Russell's basketball skills. Some Boston writers said he was too skinny, couldn't shoot, and didn't have the size or stamina to exist in the rough and tumble NBA. Red Auerbach addressed the issue at their first meeting.

"Have you been reading these stories about your inability to score?" Auerbach asked.

"It's been on my mind," Russell replied.

"I have no control over these reporters. But I can make you a promise now. When we talk contract, I will never bring up statistics." And he never did.

Russell's arrival instantly made the Celtics into a great team. No one had ever seen a player with his athleticism, rebounding, and defensive intimidation. He brought shot-blocking to a new level. Instead of swatting the ball out of bounds, he would tip it to another Celtic, and a fast-break basket would usually result.

In Russell's first year, the Celtics eliminated the Syracuse Nationals in three straight games to get to the finals. Syracuse had defeated the Celtics for three consecutive years before Russell. The final match of the championship series against St. Louis has been called one of the greatest. Boston won in double overtime 125–123, and the Celtics had their first championship. In 1958 the Celtics faced the St. Louis Hawks again but had to play the final three games without Bill Russell. He severely injured his left ankle while blocking a shot. The Celtics lost the series in six games. Over the next 11 years, the Boston Celtics compiled a record that will probably never be broken in professional sports. In 13 years, they won 11 championships, two while Bill Russell was player-coach. In 1980, sportswriters named Bill Russell, the best player in the history of the NBA.

Bill was raised in the segregated South and saw firsthand the harsh treatment of Blacks at the hands of the white establishment. Two events occurred in 1955 that made a life-long impression on him. Emmett Till, a 12-year-old boy, visiting his grandmother in Money, Mississippi, was murdered by two white men for a supposed affront to a white woman. They beat him severely, gouging out an eye before shooting him in the head and dumping his body into a nearby river.

His mother insisted that his casket be open at the funeral, so the whole world could see what had been done to her son. It may have impressed the people of Chicago, but it had no impact in Mississippi, where the two men went on trial. They were acquitted by an all-white jury, even though they had confessed to the murder.

That same year, Rosa Parks, a Black seamstress, was arrested for refusing to give up her seat to a white rider on a public bus in Montgomery, Alabama. A young minister from Atlanta, Martin Luther King Jr., led a boycott of the Montgomery bus system. For nearly a year, Blacks stayed off the buses until a 1956 U.S. Supreme Court decision outlawed segregation on the buses. Over the next few years, sit-ins ended segregation in restaurants, and Blacks who had been denied the right to vote were registered for the first time.

Prejudice against Blacks was not restricted to the South. Boston was undergoing a racial transformation when Russell arrived in 1957, primarily because of a large influx of Blacks from the South. The Black community suffered from inferior schools, overcrowded homes, and limited economic opportunities. In addition, the Boston

School Committee had deliberately segregated the city's schools, creating one system for Blacks and another for whites, separate, unequal, and unconstitutional. To achieve racial balance, some 18,000 black and white students were ordered to take buses to schools outside of their neighborhoods.

On the first day of school, hundreds of white demonstrators pelted a caravan of 20 school buses carrying students from nearly all-Black Roxbury to all-white South Boston. Police wore riot gear, and several of them were injured by bricks and debris thrown at the buses. The following day, a group of Black students and their parents gathered in the basement of a Catholic Church to listen to Bill Russell.

"We were going to meet in a high school auditorium, but the school board turned us down," Russell said. "An atmosphere of hate, distrust, and ignorance has infected our city. I lament every dilapidated, antiquated, rat-infested firetrap of a school in Roxbury. There's a fire here in Roxbury, and nobody is listening, and the fire that consumes Roxbury will consume Boston. Here's a quote from the Boston school board. 'There is no inferior education in our schools. Unfortunately, we have been getting an inferior type of student.' "We know better. Wear your color as a badge," Russell urged the students. Some of those students were lucky enough to ride to school with a 6'9" basketball player, Bill Russell, in the driver's seat.

Shortly before he was shot in the driveway of his home in Jackson, Mississippi, on June 12, 1963, Medgar Evers said: "The Negro has been here in America since 1619, a total of 344 years. He is not going anywhere else; this country is his home. He wants to do his part to help make his city, state, and nation a better place for everyone, regardless of color and race."

Despite knowing that his civil rights work could get him killed, Medgar Evers dared to keep fighting so that others might live in freedom. His words and actions had a profound impact on Russell's thinking. He challenged white bias and Black political orthodoxy and identified with Black Nationalism, racial pride, self-defense, economic autonomy, political unity, and Black unity. He teamed with Jim Brown to support Muhammad Ali and his decision not to participate in the Vietnam War. When Russell was asked if he had any objections to what John Carlos and Tommie Smith did when they raised their fists in protest at the 1968 Olympics, he said, "Just one. I didn't think of it first."

Before the famous March on Washington, Russell met with the Rev. Martin Luther King Jr. in Atlanta. Dr. King asked him to sit on stage at a pre-march rally. Russell declined, feeling he would be a distraction. Instead, he sat in the second row as Dr. King delivered his famous "I Have a Dream" speech.

Russell once described Boston as the most racist city in America. He had good reason. Shortly after the Celtics won the third title, a man walked up to him while he was sitting in a new Lincoln at a traffic light. "Hey Nigger, how many crap games did it take you to win that car?" the man shouted. Many of the same people who cheered him at Boston Garden reacted in horror when he tried to purchase a home in an all-white suburb of Reading. His wife Rose came home in tears as she watched residents sign a petition against the sale.

"We'd better forget that house," Rose said. "They don't want us there."

"I bought that house, and I'm the one making the mortgage payments. So I don't care what anyone else thinks." Russell said.

"What about our children? Who will they play with? What will our white neighbors say to them?" Rose said.

"I'm thinking about our kids," Russell replied. "I couldn't look them in the face if I put up with this kind of behavior. I won't let anyone tell me where I'm going to live."

Returning from a vacation, the Russells found their home trashed. "Nigga" was painted on the walls with excrement, and the pool table had been ripped up and covered with beer. The local police were unable to come up with any suspects. Some argue that Russell's arrogant attitude may have contributed to the home invasion.

Russell refused to pander to fans who expected athletes to be role models. "I don't think it's incumbent on me to set a good example to anybody's kids but my own. I never deviated from my principle of not playing basketball where I couldn't stay or eat. When Sam Jones and Satch Sanders were denied entry to a hotel restaurant in Lexington, Kentucky, we refused to play and flew back to Boston."

Before an exhibition game in Marion, Indiana, the mayor presented the team with keys to the city. After the game, all the Black players were denied service at a restaurant. Russell got in a cab with K.C., Sam Jones, Satch Sanders, and Tom Heinsohn and went to the mayor's home. When the startled man opened the door, Sam Jones said, "You gave us the keys to the city, but they don't open anything." All of them threw the keys into the hallway.

Nothing made a greater impression on Bill Russell than an incident involving his grandfather Jake, a sharecropper in Louisiana. After a harvest, Jake told his landlord that he would not farm the area again. "Nigger, don't tell me what you ain't gonna do," the farmer warned. After a scuffle, the white man left, threatening to be back with the Ku Klux Klan.

Jake took his family, including Russell's father, Charlie, to a neighbor, then returned and sat on his front porch with a shotgun. Several cars pulled up that night and began to empty just before Jake fired his shotgun into the darkness. The men piled into their cars and drove away. Jake never heard from the white farmer again.

One of Russell's most prized possessions as a teenager in Oakland, California, was his library card. He went there every day. One day he was reading a chapter in a book about the American Revolution. A sentence jumped out at him. "Despite the hardships they suffered, most slaves enjoyed a higher standard of living and a better life in America than they had in their primitive African homeland." He was repulsed by the idea that life could be better without freedom. It was during that time that Russell began to develop his own ideas about race. "My father, Charlie, and my grandfather, Jacob, helped shape my early views. They both preached nonviolence—until the first punch is thrown. Later I was influenced by people like Martin Luther King and Malcolm X. They had the most passion among Black national leaders, and I was drawn to both of them. I understood Dr. King's nonviolent approach but refused to reject Malcolm X's more militant view. Instead, I took ideas from both men, then mixed it with my own philosophy: "A man without integrity, belief, or self-respect is not a man. And a man who won't express his convictions has no convictions," Russell said.

"During my 13-year NBA career, I walked with Dr. King and developed friendships with people like Medgar and Charlie Evers, Roy Abernathy, Stokely Carmichael, Jim Brown, and Muhammad Ali. I made lifelong friendships with Red Auerbach, KC and Sam Jones, Satch Sanders, Tom Heinsohn, Bob Cousy, and John Havlicek. I had worthy opponents like Wilt Chamberlain, Oscar Robertson, Walter Dukes, Maurice Stokes, Earl Lloyd, Elgin Baylor, Al Attles, Bob Pettit, Rick Barry, Cliff Hagan, Ed Macauley, Billy Cunningham, and Jerry West. I have been insulted by strangers and turned down invitations from presidents."

Like no other athlete before him, Russell challenged white bias and black political orthodoxy. Instead, he identified with elements of Black nationalism, racial pride, self-defense, economic autonomy, political and Black unity.

A Family of Philanthropists

When I moved to Bristol, RI, in March 1992, my friend Ted Barrows invited me to play tennis with a local group. It was a community tennis court, but the upkeep was paid for by Alan Hassenfeld, President of Hasbro, one of the largest toy companies in the world. I played there frequently but never with or against Alan. I was aware of the Hasbro Children's Hospital in Providence, but I did not know a great deal about the family's history. Finally, Pat Conley, Historian Laureate of Rhode Island and president of the Rhode Island Heritage Hall of Fame, filled me in on the extraordinary philanthropy of the Hassenfeld family. Three family members—Merrill, Sylvia, and Alan—are members of the Rhode Island Heritage Hall of Fame.

The philanthropic saga of the Hassenfeld family is inseparable from the story of their company, Hasbro Corporation. Begun in 1923 as a cotton waste material recycling operation in Central Falls, RI, it has grown into both a massive presence and a moral and ethical beacon in the global toy industry. The Hasbro mission statement reads in part:

"We believe that all children are born with the sparkle of hope in their eyes, and sometimes, because of life's challenges, that hope has been diminished. Our mission is to assist these children in triumphing over their critical life obstacles and to bring the joy of play into their lives. Through our philanthropic programs, we work to bring 'the sparkle of Hope, the joy of Play and the power of Service' into the lives of the children who need us most."

Hasbro follows a multi-pronged approach to carry out this mission. The Hasbro Children's Foundation supports the development of direct service programs that improve the quality of life for children from birth to age 12, their families, and communities. Hasbro Children's Hospital in Providence is a leading center for the treatment of childhood diseases. The Hasbro Charitable Trust provides gifts of holiday toys to hundreds of hospitals and shelters annually. Sylvia Hassenfeld was the driving force behind developing a dedicated children's hospital at NYU Langone Medical Center, the Hassenfeld Children's Hospital that opened in 2017.

On December 7, 1988, a magnitude 8.2 earthquake devastated a large swath of northwestern Armenia, taking more than 25,000 lives. Among the survivors were many who had lost arms and legs. Some of these victims were soon on a flight to Israel, where, after decades of conflict, some of the world's most advanced prosthetic surgery and limb replacement methods have been developed.

That flight was chartered and accompanied by Sylvia Hassenfeld, working in her capacity as chairwoman of the American Jewish Joint Distribution Committee (JDC). Her mission to Armenia typified the philanthropies of the Hassenfeld family–going far beyond writing checks, important as those checks may be, into immersing themselves in the often-gruesome sights and nauseating odors of humanity devastated by disasters, both natural and manufactured.

Sylvia Hassenfeld was described as one of the most significant leaders in the American Jewish community of the 20th century. While raising her children and serving on the Hasbro Board of Directors, she became increasingly active in the Providence Jewish Federation, eventually becoming president. Her involvement with the Providence Jewish Federation led to her roles in the Council of Jewish Federations and Welfare Funds and other national and international Jewish organizations.

All of this led up to her dedication to non-sectarian humanitarian work with the Joint Distribution Committee, so vividly demonstrated by her mission to earthquake-ravaged Armenia. She oversaw social service, health, religious, and educational programs in the Czech Republic, Armenia, Hungary, Russia, Austria, Romania, Poland, and Bulgaria, among other nations.

She also represented the Joint Distribution Committee in African and Middle Eastern countries with Jewish populations when thousands of Ethiopian Jews were airlifted to Israel. In 1994 the American Jewish Historical Society awarded her its Emma Lazarus Statue of Liberty Award. In addition, she served on many Boards of Trustees, including the NYU Medical Center, Brandeis University, and the Hasbro Children's Foundation.

Sylvia's son Alan, who served as Hasbro CEO from 1989 to 2008, following his father Merrill and his brother Stephen, continues the family's calling. Any given day may find Alan pursuing his idealistic goals in eminently practical ways, anywhere in the world. As United

States Chairman of the Jerusalem Foundation, he is committed to creating a pluralistic Jerusalem, one where "East and West, old and new, everything would come together, and people would live in harmony."

Alan became acting chairman of the Foundation in 2001, believing "very idealistically" to be part of the peace process. That, he admits, was naïve. But there have been successes. The Foundation has built community centers, homes for seniors, and parks and sponsored many cultural events. His favorite Foundation project is the Hand-in-Hand School, where all classes are half Jewish and half Arab. Each class has a Jewish and an Arab teacher, and each day they teach half in Hebrew and half in Arabic. There are two principals, one Jewish and one Arab. The parent-teacher council is half and half.

"I have great hope," he says. "If you can bring people together, they can learn together, work together and create together. It is a model for peace. But if you can't get people to sit at the table because they are always fighting, taking land, or firing missiles, it won't work. You don't make change happen by knocking down walls. Change must come from within. You can't force it on people. We are desperate to keep the young people in Jerusalem, not just the religious but the very bright young people who might be going to great universities. Like many cities, the biggest problem is affordable housing for young people. You can have job opportunities and great culture, but if they can't afford housing, they are going to go elsewhere."

A University of Pennsylvania graduate, Alan has been honored for his multi-faceted efforts by universities, charitable organizations, political and religious communities, and corporate institutes. Like his mother, he has used his position on the Hasbro Board of directors to expand and intensify his philanthropic work.

Alan's lengthy visits in Israel are apt to be followed by trips to China where, as co-chairman of the International Council of Toy Industries (ICTI), he is working to improve working conditions for employees in the toy manufacturing sector. Eighty percent of global toy production comes from factories in China, and most toy buyers require that Chinese factories adhere to ICTI standards on ethical manufacturing in the form of fair labor treatment and employee health and safety. Factories are audited for compliance, but there is corruption and bribery, Alan admits.

"We've done a good job of raising the bar," he says, "but you cannot control everything. Sometimes the factories will bribe the auditor, and sometimes the auditors will solicit bribes." Back in Providence, he has been working for years with the Right Now Coalition to clean up political mismanagement issues facing Rhode Island, something in which his Hasbro affiliation is especially helpful. "Because we're not aligned with either major political party, we're able to try and make a difference in helping this community grow again," he says.

The Hassenfeld family believes that with business success comes the responsibility to give back, to make the world a better place.

The Floorwalker

My former wife, Rosemary, and I had very little in common. As I once explained to her, we did not even hate the same people. Nowhere was the gulf greater than in our respective feelings about shopping. There were few things I hated more than tramping through stores for clothes or furniture. On the other hand, there were few things that Rosemary enjoyed more.

My feelings were exacerbated by the fact that I was frequently mistaken for a floorwalker. Perhaps it was because I always wore a suit and tie and had the same bored expression as the average floorwalker. Except for the absence of a flower in my lapel, I was a perfect model for floorwalkers everywhere. It did not matter whether I was in the local W.T. Grant or a high-end store like Bergdorf & Company. Customers would approach me for directions or to complain.

In the beginning, I would answer with an abrupt "I don't work here." Later I realized that a little pretense would break up the monotony. I gave directions, heard complaints, made recommendations, and even provided interesting tidbits to inquiring customers. If they were polite and respectful, I replied in kind. Rude transgressors were sent off to departments that didn't exist or searched for products the store did not carry.

One episode stands out in my mind. Rosemary and I were shopping at Best & Company in Manhattan, a very upscale department store. We were in the children's department, shopping for clothes for our new daughter, Alicia. After looking at 20 Florence Eisman dresses that cost more than my Brooks Brothers suits, I had enough. My attention was drawn to a pram sitting on a platform in the middle of the children's department. I had never seen anything like it. The covering was made of Italian leather, and the wheels could have graced a Mercedes-Benz. The metal frame was painted gold. Curious, I looked at the price tag and was startled to learn it cost $2,700. I moved a few feet away as a young lady approached the carriage. She looked at the price tag and turned to me. "Is that price correct?" she asked, obviously mistaking me for an employee. "I can't believe it is so expensive."

"You must consider the value," I replied. "The Italian leather. The heavy-duty springs will allow your baby to sleep undisturbed in the roughest possible terrain. The value-added benefits of this pram far exceed its price."

"I can appreciate that," she said. "But it is still a lot of money."

"Granted, " I replied. "But we don't expect payment upfront. Much like a car loan, we have terms that can fit any budget. We also offer additional features, such as air conditioning and a revolutionary braking system to ensure maximum safety. Including these features brings the total cost to $3,900. But, again, we offer extended terms."

I think I had the pram sold. But Rosemary walked up at this point with a few dresses and asked my opinion. Puzzled, my prospect asked, "Doesn't he work here?" "No, he's my husband," Rosemary said. My prospect gave me a bewildered look and then faded away into the crowd.

Eventually, Rosemary and I worked out a compromise about shopping. I would hang out in a local bookstore while she attacked the department stores. It worked out well until one occasion when we were shopping at Filene's in Boston. There was no bookstore available, it was near Thanksgiving, and my feet were killing me. I spotted some empty chairs and sat down. A young lady approached and told me the chairs were reserved for job applicants for the Christmas season.

"That's exactly why I'm here," I replied.

I was 36 years old at the time, with a balding head and wearing an expensive suit. She explained that these were minimum wage jobs usually reserved for younger people. I had edited a book earlier that year on the Age Discrimination Act of 1967. I asked her if she understood the provisions the Act extended to older job applicants. She disappeared and returned a few minutes later with the head of her department. I was ushered into a private office where I completed my application.

The personnel manager looked at it and asked, "I see you are from Old Lyme, Connecticut. The jobs we are offering are here in Boston. How would you meet this requirement?"

I explained that I could take a daily train from Old Saybrook, CT, directly to Boston. The Act called for "reasonable accommodation," I said, which might require an adjustment in my schedule.

Instead of answering, she said, "You're an attorney with the Department of Labor. I can assure you we are in full compliance with the Age Discriminating Act."

There was a commotion outside the office door. It finally opened, and Rosemary stood in the doorway. "What are you doing," she screamed. "I've been looking for you for half an hour."

We exited the store quickly, and I never learned if I would be offered the job. One thing I am sure of—older applicants received special consideration when applying for jobs at Filene's that year.

THE CAVICKES

Sometimes I attend a memorial service and wonder if I'm in the right place when I hear many of the beautiful tributes given in honor of our departed friend. It isn't that my friends are not worthy of many of the wonderful things we say about them as we bid goodbye. But some of the accolades seem to go over the top. Perhaps some of us are trying to build a little credibility for our own departure.

In the case of Teddi and David Cavicke, there is no such thing as exaggeration or overstatement. Regardless of how many superlatives are used, none will truly capture the essence of this remarkable couple. David was quiet and reserved, a prominent neurosurgeon and chief of neurosurgery at Lawrence and Memorial Hospital for many years. He was also president of the hospital's medical staff and assistant clinical professor at Yale Medical School. Teddi was outgoing and always ready with a warm smile and a quick wit. She was also the kindest person I have ever known. Those of us who had the privilege of calling Teddi "friend" always knew that she would be there for us, even if the rest of the world walked out.

Dave came to life during any discussion about automobile racing. When he wasn't performing brain or spine surgery, Dave was under the hood of one of his racing cars, getting ready to compete at Lyme Rock in Lakeville, CT. As much as he loved racing cars, Teddi hated it. Her interest in auto racing took a positive turn when she learned that Paul Newman, the film actor, also raced at Lyme Park. But Teddi never got over her fear that Dave would be injured in a race. She also confided in me that she thought auto racing was loud and smelly.

So the Cavickes developed a quid pro quo. Dave continued to race at Lyme Rock, and Teddi bought a castle in France. Really! I can still remember my amazement when she returned from a European trip and told me that she and Dave had purchased a castle in Paris. She was a little concerned about the reaction from a few French historians. They objected to the fact that an American had bought a historic Paris landmark. When I asked her about the previous owner, she said, "A man by the name of Talleyrand."

Remembering my European history, I explained that Talleyrand was a priest and a leading diplomat. He worked for Napoleon during the years when French military victories brought one European state after another under French hegemony. Teddi's pleasure in finding out that the former owner of her castle was a priest diminished when I told her he fathered a child. She did understand that the French resistance to an American buying Talleyrand's former castle was similar to what many Americans felt when the Japanese bought sections of Rockefeller Center. Although I had an open invitation to visit the castle, I never did make it.

Everything changed abruptly when Dave died suddenly on May 28, 1992, at the age of 65. I will always consider it a miscarriage of justice that David was taken away far too early. Teddi continued to lead a happy life, always believing that kind words and kind deeds do not cost much. She gave smiles and favors big and small—readily. A gift sent, a meal prepared, a loaf of homemade bread, a visit made, a letter written, and transportation provided were all part of her daily routine. But she was never completely the same after she lost the love of her life.

She devoted her life to her three sons, David, Dana, and Matthew. It worked. David is a lawyer, and Dana is a doctor. Matthew never did fulfill her dream of having an opera star in the family. But he graduated from Stanford and is a very nice young man. Things came to an abrupt halt when Teddi developed Parkinson's disease. It drained her both emotionally and physically. It took away her ability to move, to talk, and it ultimately took her life.

Even now, as the reality of her death saddens me, I have a hard time keeping a smile off my face as I recall some of the wonderful stories involving Teddi. Many of them include David, the other half of a remarkable team. Dave was quiet and reserved, while Teddi was outgoing and always ready with a warm smile and a quick wit. David and Teddi Cavicke had one of the great marriages of all time.

God bless you, Teddi. And thank you for your many kindnesses to my family and me. We will never forget you.

MARY K. TALBOT | SPECIAL TO *THE PROVIDENCE JOURNAL*

Ken Dooley's articles have frequently graced the pages of *The Providence Journal* over the years. He is a brilliant storyteller and has led a fascinating life. He has written books and screenplays, run the documentary film division of a large company and traveled around the world—experiences that have introduced him to many important people and places.

Yet, when he reached out recently to talk about his wartime experiences, he didn't want to talk about any of the places he's lived or the notable figures he's interviewed. Instead, he wanted to talk about two little girls that he met once and only briefly.

Dooley, 89, was raised in Edgewood, attended La Salle Academy and headed to Providence College. He entered college as an English major and finished his freshman year before leaving to attend Air Force pilot training. He had signed up after being told that candidates needed only one year of college but "we got a surprise after we joined." Once he arrived at basic training, he found out that the rules had been changed and now the Air Force was requiring two years of college. "So, I figured, well, if they changed the contract then we could get out," he recalls with a chuckle. "But I found out very quickly that you couldn't resign from the Air Force."

"I wasn't much of a war hero," recalls Dooley. For the first three years of his service, Dooley put his writing skills to work penning articles for the Air Force Times and a newspaper in Europe and Africa where he was stationed. "My mother had six sons and five of them in harm's way," recalls Dooley. The Dooley boys served in WWII, Korea and Vietnam. One even received a Purple Heart. "She never had to worry about me. My weapon was a typewriter."

"It wasn't until the last year of my Air Force career that I did anything I considered useful," writes Dooley in a soon-to-be published book, *Dooley Noted*. "In March of 1954, I gave up my typewriter and after a short course at Kelly Air Force Base, became a 'loadmaster.' This was the person who calculated the weight and balance of an aircraft to make sure it was safe for takeoff," he explains.

It was on one of his missions with the 1700th Air Traffic Squadron that he met those two little girls. He had left Kelly AFB on a

C-54 piston-powered, four-engine aircraft. "We used to fly what they call S.A.C. or Strategic Air Command...we would transport key personnel, weapons or weapons systems." Dooley's plane landed in the Azores at Lajes Field to refuel while en route to Upper Heyford, a SAC base in England on Aug. 8, 1954.

It was late afternoon, and the flying conditions were "perfect," according to Dooley. "The Azores are very pretty, especially from the air," he remembers. It wasn't a favorite stop, however, because crew members weren't allowed to leave the base. They couldn't explore the mountains, the lush forests, or the long beaches. "We were restricted, and we couldn't even go into town so it was really boring if you got stuck there," he remembers. Fortunately, this would be an overnight stay.

Dooley and his friend, John Demetri, got off their airplane and proceeded to walk together toward the control tower where they would catch a bus to their barracks. It was late in the afternoon and Dooley remembers looking up and seeing a well-dressed woman heading towards a passenger plane with two little girls and luggage in tow. The young loadmaster and flight engineer weren't in any hurry to get to the barracks, so Dooley remembers telling his friend, "C'mon. let's help that lady" as they saw her try to navigate the "long, long steep stairway system" with kids and luggage in tow.

Although language was a barrier, the two men were able to make their intentions clear when they approached the mother and her children trying to board the plane. "She smiled at us, and I picked up one of the little girls and John [picked up] the other and we grabbed a bag too." Times and security protocols were different then so the two airmen were allowed to carry the children up the stairs and right onto the aircraft. "We put them in the seat belts and put their luggage in the overhead bins, and the little girls were all excited," remembers Dooley. "They were talking to us in Portuguese—well, of course, John and I didn't know what they were saying—but the stewardess told us that the plane was going to Brazil." The children were planning a rendezvous to see someone special. "They were telling us that they were going to see their Papa."

After the children were settled, the children's mother and the stewardess expressed their thanks to the men. Dooley and Demetri waved goodbye, left the airplane and continued to walk to the control tower. Their bus was delayed so they had to stand and wait. About 10 minutes had elapsed when "all of a sudden we heard this God-awful sound. It was terrible. We looked up and the whole mountain was on fire.

"We knew right away that nobody survived that crash."

To this day, Dooley can't understand what happened to that passenger plane with those sweet little girls. Landing at Lajes Field wasn't a particularly complicated maneuver. "When you land, the mountain was to the right and it was clear to the left. And it was the same taking off. The mountain was to the left and you just bank to the right. This guy flew the plane right into the mountain." Thinking back, Dooley now wonders if the crash was deliberate and mourns the senseless loss of life.

"I can still remember taking off the next day and flying over the wreckage. It was still smoldering." Dooley later married and had two daughters of his own but he never forgot those two little girls and their mother who lost their lives that day in 1954. He also reflects on the father they left behind. "I have often thought of that poor guy, standing at the airport, waiting, and then being told his whole family was gone."

Many jobs, marriages, births, moves, deaths and even a divorce have happened since that day when the two men witnessed the tragedy. Dooley remained close with Demetri throughout their lives. But they never spoke about the crash until about 10 years ago. Dooley remembers taking a trip to visit with his friend and his wife. As the evening wore on, Demetri's wife grew tired and excused herself and proceeded to bed. The two men were alone for just a minute or two when "all of a sudden he looked at me and said, 'Do you ever think back on what happened and those two little girls?'" No context was needed. Almost 60 years had elapsed, but Dooley knew exactly what his friend was thinking. Nothing more needed to be said. "Both of us ended up crying," Dooley shared. "That image has stayed with me all of my life," he said to his friend. Demetri responded, "Me too."

Meeting Sam Katz

In 1960, I was hired as an editor for Prentice-Hall, a publishing giant based in Englewood Cliffs, NJ. I met Seymour Katz, another editor, for the first time. I have no idea why a Jewish kid from New London and an Irishman from Rhode Island bonded quickly, but we immediately became good friends.

It didn't take me long to realize that Sam Katz was one of the great comic writers of all time. He could take an ordinary picture from any newspaper and write a new caption that would have the entire office laughing. Pope John XXIII came out with an encyclical stating that the Jews were not responsible for the death of Christ. When I arrived at my office the following day, there was a huge sign over my typewriter: "I want you to know I did it," it read. Sam Katz signed it.

I will always regret that Sam did not have an opportunity to write for comedy. Like many creative writers, he had to make a living to support himself, his wife, Eleanor, and three sons, Andrew, Matthew, and James. I became close to the entire Katz family, often babysitting when Eleanor and Sam would go out for an evening.

Sam attended the Art Students League of New York before enlisting in the U.S. Marines during World War II, where he served in China. He was called back to military service in 1950 to serve in the Korean War in the 2nd Marine Division Headquarters. After being honorably discharged, he graduated from the Boston University School of Journalism. Before joining Prentice-Hall, he was a reporter for the *New London Day*, *Norwich Bulletin*, and the *Hartford Courant.*

I took Sam and his three sons to Fenway Park for a Red Sox baseball game. We were going to eat at the famous Durkin Park before the game. Sam warned the boys that they could not have the strawberry shortcake the restaurant was famous for unless they finished their dinners. On the trip, Andrew, the oldest, began to discuss the novel, Catch 22, which he was reading. Jim, the youngest, asked what Catch-22 meant. Sam explained, but I could tell from his expression that Jim still did not understand the meaning.

Andrew and Matthew had no trouble getting through their dinners and were ready to move on to strawberry shortcake. Jim began to struggle and finally put down his fork.

"Remember, Jim," Sam said. "Unless you finish dinner, no dessert."

"But Dad," Jim replied. "If I finish dinner, I won't be able to eat the strawberry shortcake."

"Jim," Sam said—"that's Catch-22."

When I got married in 1963, Sam was one of the ushers, joining my brothers and two other friends. Sam told the priest at the rehearsal that he was Jewish. The priest told him to follow the other ushers.

I was on the altar as Sam following the other ushers up to the communion rail and knelt to receive the host. He did exactly what the priest told him to do. About two weeks after the ceremony, Sam received a greeting card congratulating him for receiving his first Holy Communion. Of course, I sent it. Sam's mother was Orthodox, and I always threatened to tell her about the wedding if Sam crossed me.

Sam left Prentice-Hall for a job with Xerox Education Publications in Middletown, CT. We always stayed in close contact. I was not surprised when Sam told me that he and Eleanor were getting divorced. Sam was an intellectual who loved classical music, especially Mozart. Eleanor had simpler tastes and always regretted publicly that she had not married a doctor, lawyer, or successful businessman.

About a year later, I met Marian, a lovely woman who became Sam's second wife. I liked her immediately, and the two of them had a wonderful life together. She was bright, intellectual, and everything that Sam ever wanted. In 2004, Sam founded the Tsorus Chorus, an organization dedicated to singing Jewish Christmas Carols. He wrote the first Jewish Carols that included The First Moyel (The First Noel); So Don't Be a Stranger (Away in a Manger); Irving, the Jewish Reindeer) (Rudolph the Red-Nosed Reindeer); The Rabbi's Lament ((O Come All Ye Faithful); Hock! The Jewish Mothers Cook (Hark, the Herald Angels Sing)

Here are three of Sam's original carols:

The First Moyel (The First Noel)

The First Moyel
He was Izzy Levine,
And he used a pair of scissors
That weren't too clean,
Moy-el, Moy-el, Moy-el, Moy-el,

A Jewish tradition that
came straight From Hell.
He snips off a piece,
That we men hate to lose,
No wonder the Baptists
Don't wanna be Jews,
Moy-el, Moy-el, Moy-el, Moy-el,
A Jewish tradition that came straight from Hell.
Won't you send us please God
Another way to atone,
We will pledge a donation
Just leave us alone,
Moy-el, Moy-el, Moy-el, Moy-el
A Jewish tradition that came straight from Hell.

Irving, the Jewish reindeer (Rudolph)
You've heard of Morris and Herman,
And Sheldon and Sherman,
But do you recall,
The most Jewish reindeer of all?
Irving the Jewish Reindeer,
He was Santa's C.P.A.
He tried to help poor Santa
Make his business pay.
Santa said, "Irving help me,
I am such a worried pup,
Unless I turn a profit,
The North Pole's going belly-up."
"Don't you worry," Irving said.
"I won't let you fail,
I called up my supplier friends,
From now on you can buy wholesale."
Oh, how the money rolled in,
And Irving made such a fuss,
The Santa made him a pottneh,
Now they're known as toys R Us.
Then one frosty Shabbos eve,

Irving gave a shout,
"Santa we will soon be rich,
Wal-Mart wants to buy us out."
Oh, how the reindeer loved him,
Each one wagged his little tail,
But Irving said, "Screw the North Pole."
And he moved to Lauderdale.

The Rabbi's Lament (O! Come All Ye Faithful)
O! Come to the Temple,
Not just on Yom Kippur,
But Shabos and holidays
The whole year long.
Come join the minyan,
That's a nice beginnyan,
O! Come on Simchas Torah,
O! Come on Lag b'Omer,
O! Come on Tu B'shevat
And Ti-isha Bav.
O! Come to the Temple
Not just Rosh Hashana,
Remember you're Jew-wish,
The whole year long...
Come ye on Sukkos,
Don't forget Shavu-u-os,
Please join our congregation,
There is no obligation,
Perhaps a small donation
See you in shul.

Sam described the chorus as a group of highly-trained vocalists, none of whom can actually sing on key. The chorus has performed in such internationally renowned venues as the Black Hole of Calcutta, Abu Graib Prison, and the Paris Sewers. Here's how Sam described "The Singers":

- Allen Silberstein announced he will discontinue the practice of proctology. "That's for assholes: he sneered. Allen says he will now specialize in testicular ailments. "It's the nuts," he said.
- Marian Katz was arrested for burglary, car theft, spousal abuse, purse snatching and blasphemy. Marian says she committed the crimes in order to run for mayor in her hometown of Waterbury. Marian says that after the election she plans to become a serial killer and run for governor.
- Richard Wrubel recently returned from a trip to Africa. He was pleased when he was greeted at the airport by natives singing "Zip-a-dee-doo-dah." Only later did he discover that "Zip-a-dee-doo-dah" in Swahili means, "Go home, Yankee bastard!"
- Marcia Wrubel said she plans to divorce Richard. She learned that when he says, "I have to go see my condos, he's really talking about a 19-year-old tenant named LaToya "Big Gazongas" Condos.

In 2009, I was invited to join the chorus with this message in the program.

"Ken Dooley is now out of prison and joins the Tsorus Chorus as a guest singer. Two elements prohibit him from becoming a permanent member: a terrible voice and his Irish Catholic heritage. On the plus side, he was elected "Goy of the Year" in New London in the years 1960 to 1965. Please don't step on his ankle bracelet as he is still on probation."

I did not see Sam and Marian as often as I wished in later years. We did get together for what turned out to be a final lunch in Mystic, Connecticut, in the summer of 2010. As usual, we spent more time laughing than we did eating or talking. Sam had lost a few steps to a worsening heart problem, and Marian was doing the driving. I walked the two of them to their car and then began to walk to mine. For some reason, I turned as I reached my car and saw that Sam was still standing staring after me. Our eyes locked, then we smiled for what was to be a final goodbye. Sam died a few months later, and Marian asked me to deliver his eulogy. San always loved to leave people laughing. He did not disappoint as I told the story of this remarkable man who played such an important role in my life for more than fifty years. Rest in peace, Sam. Every time I hear Christmas carols being sung, I think of the Tsorus Chorus.

The Pacific War

Combat in the Pacific theater in World War II is usually associated with such epic and ferocious battles as Guadalcanal and Iwo Jima. But separating these tiny points of land was an endless expanse of water and impenetrable jungle in the Western Pacific and the South China Sea, where, day after day for four years, battles were waged in the skies by skilled, dedicated and astonishingly courageous pilots, many of them too young to be served in a U.S bar.

Wars, of course, have always been cruelly reliable destroyers of young men. As the sharp tip of the American spear, these pilots of the American Fifth Air Force, charged with stopping the Japanese juggernaut advancing relentlessly down the island chains toward their goal of taking Australia out of the war, expected to be decimated, and they were. Many died in dogfights, especially in the first year of the war when the planes they flew were inferior to the vaunted Japanese Zero. But throughout the war, many more were to die in accidents and miscalculations that punctuated daily operations of all air forces at the time. Overloaded with fuel, bombs and ammunition, they flipped, crashed and exploded, attempting takeoffs on jungle runways. Operating at the extreme range of their fuel capacity with primitive navigational aids, they were often lost without a trace. Attacking at low altitudes, even marginally effective Japanese antiaircraft fire brought them down. And, if shot down and captured, they were tortured and murdered by their captors.

On May 1, 1942, a powerful Japanese fleet was steaming toward Port Moresby on the south coast of New Guinea. Capture of this critical allied base would solidify the defensive perimeter of the enormous empire Japan had conquered since bombing Pearl Harbor less than five months before and would put its air force within bombing range of northern Australia. The U.S. Navy was aware of the Japanese plan, mainly because of the same success in breaking the Japanese naval code that was to result in its great victory over the Japanese a month later at Midway. But U.S. Naval forces were believed to be too far away to stop the Port Moresby attack.

That evening at a U.S. airfield in Townsville, Australia, pilots of a squadron of P-39s were being briefed on their mission the next morning. They were to attack the Japanese invasion fleet by skipping bombs along the surface at the ships. Calculating the distance to the target, one pilot pointed out that they would not have enough fuel to get back. "Who said anything about getting back?" the general who was giving the briefing replied grimly.

In the event, the mission was unnecessary. The U.S. fleet arrived in time to inflict severe damage on the invasion fleet in what was to become known as the Battle of the Coral Sea, the first sea battle in which no surface ships exchanged fire or even came within sight of each other and all damage was the result of carrier aircraft. The Japanese gave up their invasion plans for the moment, but the incident reveals the harrowing state of allied defenses in those early days of the war. These American pilots would have been sacrificed, much as the Japanese Kamikaze pilots would be, three years later off Okinawa.

By the time Bob Thorpe and his fellow rookie pilots arrived just after Christmas in 1944, the situation in Australia had improved considerably. Threats of a Japanese invasion, a source of great anxiety but never a serious possibility because of the limits of Japanese army resources, had receded entirely. There had been damaging air raids on Darwin and other northern Australian cities, and Sydney Harbor had sustained some light damage in one largely abortive attack by submarines. And these submarines had roamed along the Australian coast, much as German U-boats had along the U.S. Atlantic coast, inflicting heavy damage on merchant shipping.

If fear of invasion had largely receded, however, a deeper dread had set in. This was due in part to deep-seated racism, evident since Australia's founding in the 18th Century as a British penal colony by a genocidal attitude to the aboriginal population. But hatred and fear of the Japanese took racism a significant step further. Since 1940, Australian troops had been sent off to fight German and Italian forces in the Middle East and Mediterranean campaigns. Battles had been won and lost. Prisoners taken by both sides were treated as humanely as conditions permitted. Of the 8,000 Australians taken prisoner, 265–less than 3 percent--died in captivity.

Those captured fighting the Japanese conquest fared far worse. This did not come as any great surprise considering the ghastly atrocities committed against civilian populations of China and Manchuria since the mid-1930s. With the onslaught across the South China Sea came reports of the brutal treatment of POWs in Singapore and Bataan. Of the estimated 22,000 Australians who would become POWs, nearly 9,000 died. And an unknown number who died without being allowed to surrender no doubt brought his total considerably higher.

Japanese brutality in the treatment of POWs came dramatically to light with the Battle of Milne Bay in August and September of 1942. During the Australian counterattack, the bodies of 36 Australian soldiers who had been tortured and executed–some of them disemboweled with bayonets–were discovered. The advancing troops also found the bodies of 59 murdered civilians, including a number of women who were sexually assaulted before being killed. The war crimes committed at Milne Bay hardened Australian soldiers' attitudes towards Japanese troops for the remainder of the war. Historian Mark Johnston has written that "the Australians' relentless killing of Japanese then and after that owed much to a determination both to retaliate in kind and to take revenge for Japanese atrocities and rumored maltreatment of POWs."

So, in the terrible complexities of human brutality, civilized standards gave way to impulsive savagery, and allied troops murdered helpless Japanese prisoners as well. An official wartime publication described how, at Wau, 50 Japanese were "hunted down and exterminated." The concepts of "hunting" and "exterminating" capture the mood of the time, which was not one of trying to bring an essentially like-minded foe to accept defeat by the rules of war, but one of seeking to annihilate an alien enemy. The killing of unarmed, sleeping, sick or wounded Japanese was common. Official pressure was put on troops to take prisoners, but Australian front-line soldiers had little desire to do so. Australian General Thomas Blamey tried to stir up hatred of the Japanese by emphasizing that the Australians were fighting to prevent both the deaths of their families and the end of civilization. The Japanese forces, which advanced along the Kokoda Trail toward Port Moresby, were described by another officer as "cocksure hordes" seeking "to glut their lust and savagery in the blood of a conquered white nation."

The Coral Sea was the 300-mile-wide moat separating the Australian population from this terrifying enemy, and the most effective force guarding this moat was the American 5th Air Force, which was established in Australia on September 3, 1942. The 5th was led by Major General George B. Kenney, who had arrived in Brisbane in late July and revealed his leadership style after a lighting tour of bases in northern Queensland. He fired the entire air command staff, getting rid of "deadwood" with the enthusiastic approval of General Douglas MacArthur,

The 5th consisted of eight bomber groups and three fighter groups at the time Kenney took command. Bob Thorpe was assigned to the 39th Fighter Squadron of the 35th Fighter Group. By late 1944 when he arrived, the 39th was already a storied unit, as tended to happen to outfits under General Kenney's command. The 52-year-old Kenney was an aggressive leader. A fighter pilot himself in World War I, with two "kills" to his credit, he had been sent to France in early 1940 as Assistant Military Attaché for Air. His mission was to observe Allied air operations during the early stages of World War II. As a result of his observations, he recommended many essential changes to Air Corps equipment and tactics, including upgrading armament from .30 caliber to .50 caliber machine guns and installing leak-proof fuel tanks. Kenney's direct reports on the superiority of the German Luftwaffe were frowned upon by much of the Air Corps brass, however, and he was sent back to a desk job in the states. But superior leadership was not to be suppressed for long in the rapid buildup to war, and soon he was to be sent off to Brisbane as MacArthur's air chief. Initially, there was a brief clash with MacArthur's chief of staff, General Richard Sutherland. After some initial disagreements over air strategy and tactics, Kenney reportedly presented Sutherland with a sheet of paper, blank except for a dot in the center. "The dot is what you know about air strategy," Kenney told him. "The rest is what I know."

Kenney won that argument, but he had to have been disheartened by the equipment available to his airmen for turning back the Japanese juggernaut. For an admirer of the then incomparable German Messerschmitt, the American P-39 was a bad joke. A poor performer at high altitudes, the only faint positive was that, by the time the American pilot had managed to reach combat altitude, the attacking

Japanese planes would usually have done their damage and left. Lieutenant Jack Frost, a fighter pilot who had arrived in Australia with the deployment of the 39th, describes the P-39 as "a beautiful airplane of limited combat quality." The plane, designed around a gun, had severe performance deficiencies. The gun was a 37 mm T9 cannon to be fired through the center of the propeller hub for optimum accuracy and stability when firing. Since the plane's primary mission was the interception of enemy bombers, H.M. Poyer, designer for project leader Robert Woods, was impressed by the power of this weapon and pressed for its incorporation. This was unusual because fighters had previously been designed around an engine, not a weapon system.

Although the T9 cannon was devastating when it worked, it had very limited ammunition, a low rate of fire, and was prone to jamming. Far worse problems resulted from having to position the engine behind the cockpit to accommodate the cannon in the plane's nose. The mid-engine placement arrangement did make possible the P-39's smooth and streamlined nose profile, achieving the "beautiful airplane" look Lt. Frost admired. The downside was that, to operate efficiently in the thin air at high altitudes, the plane needed a turbo-supercharger, which was cooled with a scoop on the left side of the fuselage. But this scoop created drag and reduced speed. The supercharger was enclosed within the plane, and, in the very tight interior space, there was no internal space left over for the turbo. As arguments over drag and speed continued, the decision was made to go into production on the P39 without the turbocharger.

Bell's true motivation for reconfiguring the plane has been argued over for decades. The darkest assertion is that the company did not have an active production program and was desperate for cash flow. Whatever the reason, the production P-39 retained a single-stage, single-speed supercharger allowing an optimum altitude of only about 12,000 feet. The cure for the drag problem turned out to be worse than the drug itself. To make matters even worse for Frost and his fellow pilots of the 39th, all of whom had trained by in the States on the P-39, the planes they were assigned when they got to Australia were nearly worn out cast-offs from the Royal Australian Air Force.

These problems and limitations figured prominently in the 39th fighting performance when the squadron was deployed from Townsville to Port Moresby in mid-May. The issue of these American fighters achieving combat altitude before attacking planes arrived over their targets was lessened somewhat by the network of coast watchers the Australians had stationed along the New Guinea north coast. The defenders now had up to 15 minutes warning of an impending attack, but it took the P-39 30 minutes to reach 20,000 feet, the attackers' altitude. So the Americans were not yet effective in fending bomber attacks, but they managed to engage some of the escorting Zeros. And, although they couldn't maneuver with the Zeros, they did work to use their higher diving speed and those devastating cannons to good effect. In the engagements between the P-39s and the Zeros, the sides were about even with some 80 losses each. The major difference was that when a Zero went down, the pilot was lost as well. But since the fighting was right over the Port Moresby area, the American pilots survived to fight again, often the following day.

Some of these survival stories were legendary. Lt. Gene Rehrer was about to engage a flight of Zeros when his engine stalled because of an interruption in fuel flow from the external tank. While he was trying to get the engine restarted, the Zeros caught up with him and shot his plane full of holes, setting his engine on fire. Another American pilot reported that Rehrer's plane went down flames and that "there was no chute." But there was a chute. With his plane burning and Japanese bullets still hitting the plane, he pulled his emergency door release lever. The P-39 did not have the conventional sliding canopy like most fighters. Instead, there were doors on either side like those on a car. A pilot in this emergency situation was expected to roll out of the seat onto the wing with the doors gone where the air stream would sweep him away and clear of the plane. But Rehrer's doors stuck, and he banged them with his knees and elbows to no avail.

Desperate, with the engine fire growing hotter behind him, he released his seat belt to have a better shot at opening one of the doors. But the plane suddenly flipped and went into a flat inverted spin. Now he was crammed against the top of the cockpit. He was helpless until the plane flipped again flung him out in midair. So now he was clear of the plane, but it occurred to him that when he released his seat belt, he must also have released his parachute harness. He reached for his chest to where the parachute "D" ring should have been–and he found it! He pulled the ring, and the chute trailed but didn't open.

"That probably saved my life," he said later. "I was still up over 15,000 feet, and the Japs would have had plenty of time to use me as target practice." With his chute still trailing, he plummeted through the overcast to about 2,000 feet when it did open. A week later, he rode into the 39th camp in an Aussie truck, some friendly natives having found and helped him. Two days later, he was flying missions again.

The combat challenges were complicated and intensified by the problems of living in an equatorial climate–Port Moresby being only 125 miles below the equator. "It stunk of rot and mold," remembers Frank Royal, a pilot who was promoted to squadron commander when they first reached Australia because, he believes, that, at 25, he was the oldest second lieutenant. "The smell permeated everything. I don't know what temperatures were, but it was hot all night and even hotter during the day, and with the tropical humidity was nearly unbearable." There was an epidemic of dysentery almost immediately, and after that the fungal sores and itches started. The men seldom wore anything more than shorts, and there was one bush that would "set their skin on fire" just by walking by it. "Jungle crud and crotch rot stated a weeping, itching mess in the moist areas of the underarms and crotch," he says. "This was mostly treated with gentian of violet, and we all looked like clowns."

Malaria took its toll too. At first, they were all given a quinine tablet each day for protection, but this caused a constant buzzing in the ears. They switched to an atibrine tablet that stopped the bussing, but everyone turned a peculiar shade of yellow. However, most did adjust to the climate, and, with frequent R&R tours to Sydney where the squadron kept an apartment, morale stayed reasonably high.

THE LAST FLIGHT OF LT. ROBERT E. THORPE

My account of the capture and execution of Bob Thorpe is based on interviews with Fred Tobi, Jack Frost, and Lew Lockhart, who flew with Bob on his final mission, flight records of the 39th Fighter Squadron, and testimony of five Japanese officers during the war crime trials in Yokohama, Japan in 1948.

The slender 20-year-old knelt before the narrow trench soon to be his grave, exhausted, filthy and clad only in a pair of blue shorts. He was in excruciating pain from bullet wounds in his legs administered as "target practice" by his captors. Imperial Japanese Naval personnel gathered around, chattering and laughing. His executioner stood behind him, preparing the sword for his ceremonial beheading, much in the manner of the fanatical ISIS militants of our day.

What was going through Bob Thorpe's mind in those last few moments before his death? The night before, May 27th, 1944, he and 15 other pilots who would be taking part in the raid met for their preflight briefing at their airbase 300 hundred miles to the south in Gusap, New Guinea. The target was the big Japanese airfield complex at Wewak. There was not much chance they would be intercepted by enemy aircraft since most Japanese planes were destroyed or damaged. But, as usual, there would be heavy ground fire.

As the pilots left the briefing murmuring, each must have calculated his odds. It was a given that the most dangerous part of any of these missions was the takeoff. Their massive, six-ton P-47s were powered by 2,000 horsepower radial engines. To carry the fuel to make the 600-mile round-trip flight, they needed an extra 400 gallons of gasoline in auxiliary fuel tanks slung beneath the wings, along with two 500-pound bombs. That weight, combined with hundreds of rounds of ammunition for their eight 50-caliber machine guns, made getting these planes off the ground over runways of metal sheets on spongy jungle earth a death-defying challenge. Some of them blew tires on the sharp edges of the metal sheets, flipped over, and burst into flames, allowing the pilots almost no chance to escape.

Once off the ground, the greatest danger they encountered was the weather. As the hot, humid air blowing in from the North Pacific

Ocean reached the Owen Stanley Mountain Range that formed the central spine of the world's second-biggest island, it rushed up toward the 15,000-foot peaks, creating massive clouds and rainstorms. With compasses and wristwatches as their only navigational aids, pilots were easily lost in this turbulent murk. Disoriented, they ran out of fuel and crashed at sea or, worse yet, in the endless jungle. There were always searches but few rescues.

All of this faced those 16 pilots as they rolled out from under the mosquito netting covering their bunks at six the following day, showered, ate breakfast, and piled into jeeps for the half-mile ride to the airstrip.

The noise on the flight line was deafening as the huge engines roared to life. One by one, the fighters taxied down the runway, gaining speed and taking off. Once in the air, they circled over Gusap until the entire sixteen-unit formation formed in four-abreast lines climbed to 15,000 feet and headed north along the Ruma River Valley toward the coast.

The river widens into a massive coastal marsh at its mouth. The formation banked west over the marsh and, dropping down to just over 1,000 feet, flying the last 150 miles to Wewak over the unbroken jungle canopy. There was less chance of the attackers being spotted over the jungle than over the coast, where the battered Japanese navy was still active. Just East of Wewak, the formation veered slightly south to avoid "sure shot Charlie," a large caliber anti-aircraft gun that had shot down several American planes.

The extensive Japanese base at Wewak was intended to block an Allied advance up the north New Guinea coast toward the Philippines. But after months of relentless air attacks, it was incapable of even providing air cover. Hundreds of wrecked Japanese planes lined its five airstrips.

Reaching the airfield complex, the first flight dropped to treetop level and began its attacks. Scores of 12.8-millimeter machine guns–the Japanese equivalent of the American 50-caliber—filled the air with metal. The American planes attacked from the East, using the morning sun to obscure the aim of the Japanese gunners.

"We attacked one-by-one, and the time over the field was only seconds," explains Lt. Jack Frost, who was on the mission when Thorpe was lost. "The first guy in is the safest. By the time the last guy made his run, all kinds of metal were coming up at him."

The field was already battered and smoking when Bob Thorpe, flying second wingman in the third flight, made his run. Damaged planes and a few buildings and vehicles were his strafing targets. When the formation finished the attack and reformed at 10,000 feet above the Wewak complex, there were just 15 planes. No one had seen Bob's plane go down.

P-47 engines were notoriously tough, often returning to base with their 18 radial cylinders shot off. The ground fire must have penetrated crucial parts of Bob's engine. Unable to gain altitude, he banked out over the water and managed to maintain enough control to set the plane down in one piece. It sank immediately, but he was able to release his harness and scramble out of the cockpit. His inflatable raft went down with the plane, but a large log was floating nearby. He swam over to it and drifted into the beach at Kairiru Island, just offshore from Wewak.

Something of a favorite today for surfers with a taste for the wild side, Kairiru is described in brochures as "an almost unbelievably picturesque setting, with the volcanic mountains rising out of the sea." On that May morning, it was sweltering, and Bob Thorpe was parched with thirst after his ordeal of ditching the plane and swimming to shore. He also undoubtedly had no illusions about what was in store for him at this point. Pilots downed in the jungle or the sea, unless quickly rescued, knew they were doomed if captured by the Japanese. As a result, some pilots regarded the side arms they carried as their tickets to instant oblivion. Whether or not Bob had considered that option, it was now moot since his pistol went down with his plane.

A patrol immediately captured him made up of "volunteers" from Formosa, under the command of Tobi Baba. Considered third-rate soldiers by the Japanese, these men were assigned only patrol and security duties. They took him into custody without any violence or cruelty. He must have seen no point in resisting, and they understood that their commanders would want him brought in quickly for interrogation. Indeed, they probably regarded the capture as a stroke of luck. Delivering him physically intact and mentally coherent for interrogation would curry favor with their Japanese overloads.

Baba turned Thorpe over to Warrant Officer Naotada Fujihira of the Twenty-Seventh Special Base Force on Muschu Island. With two members of the Takasago Unit as guards, Fujihira tied a rope around Thorpe's hands and led him on the six-mile journey, over rugged mountain trails, to his unit's headquarters. At one point, they stopped to rest, and Fujihira gave Thorpe water and a biscuit. The language barrier precluded any communication, but Thorpe may have felt some faintly reassuring sense of their common humanity at that point.

That feeling ended when they reached headquarters. Thorpe was taken to an air raid shelter and tied to a post. Sometime must have passed as he waited for what was to come next. Inside Headquarters 40 feet away, Admiral Kenro Sato, Commanding Officer of the 27th Special Base Force, was informed by Captain Kiyohisa Noto of the prisoner's capture. Sato's decision about his fate was probably instantaneous since he had just returned from Japan, where all captured American flyers were considered war criminals, and many were executed immediately. Sato ordered Noto to interrogate the prisoner and extract any useful information. Commander Kaoru Okuma, who spoke some English, was given the assignment.

Testimony at the trial after the war indicated that the interrogation began in a relatively civilized manner. Asked where he was from in the United States, Thorpe told them about the Rhode Island town of Cranston "not far from Boston." He mentioned his parents and his younger brother and sister. However, when the questions shifted to the military situation, he stubbornly stuck to the Geneva Convention requirement giving only name, rank, and serial number. As to the kind of plane he was flying, what base and squadron he was from, what the targets of the mission had been, he remained stonily silent. He did answer, however, when Okuma asked him who he thought would win the war. Thorpe replied that his country had too many resources to lose.

That infuriated Okuma, and he slapped the prisoner. By now, a dozen or more soldiers had arrived to witness the interrogation.

Okuma turned to them and said that the prisoner had insulted the Emperor and invited them to beat him. The scene turned savage. This was a group that had transitioned psychologically from dreams of triumph and control of the entire Pacific region to the grim reality of grinding defeat by overwhelming American military strength. It had been nearly two years since the Japanese Imperial Navy's catastrophic defeat in the Battle of Midway.

The triumphs at Pearl Harbor and in the Philippine campaigns were now distant and fading memories. Even large bases like Wewak were becoming strategically irrelevant, unable to adequately defend themselves, much less project power in their areas. Supply and communication lines were in tatters. Wewak's only remaining strategic significance was to block the Americans and Australians from taking control of New Guinea.

Under these circumstances, emperor worship was the only remaining unifying and motivating force for these men. That was certainly the motivation for hundreds of thousands of Japanese soldiers to sacrifice themselves fanatically in battle. What is so difficult to understand and impossible to forgive is how emperor worship could lead them to attack a prisoner tied to a post and beat him to a bloody pulp with fists and sticks.

The beating was still going on when Okuma left the scene to report the interrogation results to Noto. Okuma was ordered to execute Thorpe in any manner he chose. At 3 o'clock that afternoon, an execution party consisting of four officers—Kaoru Okuma, Tsunehiko Yamamoto, Naotada Fujihira, and Yutaka Odazawa and about 20 enlisted men led Thorpe to a native cemetery where a shallow grave had already been dug.

Odazawa carried a sword, as it had been decided that Thorpe would be ceremonially beheaded, a procedure that was intended to bestow honor on a defeated military adversary under the Bushido Code. It was seen as some ticket to paradise. But given the tattered state of the Code, any ritual value of these executions was lost in their cruelty.

It was at this point that Okuma announced that the beheading was to be preceded by "target practice" by himself, Yamamoto and Fujihira. Odazawa asked the officers to aim low to not compromise the victim with upper body wounds that would make beheading him difficult.

Fujairah fired first and missed, much to the amusement of the crowd. At his court-martial four years later, Fujihira claimed to have missed deliberately because he felt compassion for Thorpe based on their travel together over the mountain trail. Yamamoto shouted in English that "I will now shoot you with my pistol," and Thorpe staggered slightly when the bullet hit his lower leg. Okuma shot next, and blood spurted from the prisoner's other leg. He remained standing.

Complete with its shooting gallery and raucous crowd, the execution site had taken on a carnival atmosphere. Odazawa ordered some of the enlisted men to drag the prisoner to the gravesite as he filled a bottle with water. He offered it to the prisoner, then poured water on Thorpe's neck and on his heirloom samurai sword. Odazawa then performed an act as though it were from a play. He did it contemptuously, and everyone laughed.

He said in Japanese, "I, Chief Petty Officer Odazawa will now proceed to execute the prisoner." He pushed Thorpe into a kneeling position with his head bowed forward at the edge of the grave. Just before Odazawa beheaded him, Thorpe looked up and, in a calm voice, asked, "What time is it?"

Odazawa struck, and Thorpe's body fell into the grave. CWO Waichi Ogawa, a medical technician, jumped into the grave, cut open Thorpe's chest with a knife, and removed an organ, probably his liver. As the late afternoon sun set, soldiers filled in the grave. During the court-martial of the officers charged in Thorpe's execution, one of the accused drew a map showing the burial site. The court-martial records were sealed. Walter Thorpe was told that his son's remains were unrecoverable for more than sixty years.

During the war crimes trial in Yokohama in 1948, Kaoru Okuma, the man who decided to use the prisoner for target practice before the execution, described Thorpe's behavior throughout the ordeal as "magnificent."

Fifteen pilots assembled for a debriefing following the mission in which Thorpe was lost. Second Lt. James M. Robertson said, "Just as the first strafing run was started, I saw Thorpe, who was flying on my wing, peel off to make the pass. The airplane appeared to be okay."

1st Lt. Raymond Kramme conducted an aerial search for any sign of Thorpe's aircraft in the Wewak area the day of his disappearance. The results of his search were negative. Major Harris L. Denton also took off on a search mission but had to abort it when visibility dropped to zero. Denton said a search mission would be scheduled as soon as weather permitted, and he grounded the squadron.

Lt. Fred Tobi and Lt. Lew Lockhart ignored the order and flew an unauthorized mission to find Thorpe. They found no trace of him or his airplane. Tobi had lost his brother in a plane crash in 1943, and Bob Thorpe had taken his brother's place. They had gone through flight training together, and Tobi remembered meeting Nora Thorpe, Bob's mother, during the graduation ceremony when they received their wings.

They shared the same tent at Gusap and flew many combat missions together. During an interview in 2007, Tobi was asked if he had ever contacted the Thorpe family to find out what happened to Bob. "I didn't know what happened to Bob until you just told me," Tobi said. "You have to understand our thinking at the time. When a pilot went missing, we acted as if he had been transferred. Bob was my closest friend in the Air Corps. He was transferred out of the 39th, and that was it. War is hell. The scars are deep. Some losses are just too painful to think about."

The Cover-up

On December 13, 1937, a photograph of two smiling young Japanese officers, Toshiaki Mukai and Tsuyoshi Noda, appeared on the front page of the Tokyo newspaper *Tokyo Nichi Nichi*. The headline read: "Incredible Record to Cut Down 100 People–Mukia 106 and Noda 105–both 2nd Lieutenants Go Into Extra Innings."

The "people" were defenseless Chinese POWs. What is so monstrous about this story, beyond all the murders, was the acceptance, indeed the celebration, of this horror by the Japanese public. So it was to be expected that the Japanese military's savage treatment of civilians and POWs was not to be limited to the Chinese–whom they regarded as an inferior race and butchered an estimated 30 million–but would be inflicted on all of the populations and militaries they battled and conquered in Asia and the South Pacific.

The Allies were preparing to investigate these war crimes and bring the perpetrators to justice well before the end of the war. One of the most tenacious and effective of these investigators was Captain John D. Steed, a member of the Australian Board of Inquiry. An attorney, he had a reputation for toughness and thoroughness. He never raised his voice or lost his composure but simply asked question after question, recording all the answers in a notebook that never left his side.

Steed was part of a team investigating the Bataan Death March that took part in the Philippines in 1942. Approximately 75,000 Filipino and US soldiers surrendered to the Japanese under the command of General Masaharu Homma. Captives were forced to walk 100 kilometers north to Camp O'Donnell and were denied food and water for several days. Those who could not keep up were shot, beheaded, or bayoneted. Based on evidence Steed help uncover, Homma was convicted and executed on April 3, 1946.

Steed also investigated the Parit Sulong Massacre in Malaysia, 1942. Captured Australian and Indian POWs were murdered by Japanese soldiers under the command of Lt. General Takuma Nishimura, who was convicted and hanged on July 11, 1951. Steed's next assignment was the Laha Massacre, 1942. After the Battle of Ambron, more than 300 Australian and Dutch soldiers were chosen randomly and summarily executed near Laha Airfield. Steed uncovered evidence that led to the hanging of Captain Kunito Hatakeyama, who was in command of the massacre, in 1946.

Steed then investigated the Alexandra Hospital Massacre that took place during the Battle of Singapore in 1942. Japanese soldiers shot or bayoneted hospital staff members on February 14, 1942. Lt. General Saburo Kawamura and Lt. Col. Masayuki were hanged, and five other Japanese soldiers received life sentences. So Steed had a great deal of experience interviewing Japanese officers and soldiers suspected of war crimes when he arrived in New Guinea in 1945 to find out what happened to two Australians soldiers and an American pilot captured in May of 1944. He began his investigation by interviewing Kazuo Maruyama, the surgeon in charge of the hospital on Kiriku Island, who gave him the following account:

"In May or June 1944, I attended a captured fighter pilot at Naval Headquarters at Sansaria. I heard he was an American. He had come ashore near Jagur. Captain Noto sent him to live at the hospital because there was no other accommodation available. He was quite healthy when I first saw him. During the first month, he had fever once. Then he developed malaria. I gave him quinine by mouth for five days, and when he became too ill to take it, I gave him three intravenous injections. He went into a coma, however, and his brain was affected. He died about a week after he fell sick," the surgeon said.

"Two Australian prisoners were treated at the hospital around the same time. One of them had been severely injured at the time of his capture and died shortly after being hospitalized. The other, like the American prisoner, died of malaria. We had been treating him with quinine, but the disease had progressed too rapidly, and he never fully regained consciousness."

If Maruyama thought his statement would satisfy Steed, he was utterly mistaken. "You showed such compassion for these prisoners, giving them medicine while you had little for your troops," Steed challenged Maruyama. "Meanwhile, your countrymen were murdering captured prisoners throughout the South Pacific." Maruyama tried to stick to his story, but under Steed's relentless questioning, he began to contradict himself. Steed noted the inconsistencies in his notebook before turning his attention to Kiyohisa Noto, Chief of Staff of the 27th Special Base Force. Noto gave Steed a prepared statement before the first interview.

"I was Chief of Staff, 27th Special Base Force. I first went to Kairiru on March 15, 1944 and remained there until the surrender. We captured an American on Kairiru about the middle of May 1944. He was an airman, and I heard he was lieutenant. He died about 20 days after he was brought in. I think that the cause of death was malaria. I was sick with malaria myself at that time, and I do not remember details about this prisoner. I do think that he came ashore on the north side of Kairiru." Noto's explanation of the death of the two Australian prisoners matched, almost word-for-word, the story offered by Maruyama. Despite intense scrutiny by Steed, Noto stuck to his story.

The case took a different turn after Steed grilled Tsunehiko Yamamoto on the disposition of the three captured fliers and received the following sworn statement: "About that time the Australians had come to receive the remains of the prisoners and had been guided by Chief Petty Officer Kanzo Bunya to a cemetery on Kairiru Island where a grave was opened up and the remains of three Japanese who had been killed in action were handed over as being the remains of the two Australians and one American who had been executed."

Steed later confirmed that the remains were Japanese, not Australian or American. If allowed to continue the investigation, there is little doubt that he would have uncovered enough evidence to convict Yutaka Odazawa, Ogawa, Naotada Fujihira, Kaoru Okuma, and Tsunehido Yamamoto for the torture and murder of Bob Thorpe. But there were bigger fish to fry, and Steed was reassigned to the Manila Massacre, during which over 100,000 Filipino citizens were murdered.

General Tomoyku Yamashita argued that he knew nothing about the atrocities, so he could not be held accountable. Steed helped establish the Yamashita Standard, which holds that those who do not make meaningful efforts to uncover and stop atrocities are just as culpable as those who commit them. Yamashita was found guilty and executed.

Before leaving New Guinea, Steed uncovered enough evidence to try Noto as a war criminal. The man who relayed the order to execute Thorpe was found guilty of executing two Australian prisoners of war and sentenced to 20 years at hard labor at Rabaul Prison. Steed was also able to identify Ogawa as the man who actually beheaded the two Australian prisoners. When he tried to arrest Ogawa, Steed learned that the man who beheaded two of his countrymen and desecrated the body of Bob Thorpe had been allowed to return to Japan.

Steed turned over his files proving that Thorpe had also been tortured and executed by Okuma, Odazawa, Fujihira, Noto, and Yamamoto under a direct order from Admiral Sato. No action was taken by the Americans, and the suspects, with the exception of Noto, were allowed to return to Japan and resume civilian life. Meanwhile, Bob Thorpe remained buried in a shallow grave near the beach where he had been tortured, used for target practice, and beheaded.

Three years later, at the War Crimes trial held in Yokohama, Koji Kawada told the Commission that in September of 1945, about a month after the war ended, a meeting was called by Captain Kiyohisa Noto on Kairiru Island, and all company commanders attended. "I was present, as was Admiral Sato. Noto did all of the talking. He said that if any questions were asked by Australian or American authorities as to the disposition of two Australian pilots and one American, we were to say that we knew nothing about it. If perchance one of us had seen the flyer, we were to say that we had seen him and that he had been taken away and we didn't know where. We were forbidden to mention the execution." Kawada said.

"From Kairiru Island, we were taken to Muschu Island, where two meetings were held regarding two Australian and one American POW. Noto repeated what he had said at the first meeting. At a second meeting at Muschu Island, I was present when Sato explained that Chief Petty Officer Kanzo Bunya turned over some Japanese remains to the Australian Army after the war at Kairiru Island, representing them as the bodies of one American and two Australian prisoners of war. We were ordered to say that the prisoners had died of disease and had been buried with full military honors. Noto was not present at this meeting because he was being questioned by the Australians."

Amenomori submitted the following statement concerning the cover-up:

"In October or November of 1945, Admiral Sato held a conference in which he said that the Australian military authorities would conduct an investigation in the case of two Australian soldiers who were executed in 1945 and an American flier who was beheaded in 1944. He told us to tell them that the soldiers died of malaria and that services were conducted over their bodies. He also told us that even after returning to Japan we must remain quiet."

The Mission Begins

It was an exciting time to be 13 years old in 1944, especially for Gill Thorpe and me, living one street apart in Edgewood, RI. My brother Jack was fighting in the Pacific with the 1st Division of the U.S.M.C., and my brother Bill was in Europe with the 88th Blue Devils Division. Gill had a brother, Bob, a P-47 pilot with the 39th Fighter Squadron flying out of Gusap Air Base in New Guinea.

What army censors took away, Gill and I were able to replace with imagination as we exchanged stories about the exploits of our brothers. Neither one of us was the least bit worried about their safety. John Wayne was winning the war in the Pacific, and Errol Flynn, when he was not playing Robin Hood or General Custer, was handling the Nazis in Europe.

Only the bad guys got wounded or killed in the war. Nothing happened to the good guys. That thinking all changed one day in early June of 1944 when an army vehicle stopped in front of the Thorpe home. Gill was home with his sister, Nancy, when two Army officers came to the door and asked to speak to the parents of Lt. Robert Thorpe. Gill explained that his mother and father, Walter and Nora Thorpe, were playing bridge at a cousin's home.

One of the officers told Gill that his brother had been missing since May 27 and handed him a telegram to deliver to his parents. Gill called his father immediately. "Bob's missing in action," he said to his father. Gill still remembers his parents returning to the house, his mother crying softly. His father didn't say anything as he read the telegram. Word spread through the neighborhood quickly.

A few days after the official visit, an article from the Associated Press appeared in *The Providence Journal* reporting that Lt. Robert Thorpe was missing after a strafing mission against an enemy airstrip near Wewak, New Guinea. His plane was last seen as it went into a dive and was hit by enemy ground fire. The target was close to the ocean, so it was presumed that his plane had fallen into the sea. No trace was found of him or his plane, and he was officially listed as missing in action.

The news about Bob Thorpe served as a wake-up call for all of the young boys who had previously felt that war was so exciting. Good guys do get hurt in wars, Gill and I suddenly realized. We never again looked at John Wayne or Errol Flynn the same way.

Immediately after the war, Bob's designation of "missing in action" was changed to "killed in action." I remember attending a church service for him with my friends John Dinneen, Jack Swan, and Sherm Strickhauser.

On June 21, 1948, Nora Thorpe received a phone call from a woman in California offering her condolences on the death of Bob Thorpe. She had a son who was also killed in action and wanted to share her grief with another Gold Star mother. When Nora explained that Bob was "missing" and the family still hoped that he would be found, the woman told her about an article that appeared in her local newspaper. She read the article naming five Japanese officers who were going on trial for torturing and beheading her son in May of 1944. Nora called her husband at the drug store, and Walter made inquiries about the story. Before he received any formal notification, an article appeared in *The Providence Journal* on June 22, 1948, describing one of the most revolting crimes uncovered by war crimes investigators. Five Japanese officers admitted beating Lt. Thorpe, using him for target practice, beheading him, and desecrating his body.

Admiral Kenro Sato, the officer who gave the order to execute Thorpe, committed suicide in 1948 after learning that he was about to be arrested and charged in the War Crimes Trials at Yokohama. C.W.O. Waichi Ogawa, who was charged with desecrating Lt. Thorpe's body, hanged himself at Sugamo Prison shortly before the trial began. On July 6, 1948, three Japanese officers were sentenced to life imprisonment, while a fourth received a twenty-year sentence. Lt. Commander Kaoru Okuma, the officer in charge of the execution, was sentenced to death. On May 27, 1949, five years to the day of Bob Thorpe's last mission, Okuma was hanged at Sugamo Prison in Japan.

The Thorpe family accepted the news quietly and made no public comment, even after the sentences were announced and Okuma was hanged. Nora Thorpe never fully recovered from her son's brutal execution. Friends say her beautiful smile disappeared right after she learned about Bob's death, and she became withdrawn and quiet. She died prematurely in 1956 at the age of 56. Behind the scenes, Walter Thorpe never stopped in his efforts to have his son's remains returned to Rhode Island, even though he was told repeatedly they were unrecoverable. The trial records of the officers found guilty were classified as "secret," under the direct orders of General Douglas MacArthur, the Supreme Commander of Allied Powers in Japan.

Walter Thorpe never accepted this explanation, reasoning that his remains had to be buried somewhere if his son had been executed on dry land. He enlisted the aid of politicians to get some answers. All inquiries continued to be answered with a one-word comment from the military—"unrecoverable."

Walter Thorpe died at the age of 83, never entirely escaping the nagging feeling that his son's remains were out there somewhere near the beach where he had been tortured and buried. His goal of burying Bob's remains with his late wife was never achieved. Gill followed in his father's footsteps, becoming a pharmacist and, with his sister Nancy, took over the family business. Almost sixty years later, Gill decided that he had not done enough on his brother's behalf.

He began to make inquiries in 2003. He was given the name of Michael Claringbould, a historian and author of several books on the 5th Air Force, which included the 39th Fighter Squadron, Bob Thorpe's unit in New Guinea. Claringbould grew up in Papua New Guinea and became an expert at locating missing planes and aircraft downed in the Pacific in WW II.

Claringbould gave Gill a "Missing Air Crew Report" containing critical information about Bob's capture and execution, including two sketches of his burial site, only yards from the beach where he had been beheaded. Thorpe immediately contacted Sen. Jack Reed's office with the detailed maps of his brother's grave.

Bob Kerr, a columnist for *The Providence Journal*, wrote a column about Gill's efforts that attracted my attention. I had left Rhode Island in 1960 and spent the next forty years as a writer, working in Connecticut, New York, New Jersey and Pennsylvania. I had assumed Bob's remains had been returned after the trials in 1948. I called Gill, and we had our first conversation in thirty years. Gill sent me a copy of "The Missing Crewman Report" Claringbould had given him. After reading the report, I called Gill and advised him to get copies of the original court-martial records from the trials in Yokohama in 1948.

When Gill said he did not know how to go about it, I agreed to take action under the "Freedom of Information Act." That conversation started me on an eight-year journey through mission reports, letters, interviews, emails, diaries, photographs, squadron mission reports, telegrams, and records of war crimes trials. The journey was not always easy, especially when reading about the deaths of these outstanding young men. After many letters, phone calls, and trips to Washington, D.C., I finally obtained official transcripts of the trials of the five officers convicted of torturing and beheading Bob Thorpe. I read the transcripts in a hotel room, finishing it at 3 a.m. The actual details of what Bob Thorpe endured kept me up for the rest of that night and for many nights to come. I decided that morning to write a book about Bob Thorpe and the courage, conviction, and dignity he displayed on that lonely beach where he was beheaded so many years before.

I began searching for former pilots of the 39th Fighter Squadron who flew with Bob in New Guinea. I hit gold with my first contact, John Dunbar, a pilot who remembered flying with Bob Thorpe at Gusap Air Base, New Guinea. John kept a diary of his time with the 39th, providing critical information for this book. John gave me the contact information for Fred Tobi, Bob Thorpe's closest friend in the 39th Fighter Squadron. I was living in Sarasota, FL, at the time, about 45 minutes from Fred Tobi's home in Tampa.

Fred had gone through flight training with Bob Thorpe at Dove Field in Arcadia, Florida. He remembered meeting Bob's mother, Nora when the two pilots got their wings in 1943. After several interviews with Fred, Gill Thorpe flew to Tampa to meet with his brother's best friend. Now a retired fruit broker, Fred had almost total recall of his time in New Guinea. Tobi said that he and Bob always made it to their target, which was usually Wewak. When they weren't escorting bombers, they were strafing the field at Wewak. Fred remembered a mission in April 1944, when Bob had to bail out after his engine developed problems. Fortunately, he landed less than a mile from the base.

After flying 97 missions, Tobi was horribly burned when his P-47 crashed on takeoff in New Guinea in 1944. He spent the next three years undergoing extensive surgery and did not leave the hospital until 1947. Fred shared a tent in Gusap, New Guinea, with Bob Thorpe, Marcus Trout, and James Steele. Like Bob Thorpe, James Steele was captured by the Japanese and executed. Fred referred me to Captain Lew Lockhart, now 94, who flew 149 combat missions with the 39th F.S. in New Guinea. He still remembers the orientation flight he gave to Bob Thorpe, Fred Tobi, James Steele, and Marcus Trout. "All four of them had a lot more hours on the P-47 than I did when I took them on the orientation flight," Lockhart said. "The squadron had been flying P-38s until they were replaced with P-47s in late 1943. We loved the way the P-38s handled, especially with those twin engines. We didn't feel as secure with the cumbersome P-47s. Major Denton, our C.O., placed me in charge of new pilot orientation, and I still remember the drill like it was yesterday. I took the four pilots up and designated us as 'Outcast Red.' I also told them they wouldn't be seeing many enemy planes because we pretty much owned the skies in that part of New Guinea," he added.

"After takeoff, we rendezvoused at 1,500 feet, then climbed to 5,000 feet. I pointed out the Owen Stanley Mountain Range with peaks of 19,000 feet. I told them they would be flying a lot of missions over them to Wewak and Hollandia. I showed them the Finisterre Mountain Range, with peaks at 13,000 to 14,000 feet, and the Markham River. On our first mission, Bob and I were sent in a fighter sweep against Wewak, a Japanese airbase. We were deployed in four flights of four. Outcast Red was leader, with White, Blue and Green the other flights. The air and sky were clear. We flew over Wewak and observed that it was pretty beat up with wrecked aircraft and craters on the runways," Lockhart said.

Lew Lockhart spent many hours on the telephone with me, reliving his days with the 39th when his plane crashed on takeoff, and he escaped with a few minor bruises and was flying the next day. I will always remember his laughter when he told me about a trick he had discovered while ferrying P-38s from Australia to New Guinea. "I would remove the ammunition and replace it with beer for my thirsty friends in New Guinea."

Lockhart and Tobi were both on Thorpe's last combat mission on May 27, 1944. "I was leading Blue Flight, and Fred Tobi was my wingman," Lockhart said. "Bob Thorpe was the wingman for Lt. Raymond

Kramme in Green Flight. Lt. James Robertson was also on Green Flight. Major Denton, the squadron commander, was leading Red Flight. Overall, it was a successful mission, with one big negative. Bob didn't return. At the debriefing, Robertson said he saw Bob just before he made his final run, and his aircraft was in good shape. Kramme said ground fire was heavier than usual, and Bob may have been hit. Weather grounded the squadron the next morning, but Fred Tobi and I broke orders and went looking for Bob," Lockhart said. "No trace of him or the plane."

It was through Fred Tobi and John Dunbar that I made contact with Frank Royal, Roy Seher, Jack Frost, and Chuck O'Sullivan. They patiently answered all of the questions posed by a former staff sergeant who fought the Korean War in Europe and Africa with a typewriter. The memories of these men are astounding. Every time I checked their accounts of missions, squadron records, lost pilots, and planes, their recollections were highly accurate.

Lew Lockhart introduced me to a very special person by the name of Mary Morgan Martin, daughter of Captain George Morgan, who was killed in the Battle of the Philippines in 1945. Mary's mother, Mary Scott Morgan was three months pregnant when her husband and Mary's father was killed after his plane was hit by ground fire, and he was struck by the fuselage while bailing out. Mary sent me her father's wartime love letters to her mother, photos, many of them taken by her father, clippings, and daily squadron reports I would never have been able to find on my own. Mary also answered a question that had bothered me early in my research. Fred Tobi became quite emotional when I told him about the brutality of Bob Thorpe's death. He had never contacted the Thorpe family after the war to find out what happened to his best friend. He knew nothing about the trial of the Japanese officers who had murdered Bob Thorpe.

"Silence seemed to be the accepted practice," Mary Martin said. "These men were uncomfortable in discussing death, having been so close to it themselves. They did not know how their visits or telephone calls would be received. There were reports of grieving relatives verbally attacking survivors by saying things like, "Why did he die and not you?" So Mary understands why even close friends like Fred did not try to find out what happened to Bob.

MEET THE THORPES

Walter Thorpe was never one to tell war stories. Not that he didn't have plenty to tell. A World War I Yankee Division artilleryman, he had been through some of the fiercest fighting and most grueling conditions in France. There was Meuse-Argonne and the Ardennes, epic battles where many of his friends were killed or wounded. Horses literally burst their hearts, straining to pull the guns (until Walter and his battery mates stole sturdier mules from the French). There was always the filth and mud and terrible food.

"He never really said much about any of this," son Gill recalls now, some 90 years after his dad returned in the same woolen uniform, he had worn going overseas 20 months earlier, a uniform he had to line with newspapers against the cold for two winters. "What he did tell us about was getting months of back pay just before boarding the ship and gambling all the way across. At one point in the crossing, he was very wealthy. When they got to New York, someone else was."

Walter never gambled again. Even had he been so inclined, there really wasn't time. Within the next three years, he'd met and married Nora, completed training as a pharmacist, and opened Thorpe's Pharmacy in his hometown of Cranston, RI, on the shores of Narragansett Bay.

The Pharmacy was the kind of quasi-community center that thrived in so many towns in the years before the big national chains drove them out of business. There was the pharmaceutical area in the rear, counters for sundries in the center, and a 10-stool soda fountain up front where locals gathered to exchange their views on the great issues and events of the day. By the late 1930s, the economic hardships of the Great Depression were coming to an end as we transitioned into the early days of WWII.

Walter, whether filling a prescription or making up one of his renowned coffee milkshakes, made his views perfectly clear. He was adamantly opposed to the country entering another war. He'd seen enough in France, and now he suffered the awful anxiety of a parent of a military-aged son. Bob, born in 1923, was actually the Thorpes' second child. Richard, born in 1920, was a thriving three-year-old when an untended moving van rolled down a hill and crushed him to death in his playpen in the family's front yard. It was the kind of tragedy that no family ever really recovers from, and, for Walter and Nora, the thought of losing Bob as well was more than they could bear. But, by 1940, Bob was a bright, adventuresome 17-year-old, and they must have realized that if the country did go to war, the duty, challenge, and excitement of military service would be more than their son could resist.

Bob was an indifferent high school student. No one questioned his intelligence, but neither could anyone engage his interest in the subjects he was expected to study. He excelled, however, in anything that did interest him–mostly high activity pursuits like sailboat racing, fishing, and outdoor adventures with his Boy Scout troop. Scouting also seemed to bring out a commitment to civic responsibility. He spent time helping build camps, grading open space, and once disappeared from the family entirely for three days while fighting forest fires in western Rhode Island.

"He was a sight when he got home," says his brother Gill, who was eight years younger. "He was always skinny, but in his bedraggled clothes and covered with soot, he looked like a scarecrow." Gill remembers Bob as a kind and caring older brother. "I think I was six when I got a Lionel train set for Christmas," he says. "I had no idea of how to set it up. So he did the whole thing for me, and then he let me run it first."

Another time when Gill was having trouble flying kites, he remembers the special pains Bob took to help him. "He'd bought some special material for making the frames. He glued on newspaper and attached the necessary string for the bow and bridle and showed me how to make the adjustments for the tail. That kite was the best. Every kid in the neighborhood wanted one. It lasted the whole season."

Bob's interests didn't extend, however, to working at the Pharmac, much to his father's disappointment. It was very much a family operation, with Bob, sister Nancy, who was four years younger, and Gill helping out. Sweeping out in the evening was Gill's favorite chore since he was allowed to keep any change he found.

Walter had hoped that Bob would follow in his footsteps, becoming a pharmacist and eventually taking over the business. But Bob had no intention of doing so, and he worked there part-time only reluctantly.

Walter suggested that if Bob found the pharmacy so boring, perhaps he should try working in his uncle's machine shop. That lasted one day, and Bob was back sweeping out the pharmacy.

The interests of father and son finally merged when Walter bought a pickup truck for making deliveries. In driving, Bob had found the combination of work and recreation that completely appealed to him.

"You wouldn't believe how small that truck was," says Gill. "Two adults could just barely fit in the front. We kids would pile in the back. It was really cold in the winter."

Bob's range with the truck soon extended well beyond the Thorpe Pharmacy delivery area. By this time, he'd discovered girls, and he regularly visited someone up in southern Massachusetts. Also, often accompanied by a girlfriend, he would drive over to Hillsgrove airfield.

By the late 1930s, U.S. military authorities had realized they did not have a fighter plane capable of taking on the fighters of our likely enemies then lighting up the skies over Europe and China. The P-44 Rocket the U.S. then had under development was not in a class with the German Messerschmitt and the Japanese Mitsubishi. Something bigger, faster, and far better armed would be needed. In the inimitable American way, what designers at Republic Aviation came up with was in a class of its own. The P-47 Thunderbolt was the biggest, most powerful, and most heavily armed and armored fighter plane in the world.

What Bob Thorpe was watching at Hillsgrove were Thunderbolts being flown in and out on training missions from Republic's fields on Long Island. It is not hard to imagine the impression these planes must have made on him. A Thunderbolt weighed over six tons, two tons heavier than any existing single-engine fighter. To achieve the required speed and climbing performance, the designers used a 1,800 horsepower, 18-cylinder, radial engine. Since the conventional three-bladed propeller couldn't utilize all this power, four-bladed propeller 12 feet in diameter was needed. Early models were to achieve speeds of 412 miles an hour and later models over 470.

What Bob couldn't understand or appreciate gazing through the chain-link fence was the extraordinary engineering that had gone into the plane's development. For the powerful engine to operate efficiently, a super-charged duct system was needed to provide the least interrupted airflow. This supercharger was built into the rear fuselage, with a big intake for the air mounted under the engine together with the oil coolers. Exhaust gases were piped separately to the turbine and expelled through a wastegate in the bottom of the fuselage. Ducted air was fed to the centrifugal impeller and returned to the engine under pressure.

All of this precise and complex design, moreover, was to prove extremely rugged. Although Bob was to be a tragic exception, Thunderbolt pilots grew accustomed to returning home in badly shot-up airplanes. Self-sealing fuel tanks kept the fuel from burning and exploding when hit–a notorious weakness of the vaunted Japanese Zero. The cockpit was heavily armored to protect the pilot from all directions. The massive engine could keep turning even when cylinders had been shot off. One Thunderbolt survived after losing a four-foot section off one wing.

Watching these marvels roar in and out over Narragansett Bay, Bob recognized his calling, if not his destiny. Graduating from high school in June 1942, he went on a crash course to gain the weight he'd need to enlist in the U.S. Army AAF (Tactical Air Crew). "He only weighed 125 pounds when he graduated, and he had to gain 10 pounds to be inducted," says Gill. "He drank dad's coffee cabinets with malted milk powder and ate bananas every day. He also wore heavy clothing to the weigh-in. And he made it."

After basic training at Fort Devens, MA, Bob was sent for air cadet training at Dorr Field in Florida. Many of the elderly residents of sprawling Lehigh Acres, just east of Fort Meyers, are undoubtedly his contemporaries. Some of them have probably come down from the Providence, RI area to escape New England winters. But few likely realize that the land under their homes and roads was the site of a significant part of their country's crash effort to catch up with our World War II enemies' military aviator skills.

Dorr was one of five separate training fields supporting flight training at Carlstrom Field, where the Embry Riddle Academy operated a contract flight training school. Named for Stephen Dorr, a pilot killed in a midair collision in 1917, Dorr had been used to train World War I pilots, and then closed down until 1941. In 1941, as in 1917, with a

5,300-foot runway and the nearly perfect flying weather in the Southwest Florida area made it an ideal training facility.

Bob described his training in great detail in his weekly letters to his mother, which unfortunately have been lost. But we get a vivid picture of what the air cadets went through from the letters, diaries, and even some published works by fellow trainees. Flight training progressed through the three phases of Primary, Basic, and Advanced.

Primary was clearly intended to weed out those cadets who had been selected for flight training but who had no chance of completing it. William Rogers, who went through training at about the same time as Bob and who wound up in the same squadron in the Pacific Theatre, recalls that in the first two flights on the Steadman biplane trainers, the instructor flew, and the cadet went along for the ride.

The first flight on the Steadman PT-17 was fun. This primary trainer had 250 hp, a low-wing biplane with fixed landing gear. With the blue-green waters of the Gulf of Mexico stretching out to the west and the lush semitropical Florida interior to the east, it was a short and easy orientation for the majority who had never been off the ground before.

The second flight was altogether different. "That one separated the professionals from the amateurs," Rogers recalls. "The instructor wrings out the plane in acrobatics with the poor student hanging on for dear life. He gets sick and messes up the side of the plane. Now I know why the student gets the back seat."

Rogers's descriptions evoke the mindset of the instructors. All were civilians, although one of them, an instructor by the name of Litchfield, had flown with the Eagle Squadron in the Battle of Britain. There was another instructor by the name of Reilly, who was quite good, according to Fred Tobi, who went through flight training with Bob and was later stationed with him at Gusap Air Force Base in New Guinea.

The instructors had a few months to turn complete novices into fighter pilots capable of surviving and winning air battles against German and Japanese pilots, many with years of combat experience. Any slacking off in demanding the highest standards of performance would be no kindness. It could be a death sentence.

"It was a rude awakening to discover that it took tedious practice to learn to do even the simplest maneuvers," Rogers found when he got to take the controls. And it was all with the instructor's "malevolent voice" constantly "beating on my ears" in the one-way gossport, a rubber tube fitted to the trainees' helmet that the instructor spoke or yelled into: "Take your goddam foot off that rudder! Keep your nose up! Quit beating the stick. Let the damn thing fly itself! It can fly itself better than you can!"

On average, more than half of the class would "wash out" during Primary and Advance training. Jack Frost, another fellow trainee, remembers a lot of good-natured harassment by instructors. "In general, if the trainee wasn't going to make it, he'd get a lot of sympathetic treatment preparing him for other duties," Frost says.

"On the other hand," Frost continues, "if the trainee was a hot-shot, he might be visited with a variety of harassments, such as the instructor overriding the controls to see how he'd react. Some were treated with the 'gossport dosage". That is, the instructor would stick his end of the funnel into the wind stream. That blast was sure to get the trainee's attention."

Tobi recalls that the grueling routine left little time for socializing. "Everyone was too busy to worry about morale," Fred says. "But the facilities at Dorr were pretty good. It was more like a motel than a barracks. There were six cadets in double-bunked beds, laid out nicely, a swimming pool, and a P.X. The town of Arcadia wasn't much, but we didn't have time to go there anyway."

On May 2, Bob and Fred's class of cadets was transferred to Bainbridge (G.A.) Air Force Base, where they found a radical change in the military atmosphere. "We arrived by train in the middle of the night," says Fred, "and it was like being back in the service again." The commanding officer was known as the "whip." Under the whip's strict regimentation, they had intense instruction–learning, for example, how weather conditions affected flying (something that would become especially crucial when they reached New Guinea) --and they advanced to flight training with the AT-6 (Advanced Trainer). With retractable gear–the Steadman had fixed gear–and a 450-horsepower engine, this was the most maneuverable airplane that the cadets had as yet flown. Although they weren't allowed to fly them, cadets also sat in the P-39 and the P-47.

Tobi liked the P-39 because of its looks, but it was one of the worst planes during WWII. "The Russians liked it because it had a canon that could knock out German tanks," he says, "but there were lots of mechanical problems. As for the P-47, he thought it was too big and heavy. Bob, however, loved the P-47 because of his early days watching it take off and land in R.I." Minus the 20% of the cadets who had washed out at Bainbridge, the class moved on to the Marianna Air Force Base in Florida on July 2, where they entered the Advance Phase of their training. Here they continued to fly the AT-6 as they learned techniques of strafing, bombing, and dogfighting.

It was at Marianna that they were asked to list their choices of flight assignments: transports, fighters or bombers. Fred listed his selection in just that order, but Bob made fighters his first choice. Both were selected for fighters, and while they waited to be sent to the Venice Air Force Base for P-47 training, they caught up on some other skills that the rushed pilot training schedule hadn't left much time for. One was mastering the 45-caliber pistol, the pilot's sidearm. Fred qualified as a marksman, but Bob achieved sharpshooter status. "That was so typical," Fred recalls, "Bob was a quiet, reserved New Englander, but he worked with total determination at everything he did. He became one of the best pilots in the class."

As he advanced through flight training to the P-47, Bob was constantly building up his physical strength and knowledge, and skills. There was good reason for the size and weight requirements the Army had for its pilots. The force required to operate the mechanical controls of the fighter planes of the period was substantial. The P-47, particularly, could demand the strength of a wrestler. The big engine and enormous propeller exerted so much torque that an airplane could flip over on takeoff if the pilot didn't have the arm strength to hold it back. Many didn't, and they were killed. Bob did special exercises, all thorough flight training to build up his arms and wrists.

On August 30, 1943, Bob graduated from flight training and was commissioned a second lieutenant, with his mother having come to Florida to attend the ceremony. Tobi recalls meeting Bob's mother and watching as she proudly pinned the wings on her son's uniform. "Bob wanted to fly a fighter, he wanted that fighter to be a P-47 and he wanted to fly it in the Pacific theater," Tobi said.

In September of 1943, Bob and Fred were granted a 10-day leave to await assignment overseas. When he got home on leave, he found his parents were delighted with his accomplishment. For Walter, Bob winning his wings was the kind of career achievement he'd always had in mind for his eldest son. But he suggested that Bob go to Europe and fly a P-51.

"No, dad," Bob replied. "The war in Europe will be over soon. I'm going to the Pacific." Young Gill was most impressed with Bob's dress uniform. "Gabardine trousers, shiny brown shoes, starched khaki shirt with a brown olive tie and his officer bars," Gill remembers. "Wow, my big brother." There were visits with family and friends at home and the pharmacy, and soon the leave was over. Gill went with Bob to the train station.

"I have vivid memories of that," Gill says. "It was a beautiful day. Bob and I were standing outside, and some soldiers came by and saluted him. He returned the salutes, but then he took me to a less exposed area, and the saluting stopped." The train arrived. Bob boarded and waved goodbye. Gill would never see him again.

MEET THE ACCUSED

By January 1948, the war had been over for two and a half years, and Bob Thorpe's executioners had been mustered out of the Imperial Navy and returned to their homes in Japan. Living conditions were grim in the war-ravaged county. Shortages of food, fuel, and most other necessities intensified the hardship of a bitterly cold winter with snow deep in the rural communities and northern cities.

However, mitigating all of these hardships was the astonishment of the people at the calm, almost benevolent attitude and behavior of the arriving Americans. Conditioned by years of propaganda by the wartime government to expect savage, murderous occupation, the Japanese were confounded and relieved by the highly successful efforts of the MacArthur government to establish first civic and social order and then the beginnings of economic stability and development.

The Japanese did realize, however, that some retribution was coming. They had witnessed the trials and punishment of the senior military officials who had been judged to be war criminals. Justice for lower-ranking military personnel who had been discovered to have violated the rules of war had begun in the fall of 1947. It was on January 22, 1948, that notice of charges for the torture and murder of Lieutenant Robert Thorpe arrived at home of Yutaka Odazawa in Shirasawamura, a farming community in hill country 150 miles northwest of Tokyo. Crops in the area had been devastated in September by flooding from typhoon rains. What residents had feared would be a challenging, hungry winter now threatened actual starvation.

Odazawa had begun farming a three-acre plot of family-owned land when he had arrived back in the community in the summer of 1946. He was supporting a family consisting of his wife and seven-year-old son, and his bedridden mother. His mother had been severely ill since 1924, and Odazawa, then 14 years old, had begun farming to support her and a younger brother. Two older sisters had married and left the area and were unable to help.

In 1929 Odazawa had joined the Navy, apparently motivated by the promise of a somewhat better income than he could earn by farming. His civilian education had ended with primary schooling, but in the Navy, he had been able to go to gunnery school. There he learned a specialty that eventually led to his promotion to the rank of lieutenant junior grade. Along with the income, officer status earned Odazawa some prestige when he returned on leave to Shirasawamura. “He would tell me about his Navy life,” recalled his uncle, Juzaboro Matsui, proudly. “He was always performing patriotic duties honestly and conscientiously. I used to feel secure in his thorough, military spirit.”

Since his return, Odazawa had earned community respect and gratitude working as a volunteer in the village office. This work consisted mainly of distributing the meager relief supplies that were then arriving in the countryside to the poorest of the villagers and repatriates from overseas. The January summons startled and terrified the Odazawa household. Since the crop failure four months before, they didn’t know how to get through the winter. What would they do now with their breadwinner in prison?

Although he was aware of his impending arrest, Tsunehiko Yamamato continued his teaching duties at the Inatori Higher School in Shizuoka until the day before he was imprisoned. Today, Inatori is a modern five-story facility serving some 3,000 teenagers. In 1948 it was a far smaller school in an old but well-maintained building, dedicated to vocational and some college preparatory training.

Like Odazawa, Yamamato’s interests were in agriculture but as an educator rather than a farmer. He had earned his degree and teaching credentials before the war at the Tokyo Agricultural College. His choosing a teaching career was no surprise to his family since both of his parents were educators. His father had taught English at a middle school for 20 years until his retirement just before the war.

After returning to Japan in late 1946, Yomamato worked as a temporary employee for the Nippon Agricultural Association in Tokyo. He made a good enough impression on Shiro Mori, the association director, to be recommended as an agriculture teacher at Inatori. Mori also recalled that Yomamato’s curriculum for his students ranged well beyond agriculture into politics and political philosophy. “I’d often see books on his desk with titles like ‘What is Democracy?’ and ‘Protection of Liberalism,’” he said.

Kaoru Okuma’s arrest startled the employees at the Satake Works in Hiroshima, where he had been working as an engineering manager for more than a year. Today, as the Dalian Satake Chemical Equipment Co., Ltd., the company manufacturers chemical production equipment in facilities in China, Taiwan, and Korea, as well as Japan. In 1947, Satake was a struggling one-plant operation like most Japanese manufacturers at the time, and the employees believed that they owed a lot of what was being accomplished to Okuma's "strenuous services." He had been well prepared for the position. After graduating from middle school at age 17, he had gone directly to the Imperial Navy's rigorous engineering school. Graduating high in his class, he was fast-tracked to the rank of Lt. Commander at age 28.

Okuma was a brilliant engineer. Why he had entered the military rather than attending a prestigious private university, for which he was certainly qualified, is unclear. The record mentions "family reasons," which probably means financial problems. But just prior to the Pacific war, he cemented his connections with the educated classes by his marriage to a graduate of the Hiroshima College for Women.

At age 46 and a captain, Kiychisa Noto was the oldest and the highest-ranking of the accused men. He was a career naval officer, having graduated from the Officers' Training School in 1920. His service had been at sea and ashore and had included several years at the Imperial Navy headquarters in Tokyo. Noto had already been sentenced to 20 years at hard labor by an Australian military tribunal for the execution of two Australian fliers on Kairiru Island in 1945. He was released from prison in Rabaul to stand trial for Thorpe's execution with the other four defendants on June 22, 1948.

The men had been sentenced for only a few days when impassioned petitions for clemency began arriving at the War Crimes Administration Division of the U.S. Eighth Army's Judge Advocate Section. They came from families, friends, and entire communities, and organization staff. Most acknowledged the heinousness of the alleged crimes. "Japan unreservedly deserves to be blamed for her acts of atrocity during the war," wrote one of Kaoru Okuma's family members. "I have profound sympathy for the victims of the atrocities, as well as to the bereaved families," wrote another. Many referred to what they learned about what had happened to Bob Thorpe as "a horrible war crime."

Some expressed their disbelief that their loved ones could have done such a thing. "I cannot convince myself that he committed such a crime. It must have been a condition of inevitability in the whirlpool of war," wrote Noto's wife. "I cannot persuade myself to believe that such a democratic person, who had been loved and respected by his fellow teachers, students, students' parents, and others committed such a horrible crime," insisted a teacher colleague of Yamamoto. Their arguments for leniency often centered on the rigidity of the Imperial Military command structure. They cited the tradition of emperor worship and the consequent requirement that every order from a military superior had to be obeyed without question. They noted how this requirement was repeated every morning at the roll call of every military unit in the so-called "recitation of regulations."

Odazawa, the swinger of the sword, had no alternative, according to his Uncle Jusaburo: "He had a strong sense of responsibility toward his duty. This brought about a bad result only because he carried it out in a misled war. But this was a natural obligation of a Japanese subject. Therefore, I do not hesitate to say that he had no option but to take that course at that time." Jusaboro, and all the rest pleaded that the War Crimes Administration look beyond these robotic actions of the accursed and consider their humane and often self-sacrificing before and since the war. For Odazawa these involved his selfless dedication to meeting the special needs of his family and his volunteer services in community charities.

For the highly educated Tomamato and Okuma, the defenders cited interests and activities that suggested or even proved that, far from being brutal military robots, they embodied qualities that could lead to a better Japan and a better world. Tomamato sought to educate his students on democracy and personal freedom as well as agriculture. His friend Mori suggested that he had taken considerable risks in questioning Imperial authority before, as well as after, the war.

Okuma comes across in his defenders' petitions as a man struggling with his military obligation while strongly at odds with the System. An aunt of his wife recalled an incident when Okuma was at home on leave. Somehow he had met a common sailor from his unit who was in the city and had nowhere to stay. Okuma insisted the man use a spare bedroom in his home. What makes this remarkable is the vast separation between officers and enlisted personnel throughout the Japanese military. This kind of fraternization was unheard of. And Okuma went well beyond this token democratization. He was also on occasion—especially for an officer of his rank—dangerously outspoken in his questioning of, even disloyalty to, the wartime government.

"He said that he realized that this 'reckless war' would be won by the Allied Powers," recalled one petitioner, "but that he would have to go to the front and carry out his mission." Okuma's petitioners also stressed that, on the eve of his arrest, he was about to convert to Christianity. His wife's aunt, a graduate of Rumbus College, had become a Christian minister, and several other relatives had graduated from the Hiroshima Mission School. "We all, therefore, were intending to induce Kaora to become a Christian," she wrote.

The greatest irony of these petitions was the assertion that if Japan were to free itself from its aggressive, warlike past and join the community of progressive, peace-loving nations, it would need men, like those who tortured and murdered Bob Thorpe.

For the Defense

After the prosecution rested, the defense immediately made motions for findings of not guilty for all five defendants. "I think the facts of this case are relatively clear," Peters argued. "An American flier by the name of Thorpe was executed on this island. He was executed by one fell swoop of the sword. There can be no doubt in the mind of any reasonable person about what caused his death. That being true, it is impossible for anybody else to have participated in his death. Therefore, Okuma could not possibly be guilty of Specification 3 because his directing and ordering the death are covered by Specification 4. His mistreatment of the flier is covered by Specifications 1 and 2 and there is no evidence before this Commission on Specification 3.

"The evidence is so confusing as to who fired what shots, who fired first, who fired second, and which bullets hit him. We concede there is evidence that Ogawa desecrated this body, but there is no evidence that Okuma was even present at the time. All of the prosecution's evidence shows that Ogawa desecrated the body. Ogawa has tacitly admitted it by committing suicide.

"The defense asks that a finding of Not Guilty be entered for Yamamoto and Fujihira. Yamamoto did shoot him, but it was the blow by Odazawa that killed him. Fujihira shot at him, but the evidence is so confusing as to who shot first, second, or third, which bullets struck him and which didn't. There is also no evidence that Fujihira beat the prisoner.

"Odazawa willfully killed this flier, yet the testimony of the prosecution's own witness is that when Odazawa was about to behead the prisoner, he said, 'I am doing it under orders.' Odazawa had absolutely no control over what he was doing. He was ordered by Okuma on the orders of Admiral Sato and Captain Noto to execute this flier.

"It is considered appropriate to mention that in all cases where there is conflicting testimony, it is within the province of the Commission deciding the facts to weigh the testimony according to its value, accept that part which it considers of value and reject the remainder," Peters said.

Peters also cited a ruling that a Japanese lance corporal and sergeant major did not violate the customs of war because they were following the order of their commanding officer (*United States of America* vs. *Minoru Kato, 2nd Lt., et al*, December 28, 1946.)

Peters also reminded the Commission of the conditions on Kairiru Island in May and June of 1944.

"They were being bombed daily. They had an air raid while discussing Lt. Thorpe's capture. Their communications were entirely cut off, and the defenses were so bad that Fujihara had to come across there at night in a canoe from the other island. They were afraid to come out in a rowboat during the daytime. The Japanese were licked, and they knew it. They were fighting a rear action, a defense action. These few men remained on Wewak to keep it from falling into Allied hands. Suppose you had been one of those men on that island at that time. Do you think you could reason things out as you are reasoning them out here today and will tomorrow? This is war. They had to do what they thought best at that time.

"Noto, in his statement, tells you about the food conditions. They were having a hard time feeding themselves, let alone feeding another prisoner of war who had been absolutely of no benefit to them. This is probably the reason why Admiral Sato gave the order to have him executed."

Peters also accused the prosecution of "blowing hot and cold" throughout the trial.

"They have not advanced one theory and stuck to one theory. They have persistently said no, Noto didn't get an order from Sato. Then they turned right around and said, 'Noto is guilty for having transmitted Sato's order to Okuma.'

"Since Noto pleaded guilty to the charges against him, the Commission has no choice but to sentence him. He is already under a sentence of 20 years. I am asking you when you return your verdict that you specify the sentence shall run concurrently and not consecutively."

Peters acknowledged that Okuma struck the prisoner during the interrogation. He also agreed that Okuma gave permission for others to beat the prisoner.

"Captain Noto ordered Okuma to take the prisoner down to the cemetery and have him executed. He had no choice about it.

"There was one act, and one act alone which caused the death of this flier, and that was the beheading by Odazawa. All of the testimony is to the effect that the flier was shot below the knee by somebody. The prosecution says that Fujihira shot him and hit him. Other prosecution witnesses say both Okuma and Yamamoto shot and hit him.

"There is no question about the order in which the shots were fired. Fujihira fired the first shot, Yamamoto fired the second shot, and Okuma fired the third shot. Then Odazawa, who was ordered by Okuma to perform the execution, placed the flier in a kneeling position, gave him a drink of water, and washed off his sword and the prisoner's neck.

"Odazawa honored the flier by saying, 'I have no choice. This is war. I must behead you.'

"There was no animosity shown by Odazawa for this flier. He was simply following out an order and doing it in the true Bushido spirit that is the Japanese spirit of chivalry. He was honoring this man because he was a good fighter, had been shot down, and refused to give strategic information. When Okuma ordered him to go out and execute the flier and make all of the arrangements, he had no choice," Peters argued.

"Yamamoto got his pistol because Okuma ordered him to do so. He thought the execution was to be by pistol. He fired because Okuma ordered him to do so, aiming at the prisoner's legs. Fujihara lost his nerve when he fired at the prisoner, striking the ground harmlessly.

"I have tried to summarize the facts in this case and give the Commission my interpretation. These men have been given every opportunity to present their defense. They have received as fair a trial as they possibly could. I trust that when you return your verdicts, the accused will be just as thankful for their fair trial and their fair verdicts as they have up until this time," Peters concluded.

"Mr. Peters has a tough case. I wouldn't like to be in his shoes," Rand said in his final remarks. "He did the very best he could. He did try to seize on the facts that would aid the accused. Those facts are damning against each and every accused in this case.

"Did these acts violate the Rules of Land Warfare? Did they violate the general sentiment of humanity? That, I am sure, is plain. Mr. Peters stated that when I asked for the death penalty in this case, I couldn't be serious. I would like to conclude by saying that when I asked for a death penalty for all of these accused, I was never more serious in all my life."

The Commission retired for deliberation on June 30, 1948, and reconvened on July 6, 1948, to announce its findings.

Yutaka Odazawa was found guilty of murder and was sentenced to be confined at hard labor for the rest of his life.

Naotada Fujihira was found guilty of both charges against him and was sentenced to life in prison at hard labor.

Tsunehiko Yamamoto was found guilty of the same charges and also received a life sentence.

Kaoru Okuma was found not guilty of specification 5 (allowing the desecration of Thorpe's body) but he was found guilty of the other four specifications and was sentenced to be hanged.

Kiyohisa Noto was found guilty of both charges against him and sentenced to an additional 20 years, to be served consecutively, not concurrently, to a 20-year sentence imposed by a Netherlands Military Commission for murdering three Australian prisoners of war.

The defense filed a motion for modification of sentences on behalf of all five defendants. Peters claimed that the testimony conclusively shows that the five acted on the orders of Rear-Admiral Sato, commanding officer of the Naval Force Garrison at Kairiru Island.

Peters referred to a letter from General Douglas MacArthur stating:

> "Action pursuant to order of the accused's superior or of his government, shall not constitute a defense, but may be considered in mitigation of punishment if the commission determines that justice so desires."
>
> "Obedience to authority is inbred in the Japanese soldier or sailor to an extent not found in the American military force. A member of the Japanese military, when issued an order, must treat it as if it came from the Emperor himself," Peters said.
>
> "Under the supreme command of the Emperor, the voice of the officer is the voice of the Emperor. The simple soldier is taught that disobedience even to his immediate superior is virtually disobedience to His Majesty. The five accused acted under superior orders and had no moral choice but to obey such commands."

Peters went over the sentences, one by one:

Kaoru Okuma

"The accused Okuma was sentenced to death by hanging. He was charged with beating and permitting others to beat Thorpe. Okuma pleaded guilty to these charges, and the evidence sustained the findings of the Commission as to specifications one and two.

As to the shooting of Thorpe by Okuma, there is evidence that Okuma fired one shot from his pistol at the legs of Thorpe but missed.

As to the charge that Okuma ordered, caused, directed, and permitted the unlawful killing of Thorpe, the evidence proves beyond all doubt that Okuma acted in accordance with superior orders.

Okuma was guilty of slapping the prisoner of war, ordering and permitting others to mistreat the prisoner, assault with a dangerous weapon, and being present at the scene of execution. None of these constitute a capital crime.

The offenses committed do not justify other than imprisonment for a term of years."

Kiyohisa Noto

"Noto pleaded guilty to unlawfully ordering, directing, and permitting the unlawful killing of Thorpe.

But the evidence proved that Noto was ordered by his commanding officer, Rear Admiral Sato, to have the prisoner of war disposed of.

Noto knew nothing of the beating of or firing at Thorpe, and he was not present at the execution site. He committed no crime other than being chief of staff to Admiral Sato. He was a mere channel of communication, just a messenger. He is deserving of no punishment whatsoever.

Noto had been tried and convicted of a war crime and sentenced to imprisonment for 20 years at hard labor. The conviction was in no way connected with Thorpe's case.

Should the Reviewing Authority hold that Noto is deserving of some punishment, it is requested that it run concurrently with the sentence he is now serving."

Yutaka Odazawa

"Odazawa was charged with one specification—the unlawful killing of Thorpe by beheading.

Odazawa was not a volunteer; he was merely complying with an order of his superior officer. There is no evidence in the entire trial record to the contrary. These mitigating circumstances should be taken into consideration. Odazawa should receive no punishment or, at most, a token punishment."

Yamamoto and Fujihira

"The evidence sustains the finding of the Commission that these accused slapped the prisoner of war.

Both Fujihira and Yamamoto were present at the execution scene, and there is evidence that they did shoot at the prisoner. Fujihira fired but one shot and purposely missed. Yamamto fired twice, one shot hitting the prisoner below the knees. The evidence shows that the two accused fired their pistols because they were ordered to do so by Okuma. Okuma was superior to Fujihira and Yamamoto, and the two were following the order of a superior officer. Yamamoto is guilty of assault with intent to do bodily harm. Fujihira, having purposely missed, is only guilty of assault. Neither of the accused deserved so harsh a sentence as life imprisonment."

In his summary, Peters asked the reviewing authority to disapprove and modify the sentences imposed against all of the accused so that they will "receive a just and reasonable sentence commensurate with the degree of guilt." On February 11, 1949, Lt. Col. F. R. Undritz, the Assistant Staff Judge Advocate, U.S. Eighth Army, upheld the guilty verdicts but reduced the penalties of all of the accused with the following explanations:

Okuma

The accused well knew that orders had been issued for the execution of the flier before he interrogated him. He received no orders to beat the prisoner of war, yet at the interrogation, he struck him and invited others present to do likewise. He was present and in charge while the prisoner of war was beaten with hands, fists, and wooden clubs about the face and body.

After the interrogation, when he took the prisoner of war out to be executed, he further displayed his fiendish nature by personally firing live ammunition at him and permitting and directing others likewise to torture him. Then he ordered the decapitation.

The Commission sentenced the accused to death by hanging. Whereas capital punishment might well be justified for the heinous crimes the accused committed, it is believed that as a matter of policy, it should be reserved for those commanders who at the time of taking the life of another are in a position to exercise their power of command independently of any compulsion from higher authority.

The accused was ordered to execute the prisoner of war by his superior officer. He had no moral choice but to obey.

For this reason, it is recommended that the death sentence be commuted to confinement at hard labor for life.

Yamamoto and Fujihira

These accused participated in the beating of the prisoner of war at the interrogation. Later they were eager participants in the killing of the prisoner of war by firing their pistols at him before the decapitation. However, neither was in charge of the interrogation or the execution. They were encouraged to participate by Okuma, the officer in charge. Their culpability is not as great as that of Okuma, but nevertheless, justice demands they be severely punished. The Commission sentenced each of these accused to confinement at hard labor for life. It is believed a sentence of twenty years each is adequate punishment for the crimes they committed, and it is recommended that their sentences be reduced accordingly.

Odazawa

This accused was ordered to decapitate the flyer. He had no moral choice but to obey. He felt he had to comply with his orders.

However, his apparent consent to and encouragement of the barbarous acts committed by his associates upon the helpless victim whose life he was about to snuff out disclose a malignant nature.

His culpability is not as great as that of those who actually did the firing.

The Commission sentenced the accused to confinement at hard labor for life. It is believed that a sentence of ten years is adequate punishment for the crime he committed, and it is recommended that the sentence be reduced accordingly.

Noto

There was no maliciousness on the part of this accused.

He was the Chief of Staff of Admiral Sato and transmitted the latter's order for the execution to Okuma.

He knew the order was illegal, objected, and was overruled. He had no moral choice but to transmit the order.

The accused was previously tried by an Australian Commission and convicted of a similar offense committed at the same place.

For the offense of which the accused was convicted, he should be punished.

However, it is not believed that any good purpose will be served by imposing additional confinement.

It is recommended that the sentence be reduced to five years, and the unserved portion of confinement at hard labor be remitted.

Col. Allan R. Browne, Judge Advocate, U.S. Eighth Army, disagreed with Lt. Colonel Undritz's recommendations for the sentence reductions, starting with Captain Noto. He said that Noto's sentence of 20 years for participation in the killing of Lt. Thorpe was plainly inadequate. "Noto volunteered to Sato that he would have Okuma dispose of the prisoner and when Sato remained silent, Noto turned to Okuma and said, "Take the prisoner somewhere and do away with him any way you want to."

Other evidence indicates that Sato more or less permitted Noto to run the headquarters, Browne pointed out. "Even if it were assumed that Noto was only relaying an order of his superior, he had an obligation to see that the execution was carried out in a military manner. The evidence establishes that nothing was done toward this end. Those who tortured Thorpe would not have committed the various acts in the immediate vicinity of the headquarters without knowing that their actions were permitted. The beating and mistreatment of the prisoner at the interrogation, the pistol practice, the exaggerated mimicry of a Bushido execution, and the desecration of the body certainly indicate a field day by the participants," Browne said.

"After the war, Noto was active in cautioning the various participants to conceal the execution," Browne added. "When he was interrogated by the Australians on December 16, 1945, he stated that an airman had been captured and had died about 20 days later of malaria. He told them he was sick with malaria himself at the time and did not remember the details.

"He admitted in this trial that he had lied to the Australians, and he also stated that he had not been ill with malaria at the time. In view of his false statements, we have no reason to believe his unsupported statement that he had protested to Sato about the execution order," Browne added.

Browne said that Noto's sentence, although amounting to a life sentence at his age and life expectancy, was not excessive for his participation in the authorization of the execution. On March 1, 1949, the sentence of 20 years was approved.

Col. Browne also disagreed with the commutation of Okuma's death sentence to life imprisonment. "Okuma staged the killing, permitting those of vindictive mind to beat the flyer pre-death. He asked for volunteers to kill the victim. He authorized shooting at the prisoner for practice. His own father, in a clemency petition, says that the death sentence was justified.

Col. Browne refused any reduction of Yutaka Odazawa's life sentence. He said that Odazawa volunteered to behead Thorpe, and he was so eager to accomplish the killing that he cautioned the officers who were shooting at the victim to aim below the hips so that a fatal wound would not deprive him of his opportunity. Browne quoted from the testimony of Okuma in describing the execution:

"Then Odazawa took the prisoner by the back of the neck and pushed him to the ground in a kneeling position with his head bowed forward right at the edge of the grave. He then performed an act as though it were from a play. It was done in a contemptuous manner, and everybody laughed. Odazawa withdrew his sword from its sheath and in Japanese stated his own name, age, birthplace and told the prisoner in a loud voice 'You will go first to Paradise, and I will follow you later on.'

Odazawa then made a soldier fill a bottle with water from a stream ten meters away. He poured water first on the prisoner's neck, then on his samurai sword, all in the Bushido spirit of cleansing the soul. The prisoner was not blindfolded. Odazawa then swung his sword and chopped through the neck with one stroke so that the prisoner's head was attached by only a small shred of skin at the throat," Browne said. He recommended that the sentence of life imprisonment be approved.

Superior orders played no part in the action of Naotada Fujihara, Browne charged. "He showed his malice by beating the bound victim. He was sadistic and murderous. The life sentence, though inadequate, should be approved since it cannot be increased," Browne said.

The actions of Tsunehiko Yamamoto paralleled those of Fujihira,

Browne said. "He was an eager volunteer. He announced that he was practicing and told the prisoner he would kill him. He advised the others to shoot below the knees. It is difficult to understand how a sentence less than the extreme penalty could have been adjudged under facts showing such a malignant spirit as that of this man," Brown said. "Since his penalty cannot be increased, it is recommended that his life sentence be upheld."

On March 1, 1949, the Commanding General, U.S. Eighth Army, approved the sentences as follows:

Lt. Cmdr. Kaoru Okuma, death.
Captain Kiyohisa Noto, 20 years in prison.
CPO Yutaka Odazawa, life in prison.
CPO Naotada Fujihara, life in prison.
Ensign Tsunehiko Yamamoto, life in prison.

Noto was returned to his Australian Prison in Rabaul, while Odazawa, Fujihara, and Yamamoto began their life terms at Sugamo Prison. Okuma was sent to the "death row" section of Sugamo Prison to await execution.

The Asian Green Mile

Sugamo Prison had just one gallows when the Americans took over the prison but motivated by the hundreds of death sentences meted out to convicted war criminals, the capacity was expanded so that four prisoners could be executed at the same time. Considering Japan's overall brutality, the Americans were surprised when they learned that the Japanese had come up with a more humane way to hang prisoners. A cone-shaped wooden block fitted above the noose rendered the prisoner unconscious a milli-second before his neck was broken. These blocks were used during the execution of Japanese war criminals at Sugamo prison.

The first prisoner to be executed by the Americans at Sugamo, Lt. Kei Yuri, was convicted of allowing subordinates to abuse and torture prisoners and for executing prisoners on his own. The procedure used to execute Yuri on April 26, 1946, became standard for all executions at Sugamo. An old formula, developed by the English for use in Ireland, Scotland, India, and other parts of the British Empire, was used at Sugamo. Yuri's weight, height, health, age, and physical condition were considered to determine how far he would have to drop for his neck to be broken.

Yuri was informed of the date and time of his execution twenty-four hours in advance. He was asked if he had any last requests concerning the disposition of last letters, will, or personal belongings to his family.

Yuri was allowed to attend services in the chapel, which had been provided a Buddhist shrine with a Buddhist priest in attendance. Thirty minutes before the execution, he was cuffed to a body belt that went from front to back and between his legs. Fifteen minutes later, he walked into the chapel and lit incense sticks. The priest held a cup of ceremonial wine to Yuri's lips to conclude the ceremony.

He left the chapel and walked to the gallows chanting Namu-Amida-Butsu, a Buddhist prayer. Witnesses sat in a low, narrow platform opposite an elevated deck over which hung five ropes, each ending in a noose. Yuri had to be assisted up the 13 steps leading to the execution platform because the body belt made walking difficult. He walked to the first trapdoor, and a black hood was placed over his head as the ropes were adjusted and aligned with the noose coil and cone on the left side of his head.

The chief executioner called to the officer in charge that the prisoner was prepared for execution. As soon as the officer shouted "proceed," the trapdoor sprung open with a sound similar to a rifle shot. The body dangled for a few minutes, then a doctor listened with a stethoscope and called out, "I declare this man dead." The body was removed immediately, and the corpse was fingerprinted, placed in a wooden coffin, and taken to be cremated. Yuri's ashes were scattered at sea, so there could be no enshrinement by the family or the Japanese government.

During the next six months, four other prisoners were executed for killing POWs, including Isao Fukuhara on August 9, 1946; Kaichi Hirate, on August 23, 1946; Masadi Mabuchi, on September 6, 1946, and Uichi Ikegami on February 14, 1947. All of the executions were conducted at night, usually just after midnight. The first multiple executions at Sugamo occurred on July 1, 1948, one week before Kari Okuma was placed on death row, the north end of the cellblock at Sugamo. Hajime Honda, Sadamu Motokawa, Matsukkichi Muta, Sadamu Takeda, Yoschichi Takagi, Iju Sugasawa, Kazumoto Suematsu, and Masakatsui Hozumi were all convicted of murdering or allowing subordinates to murder POWs.

Although the gallows had five trap doors, only four prisoners were executed at a time. They were led to each of the first four trapdoors, the nooses were adjusted, and black hoods placed over their heads. The hangman announced that the prisoners were ready for execution, the officer screamed "proceed," and the four traps were sprung. After the four bodies were removed, the next four were led in. Ten prisoners were awaiting execution when Okuma arrived at Sugamo Prison. First Lieutentant Junsaburo Toshino was convicted of causing the death of more than thirty American and Allied POWs by refusing to restrain the military under his control from shooting them. He also ordered subordinates to kill fifteen sick prisoners.

Katutane Aihara was convicted of killing and decapitating more than twenty American prisoners while transferring them from Manilla to Moji, Japan. Chief Petty Officer Sachio Egawa was found guilty of murdering two prisoners while he was a guard at Fukuaka Prisoner of War Camp in Kyushu, Japan. Captain Sukeo Nakajima was found guilty of allowing subordinates to murder prisoners of war and executing prisoners of war on his own. Not all the condemned were from the military. Sadahara Hiramatsui, Harumi Kawate Tonatsu Kimura, Kunio Yoshizawa, Masao Michishita and Takuji Murakami were all convicted of murdering prisoners while working as civilian guards at POW camps. They were all executed on August 18, 1948.

Perhaps the most notorious of Okuma's cellmates, a medical doctor by the name of Hisakichi Toshida, had his death sentence commuted to life imprisonment. Toshida had been convicted of causing the deaths of four American prisoners of war and contributing to other deaths through medical experimentation. Toshida injected prisoners with soybean milk resulting in violent and painful deaths. Shortly after being placed on death row, Toshida became catatonic and had to be fed a liquid diet through his nose each day. Days after his sentence was commuted, Toshida regained his appetite and even asked for his medical books. He was paroled in the general amnesty in 1955 and reportedly opened a private medical practice in Tokyo.

Toshida was not the only Japanese doctor convicted of experimenting and killing prisoners of war. Five doctors were sentenced to death after being found guilty of mutilating, dissecting, and removing parts of the bodies of eight American POWs. They included Goichi Hirako, Yoshiol Mori, Yoshinao Sato, Tomoki Tashiro and Katsuya Yakamura. The incident, known as the "Kyushu University vivisection case," drew fire from the Japanese medical community, with the head of the leading medical school in Tokyo, Kenji Yoshido, stating, "Before the eyes of the world, I feel thoroughly ashamed for this disgraceful conduct of our countrymen. We desire that they be dealt with severely."

His recommendation was ignored as all five doctors had their sentences commuted to life in prison, and all were released within eight years. One other condemned prisoner escaped Sugamo's gallows. Colonel Satoshi Oie had been tried in Manila and sentenced to death by firing squad. He had returned to Sugamo to testify at war crime trials at Yokohama. On October 23, 1948, he was removed from Sugamo and placed in a bus to be transported to a nearby firing range. To the amazement of his guards, Oie fell asleep in the bus and had to be awakened upon his arrival at the execution site. He thanked everyone involved, including the six-man firing squad, walked calmly to a post, and was executed.

Things changed dramatically on death row with the arrival of the seven Class A prisoners on November 28, 1948, including Kenji Doihara, Baron Koki Hirota, Seishiro Itagahi, Heitaro Kimura, Iwane Matsui, Akira Muto, and Shigenori Tojo. Probably because of the successful suicide of Ogawa, security at Sugamo bordered on paranoia. The teeth of the condemned were X-rayed for poison implants, probably influenced by the suicide of Hermann Goring, who ingested potassium cyanide two hours before his execution. The prisoners were also forced to stand naked, facing a wall, while their cells were searched. They were watched at all times while shaving or showering. They could not go anywhere unless handcuffed to a guard. Even then, an officer would walk behind the pair.

Their cells were lit around the clock, and the prisoners were not allowed privacy at any time. They had to have their faces and hands uncovered and in full view of guards who sat outside each cell twenty-four hours a day. Okuma probably never saw any of the seven Class A prisoners because they were kept segregated, even on death row.

General MacArthur barred all photographs of the executions because they "would violate all sense of decency." On December 21, 1948, the seven prisoners were brought, one at a time, to the chaplain's office where Colonel Morris C. Handwerk, the prison commandant, informed them they would be executed in two days. With the exception of Hirota, the prisoners accepted the news calmly. Tojo was extremely pleased since he feared that they might be executed in another country.

Tojo also acted as a spokesman for the group concerning their last meal. They dined on rice, miso soup, broiled fish, and rice wine. They spent their final day writing farewell letters and in prayer with Dr. Shinsho Hanayama, the prison's Buddhist priest, who attended most of the executions at Sugamo.

Tojo wrote personal letters to his family, and then wrote a letter asking Dr. Hanayama to make public after his execution. He, like the other prisoners, gave Hanayama hair, nail clippings, glasses and even false teeth to be given to his family. An incident involving false teeth created serious problems for an American dentist. Dr. George C. Foster, a naval oral surgeon, was assigned to Sugamo Prison as chief of dental surgery. When he repaired Tojo's dental plate, he engraved the words "Remember Pearl Harbor" in Morse code on the upper dentures. Even Tojo thought the prank was funny, the Navy brass did not agree and removed Foster from his post.

At 11:30 p.m. on Dec.22, Tojo, Doihara, Matsui, and Muto were led into the chapel where Hanayama was waiting. They lit candles, burned incense, and chanted Buddhist scripture. The executions began at 12:01 a,m. on December 23, 1948. Seconds after midnight, Doihara, Tojo, Muto, and Matsui walked to the entrance of the gallows. Tojo asked Matsi to lead them in their final "Banzai." All four men turned in the direction of the Imperial Palace and shouted "Banzai" three times. Then they mounted the platform and walked to each of the four trapdoors. Black hoods were placed over their heads, and the four trapdoors sprung open immediately after the chief executioner ordered: "Proceed."

Doihara was pronounced dead at 12:07, Tojo at 12:10, Muto at 12:11, and Matsui at 12:13. Immediately after the bodies were removed, Itagaki, Hirota, and Kimura were led to the gallows. This time there was no Banzais. Itagaki was pronounced dead at 12:32, Hirota at 12:34, and Kimura at 12:35. The bodies were removed to a heavily guarded crematorium where they were reduced to ashes, then scattered to the winds. On Christmas Eve, MacArthur announced the executions of all seven Class-A war criminals held in Japan. The next mass execution was held on February 12, 1949, when eight prisoners were hanged for murdering POWs, including Yasutosi Mizuguchi, Kuratano Hirano, Yoshitako Kawane, Hideo Ishizaki, Kikuo Tomioka, Zentaro Wantanabe, Masao Kataoka, and Shoji Ito.

On May 28, 1949, exactly five years to the day when he supervised the execution of Robert Thorpe, Kaoru Okuma was executed at Sugamo. He had spent ten months on death row, a relatively long time for a class "B" war criminal. His stay on death row may have been based on the number of petitions filed on his behalf. Perhaps MacArthur was more impressed by the fact that Kaoru Okuma's father, Ichi Okuma, refused to sign a clemency petition after learning about his son's involvement with the torture and murder of Robert

Thorpe. There is no record indicating whether Kaoru Okuma went to his death with a Christian or Buddhist priest at his side.

Akiyama Yonesaku, Masaji Sekihara, Akira Yanagezawa, and Hiroshi Obinata were hanged on August 20, 1949, for torturing and murdering POWs. The last executions at Sugamo were held on April 7, 1950, when Muneo Enomoto, Otohiko Inoue, Katsutaro Inoue, Yasumasa Taguchi, Tadakuni Narisako, Matsuo Fujinaka, and Minoru Makuda were hanged for torturing and murdering POWs.

Sugamo Prison was demolished in 1971 and replaced with a shopping complex named "Sunshine City." A large stone with an engraved message marks the location of the prison gallows:

"Pray for Eternal Peace."

A Love Story in the Middle of a War

No one gave me more help in researching the book about the 39th Fighter Squadron than Mary Morgan Martin. Her father, George Morgan, was a pilot with the 39th Fighter Squadron in the early days of WWII. Her mother, Mary, was an Army nurse stationed in Australia in 1943 where she met Lt. Morgan while he was on leave.

On Thanksgiving weekend, 1942, George, with fellow pilots, came out to the 105th General Hospital in Australia to a dance. When George saw Mary he asked Patty Knapp, an army nurse soon to be married to George's friend, Captain Jack C. Mankin, if she would introduce him to Mary.

She did and they danced many dances together that night. Several days later, George called Mary and asked if she would come to a picnic the pilots were planning the following Sunday. She said yes. Mary made a notation in her diary: "George had on suntan trousers, a white T-shirt and a suntan baseball cap on the back of his head. I like what I see—he's cute."

George was back in Australia for Christmas 1942, and spent it with Mary. The letters between Mary and George started as casual, but they soon moved into the "love" stage. George sent the following letter to Mary on March 13, 1943.

Dear Mary:
Today I received your letters written on the 13th and 22nd of February. It was the frst mail I've received up here. I still have that quart of rum you gave me for Christmas. I'm saving it for a special occasion. I will let you know when I drink it. I don't think I could have enjoyed myself more while I was down there. What I'm trying to say is just being with you was fun for me. I only hope you miss me half as much as I do you.
Love,
George

In a letter to her father, Mary told her father about meeting an Air Force pilot named George.

Dear Dad:
George came down on leave on July 3rd (1943). He came to Gatton to spend his leave with me. The doctors let George have a room in their barracks. I was working, but I did get one day off while George was here which we spent in Ipswich. When I got off duty each day, we spent time together—bike riding, picnics, time in the nurses' reception lounge. If there was a dance, we danced.
Love,
Mary

It was after George returned from his July leave that he crash-landed and was reported missing in action on July 24, 1943. He had developed engine trouble while on a mission and had to land on a remote beach. Fortunately, he was not injured and was taken in by a missionary couple. Three days later, he was flying missions again.

From his letters to both his mother and Mary, it was obvious he could not tell them about the crash due to censorship of the outgoing mail. His parents learned something had happened when a telegram arrived from George telling them to "ignore all reports—am well and safe." A few days later, they received an official telegram stating that George was missing in action.

Mary learned about the episode through a letter hand-delivered by a friend of George's who was going on leave in Australia.

July 24, 1943

Dear Mary:
Eugene McGuire came in this afternoon so I am going to send this letter down by him. I had hoped you wouldn't hear of my "little" experience until you knew I was all right. It was the closest call I ever had. When I had my motor cut out, I was directly over Madang. I had to fly almost 2½ hours on a single-engine before it started to get dark. Near the place I crash-landed was a mission run by a middle-aged couple form Samoa. As you heard, they treated me very well. I couldn't make it all the way back here because of the weather. There were four of us that started out and one of the fellows, Lt. James Steele was lost in the weather and we haven't heard from him since.

The weather has been very bad, and it's always a problem of where to land when we return from a mission. Have you started knitting my red socks yet? Red is easy to keep up with. Be good and I will keep on trying to be the oldest pilot.
Love,
George

Nothing was known about Lt. Steele's fate until Japanese soldiers were questioned about him after the war. Five Japanese soldiers admitted bayoneting him to death in March of 1945.

On Nov. 8, 1943, Lt. Morgan was awarded an Air Medal for operational flight missions from May to September 1943. The citation is as follows:

For heroism in flight and exceptional and outstanding accomplishment in the face of great danger above and beyond the line of duty. These operations consisted of over 50 missions including escorting bombers and transport, aircraft, interception and attack missions and patrol and reconnaissance flights. In the course of these operations, strafing and bombing attacks were made from dangerously low altitudes, destroying and damaging enemy installations and equipment.

The depth of the romance is revealed in this letter George sent to Mary on May 11, 1944:

My Dearest
This is one letter I hate to write; I think you know why. My orders to go home were here when I arrived. I tried to get down there, but I couldn't get in touch with any of the fellows that could've helped me. I reported in thinking I might still be able to get down, but they tell me I must catch a plane tonight. If I refuse it, I don't know what would happen. I can't help but hope you will be home soon. There are times when I think I was wrong in not marrying you over here. Mary, I want you to know and remember, I love you very much. I told you how I felt when I as down there—as if I was

coming home and it was a wonderful feeling. Darling, there is very little light so I'm going to have to close. I'll write first chance I get. George

After 15 months and 149 missions, Captain George Morgan arrived back in the States on May 13, 1944. On July 20, 1944, Lt,. Mary Scott reported to Letterman General Hospital in San Francisco as a patient. She had become anemic and required hospitalization before resuming her military duties. On September 6, 1944 Captain George Morgan and Lt. Mary Scott were married at Ephrata AAB, Washington.

Just as they were setting up housekeeping in California, George received a letter ordering him to report to the commanding general, Fifth Air Force in the Pacific. Mary was pregnant when George was assigned to the 40th Air Force Squadron in the Philippines.

"I really like my P-51. It's my idea of a fighter—it's lighter and plenty fast but tricky on landing," he wrote to Mary. He assured her that the combat assignments were not much to worry about. "It's nearly all ground support, which is interesting but not dangerous."

Ground support was the squadrons mission on May 31, 1945. They were to strafe and bomb Japanese positions which were holding up the American advance. As George made his strafing run, his plane was hit by small-arms fire. He immediately pulled up, radioing to flight mates that he would land at Lingayen, which was closer than Clark, their home base.

When his damaged engine began running better, he radioed that he would try to get back to Clark. His wingman saw him suddenly turn towards Lingayen again. George radioed that the plane was not running right, and he had to get down. A few minutes later, he said he would be bailing out at 5,000 feet. His wingman watched him release the canopy but never saw his chute open.

When Captain Morgan's body was recovered, the squadron doctor reported that large cuts on the side off his body indicated that he had been hit by the stabilizer while bailing out.

Fifteen days later a telegram reached Mary:

The Secretary of War desires me to express his deep regret that your husband, Captain George E. Morgan, was killed in action on Luzon on May 31, 1945.

The starkness of the telegram stands in contrast to the poignant tragedy of George Morgan's death. His many letters to Mary and his family celebrated his joy at being an expectant father and of the life he and Mary planned together. His death, coming less than three months before the war ended, devastated them all.

Mary was born three months after her father was killed in action.

After her mother died, Mary Martin found a poem in her mother's desk. Yellowed with age, it had been cut out of a newspaper. The title is "Missing Him," and the author is listed as anonymous.

Missing Him
Missing him is all the time
Weeping
Ranting
Raving
Screaming
Shaking fist at God
Are less
But missing him is all the time.
Tears fall more gently now
From time to time
Dripping one after other
From eyes to chin.
A torrent, now and then
But missing him is all the time.
The wishes, prayers and fervent hope
That this might not be true
Come still.
But not as often now.
and with deep knowledge of the truth
Despite the wrong.
And missing him is all the time.
Life now, is altered
Very changed from what it was

No going backward, only forward.
Missing him and moving toward the future all alone
But not alone
Remembering him is all the time.

"THEY ALSO SERVE WHO STAND AND WAIT"
— John Milton

"The 39th Fighter Squadron was truly a band of brothers. Pilots, crew chiefs, ordinance, administration, medical and cooks turned it into a premier fighting force," Lt. Jack Frost told me when I interviewed him in July 2009. "We pilots got airplanes that performed, our guns and bombs worked and, our cooks made our food palatable, even though they had little to work with," Frost added.

The closeness between enlisted personnel and officers of the 39th FS started with an incident aboard the SS *Ancon*, which took the squadron to Australia in April of 1942. The ship had accommodations for about 200 people, but it was now loaded with 1,500 officers and enlisted personnel. Everyone was scrambling for bunk space and food arrangements. Lt. Frank Royal, the new CO of the 39th, called his pilots together and delivered a message that sustained the squadron through good and bad times. "We all need a place to sleep and food to eat, but our enlisted troops are lodged in the hold of this ship, and their accommodations are far worse than ours. From this point on, we will put the welfare of our enlisted crewmen first and see to it that they have a bed and food before we seek our own comfort. After all, we are headed for combat in this war, and the dedication of these men will do much to keep us alive."

"The enlisted men got the message loud and clear, and a bond, already strong, was strengthened," according to Sgt. Roy Seher, one of those untrained, warm bodies who joined the 39th when the squadron was put together in Townville, Australia, in April 1942. "I was not a member of the 39th when Col. Royal delivered that message, but I was told about it the first day I reported for duty. The influence of that message had a ripple effect and stayed with the squadron long after Col. Royal and those early P-39 pilots completed their tour and were sent home," Seher said.

"I always felt that Lady Luck smiled on me that first day with the 39th," Seher said in an interview on July 9, 2008. "We were loaded into a truck and hauled to the flight line. Orders were given, that at each revetment stop, one of us was to unload and contact the crew chief of that airplane. When my turn came, I hopped over the tailgate, walked toward the P-39 Airacobra, and came face to face with Sgt. Otto Neumann, crew chief of the CO's plane. Otto was one of those people with a firm opinion on just about everything. He could be abrasive, but he was a well-trained airplane mechanic and was willing to teach me.

"Otto hammered me with the finer points. He emphasized that you must look and analyze what you see. There's a scuffed tire, but how serious is it? That fluid streak. Is it coolant or oil? Where is it coming from? You have to know!

"During early morning run-up, the instrument readings tell you much about the health of the plane. Know what they are supposed to read and what they read now. Any deviation is a warning, and you must know why. You are entrusted with a man's life here. There is no room for screw-ups or being slipshod with any work," Neumann warned. Neumann was typical of the crew chiefs in those early days of the 39th. They watched with pride as their planes took off in the early morning sun, then waited nervously for them to return.

Lt. Lew Lockhart explained those feelings during a 2008 interview. "It was challenging when we lost a plane. The crew would stand waiting for the missing plane, hoping to see or hear a distant engine. When the plane did not appear, they waited for the debriefing. It was one thing to lose a pilot to enemy aircraft or ground fire. When the plane went missing, it affected his ground crew," Lockhart said.

"I remember the flight on May 27, 1944, when Bob Thorpe was listed as missing. "Fifteen other P-47s returned from that mission. Not one of them reported seeing Bob's plane in trouble. That's when a ground crew starts second-guessing itself. Did they overlook a possible mechanical problem? Was an error made in arming the plane? Did the gun jam or a fuel tank fail to release?" The pilots never lost faith or confidence in the men who kept their planes running in all sorts of weather and flying conditions–a decision by Capt. Lee Grosshuesch, CO of the 39th in 1944, illustrates this trust.

"In all of our flight training, we were taught to run up the engine before takeoff, check each magneto, and only then go onto the runway and take off. We were on Morotai Island, flying missions over the Philippines and Borneo, sometimes stretching our range to the limit. We would come back with only fifteen minutes of fuel and sometimes dangerously less. Every gallon of fuel was precious, and it bothered me that we used so much fuel in the magnetos check. We had a meeting of all the pilots and crew chiefs and put a new rule in place. Starting the next morning, the crew chiefs would be responsible for the run-up and mag checks. They would then shut down and top off the tank.

"The pilots would taxi out to the takeoff position. There was no hesitation by either the pilots or the crew chief to accept this transfer of responsibility. I felt that we trusted our crews with every other vital procedure. We knew that when we turned on the gun switch and pulled the trigger, all eight guns would fire. When we dropped our auxiliary gas tanks before going into a dogfight, we had faith they would release. So why shouldn't the ground crew be entrusted to check the mags? We were never let down. Our trust paid off big," Grosshuesch said.

"The runway on Morotai was on sand, and the pierced planking tended to roll up in front of the wheels, so takeoff was touchy. During the next one-month period, the other two squadrons lost a total of 25 airplanes, almost all on takeoff. During that same period, we never even had an engine falter. We also extended our range to targets over 800 miles away, allowing ourselves more time for bombing and strafing," he said. The change in the preflight protocol was seen as a great compliment and a morale builder to the ground crews.

The perfect record was broken when Lt. Fred Tobi crashed on takeoff in November of 1944. There were fifteen planes on the mission, and Tobi was taking off last and alone. He was in immediate trouble with his wing wobbling, first to the left, then to the right. Fighting it all the way, Tobi dropped both mounted fuel tanks relieving his plane of nearly 2,000 pounds of weight. It did not help. Nearing the end of the runway, the plane mushed down, the prop hit, and the plane bellied in, tearing through stumps and piles of dirt left from the building of the runway. The two fuel tanks slid along the ground following the wreckage, and there was a huge explosion. Everyone thought the pilot had to be dead, except Tobi's crew chief, Bucky Schneider, who was sitting in a jeep watching the takeoff. Schneider drove right into the ring of fire surrounding Tobi and got him into the jeep. Lt. Tobi was hospitalized with severe burns on his face, neck, and hands and was sent home to recover. He was not released from the hospital until 1947, after undergoing multiple operations on his face and hands.

That was not the end of the connection between Tobi and his crew chief. Tobi married in 1947 and lived in Tampa where he started his own apple distribution firm. Schneider started a Mom and Pop store in Buchanan, MI, and later turned it into a successful chain. Bucky bought a home in Sarasota, FL, close to Tobi's home in Tampa. They developed a warm friendship and shared enthusiasm for the game of golf. Bucky Schneider died in 2002 and Fred Tobi followed six years later.

The best example of the feelings between the officers of the 39th and enlisted personnel occurred after the squadron moved to Clark Field in the Philippines. Lt. Jack Frost tells the story in his own words:

"I had just returned from temporary duty as a forward air controller up in the Balete Pass, the main road to Baguio, Luzon, headquarters of the Japanese commanding general. It was a hectic week, with Banzai raids every night. I had just unloaded my field gear and was getting ready to clean up when I got a visit from four sergeants who said they had an urgent problem. "When the 39th moved from Lyngayen to Clark Field, space was provided for operations and recreational areas. The officers and the noncoms were each issued a building for recreational clubs. The officers were successful in scrounging furniture and appliances, but the cupboards were bare when the noncoms went looking for material. This was the first time the 39th was located in a civilized area, and the men needed a break from the bugs, sweat, and mud. I was known as 'Trader Jack' because of my reputation for putting deals together. My initial efforts were fruitless, but I got a tip that a huge load of lumber had been delivered to a supply warehouse. I drove up to the gate and asked the lieutenant in charge to let me check out the material in storage. He was most helpful as I surveyed clear grain Douglas fir in dimensional sizes and marine-grade plywood. I told the lieutenant that I would be back the next day to pick up what I needed. Frost said.

"I showed up the next day with some enlisted men on three two-and-a-half-ton trucks. I stopped the convoy about a half-mile from the gate and told all the enlisted men that all questions had to be directed to me. The lieutenant saluted as we drove into the supply area.

Some Filipino workers loaded the lumber on all three trucks. I had to suppress a giggle when the lieutenant asked me if I needed any nails. I told him a couple of kegs would be fine. I also loaded an 18-foot boat with a 25 h.p. Johnson Seahorse outboard motor. We were fully loaded and, on our way, making sure no one signed for anything and leaving no recognizable identity behind," Frost said.

"The noncoms unloaded everything into their empty building. About a week later, I was invited to see what was now the NCO Club. The lumber had been turned into tables and benches and a long bar with a metal top painted in aircraft enamel. About a month later, we received a visit from a team of investigators looking for lumber and various items taken from a depot without authority. Did anyone in the 39th know anything about this? Fortunately the one who answered the questions did not have to lie since he knew nothing. No one asked me anything.

"The interview was conducted in the NCO club, and, as we sat there, I had the feeling that the senior agent, sitting in one of the chairs made from the stolen lumber, knew what had happened, and he seemed to approve. 'That lumber was for General MacArthur's Headquarters,' he said as he left the club with a smile. "That departing grin, really a faint smile, let us know he understood where the lumber had gone, and it served its purpose well. It provided for an improved lifestyle that had been denied our men through circumstances and geography.

"Many people think this war was fought in leather jackets with white scarves in an area with watering places populated by luscious beauties. The fact is we departed civilization the day we left Townsville, Australia, for Port Moresby, New Guinea. Thick mud, unique wildlife, life-threatening diseases, and stone-age human beings awaited us. I didn't mention the enemy yet, because as a threat, they come lower than over-loaded airplanes and capricious weather." he explained.

"This observation is not to denigrate our contribution in stopping the enemy in his tracks. The determination of the enemy was constant and unremitting. The ground fire was deadly. We flew missions in P-47s that equated to a flight to Berlin, and after seven or eight hours came back sweat-soaked and fatigued. While we were away, the ground crews filled the time with worry and concern, addressing the chores that guaranteed a safe return of their pilots. The challenge to build a real recreation facility for these men was an itch I had to scratch," Frost concluded.

Alicia and Sarah

In January of 1972, I clutched a T-Bar with my 21-month old daughter, Alicia, between my legs as we ascended Haystack Mountain in Vermont. I agreed with my friends that Alicia was too young to tackle the upper levels of the mountain. But there was a good practical reason why she was there. The nursery would not take any child who was not fully toilet trained. Unfortunately, Alicia did have an occasional problem. By the time she was three, she was skiing most trails on the mountain. At age five, I could no longer ski with her. Later she became a ski instructor.

Her late toilet training was the only "slow" event in Alicia's life. She was one of the top students in the Old Lyme Public school system. When she was ten years old, I bought her one of the first Apple computers. The clerk explained that the purchase entitled her to 10 hours of instruction. When we got home, Alicia disappeared into her room with the computer. My warning that she should not attempt to do anything with it until she received her first lesson was ignored. I did not see Alicia for the rest of the weekend.

The instructor arrived for the first session, and within minutes he came to me. "Mr. Dooley, I'll stay if you want me to. But she knows more about this computer than I do." It was his first and last session. I smile when I think of that experience now. Alicia has worked as a senior programmer for Disney for the past 24 years.

In my closing remarks after being inducted into the Rhode Island Heritage Hall of Fame in 2018, I said, "If any Dooley deserves to be admitted to the Hall of Fame, it is my daughter Alicia." Her successful career at Disney had nothing to do with that remark. It is what she does with her nonprofit, Fuzzy Therapy, that is remarkable.

Alicia has five miniature horses trained as service animals, and they visit patients with Alzheimer's or other dementia problems at nursing homes. She also visits hospitals with seriously ill children and those with autism. I have accompanied her on some of those visits, and it is awe-inspiring to see how patients with memory disorders, seriously ill children, or those with autism respond to these miniature horses. During one visit, a nurse told us about a patient who had never left her room. Rommy, the star of the stable, poked his nose into the room and immediately ended her isolation. On every visit, she was the first to greet him and the last to say goodbye. When she became too ill to leave her room, Rommy would go right to her bed and place his head on her lap. On one particular visit, Rommy insisted on returning to her room for what turned out to be a final visit. She died the following day.

I was there when a five-year-old, blind and deaf, responded to Rommy when she felt his breath on her face. That smile will stay with me forever. Taking care of five miniature horses, a full-sized horse named Mo a donkey named Red, while maintaining a responsible job is no easy task. With Alicia, it is a labor of love. Fortunately, her fiancé, Trace Kicklighter, helps her every step of the way.

Alicia and I bonded from the day she was born, on April 16, 1970. She was an easy baby, a good eater, and sleeper. I loved walking around the backyard with her at our home in Old Lyme, CT. She was always so alert and observant, taking in everything around her. She walked at ten months, and, from her first day in school, she was one of the brightest students.

Unlike most of her friends, Alicia never developed an interest in dolls. She loved the pony stick horses and was "riding" around the yard before kindergarten. When she was four, her best friend was our poodle Tiffany who learned to go over the jumps Alicia set up for her. She began a love of horses that continues today.

On election night, 1980, Alicia was admitted to Yale-New Haven Hospital with Type I Diabetes. I did not know that Ronald Reagan had been elected president until two days later. She was ten years old at the time. It used to be called Juvenile Diabetes, but that name is confusing and inaccurate. I had some friends who told me that Alicia would outgrow "Juvenile Diabetes." Type I Diabetes is a lifelong, relentless disease that may result in early death. I got a glimpse into Alicia's character by the way she handled the condition.

When we returned from the hospital, I was responsible for injecting insulin into Alicia after measuring her blood sugar by testing her urine. It was not a very accurate method, and I also hated sticking needles into her, sometimes three times a day. Less than a week later, Alicia told me that she was doing her own shots. She has been on the insulin pump for more than 30 years, and a recent test shows her arteries are clear, remarkable for one who has had the disease for more than 40 years.

Alicia is always kind when she describes our relationship, saying that I was always by her side. That is not entirely true. I let her down badly when I agreed to pull her from the public school and send her to a private school. I also stood by silently when my then-wife Rosemary decided she should attend boarding school. Alicia had many friends in the Old Lyme school system and was one of the top students. I will always regret not standing up to a very unhappy woman whose own self-interests always came first.

On June 13, 1992, another young lady entered my life. She automatically went into the Pediatric Intensive Care Unit when she was born because her mother, Alicia, was a Type1 Diabetic. She weighed 8 pounds six ounces and was absolutely beautiful. Most of the babies around her were tiny, some of them in the two-pound range. A couple standing near me was admiring their new grandson, who appeared to be about three pounds. The woman looked at my granddaughter and asked, "What is wrong with her?" I replied that she was my granddaughter and explained the reason why she was in intensive care.

My granddaughter did not have a name at this point, and Alicia had this list of names that did not impress me. When I saw Alicia for the first time, I said, "Alicia, I just saw Sarah." Alicia looked at me and agreed. My choosing her name is remarkable because I had never been allowed to name ponies, horses, dogs, fish, or any other living creature. Sarah Tiffany Dooley joined us that night, and she has been with us for 29 years.

I get up at 6 a.m. and begin writing every morning by 6:30 a.m. because of those two ladies. Sarah and I bonded just as Alicia and I had in 1970. Sarah, like her mother, was a very easy baby. They lived with me in Bristol, RI, while Alicia attended Bryant College. It was among the happiest days of my life. Sarah inherited a good sense of direction from her mother. I still get lost in a closet. When she was three years old, Sarah would warn me that I missed a turn while taking her to daycare.

I have always loved classical music but cannot play one instrument or read a note. I gave Sarah a violin when she was in high school, and I was so proud when she became concertmaster of the school orchestra. She graduated from the Savannah School of Art and Design, and her work can be seen in some of my recent books. She has put smiles on my face for the past 29 years. Last year she married Josh Peacock, a very nice young man, and they seem meant for each other.

When Alicia and Sarah came to my induction into the Hall of Fame in 2018, I was at a low point physically. My Type 2 diabetes was out of control, and I had lost more than 40 pounds. I had been living alone for the past 20 years. Alicia put her foot down. "Dad, it's time." I gave up my Newport apartment and moved in with Alicia in Winter Garden, FL. Within months my Diabetes was under control, and I was back to full-time writing.

Two years ago, Alicia bought a horse farm in Savannah, Georgia. I have a separate wing of the house, which includes my bedroom, office and a large TV room. We have six horses, four cats, my dog, Sam, eight chickens, two ducks, and two turkeys. Like the White House turkeys, our two will never have to worry about Thanksgiving. Last year, a fox killed two of the chickens and injured the ducks. Trace set a trap, and we caught a fox. I remember standing near the trap and watching as the fox made threatening moves. Then Alicia arrived and began to talk to him. "Don't worry, baby. We're not going to hurt you." The fox quieted immediately, and we drove to a wooded area about 10 miles away and released him. We caught three more foxes in the next few months and followed the same procedure. We reached some form of truce because there have been no recent attacks.

At a recent birthday celebration for me, my daughter said the following:

My Dad has always had the floor, so tonight, I'm stealing it for a bit. The day I was first brought home from the hospital, my mother was worried that my lips were huge and swollen. My Dad said there was absolutely nothing wrong with me, and that's how I was raised. I was always told that I could do anything I set my mind to do. In my early years, I set my mind to avoid getting my face washed and to pet the wild ponies I was told not to sneak under the fence to see.

Sundays were always an adventure for my Mom and Dad. I was not a fan of church and tended to cry during Mass. I recall church being an experience where my Dad would read the newspaper on the playground bench outside the church while I made my way to the stars on the swing.

My Dad is always there for me. He was the one who carried me in the big, vast swimming pool when I was tiny. He caught me at the bottom of the pool slide, and he was the one I yelled at when I was four years old. I was in a ski school lesson and happened to be trapped on a broken chairlift for two hours during a nasty snowstorm. I was alone on the chair because there were six kids in the lesson, and one had to sit with the instructor because she was afraid. When we finally arrived at the bottom of the slope, Dad was waiting for me. I immediately went up to him and demanded, "Where were you?" in a shivery, teary voice. To this day, he hasn't left my side.

My Dad was there through my crazy horse phase. Wait a minute—never mind! The phase isn't over yet. He spent a lot of money on this spoiled child, woke up early to drive me to horse shows, and stood at ringside to cheer me, no matter how I rode that day. His experience as a ringside trainer has never failed him. As an adult, I took part in horseshoes, and Dad's job was to hold the video camera. If I made a mistake in the ring, I could still hear his swearing on the videotape.

When Sarah came along, Dad was immediately enamored. She went along with him on fancy dinner dates where she became the focus. She convinced him that bringing the wagon, the bicycle, the teddy bear, the shovel and pail, the ball, and other toys on their daily walk was the right thing to do. Guess who carried all those things plus Sarah on the way back home?

I'm not sure who learned the lesson in his next story, though. Sarah was dressed in her Easter best at the age of three. She walked up to Dad and asked, "Poppy, don't I look pretty?" He answered, "Yes, you do, honey, but shouldn't you wait until someone tells you that?' She looked up at him with her sparkling blue eyes and asked, "Suppose they don't?"

Dad has always been there for everything for me, so I don't know how I can ever top the things he has given me. I tried to when I bought him his first horse, a 2′7″ miniature horse named

Rascal. He has the same personality as my Dad. He loves to snuggle and bite people's ankles.

Dad, you have always been there for me, and I wish there were better words than just thank you. Dad, I love you and wish you the best 90th birthday anyone could ever have.

Meeting the Satells

In 1998, I accepted a job as an editor for Progressive Business Publications in Malvern, Pennsylvania. I thought I was getting a job—instead, I got a family. Ed Satell, the president, came to me with a problem about a month after I started with his company. He and his wife Margaret were going on a trip, and the woman who took care of their sons, Matthew and Clifford, became ill. I pinch-hit, and it became a life-changing decision.

I was certainly not qualified for the job. I didn't cook, and I was not much of a disciplinarian for my own children. But Matthew (12) and Clifford (10) and I clicked from the first day. Margaret and Ed traveled frequently, so I spent a lot of time with the boys. They had Ed's credit card numbers for White Manor, a local country club, so we ate pretty well.

Matthew and Clifford were good athletes, so much of our time was spent at baseball, basketball, or soccer events. They were both taking violin lessons, and I listened as they became excellent musicians. Ed had season tickets for baseball, football, basketball, and hockey, so we were always entertained on the weekends. More importantly, we developed a close friendship.

Both boys have grown into outstanding young men. A few years ago, I was sitting with my daughter Alicia in a restaurant in Winter Garden, Florida, on the eve of my 87th birthday. Suddenly, Margaret, Matthew, and Clifford walked through the door, surprising me to celebrate my birthday. No grandfather has stronger feelings for his grandchildren than I have for Matthew and Clifford.

For almost a quarter of a century, Margaret has always been there for me, during good times and bad, in sickness and in health, during successes such as my induction into the Rhode Island Heritage Hall of Fame, or disasters, when I lost funding for a movie two weeks before filming was to begin. She is the last person I like to talk to at night and the first one in the morning, especially when things are not going right. It is a friendship that survived divorce, mine and Margaret's, distance (I moved away from the Philadelphia area in 2002), and time. We bonded in 1998, and I have never had a better friend, socially or professionally. Our friendship was never compromised, because I continued to write for Ed Satell even after he and Margaret divorced.

Margaret proofreads every book, play, or screenplay I have written in the past 20 years. She is listed as a copy editor, but she does so much more. I described the 39th Fighter Squadron bombing New Jersey instead of New Guinea in one military book. My friends in Atlantic City would have been quite surprised if Margaret had not caught my error. That is only one example of the thousands of mistakes she has corrected over the years. She should have the title of writing partner rather than copy editor.

A few years ago, I wrote a play entitled *Love Nest*. The female lead is described as a woman who drives cancer patients to appointments, works as a hospice volunteer, sings in a community choir, and spends a lot of time and money helping the less fortunate. Other than a name change, that's a perfect description of Margaret.

She has been there for play openings and book signings, as well as for the trying times when I dealt with prostate and colon cancer. Her first question is always, "What can I do?" I've never had a kinder, more supportive friend than Margaret.

I have often said that if Margaret had been involved in the planning for D-Day on June 6, 1944, the war would have been over a year earlier. She compiles checklists every day detailing her plans for the day. I was not surprised when Margaret sent me a checklist specifying the requirements for a new man in her life. I was eliminated by requirement one, which called for a minimum height requirement of six feet. I am 5′7″ and shrinking. I took some consolation in the fact that John Glen, the great astronaut and U.S. Senator, would also have been cut by the height requirement. John was 5′10″. When Margaret visited Rhode Island for a book signing, a good friend was impressed by her beauty and brains. I advised him not to get too interested. 'You passed the first requirement but got knocked out at number two: *Must be Protestant, preferably Presbyterian*, I warned.

As the years passed, I began to wonder if any man would satisfy Margaret's qualification requirements. Then I met Doug Stay, who met all the criteria with ease. He was tall, well-educated (Colgate), a retired executive, and a member of Margaret's church. In fact, that is where they met. Doug also added qualities that were not on Margaret's original list.

Margaret is a perfectionist who can make coffee nervous, and Doug is laid-back and confident and has a knack for calming Margaret when one of her checklists is violated or ignored. On September 11, 2021, Margaret and Doug were married. I was thrilled when Margaret and Doug included me in the ceremony to deliver an Irish blessing, and I also gave the welcome address at the wedding reception. Members of both families participated in the beautiful ceremony, complete with two flower girls and ring bearer Finley Satell, Margaret's grandson.

"Grow old with me . . . . The best is yet to come," is a popular saying. "Love has no age, no limit, and no death," John Galsworthy said. Margaret and Doug both believe in love, and their bond will grow stronger with each passing day. No two people have spread more love and support to their family and friends than Margaret and Doug. It is nice to know they now have a relationship where they will be receiving as much as they give.

SWAN SONG

Three days after Pearl Harbor, most members of the Swan Club, a football team based in South Providence, RI, joined the United States Marine Corps. The list included my brother Jack, cousins Tom and Ed Dooley, Art Lowe, Joseph (Bucky) Conley, and Vin and Fred Farrelly. There were others, but I cannot remember them all.

I was ten years old at the time, and I do remember going to their football games, which they usually won. The coach was a man by the name of Sunny Jeroux. Sunny was older, so I do not know if he served in WWII or not.

I remember coming home from school one day and finding my mother crying. Fred Farrelly's mother had called and told her that her son was missing in action. His plane disappeared in an air battle with the Japanese in the Pacific and was never found. Fred was my hero. He worked for *The Providence Journal* and drove a blue Lincoln. Good looking and personable, Fred used to take us for rides in his rumble seat. In May of 1944, word went around our Edgewood neighborhood that Bob Thorpe, a P-47 pilot fighting in New Guinea, was reported as missing in action. Bob' younger brother Gill, was my good friend. I had no clue at the time that I would write a book about Bob Thorpe's capture and brutal execution by the Japanese.

In September of 1944, the Dooley family received a telegram that our brother Jack was missing in action during the invasion of Peleliu on September 15, 1944. Jack, a member of the First Marine Division, was found three days later, wounded. The attack on Peleliu resulted in a higher death toll than any other amphibious assault in U.S. military history. Peleliu's network of rocky caves, which the Japanese connected with tunnels, acted as a fortress. Jack was able to recover quickly enough to take part in the invasion of Okinawa seven months later.

In March of 1945, another Swan Club member, Bucky Walsh, a member of the Fifth Division, USMC, was seriously wounded in the invasion of Iwo Jima. Those telegrams served as a wake up call concerning my feeling about war. Up until then, I thought it was exciting, firmly believing that only the bad guys made the casualty lists. No more! I had a paper route delivering *The Providence Journal* and *The*

Evening Bulletin. Before I folded the papers and put them in my bag, I would turn to page two to check out the casualty list. I would always be relieved when I did not see the names of my brothers, Jack and Bill.

After the war, I worked at Henry's a small variety store directly across from St. Paul's Church in Cranston. Mrs. Farrelly attended daily Mass and stopped in every morning for *The Providence Journal*. We never discussed Fred, but I know her daily devotion was dedicated to him. Sadly, she died without receiving any other information than the initial telegram with the "missing in action" report. A year later, the designation was changed to "killed in action."

Bucky Conley, a cousin of Patrick T. Conley, Historian Laureate of RI, never fully recovered from the crippling injuries he sustained at Iwo Jima. Bucky, affectionately called the "Mayor of South Providence," was active in Democratic politics, and his military and political record earned him an appointment as U.S. Marshal for Rhode Island, a post he held from September 1961 until his death in 1966 at the age of forty-seven. In May 1966 the former City High School Stadium was dedicated by the City of Providence to the memory of war hero and U.S. Marshal Joseph V. "Bucky" Conley. It is now called Conley Stadium. Two of Bucky's children achieved prominent positions. His son Joseph was a pioneering coach for girls' basketball and later became Rhode Island Superior Court Administrator. His daughter Berena was a Providence school principal and the administrator of the city's Board of Licenses.

After the war, Swan Club football became active again. Sonny Giroux returned as coach, and my brother Jack took over his role as an end. Players in those days were two-way, meaning they stayed on the field for defensive and offensive snaps. Some prominent players joined the team, including Lou Gorman, who later became General Manager of the Boston Red Sox. Attrition from age and marriage took its toll. Players could not afford to risk injury while supporting families. So I do not think the Swan Club ever returned to its pre-war excellence.

Because of my brother Jack, I had the opportunity to hang around with Swan Club member before and after football games. I do not remember any of them as being particularly patriotic. I do not recall any flags hanging from cars or patriotic songs being sung. Yet most of the team enlisted to defend and fight for their country. They were not fighting for fame or recognition. They fought because it was the right thing to do.

This generation survived the worst depression this country has ever faced. Then they helped win the most destructive war in the world's history. They returned to civilian life and built the United States into the strongest and wealthiest country in the world. Tom Brokaw is absolutely right when he describes them as "The Greatest Generation."

Index